PHIL K BROOK

PROTOCOLS AND TECHNIQUES FOR DATA COMMUNICATION NETWORKS

PRENTICE-HALL COMPUTER APPLICATIONS IN ELECTRICAL ENGINEERING SERIES

FRANKLIN F. KUO, (Editor)

ABRAMSON AND KUO, *Computer-Communication Networks*
BOWERS AND SEDORE, *Spectre: A Computer Program for Circuit and Systems Analysis*
CADZOW, *Discrete Time Systems: An Introduction with Interdisciplinary Applications*
CADZOW AND MARTENS, *Discrete-Time and Computer Control Systems*
DAVIS, *Computer Data Displays*
FRIEDMAN AND MENON, *Fault Detection in Digital Circuits*
HUELSMAN, *Basic Circuit Theory*
JENSEN AND LIEBERMAN, *IBM Circuit Analysis Program: Techniques and Applications*
JENSEN AND WATKINS, *Network Analysis: Theory and Computer Methods*
KLINE, *Digital Computer Design*
KOCHENBURGER, *Computer Simulation of Dynamic Systems*
KUO (Editor), *Protocols and Techniques for Data Communication Networks*
KUO AND MAGNUSON, *Computer Oriented Circuit Design*
LIN, *An Introduction to Error-Correcting Codes*
NAGLE, CARROLL, AND IRWIN, *An Introduction to Computer Logic*
RHYNE, *Fundamentals of Digital Systems Design*
SIFFERLEN AND VARTANIAN, *Digital Electronics with Engineering Applications*
STAUDHAMMER, *Circuit Analysis by Digital Computer*
STOUTEMYER, *PL/1 Programming for Engineering and Science*

PROTOCOLS AND TECHNIQUES FOR DATA COMMUNICATION NETWORKS

FRANKLIN F. KUO, *Editor*

PRENTICE-HALL, INC., *Englewood Cliffs, New Jersey 07632*

Library of Congress Cataloging in Publication Data

Main entry under title:

Protocols and techniques for data communication networks.

Includes bibliographies and index.
1. Computer networks. 2. Data transmission systems.
I. Kuo, Franklin F., 1934-
TK5105.5.P77   001.64'404   80-13903
ISBN 0-13-731729-8

Editorial production supervision
and interior design by: James M. Chege

Cover design by: 20/20 Services, Inc.

Manufacturing buyer: Anthony Caruso

Printed in the United States of America

10   9   8   7   6   5   4   3   2   1

Prentice-Hall International, Inc., *London*
Prentice-Hall of Australia Pty. Limited, *Sydney*
Prentice-Hall of Canada, Ltd., *Toronto*
Prentice-Hall of India Private Limited, *New Delhi*
Prentice-Hall of Japan, Inc., *Tokyo*
Prentice-Hall of Southeast Asia Pte. Ltd., *Singapore*
Whitehall Books Limited, *Wellington, New Zealand*

CONTENTS

PREFACE

Computer-communication networks have come of age. At present they are being employed in a variety of different applications, including educational, commercial, and military. Since 1971, when the first major packet communication network, the ARPANET, was being tested operationally, various networks have come into being. These include the British EPSS, the French CYCLADES and TRANSPAC, the Canadian DATAPAC, the US' TYMNET and TELENET and various others in Japan and Europe. What has made packet communications practical in the 1970s is the rapidly declining cost of digital technology which has made it possible to employ minicomputers and microcomputers to control communications between two host computers.

This book is about the procedures and techniques which are employed to control the data exchange in a computer network. These procedures are called *communications protocols* and are generally implemented in software. This book is intended for the communications engineer or computer professional working with or designing networks. It can also be used for a graduate course in computer networks in either computer science or electrical engineering.

Even though the book is an edited work with individual chapters written by different authors, it is not a collection of reprints, as is the case of most IEEE books on the subject. All of the chapters are original, written especially for the book. There was considerable communication and coordination between the authors and the editor before and during the writing of each chapter. Drafts of the chapters were sent to other chapter authors for review and comments. Each chapter went through a number of revisions before it was finally declared ready for publication.

The authors are all well-known computer networks experts, and are all actively working in the field. Vinton Cerf, the author of Chapter 1 on packet communication technology, is with the Defense Advanced Research Projects Agency (DARPA) of the U.S. Department of Defense. He is best known for the internet protocol, TCP, which he jointly developed with Robert Kahn, also of DARPA. Cerf's chapter is an introduction to the packet switching concept, and shows how the concept has been applied to different communications media such as radio, satellite and terrestrial circuits.

Chapter 2 is by Carl Sunshine of the Information Sciences Institute (ISI) of the University of Southern California. Sunshine, a leading expert in internet protocols, focuses on protocols to provide general purpose, reliable, end-to-end communications between users of a computer network. These protocols are called *host-to-host* protocols in the ARPANET community and *transport* protocols elsewhere. In Chapter 3, John Day, an active researcher in protocol specifications and higher level protocols, who is now with Digital Technology, Inc. (DTI) of Champaign, IL, covers the very important higher level protocols dealing with terminal handling, file transfer, and remote job entry. These protocols are perhaps the most basic of the higher-level protocols and are often used as building blocks.

Mario Gerla, of the Computer Science Department of UCLA, is the author of Chapter 4, which deals with routing and flow control techniques for packet switched computer networks. Gerla, the coauthor of a classic 1975 paper (with D. Cantor) on routing, covers the *internal* (i.e. within the communications subnet) protocols of routing and flow-control, whose functions are to control the traffic within the network, and whose goal is the efficiency of the data transfer.

In Chapter 5, Richard Binder, a pioneer in packet satellite communications, describes some protocols that have been developed for data communications using broadcast satellites. Binder, who recently joined the Linkabit Corporation, was formerly a key member of the DARPA-sponsored Packet Satellite Working Group while at Bolt Beranek and Newman, (BBN) Inc. He has been working with packet radio and satellite technology ever since the early 1970s when he was the leading protocol specialist with the ALOHA System project at the University of Hawaii. Binder was responsible for many of the communications protocols of the ALOHANET, which was the pioneering effort that demonstrated the feasibility of packet radio and satellite systems.

Chapter 6 on mixed-media packet networks is written by two other former members of the ALOHA project, Dieu Huynh (now with the IBM Systems Communications Division, Kingston, NY) and myself. The term *mixed-media* applies to a network with both a terrestrial and a satellite component. The term *multi-media communications* also connotes a system which can handle voice, data, and graphics simultaneously, which is not what Chapter 6 is all about. It is recognized that multi-media communications are perhaps the most important applications of packet switching networks in the 1980s; but because of space limitations, the topic was not included in the present volume.

Another important protocol issue in computer networks is that of error control. In Chapter 7 the topic of coding for reliable data transmission is presented by two experts in the field, Shu Lin of the University of Hawaii who writes on block codes and Daniel Costello of the Illinois Institute of Technology, whose specialty is on convolutional codes. Lin and Costello are the authors of a new book on coding and error control to be published by Prentice-Hall in 1981. Chapter 8, by James Gray of the IBM Systems Communications Division, at Research Triangle Park, NC, is on the functions within an SNA (IBM's Systems Network Architecture) network viewed from the standpoint of synchronization among cooperating processes. Gray has made a number of important technical contributions to the development of SNA and is one of IBM's most knowledgeable people on SNA. Many of the techniques he writes about are personal contributions.

Chapter 9 is on network security and is written by Stephen Kent of the Laboratory for Computer Science of MIT. Kent, a young man in his late twenties, is already one of the leading experts in the U.S. on the subject. Network security is an ever-increasing concern on the part of both network users and designers because of applications such as electronic funds transfer and military communications. Kent's treatment of the subject in Chapter 9 is one of the most thorough and detailed yet to appear in print. In Chapter 10, the authors, James Rothnie, Nathan Goodman, and Thomas Marill of the Computer Corporation of America describe the application of computer networks to distributed data-base management (DBM). While this chapter is not on protocols per se, it nevertheless makes use of underlying protocol concepts in explaining the techniques of distributed data-base design. Two of the authors (Rothnie and Goodman) were active in the design of the system, SDD-1, which is one of the most impressive examples of distributed data-base management systems to be developed in recent years. Chapter 10 serves to point the reader to the future where applications protocols will be the dominant concern of network designers and architects.

I would like to express my gratitude to the many people whose help and cooperation made this volume possible. Particular thanks go to the contributors, whose patience, interest, and enthusiasm made this undertaking almost enjoyable.

Honolulu, Hawaii   FRANKLIN F. KUO

1

PACKET COMMUNICATION TECHNOLOGY

VINTON G. CERF

Defense Advanced Research Projects Agency
Information Processing Techniques Office

1.1 INTRODUCTION AND HISTORICAL REVIEW

This chapter is intended to be an introduction to the concept of *packet switching* and a tutorial exploration of the ways in which this concept has been applied to different communication media (e.g., radio, satellite, terrestrial circuits, coaxial and optical fiber loops).

To understand the context of the rest of this book, it is essential to appreciate what the packet-switching concept is all about. As L. Roberts puts it, in his historical review of packet switching [1]: "Packet switching technology was not really an invention, but a reapplication of the basic dynamic-allocation techniques used for over a century by the mail, telegraph and torn paper tape switching systems." In principle, the rapidly declining cost of digital technology in the late 1960s made it possible to replace manual dynamic allocation techniques with their digital counterparts. The forms in which this "new" kind of computer-controlled communication emerged in the late 1960s and early 1970s became known collectively as "packet communication technology," spanning a wide range of transmission media and specific dynamic allocation disciplines.

The basic idea is very simple. Communication between or among computers can be viewed as a "bursty" process with high peak-to-average rate requirements. For example, point-of-sale systems, inquiry-response systems, remote time-sharing services, and electronic message systems all share this bursty characteristic. In packet-switching systems, the bursts of data are called *packets*.

1

Rather than setting up a circuit, sending the burst of data, and closing the circuit, as in conventional circuit switching, a packet-switching system accepts packets from source computers, stores them in buffer memory, and then forwards them to the next packet switch, where the same store-and-forward operation occurs. The only difference between this and message switching is that the maximum length of any packet is generally very short (1000 to 5000 bits) and therefore does not require a long transmission delay to propagate through the store-and-forward network.

To provide for routing of packets through the network, each packet has a *header* containing the source and destination computer addresses, among other things. For error control, there is usually a checksum or the packet is encoded with a forward error-correction code. Typically, there is an acknowledgment scheme between adjacent packet switches so that packets not acknowledged within a certain time or packets negatively acknowledged on detection of an error are retransmitted. Figure 1.1 illustrates these simple concepts.

One advantage of the packet-switching concept is that the packets produced by the source computers can *asynchronously* time-share the communication links that connect the packet switches together. This allows traffic to be concentrated on higher-speed circuits and also supports apparent full connectivity among the source computers by virtue of the store-and-forward nature of the system. This

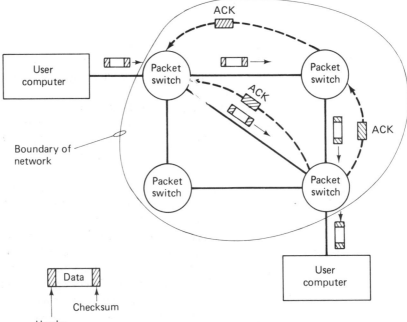

FIGURE 1-1 *A simple model of packet switching.*

efficient use of a small number of high-speed circuits (relative to a fully connected net, for instance) reduces both the cost and transmission delays in the system. Typical packet-switching systems use fewer than $3N/2$ links, where N is the number of packet switches in the net. By comparison, a fully connected net requires $N(N - 1)/2$ links.

Another common feature of packet-switching, store-and-forward systems is the capability to "alternate-route" traffic around failed links or nodes or to bypass congested links. Often, the networks realize the store-and-forward function in minicomputers separate from the mainframe computers they serve. This design is not fundamental to the packet-switching concept, but can serve to decouple the communication system operation and reliability from that of the mainframe-user computers.

Since each packet switch is a programmable computer, it is possible to make fairly elaborate decisions as to how to route packets, which packets to route next, whether to drop any packets to reduce congestion, whether to report problems to a control center, whom to bill for providing services, when to retransmit, whether to stop using a link to an adjacent packet switch because it appears not to be functioning, and so on. Many of these notions are pursued in more detail in Chapter 4.

The earliest published material on what is now known as store-and-forward packet switching came from RAND Corporation in 1964 in the form of a lengthy and thorough 11-volume design study by Baran [2]. The motivation was to provide ultrasurvivable voice and data communication by combining digital processing with a national mesh of point-to-point microwave transmitters. Operation was to be store-and-forward, with a "hot-potato" routing strategy in which all neighbors got a copy of each packet. Sequence numbering and short tables of recently forwarded packets would be used to damp duplicates and prevent congestion. The system was to be secure and each node (transceiver and digital unit) was to be very inexpensive so as to permit vast redundancy across the nation. Although this system was never implemented, it clearly anticipated the impact of low-cost digital technology on communication.

In the same year as the RAND reports were published, L. Kleinrock produced a book on queueing aspects of communication networks [3], establishing a theoretical basis for the design and evaluation of store-and-forward systems.

By 1965, D. W. Davies of the British National Physical Laboratory began, independently, to speak of packet switching using terrestrial circuits and minicomputers as the store-and-forward system. Davies is generally credited with coining the term "packet" [1]. At this time, the U.S. Defense Advanced Research Projects Agency (DARPA) began considering how the computing resources it provided for many of its research contractors could be shared among them, even though these resources were geographically dispersed across the United States. Time-sharing concepts were beginning to emerge, but the economics of providing terminal-to-computer services by direct leased lines connecting all contractor sites or through the direct dialing network did not look attractive. Furthermore, it was evident that computer-to-computer traffic for moving data files and programs would require substantial bandwidths beyond those available through the public switched telephone network. It is fair to say that the potential cost of providing the required high bandwidth, full connectivity among all the DARPA computing resources through leased circuits strongly influenced the decision to develop an alternative packet-switching system.

A two-computer experiment was conducted under DARPA support in 1966 [4]. The TX-2 computer at MIT's Lincoln Laboratory in Lexington, Massachusetts, was connected via leased circuit to the Q-32 computer at System Development Corporation in Santa Monica, California. Interactive access and data transfers between the two machines demonstrated the feasibility of connecting heterogeneous computers to share resources.

By 1968, the National Physical Laboratory was considering a prototype system consisting of a minicomputer packet switch to which several computers could be connected [5–8]. In the same year, DARPA's Information Processing Techniques Office, then under the direction of L. Roberts, issued a request for proposal to construct a packet-switching system that could interconnect many computers. The competition was won by a group led by F. Heart at Bolt Beranek and Newman in Cambridge, Massachusetts, and by late 1969, the first four nodes of the ARPANET [12] were in operation. The network grew rapidly, and by 1972, it was providing a rich environment for experimentation with heuristic and analytic packet network design concepts [13–23].

In the fall of 1972, a landmark demonstration of packet switching on the ARPANET was conducted in conjunction with the first International Conference on Computer Communication (ICCC), in Washington, D.C. Organized and directed by R. E. Kahn, one of the principal architects of the ARPANET. This demonstration established the credibility of packet switching in the computer communications community. Live, interactive terminal access to various ARPANET resources was provided via an ARPANET TIP [17] built by Bolt Beranek and Newman. For three days, conference attendees had "hands-on" access to a variety of ARPANET facilities, ranging from sophisticated text editors, computer-aided symbolic mathematical manipulation tools, and a multicomputer air-traffic-control simulator [24] to electronic message systems, network measurement, analysis and simulation tools, and interactive graphics systems.

The two primary impacts of this demonstration were, first, to show that the packet-switching network could deliver very fast response (less than 250 ms) and second, to show that standard networking protocols [15–17] supported intercommunication among a wide range of host computers. At that time, the network included Digital Equipment Corporation PDP-11s, PDP-10s, PDP-15s, IBM 360s, the General Electric 645 (later Honeywell 6180) MULTICS system, Bolt Beranek and Newman's PDP-10X (a DEC PDP-10 with a paging box), several Burroughs 6500s, Xerox Data Systems Sigma-7, and the ILLIAC IV. Even among the same hardware families, different operating systems were employed. On the PDP-10 family, for example, the TENEX, TOPS-10, and ITS operating systems were all augmented to include standard network protocols for interprocess communication.

There were two other packet-related developments that occurred in parallel with the NPL and ARPANET projects. These were the SITA high-level network and TYMNET, both of which were under construction in 1969.

The Société Internationale de Télécommunications Aéronautiques (SITA) provides an international communication network for airline reservation systems [25, 26]. Initially established in 1949, SITA developed a low-speed message switching network of teleprinters. By 1964, it was decided to augment this facility with a high-level network suitable for intercomputer communication. In 1969, SITA began to install new packet-switching computers at the high-level network centers (New York, Frankfurt, Brussels, Rome, Madrid, London, Paris, and Amsterdam). These centers were connected by leased, 2400-baud lines.

At the same time as the SITA network was installing its high-level system, TYMSHARE Corporation developed a terminal-oriented network based on small Varian minicomputers. These were interconnected by 2.4- or 4.8-kbits/s telephone circuits and acted as terminal concentrators, providing access to a number of host computers owned by TYMSHARE Corporation and other suppliers of computer services [27, 28].

In the early 1970s, a new wave of packet network development began in Europe. In 1971, the European Informatics Network (EIN) was started as a European Science and Technology Council (COST) project [31]. The project was originally called COST 11 and was ratified by 10 European countries in 1973. The network was based on datagram concepts and became operational in 1976.

In 1973, the French Institute for Information and Automation Research (Institut de Recherche d'Informatique et d'Automatique) began the CYCLADES/ CIGALE project to develop an experimental packet switching network [29]. The CIGALE packet-switching network was organized around MITRA-15 minicomputers. The full network, including host computers at major French research centers as well as CIGALE, was called CYCLADES. CYCLADES pioneered the concept of a pure *datagram* store-and-forward network in which packets are treated as independent transactions by the packet-switching network. Sequencing and flow control functions were largely left to end-to-end protocols implemented in the hosts.

The French Post, Telephone and Telegraph (PTT) Administration embarked on an experiment in packet switching in 1974. The experimental network was called RCP (réseau a communication par paquets) [30] and utilized internal *virtual circuits* to carry traffic within the network. These virtual circuits (VCs) were associated with traffic sources and sinks within host computers as contrasted with the ARPANET, which associated VCs with host pairs. RCP became a test bed for the French public packet-switched network, TRANSPAC.

In a similar way, the British Post Office developed an Experimental Packet Switched Service (EPSS) during 1973–1977 which is now being used as an experimental vehicle in the British research community as well as an aid toward development of national and international packet network services and standards. The net consists of six nodes at three sites (Manchester, Glasgow, and London) which accommodate terminal and host computer connections using a virtual-circuit protocol [32].

Since the early to middle 1970s, the PTTs have been actively developing packet-switched alternatives for data communication. In the United Kingdom, EPSS is to be replaced by PSS and IPSS (Packet Switching Service and International Packet Switching Service) in 1980. In France, the TRANSPAC network development was commissioned in late 1973. Based on concepts developed in the RCP project, TRANSPAC began operation late in 1978. The network is based on virtual-circuit services provided by a packet-switched communication network which accommodates both terminal and host interconnections [33, 34].

In 1975, the Commission of the European Economic Community (CEC) agreed to develop an information access and dissemination network, called EURONET [35]. This system was to be built for the CEC by the European PTTs, with the French PTT acting as the technical manager of the project. Based on the existing TRANSPAC system design, the EURONET software development began in 1977 and service to London, Paris, Rome, Frankfurt, Dublin, Copenhagen, Brussels, and Luxembourg is anticipated in 1980. Interconnections among the European national networks (e.g., the French TRANSPAC, the British PSS, the Nordic Public Data Network, the German Electronic Data Switching System, etc.) are also anticipated. This could make EURONET a high-level interconnection network, in addition to its original goal, which was to service the European need for access to scientific and technical information services.

In the United States, public packet switching began in late 1973 when TELENET Communication Corporation (a Bolt Beranek and Newman subsidiary until it was purchased late in 1978 by General Telephone and Electronics) filed with the Federal Communication Commission to offer a public "value-added" packet-switching service. By August 1975, TELENET was operational with seven nodes. It has grown to over 80 packet switches and provides access to about 200 host computers and also to dial-up terminal users in 156 U.S. cities.

In Canada, the DATAPAC network was developed over the 1973–1977 period, opening for service in June 1977. Four nodes are in operation in Toronto, Calgary, Ottawa, and Montreal and more are planned for 1979. DATAPAC uses a datagram communications network but provides users with virtual-circuit services. Interconnection with RCP was accomplished in 1976 and with TRANSPAC in early 1978. Other interconnections are planned with the U.K. IPSS and other national networks.

Research into packet switching at NIPPON Telephone and Telegraph (NTT) began in 1971 with the DDX-1 project. A successor project, DDX-2, was started in 1974 and combines packet- and digital-circuit-switching services. DDX-2 has been supporting experimental usage since early 1978 and is scheduled to become operational by June 1980. Based on virtual-circuit concepts, the network is designed to accommodate an array of packet-mode and non-packet-mode terminals (including host computers) [36]. Two DDX-2 packet switches have been installed at Musashino and Yokosuka Electrical Communication Laboratories. These support internal NTT usage as well as an intercomputer network between Tokyo and Kyoto universities.

The brief historical review above is incomplete in a number of respects. It does not mention a variety of packet communication research activities now under way within the U.S. Department of Defense, nor does it cover the efforts of computer manufacturers (e.g., International Business Machines, Digital Equipment Corporations, Univac, Burroughs, and NCR, to name a few). Furthermore, we have not explored the offerings of the U.S. AT&T, such as its TRANSACTION network and its proposed Advanced Communication System.

1.2   POINT-TO-POINT STORE-AND-FORWARD SYSTEMS

1.2.1   Introduction

The basic concept of store-and-forward communication has its roots in antiquity. The batching together of messages (clay tablets, papyri, etc.) to be transported long distances was an obvious means of sharing ''communication'' capacity available in the form of ship's cargo, space in saddlebags, backpacks, and the like.

More recently, electronic telecommunications made possible store-and-forward systems based on paper-tape and Teletypewriter technology. Messages were sent from one Teletype to another through a leased-line network. Intermediate Teletypes would record the messages on paper tape and forward them by electronically relaying the paper-tape messages to the next intermediate or destination Teletype.

The term *torn tape* has been used to describe such electromechanical store-and-forward systems. Messages were typically composed ''off-line'' and manually edited using paper tape. A network of Teletypewriters with automatic send/receive (i.e., paper tape) capability were configured so that some of them made up a message-switching center. The sender would dial up a message-switching center and transmit the contents of a message that had been committed to paper tape. The message-switching center would receive, punch out on tape, and acknowledge message receipt. The message center had knowledge of the topology of the entire network and could use this knowledge to decide to which Teletypewriters the message(s) should be forwarded.

As messages accumulated on paper tape at intermediate message-switching centers, they were batched together for forwarding to other Teletypewriters. Routing decisions were made manually by operators manning the teletypes.

Typically, the collection of Teletypewriters were not all part of the same electromagnetic network. Instead, many were part of a specific network, such as a circuit-switching network, a high-frequency radio network, and so forth.

The development of general-purpose computer systems made it possible to eliminate the manual torn-tape switching and forwarding. Instead, computer-controlled switching and magnetic drums or disks (or tapes) were used to temporarily store the messages in transit while on their way from source to destination.

The AUTODIN I message-switching system is an early example of such a system, built in the mid-1960s by Western Union for the Defense Communications Agency. In AUTODIN I, complete (and sometimes very lengthy) messages are entered into the switch by an operator. The messages have a very well-defined format (called JANAP 128), which is "understood" by the AUTODIN I message switches. Messages are sent from switch to switch, broken into shorter blocks for transmission between switches.

An elaborate log of messages is kept at each switch. Substantial storage is provided at each switch to buffer messages if a destination terminal is not ready to receive it. Each message is reassembled at each message switch and checked for validity before it is forwarded to another switch (if need be). In general, there are a range of priorities on each message, potentially many destinations, classification levels, and so on. The entire mechanism requires a substantial amount of computing and storage, making transit times fairly lengthy in the network.

1.2.2 Fundamental Notions and Objectives

Packet switching on point-to-point circuits (wires, point-to-point radio or satellite channels, coaxial or optical cables, etc.) is very much like the older message-switching systems except that the mechanism introduces less transmission delay and offers potentially greater flexibility to recover from intermediate switch failures.

1.2.2.1 Delay

One principal difference between packet switching and circuit or message switching is illustrated in Figs. 1.2 to 1.4. Figure 1.2 illustrates the typical delay for message delivery if a circuit must be set up before the message can be transmitted. Figure 1.3 shows that message switching can reduce this delay by allowing immediate transmission. Figure 1.4 illustrates that transit time can be further reduced by dividing the message into smaller packets and sending the smaller packets in store-and-forward fashion through intermediate packet switches to the destination. An important design issue in the last case is whether the fragmentation and reassembly of packets into messages should be done by the packet-switching system or by user computers.

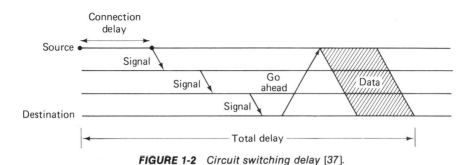

FIGURE 1-2   *Circuit switching delay* [37].

1.2.2.2 Sequencing

This latter point is related to an even more fundamental question having to do with the type of service offered by the packet network. There are two major types of packet network service:

1. Datagram.

2. Virtual circuit.

Loosely speaking, the datagram service does not provide any a priori association among datagrams in the network. Each is delivered independently of the other and there is no enforced relationship between the order in which one computer enters datagrams into the network and the order in which these same datagrams are removed from the network and delivered to the user.

It is in this sequencing domain that the greatest differences among packet networks are to be found. Most of the public or commercial networks offer a sequenced service. That is, the packet-switching computers maintain the order of packet delivery to match the order of packet entry into the network. Such a service constitutes a virtual circuit between the sender and receiver.

The main difference between a real circuit and a virtual circuit is the variable transit delay likely in a virtual circuit, which is derived from a store-and-forward packet-switching network.

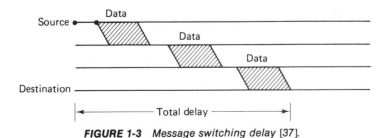

FIGURE 1-3   *Message switching delay* [37].

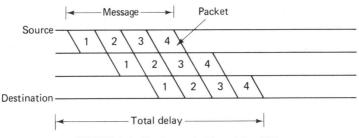

FIGURE 1-4 *Packet switching delay* [37].

In contrast, private networks often offer both a datagram and a virtual-circuit service or only a datagram service. For example, the ARPANET offers both forms of service, whereas the CIGALE network offers only datagram. The Canadian DATAPAC network offers only virtual-circuit service but builds it on top of an underlying datagram network.

1.2.2.3 Error Control

Basic facilities such as sequencing, error control, routing, fragmentation and reassembly, flow, and congestion control are often treated as if they are independent of each other. However, these concepts interact in complex ways when they are implemented in a packet-switching system.

For example, error control in point-to-point store-and-forward systems often involves a "hop-by-hop" acknowledgment procedure, such as the one illustrated in Fig. 1.1. The basic notion is that a packet sent from one node to the next will be retransmitted by the sending node if an acknowledgment for it has not been received after a "timeout" period, or if a negative acknowledgment is sent by the receiver.

The receiver may detect that a packet has been lost in several ways:

1. Packets may be numbered sequentially and detection of an "out-of-order" packet may trigger a negative acknowledgment.

2. Packets may be "checksummed" by the sender and the receiver. The sender sends the checksum in the packet, the receiver computes the checksum independently on receipt and compares this with the transmitted checksum; if they do not match, the packet is rejected.

3. Packets may even be encoded so that errors can be detected and corrected (see Chapter 7). If some errors are detected that cannot be corrected, the packet is rejected.

The actual implementation and performance of an error-detection-and-correction scheme will be influenced by the type of service to be offered, the delay, and the bandwidth characteristics of the communication circuits connecting the packet-switching nodes.

It is instructive to consider a negative-acknowledgment-only scheme to understand some of the basic design issues. Suppose that each packet is checksummed by the sending packet switch. The checksum is appended and sent with the packet. The receiving packet switch verifies the checksum and sends a negative acknowledgment if an error is detected. For simplicity, we will assume that only one packet is "outstanding" at a time.

Clearly, the source packet switch must keep a copy of the packet it sends in case a negative acknowledgment is received. When can the source discard this copy? In the absence of a positive acknowledgment, the sender must assume that after a timeout period, if it hears nothing, the packet must have arrived safely. This scheme relies on a fixed "round-trip" delay from sender to receiver and back. It is a risky scheme, since the link from receiver to sender may have broken as a negative acknowledgment was in transit. Or it may have broken before the packet arrived. Worse, the packet may have experienced so many errors that the receiver could not even tell that a packet was sent.

Most systems employ a positive acknowledgment scheme with retransmission after a timeout to avoid these uncertainties. This simple strategy may be augmented with negative acknowledgments to speed up retransmission. Sunshine has analyzed many of the performance issues in [38].

Typically, the product of average round-trip time and communication link bandwidth makes any "single-packet-outstanding" strategy very inefficient in terms of channel utilization. To improve utilization, it is common to transmit more than one packet before expecting a response. This keeps the "pipe" full of packets. However, this strategy introduces the need for unique identification of each packet so each can be positively or negatively acknowledged.

The design of an error-control strategy that works with multiple outstanding packets is usually influenced by the way in which sequencing is to be dealt with. For example, the TYMNET system maintains the sequence of packets on a hop-by-hop basis as they move from source to destination[1] [27, 28]. If a packet is received in error, or one is missed, the receiver sends a negative acknowledgment and does not forward any subsequent packets until the missing packet is received.

At the implementation level, one could queue up packets received successfully after the one(s) missed or one could discard them and rely on the source to retransmit all packets, including and after the one(s) in error. The trade-off is between buffer space and recovery delay. If only one packet needs to be retransmitted, queueing of the others will speed up recovery.

Other networks implement sequenced delivery on an end-to-end basis (source-to-destination packet switch) and do not try to maintain sequence during store-and-forward transit. The ARPANET and CIGALE are of this type. To allow

---

[1]   Actually, TYMNET employs a special multiplexing scheme in which packets are batched together in a "frame" for checksumming purposes, but we will ignore that detail for the moment.

multiple packets to be in transit from switch to switch, these networks divide the physical link between switches into a set of logical links (typically 8, although for very long delay channels, these might be 16, 32, or even 64 logical links).

The sending packet switch assigns a packet to a logical link that is not in use. Upon assignment, the logical link becomes busy. The logical-link number is carried in the packet so that it can be uniquely acknowledged. Only one packet at a time occupies a logical link, but the many logical links allow the sender to transmit many packets before having to receive an acknowledgment.

The receiver can acknowledge any number of logical-link receptions at once by sending back an 8-bit (or 16- or 32- or 64-bit) word with bits set to show which logical links are being acknowledged. Since these networks do not maintain hop-by-hop sequencing, it is possible to reuse a logical link as soon as it has been acknowledged, independent of the status of any other logical links.

In fact, things are slightly more complex, since it is possible for more than one copy of the same packet to be sent to the receiver on a given logical link. The receiver must be able to detect this to avoid accidentally treating a duplicate as a new packet. Conceptually, this is achieved by labeling a packet with both its logical-link number and a "color." Suppose that a logical link is idle and a packet is sent on it. The packet is labeled with the link number and is colored "blue." This blue packet is transmitted and retransmitted until an acknowledgment is received for a blue packet on that particular logical link. The logical link becomes idle. A new packet may be sent on the logical channel. As before, the packet is labeled with the logical-channel number, but this time it is colored "pink." If an extra blue acknowledgment arrives at the sender, it will be ignored since the sender is now awaiting a pink acknowledgment. If an extra blue packet arrives at the receiver, it can acknowledge it, but discard it.

Of course, in fact, the packets are simply labeled "even" and "odd" or "zero" and "one" rather than "pink" and "blue." The mechanism does not preserve the relative order of all packets sent on the physical channel, since each logical link is treated independently.

There are now international standards for line-control procedures whose basic purpose is to reliably transport "frames" of data from one computer to another. One such standard is called High Level Data Link Control (HDLC) procedure. This standard was developed by the International Standards Organization (ISO) and is documented in [39]. This standard is closely related to the IBM Synchronous Data Link Control (SDLC) procedure from which it is derived, and is known as the Advanced Data Communications Control Procedure (ADCCP) in the United States.

The basic format of an HDLC frame is shown in Fig. 1.5. A frame is signaled or flagged to the receiver by the presence of the flag sequence, labeled FLAG in the figure. The transmission hardware protects against the unintentional signaling of the FLAG sequence by "stuffing" a zero into the data stream after any sequence of five 1 bits. The receiving hardware deletes a zero which follows five 1 bits, once it detects the occurrence of an incoming FLAG sequence.

The end of a frame is detected when a second FLAG sequence occurs. A

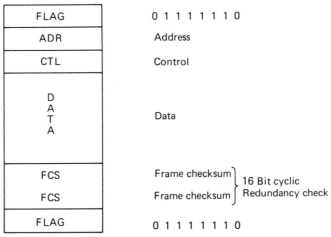

FIGURE 1-5 *Basic HDLC frame format.*

storage register preserves the preceding 16-bit frame checksum, and its value is compared against the checksum which the receiving hardware generates as the frame arrives. The basic bit-stuffing and checksum verification procedures are available from a number of manufacturers in the form of dual-in-line-package (DIP) chips at modest cost.

The HDLC procedure consists of much more than bit stuffing and checksumming of frames. Error control, sequencing, and flow control are also a part of the design. There are other details of the HDLC procedure, such as link setup (initiation) and disconnect, which utilize the Set Asynchronous Response Mode (SARM) command, the Unnumbered Acknowledgment (UA) response, and the Disconnect (DISC) command. The poll/final (P/F) bit serves a function in both commands and responses. In command frames it is called the Poll (P) bit, and when set it demands a response. In response frames it is called the Final (F) bit and acknowledges the command poll.

The basic mode of operation in HDLC is an asymmetric primary–secondary mode in which one side issues commands and the other responds. However, there is an asynchronous balanced mode (ABM) in which both sides act as primary and secondary, each issuing and responding to commands from the other.

Further details about HDLC are beyond the scope of this chapter, but the interested reader is referred to [37, 39] for more information.

1.2.2.4 Flow Control

At the lowest level in a store-and-forward packet switching net, there is a need to control the rate at which packets flow from one packet switch to the next. Line-control procedures such as HDLC are designed to achieve this by limiting the number of packets that can be outstanding (i.e., unacknowledged).

The control field (CTL, see Fig. 1.5) of HDLC is organized as shown in Fig. 1.6.

Each information frame carries two numbers, N(S) and N(R). N(S) is a number between 0 and 7 which identifies the frame number in a repeating modulo 8 sequence. N(R) is the frame number of the next frame expected. Frames are expected to arrive in sequence, so N(R) is not incremented if the expected frame does not arrive. Since both N(S) and N(R) are carried in information frames, acknowledgments N(R) are carried piggyback on information frames. If a receiver has no outgoing information frame to send, a receiver ready (RR) supervisory frame can be sent, indicating which frame is expected next.

If a frame number that is unexpected arrives, the receiver can respond with a supervisory reject (REJ) response, indicating the number of the frame expected.

The HDLC procedure also allows the receiver to stop all transmissions from the sender by emitting a Receiver Not Ready (RNR) response. This response indicates which frame is next expected (to acknowledge all those which preceded it and which have arrived successfully), but it tells the sender not to send any more. This condition is terminated by sending an RR frame. Then there are two basic flow control mechanisms—the RNR control and the basic limitation of seven outstanding frames. There are provisions for extended numbering (up to 127 outstanding frames) if the round-trip delay and transmission bandwidth require it, to keep the channel busy.

The logical-channel error-control scheme described in Sec. 1.2.2.3 also limits the number of packets outstanding to the number of logical channels. If buffering problems at the receiving side prevent a packet from being accepted, it is simply discarded without acknowledgment. The sender will retransmit later. This scheme does not explicitly stop the sender from sending new packets, so some processing time to discard new packets is traded off for a simpler line-control mechanism.

Format	Commands	Responses	Encoding							
			1	2	3	4	5	6	7	8
Information	I			N(R)		P	N(S)			0
Supervisory		RR		N(R)		F	0	0	0	1
		RNR		N(R)		F	0	1	0	1
		REJ		N(R)		F	1	0	0	1
Unnumbered	SARM		0	0	0	P	1	1	1	1
	DISC		0	1	0	P	0	0	1	1
		UA	0	1	1	F	0	0	1	1
		CMDR	1	0	0	F	0	1	1	1

Poll/final

FIGURE 1-6 Basic HDLC control field formats.

One potential disadvantage of HDLC as a line-control procedure for internal packet network operation is the artificial imposition of a sequencing relation on packets being transported from one packet switch to another. In networks that do not seek to preserve packet sequence on a hop-by-hop basis, this artificial constraint can impose unnecessary additional transit delays when errors occur.

Flow control is generally regarded as a procedure for protecting the receiver's resources and for enforcing some policy for allocating the flow of packets through the network. While it is generally necessary to control the rate at which new packets are sent on a hop-by-hop basis, there may also be a need to control introduction of packets into the network bound for particular destinations from a given source. This can be considered an end-to-end flow control, where the ends lie within the packet network at the source and destination packet switches. The critical resource is usually buffer space at the destination, so intranet flow control typically consists of limiting the number of packets a source can introduce into the network bound for a given destination.

These limitations can be dynamic in nature, in which case the destination packet switch sends "permits" to the source packet switch. Or they can be more static, in which case buffers are reserved during the lifetime of a virtual circuit, for example. In some networks, such as TRANSPAC and TELENET, buffer reservations are assigned along a fixed route, while in others, the reservations are only made at the destination packet switch (e.g., ARPANET). We will return to this topic when we discuss the subject of routing.

It is generally the case that flow control is enforced through the allocation of permits to send packets and the reservation of buffers to receive them. In some instances, the buffers are only "virtually" reserved. That is, a pool of buffers are shared, and statistical assumptions are made as to the amount of flow that can be supported with a given size buffer pool.

In fact, flow control should really be dealt with by metering the rate of flow of packets into the network bound for given destinations. But for asynchronous systems, the measurement and control of rate of flow is very difficult to implement. This is still very much a research topic, and the problem arises at levels of protocol beyond (outside) the basic packet-switching network. Excellent sources of primary material on flow control may be found in [57] and in Chapter 4.

1.2.2.5 Congestion Control

We make a distinction between flow control and congestion control. *Flow-control* methods generally apply to point-to-point procedures between adjacent packet switches or source/destination packet switches. *Congestion control*, on the other hand, is an inherently multipoint problem, designed to protect the aggregate network resources from becoming oversubscribed. A simple "thought experiment" illustrates the distinction. Suppose that a source and destination packet switch are attached to very high capacity host computers. The basic flow-control mechanism may indicate that substantial bandwidth can be supported between these two end packet switches. However, the store-and-forward resources of the rest of the network may be incapable of supporting the desired flow. Indeed, each individual source/destination flow may be accommodated, but the aggregate may overtax the total network resources.

This is again a major research area. A number of techniques have been studied and even implemented, but there is still no guaranteed foolproof technique that is both efficient in its use of resources and effective at avoiding congestion. A congestion-prone system has throughput–delay behavior as shown in Fig. 1.7. Throughput rises with offered traffic and delay grows until throughput reaches a maximum. At this point, the system is saturated. In an ideal system, the throughput would remain constant, although delay would increase, with increasing offered load. In a congestion-prone system, the throughput drops with increased load until it reaches zero and delay becomes infinite. This phenomenon is a familiar hazard to freeway commuters during rush hour.

A variety of methods have been proposed to deal with this problem. One method, proposed by D. Davies [40, 52], is called "isarithmic" congestion control. In this technique, the network contains a fixed number of packet-carrying crates. No packet switch can accept a packet from the outside world without having an empty crate to put it in. Crates are emptied at destination packet switches after the packet has been delivered to the destination host.

One immediate problem with this idea is how to distribute empty crates to packet switches which need them. This is similar to the problem of car rental agencies which find many cars available at major cities but few are available when needed at small towns. Taxi systems also have this problem. The proposed solution for the isarithmic network is to treat crates like taxis. About half of the empty crates are allowed to queue up idling at packet switches. The rest must shuttle at random to other packet switches. Obviously, this creates overhead within the network.

The isarithmic scheme is elegant on paper and in simulations, but has a fatal flaw. If a packet switch crashes and loses some empty crates, it is not clear how

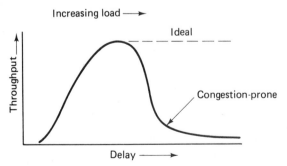

FIGURE 1-7 *Performance in congestion–prone systems.*

to generate replacements. If new crates are created, how can it be guaranteed that no more than the correct fixed number are present in the network? Even an attempt to keep the number constant on the average is impossible (or too expensive) to achieve, since a distributed counting mechanism that accurately assesses the number of crates is needed, even in the presence of dynamic failures. This scheme has been simulated but never implemented in a live packet-switching network.

Apart from the obvious problem, the basic idea may still be flawed if traffic flows create local congestion. This raises the issue of the relationship between routing and congestion control, which is discussed in the next section.

Another strategy was implemented in the CYCLADES/CIGALE network: drop packets when buffers begin to fill up! Although very simple to implement, the method produces bizarre performance results when congestion strikes.

In a simulation study, Irland [41] showed that when the first link between some pair of packet switches saturates, the network begins to congest. Packet discard rates as high as 40% were observed. Since all discarded packets must be retransmitted, the delay increases and throughput decreases in the classical curve of Fig. 1.7.

Another attack on the problem has been proposed by Raubold and Haenle [42]. In this method, the store-and-forward buffers of each packet switch are partitioned into N classes, where N is the maximum number of hops that will ever be required to forward a packet from source to destination. Obviously, it is important for the routing algorithm to avoid loops or it will be impossible to enforce the upper limit on hops. Packets are divided into equivalence classes according to the number of hops they have traversed so far.

The basic idea is to "protect the investment" in hops expended on a given packet. If a packet has traversed through H hops, it has access to all buffers in classes H and smaller. Assuming that the number of buffers in each switch is at least N, that each partition contains at least one buffer, and that there are no loops in the routing, the system should not deadlock. However, implementing this strategy in a way that is robust in spite of node failures is quite a challenge. Generally, the implementations thus far have restricted themselves to essentially fixed routing algorithms.

Pouzin offers a range of comments and suggestions on this topic in [43]. Pouzin and Zimmermann review the issues in the context of protocol design in [44]. The options range from excessively conservative schemes in which buffers are reserved but are not well utilized (fixed preallocations, for example) to highly adaptive, but not necessarily free of deadlock.

In [45], Kleinrock summarizes the basic lesson: "To date there is no satisfactory theory or procedure for designing efficient flow control procedures, much less evaluating their performance, proving they contain no deadlocks, and proving they are correct." Kleinrock treats the subject in a very general way in [46]. He introduces the concept of the "power" of a network as its throughput divided by its delay. Under simple assumptions about the statistics of the input demand, power is maximized if the network is operated at half its maximum throughput and twice its minimum delay.

No discussion of congestion control would be complete without mention of *deadlock*. Deadlock is the ultimate performance degradation. All throughput stops and the system simply crystallizes. An obvious example is the so-called "head-on" or "store-and-forward" deadlock. If the routing algorithm causes traffic flowing in opposite directions to flow through two adjacent packet switches, and each switch fills to capacity with packets destined for the other, the two become deadlocked.

Some of the earliest investigations in this area were reported by Kahn and Crowther [47] in their work on the ARPANET. Even if deadlocks are avoided, there may still be degradations in performance which result from poorly conceived or tuned congestion control algorithms, ill-behaved routing algorithms, and so on. Some of the more spectacular effects are detailed in [48] by Opderbeck and Kleinrock, and in [49] by Danthine and Eschenauer.

Opderbeck and Kleinrock identified degradations resulting from unnecessary retransmissions for single packet messages in the ARPANET. Danthine and Eschenauer observed that asymmetric traffic (long packets in one direction and short ones in the other) could lead to substantial throughput degradation in the short-packet direction. In essence, acknowledgments are delayed in the long-packet direction by the long packets, even with piggybacking of acknowledgments on return traffic. If the basic congestion control scheme is to impose a fixed limit on the number of packets outstanding in each direction, the short-packet side will underutilize the channel. The maximum number of packets outstanding are quickly transmitted and until acknowledgments are returned on the long-packet direction, the short side must continue to retransmit short packets and cannot keep the "pipe" filled with new traffic.

Most of these problems emerge as poor implementation choices, but many turn out to be fundamental congestion or flow-control hazards that must be dealt with. The present state of the art is woefully weak.

1.2.2.6 *Routing*

A fundamental notion in all store-and-forward systems is routing. The basic objective is simply stated. In a network that is not "fully connected" (i.e., not all packet switches have direct communication links to all other switches), what is the "best" sequence of switches through which a packet should be forwarded to reach the desired destination? The problem is to determine what "best" means. This is particularly formidable if the value of the metric changes with time. Typically, most packet-switched networks attempt to minimize delay or the number of "hops" needed to reach the destination.

A variety of terms for describing routing have accumulated in the literature. "Fixed routing" means that a route is preselected, possibly when the network is designed, and is never or only rarely changed. The SITA network employs a fixed routing strategy. To accommodate adaptation to failures, a set of routing tables are computed, one for each possible failure. Upon detection of a link or switch failure, the appropriate routing table is loaded from a local disk or drum memory.

The TYMNET system selects a route when a customer first "logs in" to the system. A central supervisory computer surveys the current routings already in operation and tries to optimize the traffic flow and minimize the delay for the new traffic source. In the event of a failure, customers log in again and a new route is selected [54].

In the TELENET and TRANSPAC systems, a route is selected when a customer requests that a virtual circuit be set up. The route selection is distributed in the sense that the hop-by-hop routing of the virtual circuit setup request determines the route of the virtual circuit. If a failure occurs, the virtual circuit is reset and the customer requests that a new one be set up.

In the ARPANET and in DATAPAC, routes are dynamically selected on a hop-by-hop and packet-by-packet basis. The packet switches exchange delay and traffic load information among themselves and change their routing decisions accordingly. This is sometimes referred to as dynamic or adaptive alternate routing. Nondynamic alternate routing usually confines itself to recovering from failures.

The more dynamic the routing scheme, the more prone the scheme may be to anomalies such as loops in the routing mechanism. Various strategies have been put forward for dealing with the looping problem. Naylor proposed a testing technique in [50] that would verify loop-free routes before assigning them. This is a complex procedure and it was not clear that the testing procedure cycle time would be compatible with the rate at which the routing algorithm might have to change to achieve any sort of optimality.

Another strategy, based on theoretical considerations, was proposed by Gallager in [51]. In this technique, the rate of change in delay was used as the decision variable for making routing changes. The difficulty with this scheme is that it requires that the rate of change be smooth and measurable. In practice, it appears that the absolute delay and its rate of change vary rapidly and any implementation would tend to "thrash" with regard to route selection. Nevertheless, the analysis offers a benchmark against which practical algorithms can be compared.

Early work by Fultz and Kleinrock [53] explored adaptive algorithms that would bifurcate traffic, allowing multiple routes to be used simultaneously to increase effective bandwidth. For this strategy to be effective, it must be known whether there really does exist more than one route from source to destination— not easy to determine in the presence of line and switch failures.

One of the earliest routing strategies, called "hot-potato" routing, was proposed by Baran, Boehm, and Smith in their seminal work on packet switching

[2]. Packets were routed to all neighbors and duplicates were filtered through the use of tables recording the identity of recently forwarded packets. This was never seriously considered for any networks actually implemented.

McQuillan has conducted a considerable amount of research in this area [37, 55, 56], including substantial experimentation with the ARPANET routing algorithms. The primary conclusions reached in the measurement effort were that the measurement of delay or queue length at a given packet switch provided only very "noisy" (i.e., high variance) information on which to base any routing decisions. Furthermore, the basic ARPANET routing algorithm showed evidence of a built-in potential for oscillation. Most surprising, it turned out that the fundamental procedure for deciding whether a line was up or down introduced severe oscillations in network behavior, especially when congestion occurred.

It is sometimes the case that alternate or adaptive routing algorithms, which take into account delay caused by local congestion, are considered to be congestion avoidance mechanisms. This is only partly correct. If congestion is indeed local, then routing around it may be exactly the proper thing to do. On the other hand, if the congestion is a sympton of excessive traffic entering the entire network, alternate routing merely spreads the infection. It is not easy to distinguish between the two cases if the bulk of the information available at a local packet switch is local and not global.

When a distributed routing algorithm is adopted, there is always a question as to the basis for making decisions. McQuillan, in [37], defines four categories:

1. Deterministic control.

2. Isolated control.

3. Distributed control.

4. Centralized control.

Roughly speaking, deterministic control implies fixed routes. The SITA network uses this strategy, but has precomputed tables which can be manually selected to deal with line or node outages. Isolated control involves decision making based solely on local information (i.e., not even sharing information with adjacent packet switches). Distributed control allows each packet switch to make its own decision but tries to propagate information of global importance to all the nodes. Centralized control leaves route-making decisions to a single central authority (possibly backed up by alternate centers, in case of failure).

The ARPANET and DATAPAC use the third type of algorithm, while TYMNET uses the fourth type. The fundamental issue in devising a routing scheme that is stable (e.g., does not introduce loops) is to find some efficient way of propagating the required information to the place(s) that must make routing decisions. The fundamental barrier is time: time to deliver routing information to or among the packet switches before conditions have changed and have made the information obsolete.

The various points of view on this subject sometimes reflect specific costs in particular networks for propagating the routing information around the network. Regardless of whether centralized or distributed control is used, there is a cost in time, bandwidth, buffer space, and other network resources to move routing information from the locations where routing policies are selected to the locations where the policies are enforced.

Routing mechanisms can adversely interact with the flow and congestion control objectives, so these mechanisms and strategies cannot be designed independently of each other. For example, a routing algorithm that causes loops to be formed can lead to network congestion. Inefficient routing algorithms that require substantial network resources for their implementation and operation can render the network useless for carrying any "paying" traffic. If there is a message here, it may be that the old "divide-and-conquer" adage is misapplied in network design if one tries to design and build independent techniques for flow and congestion control and routing which do not take their interrelation into account.

1.2.2.7 *Protocol Layering*

In spite of the cautionary words in the preceding section regarding the "divide-and-conquer" approach to network organization, there is a certain amount of decomposition which can help. For instance, it is helpful to consider a horizontally partitioned layering of functions which must be performed to realize any particular application running on a computer attached to a store-and-forward network.

In a networking environment, the term *protocol* has come to mean both a format and a set of procedures that are commonly agreed to for the purpose of achieving communication. Layering of protocols is the result of a stratification of function among parts of the system.

One of the more comprehensive attempts to use layering to define a communication systems architecture can be found in the notes of the International Standards Organization (ISO), Technical Committee 97, subcommittee 16 on Open Systems Architecture. The objective of TC97/SC16 is to define the function and layering of a set of protocols so as to permit the interoperation of systems which are built independently but to the same architectural standard.

The protocol layers proposed by SC16 are illustrated in Fig. 1.8. The layers are representative of the software and hardware needed to obtain service from a packet-switching network. At the lowest level is the physical or electrical standard—the type of connector, the voltage levels, the meaning of each connector lead, and so on. The link level is representative of a procedure like that described in Secs. 1.2.2.3 and 1.2.2.4 (HDLC). This layer of protocol is

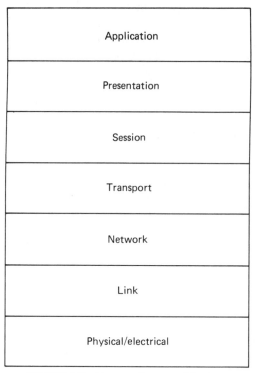

FIGURE 1-8 *Open systems architecture.*

used to move blocks of data reliably from data termination equipment (DTE) to date communication equipment (DCE). For our purposes, we can think of host computers as DTEs and packet switches as DCEs. The protocol hierarchy shown in Fig. 1.8 is in the DTE, some of it is reflected in the DCE, as shown in Fig. 1.9.

The network protocol is the set of procedures that permits the host to send and receive packets on the network. It typically includes provisions for addressing, network control messages, setting up of virtual circuits (if such services are available), and so on. Depending on the communication medium and network implementation, the services provided by any particular network may vary considerably.

Transport layer is intended to provide DTE-to-DTE services such as flow control, end-to-end error control, sequencing, duplicate detection, multiplexing, and so forth. Depending on the ultimate applications, the services required at this layer may range from virtual-circuit service to pure datagram service.

The session layer of protocol is intended to model the notion of controlled access to host services. This is the layer that implements user "LOGIN" to a system, for example. The presentation layer provides mechanisms for mapping between specific user terminals to generic or "virtual" terminal characteristics, for example. Finally, the application layer deals with specific applications such as text editing, message handling, query/response, and so on.

It would be a mistake to think that all store-and-forward networks can, should, or do provide exactly the same set of functions in the same set of protocol layers. At best, the open systems architecture provides a model against which to compare a network design, and this can be very helpful indeed when trying to determine opportunities for making different networks interoperate.

1.2.2.8 *Addressing*

At each protocol layer there is usually a need to identify at least the destination of a unit of data. This destination identification is needed because at nearly all layers except, perhaps, the physical layer, there may be more than one potential destination. The most common approach to addressing in systems with a layered architecture is to create a hierarchical address space. For example, a DTE (host) may be physically attached to a DCE (packet switch) via a shared local loop, so it has a unique link address. The interface between the packet

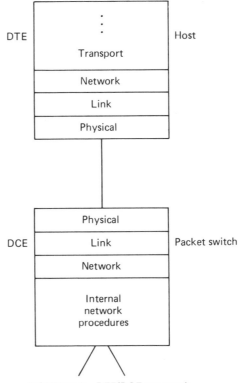

FIGURE 1-9 *DTE/DCE protocols.*

switch and the local loop is one of many in the system, so both the interface and the packet switch must have identifiers.

Within a host, there may reside a number of running programs or processes. These processes have logical input/output channels or ''ports'' which must be addressed if the data communicated across the network and through many protocol layers are to reach the desired destination. There may be more than one network, so these may need distinct identifiers to allow for multinetwork operation. In general, the hierarchical address schemes might partition the global address space into

NETWORK.HOST.PROCESS.PORT...

Discussions about addressing often lead to strong and lengthy arguments, owing to the confusion of three concepts: names, addresses, and routes. J. Shoch deserves credit for making clear the distinction among these concepts. A *name* is used to identify WHAT something is. It might identify a service (e.g., an electronic message service, inquiry retrieval service, LOGIN directory, etc.) or a particular host computer or a network. An *address* identifies WHERE something is (which switch a host is attached to within a net, for instance). A *route* identifies HOW TO GET THERE.

The assignments of names, addresses, and routes may be static or dynamic: usually more static on the name side and dynamic on the route side. Networks usually provide one of two types of addresses: virtual or physical addresses. In a physically addressed network, such as ARPANET, the address identifies which packet switch the host is attached to and which port of that packet switch. For instance, host number 1 at IMP number 22 (address 1/22) is named USC-ISIA (University of Southern California, Information Sciences Institute, host A). The ARPANET internally assigns routes to address 1/22 dynamically. If this host were reattached to a different IMP or port number, the host address would change.

In a virtually addressed network, the packet switches maintain correspondence tables between virtual addresses and physical ones. This permits hosts to be attached to more than one physical address while retaining only one virtual address. Alternatively, more than one virtual address can map to the same physical address, allowing several virtual hosts to be emulated by one physical host. The cost of such a scheme is larger routing tables in each packet switch.

1.2.2.9 Standards

A thorough exploration of the efforts now under way to standardize various aspects of packet-switching and data communication technology would require another chapter or even another book! The primary international organizations responsible for standards making are the International Telecommunications Union (ITU), which has a consultative committee for international telegraphy and telephone (CCITT). The CCITT is charged with developing voluntary international standards for communication. Another organization, the International Standards Organization (ISO), has responsibility for developing computer and data-processing standards.

Within U.S. national boundaries, such agencies as the American National Standards Institute and the National Bureau of Standards provide technical representation to CCITT and ISO as well as formulating standards for use by the federal government (in the form of Federal Information Processing Standards— FIPS—for example).

One of the most widely known packet-switching standards is the CCITT X.25 standard, which actually includes three protocol layers: electrical, link control, and network interface.

The lowest level, physical/electrical interface, in X.25 follows the CCITT X.21 digital interface standard. The second level is compatible with HDLC, although provision has been made for the older binary synchronous protocol (BISYNC) developed by IBM and representing a de facto standard for many years.

The third level of X.25 is the packet or virtual-circuit level. The basic procedures at level 3 of X.25 are aimed at the creation, termination, and use of virtual circuits which logically connect host computers to one another across a packet-switched network.

The basic X.25 packet format, illustrated in Fig. 1.10, shows how logical channels (virtual circuits) are identified in information packets which are moved from host to packet switch by means of the level 2 HDLC protocol.

As can be seen in Fig. 1.10, the packet level of X.25 uses a flow control scheme much like the one used at level 2. The P(R) and P(S) fields identify the sequence number next expected to be received and the one being sent, respectively. The "M" bit indicates that there are more data to be sent, which should be logically associated with this data packet. This permits users to send sequences of packets to the destination, which can be logically grouped together on receipt.

Logical channels are full duplex streams of packets. They are set up by requests from hosts to packet switches, using call setup packets, as illustrated in Fig. 1.11. The call setup packet provides 14 digits of addressing each for source and destination DTE. Destination-only addressing is allowed, although most systems will probably want to know "who is calling" before accepting an incoming call. Space has been provided for special facility requests, such as reverse charging, closed user groups, bandwidth requirements, and so on.

There are other special packets for accepting calls, sending out-of-band interrupts on a virtual circuit, closing virtual circuits, resetting virtual circuits, restarting the X.25 level 3 protocol, and starting or stopping flow on a given virtual circuit.

X.25 represents an important step in the direction of international standardization of packet-switching services. It has not, as of this writing, penetrated deeply into the computer manufacturing community but is getting considerable

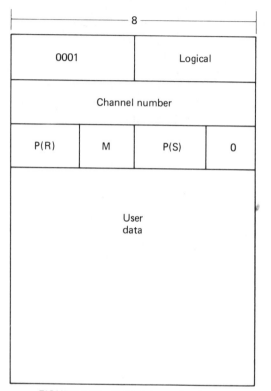

FIGURE 1-10 *X.25 data packet format.*

attention. In the research community, there is strong concern for the complexity of the protocol and its potential performance impact on real-time, transaction-oriented systems. An augmentation of the basic virtual circuit X.25 protocol to provide for a simpler datagram mode of operation is under consideration by CCITT. In the long run, both modes of operation are needed to support different types of applications.

1.2.3 Design Considerations

Apart from the many protocol-related issues raised in Sec. 1.2.2, there are a variety of theoretical and practical problems that must be solved to build packet-switched networks. Among the hardest problems are the *choice of topology* and *assignment of communication link capacity* for the system.

The capacity problem is influenced by the expected traffic demand and the routing discipline. The routing discipline is affected by the choice of topology; and the choice of topology is influenced by the traffic demand! So we have a classical optimization problem. In the literature, the problem is usually partitioned into four groups, arranged in increasing order of difficulty [58].

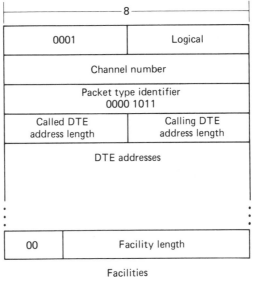

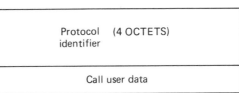

FIGURE 1-11 *X.25 call set-up packet.*

1. A capacity assignment problem (CA).

2. A flow assignment problem (FA).

3. A capacity and flow assignment problem (CFA).

4. A topology, capacity, and flow assignment problem (TCFA).

The *capacity assignment problem* can be simply stated:

> Given the topology, traffic requirement matrix, and the routing strategy, select a capacity assignment that minimizes the average delay given a cost function relating cost to units of capacity.

The minimization might be subject to a maximum cost, or perhaps throughput might be maximized, subject to delay; other formulations are possible.

The *flow assignment problem* is closely related to the problem of selecting a routing strategy since, for a given topology, a fixed routing assignment results in certain flows over each link in the network. If link capacity cannot be arbitrarily assigned but is constrained to fall into a fixed set of assigned values, the routing strategy has to be adjusted.

The *capacity and flow assignment problem* asks that:

Given the topology, traffic requirement matrix, and cost of capacity function, minimize cost over the various flow assignments which meet the traffic requirements and which limit delay to be less than some allowed maximum.

This problem usually exhibits a number of local minima, making global solutions very hard to find, even if simplifying assumptions such as linear cost for capacity are made.

The hardest problem is to solve all three problems at once:

Given a traffic requirement matrix, minimize the cost of capacity, subject to satisfying the traffic requirement, restricting average delay, and finding a feasible flow, assuring that the topology found also guarantees a network that is at least two-connected for reliability.

A summary of techniques for dealing with these problems may be found in [58] together with an extensive bibliography. In general, only heuristic methods have been identified for solving the most complex (TFCA) of these problems, such as the ''branch exchange'' method [13, 59], in which links are inserted or eliminated to see if cost can be reduced while continuing to meet all other requirements.

Another strategy is called the *cut saturation method* [60–62], in which set of links called ''cut set'' are examined to see if they are operating at capacity. The ''cut set'' of links, if removed, would disconnect the network into two or more parts. A cut is saturated if each link in the cut is operating at capacity. If the cut is not saturated, the algorithm can try to assign additional traffic on the unsaturated cut. Once saturation is reached, assign the most cost-effective link to join the two parts of the net separated by the cut and eliminate the least cost-effective link from each component.

1.3 OTHER COMMUNICATION MEDIA

Section 1.2 has dealt primarily with problems related to the design and implementation of store-and-forward packet-switching systems using dedicated communication media. There is another class of packet-switching systems exhibiting a different range of problems and behavior: multiaccess-media packet-switching systems.

The earliest example of such a system is the ALOHA system built by Abramson and Kuo at the University of Hawaii [63]. In this system a collection of microprocessor-controlled transmitters shared a single frequency band, F1, while the central computer transmitted on frequency band F2. Packets sent on F1 were acknowledged on F2. If a ''collision'' occurred and no acknowledgment was forthcoming, the transmitter would retransmit at some random time later. In this system, the terminals used the F1 band and the mainframe central computer used F2. Only F1 was subject to multiaccess collisions.

This appealing idea—the sharing of a common, multiple-access resource—has been extended to the satellite domain, as explored by Binder in this book, to coaxial cable, as explored by Metcalfe and Boggs in [64] and to packet radio as explored by Kahn et al. in [65, 66].

Although each of these media shares the common characteristic that multiple transmitters may be attempting to operate at once in the same channel, there are other characteristics that distinguish them and present challenges to the packet-switching system designer.

The ETHERNET uses a coaxial cable which is usually nor more than a kilometer or two in length. It may have a "dendritic" or treelike topology. The propagation delays in the cable are very short, so transceivers can be designed that detect collisions by comparing outgoing and incoming signals. All transmitters stop when collisions are detected.

In a satellite system, the delay for one-way propagation through a synchronous satellite is roughly 250 ms. The collision-detection mechanism for a satellite system requires the efficient use of a shared transponder channel, which suggests that the ground stations cooperate with one another to permit many packets to be "in flight" at a time. In Chapter 5, Binder describes how this can be achieved. Basically, each ground station can hear whatever is sent by the others, since the system is broadcast in nature. Each ground station can announce its channel requirements to the others and, since they all have the same information to work with, they can each independently compute the same schedule for access to the channel.

In the packet radio system, propagation delays fall between those in the ETHERNET and in the satellite case. However, the packet radio system is a store-and-forward network whose topology changes as the nodes move around. Thus, not all nodes hear every transmission. It is fair to say that the packet radio system combines all of the most challenging features of multiple-access and dedicated store-and-forward systems. The packet radio units can often detect when the common radio channel is in use and not transmit during that time (a "carrier sense multiple access" mode), but since some radios are hidden from others, this CSMA method cannot be relied upon to eliminate the effects of collision. The reader interested in learning more about this fascinating system is urged to read Refs. [64] and [65].

1.4 CONCLUSIONS

The first conclusion one can draw is that packet switching has proved itself as a useful and important computer communication technology. Second, there is clearly a great deal more to be said about the current state of the art and future directions than could be included in this brief chapter.

Third, the extension of packet-switching concepts to other media has already provided formidable challenges to analysts, system designers, and engineers. One can foresee the possibility of multiple satellite systems operating in asynchronous orbit, using packet radio techniques for satellite-to-satellite communication. The use of packet-switched satellites with spot-beam techniques will provide another challenging variation on the same theme.

REFERENCES

[1] ROBERTS, L. G., "The Evolution of Packet Switching," *Proceedings of the IEEE*, **66**(11), p. 1307, November 1978.

[2] BARAN, P., S. BOEHM, and P. SMITH, "Distributed Communications," *Memo RM-3097-PR*, The Rand Corporation, Santa Monica, Calif., 1964.

[3] KLEINROCK, L. *Communication Nets—Stockastic Message Flow and Delay*, McGraw-Hill Book Company, New York, 1964.

[4] MARILL, T., and L. G. ROBERTS, "Toward a Cooperative Network of Time-shared Computers," *Proceedings of the AFIPS Fall Joint Computer Conference*, **29**, 1966.

[5] DAVIES, D. W., K. A. BARLETT, R. A. SCANTLEBURY, and P. T. WILKINSON, "A Digital Communication Network for Computers Giving Rapid Response at Remote Terminals," *ACM Symposium on Operating Systems Principles*, 1967.

[6] DAVIES, D. W., "The Principles of a Data Communication Network for Computers and Remote Peripherals," Hardware Paper D11, *Proceedings of the IFIP*, Edinburgh, 1968.

[7] DAVIES, D. W., "Communications Networks to Serve Rapid-Response Computers," *Proceedings of the IFIP*, Edinburgh, 1968.

[8] SCANTLEBURY, R. A., P. T. WILKINSON, and K. A. BARTLETT, "The Design of a Message Switching Center for a Digital Communication Network," Hardware Paper D26, *Proceedings of the IFIP*, Edinburgh, 1968.

[9] ROBERTS, L. G., "Multiple Computer Networks and Intercomputer Communication," *ACM Symposium on Operating Systems Principles*, 1967.

[10] ROBERTS, L. G., and B. D. WESSLER, "Computer Network Development to Achieve Resource Sharing," *Proceedings of the AFIPS Spring Joint Computer Conference*, **36**, pp. 543–549, 1970.

[11] HEART, F. E., R. E. KAHN, S. M. ORNSTEIN, W. R. CROWTHER, and D. C. WALDEN, "The Interface Message Processor for the ARPA Computer Network," *Proceedings of the AFIPS Spring Joint Computer Conference*, **36**, pp. 551–567, 1970.

[12] BBN, "Specifications for the Interconnection of a Host and an IMP," *Report* 1822, Bolt, Beranek and Newman, Inc., Cambridge, Mass., 1969.

[13] FRANK, H., I. T. FRISCH, and W. CHOU, "Topological Considerations in the Design of the ARPA Computer Network," *Proceedings of the AFIPS Spring Joint Computer Conference*, **36,** 1970.

[14] KLEINROCK, L., "Optimization of Computer Networks for Various Cost Functions," *Proceedings of the AFIPS Spring Joint Computer Conference*, **36,** 1970.

[15] CARR, S., S. CROCKER, and V. CERF, "HOST–HOST Communication Protocol in the ARPA Network," *Proceedings of the AFIPS Spring Joint Computer Conference,* **36,** 1970.

[16] CROCKER, S. D., J. F. HEAFNER, R. M. METCALFE, and J. B. POSTEL, "Function-oriented Protocols for the ARPA Computer Network," *Proceedings of the AFIPS Spring Joint Computer Conference*, **40,** pp. 271–279, 1972.

[17] POSTEL, J., and J. FEINLER, eds., *The ARPANET Protocol Handbook*, Defense Communications Agency, Washington, D.C., January, 1978.

[18] ORNSTEIN, S. M., F. E. HEART, W. R. CROWTHER, H. K. RISING, S. B. RUSSELL, and A. MICHEL, "The Terminal IMP for the ARPA Computer Network," *Proceedings of the AFIPS Spring Joint Computer Conference,* **40,** pp. 243–254, 1972.

[19] MCQUILLAN, J. M., W. R. CROWTHER, B. P. COSELL, D. C. WALDEN, and F. E. HEART, "Improvements in the Design and Performance of the ARPA Network," *Proceedings of the AFIPS Fall Joint Computer Conference*, **41,** pp. 741–754, 1972.

[20] KAHN, R. E., "Resource-sharing Communication Networks," *Proceedings of the IEEE*, **60**(11), pp. 1397–1407, November 1972.

[21] KAHN, R. E., and W. R. CROWTHER, "Flow Control in a Resource-sharing Computer Network," *Proceedings of the 2nd Symposium on Optimization of Data Communication Systems,* 1971, pp. 108–116. [Also in *IEEE Transactions on Communications,* **COM-20**(3), pp. 539–546, March 1972.]

[22] WALDEN, D., "A System for Inter-process Communication in a Resource-sharing Computer Network," *Communications of the ACM*, **15**(4), pp. 221–230, April 1972.

[23] HEART, F., A. MCKENZIE, J. MCQUILLAN, and D. WALDEN, "ARPANET Completion Report," Defense Advanced Research Projects Agency, Information Processing Techniques Office, Washington, D.C., January 1978.

[24] THOMAS, R. H., and D. A. HENDERSON, "McRoss—A Multi-computer Programming System," *Proceedings of the AFIPS Spring Joint Computer Conference*, **40,** pp. 281–293, 1972.

[25] DAVIES, D. W., and D. L. A. BARBER, *Communication Networks for Computers*, John Wiley & Sons, Inc., New York, 1973, pp. 295–300.

[26] CHRETIEN, G. J., W. M. KONIG, and J. H. RECH, "The SITA Network," in *Computer Communication Networks* (R. L. Grimsdale and F. F. Kuo, eds.), NOORDHOFF, P., N. V. LEYDEN, Netherlands, NATO Advanced Study Institute Series, pp. 373–396, 1975.

[27] TYMES, L., "TYMNET—A Terminal Oriented Communications Network," *Proceedings of the AFIPS Spring Joint Computer Conference,* **38,** pp. 211–216, 1971.

[28] RINDE, J., "TYMNET: An Alternative to Packet Technology," *Proceedings of the*

3rd International Conference on Computer Communications, Toronto, pp. 268–273, August 1976.

[29] POUZIN, L., "Presentation and Major Design Aspects of the CYCLADES Network," *Proceedings of the 3rd Data Communications Symposium*, Tampa, Fla., pp. 80–85, November 1973.

[30] DESPRES, R. F., "A Packet Network with Graceful Saturated Operation," *Proceedings of the International Conference on Computer Communications,* Washington, D.C., pp. 345–351, October 1972.

[31] BARBER, D. L. A., "The EIN Project: The End of the Beginning," *Proceedings of the 4th International Conference on Computer Communications, Evolutions in Computer Communications*, pp. 33–38, September 1978.

[32] HADLEY, D. E., and B. R. SEXTON, "The British Post Office Experimental Packet Switched Service (EPSS)—A Review of Development and Operational Experience," *Proceedings of the 4th International Conference on Computer Communications,* pp. 97–102, September 1978.

[33] DANET, A., R. DESPRÈS, A. LEREST, G. PICKON, and S. RITZENTHALER, "The French Public Packet Switching Service: The TRANSPAC Network," *Proceedings of the 3rd International Conference on Computer Communications*, Toronto, August 1976.

[34] BERTIN, C., J. C. ADAM, P. GUINAUDEAU, and Y. MATRAS, "Development of a Packet Switching Node Prior to Opening of the French PTT Network, to Help Future Users Debug Their Network Access Software," *Proceedings of the 4th International Conference on Computer Communications*, pp. 589–594, September 1978.

[35] DAVIES, G. W. P., J. Y. GRESSER, P. T. F. KELLY, and J. R. THOMAS, "The EURONET Telecommunication and Information Network," *Proceedings of the 4th International Conference on Computer Communications*, pp. 189–194, September 1978.

[36] MATSUMOTO, M., J. MIZUSAWA, and H. OHNISHI, "DDX Packet Switched Network and Its Technology," *Proceedings of the 4th International Conference on Computer Communications,* pp. 583–588, September 1978.

[37] MCQUILLAN, J. M., and V. G. CERF, "A Practical View of Computer Communications Protocols," *IEEE Publishing Services, EHO* 137-0, 1978.

[38] SUNSHINE, C., "Interprocess Communication Protocols for Computer Networks," *Digital Systems Lab Technical Report* 105, (Ph.D. thesis, Stanford University), December 1975.

[39] ISO, "High Level Data Link Control (HDLC)," *DIS* 3309.2 and *DIS* 4335, International Organization for Standardization, Geneva.

[40] DAVIES, D. W., "Flow Control and Congestion Control," *COMNET* 77, *Proceedings of the John von Neumann Society*, Budapest, Hungary, pp. 17–36, September 1977.

[41] IRLAND, M., "Simulation of CIGALE," *Proceedings of the 4th Data Communications Symposium,* Quebec City, Canada, pp. 5–13, October 1975.

[42] RAUBOLD, E., and J. HAENLE, "A Method of Deadlock-free Resource Allocation and Flow Control in Packet Networks," *Proceedings of the 3rd International Conference on Computer Communications*, Toronto, Canada, pp. 483–487, August 1976.

[43] POUZIN, L., "Flow Control in Data Networks: Methods and Tools," *Proceedings of the 3rd International Conference on Computer Communications*, Toronto, Canada, pp. 467–474, August 1976.

[44] POUZIN, L., and H. ZIMMERMANN, "A Tutorial on Protocols," *Proceedings of the IEEE, Special Issue on Packet Communication Networks*, **66**(11), pp. 1346–1370, November 1978.

[45] KLEINROCK, L., "Principles and Lessons in Packet Communications," *Proceedings of the IEEE, Special Issue on Packet Communication Networks*, **66**(11), pp. 1320–1329, November 1978.

[46] KLEINROCK, L., "On Flow Control," *Proceedings of the International Conference on Communications*, Toronto, Canada, pp. 27.2-1 to 27.2-5, June 1978.

[47] KAHN, R. E., and W. R. CROWTHER, "Flow Control in a Resource-sharing Computer Network," *Proceedings of the Second IEEE Symposium on Problems in Optimization of Data Communication Systems*, Palo Alto, Calif., October 1971, pp. 108–116. [Reprinted in *IEEE Transactions on Communications*, **COM-22**(6), pp. 539–546, June 1972.]

[48] OPDERBECK, H., and L. KLEINROCK, "The Influence of Control Procedures on the Performance of Packet-switched Networks," *National Telecommunications Conference Record,* San Diego, Calif., pp. 810–817, December 1974.

[49] DANTHINE, A., and E. ESCHENAUER, "Influence on Packet Node Behavior of the Internode Protocol," *IEEE Transactions on Communications*, **COM-24**(6), pp. 606–614, June 1976.

[50] NAYLOR, W., "A Loop-free Adaptive Routing Algorithm for Packet-switched Networks," *Proceedings of the 4th Data Communications Symposium*, Quebec City, Canada, pp. 7.9–7.14, October 1975.

[51] GALLAGER, R., "A Minimum Delay Routing Algorithm Using Distributed Computation," *IEEE Transactions on Communications*, **COM-25**(1), pp. 73–85, January 1977.

[52] DAVIES, D. W., "The Control of Congestion in Packet Switching Networks," *IEEE Transactions on Communications*, **COM-20**, pp. 546–550, June 1972.

[53] FULTZ, G. L., and L. KLEINROCK, "Adaptive Routing Techniques for Store and Forward Computer Communication Networks," *Proceedings of the International Conference on Communications*, Montreal, Canada, pp. 39-1 to 39-8, June 1971.

[54] RINDE, J., "Routing and Control in a Centrally Directed Network," *Proceedings of the AFIPS National Computer Conference*, pp. 603–608, June 1977.

[55] McQUILLAN, J. M., "Routing Algorithms for Computer Networks—A Survey," *Proceedings of the National Telecommunications Conference*, pp. 28:1-1 to 28:1-6, December 1977.

[56] McQuillan, J. M., "Adaptive Routing Algorithms for Distributed Computer Networks," *BBN Report* 2831, (Ph.D. thesis, Harvard University), May 1974.

[57] Grange, J. L., and M. Gien, eds., "Flow Control in Computer Networks," *Proceedings of the International Symposium on Flow Control in Computer Networks*, Versailles, France, February 12–14, 1979, North-Holland Publishing Co., New York, 1979.

[58] Inose, H., and T. Saito, "Theoretical Aspects in the Analysis and Synthesis of Packet Communication Networks," *Proceedings of the IEEE, Special Issue on Packet Communication Networks*, **66**(11), pp. 1409–1422, November 1978.

[59] Stieglitz, K., P. Wiener, and D. J. Kleitman, "The Design of Minimum Cost Survivable Networks," *IEEE Transactions on Circuit Theory*, **CT-16**(11).

[60] Frank, H., R. E. Kahn, and L. Kleinrock, "Computer Communication Network Design—Experience with Theory and Practice," *Proceedings of the AFIPS Spring Joint Computer Conference*, **40,** pp. 255–270, May 1972.

[61] Boorstyn, R. R., and H. Frank, "Large Scale Network Topological Optimization," *IEEE Transactions on Communications*, **COM-25**(1), pp. 29–47, January 1977.

[62] Gerla, M., H. Frank, W. Chou, and J. Eckl, "A Cut Saturation Algorithm for Topological Design of Packet Switched Communication Networks," *Proceedings of the National Telecommunications Conference*, pp. 1074–1085, December 1974.

[63] Abramson, N., "The ALOHA System," in *Computer-Communication Networks* (N. Abramson and F. F. Kuo, eds.), Prentice-Hall, Inc., Englewood Cliffs, N.J., pp. 501–518, 1973.

[64] Metcalfe, R. M., and D. R. Boggs, "ETHERNET: Distributed Packet Switching for Local Computer Networks," *Communications of the ACM*, **19**(7), pp. 395–404, July 1976.

[65] Kahn, R. E., "The Organization of Computer Resources into a Packet Radio Network," *IEEE Transactions on Communications*, **COM-25**(1) January 1977.

[66] Kahn, R. E., S. A. Gronemeyer, J. Burchfiel, and R. C. Kunzelman, "Advances in Packet Radio Technology," *Proceedings of the IEEE*, **66**(11), November 1978.

However, it is important to note that acknowledgment for error-control purposes is *not* identical to granting new flow-control credits. In protocols such as X.25 (see Sec. 2.4.4), where the window size must remain fixed, acknowledgments and new credits are synonymous. In more flexible protocols, such as TCP (see Sec. 2.4.1), acknowledgments and credits are independent. A packet may be acknowledged without granting new credit by advancing the acknowledgment sequence number and reducing the window size by a corresponding amount, thus leaving the upper edge of the window in a fixed position. New credits may be granted without acknowledging any received packet by increasing the window size but leaving the acknowledgment sequence number unchanged.

The time at which to grant new credits and the number of credits to allow are important factors in protocol performance. If too many credits are granted, arriving packets may have to be discarded for lack of buffer space, causing excessive retransmissions. Hence, the granting of credits is often tied to the availability of buffer space. A "conservative" flow-control strategy delays advancing the window until buffers for the promised space are available [11, 36].

But conservatism has its own costs. By limiting the window size, it may constrain the sender to a lower transmission rate than the receiver could support [4]. Under ideal conditions, when packets arrive at regular intervals and in order, minimal buffering is needed to handle an arbitrarily large window size and throughput. Under these circumstances, an "optimistic" flow-control strategy returning a larger window size than the buffer space available may improve performance. These questions are discussed further in Sec. 2.3.1.

Flow control, which is an end-to-end function between sending and receiving portions of a transport protocol, should not be confused with *congestion control*, which is the mechanism by which the communication network protects itself from excessive traffic (see Chapter 4). Congestion control is needed in addition to flow control because a combination of connections, each within its own flow-control constraints, may together exceed the capacity of the network. Although flow-control constraints are normally imposed by the receiver, the sending transport station may also limit the flow over one connection for fairness considerations (i.e., to provide a fair share of service to other connections).

Although the cost of memory continues to drop, limited buffer space remains a fact of life in protocol design. Transport protocols require significant buffer space for two main purposes: storing out-of-order arrivals and matching uneven sending and receiving rates. When packets arrive out of order, it is desirable to store them until their predecessors arrive rather than discarding them and requiring retransmission from the source. Mismatched scheduling of sender and receiver, variable transmission delays, and differing production and consumption rates all lead to uneven arrival and receiver acceptance times which require buffering to prevent unnecessary blocking. Since flow control is closely tied to buffer availability, the amount of buffer space needed for efficient operation under different circumstances is an important factor in protocol performance. This is discussed further in Sec. 2.3.1.3.

2.2.6 Synchronization

Since delay is highly variable in a packet-switching network, packets may arrive with much different timing than that in which they were submitted, or even out of order. Sequence numbers allow the receiver to reestablish the proper order of packets but not their exact relative timing. Some applications with real-time constraints, such as packetized speech, graphics, or some forms of teleconferencing, may require data to be delivered with correct timing. This requires an addition of a *time stamp* to the packet header information, giving the time at which the packet was produced or emitted. The time stamp is then used by the receiving transport protocol to deliver packets at the proper real time. The clocks at the receiver and the sender must be running at the same rates, although not necessarily showing the same time, in order for the correct time spacing of packets to be reproduced. The delay in delivering the first packet determines the delay for all succeeding packets and the amount by which the delivery time of the data stream lags the production time [10].

Because transmission delay varies widely, it is possible that a packet will not have arrived at its destination at the moment it should be delivered. To minimize this difficulty, the receiver normally delays a moderate amount after receiving the first packet of a real-time data stream in order to provide "time buffering." Packet-switching networks may have to adopt some form of path setup or resource allocation mechanisms to support such traffic within acceptable delay bounds.

In some cases, the proper timing of data may be more important than its completeness (i.e., in packet speech). In these cases time stamps may completely control the acceptance and delivery of information, while sequence numbers are omitted and long-delayed packets are simply dropped. The normal acknowledgment and retransmission mechanisms may be dropped if the application can tolerate occasional lost packets [10].

Another requirement for timing information comes when multiple data streams must be synchronized with each other. This might occur, for example, in multimedia teleconferencing when speech and text display or graphics must be transmitted over parallel data streams and replayed in proper synchronization. This requirement again calls for the introduction of time stamps or some other synchronization markers into the control information of each data stream.

2.2.7 Priority

The ability to send a small amount of data or an attention signal that sidesteps the normal data stream is a useful communication facility found in many interprocess communication schemes. To provide this facility over a network, the transport protocol must provide an "out-of-band" channel which is not constrained by the flow-control mechanisms applied to normal data. This may be achieved by a special "interrupt" type of control packet, which carries a small amount of data (e.g., 8 bits in X.25) or an attention signal. The interrupt information may also be sent along with a normal data packet if one is pending. The sending protocol requests priority transmission from the transmission medium for such packets if available, and the receiving transport protocol processes them as soon as they arrive. The interrupt or out-of-band signal is then passed to the receiving process to handle appropriately.

In addition to carrying a small amount of interrupt information, the out-of-band signal may also indicate where in the normal data stream the signal was generated. This is useful when the action prompted by the signal involves the data stream as in a "flush input" request. The out-of-band signal may itself carry a reference to the data stream, or a special "mark" code corresponding to a signal with no reference may be sent in the data stream [19]. In other cases, the signal has a meaning independent of the data stream as in an "are you there?" request, and no reference is needed.

A typical use of such out-of-band signals is for a sender to gain the attention of a receiver who has been slow in accepting or processing previously sent data. Since the interrupt signal goes ahead of any data that may be waiting, it hopefully gains the prompt attention of the receiver. In this case, the receiver may wish to purge or discard data up to the point at which the interrupt was generated or may enter some special fast scanning mode for rapidly examining waiting data (see Chapter 3). Since the desired processing of interrupts may vary from application to application, transport protocols themselves do not normally include such additional processing of interrupts. However, owing to the frequent utility of the "purge" operation in association with interrupts, this facility may be optionally requested along with an interrupt in some protocols.

2.2.8 Security

Although sequence numbers and checksums provide protection against normal transmission-medium behavior, they do not protect against "malicious intruders" who can examine data in transit, replay old data at arbitrary times, or fabricate spurious data. Protection against these and related difficulties is normally provided by encrypting data to be transmitted. This requires establishment of a common encryption key at both sender and receiver before data transfer begins. Authorization for communication and distribution of the keys must themselves be done in a secure fashion. Once the keys are distributed, all data may be encrypted while only necessary control information, such as addresses and sequence numbers, appears in the clear. When damaged or spurious information is decrypted by the receiver, its checksum or sequence number will be incorrect, allowing it to be discarded. Further discussion of this topic may be found in Chapter 9.

2.2.9 Initialization and Crash Recovery

Several of the mechanisms described above, such as flow-control windows, encryption keys, and particularly sequence numbers, require proper initialization between the two transport stations supporting a conversation. It is vital that the receiving module of one transport protocol and the sending module of the other transport protocol coordinate properly the sequence numbers to be used in transmitting and accepting packets. Since a TS needs a significant amount of state information and processing to support each conversation, it is desirable to maintain this information only while partners are actively communicating, and to release TS resources when the conversation is finished.

This leads to the idea of establishing a connection in order to initialize control information necessary for reliable communication between two transport stations. The connection must be established (control information initialized) before data communication can begin and must be terminated (TS resources released) when communication is finished. Special control packets for establishing and terminating connections are part of most transport protocols. Other functions, such as the name lookup described in Sec. 2.2.3, may also be performed during connection establishment.

Although transport protocols are able to recover from the full range of transmission-medium errors, they must also handle a failure by one or both transport stations. When the computer supporting a TS crashes and is restarted, some or all memory of connections in progress may have been lost. Under some circumstances, it may not be possible to avoid either loss or duplication of data that were in transit at the time of failure. However, the newly restarted TS must cooperate with the TSs on the other side of previously active connections to signal the failure and then restart reliable communications. Mechanisms for connection establishment, termination, and crash recovery are discussed further in Sec. 2.3.

2.2.10 Internetworking

As networks proliferate it becomes increasingly desirable for users on different nets to be able to interact. Although the general problems of network interconnection are beyond the scope of this chapter, we will consider the basic alternatives for providing virtual-circuit service between users on different networks.

If networks already have or are willing to adopt a common transport protocol, a fully end-to-end service may be provided with minimum requirements on the interface or "gateway" between networks. Only basic datagram facilities are needed across nets, since the common transport stations on either side provide the additional functions, just as in a single net. This "endpoint" approach provides full flexibility of alternate routing and error tolerance at all points between the end users, including the gateways. It has been successfully employed in ARPANET and the European Informatics Network [14].

If it is not possible to adopt a common protocol, each net maintains its own local protocol and the gateway is required to join the two virtual circuits to each other. This "stepwise" approach leads to a more complex and costly gateway, and may not be fully successful if incompatible features (e.g., for priority or flow control) occur in the two nets. The resulting service is not fully end to end, but rather the concatenation of independent virtual-circuit segments. Nevertheless, it does allow two dissimilar nets to interconnect with some degree of success, and may have some advantages for accounting and congestion control that appeal to public networks. A more complete treatment of these issues may be found in [18, 37, 40].

2.2.11 Multidestination Communication

Most of the protocol mechanisms discussed above are suitable for point-to-point communication between two parties. With the advent of broadcast communication technology using satellites, radio, and cables, it becomes possible for many or all computers on the network to hear a transmission. Broadcast or *multidestination* communication is useful in such applications as electronic mail (the same message may go to many people) or distributed systems where bids for service or action commands may be broadcast to many servers. Without knowing the exact number or even the identities of all destinations, the normal sequencing and acknowledgment mechanisms used in point-to-point transport protocols are not applicable. Effective use of broadcast technology and the feasibility of reliable multidestination communication remain important research questions.

2.3 PROTOCOL MODELING AND ANALYSIS

Section 2.2 described the problems that a transport protocol must solve and the mechanisms used in dealing with those problems. This section discusses the performance of transport protocols in greater detail and introduces techniques for predicting or optimizing protocol performance. The two main aspects of protocol performance are efficiency and reliability. *Efficiency* concerns throughput, delay, buffering requirements, overhead, and other quantitative measures. *Reliability* concerns the correct operation of the protocol in managing connections and transferring data.

In both areas, transmission-medium characteristics play an important role in determining protocol performance. To avoid overly complex models and successfully analyze transport protocol performance, transmission-medium behavior must be abstracted into a small set of relevant characteristics. For example, rather than modeling the detailed store-and-forward delay of the packet as it travels through successive switching nodes of the network, end-to-end delay may be modeled as a random variable coming from a particular probability distribution. This process of abstraction transforms a detailed transmission medium into a "black box" with specified characteristics which connects two transport stations. The relevant characteristics include delay distribution (including maximum packet lifetime), bandwidth, packet-size limits, and probability of loss, damage, or duplication of packets.

A basic task in protocol design or analysis is specification. As a minimum, protocols must be clearly described for purposes of human understanding and implementation. If protocol performance is to be analyzed beyond debugging errors after they occur, suitable specifications of both the protocol and the services it is intended to provide must be developed to facilitate simulation, correctness proofs, exhaustive case studies, and other forms of analysis [20, 35, 38]. Since the questions to be answered and techniques used to answer them are quite different for reliability and efficiency, these two areas are considered separately in Secs. 2.3.1 and 2.3.2.

2.3.1 Efficiency

The main efficiency performance measures of interest are traditionally throughput and delay. For transport protocols, *throughput* is the transmission rate of useful data between processes, excluding any control information or retransmissions that the protocol requires. *Delay* is the time from starting to transmit a packet at the sender to successful arrival of the entire packet at the receiver, or arrival of an acknowledgment at the sender in the case of round-trip delay. Other measures of interest include number of retransmissions, line efficiency (the ratio of useful traffic to total traffic), and buffer requirements. Although much has been written concerning these problems within communication networks, very little research has been reported on the efficiency of transport protocols.

Transport protocol performance is limited on one side by transmission-medium characteristics and on the other side by user process behavior. Within these constraints, the main protocol parameters that determine performance are retransmission interval, flow-control strategy, buffering, acknowledgment scheme, and packet size. Understanding how these parameters affect performance and determining optimal values for them is the purpose of this section.

We will focus on performance determining factors for a single end-to-end connection rather than the competition for resources among many connections. Although the management of demand from many sources is a major problem within transmission networks, a transport station must also try to share its resources fairly among all connections [11, 23]. Controls to achieve this are applied in addition to the perconnection controls we shall discuss.

Two basic features of transport protocol operation largely govern protocol efficiency: overhead and retransmission. Overhead results from the control information, including checksum, address, sequence number, length, window, acknowledgment, and so on, which must be carried in packet headers or separate control packets to achieve reliable communication. These header fields provide useful services and reliability but lead to increased delay and reduced throughput. Retransmission leads to a different kind of overhead, in that the data group itself must be transmitted more than once, thereby using up channel capacity. Flow control causes a third type of degradation, in that the channel is forced to remain idle when it could be carrying useful data because of the flow-control constraints. Each of these basic factors is discussed in a following section.

2.3.1.1 Packet Size

In transmitting large amounts of information between processes, a transport protocol may package the data in a varying number of packets. Transmission delay in a store-and-forward network will be lower for smaller packets because the transmission time on each hop between switching nodes is proportional to the packet length [11] (although some networks either fragment or combine submitted packets before internal transmission). Unfortunately, overhead for short packets increases, since each packet carries a fixed-length header, and more acknowledgment and general processing for the same amount of data will be necessary. Hence, maximum throughput attainable decreases while line efficiency (and total cost in bits transmitted) increases for shorter packets. Longer packets reduce overhead and allow higher throughput at the cost of increased delay [24, 36].

To illustrate some of these trade-offs, Fig. 2.4 shows the total time to transmit a large block of information using different packet sizes, assuming typical network characteristics and a delay proportional to packet length. Using the smallest packets, throughput is so low that total delay is high. For very large packets the increasing delay per packet also leads to high total delay. The optimal value for this application is an intermediate packet size.

Other applications may have other priorities for cost, throughput, and delay performance. Real-time or interactive applications may select short packets to achieve low delay at somewhat higher cost. Applications desiring minimum cost or maximum throughput and willing to tolerate larger delays may use long packets [11]. Hence, to provide optimal service the transport protocol must be given an indication of the type of performance the user desires.

2.3.1.2 Retransmission

As described in Sec. 2.2, transport protocols overcome loss or damage of packets in the transmission medium by retransmitting the packets if no positive acknowledgment is received. The interval R at which packets are retransmitted has a major impact on protocol efficiency. In general, a large R allows higher

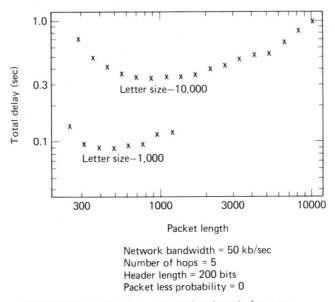

Network bandwidth = 50 kb/sec
Number of hops = 5
Header length = 200 bits
Packet less probability = 0

FIGURE 2-4 *Total delay vs packet length for two block (letter) sizes.*

throughput, since no bandwidth is "wasted" on unnecessary retransmission, while a small R reduces mean delay because lost or damaged packets are retransmitted sooner.

To quantify these general observations, packet transmission delay through the network may be modeled as a probability density function $f(t)$, which typically has a high peak around the nominal delay and a long tail representing the possibility of occasional long delays. The probability LS of lost or damaged packets can be included in $f(t)$ as an impulse at $t = $ infinity with value LS (the probability that a packet never arrives).

The function $f(t)$ and its associated cumulative distribution $F(t)$ model the delay for a single transmission of the packet, while we wish to find the probability distribution for the first *successful* delivery of possibly many retransmissions, called $G(t)$. Assuming that packets are retransmitted at intervals R and that $f(t)$ is identical for each retransmission of a packet, $G(t)$ is given by the following expression:

$$G(t) = \text{Prob}\{\text{at least one successful delivery by time } t\}$$

$$= 1 - \text{Prob}\{\text{no success by time } t\}$$

$$= 1 - \prod_{i=0}^{n-1} [1 - F(t - i \cdot R)] \qquad n = \lceil t/R \rceil$$

52

$G(t)$ provides the basis for computing the mean delay until first successful delivery and the mean number of retransmissions required. This also gives a measure of the mean throughput attainable, which is proportional to the inverse of the number of retransmissions [36].

Figure 2.5 shows a plot of delay versus throughput for varying retransmission interval R and a typical $f(t)$ with mean of 1. Small R yield points toward the left of the curves and large R yield points toward the right. High packet-loss probabilities LS are used for a more graphic illustration. The definite "knee" in the curves for nonzero LS indicates an optimum value of R. For larger R, delay is increased with little savings in throughput. For smaller R, throughput is reduced (because of excessive retransmission) with little improvement in delay. This optimal value of R occurs for $R = t$ such that the $f(t)$ curve indicates that most single transmissions would have arrived by this time if they were going to arrive.

If the transport protocol is sequencing packets as well as doing error correction, the assumption of independent identically distributed transmission delays for successive packets must be modified. This is because loss of a packet or its acknowledgment causes acknowledgment of all subsequent packets to be delayed until the earlier error is corrected, even though other packets are successfully received. In this case, negative acknowledgments may improve performance by forcing prompt retransmission of the damaged packet. Even with negative acknowledgment, the general effect of sequencing is to increase apparent delay so that a larger R should be used for optimal performance. The amount of this increase depends on the variance in $f(t)$ and hence the amount that packets are likely to arrive out of sequence [36].

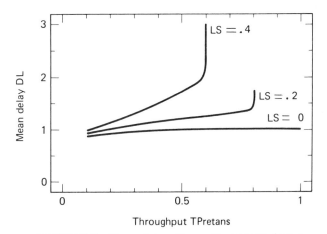

FIGURE 2-5 *Mean delay DL vs throughput factor TPretrans for Erlangian network transmission delay with mean = 1 and k = 16.*

2.3.1.3 Flow Control and Buffering

Transmission of new packets from a sender is limited by the number of credits granted by the receiver. Since round-trip delay is typically an order of magnitude greater than host-to-packet-switch transmission time in a packet-switching network, several packets must be in transit simultaneously to achieve high throughput. On the other hand, the receiver may wish to limit the sender's transmission rate by granting few credits. In either case, the number of credits or window size to be used to achieve the desired throughput must be determined.

A simple closed queueing model with the transmitter as one server and the network and receiver as the other server provides a first-order answer to this question. Service time 1 at the transmitter (T_{local}) is the host-to-network transmission time for a packet, while service time 2 (T_{net}) includes propagation of a packet through the network, receiver processing, and return of an acknowledgment, or approximately the round-trip delay. The second server is an infinite server, since packets can proceed in parallel through the network (see Fig. 2.6). The window size N_{win} defines the number of customers (packets) in the system. Let N be the ratio of service time 2 to service time 1.

The utilization of server 1 is the fraction of time that the transmitter is active with a given window size and hence provides a good indication of throughput attainable. Standard results from queuing theory show that throughput rises linearly with window size to a maximum value at a window size of N when round-trip delays are fairly constant [2, 36]. A somewhat larger window size will

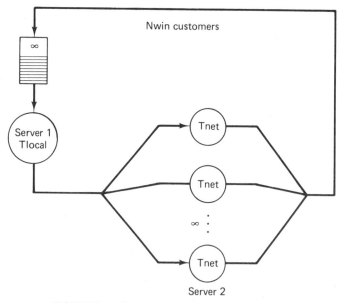

FIGURE 2-6 *Queueing model of flow control.*

be required to obtain maximum throughput if the round-trip delay is highly variable. To limit the throughput to a fraction F of the nominal bandwidth available, a window size of $F \cdot N$ should be used.

As long as packet loss and damage probabilities remain low, the foregoing analysis shows that throughput will be flow-control-limited by a small window size. In networks where transmission errors are more likely, throughput may become retransmission-limited because retransmissions of pending packets have priority over new transmissions. In general, achievable throughput will be the minimum due to either flow control or retransmission constraints. Further transmission restrictions may be imposed by the source transport station in order to share its communication resources fairly among all connections.

As noted in Sec. 2.2.5, flow-control policy is often tied to buffer availability. The amount of destination buffer space required for efficient operation depends on the relative rates and timing of packet arrival and consumption. Let M be the ratio of arrival rate to consumption rate. If $M \gg 1$, simple queueing models show that no matter how many buffers are available, nearly all will be filled in the steady state, and most arriving packets will have to be discarded. Throughput is limited by the receiver's acceptance rate, and a conservative strategy with small window size and few buffers will avoid wasting resources. If $M \ll 1$, very few packets will be discarded and little buffer space is needed. Throughput is limited by the sender's production rate.

When $M = 1$, the smoothness or relative timing of packet arrival and consumption becomes the dominating factor. The transmission system may be the main contributor to variation in delays, or the sender and receiver may themselves produce or consume packets at uneven rates (e.g., because of periodic scheduling in multiprogramming systems). Smooth arrival and consumption behavior requires minimal buffering. More uneven behavior requires more buffering for arriving packets, and a conservative policy with window size tied to buffer availability is more effective.

2.3.2 Reliability

The object of reliability analysis is to demonstrate that a protocol meets specified performance goals concerning correct operation. This requires a clear formulation of performance goals which cover the features of operation to be verified, such as proper delivery of data and avoidance of deadlocks. Assumptions about transmission-medium characteristics and protocol mechanisms must also be specified. From this starting point, a proof or convincing demonstration that the protocol meets the desired performance goals must be constructed.

Since the data-transfer and connection management elements of transport protocols address different problems, they are frequently treated separately. Once a connection is established, the protocol operates cyclically, transmitting one data packet after another, and the main performance goals concern correct data transfer. In connection establishment, on the other hand, the objective is to move from an unsynchronized initial state to a properly synchronized final state (e.g., sequence numbers properly initialized). Other connection management functions, such as terminating connections and recovering from failures, also involve transition from an initial state to a desired final state. Hence data transfer and connection management are treated in separate sections below.

2.3.2.1 Data Transfer

The basic model of data transfer through a transport protocol is a stream of data, provided by a source process, which are packaged into packets by the source transport protocol, sent through a transmission medium, and reconstituted into a stream of data for the destination process (see Fig. 2.7). Since the main cause of difficulties is transmission-medium behavior, we shall assume that the packetizing and reassembly functions work properly and focus on any differences in the delivered packet stream from the submitted packet stream.

We shall call the protocol elements on the sending side a "sending discipline" and those on the receiving side a "receiving discipline." Of course, a full duplex connection has sending and receiving disciplines on each side, and for greater efficiency, acknowledgment information may be carried along with data in the reverse direction. However, for purposes of analysis, the two directions of information flow may be considered logically separate.

Detailed performance goals may be formulated in terms of the submitted and delivered stream of packets [34]. These concern the possibility for damage, loss, duplication, or out-of-order delivery of packets by the transmission medium. Each submitted packet must not be lost (not delivered), delivered in a damaged condition, delivered more than once, or delivered in a different order than submitted.

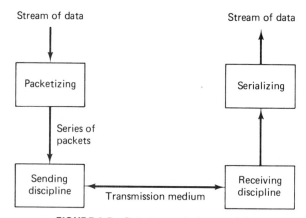

FIGURE 2-7 Data transmission model.

The sending and receiving disciplines may be specified as follows:

SENDING DISCIPLINE

The sending discipline maintains a variable called *next sequence number* (NSN). Each packet submitted has NSN attached and then NSN is advanced to its successor.[1] The packet with NSN and a checksum is transmitted, a timer is started, and a copy retained in a "pending" queue.

Arriving acknowledgement packets (ACKs) are checked for errors and damaged ones are discarded. ACKs for discarded packets are ignored.

When an ACK referencing the sequence number of a pending packet is received, the pending packet is discarded (and the sender notified of success). If no ACK is received for a pending packet within the retransmission interval R, the pending packet is retransmitted and the timer is restarted.

RECEIVING DISCIPLINE

The receiving discipline maintains a variable called the *expected sequence number* (ESN). Each packet received is checked for errors and discarded if damaged. If not damaged, the packet sequence number (PSN) is compared with ESN and action is taken as follows:

If less, transmit an ACK referencing PSN and discard the packet as a duplicate.

If equal, transmit an ACK, deliver the packet to the process, and advance ESN to its successor.

If greater, discard the packet as out of order.[2]

The foregoing protocol definitions assume that all damage to packets or acknowledgments will be detected. In fact, it is not possible to detect all transmission errors, resulting in occasional acceptance of a faulty packet or

---

[1] The simplest and most widely used successor function is to increment by one, although others may be used based on the length (in bytes or other units) of each packet.

[2] For greater efficiency, the receiving discipline may choose to keep some number of out-of-order packets for a time.

ACK. However, the probability of an undetected error can be made extremely small by the use of modest-length checksums [13], so we will ignore this source of error.

We also assume that the protocol is properly initialized (i.e., the connection is established). This means that NSN in the sending discipline is equal to ESN in the receiving discipline on the other side of the connection and that no data packets have been sent. Connection establishment is itself a difficult problem discussed later in this section.

The definitions also assume an infinite sequence number space and that the protocol will go on trying to retransmit an unacknowledged packet forever. Relaxation of these assumptions is discussed below. Flow-control constraints and the possible use of negative acknowledgments are also ignored, since they will affect the efficiency but not the correct operation of the protocol.

With these assumptions in mind, we construct an informal proof that the performance goals are met by considering each possible type of error.

- *Duplication.* No duplicate packet generated by the sending discipline or the transmission medium will ever be delivered to the receiving process because the receiving discipline advances its ESN after delivering the first copy. Hence, all other copies will be detected as old duplicates and discarded by the receiving discipline.

- *Damage.* Any packet damaged by the transmission medium will be detected and discarded by the protocol (this is an assumption).

- *Loss.* Any data packet lost by the transmission medium will not be acknowledged and hence will be retransmitted by the sending discipline. A lost acknowledgment will result in retransmission of the data packet by the sending discpline and a later acknowledgment from the receiving discipline.

- *Sequencing.* If a packet arrives at the receiving discipline before one of its predecessors, the ESN check will cause it to be discarded. Only the next packet in order can be accepted by the receiving discipline for delivery.

In reality, sequence numbers must be finite in length and hence eventually wrap around to previously used values. If packets could persist an arbitrarily long time in the transmission medium, old packets could arrive at the receiving discipline and be accepted instead of new packets with the same sequence numbers. Acknowledgments may also be delayed, causing the sending discipline to think a packet has been transmitted successfully when in fact it has not been. This leads to the constraint expressed in Sec. 2.2—that sequence numbers must not wrap around within a maximum packet lifetime. More specifically, a data packet must not be transmitted with a given sequence number until any previous data packet or acknowledgments carrying that sequence number are certain to be absent from the transmission medium. This is normally ensured by providing a large enough sequence number size for the highest anticipated transmission rate and packet lifetime. A more formal derivation of this constraint may be found in [26].

Failure Consequences: The foregoing analysis assumes that sending and receiving disciplines continue to operate correctly without loss of memory throughout the lifetime of a connection. It is also important to consider the consequences when one side of a connection fails with loss of memory, as would occur in a host crash. Under these circumstances, packets that have been transmitted but not yet acknowledged will lead to either loss or duplication of information.

The details of this situation are as follows. Suppose that a sending discipline A has accepted a packet and transmitted it but has not yet received an acknowledgment or reported successful delivery to its user. If the receiving discipline B has accepted the packet and then fails and restarts with an incorrect ESN, it may accept the packet a second time. Alternatively, B may reject all packets after restarting and signal its predicament to A. If A resends the packet after recovery is complete, it will again be delivered twice. If A chooses not to resend the packet, it may never have been delivered if B did not receive it before failing. Failure of the sending dicipline results in a similar set of cases, leading either to duplicate delivery or failure to deliver a packet. Deadlock is another possible failure consequence, since no packets will be accepted by the receiving discipline if NSN and ESN are not properly synchronized.

This analysis shows a fundamental limitation of transport protocols. As long as they continue to function normally, they successfully mask all errors by the transmission medium. But when part of the protocol itself is violated, owing to failure of sending or receiving disciplines, they can no longer guarantee reliable transmission, and either loss or duplication of information may result [3, 34]. The safest course of action is to signal the uncertain state of data in transit at the time of failure to the users of the protocol, who must recover from the error with higher-level mechanisms outside the transport protocol. Another approach is to reduce the rate of protocol failures to an acceptable level by use of backup storage, redundant machines, or other means.

2.3.2.2   Connection Management

Connection management provides for the initialization and subsequent release of the resources needed for reliable data transfer. This includes connection establishment, termination, and failure recovery as described in Sec. 2.2.9. Connections follow a life cycle starting in a nonactive state, passing through intermediate opening states to an established state where data transfer takes place, and finally returning to the nonactive state through some intermediate closing states. Each of these phases is discussed in the following sections. The greatest difficulties surround connection establishment, since it must be accomplished over an unreliable transmission medium with no prior synchronization of sender and receiver.

Connection Establishment: The main function of connection establishment is to initialize the next sequence number (NSN) used by the sending discipline and the expected sequence number (ESN) used by the receiving discipline for subsequent data transfer. The simplest approach to this problem might be to use a fixed value (e.g., 0) for these variables every time a connection is started. Unfortunately, this simple scheme can easily lead to violation of the constraints on sequence number reuse described above with the consequent duplicate delivery of data. Figure 2.8 shows two successive connections between the same pair of processes *A* and *B*. If a duplicate packet from the first connection is delayed in the network until the second connection has started, it may look like a valid new data packet and be accepted.

One solution to this problem is to wait at least a maximum packet lifetime before starting a new connection between the same pair of processes (with the same ports), guaranteeing that all old packets are gone. This may not be acceptable in large systems with long packet lifetimes. In some networks a user may explicitly request destruction of any remaining packets on a connection (a "reset"), but this is only possible if the network has knowledge of transport connections (i.e., can locate and distinguish packets of a particular connection from all others).

```
A                                                    B

OPEN                                                 LISTEN
Opening                                              Listening
-->        <Seq 0> <data ABC>                        -->
|                                                    accept
<--                     <Seq 0> <ACK 3>              <--
-->        <Seq 3> <data DE>                         . . . . .        Delayed
-->        <Seq 3> <data DE>                         -->              retransmission
<--                     <Seq 0> <ACK 5>              <--              terminate connection
CLOSE                                                CLOSE
Not Active                                           Not Active
|                                                    |
|                                                    |
|                                                    |
OPEN                                                 LISTEN            start new connection
Opening                                              Listening
-->        <Seq 0> <data GHI>                        -->
                                                     accept
<--                     <Seq 0> <ACK 3>              <--
-->        <Seq 3> <data JK>                         . . . . .        new data delayed
. . . . .  <Seq 3> <data DE>                         -->              old duplicate arrives
<--                     <Seq 0> <ACK 5>              <--
|                                                    Old data accepted
```

FIGURE 2-8 *Old data delivered instead of current data.*

Other solutions require a more careful selection of the initial sequence number (ISN) used for a new connection. This may involve adding additional control information to distinguish packets from different connections, such as an *incarnation number,* which is incremented for each new connection [17], or generating unique addresses for each connection [39].

If the sequence number alone is used to distinguish packets from different connections, it must be carefully selected based on memory of previous connection sequence numbers or based on a clock. In the memory approach, the ISN is set to the last sequence number used in the previous connection plus one. This requires maintaining state information for inactive connections at least for a maximum packet lifetime. In the clock approach, the ISN is set from a single clock for all connections at a host [41]. This minimizes the state information to be maintained for inactive connections or through host crashes, but requires resetting the sequence number on an active connection if the clock is about to catch up with the sequence numbers in use [39].

Once ISN is selected, it must be transmitted to the receiving discipline in a special synchronization control packet (SYN). The receiver uses the sequence number in the SYN packet to set ESN in his receiving discipline and replies with an SYN packet, giving his or her own ISN. Each SYN packet must be acknowledged. When a transport station has received an acknowledgment for its own SYN and received its partner's SYN packet, the connection is established.

Unfortunately, errors may still occur if SYN packets from old connections are delayed and delivered just as a new connection is being opened. The careful selection of ISN prevents data from an old connection from being accepted on a new connection but does not protect against SYN packets themselves being duplicated. As shown in Fig. 2.9, an old SYN may arrive at B just at the moment when B is ready to establish a new connection; B will accept the SYN as a new connection request, reply with its own SYN, and consider the connection

```
A                                                    B

Listening                                            Listening
. . . . .        <Seq z> <SYN>                       -->              Old connection request
|                                                    Set ESN = z + 1
<--                            <ACK z + 1>           <--
Discard                                              |
|                                                    Pick ISN = y
<--                            <Seq y> <SYN>         <--
Set ESN = y + 1                                      |
-->              <ACK y + 1>                         -->
|                                                    Established
Pick ISN = x                                         |
-->              <Seq x> <SYN>                       -->
|                                                    Discard
<--                      <Seq y + 1> <ACK z + 1>     <--
Discard                                              |
```

FIGURE 2-9 *Deadlock with simple connection establishment.*

established. As a result, *A* will receive the replying SYN and interpret it as a new connection request. *A*'s attempt to reply will be discarded by *B*, who thinks the connection is already established, causing a deadlock that prevents data transfer.

To avoid this problem, a more reliable means of transmitting a new connection request to the remote transport station must be used. The transport station receiving the request asks for verification of the request at the same time it sends its own ISN. The initiating transport station then acknowledges the verification request, as shown in Fig. 2.10. This "three-way handshake" mechanism was suggested in [41] and has been successfully used in TCP [8].

Connection Termination: A simple mechanism for terminating connections is for each user to tell his or her transport station to close the connection. The transport station then immediately halts all operation on behalf of that connection and frees all resources. This requires agreement between the users at a level above the transport protocol on a safe time to terminate the connection.

Alternatively, the transport protocol itself may provide a mechanism by which one of the processes can inform the other that communication over this connection is to cease. A special control packet indicating that the conversation is finished (FIN) may be used to accomplish this. The FIN packet carries a sequence number just like a normal data packet. Several procedures for exchanging FIN packets are possible. In the simplest, the FIN is acted upon as soon as it is received and another FIN packet is returned. If a FIN arrives before some preceeding data packets (e.g., out of order), those data will not be delivered before the connection is terminated.

To "gracefully" close a connection, a FIN must be processed only after all preceding data. This allows any data in transit to be delivered first. When the user asks the transport station to close a connection, he or she may not transmit any further data but must be willing to receive any arriving data until his or her partner complies with the close request.

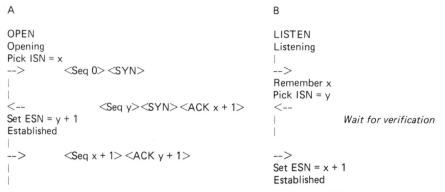

FIGURE 2-10 *"Three-way handshake" connection establishment.*

Failure Recovery: When a transport station or the host computer supporting it fails and then subsequently restarts, knowledge of connections in progress may have been lost. In this case, connections that were established become "half open," with the failed side thinking they are not active and the other transport station believing the connection is still established.

Since the established side is consuming resources, it is desirable to reset half-open connections promptly. One way to close half-open connections is to have a watchdog timer in each transport station that goes off if an established connection has not actively received any correct packets for some time or if a retransmission counter exceeds some specified value. The occurrence of such events will cause the transport protocol to unilaterally close its side of the connection.

To recover more promptly, another type of control packet, indicating that the connection should be reset (RST), may be used. If the failed side of the connection restarts and receives data packets, it returns an RST packet, referencing the sequence number of the data packet. When the RST reaches the established side, it is checked for validity and the connection may be immediately terminated. An old duplicate RST packet would not pass the validity check and hence would have no effect. Attempts to establish a new connection from the failed side to an already established side are cleared in a similar fashion.

2.3.3 Formal Verification

An informal narrative type of analysis such as that performed above is very valuable in providing motivation for and intuitive understanding of transport protocol mechanisms. However, the number and complexity of control procedures used in transport protocols require more rigorous analysis if their correct operation is to be demonstrated with a high degree of certainty.

This requires a precise model of the protocol whose detailed operation can be analyzed. This model typically consists of a pair of protocol machines connected by a transmission medium. The machines receive commands from their respective users, and messages from each other via the transmission medium. The transmission medium is itself a simple kind of machine that may introduce errors, delays, and other perturbations between its input and its output.

Attempts at rigorous verification have followed two main approaches: program proofs and state models [38]. In the former each machine is described algorithmically, and assertions that reflect the desired reliability goals must be formulated and proved. This approach has been effectively applied to verifying the data-transfer features of transport protocols where large or infinite numbers of interaction sequences are possible due to large sequence number spaces and retransmissions.

The state modeling approach has used such formalisms as Petri nets, state diagrams, state transmission matrices, flowcharts, and programs to define the protocol machines. Some form of reachability analysis is then performed to generate all possible interactions of the machines, followed by a check for undesirable states. This approach has been successful in verifying data-transfer features where simplifying assumptions are made to keep the number of states tractable, but is most applicable to connection management where the number of states is inherently small.

Some of the most fruitful work has involved a mixture of both techniques, where a relatively small state model of the basic features of the protocol is combined with additional context information or variables which reflect such information as sequence numbers [35, 38]. Rather than attempting a cursory survey of this complex area, we present a moderately detailed example which illustrates the flavor of the approach. The example shows the technique used in [34] to formally verify portions of an early version of the TCP connection management procedures.

Each transport station is modeled as a classic state machine with an input set, an output set, a set of internal states, and functions giving the next state and output for each combination of input and current state. Inputs consist of user commands, messages from the other protocol machine (or the network), and internally generated events such as timeouts. The two machines operate independently, with synchronization achieved by one machine waiting for a particular type of packet from the other machine.

We define the composite state of the system as the state of the protocol machine on each side of the connection, plus any relevant packets in the transmission medium between them. Transitions from one composite state to another are derived from the state transitions of the individual protocol machines by including all possible transitions of either protocol machine, given the state of the transmission medium.

The number of composite states is then the number of protocol machine states squared times the number of different states of the transmission medium. In a "pure" state machine approach, this would quickly lead to an unworkable number of states. This potential state explosion may be limited in two ways: by reducing the number of protocol machine states, and by treating as equivalent different sets of packets in transit.

For TCP, only four states are used to model the basic steps of connection establishment: *Not Active*, *Established*, and two intermediate steps representing the initiation or reception of a new connection request (*SYN-Sent* and *SYN-Received*). Additional information used in determining the processing of packets (such as used or expected sequence numbers) is kept as separate "context" variables. To limit the number of transmission-medium states, worst-case assumptions are made about delayed duplicate arrivals. All types of "old" packets are allowed to arrive in any state, so that no acknowledged packets need to be explicitly represented in the composite state [39].

By taking advantage of these reductions, a relatively compact model of connection establishment in TCP may be developed (Fig. 2.11). Each composite state is represented by a pair of process states and a list of packets in the transmission medium. Some context is represented along with the basic state of each process. This consists of the sequence number for outgoing packets in the SYN-Sent, SYN-Received, and Established states, and also a received sequence number for incoming packets in the Established state. This allows us to determine whether the protocol has correctly initialized sequence numbers when the Established state is reached.

Packets are represented by their packet types, with a subscript giving their own sequence number if relevant, followed by the sequence number of another packet they may refer to (in parentheses). An arrow above the packet shows its direction of travel. Symmetric states (identical except for switching process identities and packet directions) have been eliminated to simplify the figure. Transitions to the same state, such as retransmissions, are not shown. Composite transitions resulting from simultaneous transitions of both protocol machines are perfectly legal but are shown as sequential individual transitions to reduce the number of arrows.

This composite state model demonstrates several aspects of protocol correctness for the normal case where both protocol machines start in the *Not Active* state and function according to their definition (no failures). This includes safety considerations (absence of deadlocks, correctness of outcome), and viability considerations (progress and eventual termination), as follows.

The only terminal state shows both machines in the Established state, with sequence numbers for both directions properly initialized. Hence, there is no deadlock in the procedure for connection establishment. All paths leading back to the Not Active state for either machine are caused by collisions (simultaneous open requests), which will cause a later retry to establish the connection. (The need for retries was avoided in a later version of the TCP.) Assuming that perpetual collisions are avoided by the random retry timeout, and that the transmission medium provides a nonzero probability of delivering any packet, the protocol will eventually succeed in establishing a connection.

A great deal of other work on formal verification has begun to appear in the literature (see [38] for a partial survey), and there is every indication that this will remain an active research area until more automated techniques, which can handle more complex protocols, are developed.

2.4 HISTORY AND STANDARDS

Up to this point we have described transport protocol design and analysis from a general point of view, largely avoiding the details of particular protocols. Such a presentation brings together the lessons learned in many separate research and development efforts. In this section we briefly present some of the history of transport protocol development, various protocols that have resulted from these efforts, and the status of standardization efforts. For each protocol, the approach

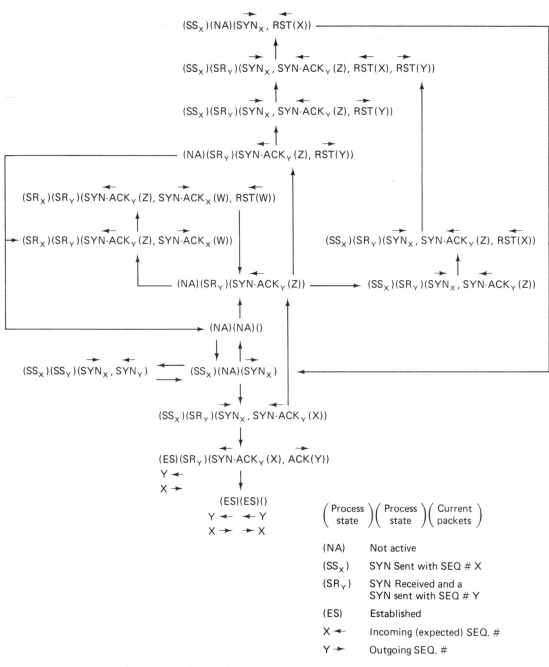

FIGURE 2-11 Composite state diagram for "three-way handshake".

66

taken in providing major transport functions (see Sec. 2.2) is described, allowing a comparison of different protocols.

The first transport protocols were developed as part of scientific research projects. These were the host–host protocol in the ARPANET [5] (with its implementation in the network control program or NCP), and the transport protocol of the French Cyclades network [42]. Further adaptations of these pioneering efforts are being used in other research environments, and more recently have been applied to particular commercial applications such as banking or utilities networks. Computer manufacturers and public data communication networks have also found a need to provide virtual-circuit-type services. As networks proliferate, the need to provide these services across multiple networks becomes ever more complex but necessary. Developments in each of these areas will be outlined in the following sections.

2.4.1 ARPANET

The ARPANET provided the environment for the earliest transport protocol. Since the communications subnet of switching computers provided a datagram or individual message-oriented communication service, the need for additional connection-oriented services was felt at an early date (see Chapter 1). Since the network provided highly reliable and sequenced message delivery, the host–host protocol focused on flow control, interrupt, multiplexing, and convenient addressing. In combination with the initial connection protocol (ICP), it provided a set of well-known addresses and procedures by which many connections to various services could be supported.

The ARPANET host–host protocol established an important principle of protocol specification. While the format and procedures for message exchange between protocol machines was exactly and completely specified, the interface between the user and the protocol was only functionally specified. The basic functions included open, close, send, receive, and interrupt operations. This allowed implementations of the protocol (the NCPs) and particularly the user interfaces to them to be successfully tailored to different machines, while NCPs for different machines were all guaranteed to be able to talk to each other.

The user interface to the NCP was stream-oriented, with flow control in both bits and messages provided by incremental ''allocate'' control messages between NCPs. Interrupt signals were not synchronized with the data stream. Control messages for all connections between a pair of NCPs were sent over a single control connection, while data messages were sent on their individual connections.

2.4.2 Research Nets

The French Cyclades network, designed somewhat later than the ARPANET, employed a simpler communication subnet with less responsibility for reliable transmission of packets. Hence the transport station (TS) developed for the

Cyclades net included procedures for error detection and recovery as described in Sec. 2.2. The user interface was record-oriented with the TS handling letters. Error control was on letters, with a complete letter being retransmitted in case of any error. Sequencing and flow control were also on a letter basis with agreement on maximum letter size forming part of connection establishment.

In parallel with the Cyclades TS, a second-generation ARPANET protocol was developed. This internet protocol [6], soon came to be called TCP, after its implementation in a *transmission control program* [7]. As the name implied, its goal was to provide fully reliable virtual-circuit service across many networks. Unlike the NCP, full error-detection and recovery procedures were included in TCP with the anticipation that some networks in a multinetwork system might not provide full reliability. Postel [27] provides a more detailed comparison of NCP and TCP.

To allow fine-grained flow control and more efficient error recovery, TCP sequence numbers were in units of bytes. This also allowed repeated fragmentation of data into arbitrary-length packets if necessary between networks with varying packet sizes. The user interface to TCP was record-oriented, as in the Cyclades TS, but error and flow control were performed on a byte basis.

While the original TCP had long sequence numbers and highly reliable procedures for data transfer once a connection was established, the procedures for first establishing a connection were rather simple. Several weaknesses in these simple connection management procedures were identified in the course of TCP development, leading to invention and adoption of the more sophisticated techniques described in Sec. 2.3.2. In particular, techniques for initial sequence number selection, the three-way handshake for connection establishment, and resynchronization for clock-based sequence numbering were proposed and implemented.

More recently [8], some TCP functions, including fragmentation/reassembly and TS addressing, have been moved into a separate "internet" protocol, which is essentially a multinet datagram protocol. For a priority mechanism, the original short interrupt packet has been dropped in favor of an "urgent pointer" that indicates a place in the normal data stream requiring urgent attention (see Chapter 3). An optional block-oriented flow control has also been adopted.

From an early date, the Internetwork Working Group (INWG, Technical Committee 6.1) of IFIP (the International Federation for Information Processing) has played an active role in transport protocol development. From the combined experience of ARPANET, Cyclades, and other networks represented by researchers in the group, several proposed transport protocol standards, most notably INWG 96 (known by its report number) [21], have been prepared and are periodically revised and updated. The latest revision specifically provides for adaptation of the transport protocol to the characteristics of the underlying transmission medium. In particular, greater efficiency may be achieved with networks providing a high level of service by negotiating the omission of procedures at the transport protocol level that are already provided by the network, such as flow control. This may be particularly useful for public networks with X.25 interfaces as described below.

Numerous adaptations have grown out of the early ARPANET, Cyclades, and INWG protocols. The European Informatics Network (EIN) provides a test bed for INWG protocols in a multinetwork multinational environment [14]. The MIT Laboratory for Computer Science has developed a TCP-like protocol called DSP, optimized for use in a local network environment. DSP uses unique addresses, which may never be reused, to help distinguish packets from different connections. Xerox Palo Alto Research Center has developed transport protocols and a wide range of other protocols based upon them for use in a local network office automation system. At Lawrence Livermore Laboratory, a very high bandwidth local network with small maximum packet lifetimes has led to a TCP-like protocol with connection establishment based on timers and memory of sequence numbers [16].

Some commercial applications of these protocols have also appeared. The U.S. Defense Communications Agency has adopted a TCP-like protocol that includes additional procedures to support military security and priority for its AUTODIN II common user data network. A large French gas and electric utility network has adopted a modified TS protocol [9]. A large Belgian bank has added encryption to a TS-like protocol for use in its banking network [15]. The strong similarity of these systems and their lack of interoperability due to small differences argues strongly for the early standardization of a common transport protocol from this family. Such a standard is being developed in INWG for presentation to ISO (TC97 SC16) and other relevant standards bodies.

2.4.3 Computer Manufacturers

With few exceptions, computer manufacturers' "networks" have been oriented toward connecting terminals to a large central computer. A variety of such network products have been announced in recent years. Despite the inherent asymmetry of the terminal-to-computer relationship, a protocol layer providing the functions of a transport protocol may usually be identified in these systems. We briefly describe Digital Equipment Corporation's DECNET and IBM's SNA as representative examples.

2.4.3.1 *DECNET*

DECNET followed the ARPANET approach of strong protocol layering with a data link control level, a logical connection or virtual-circuit level, and a user or application-level protocol. The network services protocol (NSP) is the DEC-NET equivalent of a transport protocol. Unlike the ARPANET, there is no strict distinction between host computers and switching nodes in DECNET, and both functions may be implemented in the same machine. One portion of NSP is concerned with routing packets and maintaining current routing information. The remainder of NSP forms a transport protocol concerned with opening and closing connections and sending and receiving data packets or interrupts. As with the INWG 96 protocol, various elements of procedure, such as flow control, sequencing, and acknowledgments, may be selected by the user. This allows the full range of transport protocol mechanisms to be used when needed, or lesser services to be used when they are adequate (e.g., across single physical link) with a minimum of transport protocol overhead.

Addressing in DECNET may be to specific numeric ports which are known to the routing algorithms, or generic names which must be looked up at either source or destination when the connection is established. Connection establishment also involves an exchange of version numbers between the protocol modules to ensure protocol compatability. Error control and flow control are on a message basis, with source and destination having to agree implicitly on message size limits. Flow control, when enabled, is "conservative," with the sender granted credits only for the number of buffers the receiver has made available. Connection termination procedures are "ungraceful," any pending data messages being discarded. All connections start with the fixed sequence number 0. Messages may be broken into up to 16 segments by the source, but no further fragmentation at intermediate nodes is allowed. Addressing may be single level for small networks or hierarchical for larger systems.

2.4.3.2 IBM Systems Network Architecture (SNA)

Like most computer manufacturers' networks, IBM's SNA is oriented toward secondary terminal nodes accessing a single or small number of primary main computer nodes, rather than arbitrary nodes conversing with each other on a more equal footing. This asymmetry permeates many of the SNA protocols.

Transport protocol functions are provided primarily by the *transmission control* (TC) layer of SNA (see Chapter 8 for further details on SNA). Connections (called *sessions*) are established between TCs (actually between "service managers," which correspond to what we have called connection machines in each "network addressable unit") with the help of a third party, the *system services control point* (SSCP). The SSCP converts names to addresses, checks access permission, optionally queues requests, and returns initialization information to the TCs on each side of the session. The primary TC then actually initiates a connection to the secondary TC, avoiding any possibility for race conditions. Connection termination is also mediated by the SSCP, and may be either immediate or graceful. An SNA system may have more than one SSCP.

Blocks of information are formed into a series (called a chain) of *request units* (RU) and sequencing is performed by the level above TC. Flow control is performed by TC on request units, but acknowledgments and error recovery are on entire chains at a higher protocol level. As in the ARPANET NCP, error control relies primarily on the hop-by-hop link error-detection mechanisms below the transport level. Two logical full duplex connections are provided in each session: normal and expedited. The expedited channel provides for out-of-band signaling between processes, and also carries all control messages. Flow control (called *pacing*) is only provided on the normal channel and uses an essentially fixed window size determined at session establishment.

2.4.4 Public Networks

As packet switching proved itself in the research environment, interest in providing public data communications service using packet switching has grown. Networks providing public service are already in operation in the United States, Canada, and the United Kingdom, and are in advanced stages of development in Japan, France, and several other countries. These networks are operated either by government postal, telephone, and telegraph authorities, or by regulated private companies.

In an effort to provide standardized and compatible services throughout the world, these organizations cooperate through the International Telephone and Telegraph Consultative Committee (CCITT) to formulate "recommendations" for providing various types and levels of service. Several recommendations for packet-switching network operation have been adopted in recent years, most notably the X.25 recommendation specifying the interface or protocol to be followed by subscribers accessing public networks.

An important feature of X.25 is that it specifies only the interface between the customer's computer (*data terminal equipment or DTE*) and his local attachment point to the network (a switching node or *DCE*). X.25 includes a protocol for managing the physical link between customer and network which is a version of the ISO HDLC protocol, and a higher-level virtual circuit protocol which provides for many simultaneous virtual circuits over the physical link. This latter packet-level or level 3 protocol has many features of a transport protocol but operates only between the subscriber computer on one side and the local network switching node on the other side (but see below).

To achieve end-to-end service between two subscribers, the network must establish connections and transmit data between source and destination DCEs using an internal protocol not specified in X.25. The destination node provides a third portion of a virtual-circuit path by using X.25 with the destination subscriber (see Fig. 2.12). In some networks, the internal protocol uses a single virtual circuit between source and destination nodes, while in others an independent virtual circuit between each intermediate node is used. Hence, end-to-end service is provided by a concatenation or series of at least three independent virtual circuits. The outer two links are governed by the X.25 protocol while the inner link or links are implemented as desired by each local network.

The X.25 level 3 protocol performs sequencing and flow control on a packet basis. Two logically separate full duplex data streams are provided in each connection, a normal stream and a "qualified" stream, but both are sequenced and flow-controlled together. Flow control uses a window mechanism with a size

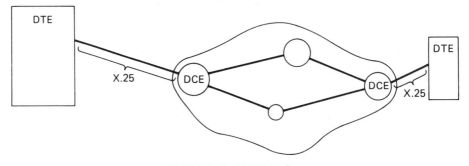

FIGURE 2-12 *X.25 interface.*

of one to eight packets. The window size is fixed at the time the connection is established, based on the class of service requested. No checksums or acknowledgments are used at level 3 (the "acknowledgment" actually serves to advance the flow-control window), but the link-level protocol provides common error detection and correction for all virtual circuits. An out-of-band signal or interrupt of 8 bits is provided which must be acknowledged by the destination subscriber before a second interrupt can be transmitted.

Connections are established by a special *call request* packet, specifying the destination address and optional service features required. The request is forwarded through the network to the destination subscriber, who returns an accept or reject packet. Simultaneous requests by a pair of subscribers to call each other may result in 0, 1, or 2 calls being set up, depending on local network procedures. Connections may be terminated ("cleared") at any time, with any data in transit discarded. The user or network may also "reset" a virtual circuit under unusual circumstances, causing discard of any data in transit and reset of sequence numbers and flow control, but not closing the connection.

Although, strictly, X.25 specifies only the *interface* between customer and network, it provides a basis for inferring the subscriber-to-subscriber service that will be offered by public networks. Some of the level 3 protocol features, such as interrupt and call establishment, are defined to have end-to-end significance. Other features, such as sequencing and flow control, are only required to have local significance (as in TRANSPAC), but may also be implemented to have end-to-end significance (as in DATAPAC). Thus, when a receiving subscriber advances the flow-control window, the effect on the sending subscriber's flow-control window is uncertain and depends on local network implementation. Call clearing and resets may also be handled either way. Hence, the end-to-end service characteristics of public networks require further definition beyond X.25 and will vary from network to network.

Because there is no end-to-end error control in X.25 and because resets may occasionally occur, users with high-reliability requirements may need to implement their own error-control procedures in an end-to-end protocol on top of X.25. The uncertainty of X.25 flow control may also require end-to-end flow-control procedures. Some public network subscribers thus find themselves in need of end-to-end transport protocols on top of X.25 [9, 15]. To reduce the inefficiency of similar mechanisms being used at both levels, two approaches are possible. The transport protocols may be streamlined and adapted to take advantage of the high grade of service offered by X.25 [15, 19, 21], but some duplication is inevitable.

Alternatively, public network interfaces may be expanded to include a simpler datagram-type service without connection establishment, sequencing, or error control [22, 31]. These functions could then be provided by an end-to-end transport protocol. Such a datagram service should be cheaper to provide and would also be useful to point-of-sale and other transaction-oriented users who do not need virtual-circuit service. During the original development of public packet networks, it was strongly argued that datagram and not virtual-circuit service should be the basic service provided, with transport functions left to the users, and an initial version of DATAPAC did operate in this way.

When public packet-switching networks are interconnected, the uncertainties concerning end-to-end service characteristics are multiplied. A CCITT recommendation for the interface between networks (numbered X.75) has been formulated. X.75 closely resembles X.25 and specifies a virtual-circuit-type protocol for the link between networks with a separate virtual circuit for each internet call. Although like X.25, X.75 addresses itself only to the link between networks and not to end-to-end architecture, it seems clear that the overall architecture will be a series of concatenated virtual circuits through each local network and across each internetwork link, as shown in Fig 2.13 [18, 40]. This increases the number of elements that must operate reliably and increases the number of intermediaries participating in virtual-circuit functions, raising doubts about the optimality of this approach [18]. Quality of service resulting from this architecture will have to be assessed when multinetwork operations using X.75 become a reality.

2.4.5 International Standards Organization (ISO)

The most recent major development in protocols has been the formation of the ISO TC97 SC16 to study "open systems interconnection." The goal of this group

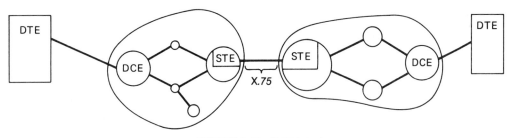

FIGURE 2-13 *X.75 interface.*

is to define an overall architecture for all levels of protocol in "open" systems of interconnected computers, and a preliminary architecture with seven levels has already been proposed [1]. Level 4, called the transport level, appears to contain most of the functions of traditional transport protocols. However, some functions, particularly concerning addressing of multiple processes within a system, have been placed in level 5, called "session control."

Initially, ISO is focusing on defining the services provided at each level rather than designing specific protocols at any level. However, this work will undoubtedly have a strong impact on the future development of transport protocols.

REFERENCES

[1] BACHMANN, C. W. and others, "Session 8: Standard Interfaces and Protocols for Distributed Systems" (3 papers), *Proceedings of the 7th IEEE Computer Society International Conference·(COMPCON),* Washington, D.C., pp. 139–156, November 1978.

[2] BELSNES, D., "Flow Control in Packet Switching Networks," *Proceedings of the European Computing Conference on Computer Networks*, (Online Conferences, Uxbridge, England.) pp. 349–361, 1975. Also *INWG Note* 63.

[3] BELSNES, D., "Single Message Communication," *IEEE Transactions on Communications,* **COM-24**(2), pp. 190–194, February 1976.

[4] BENNET, C. J., and A. J. HINCHLEY, "Measurements of the Transmission Control Program," *Proceedings of the Symposium on Computer Network Protocols*, Liège, Belgium, February 1978, pp. G1:1–11, February 1978. Also in *Computer Networks Journal*, **2**(4/5) 1978.

[5] CARR, S., S. CROCKER, and V. CERF, "Host/Host Protocol in the ARPA Network." *Proceedings of the AFIPS Spring Joint Computer Conference*, **36** pp. 589–597, 1970.

[6] CERF, V. G., and R. E. KAHN, "A Protocol for Packet Network Intercommunication," *IEEE Transactions on Communications*, **COM-22,** pp. 637–648, May 1974.

[7] CERF, V. G., Y. DALAL, and C. SUNSHINE, "Specification of Internet Transmission Control Program," *INWG Note* 72, December 1974.

[8] CERF, V. G., and J. B. POSTEL, "Specification of Internetwork Transmission Control Program Version 3," unpublished report, January 1978.

[9] CHESNEAU, C., and others, "Normalisation des Fonctions de Communication à Travers un Réseau de Transmission de Données à Commutation de Pacquets à Electricité de France et Gaz de France" (in French), *Proceedings of the Symposium on Computer Network Protocols,* Liège, Belgium, pp. B2:1–15, February 1978.

[10] COHEN, D., "A Protocol for Packet Switching Voice Communication," *Proceedings of the Symposium on Computer Network Protocols*, Liège, Belgium, February 1978, pp. D8:1–9. [Also in *Computer Networks Journal*, **2**(4/5), 1978.]

[11] Crowther, W., and others, "Issues in Packet Switching Network Design," *Proceedings of the AFIPS National Computer Conference,* pp. 161–175, 1975.

[12] Danthine, A., and F. Magnee, "End-to-End Protocol Performance," *Proceedings of the Conference on Computer Performance Evaluation,* (Online Conferences, Northwood Hills, England), pp. 569–587, 1976.

[13] Davies, D. W., and D. L. A. Barber, *Communication Networks for Computers,* John Wiley & Sons, Inc., New York, 1974.

[14] Deparis, M., and others, "The Implementation of an End-to-End Protocol by EIN Centers: A Survey and Comparison," *Proceedings of the 3rd International Conference on Computer Communications,* Toronto, Canada, pp. 351–360, August 1976.

[15] Eschenauer, E., and V. Obozinski, "The Network Communication Manager: A Transport Station for the SGB Network," *Proceedings of the Symposium on Computer Network Protocols,* Liège, Belgium, pp. C2:1–21, February 1978. [Also in *Computer Networks Journal,* 2(4/5), 1978.]

[16] Fletcher, J. G., and R. W. Watson, "Mechanisms for a Reliable Timer-based Protocol," *Proceedings of the Symposium on Computer Network Protocols,* Liège, Belgium, pp. C5:1–17, February 1978. [Also in *Computer Networks Journal,* 2(4/5), 1978.]

[17] Garlick, L. L., and R. Rom, "Reliable Host–Host Protocols: Problems and Techniques," *Proceedings of the 5th Data Communications Symposium,* Snowbird, Utah, pp. 4:58–65, September 1977.

[18] Grossman, G. R., A. Hinchley, and C. A. Sunshine, "Issues in International Public Data Networking," *Computer Networks Journal,* 3(4), pp. 259–266, September 1979.

[19] Hertweck, F., E. Raubold, and F. Vogt, "X25 Based Process–Process Communication," *Proceedings of the Symposium on Computer Network Protocols,* Liège, Belgium, pp. C3:1–22, February 1978. [Also in *Computer Networks Journal,* 2(4/5), 1978.]

[20] "Systems Network Architecture Format and Protocol Reference Manual: Architectural Logic," *IBM Corp. Document SC30-3112-1,* June 1978.

[21] "A Proposal for an Internetwork End to End Protocol," *INWG Note* 96, July 1975. (Revised version in *Proceedings of the Symposium on Computer Network Protocols,* Liège, Belgium, pp. H:5–25, February 1978.)

[22] Jacquemart, Y. A., "Network Interprocess Communication in an X25 Environment," *Proceedings of the Symposium on Computer Network Protocols,* Liège, Belgium, pp. C1:1–6, February 1978. [Also in *Computer Networks Journal,* 2 (4/5), 1978.]

[23] Kleinrock, L., and H. Opderbeck, "Throughput in the ARPANET—Protocols and Measurement," *Proceedings of the 4th Data Communications Symposium,* Quebec City, Canada, pp. 6:1–11, October 1975.

[24] Kleinrock, L., W. E. Naylor, and H. Opderbeck, "A Study of Line Overhead in the ARPANET," *Communications of the ACM,* 19(1), pp. 3–13, January 1976.

[25] Le Lann, G., and H. Le Goff, "Verification and Evaluation of Communication Protocols," *Computer Networks Journal*, 2(1), pp. 50–69, February 1978.

[26] Merlin, P. M., and D. J. Farber, "Recoverability of Communication Protocols—Implications of a Theoretical Study," *IEEE Transactions on Communications*, COM-24(9), pp. 1036–1043, September 1976.

[27] Postel, J., "An Informal Comparison of Three Protocols," *Computer Networks Journal*, 3(1), pp. 67–76, 1979.

[28] Pouzin, L., "Basic Elements of a Network Data Link Control Procedure," *INWG Note* 54, January 1974. [Also in ACM SIGCOMM *Computer Communication Review*, January 1975.]

[29] Pouzin, L., "Virtual Call Issues in Network Architectures," *Proceedings of the European Computing Conference on Communication Networks* (Online Conferences, Northwood Hills, England), pp. 603–618, September 1975.

[30] Pouzin, L., "Network Protocols," in *Computer Communication Networks* (R. L. Grimsdale and F. F. Kuo, eds.), Nato Advanced Study Institute Series, P. Noordhoff N.V., Leyden, Netherlands, pp. 231–255, 1975.

[31] Pouzin, L., "Virtual Circuits vs. Datagrams—Technical and Political Problems," *Proceedings of the AFIPS National Computer Conference*, New York City, pp. 483–494, June 1976.

[32] Pouzin, L., "Flow Control in Data Networks—Methods and Tools," *Proceedings of the 3rd International Conference on Computer Communications*, Toronto, Canada, pp. 467–474, August 1976.

[33] Stenning, N. V., "A Data Transfer Protocol," *Computer Networks Journal*, 1(2), pp. 99–110, September 1976.

[34] Sunshine, C., "Interprocess Communication Protocols for Computer Networks," *Digital Systems Lab, Technical Report* 105 (Ph.D. thesis, Stanford University), December 1975.

[35] Sunshine, C., "Formal Techniques for Protocol Specification and Verification," *Computer* 12(9), pp. 20–27, September 1979.

[36] Sunshine, C., "Efficiency of Interprocess Communication Protocols for Computer Networks," *IEEE Transactions on Communications*, COM-25(2), pp. 287–293, February 1977.

[37] Sunshine, C., "Interconnection of Computer Networks," *Computer Networks Journal*, 1(3), pp. 175–195, February 1977.

[38] Sunshine, C., "Survey of Protocol Definition and Verification Techniques," *Proceedings of the Symposium on Computer Network Protocols*, Liège, Belgium, pp. F1:1–4, February 1978. [Also in *Computer Networks Journal*, 2(4/5) 1978.]

[39] Sunshine, C., and Y. Dalal, "Connection Management in Transport Protocols," *Computer Networks Journal* 2(6), pp. 454–473, December 1978.

[40] Sunshine, C., "Current Trends in Computer Network Interconnection," *Advances in Data Communications Management*, Heyden & Sons, Philadelphia, Penna., 1980.

[41] TOMLINSON, R. S., "Selecting Sequence Numbers," *INWG Protocol Note* 2, August 1974. Also in ACM SIGCOMM *Operating Systems Review*, **9**(3), July 1975.

[42] ZIMMERMAN, H., "The CYCLADES End to End Protocol," *Proceedings of the 4th Data Communications Symposium*, Quebec City, Canada, pp. 7:21–26, October 1975.

3

TERMINAL, FILE TRANSFER, AND REMOTE JOB PROTOCOLS FOR HETEROGENEOUS COMPUTER NETWORKS

JOHN D. DAY

Digital Technology Incorporated

3.1 INTRODUCTION

Terminal, file transfer, and remote job entry protocols provide basic services for the users of computer networks. Terminal protocols establish mechanisms that allow efficient and flexible terminal access to networks. Terminal protocols not only allow a user to access a time-sharing service through the network, but can also be used as a character-oriented network interprocess communication facility. File transfer protocols allow users to manipulate remote file systems and to transfer files or parts of files from one host system to another. Remote job entry protocols provide users with a mechanism for submitting jobs to various batch services on a network. Many of the problems encountered in these protocols recur in more complex forms in the more sophisticated protocols (e.g., net mail protocols, distributed-data-base protocols) which may be built on top of them.

In this chapter, we will be concerned primarily with protocols for heterogeneous networks. Protocols for homogeneous networks generally are a subset of the heterogeneous network protocols in terms of the scope and of the mechanisms they use. To expose the reader to as wide a variety of the problems found in these protocols as possible and to do it in a reasonable amount of space, we will restrict our discussion to heterogeneous network protocols.

A computer communications protocol is typically designed as one of several successive protocol *layers*. Protocols are layered for many of the same reasons that large software systems are organized into layers. The layers provide a means to aggregate related functions. In addition, a protocol layer provides a *transparent* service for the next higher level, so that modifications to a lower level do not affect a higher level. In much of the protocol literature the terms ''lower level'' and ''higher level'' are used to denote the absolute (rather than relative) position of the protocol. In this usage, the term ''lower level'' is applied to protocols concerned primarily with the reliable transfer of data across the network. These are the protocols dealt with in Chapters 1, 2, and 6. The term ''higher level'' is applied to protocols concerned primarily with performing remote operations. These are the protocols dealt with in this chapter and in Chapter 10. More descriptive labels might be ''communications protocols'' (for lower-level protocols) and ''resource-sharing protocols'' (for higher-level protocols).

3.2 TERMINAL PROTOCOLS

3.2.1 Terminal Access

Probably the most common computer communications requirement today is for terminal access. Terminal access is commonly provided by terminal-concentrator networks. These networks are organized into a *star* or a *tree* topology. Terminals and terminal concentrators are connected by point-to-point lines to the central data processing center. The point-to-point lines and in some cases the terminal concentrators of a terminal-concentrator network can be replaced with a packet-switched network (Fig. 3.1). Replacing a terminal-concentrator network by a packet-switched network can significantly reduce costs and also increase reliability.

Terminal access to a network may be provided in one of three basic ways: through a large computer, through a network access machine or ''mini-host,'' or through a direct interface (Fig. 3.2).

When a large computer (or host) is connected to a network, terminals attached to the large computer may access the network using special network access software in the host. The terminal user executes a program on the host that allows connections with other hosts to be opened and closed. Since the host can support complex software, this technique can provide a sophisticated network terminal user environment.

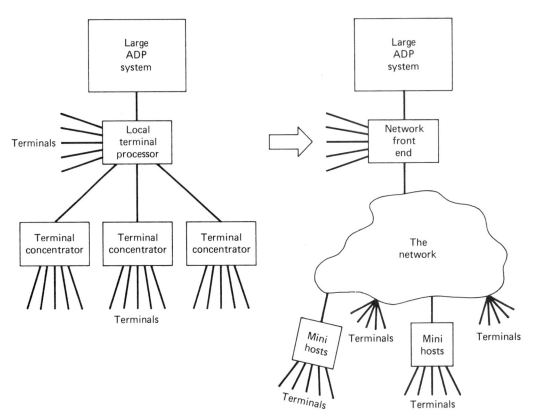

FIGURE 3-1 *Typical method for using a network to replace point-to-point lines.*

In the second approach, a minicomputer is dedicated to providing many of the network terminal user services available to the terminal user accessing a network through a large computer, but at considerably less cost. Several of these mini-host systems [2, 7, 12, 39, 40] have been developed. Some are oriented to providing a convenient human interface [12, 39]. Some support-specialized peripherals, such as graphics displays or plotters [7] and digital voice equipment [40]. Others use artificial intelligence-based systems to provide very sophisticated user facilities [2].

In a third approach, the network itself provides a facility through which terminals can be directly connected to the network via dial-up or permanent connections. Once connected, the terminal user then issues commands to the network. The command language allows the user to open and close connections to host computers and to set certain terminal-specific parameters. In the AR-PANET, this facility was called the *Terminal Interface Processor* [36], or TIP. In the nomenclature of the CCITT (Consultative Committee for International

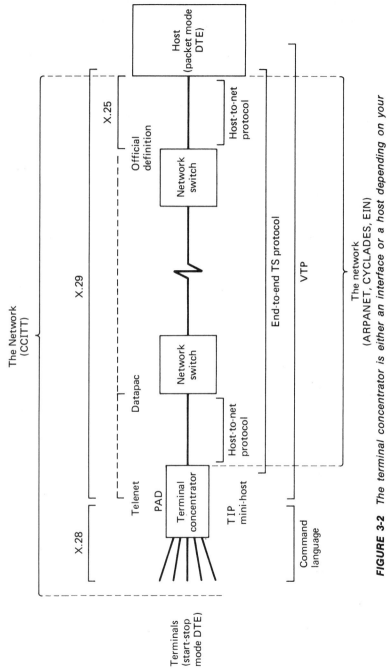

FIGURE 3-2 *The terminal concentrator is either an interface or a host depending on your point of view.*

81

Telegraphy and Telephony), it is called the *Packet Assembler/Disassembler* [11], or PAD. The command languages provided by the TIP and the PAD are cryptic and primitive. The TIP and the PAD are functionally almost identical, but are architecturally distinct. In the ARPANET, the TIP is considered logically to be a host (with very limited capabilities). Although the TIP software resides in the packet switch, it appears to all other hosts and to the switching software as a host connected to the network. The CCITT, on the other hand, considers the PAD to be a part of the network, an interface between two kinds of data terminating equipment (DTE): the packet-mode DTE (or the computer) and the start/stop-mode DTE (or the terminal). There is considerable controversy surrounding these two viewpoints. Although the first appears to be conceptually clean and efficient, it has been argued that the second provides certain economic and growth advantages for some networks.

3.2.2 Characteristic Problems of Terminals and Networking

Terminal handling has always been problematic, but with networks the problem is further complicated. If a network were no more than a different technology providing the equivalent of point-to-point lines, networking would not compound the terminal handling problem. Data generated by a terminal could simply be "packaged" and transferred over the network to the computer, and vice versa. However, one of the major advantages of networking is that a terminal user can potentially establish communication with any computer attached to the network. Conversely, then, each computer on the network must be prepared to handle every kind of terminal that may access the network at large.

Although terminals exhibit broadly similar characteristics, they differ in very significant ways. Most operating systems require a separate piece of software to handle each kind and make of terminal attached to it. Since most computer installations support only a few kinds of terminals, this variety does not represent an undue burden. However, if this approach were carried over to the network, each host would have to support all n kinds of terminals, supported by each of the m hosts on the network. Thus each host must potentially be able to support $m \times n$ terminals in order to allow any user to connect to it. Clearly, this is impractical.

Terminal-oriented protocols are designed to reduce this "$m \times n$" problem to a manageable size by establishing conventions for handling all the terminals on the network. There are several aspects of terminal handling that a terminal protocol must consider.

1. *Attentions*. Most terminals provide a means of sending an expedited signal out-of-band or outside the normal flow of data. These signals are not flow-controlled and are always given priority in transmission. The meaning attached to the signal may depend on how it was generated

(what keys were pressed), or the program the terminal was communicating with, or data in the data stream.

2. *Control of the terminal handling.* Associated with each terminal are certain parameters that affect the local handling of the terminal. Examples are the amount of padding after format effectors, such as carriage return, local flow control, and so on. These parameters will not be known at the point of network access if the terminal is not permanently connected (e.g., a dial-up). Therefore, the user or the remote host must be able to set them.

3. *Dialogue mode.* Some systems are oriented around half-duplex or line-at-a-time operations. Others are full-duplex operations and respond without waiting for a full line of text. Methods must be provided for selecting and efficiently providing each mode.

4. *Terminal data structure.* Data flowing to a terminal are placed in a data structure. The complexity of this data structure varies with the sophistication of the terminal. For a typical scroll terminal such as a Teletype Model 33, the data structure is a one-dimensional array. For paged terminals, it is a two-dimensional array. All terminals have commands for manipulating this data structure. For scroll-mode terminals there is the command to generate a new line. For more sophisticated terminals, commands may exist for addressing the data structure (cursor addressing), modifying it (line delete or insert), or assigning special attributes to parts of it (highlighting, or field protection). Different terminals encode these commands differently. Also, different encodings for character data may be generated by terminals and hosts.

5. *Symmetry.* A terminal protocol should not only allow a terminal to interact with an application process on a host (PT), but it should also allow process–process (PP) and terminal–terminal (TT) interactions. Although a majority of the connections established will be of the PT form, the symmetrical forms can be very useful. For example, one may find that the easiest way for a program on one host to use a program on another is for each one to appear to be a terminal user of the other. A classic example of this occurred in the ARPANET. A system in California for numerically evaluating and graphing equations was allowed to use an algebraic-manipulation system at MIT [37]. With this combination a user could first simplify a problem using the algebraic-manipulation system at MIT and then evaluate and plot the resulting equations using the system in California. Since both systems were designed for terminal use, the simplest way to connect them was for each to appear to the other as a terminal user.

6. *Negotiations.* Since it is neither possible nor desirable to legislate away

the differences between terminals, it is necessary to provide some mechanism for each side of a connection to negotiate dynamically the facilities and parameter values it requires or is capable of providing.

7. *Extensions*. The ultimate terminal has yet to be built. Not only are terminals becoming more and more sophisticated [1, 2], but they are also being specialized to serve very specific functions, such as point-of-sale or banking. Therefore, the protocol must be open-ended so that new terminal types and capabilities can be accommodated easily and efficiently.

3.2.3 Approaches to Terminal Protocols

Two basic approaches to terminal protocols have emerged. One approach [11, 49] attempts to parameterize the differences between terminals. The protocol is used by the host to set the various terminal parameters to the requested values. The other approach [3, 6, 14, 28, 47, 49] defines a *network virtual terminal (NVT)*. The terminal side of a connection maps the output of its terminal into the NVT format for transmission to the host. The host then maps the NVT format into its local form. This reduces the "$m \times n$" problem to an "$m \times 1$" problem. Each host on the network must support one new terminal type (the NVT) when it joins the network. The next two sections will discuss the parametric and virtual terminal approaches in more detail.

3.2.3.1 *Parametric Terminal Protocols*

The parametric approach has been pursued primarily by the national PTTs (postal, telegraphy, and telephone ministries) within the CCITT and in the United States by the Telenet corporation. The CCITT has approved protocols to define a Packet Assembler/Disassembler (PAD). These have been designated X.28 and X.29. Recommendation X.28 defines the protocol for use between the start/stop mode DTE (the terminal) and the PAD. Recommendation X.29 defines the protocol for use between the PAD and the packet-mode DTE (PDTE) (the host). (There is also a Recommendation X.3, which defines the PAD.)

CCITT Recommendation X.25 defines the protocol for data transfer between the packet-mode DTE (the host) and the data communicating equipment or DCE (the network). X.29 uses the user data fields defined by X.25 to exchange control information and user data between the PAD and the host. It may seem that X.29 is being used in an end-to-end fashion on top of the X.25 protocol. From the point of view of the CCITT, this is not the case. The PAD is part of the network or DCE. Thus, X.29 is not being used end to end, even though the PAD may be some distance from the computer; X.29 is an interface.

X.29 provides several PAD messages which are used to control the PAD and to indicate certain conditions. The PAD parameters can be inspected and modified by the use of the READ, SET, and SET AND READ messages. For example, a PDTE may send a SET PAD message to a PAD to set the line-length parameter. The SET message has as an argument a list of pairs of parameter codes and parameter values. The parameter code indicates which parameter is to be modified and the parameter value contains the new value of the parameter. This <CODE, VALUE> pair is repeated for each parameter that is to be modified. The PAD replies to one of these messages with a PARAMETER INDICATION message, which gives the current or new values of parameters in the same format as the SET or READ. A list of the PAD parameters defined as of January 1979 is provided in Table 3.1.

When the terminal user generates a ''break'' character at that terminal, the PAD will send an X.25 Interrupt, followed by an INDICATION OF BREAK PAD message. The Interrupt packet travels outside the normal data flow. The exact semantics of the ''break'' condition are determined by the PAD parameters. Its primary purpose is to allow the terminal to abort an operation or discard output. Other PAD messages are provided for indicating errors, resetting the PAD, and clearing the PAD.

The PAD protocols provide no generic functions. The data stream consists of IA5 characters. (ASCII is essentially IA5 with national options.) It is assumed that the application in the host knows what the terminal will do with the

TABLE 3-1: *PAD parameters according to CCITT proposed recommendation X.3.*

PAD Recall	Provides the means to leave data transfer state and return to PAD command state.
Echo	Determines whether or not the PAD echos characters received from the terminal.
Data Forwarding Signals	Allows the terminal or host to specify when buffered characters are to be transmitted to the host.
Idle Timer Selection	Allows the terminal or host to specify a time interval for buffered characters to be transmitted if no forwarding signal has been received.
Ancillary Device Control	Provides flow control between the PAD and the terminal (with PAD as receiver of data).
Suppress PAD Signals	Allows PAD service signals to be suppressed.
Break Signal Semantics	Allows the terminal or host to select the action of a break signal.
Discard Output	Allows the PAD to discard all data received from the host.
Carriage Return Padding	Allows the terminal or host to specify the number of padding characters after a carriage return.
Line Folding	Allows the PAD to automatically fold lines greater than a specified length.
Flow Control	Provides flow control between the PAD and the terminal (with the terminal as a receiver).

characters. It is also assumed that the terminal will do what was intended. At present, the PAD has only been defined for scroll-mode terminals. It is unclear how it will be used to support more sophisticated devices. Experience with X.25 has shown that to ensure reliable communications, an end-to-end transport protocol is required on top of X.25 or that equivalent end-to-end facilities be added to X.25 [26, 29]. It is very unclear how the use of an end-to-end protocol on top of X.25 can be extended to use with X.29 in a consistent manner. Another aspect of X.29 which exacerbates this problem is that X.29 uses a facility (the Z-bit) of the lower-level X.25 protocol to distinguish PAD control messages from data. It may be difficult for some systems to support this mixing of levels. Currently, there are no plans within CCITT to provide end-to-end facilities in either X.25 or X.29.

The Interactive Terminal Interface (ITI) [49] used by Telenet is very similar to X.29. The are two major differences between the two. First, Telenet supports a much more extensive set of parameters (Table 3.2). To some degree ITI indicates the kinds of additions to X.29 we can expect in the future. Second, Telenet's ITI supports what is called a *virtual terminal* (VT) *mode*. The Telenet VT described is not as fully developed as the ones we will discuss below. This VT supports only a very primitive scroll terminal. The only generic functions provided by ITI are a go-ahead (for half-duplex operation), an interrupt process, an abort output, and a break.

The parametric approach is most successful when the primary purpose is to handle existing terminals [3]. The PAD provides a basic, transparent mode of operation, which places most of the burden of terminal handling on the PDTE or the host. The PAD parameters allow the PDTE to shift some of this burden to the PAD. As the PAD is used to support more and more complex terminals, the number of parameters required increases rapidly. X.29 has 12 parameters; Telenet's ITI now has more than 50. The PAD protocols do not allow PAD to PAD communication, and it is unlikely that it will allow the PDTEs to use the PAD protocols for communication between themselves. However, symmetrical operation has been mentioned as a point of further study. Many of these problems can be avoided by using the virtual terminal approach.

3.2.3.2 *Virtual Terminal Protocols (VTPs)*

The VTP approach has been used by the ARPANET in the United States [14, 18], by the CYCLADES network in France [33, 46], by the GMD network in West Germany [47], by the European Informatics Network (EIN) built for the European Economic Community (EEC) [3, 4, 42, 44, 45], and has been proposed for the Belgian University Network [6]. Some vendors of networks advertise that they provide a virtual terminal protocol. However, on closer inspection one finds that their "virtual" terminal is identical to the terminals sold by these vendors. Also, these protocols often do not provide any means for extensions or negoti-

TABLE 3-2: *Telenet interactive terminal interface parameters.*

Parameter id	Interactive Terminal Parameter
0	Connection Mode
1	Linefeed Insertion
2	Network Message Display
3	Echo
4	Echo Mask
5	Transmit Mask
6	Buffer Size
7	Command Mask
8	Command Mask
9	Carriage Return Padding
10	Linefeed Padding
11	Tab Padding
12	Line Width
13	Page Length
14	Line Folding
15	(Reserved)
16	Interrupt on Break
17	Break Code
18	Virtual Terminal Options
19	2741 Initial Keyboard State
20	Half/Full Duplex
21	Real Character Code
22	Printer Style
23	Terminal Type
24	Permanent Terminal
25	Manual/Automatic Connection
26	Rate
27	Delete Character
28	Cancel Character
29	Display Character
30	Abort Output Character
31	Interrupt Process Character
32	Automatic Disconnection
33	Flush Output
34	Transmit on Timers
35	Idle Timer
36	Interval Timer
37	Network Usage Display
38	Carriage Return Padding
39	Padding Options
40	Insert on Break
41	DCE-to-DTE Flow Control
42	DCE XON Character
43	DCE XOFF Character
44	Generate Break

TABLE 3-2: *Telenet interactive terminal interface parameters. (continued)*

Parameter id	Interactive Terminal Parameter
45	APP on Break
46	2741 Input Unlock Option
47	2741 Input Unlock Timer
48	2741 Input Lock Character
49	2741 Output Lock Option
50	2741 Output Lock Timer
51	2741 Output Unlock Option
52	Defer Echo Mask
53	Break Options
54	DTE-to-DCE Flow Control
55	DTE XON Character
56	DTE XOFF Character
57	Connection Mode
58	Command Mode Escape

ations. These protocols are intended for homogeneous systems and will not be considered here. In the VTP approach, the user composes input at the terminal. Before this input is transferred across the network, it is translated into the NVT format. When the host receives the data from the network, it then translates this NVT form into the form expected by its terminal handling software. The application then receives the data as if they had come from a local terminal. The major advantage of this approach is that it avoids the $m \times n$ problem while allowing relatively sophisticated terminal usage. Many conventional operating systems, such as the Burroughs MCP and Honeywell MULTICS, have used this canonical-form approach for many years with great success. Depending on the detail with which the NVT is defined, applications may use network terminals without any loss of sophistication.

The ARPANET TELNET protocol [24, 48] was the first Virtual Terminal Protocol (VTP) and has been remarkably successful. TELNET is a very simple protocol intended for use by scroll-mode terminals. It is based on three principles: the concept of the network virtual terminal, the concept of negotiations (or negotiated options), and a symmetrical view of terminals and processes. The latter two principles are generally viewed as the major design successes of TELNET. The scroll-mode VT was adequate for most ARPANET applications. Further development of the VT was left for later.

The model used by TELNET consists of two NVTs connected back to back. Each user end, whether terminal or process, considers itself to be dealing with an NVT. The keyboard of one NVT is connected to the presentation unit or screen of the remote NVT, and vice versa. When data is sent to the NVT by an application or user, it is not entered into the local presentation unit unless certain echo-control negotiations have occurred. The primary advantage of this model is that it easily allows the protocol to be used for terminal-to-terminal and process-to-process applications as well as the more common terminal-to-process ones. This attribute is probably the most important contribution of the TELNET protocol. The TELNET model also allows a considerable amount of asynchrony to exist in the protocol. In addition, it avoids the delays and inefficiencies of attempting to synchronously share a data structure across a network.

The option negotiation mechanism allows the user to set terminal parameters to values other than the default or to negotiate more sophisticated facilities. The TELNET protocol negotiation mechanism can be initiated by either side. Besides negotiating whether or not a particular option is to be in effect, the mechanism also allows one to specify, when appropriate, which side is to perform the function. For example, a user may negotiate the Echo option and specify whether echoing is to be done locally or remotely to the initiator of the negotiation.

Four commands support option negotiation (DO, DONT, WILL, and WONT). WILL <option name> is sent by either party to indicate that party's willingness to begin performing the option. DO <option name> and DONT <option name> are the positive and negative acknowledgments. Similarly, DO <option name> is sent to request that the other party begin performing the option. WILL <option name> and WONT <option name> are the positive and negative acknowledgments (see [14] and [48] for a more complete description).

The TELNET protocol has several severe shortcomings. The scroll-mode terminal is the only terminal model that TELNET can efficiently support. Experiments with extending TELNET to handle more complex terminals have shown that major inefficiencies develop (see, e.g., [19]). The only reasonable way for new terminal commands or primitives (e.g., position the cursor) to be introduced without modifying the protocol is to use the subnegotiation mechanism. This means that each new terminal command requires a minimum of six octets (octet = 8 bits) to be represented. Because the protocol is stream-oriented, a TELNET implementation must scan every octet of the data stream to find control sequences, such as negotiations. Additional inefficiencies are introduced by the encoding of negotiations. TELNET only provides for extensions to the protocol along one axis. Although they are not explicitly constrained by TELNET as such, the negotiable options are primarily terminal-related parameters. The ability to negotiate the use of new terminal commands or to negotiate new terminal classes to modify the basic NVT model is not provided by the protocol.

The success of TELNET in the ARPANET can be attributed to three factors: (1) for a first try, it is a very good design of a VTP; (2) very few sites actually use the options, so that many of Telnet's facilities have never been tested; and (3) the limits of TELNET have not been tested outside the rather specialized research environment found in the ARPANET. For a VTP to be successfully used in a general environment, the virtual terminal must be very well defined. Otherwise, programs that use the terminal in more sophisticated applications such as displaying and updating fields on a CRT will not be able to format their output deterministically without considerable knowledge of the real terminal being used. Also, for a VTP to be generally applicable, it must restrict itself to terminal functions. TELNET mixes protocol layers considerably. A glance at the list of options (Table 3.3) will show that there are not only terminal options, but also options that deal with lower-level, terminal-handler parameters (Message Size, Output Formfeed Disposition, etc.) and options that are concerned with time-sharing system functions (Reconnection, Logout, etc.). Protocol research in the ARPANET terminated in 1973, so that many of the improvements that were intended were never made. Since that time almost all protocol research has been done in Europe.

3.2.4 European VTP Research

While TELNET focused primarily on the symmetry and negotiation issues, the Europeans have focused their attention on the definition of a virtual terminal model that could be used in a wider range of applications. There are several centers in Europe that have been investigating the design of VTPs: Schicker and Duenki in Zurich [45], Bauwens and Magnee at Liege [6], Schulze and Borger at Darmstadt [49], Higginson at University College London [28], and Barber at the National Physical Laboratory in England [3, 4]. Two basic VTP organizations have emerged in this research. In the earlier work [42, 46], symmetric operation was ignored. This led to a model in which the combination of the real terminal and the software to convert to the protocol appeared as a virtual terminal to the

TABLE 3-3: *ARPANET Telnet protocol options.*

0	Binary Transmission
1	Echo
2	Reconnection
3	Suppress Go Ahead (Dialogue Control)
4	Message Size
5	Status
6	Timing Mark
7	Remote Controlled Transmission and Echoing
8	Output Line Width
9	Output Page Size
10	Output Carriage-Return Disposition (Padding)
11	Horizontal Tab Stops
12	Horizontal Tab Disposition
13	Output Formfeed Disposition
14	Output Vertical Tabstops
15	Vertical Tabstops Disposition
16	Linefeed Disposition
17	Extended ASCII
255	Extended Options List
18	Logout
19	Byte Macro
20	Data Entry Terminal

application program. Later, Schulze and Borger [49] proposed the use of a shared communications variable as the basis of a common data structure. Although this approach allows symmetric operation, it does so with considerable loss of asynchrony and efficiency. Recently, a more flexible approach [28] has been used to provide symmetrical operation without the use of a common data structure. This protocol uses an organization much like the two-NVT organization found in TELNET.

The European investigations into VTPs have made two major contributions: (1) a well-defined virtual terminal and (2) the development of a model for attentions or interrupts. Both are crucial in a general environment VTP. The model used by most of these VTPs is shown in Fig. 3.3. The protocol commands change the state of the control unit and the contents of the data structure. (The adaptation unit maps the state of the VT onto the real terminal.) The data structure is a representation of the data that are accessible and may be displayed to the user. In order to model more efficiently the wide variety of terminals

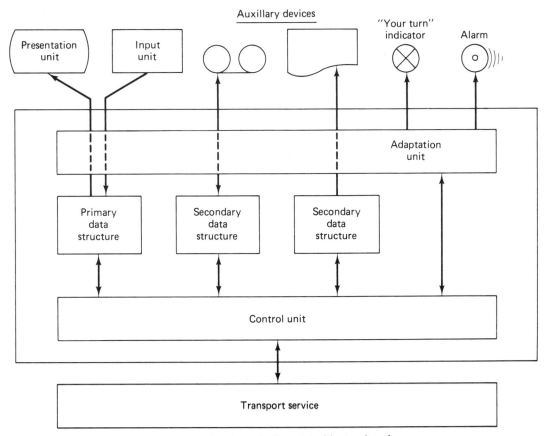

FIGURE 3-3 *Virtual terminal model with user interfaces.*

available, most VTPs adopt the concept of *terminal classes*. The VTP defines a basic framework for the virtual terminal, and classes of virtual terminals are defined that correspond to the classes of real terminals available (e.g., scroll mode, paged, data entry, banking, point of sale). Each class uses the basic model and adds to it the facilities and structures required. For example, the page-terminal class uses the basic scroll-mode terminal model but makes the data structure a two-dimensional array and adds a parameter to denote page size. The data-entry-terminal class takes the paged model and adds the ability to define fields in the array and to assign attributes to them. (It is not necessary that each class be a proper subset of the next.) Thus, the use of terminal class avoids requiring all implementations to support the most sophisticated terminal functions and allows the characteristics of the VT to more closely resemble the real terminal being used. The best descriptions of this aspect of VTs may be found in [6, 28, 45]. The negotiation mechanisms in the European VTPs differ from the TELNET mechanism in two significant ways: (1) since European VTP models consist of a single virtual terminal or two VTs that are more tightly coupled, the negotiation mechanisms do not specify which side is to perform the function; and (2) the specification of each TELNET option defines how the negotiation is to be terminated (e.g., how to avoid endless offer and counteroffer). In the European designs, a general rule is defined for terminating all negotiations. Of lesser importance, the European designs also provide commands for one side to request of the other what options and what range of parameters it supports and for the requested side to report what it supports.

There are two kinds of VTP commands: commands used to control the virtual terminal and to establish its parameters, and commands used to modify the data structure. The control-related commands are used in the negotiation sequence and to control auxiliary devices. The data-structure-related commands are used to format and enter text in the data structure (see Table 3.4). The list of data-structure-related commands could be almost as varied as the number of terminals available. The choice is mediated by the following minimum guidelines:

1. Include only those commands which represent the terminal class being defined. Do not include commands that could be considered ''bells and whistles.''

2. Do not use two commands where one will do.

3. Do not include a command if the same function can be performed by a short sequence of existing commands.

4. When confronted with a choice of two or more ways to do the same thing, choose the one that can be most easily transformed into the others or will be the least ambiguous if some state information is lost. For example, in the case of relative vs. absolute cursor addressing, it is as difficult to convert relative cursor addresses to absolute ones as it is to

TABLE 3-4: *Minimum parameters and primitives required by the INWG VTP*

	Primitives	*Parameters*
Scroll Mode		
	Agree	Terminal Class
	Disagree	Line Length
	Request	Erase/Overprint
	Indicate	Dialogue Mode
	New Line	Auxiliary Data Structure
	Start of Line	
	Text Segment	
	Purge	
	Asynchronous Attention	
	Synchronous Attention	
Paged Mode		
	Scroll Mode Primitives	Scroll Mode Parameters
	Delete All	Page Size
	Position	
Data Entry Terminal Mode		
	Paged Mode Primitives	Paged Mode Parameters
	Attribute*	
	Delete Attribute	
	Erase Unprotected	
	Next Unprotected Field	

*Attributes are protected/unprotected fields, and three levels of display: Nondisplay, Normal, and Intensified.

convert absolute ones to relative ones. However, if the receiver loses the state of the virtual terminal, absolute addresses convey more information. Since the data being displayed to the user may be intact, this means that although the VT may not be sure, it knows what is happening. The user still sees everything (or almost everything) as it was intended.

3.2.5 Attentions

The use of attentions, or out-of-band signals, has also been a question of much concern to designers of VTPs. There are essentially two kinds of attentions that are required in a VTP: the asynchronous attention, which is independent of the data stream, and the synchronous attention, whose action must be coordinated with a point in the data stream. The first poses no problems, but there are certain race conditions that make providing the second more difficult. An excellent solution to this problem was first proposed in [21] and later developed in detail by Bauwens and Magnee in [5].

The basic issues that the attention mechanism must address are:

1. Whether or not data is to be purged.

2.   The dialogue mode after the attention (full- and half-duplex).

3.   If half-duplex, which side has the turn.

In the Schicker and Duenki scheme the attention carries these pieces of information, which provide the remote user with a means to flush data, to request that the "turn" be given to it, and to send other out-of-band signals. (In addition, most of the VTPs provide about 8 or 16 bits for the terminal classes or user applications to define.)

The mechanism described by Schicker and Duenki assumes that the transport service provides reliable delivery of out-of-band signals, often called telegrams. In addition, only one attention from either side may be outstanding. The attention mechanism consists of the telegram sent out-of-band and a data mark that is sent in the normal data stream. The mark acknowledges that an attention has been received and also indicates the point in the data stream at which the attention phase ends and a new data phase begins. As seen by the initiator of an attention, the procedure goes as follows (Fig. 3.4):

The initiator

- Stops accepting keyboard and network messages.

- Transmits an attention telegram specifying dialogue possibilities, purge information, and so on.

- Awaits a responding attention telegram with the remote partner's request specifying the same information.

- Reevaluates the dialogue mode and location of the turn according to a distributed algorithm.

- Transmits a "mark" which carries the confirmation of this "negotiation" and signals the beginning of the next data phase.

- Accepts incoming messages, discarding or displaying them according to the attention information received until a mark is received.

- Reinitializes the dialogue mode and continues processing.

The sequence for the receiver of an attention is very similar:

- Respond with an attention telegram.

- Issue a mark in the data stream.

- Wait for the incoming mark, discarding or displaying data according to the parameters of the attention telegram.

- Continue normal processing when the mark arrives.

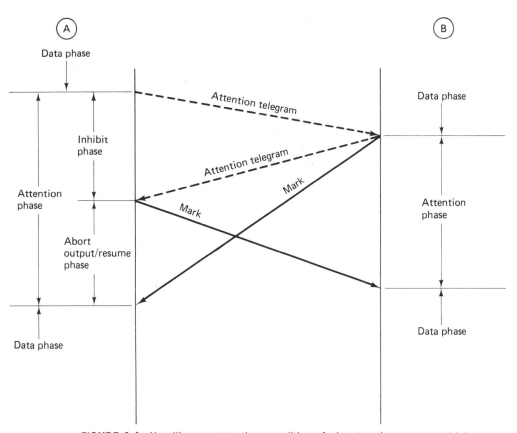

FIGURE 3-4 *Handling an attention condition: A denotes the process which initiated the attention; B denotes the process which receives the attention (after Bauwens and Magnee [6]).*

The foregoing procedure was freely adapted from the Duenki and Schicker paper [21]. For a detailed discussion showing how various deadlocks and races are avoided by this scheme, the reader should consult the paper by Bauwens and Magnee [5].

3.2.6 VTP Architecture

The major difference between the VTPs described here lies in how the virtual terminal is viewed. In the ARPANET TELNET protocol there are two virtual terminals organized so that the keyboard of one and the display of the other belong to one user, and similarly on the other side. The two VTs are essentially independent. This structure is very flexible and allows the symmetrical terminal–terminal or process–process applications. (One of the design goals of the

TELNET protocol was to provide a general character-oriented interprocess communication facility.)

In the VTPs described by Bauwens and Magnee [6] and by Schicker and Duenki [42], there is one VT (see Fig. 3.5). These VTPs are asymmetrical and only support process–terminal applications. The virtual terminal is considered to be the combination of the real terminal and the software to convert to the VT format. From the point of view of the host, it merely has to support this remote VT. Schulze and Borger [49] suggest a VTP based on the "shared communication variable." The essence of this approach is to transplant the "single-site" model into the network environment. In this VTP, each side takes turns accessing a single virtual data structure. This virtual data structure is provided by a lower-level protocol. This protocol is able to give the illusion of a single data structure by having a copy of the data structure at each host and restricting access to only one user at a time. This approach cannot support the asynchronous, full-duplex dialogues found in many systems. By taking a centralized approach rather than a distributed approach and not allowing asynchrony, this approach can incur considerable overhead in resolving contention for the data structure. (Other flaws in the "shared communication variable" approach appear when it is applied to broadcast protocol applications or distributed data bases, e.g., maintaining multiple copies of the "shared variables" reliably and consistently.)

In the INWG VTP [29] each side has a VT which represents that side's view of the state of the VT session. This model explicitly recognizes the asynchronies present in the network. Input from the local user is written on the local data structure and transmitted over the network to be entered in the remote data structure. In the asynchronous full-duplex or "free-running" dialogue mode, the contents of the two data structures may be different owing to the concurrency of the applications and variable network delays. (The same data are written on both, but the order may differ.) This free-running dialogue mode can provide greater efficiency by allowing messages to be sent at any time. In fact, for some applications it may even be desirable that the two data structures be different.

3.2.7 PAD Protocols and the VTPs

The PAD protocols are more concerned with the support of current telecommunication requirements, while the VTPs are aimed at the more general com-

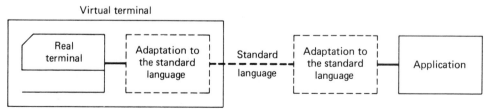

FIGURE 3-5 *Asymmetrical VTP architecture (after Bauwens and Magnee [6]).*

munications environment likely to evolve in the future. Currently, most users of computer networks use one host. In essence, the network is replacing point-to-point lines. The PAD protocols are designed for this environment. The PAD protocols parameterize basic terminal handling characteristics; but assume that the host knows how to manipulate the presentation unit. In the future, we can expect users to use several hosts of different manufacturers. The VTP will then become a necessity as users break out of essentially closed groups. However, this does not mean that the PAD and VTP approaches are diametrically opposed. The VTP is primarily concerned with manipulating the presentation unit, which the PAD is not. Compatibility between the PAD and VTP can be achieved by making the virtual terminal one of the kinds of "terminals" a PAD can support. Or if the "real terminal" is sufficiently sophisticated, it can implement the VTP directly and use the PAD protocols as a more sophisticated transport service.

3.3 FILE TRANSFER PROTOCOLS

A *File Transfer Protocol* (FTP) defines the set of rules for the transfer of files from the file system on one host to the file system on another. In heterogeneous networks the purpose of an FTP is to establish a network virtual file system (NVFS). The network virtual file system allows a process in a local host to access data stored in any remote host as if the data were stored locally. To accomplish this, an FTP is concerned with three kinds of functions:

1. File transformation.
2. File transfer.
3. File manipulation.

The *file transformation* function of an FTP attempts to provide canonical, or at least compatible, representations of the data contained in a file. These transformations convert the file into a form that is usable at the destination. In the classical case, an FTP will define several virtual file formats. The source will map the file into the proper virtual form, and the destination will map the received virtual form into the proper local format.

The *file transfer* functions of an FTP enable the user to open a file by name, address data within the file, and to transfer data to and/or from the file. These operations take place under an access control mechanism which defines and enforces access permissions on a per-user, per-operation, and per-file basis. File transfer functions may allow all or part of the file to be moved. (In the current literature, file transfer generally refers to the transfer of whole files only, while file access refers to the ability to transfer parts of a file as well as whole files.)

The *file manipulation* functions of an FTP enable the user to create, delete, rename files, and perform other operations on the information the file system maintains about the files. Access controls and directory information such as creation date, file name, and so on, are good examples of this information.

In a VTP the data structure models a canonical presentation unit. The canonical file formats defined in an FTP are an extension of the data structure concept. In heterogeneous networks, the file transfer protocol defines canonical data representations, canonical file structures, and canonical file operations. These canonical forms make possible the network virtual file system. They relieve each host of the burden of recognizing the local data representations, file structures, and file operations of all other hosts. Each host need only be able to translate between its local forms and the canonical, network forms. The design of the canonical forms, the efficiency of the transformations, and the veracity with which these canonical forms represent local forms are the major issues in FTP design.

Most of the communication aspects of file transfer are dealt with at lower levels. However, the larger the amount of data to be transferred between hosts, the more likely it is that the transfer will be interrupted by a network failure. To avoid the need for the retransfer of a large amount of data in the event of such a network failure, an FTP must provide some sort of mechanism for restarting the transfer from an intermediate point.

In the next section, we will survey some of the file transfer protocols that have been proposed or implemented. We will discuss the ARPANET FTP in some detail since it is fairly representative. The discussion of the other FTPs will primarily deal with unique facilities or the different approaches to a problem these protocols use. Following this survey we will review the various aspects of an FTP and the successes and failures of the protocols.

3.3.1 ARPANET FTP

The ARPANET FTP [34, 35] was defined in early 1973 by the ARPANET Network Working Group. The FTP consists of a user FTP, which generates commands, and a server FTP, which acts on these commands and generates the replies. Although this FTP could be used by a program, the protocol is very much oriented toward an interactive environment. In most ARPANET implementations, a human user directly monitors transfers of files. The model for the ARPANET FTP is shown in Fig. 3.6. The user enters requests to the user interface in a local command language. These requests are then translated into FTP commands which are sent to the server by the *User Protocol Interpreter* (PI). The *Server Protocol Interpreter* (PI) attempts to perform the operation indicated by the command and sends back a reply indicating its success or failure.

The user and server PIs are only concerned with the control of the FTP. Data transfer is mediated by the *Data Transfer Process* (DTP) of each implementation. When an FTP command that causes a file to be transferred is generated by the

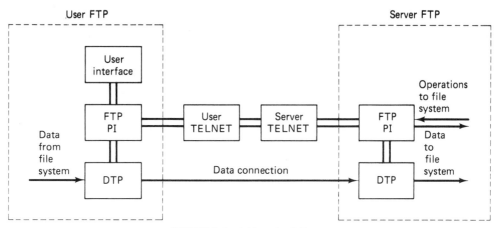

FIGURE 3-6   ARPANET FTP model.

user FTP PI, it will cause its DTP to "listen" for a data connection on the appropriate network port. When the server FTP PI receives the command, it causes its DTP to initiate a data connection to the previously specified socket (i.e., network port), usually at the user's host. The DTP is responsible for all data translation and formatting.

The ARPANET FTP design provides for "third party transfers," i.e., it allows a file to be transferred from host A to host B with the user at host C. The procedure for this is as follows (see Fig. 3.7): after the user PI has established the control connection and logged in, SOCK commands are sent to each server to notify it of the sockets to be used for data transfer. A PASV command is sent to one server, indicating that it should passively wait for a connection on its data-transfer sockets. The STOR command indicates to A where the data from the data connection is to be stored. The RETR command indicates to B the file from which data is to be transferred to the data connection.

The FTP control connection is a TELNET connection. Therefore, the user and server PIs appear as network virtual terminals to each other. All FTP commands and replies consist of ASCII strings that can be generated or interpreted by a user at a terminal. One of the design constraints placed on the Network Working Group was that it be possible for a user at a TIP to be able to use FTP in some form even if rather primitive. Each FTP command (Table 3.5) consists of a four-character command, a space, and one or two arguments terminated by a "carriage return-line feed" sequence. FTP replies (Fig. 3.7 and Table 3.6) consist of a three-digit reply code followed by arbitrary text. The reply code provides sufficient information for a program to intelligently use FTP, while the text provides server–host-specific text to human users. Although a program using FTP or the user FTP PI may only be interested in success or failure, a human being may wish to see more information that can best be given in a prose form, specific to a server's file system.

TABLE 3-5: *ARPANET FTP commands*.

Access Control Commands

USER	<user code>	These commands are used for logging
PASS	<password>	the user onto the system
ACCT	<account number>	
REIN		Reinitialize the FTP session.
BYE		Logout or terminate the session.

Transfer Parameter Commands

BYTE	<byte size>	Specifies byte size on the connection.
SOCK	<host>,<socket>	Specifies socket for data transfer.
PASV		Specifies which side is to wait for data connection
TYPE	<data type>	Specifies data type ASCII, IMAGE, and so on.
STRU	<file structure>	Specifies file structure as file or record.
MODE	<transfer mode>	Specifies transfer mode as stream, blocked or compressed.

FTP Service Commands

RETR	<pathname>	Retrieve a file from server to user.
STOR	<pathname>	Store a file from user to server.
APPE	<pathname>	Append to a file.
ALLO	<file size>, <record size>	Allocate file space.
REST	<marker>	Restart transfer at marker.
RNFR	<pathname>	
RNTO	<pathname>	Used to rename a file.
ABOR		Abort a file.
DELE	<pathname>	Delete a file.
LIST	<pathname>	Directory list or file status.
NLST	<pathname>	Directory list.
SITE	<string>	Executive site specific command.
STAT	<pathname>	Status.
HELP		System specific documentation.
NOOP		No operation.

The ARPANET FTP supports four basic file formats: ASCII, EBCDIC, Image, and Local Byte. The first two of these are concerned with character files. ASCII and EBCDIC file types can have one of three internal formats: nonprint, TELNET format controls, or ASA carriage controls. It is beyond the scope of the ARPANET FTP to define truly canonical file formats. These file formats provide a means of transferring a file in such a way that it can be used by the most common applications on the destination host. If the file is to be stored or used by a program as input, the nonprint format is used. This format does not require vertical format information and assumes that local conventions will be used for spacing and margins. For files that are to be printed, either the TELNET or ASA formats are used. The TELNET format is used by files that contain ASCII carriage control information, such as formfeed, vertical tab, carriage return, and so on. Since ASA carriage control is fairly common in many systems, it is provided as an alternative means of formatting print files. In addition to print files, the FT provides an Image and a Local Byte Size file type for transferring

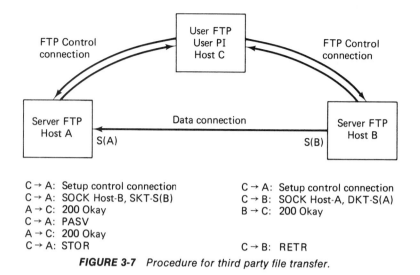

C → A: Setup control connection	C → A: Setup control connection
C → A: SOCK Host-B, SKT-S(B)	C → B: SOCK Host-A, DKT-S(A)
A → C: 200 Okay	B → C: 200 Okay
C → A: PASV	
A → C: 200 Okay	
C → A: STOR	C → B: RETR

FIGURE 3-7 *Procedure for third party file transfer.*

non-character data between hosts. Two file structures are also provided: a *stream-structured* file, which is simply a one-dimensional stream of bytes, and a *record-structured* file, which is two-dimensional. (Variable-length records are allowed.)

In order to provide greater integrity and efficiency for the data transfer, the FTP provides three transfer modes. The simplest is *stream*. This is the default

TABLE 3-6: *ARPANET FTP reply structure and examples.*

1yz	Positive preliminary reply—requested action initiated; expect another reply before sending a new command.
2yz	Positive completion reply—requested action was successfully completed.
3yz	Positive intermediate reply—command accepted, more information required, send another command.
4yz	Transient negative completion reply—command not accepted, but error condition is temporary. Examples would be an unavailable file or temporary shortage of resources.
5yz	Permanent negative completion reply—command unacceptable.
x0z	Syntax-related reply
x1z	Informational reply
x2z	Connection-status-related reply
x3z	Authenication and accounting reply
x4z	Unspecified
x5z	File-system-related reply
xy0–xy9	Used to enumerate replies of one category

Examples:

200	Command okay
212	Directory status
450	Requested file action not taken: file unavailable
125	Data connection open; starting transfer

mode and is provided for minimal implementations. Data transferred in this mode
are simply sent to the foreign host with no additional information. Completion of
a transfer is signaled by closing the data connection. A *blocked* mode is also
provided, which provides considerably more integrity. This mode sends each
piece of the file in a block with a count of the number of bytes in the block, flags
to note end-of-record and end-of-file, and possibly a restart marker. To increase
transfer efficiency, a *compressed* mode is also provided. This data compression
mode can be used on both binary and character data.

When the current version of the ARPANET FTP was defined, most of the
designers assumed that one major revision would be required. In early 1973 an
understanding of the place of file transfer in the network and the nature of the
network virtual file system was just beginning to emerge. There are several issues
that the designers of this protocol chose to avoid. Among these are questions of
access control, more sophisticated file structure and data formats, and network
architecture.

3.3.2 File Access Protocol

Later in 1973, this author proposed two basic modifications to the ARPANET
FTP [15]. First, it was noted that FTP contained two basically independent
functions. FTP has one set of operators for file transfer and another set for file
manipulation. By separating these into two separate protocols, a File Access
Protocol (FAP) and a File Management Protocol (FMP), a greater degree of
efficiency, modularity, and even security could be attained. Many network
applications require only the ability to move a file. These applications should not
be encumbered with facilities they do not require. Since protocol organization
generally has implications for the software, this organization would allow more
efficient implementations. Also, this organization allows better access control.
By partitioning the file access and file management functions, it is possible to
require separate user authentication for each. Thus, an application that only
transfers files can be given access to the FAP, but not the FMP. It is often easier
to provide access control by not giving the user access to the operations than
trying to restrict the use of the operations. Thus, an RJE protocol or data-base
protocols could be allowed to use the FAP to access files and transfer data but
would not be able to modify file access controls, delete files, or modify directory
information.

The second basic change proposed in RFC 520 [15] was that FTP should be
modified to allow access to parts of a file. The ARPANET FTP only allows for
the transfer of entire files. This is uneconomical and would be unacceptable in a
non-research environment. Many data-base applications that would be built on
top of the file transfer service would require the ability to access portions of a
file. RFC 520 proposed that a byte pointer be defined that could be moved within
the file. A user process would move the pointer to the desired location within the
file using FTP commands for that purpose. Then a read or write command would

be performed that would transfer data to or from the place in the file referred to by the byte pointer. Special values of the pointer would be provided to specify the beginning and end of the file. The obvious generalizations of the byte pointer could be used to address record-oriented files or more complex file structures.

Since 1973 marked the end of higher-level protocol development in the ARPANET, these and other ideas were never explored further. However, as we will see below, similar protocol organizations are receiving considerable investigation in European networks.

3.3.3 File Transfer in the National Software Works and RSEXEC

There have been two other efforts within the ARPANET community to investigate distributed file system operations: the RSEXEC system [50, 51], developed by Bolt Beranek and Newman, and the National Software Works [32], developed in part by Massachusetts Computer Associates. RSEXEC provides a distributed file system on several ARPANET PDP-10 TENEX hosts. (RSEXEC has been implemented in two non-TENEX hosts, but the implementers encountered TENEX-specific problems with the RSEXEC protocols.) The distributed file system allows the user to maintain files on several hosts in a fairly transparent manner. A user need not remember where a file is stored, but can reference it by name. Also, RSEXEC attempts to use the distributed file system to increase the availability of files by allowing a user to maintain multiple copies of a file. Many RSEXEC file management operations take into account that a file exists at several places and aids the user in dealing with them. For example, when a user asks to delete a multicopy file, RSEXEC asks if all or only some of the file should be deleted. This sort of ''aid'' is very useful at our present state of development. Since we lack experience with distributed file systems, it is not clear what they should do and should not do automatically. Most of the RSEXEC file functions can be classified as file management functions. It uses the ARPANET FTP for transfers.

The National Software Works [32] is an ARPA-funded research project investigating the problem of providing support for the ''construction, use, maintenance, modification, verification, and storage of programs'' and their data in an environment where the ''hardware, software, and human resources may be geographically and administratively dispersed.'' One aspect of the design of NSW has been the development of a distributed file package. The NSW approach essentially imposes an NSW file system on a subscriber host in addition to the local file systems of the hosts. Although this file system could be used as a canonical form, it is not. Files in the NSW file system are not directly accessible to the local host file system. Thus, NSW avoids many of the compatibility problems between different file systems by simply legislating a new file system. However, in the area of file or data formats, NSW goes to great lengths to try to achieve a canonical form that can be easily translated and used on different host computers. NSW is more concerned with issues of access control and file and directory management in network systems.

3.3.4 DEC's Data Access Protocol

Digital Equipment Corporation has defined a file transfer protocol [20, 38] called *Data Access Protocol* (DAP) for use with its DECNET product. This protocol differs from the ARPANET FTP in several distinct ways. First, DAP uses a single full-duplex connection for both control and data. Second, rather than using a standard representation for files, DAP provides a collection of basic elements from which a file system may choose to tailor the protocol. This approach allows like systems to transfer files without unnecessary conversion while allowing unlike systems to choose some form that is compatible or usable by each. The primary danger with this approach is that if care is not taken in choosing elements, one is faced with a proliferation of "basic" elements that will make the protocol unwieldy and inefficient. A good choice of basic elements must reflect the best traits of both a standard representation and the diversity of forms found in contemporary file systems.

Unlike the ARPANET FTP, DAP allows the user to address records within a file and to transfer parts of a file. However, this is only possible with records and cannot be used with arbitrary strings of bytes. The DAP procedure for a third-party file transfer contains a rather severe security problem. If host A wishes to transfer a file from host B to host C, A first logs on to B, then A sends B the user's user code and password for host C and B logs in to C. A similar problem is found in the ARPANET RJE protocol.

DAP occupies a middle ground between being designed for a homogeneous or a heterogeneous network. Although the various DEC operating systems differ, there are considerable similarities between them. Therefore, some of the solutions found in DAP may not be applicable in general.

3.3.5 European FTP Developments

There has been considerable work on the design of file transfer protocols by European investigators. A preliminary file transfer protocol [22] has been defined for the British Post Office's EPSS network which borrows much from the ARPANET. A major innovation in the EPSS FTP is the use of a *window* for restart markers. This window is very similar to the flow-control window found in transport protocols (see Chapter 2). The sender of the file establishes the width of this restart window. The sender inserts restart markers in the data sent to the destination. The destination acknowledges these markers when it has received the data and written them into the file. When the source receives a restart marker acknowledgment, it advances the right window edge accordingly. The source stops sending data if it should send a full window's worth of restart markers without receiving a reply. Thus, the restart window allows the source to limit the amount of restart information it must maintain and the amount of data that may need to be buffered.

A group of investigators at ETH in Zurich have proposed a Bulk Transfer Function (BTF) [41] for the European Informatics Network. The best features of this protocol are that it attempts to provide only the data-transfer functions and does not attempt to combine file transfer, file management, and even remote job entry functions (as DAP and EPSS FTP do) in one protocol. This protocol adopts the same organizational position as the File Access Protocol (see Sec. 3.3.2) and attempts to provide basic file transfer service in an efficient manner. BTF also entertains the problems involved in providing a standard data representation.

An excellent FTP [23] has been proposed for the French CYCLADES network that embodies the architectural considerations of both the FAP/FMP and BTF proposals. This protocol is organized in such a way that several levels of support can be provided, depending on the sophistication of the protocol implementation. This is an important factor, since not all hosts have the resources to implement sophisticated network software. This protocol proposes a basic structure within which both file access and file management functions may be defined in an independent manner. In its early stages of development some parts have been left unspecified.

3.3.6 Current Issues of File Transfer Protocol Development

The European work on FTP seems to be much more sensitive to the requirements of the general user than previous U.S. work. However, considerable work remains to be done on file transfer protocols before they can be generally used outside the research environment. In the remainder of this section we will review some of these areas.

One of the areas of interest is the necessity of an explicit restart mechanism. It can be argued that if an FTP allows for transferring parts of a file, an explicit restart mechanism is not needed. The argument is as follows. To implement restart, one requires the ability to start writing and reading the file at a place other than the beginning. One also needs a way of telling the other side where in the file to restart. The restart markers serve this purpose. An FTP that allows the transfer of parts of a file (i.e., a File Access Protocol) already provides both of these facilities. In a File Access Protocol, if a transfer is interrupted by a network failure, the receiver of the file need only determine the file address (in whatever address space the protocol uses) of the last item of data written on the file. The protocol can then be used to position the reestablished FTP session to begin a transfer at that position.

The only advantage restart markers have over file addresses in a File Access Protocol is that restart markers do not have to be universally recognizable. Although a restart marker represents a file address, only the system that generated the marker needs to be able to decode the marker into a file address. All current FTP protocols use this fact to define (or not define) their markers. For example, the ARPANET FTP definition states: "The marker information has meaning only to the sender. . . . The marker could represent a bit-count, a record count, or any other information by which a sender may use to identify a data checkpoint.'' This is a typical definition of a restart marker. However, some constraints must be placed on the granularity of the restart marker if restart deadlock is to be avoided.

A restart deadlock can occur in the following way. Suppose that a record-oriented host such as an IBM 370 wishes to retrieve a record-oriented file from a stream-oriented host such as a PDP-10. Furthermore, let us assume that the FTP implementation on the record-oriented host will only acknowledge restart markers that fall on record boundaries. (None of the protocols described above place restrictions on when markers can and cannot be inserted.) Since it is sometimes very difficult on record-oriented hosts to write or update partial records, it is not unlikely that an implementor would make the implementation simpler by putting markers on record boundaries. However, the FTP on the stream-oriented host does not recognize that not all files are streams and inserts a marker every X number of bytes. Eventually, X and the record size on some file transfer will be relatively prime. In the EPSS FTP this means that a deadlock will occur, because the receiver will never acknowledge a marker after the sender has sent a window's worth of markers. In the ARPANET FTP, this means that no markers will be acknowledged and a restart would commence at the beginning of the file.

None of the protocols with explicit restart mechanisms discussed above treat this problem. Some, such as DAP, may avoid it by only allowing record addressing of a file. This is a small problem that can be avoided by further refinement of the definition of the restart mechanism. There are two ways of avoiding the problem. Either the protocol must state that implementations must be prepared to restart transmission in the middle of a record, or the protocol must define the lowest level of granularity a restart marker may address. The result of either is almost the same. The protocol must define some universal addressing unit that can be applied to all files. This is paramount to defining a File Access Protocol. Thus, it would appear that protocols that allow file access do not require an explicit restart mechanism. And protocols that do not allow file access but have an explicit restart mechanism have virtually all the machinery required to provide file access, but do not make it available to the user.

The file systems found in current computer operating systems exhibit considerable variety and diversity. If an FTP is to be truly successful, it must allow data to be transferred efficiently between hosts and in a form that can be readily used. Considerably more work needs to be done on the problems of data formats, file structures, and access control mechanisms. Research on these areas will probably generate a solution intermediate between a standard representation and a catalog of all existing forms. In fact, as yet there is no good understanding of exactly how diverse the data formats, file structures, access control systems, and even file operations found in current file systems are, although it is apparent for most data-base applications that automatic translation from one data structure to another will be virtually impossible.

Although early FTP designs took a monolithic approach by combining all aspects of the file system into one protocol, later designs seem to recognize the advantages of partitioning FTPs into at least two separate protocols: a data-transfer portion and a file management portion. Such an organization as mentioned above enhances the security aspects of the protocol by allowing access to be effectively compartmentalized. It enhances software modularity and increases the efficiency of the protocol. Data-transfer applications are not burdened with using protocol implementations that must be able to perform functions unnecessary to the application.

By not using a monolithic design, it is easier to off-load an FTP to a network front-end. In addition, this approach yields a greater advantage in terms of saving host resources than the monolithic approach. Off-loading studies [18] have shown that when a protocol like the ARPANET FTP (a monolithic design) is off-loaded, the primary division of labor between the front end and the host is for the front end to do the data-transfer tasks and the host to do the file management tasks.

3.4   REMOTE JOB ENTRY PROTOCOLS

Remote job entry may be the next most important network requirement (after remote terminals) of users in the current data-processing environment. Most of the communications requirements of production-oriented data-processing shops are for interactive terminals or remote job stations. Remote Job Entry Protocols (RJEP) provide the network user with the flexibility to use one implementation of RJE software with a variety of batch systems. Thus, if people within an organization wish to use batch software facilities on, for example, an IBM 370, a UNIVAC 1110, and a CDC 7700, it is not necessary to have three RJE systems or packages. The benefit to the host providing the batch facilities is that a service host that can provide better service (cheaper, faster turnaround, etc.) can make it easier for potential customers to switch to it.

Protocols for remote job entry have been proposed and implemented in several networks [8, 10, 24]. An RJEP provides the user with the basic functions found in most batch systems:

- Commands for user identification and job submission.

- Commands for retrieving output.

- Commands for determining job status and for allowing some degree of modification (i.e., canceling).

- Commands for controlling the transfer of jobs and output across the network.

These protocols do not specify a ''network'' job control language, such as that described by Schicker and Duenki [43]. RJEPs are only concerned with remote job functions. Job control is a higher-level function which is "data" from the point of view of the RJEP. In the RJEPs discussed here, it is assumed that the job uses the job control language native to the particular host. However, this is not required. Since protocol levels provide transparent data transmission, a network job control language could be added without modifying the RJEP. However, it should be noted that most network job control languages (NJCL) entail a much more general environment than that supported by the typical RJEP. Thus, while an NJCL could be used on top of an RJEP, the RJEP would not support the whole of the control language. Needless to say, an RJEP does nothing to lessen the differences in the language implementations (i.e., Fortran on a Burroughs system is not exactly Fortran on an IBM system).

The two protocols discussed in the previous sections provided what might be termed basic services. Handling remote terminals and transferring files are not only the basic services a user needs but also represent two major classes of network traffic. Terminals generate bursty traffic where short delays or response times are important. File transfers generate constant long-duration traffic, where high bandwidth or throughput is important. Response time and throughput are generally the major design factors in flow-control and buffering schemes. RJEPs are also basic user services, but combine the terminal aspects with the bulk transfer aspects. Therefore, they do not easily fall into one of the two traffic classes. An interesting aspect of the RJEPs surveyed here is how well they provide the inexpensive and efficient service required of a basic user facility while utilizing the traffic-oriented facilities provided by the lower-level VTP and FTP services.

In the remainder of this section, three RJEPs are surveyed: (1) the UCLA-CCN NETRJS protocol [8], (2) the "official" ARPANET NETRJE protocol [10], and (3) an RJE protocol proposed by Day and Grossman [17] to solve some of the problems experienced with the first two.

3.4.1 UCLA's NETRJS

In the early days of the ARPANET there was considerable demand for RJE access to UCLA's IBM 360/91. Many user groups on the network had large computation problems that were especially well suited to the 360/91. To meet this demand the staff at UCLA's Campus Computing Network (CCN) developed the NETRJS protocol (network remote job service). The server side of this protocol was implemented during the summer of 1971 at UCLA. User NETRJS implementations appeared at various sites on the ARPANET over the next few years. This service is still used heavily by the ARPANET community. Although, the NETRJS is sufficiently general to accommodate different batch systems, no other server NETRJSs were implemented. This can be traced to two main causes:

1. NETRJS was superseded about a year and a half later by the official ARPANET RJE protocol.

2. The lack of large batch-oriented computers with excess capacity on the network. This was probably the greatest contributing factor.

The protocol is designed around the concept of a virtual remote batch terminal (VRBT) that may have card readers, line printers, and card punches attached to it. The server side of the protocol interfaces the VRBT to the local batch system. The user side maps a specific remote batch terminal (or collection of peripherals attached to a host) into the VRBT format. The VRBT is assumed to be controlled by the user's terminal. This terminal fulfills the function of the RJE terminal operator. The VRBT may also have associated with it one or more sources of input or output. These fulfill the functions of readers, punches, or printers.

The user of NETRJS establishes communication with the server using the Initial Connection Protocol. This procedure sets up a full duplex TELNET connection (Fig. 3.8). (In ARPANET, this requires two separate simplex connections.) This Telnet connection represents the terminal portion of the VRBT. The user's NETRJE commands for logging on, determining the status of jobs, and so on, are sent over this connection. When a job is to be submitted, a separate simplex connection is open to the server and the input is transmitted on this connection. This simplex connection represents the "virtual card reader" of the VRBT. Similarly, when the user wishes to retrieve its output, a simplex connection is opened from the server and the output is transmitted to the user. This is the "virtual line printer." These simplex connections for input and output are associated with the terminal connection in the following way. When the TELNET connection is established, a block of sockets (usually eight) are reserved. The connection uses the lower two of these. The sockets to be used for the three possible simplex connections (printer and punch) are defined to be fixed offsets from the base TELNET sockets). These simplex or data-transfer connections can be left established all the time or opened only when needed.

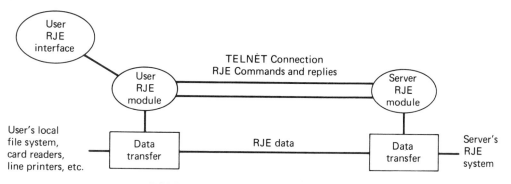

FIGURE 3-8   *The UCLA-CCN NETRJS protocol.*

The data-transfer portion of the protocol provides data compression and some error control (sequenced messages). The restart facilities that are available are a function of the indigenous batch system and are not part of the protocol.

3.4.2 ARPANET NETRJE Protocol

The NETRJS protocol was intended to be a starting point for the development of an ARPANET RJE based on TELNET and the Data Transfer Protocol (DTP). Therefore, many issues were not addressed in this early version. Unfortunately, the DTP was never specified and the current FTP was developed instead. Thus, the ARPANET RJE protocol, called NETRJE, was designed to be based on TELNET and FTP.

The NETRJE protocol provides for a "hot" line printer or card reader. This means that it would be possible for the user to set up the TELNET connection as in the NETRJS protocol. Then by placing special NETRJE cards in front of the deck, a user could submit jobs to the remote host by just putting the card deck in the reader. Similarly, when the job was completed the server would automatically print the output on a line printer at the host specified by the user. (It is possible in this protocol for a user at host A to use a server at host B; specify that input was to be from host C and the output was to go to host D.) In Sec. 3.3.6 it was pointed out that the ARPANET FTP was designed primarily as an interactive system and not for use by other network services. This combined with the "hot" line printer concept make NETRJE fairly cumbersome. Not only does it require considerable resources to implement and operate, but it also has a major security problem.

To use NETRJE, the user first establishes a NETRJE TELNET connection (Fig. 3.9) between the user RJE and server RJE processes. This connection is

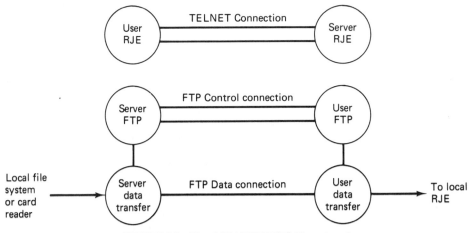

FIGURE 3-9 *The ARPANET NETRJE protocol.*

used much like the TELNET connection in NETRJS. Log on, status, and other such commands are sent on this connection. To submit a job the user must send an INPUT command (Table 3.7) to the server NETRJE process. The server NETRJE then initiates an FTP on the other host. The input file or card deck is then transferred over the network using FTP. To return the output, a similar sequence occurs. The server NETRJE uses its FTP to move the output to the host specified. The File Transfer Protocol requires a separate log on. From the point of view of the user NETRJE host, the NETRJE and FTP functions are completely independent. In fact, the output may be destined for a host other than the user's. To provide the "hot" line-printer feature, the user must store the user code and password for the host to receive the output on the server NETRJE host. This is a very severe security problem. Because of the desire to provide the hot line printer, NETRJE requires the NETRJE server and only the NETRJE server to use user FTP to transfer input and output. The only way for the user to avoid this problem is to FTP the input to a file on the server host; use NETRJE to submit the job and route the output to a file on the server host. When the job is complete, the user can then FTP the output to wherever it must go. Of course, such a procedure makes the use of NETRJE almost superfluous.

The desire to provide the hot line printer and to use the FTP causes the NETRJE protocol to be overly complex. To support the NETRJE protocol, a user must implement user TELNET, server FTP, and user NETRJE, while a server must implement server TELNET, user FTP, and server NETRJE. A server FTP implementation requires considerably more resources both in per-

TABLE 3-7: *Brief overview of ARPANET NETRJE commands*.*

REINIT	Reinitializes the state of the RJE server.
USER<user-id>	Logs the user into the server.
PASS<password>	Password for user log on to the server.
BYE	Terminates the server session.
INID/INPASS	Used to specify user code and password for retrieving input.
INPATH/INPUT	Specifies the host and path name of the input as well as the format for transfer.
ABORT	Used to abort input or output transfers.
OUTUSER/OUTPASS	Used to specify user code and password for storing output.
OUT	Specifies what is to be done with the output of the completed job: store locally, or FTP to some host.
CHANGE	Allows output disposition to be modified.
RESTART	Restart transfer from the beginning.
RECOVER	Restart transmission from last file transferred.
BACK	Backup the output "count" blocks.
SKIP	Skip the output forward "count" blocks.
STATUS	Requests status of session, a particular job or a transfer.
CANCEL/ALTER	Allows jobs to be canceled or to have site-specific parameters altered.
OP	Sends a message to the operator.

*These are typical of the protocols discussed here.

sonnel and software than a user FTP. In addition, when an RJE session is in progress all three of these protocol implementations will be executing for most of the life of the session. This could entail considerable burden for some systems. Although it may be acceptable to require a *service* to shoulder such burdens, it is not acceptable to require a user to assume them in order to gain a rather basic service. Most user installations are oriented toward meeting their user's needs, not toward implementing large amounts of network software.

This protocol has met with a rather underwhelming response from the ARPA network users and servers. The server side of the protocol was implemented at two or three sites. Two of these UC–San Diego and UC–Santa Barbara have since left the network. Very few, if any, user NETRJE's were ever implemented.

3.4.3 Day and Grossman Proposal

In early 1977, Gary Grossman and this author proposed an RJE protocol [17] that avoids the problems found in NETRJE. The functions required of an RJE system are fairly common and do not require much improvement. Our purpose was to use the RJE model to illustrate a solution to a more general problem. A network RJE facility should, in the interests of modularity, be based on a virtual terminal service and a file transfer service. However, RJE is such a basic user service that its implementation should not be overly expensive. It cannot be assumed that all users will be able to afford the resources to implement a fully general system. Our proposal provides a consistent structure within which a user may choose a method for attaining RJE service suitable to the available resources. This is a problem that recurs over and over again in the development of higher-level protocols.

This protocol is built around three distinct models, each one more sophisticated and with fewer shortcomings than the previous. It is assumed that a system which adopts one of these is willing to trade off sophistication for lower resource requirements, such as time, manpower, and computer resources. The three models can be characterized as: (1) RJE using TELNET only, (2) RJE using TELNET and data transfer, and (3) RJE using TELNET and FTP. (To be consistent with the original paper, terms from the ARPANET will be used in this description. They indicate only functional requirements.) The user may use the different models separately or in any consistent combination. Servers that provide a more sophisticated model are assumed to also provide all lesser models.

The first model (Fig. 3.10) uses only TELNET to provide the RJE service. This is a "quick and dirty" form of the protocol. Transfers of card decks and printer output are multiplexed on this connection. The user must provide software to demultiplex the commands and output on this connection. This technique has been used successfully in several ARPANET access systems. It has the advantage of being easier for a naive user, since the user does not have to remember non-

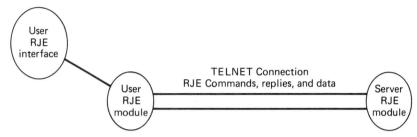

FIGURE 3-10 *Day and Grossman RJE protocol using only a TELNET connection.*

mnemonic port numbers. The major disadvantage of this model is that commands and replies may not be acted upon promptly because they become queued behind some card input or printer output. This is the price one pays for using this model.

The second model (Fig. 3.8) avoids the problem of delaying commands and replies by using separate connections for data transfer. This model is intended to closely resemble the NETRJS model described above. This model is capable of supporting all RJE functions with the exception of the transfer of input and output between hosts other than the user and server hosts. This model also meets all modularity requirements. RJE using only two hosts probably meets the requirements of the great majority of users.

The third model (Fig. 3.11) uses TELNET and FTP. The only major advantage of this model is that "third-party" transfers can be accomplished without divulging user code and password unnecessarily. The third-party transfer or server–server interaction described in Sec. 3.3 allows the user to route input and output to a third host in such a way that the user only has to send the user code

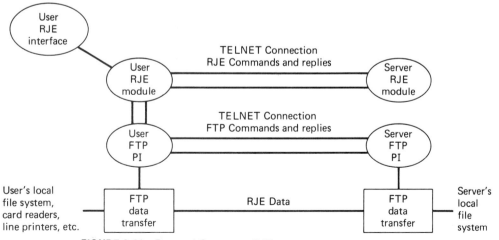

FIGURE 3-11 *Day and Grossman RJE protocol using TELNET and FTP.*

and password directly to the third host. A network is not required to have an ARPANET-like FTP. However, something like the ARPANET FTP's third-party transfer is required to provide this facility in such a way as to not divulge passwords.

This protocol avoids the security problem without sacrificing any of the generality of the NETRJE. However, if the user wishes to exercise some of the more sophisticated facilities, the user is required to shoulder some of the burden. For example, a hot line print can be provided, but it requires the user to provide the software to implement it. The server notifies the user when a job has completed (assuming that the user leaves the connection open). It is then the task of the user software to retrieve the output. Or the user can periodically establish an RJE connection, and retrieve the output of completed jobs. However, the burden for automatically printing output or submitting input is placed on the user's system. This approach allows the user to decide how important a hot printer or reader is.

Space does not permit a description of the commands used with the models. The commands and their syntax are organized in such a way that the forms used with the more sophisticated models are consistent with the forms used for the simpler models.

3.4.4 Summary

The purpose of this section has been to give the reader a general idea of the nature of Remote Job Entry Protocols. The commands and functions provided by the various RJEPs do not vary significantly. However, the protocol architecture within which these facilities are provided does vary. These differences allow considerable flexibility in the level of sophistication to be provided and in the cost of developing and using the protocol.

Remote Job Entry Protocols allow a user to execute a job on one of several computers. RJE in a network with more than one server host provides a rudimentary form of loadsharing. (The decision to perform a job on a different system is made by a human being rather than automatically.) Many proponents of networking speak in glowing terms of the advantages to be gained by being able to loadshare. There are three major reasons for executing a program on a remote host: (1) less cost or faster turnaround; (2) the existence of special packages or other software on the remote host; or (3) the program is simply too large to be executed locally. The last two are examples of accessing special facilities via a network. However, the first requires further consideration. Recent modeling and analysis [16, 31] indicates that rather sizable cost differentials (i.e., an order of magnitude) must exist for loadsharing to be feasible. With current technology, the cost of transferring an entire job from one host to another and then transferring the output back is high. The overriding cost is not the cost of the network itself, but the cost of network software in the individual hosts. Of course, this analysis assumes that there are no major problems with programs from one system executing on another. There are circumstances in which loadsharing is economical, but one should carefully consider each case before claiming that one of the major advantages to be gained by networking is loadsharing. A general rule might be that if functions can be shared (i.e., resident on several hosts) such that a small transfer of data generated a large amount of computation, then an economically feasible situation can exist.

3.5 CONCLUSIONS

In this chapter we have discussed three major classes of higher-level protocols: terminal, file, and remote job entry. In a sense these protocols are the most basic of the higher-level protocols. These protocols are often used as building blocks for more sophisticated network services such as distributed data-base systems (see Chapter 10) and network mail protocols. We can expect the number and kinds of higher-level protocols in use to rise rapidly. Most network users will not develop low-level communications protocols. They will either use one of the international standard protocols or use a protocol provided by their communications vendor. However, it is very likely that corporations, consortiums, special-interest groups (such as libraries), and so on, will find it necessary to develop specialized high-level protocols for their own use. Unfortunately, at the present time high-level or resource-sharing protocols are much more poorly understood than communication protocols. It is fairly well recognized that there is a qualitative difference in the two categories. More work is required to gain a better understanding of the nature of the intermediate models that are the heart of these protocols. Rigorous specifications are even more critical in resource-sharing protocols than in communication protocols. For resource-sharing protocols it is necessary to describe not only the behavior of a protocol implementation, but also the effects of certain protocol operations on the host system and its services, and the subsequent behavior of the host. The lack of rigorous specifications of protocols for heterogeneous networks can have catastrophic and costly results. At the present time, there is no rigorous specification methodology for higher-level protocols.

Recently, the International Standards Organization has begun a program of work that is rapidly adding to our understanding of resource-sharing protocols. ISO's Technical Committee 97 has established Study Committee 16 to develop an architecture for open-systems interconnection. An "open system" is one that is capable of interconnecting systems of different manufacture (i.e., heterogeneous). SC16 is developing a network architecture within which standard international protocols can be developed. The SC16 architecture [30] consists of seven layers: four concerned with lower-level communications services and three with higher-level resource-sharing services. One of the major benefits of the discussions among the experts from all over the world who are drafting this Open System Architecture is that many general principles of network protocol design and specification have begun to emerge. However, much work remains to be done before this aspect of computer networks is reasonably understood.

Acknowledgments

I would like to thank Ed Feustal and Fred Reucking of Rice University, Carl Sunshine of the RAND Corp., and Richard Howe of DTI for their help and advice in getting the rough draft into final form. I would also like to express my gratitude to Mike Williams of SDC and Peter Alsberg of DTI, who provided encouragement and direction, and to Frank Kuo for his patience.

GLOSSARY

ARPA: Advanced Research Projects Agency of the Department of Defense.

ARPANET: One of the earliest of the packet-switched networks; developed and funded by ARPA.

BTF: Bulk Transfer Facility; a file transfer protocol developed by a group at ETH Zurich.

CCITT: Consultative Committee for International Telegraphy and Telephony; sets international standards between communications carriers and for interfaces to them.

DAP: Data Access Protocol; a file transfer protocol developed by Digital Equipment Corporation.

DCE: Data communication equipment; CCITT nomenclature for anything owned by a communications carrier.

DTE: Data terminating equipment; CCITT nomenclature for anything owned by a subscriber that attaches to equipment owned by a carrier.

EPSS: Experimental Packet Switched System; a packet-switched network developed by the British Post Office.

ETH: Eidgenossishe Technische Hochscule, Zurich.

FAP: File Access Protocol; a file transfer protocol that allows parts of a file to be transferred. Also used as a generic term for only the transfer portion of an FTP.

FMP: File Maintenance Protocol; a generic term for the higher-level aspects of an FTP, such as directory management, renaming, and so on.

FTP: File Transfer Protocol; a network protocol for moving files from one host to another.

GMD: Gessellschaft for Mathematic und Daten verarbeitung, Darmstadt.

IFIP: International Federation for Information Processing.

INWG: International Network Working Group, IFIP Working Group 6.1.

ISO: International Standards Organization.

ITI: Interactive Terminal Interface; a Telenet product.

NETRJE: Network Remote Job Entry protocol in the ARPANET.

NETRJS: Network Remote Job Entry Service; developed by UCLA for the ARPANET.

NJCL: Network Job Control Language; a generic term.

NSW: National Software Works; an ARPA project to develop a distributed heterogeneous system for software development.

NVT: Network Virtual Terminal.

NWG: Network Working Group; a committee drawn from members of the ARPANET which designed the higher-level protocols for the ARPANET.

OSA: Open System Architecture; the reference model developed by ISO/TC97/SC16.

PAD: Packet Assembler/Disassembler; CCITT nomenclature for a device attached to a public data network which directly interfaces start–stop terminals.

PDTE: Packet-mode Data Terminating Equipment; a DTE that generates packets as opposed to characters.

PI: Protocol Interpreter.

RJEP: Remote Job Entry Protocol.

TELNET: Telecommunications Network; the ARPANET virtual terminal protocol.

TENEX: Operating system for a PDP-10 funded by ARPA and developed by Bolt Beranek and Newman.

TIP: Terminal Interface Processor; a specialized ARPANET switch that allows terminals to be directly connected to the network.

VTP: Virtual Terminal Protocol.

X.3:   CCITT recommendation that defines the PAD.

X.25:   CCITT recommendation that defines the interface between a packet-mode DTE and a packet-mode DCE.

X.28:   CCITT recommendation that defines the interface between a start/stop-mode DTE and the PAD.

X.29:   CCITT recommendation that defines the interface between a packet mode DTE and the PAD.

REFERENCES

Items in the bibliography marked with a NIC number have been archived by the ARPA Network Information Center, Stanford Research Institute, Menlo Park, CA 94025. Items marked with an RFC number are a series of Requests for Comments maintained at the

NIC by the ARPA Network Working Group. The *ARPANET Protocol Handbook* is edited
by Elizabeth Feinler and Jon Postel and is produced for the Defense Communication
Agency. Copies are available from the NIC or Defense Communications Agency, Code
535, Washington, D.C. 20305. Items marked with INWG numbers are the working papers
of IFIP Working Group 6.1 (International Network Working Group) and can be obtained
from Alex McKenzie, Bolt, Beranek and Neuman, 50 Moulton Street, Cambridge, MA.
02138

[1]   ALSBERG, P. A., J. F. BAILEY, D. S. BROWN, and J. R. MULLEN, "Intelligent
      Terminals as User Agents," *Trends and Applications 1976: Micro and Mini
      Systems,* IEEE 76Ch1101-5C, Gaithersburg, Md., 1976.

[2]   ANDERSON, R. H., "Advanced Intelligent Terminals as a User's Network Interface,"
      Proceedings of the 11th IEEE Computer Society Conference, 1975.

[3]   BARBER, D. L. A., "The Role and Nature of a Virtual Terminal," *Computer
      Communications Review*, **7**(3), p. 5. Also in *Proceedings of the AFIPS National
      Computer Conference*, 1976.

[4]   BARBER, D. L. A., "The Real Virtual Terminal," *INWG Protocol Note* 64, 1977.

[5]   BAUWENS, E., and F. MAGNEE, "Remarks on Negotiation Mechanism and Attention
      Handling," S.A.R.T. 77/12/13, *INWG Protocol Note* 72, 1977.

[6]   BAUWENS, E. and F. MAGNEE, "The Virtual Terminal Protocol for a Belgian
      University Network," " *Proceedings of the Symposium on Computer Network
      Protocols*, Liège, Belgium, February 1978.

[7]   BOUKNIGHT, W. J., G. R. GROSSMAN, and D. M. GROTHE, "The ARPA Network
      Terminal Service—A New Approach to Network Access," *Proceedings of the 3rd
      Data Communications Symposium*, 1973.

[8]   BRADEN, R., "Interim NETRJS Specifications," *ARPANET RFC* 189, NIC 7133,
      1971.

[9]   BRADEN, R. T., "NETCRT—A Character Display Protocol," *ARPANET RFC*
      205, 1971.

[10] BRESSLER, R., R. GUIDA, and A. McKENZIE, "Remote Job Entry Protocol,"
      ARPANET RFC 407, 1972.

[11] CCITT, "Proposals for Draft Provisional Recommendations for Interworking be-
      tween Non-packet Mode and Packet Mode DTE," *CCITT Study Group VII
      Temporary Document 62-E,* Geneva, 1977.

[12] CHESSON, G. L., "The Network UNIX System," *Proceedings of the 5th Symposium
      on Operating System Principles*, Austin, Tex., 1975.

[13] COSELL, B., and D. WALDEN, "Telnet Issues," *ARPANET RFC* 435, 1973.

[14] DAVIDSON, J., W. HATHAWAY, J. POSTEL, N. MIMNO, R. THOMAS, and D.
      WALDEN, "The ARPANET Telnet Protocol: Its Purpose, Principles, Implemen-
      tation, and Impact on Host Operating System Design," *Proceedings of the 5th
      Data Communications Symposium*, 1977.

[15] DAY, J. D., "A Proposal for a File Access Protocol," *ARPANET RFC* 520, 1973.

[16] DAY, J. D., and G. G. BELFORD, "A Cost Model for Data Distribution," *CAC*

Document 179, Center for Advanced Computation, University of Illinois, Urbana, IL., 1975.

[17] Day, J. D., and G. R. Grossman, "An RJE Protocol for a Resource Sharing Network," *ARPANET RFC* 725, 1977. [A shorter version appears in *Computer Communications Review*, 7(3).]

[18] Day, J. D., "Offloading ARPANET Protocols to a Front End," *CAC Document* 230, Center for Advanced Computation, University of Illinois, Urbana, IL., 1977.

[19] Day, J. D., "TELNET Data Entry Terminal Option," *ARPANET RFC* 731, 1977.

[20] *Digital Network Architecture Design Specification for Data Access Protocol*, Digital Equipment Corporation, Maynard, Mass., July 1975.

[21] Duenki, A., and P. Schicker, "Symmetry and Attention Handling: Comments on a Virtual Terminal," EIN/ZHR/77/03, *INWG Protocol Note*, 1977.

[22] EPSS Liason Group, Study Group 2, "A Basic File Transfer Protocol," HLP/CP (75) 3, Issue 2, *INWG General Note* 93, 1975.

[23] EPSS Liason Group, "An Interactive Terminal Protocol," HLP/CP (75) 2, *INWG General Note* 94, 1975.

[24] Gien, M., "A File Transfer Protocol (FTP)," *Proceedings of the Symposium on Computer Network Protocols*, Liège, Belgium, February 1978.

[25] Heinze, W., B. Struif, and M. Wilhelm, "The PIX–RJE Protocol," PIX/RJE/TAG/77, GMD-IFV, Rheinstrasse 75, D-6100 Darmstadt, 1977.

[26] Heinze, W., and B. Butscher, "File Transfer in the HMI Computer Network," *Proceedings of the 3rd European Network User's Workshop*, IIASA, Laxenburg, Austria, p. 13, April 1977.

[27] Hertweck, F. R., E. Raubold, and F. Vogt, "X.25 Based Process–Process Communication," *Proceedings of the Symposium on Computer Network Protocols*, Liège, Belgium, February 1978.

[28] Higginson, P. L., "Restructured Version of ESP 25—Part C; Chapter 2—Packet Assembler Disassembler for the Adaptation of Asynchronous Character Terminals to the Virtual Terminal," *INDRA Note* 640, Department of Statistics and Computer Science, University College, London, 1977.

[29] IFIP WG 6.1, "Proposal for a Standard Virtual Terminal Protocol," *INWG Protocol Note* 91, 1978. (Also in *Proceedings of the Symposium on Computer Network Protocols*, Liège, Belgium February 1978.)

[30] International Standards Organization, "Reference Model for Open System Architecture," *ISO/ TC97/SC16/N227* revised, 1979. (Available from National Standards Bodies.)

[31] Jacquemart, Y., "Network Interprocess Communication in an X.25 Environment," *Proceedings of the Symposium on Computer Network Protocols*, Liège, Belgium, February 1978.

[32] Luca, R., "Zones—A Solution to the Problem of Dynamic Screen Formatting in CRT-based Networks," *Proceedings of the 4th Data Communications Symposium*, Quebec, October 7–9, p. 1-1, 1975.

[33] MANNING, E., Personal communication, 1976.

[34] MUNTZ, C. A., and P. M. CASHMAN, "File Package: The File Handling Facility for
      the National Software Works (preliminary)," *Massachusetts Computer Associa-
      tion Document CADD-7602-2011, 1976.*

[35] NAFFAH, N., "Protocole appareil virtuel-type écran," TER 536, *Réseau CY-
      CLADES, IRIA,* Rocquencourt, France, 1976.

[36] NEIGUS, N., K. POGRAN, and J. POSTEL, "Revised FTP Reply Codes," *RFC* 640,
      1974. (Also in the *ARPANET Protocol Handbook*.)

[37] NEIGUS, N., "File Transfer Protocol," *RFC* 542, 1973. (Also in the *ARPANET
      Protocol Handbook*.)

[38] ORNSTEIN, S. M. *et al.* "The Terminal IMP for the ARPA Computer Network,"
      Proceedings of the AFIPS Spring Joint Computer Conference, **40,** 243–254, 1972.

[39] PARRISH, W., and J. R. PICKENS, "MIT-Mathlab Meets UCSB-OLS," *ARPANET
      RFC* 525, 1973.

[40] PASSAFIUME, J. J., and S. WECKER, "Distributed File Access in DECNET,"
      *Proceedings of the 2nd Berkeley Workshop on Distributed Databases and Net-
      working,* Lawrence Berkeley Laboratory, Berkeley, Calif., 1977.

[41] PYKE, T. N., JR., "Network Access Techniques: Some Recent Developments,"
      Proceedings of the 3rd Texas Conference on Computing Systems, Austin, Tex.,
      1974.

[42] RETZ, D. L., "ELF—A System for Network Access," *IEEE Intercon Conference
      Record,* New York, 1975.

[43] SCHICKER, P., A. DUENKI, and W. BAECHI, "Bulk Transfer Facility," EIN/ZHR/
      75/20, *INWG Protocol Note* 31, 1975.

[44] SCHICKER, P., "Virtual Terminal Protocol (Proposal 2)," EIN/ZHR/75/5, *INWG
      Protocol Note* 30, 1975.

[45] SCHICKER, P., and A. DUENKI, "Network Job Control and Its Supporting Services,"
      Proceedings of the 3rd International Conference on Computer Communications,
      Toronto, Canada, August 1976.

[46] SCHICKER, P., and A. DUENKI, "Virtual Terminal Definition and Protocol," EIN/
      ZHR/76/019a, *INWG Protocol Note* 51, 1976.

[47] SCHICKER, P., and A. DUENKI, "The Virtual Terminal Definition," EIN/ZHR/77/
      0186, submitted to *Computer Networks,* 1977.

[48] SCHICKER, P., and H. ZIMMERMAN, "Proposal for a Scroll Mode Virtual Terminal,"
      EIN/CCG/77 02, *INWG Protocol Note* 62, 1977.

[49] SCHULZE, G., and J. BORGER, "A Virtual Terminal Protocol Based upon the 'Shared
      Communication Variable' Concept," *Proceedings of the Symposium on Computer
      Network Protocols,* Liège, Belgium, February 1977.

[50] TELNET Protocol Specification, NIC#18639, 1973. (Also in the *ARPANET Pro-
      tocol Handbook, 1973*.)

[51] Telenet Corp. Interactive Terminal Interface Specification, Telenet Corp., Washington, D.C., 1977.

[52] THOMAS, R. H., "Distributed Computation Research at BBN," *Report* 2976, Bolt, Beranek, and Newman, Inc., Cambridge, Massachusetts, 1974.

[53] THOMAS, R. H., "A Resource Sharing Executive for the ARPANET," *Proceedings of the AFIPS National Computer Conference*, 1973.

4

ROUTING AND FLOW CONTROL

MARIO GERLA

University of California, Los Angeles

4.1 INTRODUCTION

A computer network consists of computer and communications resources and customers that want to use them. The resources are generally sharable, and therefore coordination is required among the customers for their efficient and fair use. This coordination is obtained via network procedures or protocols, which are rules governing the access to resources, the establishment of connections, and the exchange of data through the network.

In this chapter we restrict our analysis to the communication resources, that is, the resources required for the transfer of data from the entry to the exit point in the network. These resources are the channels, the switching processors, and the data buffers; together with the protocols that govern them, they form the communication *subnet*. Since one of the key motivations for data networking (as opposed to dedicated, point-to-point connections) is the efficient sharing of common facilities among a large population of (typically "bursty") users, it is natural that the protocols supervising the sharing of such resources play a major role in the design and operation of a data network. These protocols are often referred to as "internal" protocols (i.e., operating within the subnet boundaries) to distinguish them from the network access and end-to-end protocols, which involve external processes. Examples of end-to-end protocols were discussed in Chapters 2 and 3. In this chapter we discuss two internal protocols, routing and flow control. Other examples of internal protocols are presented in Chapters 5 and 6.

The function of routing and flow-control procedures is to control the traffic within the network. The goal here is the *efficiency* of the data transfer. It is assumed that the *integrity* of the data transfer (e.g., error protection, sequencing, duplicate detection, security, etc.) is provided by other protocols.

The goal of the *routing* protocol is to provide the best collection of paths between source and destination, given the traffic requirements and the network configuration. The definition of best path may vary depending on the nature of the traffic (e.g., interactive, batch, digitized voice) and the existence of contraints not necessarily related to performance (e.g., political, legal, policy, and security issues). In this chapter, however, best paths will be generally regarded as the paths of minimum delay. Since traffic requirements and network configuration change in time (the latter, for example, because of link and node failures), the routing protocol must be "adaptive," that is, it must be able to adjust the routes to time-varying network conditions.

The routing protocol attempts to optimize to network resource utilization as long as the offered traffic is "feasible" (i.e., it can be accommodated by the network). When the offered traffic exceeds network capacity, network inputs must be regulated so as to reduce total load to an acceptable level. This input regulation is provided by the *flow-control* procedure. More precisely, the goal of flow control is to control the admissions to the network so that resources are effciently utilized and, at the same time, user performance requirements are satisfied. This control is very critical, since the throughput in an uncontrolled network tends to increase steadily for increasing offered traffic, up to capacity. Beyond capacity, the uncontrolled network may suddenly collapse, leading to severe performance degradation and possibly deadlocks. An essential function of flow control is therefore the prevention of deadlocks that may arise as a consequence of congestion.

A network function closely related to flow control is the detection of inaccessible nodes. These are the nodes that cannot be reached from a given node either because they have failed or because all the links leading to them have failed and therefore are isolated. Prompt detection of inaccessible nodes is essential to avoid network congestion due to undeliverable packets.

In this chapter "flow control" is intended as a synonym for "congestion control." Some authors extend the definition of flow control to include higher-level functions, such as error protection, duplicate detection, and so on [5]. This is not surprising since, as we will see later, congestion control is the result of the cooperation of several levels of protocols, starting at the link level and going all the way up to the end-to-end level. Each one of these protocols contributes to flow control while performing other functions, such as link error protection, packet sequencing, and so on. In this chapter we attempt to isolate the congestion control features from the other features, and reserve the term "flow control" for those functions (of the protocols) that promote and protect the efficient use of shared resources.

So far we have presented the routing protocol and the flow-control protocol as separate functions: flow control determines when to block (or drop) data traffic either at the entrance or within the network, while routing selects the best path to destination. Strong interaction between the two protocols actually exists in some types of packet subnets. In virtual-circuit subnets, for example, where a path is preestablished (and resources along the path are preallocated) at connection setup time, the routing protocol is responsible for finding the best path with sufficient resources to support the connection. If no such path is found, the connection is refused. So, routing and flow control work in concert in virtual-circuit nets. In datagram networks, on the other hand, these functions are to a large degree independent.

The purpose of this chapter is to identify the objectives and review the existing implementations of routing and flow-control procedures. Section 4.2 introduces the routing problem in two different environments: the *static* (or quasistatic) traffic environment and the *time-varying* traffic environment. Section 4.3 reviews the solutions for static (and quasistatic) routing and discusses important applications of such solutions to network design. Section 4.4 deals with adaptive routing (for rapidly varying traffic requirements) and proposes a classification of adaptive routing policies. This classification is used to introduce and compare several policies that have been described in the literature and/or implemented in real networks.

Section 4.5 discusses flow control. The various levels at which flow control operates—node to node, network access, entry to exit, and virtual circuit—are identified and are illustrated with examples of actual implementations.

Section 4.6 deals with the detection of nodal failures and isolations and presents a simple algorithm to detect unreachable nodes.

Finally, Section 4.7 discusses the extension of the traditional concepts of routing and flow control in new network environments, including large networks, multiple net interconnections, and hybrid packet and circuit networks.

4.2 THE ROUTING PROBLEM

4.2.1 The Objective

We assume that a traffic pattern $r(i, j)$ (packets/s) from source i to destination j, $i = 1, \ldots, N; j = 1, \ldots, N$, where N is the number of switching nodes, is presented to the network. The value $r(i, j)$ therefore represents the sum of all the traffic requirements from terminals and computers connected to node i to terminals and computers connected to node j. We also assume, for the moment, that this traffic pattern is feasible (i.e., it can be accommodated by the network). The objective of the routing procedure is to transport packets on minimum-delay paths from source to destination. In optimizing packet delays we can use two different criteria:

1. Optimization of an average system delay, averaged over all node pairs (system optimization).

2. Optimization of the individual delay for each source-to-destination traffic requirement $r(i, j)$ (user optimization).

Using system optimization, the paths between all source-to-destination pairs are optimized jointly according to a common objective, the overall average delay. With user optimization, on the other hand, each source-to-destination requirement is optimized independently (''selfishly,'' we may say) until a competitive equilibrium is reached. It turns out that the routing solutions obtained using these distinct criteria are not very different, especially for large networks with uniform requirements. Conceptually, however, it is important to distinguish between the two approaches.

The system optimization approach is generally used in static routing problems, with centralized decision, while the user optimization concept is most common in adaptive routing problems with distributed decision. It is possible, however, to produce user optimal solutions with centralized routing algorithms, and, likewise, system optimal solutions with distributed algorithms, as will be discussed later.

4.2.2　Static versus Adaptive Routing

In discussing routing policies for computer networks, an important distinction must be made between static and adaptive policies. This distinction depends on the environment in which a policy is designed to operate. If network topology is not subject to changes (due to failures, modifications, growth), and traffic inputs are stationary (e.g., characterized by Poisson processes with constant mean), then the optimal routing solution is a *static solution* consisting of a set of fixed paths between all node pairs. The traffic between each source—destination pair may be distributed on several paths simultaneously in well-defined proportions, where the proportions are fixed in time.

In a real network environment, however, the topology changes with time and the user traffic requirements tend to fluctuate more-or-less rapidly in time. To minimize delays it is then necessary to implement an *adaptive* routing policy that can react and adjust to various changes. The adaptivity of a policy can be measured in terms of its response time (i.e., the rate of change that it can efficiently track and adjust to). If the rate of change is sufficiently low (with respect to network transmission rates), a reasonable solution is a periodically refreshed static solution. Indeed, there is a continuum of solutions between the two extremes—static and adaptive—characterized by different response times and used for different applications. Recently, a gamut of alternatives that combine static and adaptive routing features have been experimentally evaluated, with encouraging results [59].

Beside the use in operational networks, static routing policies find an important application in the network design process. During this process, we need to predict the throughput and delay performance of a given topology, for a given traffic pattern. The routing policy clearly has a major impact on such performance. Most routing implementations are adaptive, and, unfortunately, the analysis of adaptive routing policies is an extremely difficult task. To simplify the problem, the traffic pattern is usually approximated with a stationary pattern, and the routing policy with a static routing policy. The static policy evaluation is then carried out very efficiently using the computational techniques discussed in Section 4.3.

4.3. STATIC ROUTING

4.3.1 Routing-Table Representation

A static routing policy is represented by a set of routing tables, one for each node, indicating how the traffic arriving at that node must be routed on the outgoing links, depending on its final destination. The routing table for node i is an $N \times A_i$ matrix $P^{(i)}(\cdot, \cdot)$, where N = number of nodes in the network and A_i =

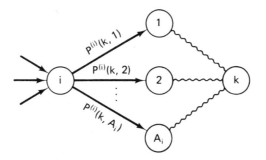

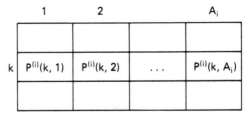

FIGURE 4-1 *Routing table* $p^{(i)}$ *at node* i.

number of neighbors of node i. $P^{(i)}(k, j)$ is the fraction of traffic directed to k which, upon arrival at node i, is routed through neighbor j (Fig. 4.1). Clearly, by definition,

$$\sum_{j=1}^{A_i} P^{(i)}(k, j) = 1 \qquad \forall\, i \tag{4.1}$$

The actual distribution of the incoming traffic to outgoing links may be done randomly using as probability weights the values $P^{(i)}(k, j)$. If for any node i there is only one permissible outgoing link from i to any destination k, that is,

$$P^{(i)}(k, j) = \begin{cases} 1 & \text{for } j = j_{ik} \\ 0 & \text{for } j \neq j_{ik} \end{cases} \tag{4.2}$$

then the routing policy is referred to as a *fixed* (or single-path) routing policy, since only one path is used from any node i to any destination k. In general, however, the optimal static routing solution is a *multipath* solution, allowing for the simultaneous use of several routes in order to minimize delays.

The routing-table representation may also be used, as we will see later, for adaptive policies. In that case, the entries $P^{(i)}(k, j)$ will vary with time, following the changes in network conditions.

Before presenting the routing problem, we introduce the concept of link flow vector $\mathbf{f} = (f_1, f_2, \ldots, f_b)$, where b is the total number of (directed) links in the network and f_i is the average data flow (in bits/s) carried on link i and due to the contribution of all packets transmitted over link i. Clearly, $\mathbf{f}$ is uniquely defined, given the traffic requirements and the routing policy. Conversely, not any generic vector $\mathbf{f}$ corresponds to a realizable routing policy and requirement matrix. If it does, then $\mathbf{f}$ is a multicommodity (MC) flow for that particular requirement matrix. An MC flow results from the sum of single commodity flows $\mathbf{f}^{jk}$ ($j, k = 1, 2, \ldots, N$), where $\mathbf{f}^{jk}$ is the average flow vector generated by packets with source node j and destination node k, and N is the number of nodes.

4.3.2   Problem Formulation

Consider a packet-switched computer communication network. In such a network, messages are segmented into packets, and each packet traveling from source i to destination j is "stored" in a queue at each intermediate node k, while awaiting transmission, and is sent "forward" to l, the next node in the route from k to j, when channel (k, l) is free. Thus, at each node there are several queues, one for each output channel. Packet-flow requirements between nodes arise at random times and packets are of random length; therefore, channel flows, queue lengths, and packet delay are random variables.

Under appropriate assumptions,[1] it is possible to relate the average delay T of a packet traveling from source to destination (the average is over time and over all pairs of nodes) to the average flows in the channels. The result of the analysis is [42]

$$T = \frac{1}{\gamma} \sum_{i=1}^{b} \frac{f_i}{C_i - f_i} \tag{4.3}$$

where T = total average delay per packet (s/packet)

N = number of nodes

b = number of (directed) links

r_{ij} = average packet rate from source i to destination j (packets/s)

$\gamma = \sum_{i=1}^{N} \sum_{j=1}^{N} r_{ij}$ = total packet arrival rate from external sources (throughput) (packets/s)

f_i = total flow on channel i (bits/s)

C_i = capacity of channel i (bit/s)

The expression of T becomes more complicated when more details are included in the model [25]; the method proposed here also applies to those more general models.

A static routing problem can be defined as the problem of finding the static routing policy which minimizes the average delay T. Considering the relationship between routing policy and link flows, we may formulate the problem as follows:

given: (a) Topology
(b) Channel capacities C_i
(c) Requirement matrix R

minimize:

$$T = \frac{1}{\gamma} \sum_{i=1}^{b} \frac{f_i}{C_i - f_i} \tag{4.4}$$

over the design variable: $\mathbf{f} = (f_1, f_2, \ldots, f_b)$

---

[1] Assumptions: Poisson arrivals at nodes, exponential distribution of packet length, independence of arrival processes at different nodes, independence assumption of service times at successive nodes [42].

subject to: (a) **f** is a multicommodity flow satisfying the requirement matrix
             R
             (b) **f** ≤ **C**

From formulation (4.4), we notice that the routing problem is a convex MC flow problem on a convex constraint set; therefore, there is a unique local minimum which is also the global minimum and can be found using any downhill search technique [3].

4.3.3 Solution Techniques

Several optimal techniques for the solution of MC flow problems are found in the literature [15, 67]; however, their direct application to the routing problem proves, in general, to be cumbersome and computationally not efficient. Consequently, considerable effort was spent in developing heuristic suboptimal routing techniques [8, 22, 69]. Satisfactory results were obtained and computational efficiency was greatly improved. However, all these techniques are affected by various limitations and may fail in some pathological situations.

A new downhill search algorithm, called *flow deviation* (FD), was recently developed by Fratta, Gerla, and Kleinrock [21]. The FD algorithm finds the optimal solution and is computationally as efficient as the heuristics. To place the FD algorithm in the proper perspective we first introduce the most popular among the heuristic algorithms—the *minimum link algorithm*—and compare it to the FD algorithm.

A. Minimum Link Algorithm [8]

We begin by giving an outline of the heuristic algorithm reported in [8].

Algorithm:

- Step 1. For a given source j and destination k, determine all paths Π_{jk} with the minimum number of intermediate nodes. Such paths are called "feasible" paths.

- Step 2. Choose, among the feasible paths, the least utilized path (or the path with maximum residual capacity).

- Step 3. Route the requirement γ_{jk} along such a path.

- Step 4. If all source destination pairs have been processed, stop; otherwise, select a new pair and go to 1.

Step 1, repeated for all node pairs, corresponds to the evaluation of all shortest paths between all pairs of nodes, assuming unitary link length. Such a computation requires from $O(N^2)$ to $O(N^2 \log N)$ operations, depending on network connectivity. It can be shown that the total amount of computation required by the algorithm has proportion between $O(N^2)$ and $O(N^2 \log N)$.

The minimum link algorithm is conceptually simple and computationally very efficient. Its major drawback is that of being rather insensitive to queueing delays and therefore possibly far from optimum in heavy traffic situations.

B. Flow Deviation Algorithm [21]

Before introducing the flow deviation algorithm, we mention the following properties of the optimal routing solution.

- Property 1. The set of MC flows **f** satisfying the requirement matrix R is a convex polyhedron. The extreme points of such a polyhedron are called "extremal flows" (or "shortest-route flows") and correspond to shortest-route policies. A shortest-route policy is a single-path policy that routes each (j, k) commodity along the shortest path, evaluated under an arbitrary assignment of lengths to the links. To each such assignment there corresponds an extremal flow. Any MC flow can be expressed as a convex combination of extremal flows [3].

- Property 2. For a given MC flow **f,** let us define link length as a function of link flow of the form $l_i \triangleq \partial T / \partial f_i$. Let ϕ be the shortest-route flow associated with such link lengths and let $\mathbf{f}' = (1 - \lambda)\phi + \lambda\mathbf{f}$ be the convex combinations of ϕ and **f** minimizing the delay T. If $T(\mathbf{f}') = T(\mathbf{f})$, then f is optimal[3].

Property 2 provides a way of finding a downhill direction if it exists. Based on such property, we may now state the *flow deviation algorithm* as follows.

Algorithm:

- Step 0. Let $\mathbf{f}^{(0)}$ be a starting feasible flow. (A starting feasible flow can be obtained using a modified version of the FD algorithm [21].) Let $p = 0$.

- Step 1. Compute $\phi^{(p)}$, the shortest-route flow corresponding to $l_i^{(p)} = [\partial T / \partial f_i]_{f = f^{(p)}}, \forall i = 1, \ldots, b$.

- Step 2. Let $\bar{\lambda}_p$ be the minimizer of $T[(1 - \lambda)\phi^{(p)} + \lambda\mathbf{f}^{(p)}], 0 \le \lambda \le 1$. Let $\mathbf{f}^{(p + 1)} = (1 - \bar{\lambda}_p)\phi^{(p)} + \bar{\lambda}_p\mathbf{f}^{(p)}$.

- Step 3. If $|T(\mathbf{f}^{(p + 1)}) - T(\mathbf{f}^{(p)})| < \epsilon$, stop: $\mathbf{f}^{(p)}$ is optimized to within the given tolerance. Otherwise, let $p = p + 1$ and go to step 1.

A geometric representation of the FD algorithm is given in Fig. 4.2.

Step 1 is the most time-consuming operation of the algorithm and requires an

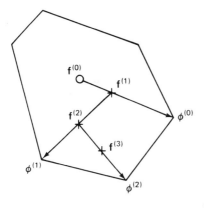

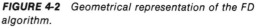

FIGURE 4-2   *Geometrical representation of the FD algorithm.*

amount of computation between $O(N^2)$ and $O(N^2 \log N)$. Therefore, the amount of computation required by the minimum link algorithm and the FD algorithm are comparable.

We have shown how to obtain the optimal flow **f**. To construct the optimal routing tables $P^{(i)}(k, j)$, some additional bookkeeping is required. In particular, we need to keep track, during the execution of the FD algorithm, of the "destination" flows $\mathbf{f}^{(k)}$, $k = 1, \ldots, N$, where k is the generic destination and $f_m^{(k)}$ represents the average data flow on link m due to all the contributions directed to destination k. Destination flows $\mathbf{f}^{(k)}$ are actually a by-product of the FD algorithm. From the destination flows the routing tables are simply derived as follows:

$$P^{(i)}(k, j) = \frac{f_{i,\,j}^{(k)}}{\sum\limits_{l=1}^{A_i} f_{i,\,l}^{(k)}} \qquad (4.5)$$

where (i, j) indicates the directed link from i to j, and A_i = number of neighbours of node i.

4.3.4 Distributed Solution Approach (Gallager [24])

In previous sections we have shown algorithms for the *centralized* computation of optimal routes (i.e., one computer center knows the topology and the traffic requirements and does all the processing to generate the routing tables). In this section we show that the optimal solution can also be obtained via a distributed process, where each node in the network participates in the routing computation. This is clearly of interest when the static policy is used as an operational protocol. In this case, reliability is greatly enhanced by a distributed implementation.

In order to illustrate the distributed computation mechanism, we begin with a simple routing problem. For an arbitrary, connected topology, we define $d(i, j)$ to be the length of link (i, j) [where $d(i, j) > O$]. We wish to find the shortest paths from each node to all the destinations. We assume that each node: (1) has some processing capability, (2) knows the length of its outgoing links, and (3) can exchange information only with its neighbors. A simple distributed algorithm that satisfies such assumptions is described below.

Let us assume that each node i ($i = 1, \ldots, N$) has an $N \times A_i$ matrix $DT^{(i)}$, called a *distance table*, whose entry $DT^{(i)}(k, l)$ is the estimated minimal distance from node i to destination k if l is chosen to be the next node in the route to k. Furthermore, from $DT^{(i)}$, an N-dimensional vector $MDV^{(i)}$ (the minimum-distance vector) is derived as follows:

$$MDV^{(i)}(k) = \operatorname*{Min}_{l \, \epsilon \, A_i} DT^{(i)}(k, l) \tag{4.6}$$

$MDV^{(i)}(k)$ represents the minimum estimated distance from i to k. We now introduce the distributed procedure for the calculation of minimum-distance routes. Each node periodically updates its own distance table by using the knowledge of length values on its outgoing links and the information received from the neighbors. More precisely, during every interval δ, each node transmits to (and receives from) its neighbors the vector MDV. Upon reception of vectors $MDV^{(l)}$, $l \, \epsilon \, A_i$, node i updates $DT^{(i)}$ as follows:

$$\begin{cases} DT^{(i)}(k, l) = d(i, l) + MDV^{(l)}(k) & k \neq i \\ DT^{(i)}(k, l) = 0 & k = i \end{cases} \tag{4.7}$$

Initially, we let

$$DT^{(i)}(k, l) = 0, \qquad \forall \, k, l \tag{4.8}$$

It can be shown that if the topology is connected, this procedure leads in a finite number of steps to a final set of tables $DT^{(i)}(k, l)$, where all the entries are $< \infty$. The vector $MDV^{(i)}(k)$ calculated from the final table DT is the shortest distance from i to k and the neighbor l^* such that

$$DT^{(i)}(k, l^*) \leq DT^{(i)}(k, l) \qquad \forall \, l \, \epsilon \, A_i$$

is the next node on the shortest path from i to k.

If the distance along link (i, j) is defined to be $d(i, j) = 1$ for all the links in the network, the algorithm becomes the well-known minimum-hop routing algorithm, producing minimum-hop distances to all destinations (we will see an important application of this algorithm in the study of isolation-detection procedures in Section 4.6).

We now return to the routing problem in packet networks. The minimum-delay routing problem found in packet networks is more complex than the shortest-path problem, but it can still be solved using distributed computation. Here we report an elegant distributed algorithm due to Gallager [24], which in many ways resembles the shortest-path algorithm. We define the link length to be

$$d(i,j) = \frac{\partial T}{\partial f_{ij}} = \frac{1}{(C_{ij} - f_{ij})^2} \tag{4.9}$$

where C_{ij} = capacity of link (i, j)

f_{ij} = average flow on link (i, j)

Clearly, $d(i, j)$ is intended to approximate the incremental delay due to a unit increment of flow on link (i, j). Each node i ($i = 1, \ldots, N$) stores a matrix $\mathrm{IDT}^{(i)}$, called the incremental delay table, whose entry $\mathrm{IDT}^{(i)}(k, l)$ represents the estimated incremental delay produced by routing a unit of k-traffic (i.e., traffic with final destination k) through neighbor node l. Also stored in node i is the routing table $P^{(i)}$, whose entry $P^{(i)}(k, l)$ represents the fraction of k-traffic that is routed through neighbor l. From $\mathrm{IDT}^{(i)}$ and $P^{(i)}$, the vector $\mathrm{IDV}^{(i)}$ (incremental delay vector) is computed as follows:

$$\mathrm{IDV}^{(i)}(k) = \sum_{l \in A_i} P^{(i)}(k, l)\mathrm{IDT}^{(i)}(k, l) \tag{4.10}$$

$\mathrm{IDV}^{(i)}(k)$ represents the incremental delay produced by injecting a unitary increment of k-traffic into node i.

Now, each node periodically exchanges IDVs with the neighbors. After the exchange, the $\mathrm{IDT}^{(i)}$ tables get updated in the obvious way:

$$\mathrm{IDT}^{(i)}(k, l) = d(i, l) + \mathrm{IDV}^{(l)}(k) \tag{4.11}$$

The routing tables $P^{(i)}$ are also updated. The idea is to deviate the flow from high incremental delay routes to low incremental delay routes. Clearly, this deviation will produce a net delay saving. Thus, letting l^* be the minimizer of $\mathrm{IDT}^{(i)}(k, l)$, for $l \in A_i$, we update the routing tables as follows:

$$\begin{aligned} P^{(i)}(k, l^*) &= P^{(i)}(k, l^*) + \delta' \\ P^{(i)}(k, l) &= P^{(i)}(k, l) - \delta'' \qquad \text{for } l \neq l^* \end{aligned} \tag{4.12}$$

where δ' and δ'' are small positive quantities properly selected so as to satisfy the constraints:

$$\left\{ \begin{array}{c} \sum_{l \,\epsilon\, A_i} P^{(i)}(k, l) = 1 \\[2em] P^{(i)}(k, l) \geqslant 0 \end{array} \right. \tag{4.13}$$

In order to prevent loops during the update process, some additional rules must be observed. In particular, the updating must start from the destination node (say, k) and propagate back to the origins; that is, a node cannot update its tables until it has received the IDVs from all its downstream neighbors (i.e., all the neighbors to which it is sending traffic with final destination k). After a node has completed the update, it will broadcast its IDV to *all* the neighbors.

When the rules are carefully followed, this procedure converges to the optimal (system optimizing) solution found by the FD method. An important feature of this distributed procedure is that the routing tables are loop-free not only in the final solution, but also during the entire updating process.

4.3.5 System Optimization versus User Optimization

We have seen in Sec. 4.2 that two different objectives can be pursued in the solution of the routing problem:

1. Minimization of total average delay (system optimization).

2. Minimization of individual source-to-destination delays until competitive equilibrium is reached (user optimization).

The minimum link and the flow deviation solutions, as stated in Section 4.3.3, are examples of *system optimization* obtained with centralized approaches. The distributed algorithm in Section 4.3.4 also yields a system-optimizing solution. It is of interest now to obtain also the *user-optimizing* solution, especially since we intend to approximate adaptive routing policies (which are generally user-optimizing) with the more easily analyzable static policies. It turns out that a simple modification to the objective function in the FD procedure will do the trick! Namely, it suffices to use a new objective function D, where D is defined as follows [26]:

$$D = \sum_{i=1}^{b} \log\frac{1}{1 - f_i/C_i} \qquad \text{where } b = \text{number of links} \tag{4.14}$$

If the objective D is used in the FD method, the link length becomes (see 4.9)

$$l_i = \frac{\partial D}{\partial f_i} \equiv \frac{f_i}{C_i - f_i} \equiv T_i(f_i) \tag{4.15}$$

That is, the link length is proportional to the delay incurred on the link; consequently, the shortest path is exactly the minimum-delay path—the path that would be chosen by a "selfish" user to send his or her own traffic down to the destination. A user concerned about overall system performance and, in particular, about the impact of his or her traffic on the rest of the community would instead use the minimum-*incremental*-delay paths, which minimize $\sum_{i=1}^{b} \partial T/\partial f_i$.

We will come back to these "social" issues in adaptive routing in Section 4.4. Here we want to report on some comparisons between user-optimizer and system-optimizer performance. For a medium-sized network (21 nodes), with two-connectivity, uniform capacities, uniform traffic requirements, and 65% loading, we found that the difference between the two traffic patterns was insignificant (less than 1%). This corroborates an earlier conjecture that the optimal traffic pattern is not so sensitive to the actual form of the objective function, as long as this function reflects the asymptomatic behavior for f_i approaching C_i [25].

4.3.6 Application of Static Routing to Network Design

Static routing finds numerous applications in computer network design. During the design, we are not generally interested in the actual routing tables that produce the minimum-delay selection. Rather, we want to determine whether a given traffic pattern can be accommodated by the network, and, if it can, what the average delay will be. In fact, the network topology is generally designed interactively by producing small perturbations (such as addition/deletion of a few links or reduction/upgrading of a few link capacities), observing the effect of such perturbations on throughput and delay performance and trying to find improving directions. This performance evaluation is accomplished using a static routing algorithm.

A method that applies this process is the cut-saturation algorithm for the topological layout of packet switched networks [29]. A *cut* is a set of lines whose removal will disconnect the network. A cut is *saturated* if the traffic load in every line of the cut equals the line capacity. There are, in general, a large number of cuts in a network. When traffic load grows, one of the cuts approaches saturation. The only way the network capacity can be increased, then, is to increase line capacities along the cut or add additional lines to the cut. This principle is the basis of the *cut saturation* (CS) *algorithm*. The algorithm attempts to keep network throughput within specified bounds while iteratively reducing overall line cost and verifying capacity, delay, and reliability constraints.

The heart of the CS algorithm is its routing algorithm. The routing algorithm employed is an adaption of the flow deviation method, which provides optimal link flows for a given network topology, link capacity allocation, and traffic requirement. (For simplicity, we assume that the traffic requirements between all pairs of nodes are identical and equal to the quantity RE.)

The object of the optimization is to achieve a desired network throughput at the lowest possible cost. Given a typical network configuration (usually, at least two-connected, but much less than three-connected) subject to the network constraints, the routing algorithm can be applied to obtain optimal link flows. With these link flows, some links will be highly utilized (80 to 90%), while others will be underutilized. If the links are ordered according to their utilization and then successively removed, the network will eventually be partitioned in two *disjoint components* of nodes. The *minimal* set of these highly utilized links that disconnect the network is called a *saturated cut set*.

Through numerous experiments, it was continuously observed that the total traffic between these two components was usually very close to the sum of the flows in the saturated cut-set links. In other words, if ND_i = number of nodes in component i for $i = 1, 2$; NC = number of links in the cut set separating the two components; and f_k = flow in cutset link k, then

$$ND_1 \times ND_2 \times RE \simeq \sum_{k=1}^{NC} f_k \qquad (4.16)$$

Clearly, the saturated cut set imposes a physical limitation on the network throughput, and an increase in throughput RE can be obtained only by increasing the traffic $F = \sum f_i$ across the cut set. This can be achieved by adding capacity and/or new links to the cut set.

From the link flow solution provided by the FD method we can easily identify the cut set as the minimal set of most utilized links. Furthermore, we can identify the links that are good candidates for deletions, since these are the links with low utilization.

Each iteration of the cut saturation algorithm consists of several basic steps:

1. Routing (performed after each network modification to generate new optimal link flows).

2. Saturated Cutset Determination (performed at each stage of routing).

3. Add-Only (selects the "best" link to join the two components across the cut set).

4. Delete-Only (selects the best link for deletion from the topology).

5. Perturbations (combines Add-Only and Delete-Only operations).

For each cut saturation algorithm iteration, steps 1 and 2 are performed sequentially. Then either step 3 or 4 or 5 is selected (i.e., links are added, or deleted, or added and deleted) depending on the present level of throughput RE as compared with the desired throughput.

4.4 ADAPTIVE ROUTING

4.4.1 Objectives and Problem Formulation

In discussing static policies, we focused on the computational aspects of the algorithms and (for distributed implementations) on the type of information exchanged between nodes. We did not consider the amount of overhead (line and CPU) introduced by the routing message exchange and the routing table computation; nor did we concern ourselves with the time required to converge to the optimal solution; nor did we investigate the impact of line/node failures on the convergence of the algorithm. These factors can be disregarded in a static (or quasistatic) routing environment, where the time between traffic pattern changes is infinitely larger than the average network transmission time, and therefore the routing computation can be performed in the background mode, at a very slow rate, without overtaxing lines or processors.

In a dynamic network environment we remove those assumptions and allow the time between traffic changes to be comparable to the time required to measure such changes, to compute new routes, and to implement such routes in the nodes. Furthermore, we are concerned about failures, and require prompt recovery from them. We still insist, however, that at steady state the adaptive algorithm performs as well as the optimum static algorithm (except, of course, for the additional overhead introduced by the routing message exchange).

Based on the foregoing considerations, the objectives of the adaptive routing policy are stated as follows:

1. At steady state, the adaptive policy must converge to the optimal static policy corresponding to the existing traffic pattern

2. In time-varying traffic conditions, the policy must adjust to load fluctuations so as to yield minimum delay.

3. After failures, the policy must minimize the time to recover to a stable condition.

The adaptive routing problem consists, therefore, of defining a procedure that dynamically updates routing tables according to changes in the network. This procedure will include several functions: the acquisition of the status of the network (e.g., by measurement of link queue lengths or link idle time); the computation of the routes; and the implementation (distribution) of the routing tables. Critical issues in the design of the adaptive procedure are line and processor overhead. The overhead poses a constraint on the frequency of routing updates, and therefore on the performance during transient traffic conditions and the time to recover from failures.

4.4.2 Classification

An adaptive policy consists of several functions (status acquisition, route computation, information exchange, etc.), each of which can be implemented in several different ways. The number of possible combinations is very large; thus a preliminary classification is helpful before engaging in a discussion of the basic functions and the survey of existing and proposed policies.

Numerous classifications have been proposed [23, 26, 49, 59,]. In this study we choose to classify adaptive policies on the basis of the location(s) where the routing computation is performed and the type of network status information required. Four classes are identified:

1. *Isolated policies.* The routing computation is performed by each node independently, based on local information. No exchange of status or routing information among the nodes is provided.

2. *Distributed policies.* The routing computation is performed in parallel by all the nodes, in a cooperative manner, based on partial status information exchanged between the nodes.

3. *Centralized policies.* The network routing center (NRC) assembles the global state of the network, computes minimum delay routes, and distributes routing tables (or routing commands) to all the nodes.

4. *Mixed policies.* These policies derive and combine features from some or all of the previous classes. A typical example is the integration of centralized and isolated routing computation.

4.4.3 Functions of an Adaptive Routing Policy

In spite of the substantial differences that clearly exist between the various types of routing policies, it is possible to identify some basic functions that may be regarded as the "building blocks" of all the possible policies. These functions are:

1. Network status monitoring.

2. Network status reporting.

3. Route computation.

4. Route implementation.

5. Packet forwarding.

The following sections define each one of the foregoing functions and review some of the alternative implementations.

4.4.3.1 *Monitoring Network Status*

The network status variables of interest in the routing computation are the topological connectivity, the traffic pattern, and the delay. We distinguish among *local*, *global*, and *partial* status. In order to acquire local connectivity, each node monitors the status of adjacent lines and/or nodes by monitoring line traffic or (in the absence of traffic) by periodically interrogating the neighbors. Local traffic load is monitored by measuring average (or instantaneous) queue lengths, or average flow on outgoing links, or incoming traffic from external sources. Global status consists of the full network connectivity and traffic pattern information, and may be acquired by collecting and carefully correlating the local status information from all the nodes in the network. Partial status (relative to a given node) is at an intermediate level between local and global status. It is the status of the network "as seen by the node" and it includes all the elements necessary for the routing decision at that node. As an example, the partial status may include the local status, the list of reachable nodes, and the estimated delay (or hop distance) to each of these nodes.

We will see later that there is a close correlation between network status information techniques and routing classes as introduced in Section 4.4.2. Briefly, the isolated routing policy is based on local status information; the distributed policy is based on partial status information; and the centralized policy requires local status acquisition at all nodes and global status information at the NRC.

4.4.3.2 *Network Status Reporting*

Network status measurements may be processed locally or may be forwarded to a collection center for further processing. In the centralized routing case, local measurements are periodically reported to the NRC and are there integrated to produce the global status. In the distributed case, the local measurements are combined with the information received from neighbors to update the partial status of the network (as viewed by that node); then the partial status is communicated to the neighbors. In the isolated case, measurements are processed and used locally; no exchange of status information occurs between nodes.

4.4.3.3 Route Computation

As a general rule, route selection follows the criterion of minimum delay to destination, based on the network status information available at the node. In an isolated routing policy each node knows the state of its own queues. It also stores a precomputed list of preferred output links (ranked in priority order) for a given destination. A typical strategy consists of routing packets to the highest-priority link, until the queue exceeds a given threshold. Then the second-best link is used, and so on. In a distributed policy, each node computes from the partial status information the minimum-delay route to each destination. This route is then used for future traffic to that particular destination (in more sophisticated implementations, the node may decide which fraction of the total traffic to that destination should be forwarded along the chosen route). In a centralized policy the NRC maintains global network status and periodically constructs the best routes between all node pairs; no routing computation is required at the nodes.

4.4.3.4 Route Implementation

There are several possibilities for storing the routing information in the nodes. The most general solution consists of storing at node i (for $i = 1, \ldots, N$) an $N \times A_i$ matrix (where N = total number of nodes and A_i = number of neighbors of node i) whose entries are the fractions of the total traffic to a given destination that must be distributed among the various neighbors (multipath routing). This solution reduces to single-path routing if only one output link per destination is used. The routing tables are either computed locally (distributed routing) or are provided by an NRC (centralized routing).

One problem with the foregoing routing-table implementation is that packets in the same end-to-end user session may follow different paths. To maintain sequencing, several approaches are possible. One is the virtual-circuit approach, in which routes are selected on a session-by-session basis (depending on link utilization and topological connectivity criteria) and are implemented by loading the proper routing maps in the intermediate nodes on the route. This approach is used in Tymnet [58] and Transpac [14]. Another approach is the "explicit path routing" scheme implemented in the IBM Standard Network Architecture [36], in which each node computes (using a distributed algorithm) the K shortest paths to each destination. At the opening of a session the origin node selects an appropriate path to destination (based on load considerations) and stamps in the header of each packet the selected path ID and the destination node ID. The next node on the path uses this information and its own path table information to map the original path into one of its own paths and to stamp this new path ID in the packet before forwarding. In this fashion, all packets follow the route selected by the origin node, with no need for specific routing instructions at the intermediate nodes for each session as required by the virtual-circuit approach.

In another scheme, called "source routing," the source node has the knowledge of the complete paths to all destinations and stamps the entire route (i.e., the list of intermediate-node IDs) in the header of each packet [65]. When multiple paths are available, the source node may balance the load by distributing packets on different paths or, if desired, may route the packets belonging to the same session all on the same path, as in the explicit path scheme.

4.4.3.5 Packet Forwarding

Packet forwarding is the process that takes place at each intermediate node on the path and involves the inspection of the header of each incoming packet, the consultation of proper tables (if necessary), and the placement of the packet on the proper output queue. We distinguish between virtual-circuit and datagram forwarding mechanisms. In the *virtual-circuit* mode, the packet carries in the header the ID of the connection to which it belongs. At each intermediate node a routing table provides a mapping between the ID number and the route to be used. ID number and route are fixed at connection setup time. In the *datagram* mode we have two further possibilities: (1) the complete route (i.e., the intermediate-node IDs) is *prestamped* in the routing label of each packet header at the entry node and node IDs are "peeled off" from the routing label while the packet progresses along the path; or (2) only the destination node is carried in the header, and the next hop is determined by routing-table inspection.

4.4.4 Isolated Routing Policies

In an isolated implementation, a node can derive useful routing information only from the length of its local queues. The simplest policy aimed at minimizing delay consists of choosing the output link with the shortest queue, regardless of the final destination of the packet. This is the essence of Fultz's *shortest queue and zero bias algorithm* [23], and Baran's *hop potato* algorithm [1].

An even more simple-minded, isolated policy is the *flooding* policy [23]. Here the node disregards even the locally available delay information and routes one copy of each transit packet to all neighbors (except for the neighbor from which the packet was just received). A hop count is incremented in the packet header after each transmission. Packets are "absorbed" by the intended destination or are discarded after a maximum hop number is reached.

The foregoing schemes have some adaptivity to load fluctuations and to failures. The flooding algorithm, in particular, is extremely robust to failures in that it will always deliver a copy of the packet to a reachable destination. Major drawbacks, however, are poor line efficiency (especially in flooding) and the presence of loops.

To improve line efficiency and reduce looping, one may combine the local adaptive policy with a static routing policy. The static policy is used to establish a priority ordering among the outgoing links that may be used to reach a given destination. For example, the static FD solution discussed in Section 4.3 may be used to assign relative frequencies $P^{(i)}(k, l)$ to links out of node i to destination k. The link with highest frequency is the "primary" (or preferred) link. Links with lower frequencies are the "alternate" links, ranked in order of priority. Another static policy frequently used for this purpose is the combination of minimum hop route (for the primary) and second shortest route (for the "alternate") [59].

When the isolated, adaptive policy is used in conjunction with an underlying, static policy, the traffic is distributed among primary and secondary routes according to queue lengths rather than following fixed proportions as in the static, multipath policy. For example, all the packets might be routed along the primary path until the queue exceeded a given threshold Q_1. Then, the second-best path would be used until a threshold Q_2 was reached, and so on.

These combined static and local adaptive policies are very efficient, and have recently been the subject of several analytical and simulation studies [69]. The results show that the adaptivity to load fluctuations is very good. The adaptivity to failures, on the other hand, is rather poor, owing to the fact that the underlying policy is static. During failures, the major problem is looping. This weakness can be corrected, however, by replacing the static policy with an adaptive, globally optimal policy. More on the combination of isolated policies with other policies is found in Section 4.4.7.

4.4.5 Distributed Routing Policies

Distributed, adaptive policies assume distributed routing computation and routing information exchange among neighbor nodes. In this respect they are very similar to the distributed, static policies discussed in Section 4.3. The main difference is that the adaptive policies must be capable of rapidly adjusting to changes in network topology and traffic pattern (we recall that for static policies, the goal was the optimal routing solution, independent of the time required to reach it).

Let us first briefly reanalyze the static policies presented in Section 4.3, to determine whether they can be used in a dynamic environment. We start with the *minimum-hop policy* and recall that such a policy yields minimum-hop distances to all destinations if the tables are initially set to zero. Now, it can be shown that with a slight modification of the procedure, the convergence to the optimal solution is maintained even if the tables are initialized to arbitrary values. This is indeed the situation we would find immediately after a topological change (link or node failure, or link or node insertion) when tables reflect preexisting minimum hop distances. The algorithm will drive the tables to the new optimal values, regardless of their starting conditions, in a number of updates approximately equal to the diameter of the network (i.e., the maximum-hop distance between any two nodes). For a typical medium-sized network (say 5 to 20 nodes;

9.6 kbits/s line speed) the algorithm will converge in a few seconds. This is certainly an adequate response time, considering that the interval between failures may be on the order of hours.

Next, we consider the *distributed algorithm* used to find the optimal static routing solution. In this case the conversion of the static (or, better, quasistatic) algorithm to dynamic operations presents some difficulties. First, the table updating must be coordinated among nodes so that it proceeds sequentially from the destination to the origins. A node cannot update its tables until it has heard from all its downstream neighbors. This proper sequencing of updates may fail in the presence of line errors and link/node failures. In this case loops in the traffic flow, and therefore deadlocks, may occur [24]. A second, major problem is the slow convergence. At each update, only a small increment of the total traffic can be "deviated" from the old routes to the new shortest route. Larger increments may be used to speed up the update process; but they may then compromise the optimality of the solution. As a result, the quasistatic distributed routing policy is not suitable for dynamic operations when the traffic fluctuation period is comparable to the routing update cycle and when link and node failure rates are not negligible.

The success of the minimum hop algorithm in contrast with the failure of the optimal multipath algorithm for dynamic network operations indicates that it is relatively easy to compute and dynamically update *single* shortest paths from each node to all destinations, while it is very difficult to compute and adaptively maintain *multiple* paths on which traffic should be distributed. This finding suggests the following suboptimal solution to the minimum-delay problem: each node periodically recomputes the minimum-delay path to each destination using a distributed shortest-path technique similar to the minimum-hop technique, except that the length of each link, instead of being unity, is defined to be the current delay (sum of transmission and queueing delay) on that link. All the traffic is then routed along the minimum-delay path. Clearly, in sustained loads, this solution is not stable, since queues on the minimum path will build up, causing delays to increase. Consequently, at the next update iteration, another path will be found to be the minimum path and all the traffic will be deviated to it. So the routing solution may show an oscillating behavior, where several routes are used cyclically, even when the external traffic pattern is stationary (this is in contrast with the optimal routing solution, where multiple routes are used simultaneously). Of course, the minimum-delay-path policy would approach the optimum solution if the routing updates are carried out very frequently (in the limit, on a packet-by-packet basis). Unfortunately, this is not possible, owing to the line and processor overhead involved in the updating process.

The minimum-delay-path algorithm described above is the basis of the most popular of all adaptive routing algorithms, the ARPA network "shortest queue + bias" algorithm [23, 49]. The data structure and the update process are identical to those implemented in the distributed shortest-path algorithm (see Section 4.3). Each node i ($i = 1, \ldots, N$) maintains a delay table $DT^{(i)}$, whose entry $DT^{(i)}(k, l)$ is the estimated delay from node i to destination k if l is chosen as the next node in the route to k. From $DT^{(i)}$, a vector $MDV^{(i)}$, the minimum-delay vector, is obtained as follows:

$$MDV^{(i)}(k) = \min_{l \in A_i} DT^{(i)}(k, l) \tag{4.17}$$

where A_i is the set of nodes adjacent to node i. $MDV^{(i)}(k)$ represents the minimum estimated delay from i to k. The adaptive policy attempts to send packets on minimum-delay routes; therefore, packets directed to k are sent to neighbor l_s such that

$$DT^{(i)}(k, l_s) = \min_{l \in A_i} DT^{(i)}(k, l) \tag{4.18}$$

Each node periodically updates its own delay table using the delays measured on its output lines and delay information received from neighbor nodes. In fact, every fraction of a second each node transmits asynchronously to its neighbors the vector MDV. Upon reception of vectors $MDV^{(l)}$, $\forall\ l \in A_i$, node i updates $DT^{(i)}$ as follows:

$$DT^{(i)}(k, l) = d(i, l) + MDV^{(l)}(k) + D_P \tag{4.19}$$

where $d(i, l)$ is the measured delay (queueing + transmission) on channel (i, l) and D_p is a "bias" term optimally adjusted to reduce looping effects [23].

The ARPA net routing algorithm has been the subject of several simulation and measurement studies [10, 23, 51]. The major weakness found in the course of these studies was the incapability of effectively splitting the traffic on multiple paths during sustained loads. Let us assume that heavy traffic exists between two nodes, requiring the simultaneous use of more than one route, and suppose that two disjoint routes are available. The ARPA policy can select only one route at a time between subsequent updates. Within each update interval, one of the routes is alternatively filled up to saturation, while the other route is idle, thus causing inefficient use of resources and, possibly, loops.

4.4.6 Centralized Routing Policies

The heart of a centralized routing policy is the network routing center (NRC), which is the center responsible for global network status collection, route computation, and route implementation. The NRC may be a nodal processor equipped with specialized software, but more commonly it is a host computer with adequate storage and processing capability as required to store the network topology and traffic information and to compute the optimal routes.

Different versions of centralized policy exist depending on the type of network information stored in the NRC, the route computation algorithm, and the route implementation technique. In particular, two alternatives are possible for route implementation:

- Periodical distribution of routing tables from the NRC to all the nodes.

- Implementation of individual paths on a call-by-call basis (virtual-circuit approach).

In the following we describe two centralized policies implemented in existing networks. The first policy is a virtual-circuit policy currently operating in TYMNET, the packet network supporting the communications requirements of TYMSHARE [58]. The second is a routing-table distribution policy operating in the experimental Packet Radio Network sponsored by the Advanced Research Project Agency (ARPA) and deployed in the San Francisco area [20].

In TYMNET, for each connection request between a user and a remote host, a control packet is first sent by the origin node to the network routing center (the supervisor) carrying the information of source, destination, and password. After password verification, the supervisor computes the minimum-cost path for the virtual circuit. Each link in the network has a cost associated with it. This cost is a function of link bandwidth and load condition (Table 4.1). The link is said to be in normal or overload conditions, depending on whether the number of virtual circuits carried on it is below or above a specified threshold.

Once the path has been computed, the supervisor allocates buffers and sets up mappings (permuter tables) at each intermediate node on the path to create the virtual circuit. User blocks flowing on a given virtual circuit are identified by a connection ID number carried in the header and are routed according to the permuter table information. After receiving the permuter table entries, each node sends an acknowledgment to the supervisor. Once all the acknowledgments are in, the supervisor informs the end users that the connection has been established and data transfer can start.

To compute minimum-cost routes, the supervisor must have knowledge of the network topology and link loads. While link load information is incrementally updated by the supervisor after each circuit allocation/deallocation, network topology must be initially acquired with a special procedure called "network

TABLE 4-1: *Link costs in TYMNET.*

Line speed (bits/s)	cost normal	cost overloaded one way	cost overloaded both ways
9600	10	26	42
7200	11	27	43
4800	12	28	44
2400	16	32	48

takeover." In the takeover phase, the supervisor first sends a takeover command to its own node, and learns that node's capacity, the capacity of its links, every permuter table entry in that node, and the neighbors of that node. After this first step is completed, the supervisor sends takeover commands to the neighbors of the node just taken over, and the procedure continues until no more nodes are discovered. After takeover, if link failures occur, they are reported by adjacent nodes to the supervisor, and the topological map is updated. From the map, nodal failures and isolations can be detected by the supervisor and taken into account in future connection establishments. However, the existing virtual circuits that have been disrupted by a failure are not automatically rerouted by the supervisor; rather, they must be reinitialized by the users.

In the Packet Radio Network, the role of network routing center is played by the station [20]. The station learns about network connectivity via an initialization procedure very similar to the takeover procedure in TYMNET. When network topology is completely mapped, optimal routes from each node to the station are computed using hop distance and traffic load as criteria. (*Note*: Only the routes to and from the station are of interest, since in the first version of the experimental Packet Radio Network the station acts as a store-and-forward center for all the traffic.) Next, routing labels are assigned from the station to all the nodes. A routing label for a given node is a string containing the IDs of all the nodes on the optimal path from that node to the station. The originating node stamps the routing label in the header of the packet before transmission. Subsequent nodes on the path recognize the packet as directed to them, and progressively "peel off" their IDs from the routing label.

The foregoing routing label procedure was designed for a centralized traffic pattern, but clearly could be extended to the distributed traffic pattern case, in which a node wishes to establish direct connections with several different destinations without going through the station. In this case, a node must be equipped with a distinct routing label for each destination. For large networks, however, this procedure may become too costly because of storage overhead (to store the routing labels) and traffic overhead (to distribute labels from the station). Thus, distributed routing schemes become more attractive beyond certain network sizes.

A centralized policy enjoys some distinct advantages over distributed and isolated policies: it eliminates routing computation requirements at the nodes (this was an important reason for choosing a centralized policy in the Packet Radio Network, where the nodes have very limited processing capabilities); it permits a more accurate optimization of the routes, eliminating loops and oscillations that may occur when network state is not completely known; and it allows some form of flow control on the incoming traffic. The last property is especially attractive: in TYMNET, for example, the supervisor constantly monitors loading in the network and therefore can reject calls when a load threshold is exceeded. We will see in Section 4.5.4 that this flow-control capability is considerably more difficult to implement in distributed controlled networks.

On the negative side, there are two problems that limit the applicability of centralized policies to operational networks. One is the increased traffic overhead in the proximity of the NRC due to the periodic collection of status reports from all the nodes and the distribution of routing commands from the NRC to the nodes [13]. The other, more serious problem is reliability. If the NRC fails, the entire network goes out of control. This problem is partially corrected by using a hierarchy of NRCs (four in TYMNET) which continuously monitor each other; when the senior NRC fails, the next in line takes over. This solution is costly, however, and not always satisfactory: in a military environment, for example, the NRCs may become very vulnerable targets.

To compensate for the deficiencies (and combine the advantages) of the various routing schemes, one may wish to use more than one policy simultaneously. This approach is possible and is discussed in the next section.

4.4.7 Mixed Routing Policies

In principle, it is possible to combine any type and number of routing strategies in the same network, as long as precise rules are defined at each node for the selection of one of the policies, depending on the type of traffic and load and connectivity conditions. In practice, line and processor overhead considerations restrict the number of policies that can be combined in a mixed strategy to two or at most three policies (in the latter case one policy should be a low-overhead, isolated policy). The idea, of course, is to find policies that can compensate for each other's deficiencies. Although no mixed policy has ever been implemented, several proposals exist, and are briefly discussed below.

The *delta-routing* strategy proposed by Rudin [59] combines centralized and isolated routing. Initially, a set of alternate paths between each source–destination pair is computed by the NRC (or as a function of topology) and distributed to the nodes. Then, as part of the centralized routing policy, average link delays are periodically reported from each node to the NRC. The NRC assembles the global state of the network and evaluates delay on the previously computed paths. If the differences between the delays on the alternate paths for a given source–destination pair are within a value δ (hence the name "delta routing"), no routing instructions are sent from the NRC to that source for that particular destination: routing responsibility is delegated to the isolated policy implemented in the node. If, on the other hand, the delay differences are larger than δ, the NRC intervenes and instructs the node to use the lowest delay route. The isolated routing policy locally implemented at each node chooses the route with lowest queue among the alternate routes initially supplied by the NRC. The isolated policy is activated only if specific routing instructions were not received by the node from the NRC in the previous update interval.

The delta-routing strategy combines the capability of the isolated policy to promptly react to local traffic buildups and failures and the long-term optimality of the centralized policy. The delta criterion effectively reduces traffic overhead, since routing information is sent to the nodes only when needed (i.e., when topological changes or load fluctuations require NRC intervention).

Another proposal for mixed strategy was discussed by the author in [26]. As a difference from the Rudin's scheme, this scheme combines a centralized policy with a distributed policy (the minimum-hop policy). The NRC periodically collects network information, computes routing policy corrections according to such information, and transmits routing update messages to all nodes. For additional failure protection, the nodes are also equipped with minimum-hop tables. Following is a more detailed description of the policy.

During normal operating conditions, only the centralized policy is active. Under the centralized policy each node transmits to NRC asynchronously, every 0.5 s, the following information:

- Number of packets transmitted on each output channel in the past 0.5 s.

- For each destination k, the number of packets directed to k, which were received from external sources (host computers, terminals, etc.) in the past 0.5 s.

Using the information received from the nodes, the NRC evaluates channel and external input rates averaged over the past 10 s. Every 10 s the data are fed to a routing program that is resident in core memory. The routing program can be the flow deviation algorithm (see Section 4.3.3): in such a case, the program computes, on the basis of channel traffic and external requirement, for each node–destination pair, the new route on which a fraction of the traffic, say α ($0 \leq \alpha \leq 1$), must be "deviated" in order to improve network performance. At the end of the computation, which typically requires 100 to 300 ms, NRC delivers to each node a routing "correction" message which contains:

- A vector of "next nodes," one per destination, to which a fraction α of the incoming traffic must be deviated.

- The parameter α.

No routing correction is sent to a node if $\alpha < \alpha_0$, where α_0 is an appropriate threshold value. Upon reception of the routing message, each node updates its routing table. Since the flow deviation algorithm is an optimal routing algorithm, the centralized adaptive policy converges to the deterministic policy in steady network conditions.

The minimum-hop policy is only used as a backup during failures. As soon as a node experiences the failure of an output line or neighbor node, (1) it modifies its minimum-hop numbers, according to the failures; (2) it immediately transmits the minimum-hop table to the neighbors; and (3) it switches from a centralized to a minimum hop mode of operation (i.e., it routes the packets along minimum-hop routes). Gradually, all nodes switch to minimum-hop policy, until the NRC learns about the failure. New tables are then computed, which account for the failure, and the centralized adaptive policy is gradually restored. During the transient period following the failure, minimum-hop and centralized policy coexist in the network. It can be easily seen that such a situation is logically acceptable and does not create severe performance degradation.

The use of the minimum-hop policy as a supplement to the centralized policy offers several advantages. First, the minimum-hop policy may be used for the detection of isolated nodes (as discussed in Section 4.6), and therefore its cost may be justified by other reasons beside routing. Second, if all the NRCs fail, or a portion of the network becomes disconnected from NRCs, the minimum-hop policy provides a basic, reliable routing capability not present in the delta-routing scheme.

4.5 FLOW CONTROL

4.5.1 Flow Control: Problems and Approaches

Let us come back for a moment to the model of the packet network as a pool of resources (channels, buffers, switch processors). Each user must acquire a subset of these resources (in a proper sequence) to accomplish its task, which typically is the transfer of data from source to destination. If the competition for the resources is unrestricted and uncontrolled, we may encounter three types of problems: inefficiency, unfairness, and congestion.

Network operation becomes *inefficient* when resources are wasted, either because of conflicts between two or more users, or because a user acquires more resources than strictly needed, thus starving other users. A typical example of wastage due to conflicts occurs in random-access schemes (e.g., ALOHA): when two users transmit simultaneously on a random-access channel, the data are garbled and *the channel is wasted* (channel interference).

Another example of wastage, this time due to unnecessary acquisition of buffer resources, is given by the situation depicted in Fig. 4.3. We have a two-node network with three host-to-host connections (A, A';B, B'; and C, C'). Line speeds are as indicated in Fig. 4.3. Assume that the pair (A, A') is initially silent; then up to 20 units of throughput can be accommodated from B to B' and from C to C'. Let us now introduce a file transfer requirement from A to A'. Because of the mismatch between line speeds along the path, the buffers at the intermediate nodes are rapidly filled by (A, A') traffic. Consequently, packets from B and C are rejected by the switches (buffer overflow) and throughput from B to B' and C to C' is reduced to zero. The introduction of new traffic causes a total throughput decrease from 20 to 10 units! This decrease in efficiency is due to *buffer wastage* by (A, A') traffic (buffer capture).

Unfairness is a natural by-product of uncontrolled competition. Some users, because of their relative position in the network, may be able to capture a larger share of resources than others and thus enjoy preferential treatment. An obvious example of unfairness is offered by the network in Fig. 4.3, where the pair A, A', because of the higher value of some of the line speeds along its path (100 instead of 10), tends to capture the buffer pools at the intermediate nodes. Similar examples of unfairness are discussed in [34].

A network is defined to be congested if an increment of offered (external) traffic causes a decrease in effective throughput [45]. Congestion is a direct consequence of wastage. Since wastage (in an uncontrolled network) increases proportionally to offered traffic rather than to useful throughput (as demonstrated by the random-access and buffer capture examples mentioned before), there must exist an optimum offered load beyond which the wastage is higher than the potential gain in throughput. Beyond such an optimum, the network is congested.

It is undesirable to operate the network in *congested* conditions for two reasons: inefficiency and deadlocks. We already discussed inefficiency. As for *deadlocks*, these occur when each user in the network has acquired part of the resources necessary to complete a task and does not want to release them, while waiting for the remaining resources to become free. When a deadlock develops, throughput clearly drops to zero, since no task can be completed. A simple example of deadlock created by heavy offered load is illustrated in Fig. 4.4. Here heavy traffic between A and B may cause the packets directed from A to B to fill up the buffers in A; similarly, packets from B to A will fill up B. In this situation, the throughput between A and B falls to zero since packets currently in A cannot be transfered to B for lack of free buffers in B ready to receive them, and vice versa.

The solution to this problem and, more generally, to all problems related to

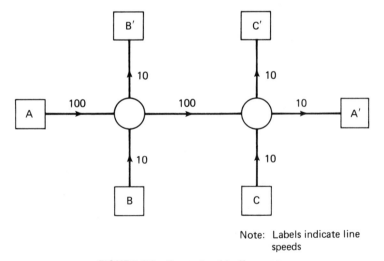

Note: Labels indicate line speeds

FIGURE 4-3 *Example of buffer capture.*

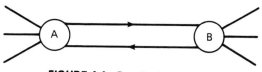

FIGURE 4-4 *Deadlock example.*

congestion is *flow control*. Flow control is a protocol, or more generally, a set of protocols whose goals are:

- To maintain efficient network operations.

- To guarantee fairness in resource sharing.

- To protect the network from congestion.

These goals are achieved by properly regulating and (if necessary) blocking the flow of packets internally in the network as well as at network entry points. Actually, different flow-control procedures operate at different levels in the network, as discussed in the following section.

Flow control (as any other form of control in a distributed network) may require some exchange of information between nodes (to select the control strategy) and, possibly, some exchange of commands (to implement that strategy). This exchange translates into channel and processor overhead. Furthermore, flow control may require the reservation of resources (e.g., buffers, bandwidth) to individual users or classes of users, thus reducing the statistical benefits of complete resource sharing. Therefore, there is a trade-off between gain in efficiency (due to controls) and loss in efficiency (due to limited sharing and overhead) that must be carefully considered in designing flow-control strategies. This trade-off is illustrated by the curves in Fig. 4.5, showing the effective

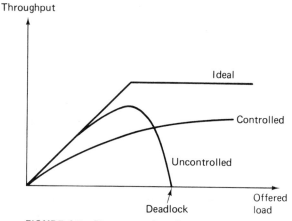

FIGURE 4-5 *Flow control performance tradeoffs.*

151

throughput as a function of offered load. The ideal throughput curve corresponds to perfect control, with global information and zero overhead. Ideal throughput increases linearly until it reaches a horizontal asymptote corresponding to the theoretical network throughput. The controlled throughput curve is a typical curve that can be obtained with an actual control procedure. Throughput values are lower than in the ideal curve because of control overhead. The uncontrolled curve follows the ideal curve for low offered load; for higher load, it quickly collapses to a deadlock. Clearly, controls buy safety at high offered loads, at the expense of reduced efficiency. The reduction in efficiency is measured in terms of higher delays (for light load) and lower throughput capacity (at saturation).

In the following sections we first define the various levels at which flow control may be applied in a packet network. For each level we then define the specific congestion and deadlock problems that may be encountered, and present various flow-control solutions to solve them.

4.5.2 Levels of Flow Control

Since flow-control levels are closely related to network protocol levels, a brief review of network protocols is in order (see also Chapters 2 and 3).

Figure 4.6 depicts the typical protocol-level structure implemented in a packet network. At the lowest level we have the *link protocol*, which serves the purpose of transporting packets reliably across physical links. One of the functions of this protocol is related to flow control and consists of dropping a packet if the receiving node is not ready (because, e.g., it is congested). The sender will then retransmit the packet after an appropriate timeout. In some protocols, a congested receiver may stop the sender using appropriate commands (e.g., RNR≡Receiver Not Ready, in HDLC and SDLC). We distinguish two types of physical links: the internal (or node-to-node) links and the network access links. Correspondingly, we have (at the same level in the protocol hierarchy) the *network access protocol* and the *node-to-node protocol*. Typical examples of link protocol implementation are HDLC, SDLC, and X.25 level 2 (which is a subset of HDLC).

At a higher level we have the *entry-to-exit (ETE) protocol*. The objective of this protocol is the reliable transport of single- and multi-packet messages from entry to exit node. At this level, important issues related to flow control are the sequencing and reassembly of multipacket messages at the exit node and the regulation of input traffic using buffer allocation and windowing techniques.

The highest level of network protocol is the *process-to-process* (or transport) *protocol*, which provides for the reliable delivery of packets on a "virtual" connection between two remote processes. The study of this protocol is the subject of Chapter 2. One of the functions of this protocol is flow control. The goal is to regulate the flow so as to make the most efficient use of network resources while avoiding buffer overflow at the destination. An effective solution

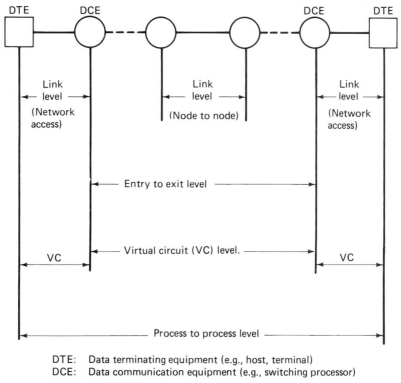

DTE: Data terminating equipment (e.g., host, terminal)
DCE: Data communication equipment (e.g., switching processor)

FIGURE 4-6 *Network protocol levels.*

towards this objective is the window scheme, discussed extensively in Chapter 2.

In virtual-circuit networks, yet another level of protocol exists, just below the process-to-process level: the *virtual-circuit protocol*. We recall that in virtual-circuit networks, a "virtual" circuit must be set up between a pair of users (or processes) wishing to communicate with each other *before* data transfer can be started. The establishment of this circuit implies dedication of resources of one form or another along the network path. A typical virtual-circuit implementation, used in Transpac [14], consists of assigning a fixed path to each connection at setup time. A virtual-circuit ID number, stamped in the packet header, uniquely identifies the packets belonging to a connection and is used to route packets to their destination using routing maps implemented at the intermediate nodes at setup time.

As a difference from virtual-circuit networks, *datagram* networks do not require any circuit setup before transmission. Each packet is independently submitted to the network and carries all the information required for its delivery to destination [55].

The virtual-circuit protocol specifies the rules for establishing, maintaining, and closing virtual circuits. Most important, from the flow-control point of view, the protocol permits *selective* flow control to be exercised on a connection-by-connection basis. Selective flow control is not available in datagram networks, since in such networks the information regarding each connection is embedded into the transport protocol portion of the header and is not inspected by transit nodes.

The foregoing network protocol review has identified various flow-control functions and capabilities built into different levels of protocols and has brought to our attention the fact that each protocol level has its own distinct flow-control responsibilities. Based on this fact, we propose a classification of flow-control procedures that parallels the classification of network protocols. We define the following levels of flow control:

1. Node-to-node level.

2. Network access level.

3. Entry-to-exit level.

4. Virtual-circuit level.

5. Process-to-process level.

The specific functions and the various possible implementations of the levels listed above are described in the following sections, with the exception of the process-to-process level, which is treated extensively in Chapter 2.

4.5.3 Node-to-Node Flow Control

Node-to-node flow control (or hop flow control, or store-and-forward flow control) has the function of blocking the store-and-forward traffic to a node that is congested. The blocking function is a provision of the link protocol, which automatically discards packets at the receiver end (if the receiver is congested) and retransmits them later, after a timeout. For all purposes the link behaves as if it were blocked, until the nodal congestion clears. In some protocols (e.g., HDLC and SDLC) the congested receiver instead of discarding packets will block transmission from the sender using an RNR (≡ Receiver Not Ready) command. After the congestion is cleared, the receiver issues an RR (≡ Receiver Ready) command to reopen transmissions.

The various node-to-node flow-control procedures differ one from the other depending on the definition of nodal congestion used to trigger the blocking. In the simplest case, a node is congested if it has no free buffers. Thus, packets are indiscriminately accepted until all buffers are full. This strategy may, however, lead to deadlocks as shown in the example in Section 4.5.1. For completeness, the example is presented again in Fig. 4.7. If node *A* is full with packets directed to *B*, and node *B* is full with packet directed to *A*, no traffic can move on link

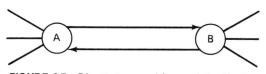

FIGURE 4-7 *Direct store and forward deadlock.*

(A, B). Deadlock! This deadlock is often referred to as *direct* store-and-forward deadlock [39].

The straightforward solution to this deadlock problem consists of introducing a *selective* definition of congestion: if queue length on link i is $\geq Q_{max}$ (where $Q_{max} <$ total number of node buffers), the node under consideration is defined to be congested for all the incoming traffic directed to link i. (In other words, link queues are upper-limited by Q_{max}.) This strategy (called "channel queue limit" strategy) clearly eliminates direct deadlocks since the packets in A directed to B (see Fig. 4.7) cannot occupy the entire buffer pool in A. The channel queue limit strategy has been implemented in the ARPANET [48] using $Q_{max} = 8$.

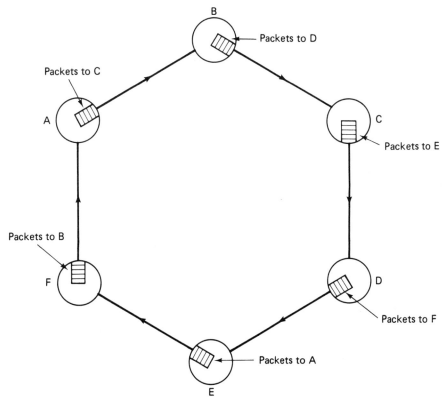

FIGURE 4-8 *Indirect S/F deadlock.*

There is another form of deadlock that can arise in packet networks, the *indirect* store-and-forward deadlock. Figure 4.8 illustrates a typical deadlock situation. Suppose that adverse traffic conditions in the ring topology shown in Fig. 4.8 cause each queue to be filled at one point with Q_{max} packets (i.e., the limit imposed by the channel queue limit strategy). Furthermore, assume that the packets at each node are directed to a node two or more hops away [e.g., all packets queued on link (A, B) are directed to C]. In these conditions no traffic can move in the network since all queues are $= Q_{max}$. So we have a deadlock in spite of the fact that the network is equipped with direct store-and-forward deadlock-prevention mechanisms (i.e., channel queue limit strategy). But this, of course, is a different type of deadlock, *indirect store-and-forward deadlock*. A solution to indirect store-and-forward deadlock is offered by the "structured buffer pool" strategy proposed by Raubold et al.[57]. In this strategy, nodal buffers are organized in a hierarchical structure, as shown in Fig. 4.9. At level zero we have a pool of unrestricted buffers. From level 1 to level H_{max} (where H_{max} is the maximum number of hops on any network path) buffers are reserved for specific classes of packets; in particular, buffers at level i are reserved for packets that have covered $\geq i$ hops. Thus, in heavy load conditions, buffers fill up progressively from level 0 to level H_{max}. When in a node the buffers at levels $\leq i$ are all filled up, arriving packets that have covered $\leq i$ hops are discarded. It can be shown [57] that this strategy eliminates store-and-forward deadlocks both of direct and/or indirect type. This protection does not, of course, come for free, the cost here being represented by a large buffer requirement (H_{max} could be as high as $N - 1$) and by extra processing required at each node to maintain the structured buffer pool and to check for buffer availability.

Another strategy for recovery from indirect store-and-forward deadlocks was presented in [37]. In that strategy each node is equipped with two "overflow

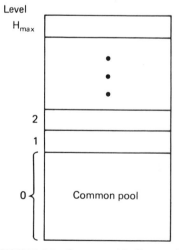

FIGURE 4-9 *Structured buffer pool.*

buffers'' to be used only when a deadlock is detected. In the deadlock-recovery mode of operation (which follows deadlock detection) each node randomly selects a packet from its queues, stamps it with a random number, and delivers it to the ''overflow net'' (i.e., the net supported by the overflow buffers). Packets will now compete for the overflow buffers, but the contention between two packets is resolved by giving the buffer to the packet with the lower stamp and by dropping the higher stamp packet. The two overflow buffers per node are needed for simultaneous reception and for transmission. With the foregoing procedure it is clear that the lowest-numbered packet will eventually be delivered to destination, thus freeing a regular buffer and resolving the deadlock, since traffic will then move through the network using regular buffers. As the previous strategy did, this recovery strategy also introduces some buffer wastage and some processing overhead during the overflow mode of operation.

Node-to-node flow control prevents deadlocks but does not prevent network overload, since it takes effect only after internal queues have become relatively large. Thus, network operation, although deadlock-free, may still be inefficient when external demands exceed network capacity. A more effective strategy, in this case, is the control of new admissions into the network. This strategy, called network access flow control, is discussed next.

4.5.4 Network Access Flow Control

The network access flow control has the objective of regulating the input of packets into the network based on local or global congestion measurements. As in the case of node-to-node flow control, this control is supported by the network access link protocol through a mechanism of packet discard (when the network is congested) and retransmission, or through an RNR, RR mechanism.

The simplest access control scheme consists of admitting (or rejecting) input traffic based on the amount of free storage available at the entry node. One such scheme is the input buffer limit control proposed by Lam [45]. Each node has a pool of N_T buffers, all of which may be occupied by transit traffic. However, no more than N_I ($\leq N_T$) buffers can be occupied by input packets. The ratio N_I/N_T is the input buffer limit for this node and is shown to have a critical impact on network performance. More precisely, given the network topology and the traffic characteristics, there exists an optimal value of N_I/N_T which maximizes throughput. Another access control scheme operating on the basis of entry node buffer availability is the *local threshold* scheme proposed and experimented for the NPL (National Physics Laboratory) network [60].

Entry node congestion is not the most effective criterion for access control. Although any congestion in the network will eventually propagate upstream to the entry nodes (via the ''back-pressure'' mechanism of the node-to-node control), it is nevertheless to our advantage to be able to anticipate congestion using buffer occupancy information collected from various nodes in the network.

We present here two distributed strategies—the permit scheme, and the congestion table scheme—which attempt to achieve this objective.

In the *permit* scheme there is a fixed number of permits in the network, which are circulated among nodes in a random fashion or according to well-defined rules. A packet can leave the entry node only when it captures a permit passing through it. The packet then carries the permit through the network and releases it at the destination. This scheme was proposed for the NPL network [15, 60]. A major weakness of the permit scheme is "starvation" (i.e., the lack of permits at an entry node). The problem of starvation is related to the difficulty in supplying high-bandwidth users with enough permits to satisfy their demands and yet maintaining fairness.

In the *congestion table* scheme [53] each node regulates its input packet rate on the basis of the information contained in congestion control tables. These tables keep the count of buffers available at each node and are periodically updated by an information exchange process between neighbor nodes, much in the way routing tables are updated in the distributed routing algorithm. The information on the number of buffers available at the destination and along the path is used at the entry node to regulate the input rate to such destination. In addition, the sum of the buffers available at all nodes is used to evaluate overall network congestion.

SNA uses end-to-end (PLU to SLU) sessions to provide network flow control as well as access control. The "pacing" responses are, in effect, permits that are dedicated to the use of a single user (see Chapter 8 for more details).

When we compare the access control schemes with the node-to-node control schemes we notice a substantial difference in goals as well as results. In particular, node-to-node control does not protect from overload, while access control does not protect from deadlocks. Thus, the schemes are complementary and are both necessary for efficient and safe network operation.

4.5.5 Entry-to-Exit Flow Control

One of the most common trouble spots in a packet network is buffer congestion at the exit node. Exit buffers must absorb the mismatch between sender and receiver speed and, in some cases, must provide for reassembly of packets into messages and for message sequencing. These requirements motivate the development of a special flow-control scheme, the entry-to-exit scheme, whose goals are to avoid the overflow of exit buffers (by regulating inputs at the entry node) and to guarantee reassembly room at the exit node (by allocating exit buffers as needed).

If message reassembly and sequencing is not a requirement (as in the case of most datagram networks), the entry-to-exit scheme is not strictly necessary, since node-to-node and network access schemes to some extent already protect the exit buffers from overflow. Entry-to-exit flow-control implementation then becomes an issue of efficiency.

If message sequencing and/or reassembly, on the other hand, are required (as in ARPANET, for example), the entry-to-exit scheme is necessary to avoid deadlocks at the exit node. Figure 4.10 illustrates a typical reassembly deadlock situation (similar considerations can be used to identify and study the sequencing deadlock). Suppose that, for the network example shown in Fig. 4.10 node-to-node control is provided by the channel queue limit scheme (with $Q_{max} = 4$), message size is four packets, and four buffers are available for message reassembly at the exit node. Consider the situation depicted in Fig. 4.10 of messages A, B, and C traveling to destination host 1. Message A has seized the reassembly buffer at node 3 but is missing packet A_2 (which is waiting in the node 1 queue) and therefore cannot be delivered to the host. Packets in node 2 cannot move, since no reassembly buffers are available in node 3. Similarly, packets in node 1 cannot move, since there are no free store-and-forward buffers in the node 2 queue. Thus, packet A_2 cannot reach node 3. Deadlock!

The possibility of reassembly deadlocks in packet networks was first discovered by Kahn and Crowther during their early work on ARPANET protocols [37]. They pointed out a solution that was later used as a basis for the ARPANET entry-to-exit protocol described below. In ARPANET, reassembly buffers are allocated at the exit node via reservations (explicit or implicit) made from the entry node. Reassembly buffer reservation therefore prevents buffer overflow of multipacket messages at the exit node. In addition, we must protect the destination node from congestion caused by single-packet messages, since these do not require reassembly reservations (at least, at the first transmission attempt). In ARPANET, single-packet message congestion control is obtained via a window mechanism which limits the aggregate of all messages in flight from a given source host to a given destination host to be less than eight. A more detailed description of the protocol is given below [48].

1. *Reservation for Multipacket Messages.* The source IMP (interface message processor), upon receiving the first packet of a multipacket transaction from the host, sends a control message to the destination IMP requesting the allocation of eight reassembly buffers. If buffers are available, the destination IMP reserves the buffers and notifies the source IMP, which can then start transmission of the message. If no buffers are available, the source must repeat the request until successful. After all the packets in the message have arrived and have been fully reassembled, the destination IMP delivers the message to the destination host. At the

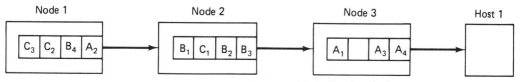

FIGURE 4-10 *Reassembly buffer deadlock.*

same time, it reserves eight more buffers and sends an acknowledgment, called RFNM (Request For Next Message) to the source IMP to announce the delivery of the previous message and to confirm the buffer reservation for the next message. If the transaction has been completed, or if the source host is not responsive, the source IMP cancels the reservation. Otherwise, it sends the next message.

2. *Reservation for Single-Packet Messages.* A single-packet message is transmitted to its destination immediately after a source IMP receives it while a copy is kept at the source (no buffer reservation at the destination IMP is needed at the first try). If there is space at the destination, the packet is accepted and passed on to the host and a RFNM is returned. If no buffers are available at the destination, the message is discarded, a request for a single buffer allocation is queued, and when space becomes available the source IMP is notified that the message may now be retransmitted.

3. *Flow and Sequence Control* (same for all messages). Message numbers are sequentially assigned to all messages between any source–destination host pair. The sequence number is checked at the destination IMP. At most, eight messages are allowed to be outstanding between a given host pair. Messages arriving with out-of-bound sequence numbers are discarded.

4.5.6 Virtual-Circuit Flow Control

This component of flow control is available only in virtual-circuit networks and is intimately associated with the virtual-circuit protocol. The virtual-circuit protocol generally consists of the concatenation of two network access segments and one entry-to-exit segment, all operating at the same level but independent of each other (see Fig. 4.6). The entry-to-exit segment may, in turn, consist of the concatenation of independent virtual circuits, one for each physical link on the path [14]. A standard protocol, X.25, has recently been recommended by CCITT for network access in virtual-circuit networks (see Section 2.4.4). No standards have yet been set for the intermediate segment of the virtual circuit, although some networks have also elected to use X.25 for this function [14].

The virtual-circuit structure gives a powerful handle on flow control, at least in two respects:

1. At connection setup time, the network may compare available resources with the requirements declared by the user (see throughput class declaration in the X.25 protocol [4]). It may refuse the connection if the requirements cannot be met. It may dedicate some of the resources if the connection is accepted [14].

2.   After the establishment of the connection, the network can exercise
     selective flow control on each connection. In particular, if a resource
     becomes congested (because of a failure, for example), the connections
     that use that resource can be promptly traced back to their origins and
     regulated at the network access level rather than allowing congestion to
     build up before taking any action (as in the datagram case).

The flow-control advantages deriving from these features are quite obvious.
If users are disciplined and correctly declare their expected bandwidth and delay
requirements at setup time, the probability of network overload due to bursts in
external demands is greatly reduced, since the network refuses connections that
exceed its current capacity or, alternatively, reduces the throughput on low-
priority connections to satisfy high-priority demands. Furthermore, if congestion
occurs, the recovery is more prompt and fair than in datagram networks because
of selective flow control. For example, if a region of the network becomes
temporarily congested, the virtual-circuit level of the network access flow control
will, upon learning about the congestion, selectively block further inputs from
connections directed to the congested area, while other traffic can proceed
undisturbed. If the virtual-circuit level were not implemented (as in the case of
datagram networks), the link level of the network access flow control would
eventually take over, blocking all input traffic indiscriminately.

In Section 4.5.1 we proposed three criteria for the evaluation of a flow-control
scheme: protection against congestion, fairness, and efficient utilization of
resources. From the previous arguments it is clear that the virtual-circuit flow-
control mechanism more than satisfies the congestion prevention criterion.
Fairness is also improved by a virtual-circuit implementation. It is well known,
in fact, that in a datagram network, source–destination pairs that are at short
hop distance tend to capture a larger share of the bandwidth than pairs that are
far apart [55]. Furthermore, in a datagram network undisciplined users may
attempt to increase their own throughput at the expense of everybody else's by
choosing more favorable end-to-end protocol parameters (e.g., larger window
size and smaller timeout than the average user). In virtual-circuit systems the
unfair allocation of resources due to capture (either nonintentional or malicious)
is minimized by the fact that internal network resources are preallocated at call
setup time and are guaranteed thereafter (at least in a statistical sense). Presumably, the connection cost to the user is proportional to the amount of resources
consumed.

The third consideration—efficiency—is perhaps the weakest and most contro-
versial point of the virtual-circuit implementation. As argued by Manning in [47],
"the fixed allocation of buffer resources to virtual circuits is appropriate if the
traffic is highly predictable (i.e., smooth), but may result in overcommitment and
unnecessary blocking if the traffic is bursty." Furthermore, the efficiency of
adaptive routing is lost, since paths are fixed at call setup time. Finally, the
connection setup procedure may introduce traffic overhead and response-time

delays that are intolerable in some applications (e.g., inquiry–response transactions). Similar points of view are expressed by Pouzin in [55]. Other authors, of course, stress the advantages of the virtual-circuit approach [14].

After considering the various pros and cons one comes to the conclusion that virtual circuit is more efficient for steady flow connections (e.g., file transfers, digitized voice; facsimile) while datagram is more efficient for bursty connections. This would then indicate that networks with diversified requirements should actually implement both types of protocols, virtual circuit and datagram. The virtual-circuit users would then pay a higher price for the added flow-control benefits. This possibility of dual implementation is now being considered by CCITT [4], and is favored by various data communications carriers.

4.6 NODAL FAILURE AND ISOLATION DETECTION

Link and/or node failures may create sets of nodes that are not reachable from the rest of the network. The network must promptly recognize unreachable destinations in order to discard packets directed to them. Failure to do so would result in an increasing number of undeliverable packets circulating in the network, eventually leading to congestion.

A protocol for the detection of failed or isolated (i.e., unreachable) nodes is therefore necessary. This protocol, although distinct from both routing and flow-control protocols, is discussed here since it employs mechanisms similar to those used in the routing procedures, and it attempts to prevent network congestion in the same way as flow-control procedures do.

We may define centralized or distributed isolation detection procedures, in much the same way as we have centralized and distributed routing procedures. Centralized procedures are typically implemented in centrally controlled networks. An example of centralized detection is offered by TYMNET [58], in which the supervisor recognizes that a node (or a set of nodes) is unreachable when no reports are received from it in a period of time. Future connection requests to such node are rejected by the supervisor. Other centralized schemes may provide for the distribution of the reachable node list from the control center to all the (reachable) nodes. This enables each node to immediately determine whether input traffic directed to a given destination can be accepted or not.

The disadvantages of centralized isolation detection procedures are quite similar to those found in centralized routing policies: multiple centers are required in order for the procedure to be reliable and protected from failures of the centers; furthermore, if a section of the network becomes disconnected from all the centers, this section cannot determine which destinations are reachable and which are not, and therefore will inevitably become congested with undeliverable packets.

To overcome these limitations, a distributed approach can be used. An elegant solution to this problem is based on distributed minimum hop distance computation and was first implemented in ARPANET [48]. As discussed in Sec. 4.3.4, the minimum-hop algorithm is a distributed algorithm that produces in each node the minimum hop distance (and corresponding minimum hop path) to each destination. If a destination is not reachable, the hop distance to it is infinity. If during network operation a node goes down or becomes unreachable, the hop distances to it progressively grow in each node during the update process. When the hop distance to a destination becomes $\geq N$, where N is the number of nodes in the network, that destination is unreachable since no path without loops (and therefore no shortest path) in an N node network can have more than $N - 1$ hops. Thus, when the hop distance to a given destination exceeds $N - 1$, the destination is declared unreachable and all the packets to it are discarded. The procedure also works in the case in which an entire section of the network becomes disconnected. In this case the distances to nodes lying in disconnected partitions of the network become infinity.

When a node recovers from failure or becomes reconnected to the network, a new update process takes place, which restores the original hop distances to that node. In this update process, whenever the distance to a previously unreachable node drops below N, the node is declared to be reachable again and traffic to it can be accepted.

4.7　CONCLUSIONS AND FUTURE PRESPECTIVES

Having discussed the main issues in routing and flow control, and having presented and compared a number of solution techniques, we conclude this chapter with some considerations on the selection of the best strategy for given user requirements and with the identification of new trends in networking that will impact on future routing and flow-control designs.

4.7.1　Issues in Routing

4.7.1.1　Selecting the Routing Strategy

There is no universally optimal routing strategy. Rather, the best strategy will depend on many parameters, including traffic characteristics, user delay and throughput requirements, network topology, nodal storage, and processing capabilities. If the traffic, for example, is predominantly batch-oriented and characterized by long connect times and steady flow on each connection, steady-state efficiency in the routing solution becomes more important than quick response to traffic fluctuations. Thus, a centralized scheme, or an optimal distributed scheme providing efficient multipath routing, is the recommended choice. In a transaction-oriented environment, on the other hand, the traffic fluctuations may be so unpredictable and so rapid that only local, isolated routing strategies can achieve efficient load leveling on multiple paths. As another example, if the nodes are very vulnerable (as in the case of some military applications), a minimum hop strategy may be preferable because of its capability of prompt recovery from failures.

The best of all worlds is, of course, the mixed strategy combining the advantages of many schemes. Mixed implementations are becoming particularly interesting in large networks (both public and private) which plan to cater to very diversified traffic environments and therefore require multipath efficiency as well as prompt response to fluctuations. As discussed in Section 4.4.7, a mixed strategy should include a slowly adaptive component providing optimal routes at steady state (this could be a centralized scheme or a distributed optimal scheme); an isolated component providing local queue balancing; and possibly a minimum-hop component providing rapid recovery from nodal failures.

4.7.1.2 Large Networks

When networks grow large, the conventional routing strategies become inefficient because the increased size of the routing tables (proportional to the number of nodes) causes higher line overhead (due to routing-table exchanges) and higher storage overhead. The obvious solution to this problem is the hierarchical routing implementation [9, 26, 39]. In a hierarchical implementation, the network is partitioned into regions, and routes within each region are efficiently computed using a regional strategy. The regions are interconnected by a "national" network governed by a national routing strategy. The route connecting nodes in different regions is then the concatenation of three locally optimal routes (one national and two regional). In [39] algorithms for network partitioning are presented, and the performance of hierarchical routing is compared with that of optimal routing.

Related to the issue of hierarchical routing in large networks is the issue of internet routing. When local networks are interconnected via gateways [65], local routing is accomplished using the preexisting routing strategies, while intergateway routing may be provided by a gateway-to-gateway routing procedure which resembles the national routing procedure proposed for hierarchical networks. With this scheme the gateways must have the knowlege of all host addresses. To simplify gateway design, "source" routing with route prestamped in each packet header can be implemented (see Section 4.4.3).

4.7.1.3 Heterogeneous Network Environments

To improve efficiency and reduce cost, modern network environments are becoming increasingly heterogeneous, combining different types of traffic, different transport mechanisms, and even different media. This departure from homogeneity often requires changes in the conventional routing schemes.

In packet-switched networks carrying both data and real-time traffic (e.g., digitized voice, facsimile), it is apparent that different routing criteria should be applied to data and real-time traffic. Forgie [18] proposes a virtual-circuit routing approach for voice connections (as in TYMNET), where voice is carried on fixed paths for the entire duration of the session and a voice call may be refused if link utilization along the path exceeds a given threshold. Data packets, on the other hand, are routed using a datagram approach. A more complete discussion of real-time traffic transmissions in a packet network and a proposal for a protocol for packet-switching voice communications are found in [11].

Another case of heterogeneous network environment is represented by the integration of packet-and circuit-switching transport mechanisms [12,31]. Hybrid packet and circuit schemes are most advantageous in diversified traffic environments, comprising, on the one hand, file transfer and real-time traffic (for which the circuit mode is appropriate) and, on the other hand, transactional traffic (for which the packet mode is appropriate). In a hybrid network, the objective of the routing protocol is to find feasible, minimum blocking paths for circuit-switched requests, and minimum-delay paths for packet transmissions. These objectives may be achieved with separate routing algorithms, but this may lead to inefficiencies due to high line and processor overhead and lack of proper coordination. The design of a unified routing algorithm, on the other hand, is a challenging problem, since it is not obvious that the best route for packet transmission is also efficient (or even feasible) for circuit establishment. A unified algorithm based on distributed computation was proposed in [32]. This algorithm computes at each node the set of paths to each destination, and ranks them by increasing values of residual bandwidth and increasing delay. Packets are always routed on minimum-delay paths, while circuits are routed on paths with sufficient residual bandwidth to satisfy the bandwidth requirement.

A third type of heteregeneous configuration is the *mixed-media* network, employing different communications media to connect nodes within the same network. In a mixed terrestrial and satellite network, for example, the nodes (generally distributed over a wide geographical area) are interconnected by a terrestrial network. In addition, a subset of the nodes communicate with each other via a multiple-access satellite channel [28, 33]. The challenging issue of determining which traffic to route via the terrestrial path and which to send via satellite is discussed in the references cited above.

4.7.1.4 *Performance Evaluation*

Performance evaluation tools are necessary for the design of a particular routing policy as well as for the selection of the best policy among a set of candidates. The typical performance measure is delay, but other measures (throughput, overhead, etc.) can be proposed.

For the static and quasistatic routing policies [3, 24], analytical methods exist to find the steady-state value of the delay and to prove that it is optimal (i.e., minimal). For adaptive policies, on the other hand, the analysis has not been so successful. This is in great part due to the fact that, considering the network of queues associated with the packet-switched network, the transition probabilities from one queue to another are no longer fixed (as they were in the static routing policy) but are dependent on the state of the network (e.g., length of some of the queues). This dependence prevents the use of the product form solution for networks of queues [2], which states that each queue can be studied as if it were independent (we recall that the product form solution is the fundamental result on which the static routing analysis is based [42]). Because of the difficulty of the analytical solution, most of the evaluation and comparison of adaptive routing schemes has been traditionally based on simulation and measurement results.

Very recently, however, there has been a renewed interest in the development of analytical models for adaptive routing schemes [19, 61, 63, 69]. Some success in evaluating simple networks of small size has been reported [69]. We expect that powerful analytical tools, when (and if) available, will have major impact on the design of adaptive routing algorithms.

4.7.2 Flow-Control Issues

4.7.2.1 Selecting the Best Flow-Control Strategy

The design of the best flow-control strategy is even more application-dependent than the design of the best routing strategy. In choosing the proper flow controls, we not only have to take into account response-time and bandwidth requirements of the specific applications; we also have to fit our proposed strategy within the existing protocol structure, using the flow-control facilities made available by the various protocol layers. For example, the selection of the node-to-node protocol may differ, depending on whether we use a virtual-circuit or a datagram transport mechanism. With a virtual-circuit mechanism [14], buffers are preallocated along the path, so there is no danger for direct or indirect store-and-forward lock ups; while with datagram, these lockups may occur and some protection must be built in. As another example, if the end-to-end (or transport) protocol is sensitive to the congestion in the subnet (e.g., it receives periodical status messages from the subnet), it may effectively reduce input flow into the network (by reducing window size, for example) at the first symptoms of subnet congestion. A strong and disciplined end-to-end protocol clearly permits us to relax some of the requirements for internal flow control.

If traffic components of different nature coexist in the same network, different types of controls (much in the same way as different routing schemes) may be required for different components. If data traffic is mixed with voice traffic, for example, it may be more appropriate to drop voice packets when a node becomes congested rather than using a complicated buffer pool structure, as Raubold [57] does, or an overflow network, as suggested by Kahn [37].

Finally, we have identified several possible congestion and deadlock situations in a network and have showed techniques to prevent or resolve them. However, the designer should first investigate the frequency with which these situations will occur in his or her network, and consider the possibility of recovery via operator intervention if the likelihood of such deadlocks is extremely low and if automated prevention and recovery mechanisms are very costly to implement. Kahn, in his discussion of indirect store-and-forward deadlocks in [37], suggests that although it is important conceptually to understand the nature of these deadlocks, in practice it may be more cost-effective to recover from them manually. In support of this argument, we may mention that the ARPANET is not protected against indirect deadlocks, and yet has not crashed because of an indirect lockup in 10 years!

4.7.2.2 Random-Access Networks

In terrestrial packet networks we have shown that congestion was caused by (or associated with) buffer contention and buffer wastage. A packet cannot advance in the path because there are no free buffers in the next node, and at the same time it holds buffers in the present node, preventing the acceptance of other packets. In random-access networks (e.g., packet satellite [33, 41], packet radio [38], and packet cable [50]) an additional cause of congestion is the channel wastage due to collisions. It can be shown that if packet transmission rates exceed a given threshold (which varies from scheme to scheme), the throughput of the random-access channel very rapidly decreases and becomes zero (instability problem) [41]. To prevent congestion due to conflicts, stability control procedures are implemented which generally consist in controlling the transmission rate (or scheduling future transmissions) as a function of channel load. The stability procedure based on transmission and retransmission control is essentially part of the link protocol and therefore can be viewed as a form of node-to-node flow control. For references on stability control procedures in various random-access networks, see [30, 43, 66].

4.7.2.3 Fairness

Fairness is an issue that has not been given the attention that it deserves in past flow-control studies and proposals, probably in part because it is difficult to give a precise definition of fairness. Another reason is the fact that fairness and capture issues have become very obvious and very critical only in recent packet satellite studies [43, 46]. For terrestrial-type networks, some instances of unfairness, mostly related to the different ways of allocating buffers to external traffic and transit traffic in a packet-switched node, are reported in [45, 56] and methods to correct this unfairness are proposed. The issue of fairness, however, is much more general than the discrimination between external and transit traffic. It is conceivable, for example, that in a heavily loaded network, some users may be able to capture a larger share of resources than average because of geographical advantages (e.g., fewer hops on the path) or because of higher sophistication (e.g., more powerful end-to-end protocol, more buffers, etc.). This situation must be clearly disciplined in public networks advertising equal service to all users.

4.7.2.4 Large Nets

Large networks implemented with a hierarchical structure or resulting from the interconnection of several networks require special flow-control mechanisms in addition to the ones implemented in each individual network. A key role in internet control is played by the gateway [6, 64]. Gateways throughout the network may exchange information regarding the congestion in the respective networks, and may stop traffic (i.e., drop datagrams, refuse virtual circuits) when the final destination is congested. The gateway flow control is particularly critical when some of the networks are of random-access type (and therefore more prone to congestion), such as a packet satellite network used at the "national" level [35] or a packet radio net used for local access [38].

4.7.2.5 Heterogeneous Environments

As already seen for the case of routing, heterogeneous environments also require special attention in the design of flow-control procedures. In mixed traffic environments, for example, batch traffic may be prevented from entering the network during peak hours. More generally, if there is a priority structure, low-priority traffic will be refused first. But even in the absence of priorities, stream traffic (e.g., digitized voice) should be handled differently from data traffic. In fact, before accepting a voice call, the entry node should know with some certainty that bandwidth throughout the network will be available for it [18]. Failure to do so may cause unacceptable degradation of the existing voice connections.

In hybrid networks combining packet and circuit switching, flow control problems are more complex than in separate packet and circuit implementations, since the network must decide how to dynamically share its resources between the packet and the circuit component. Furthermore, a user-refused circuit-switched bandwidth may come back as a packet user, and vice versa; or the network may reduce the rate (and therefore the bandwidth) on existing circuit connections to free resources for new traffic. At this moment, flow control in hybrid networks is still an open problem.

4.7.2.6 Performance Evaluation

Some of the comments that were made for the performance evaluation of adaptive routing apply also to flow control: the complete model of a flow-control structure in a packet network is so complex (involving, as it does, several layers of protocols) that the analytical approaches are scarce and the most common attack is via simulation or measurements.

In recent years, individual components of a flow-control strategy have been attacked analytically, with some success. The end-to-end flow-control model based on a fixed window was studied in [7, 40, 52, 68]. Kermani in [40] also discusses the optimal control of the window as a function of network load. Network access flow control was studied by Lam in [45]. Store-and-forward buffer allocation policies implemented in the node-to-node flow control were addressed by Irland in [34]. Fayolle et al. analyze the performance of the "send and wait" protocol in [17].

This is an encouraging start, but we are still far from having an analytical model of flow control that reflects the interactions of the various layers of protocol. For example, a question of great practical importance for which there is no analytical answer is the following: In preventing network congestion, what should be the share of responsibility of end-to-end protocol, access protocol, node-to-node protocol and (if present) virtual-circuit protocol, respectively? In other words, is it more cost-effective to enforce strict controls at the network access and node-to-node level and relax the flow-control requirements at the end-to-end level; or vice versa, is it better to permit uncontrolled sharing of the internal network resources and push back to the user all the flow-control responsibilities? The answer, of course, would depend on many factors, some of which may not be of technical nature. However, the issues are important, and some guidance from analytical solutions would be extremely useful for the design and interpretation of more detailed simulation and measurement experiments.

An interesting step in the direction of the development of models combining multiple levels of protocols is represented by [68]. In this paper, the interaction of end-to-end protocols and the isarithmic protocol (which is a form of network access flow control) is studied using a network of queues model with multiple classes of customers. One of the important results of this study is the fact that network access control can effectively prevent one single user from "capturing" a larger share of network resources than everybody else.

Models such as the one developed in [68] will greatly enhance the understanding of the basic flow-control issues and will contribute to the design of more-protected as well as more-cost-effective networks.

REFERENCES

[1] BARAN, P. "On Distributed Communications," series of 11 reports, The Rand Corporation, Santa Monica, Calif. August 1964.

[2] BASKETT, F. et al., "Open, Closed and Mixed Networks of Queues with Different Classes of Customers," *Journal of the ACM*, **22**(2), 248–260 April 1975.

[3] CANTOR, D., and M. GERLA, "Optimal Routing in a Packet Switched Computer Network," *IEEE Transactions on Computers*, June 1975.

[4] CCITT Recommendation X.25, "Interface between DTE and DCE for Terminals Operating in the Packet Mode on Public Data Networks," 1976.

[5] CERF, V., and R. KAHN, "A Protocol for Packet Network Intercommunication," *IEEE Transactions on Communications*, **COM-22**(5) May 1974.

[6] CERF, V., and P. KIRSTEIN, "Issues in Packet Network Interconnection," *Proceedings of the IEEE,* November 1978.

[7] CHATTERJEE, A., N. GEORGANAS, and P. VERMA, "Analysis of a Packet Switched Network with End-to-End Congestion Control and Random Routing," *Proceedings of the 3rd International Conference on Computer Communications*, Toronto, August 1976.

[8] CHOU, W., and H. FRANK, "Routing Strategies for Computer Network Design," presented at the *Symposium on Computer Communications Networks and Teletraffic, Polytechnic Institute of Brooklyn*, Brooklyn, N.Y., April 4–5, 1972.

[9] CHU, W., and M. SHEN, *A Hierarchical Routing and Flow Control Policy (HRFC) for Packet Switched Networks,* in *Computer Performance* (K. M. Chandy and M. Reiser, eds.), North-Holland Publishing Company, Amsterdam, 1977.

[10] COLE, G. C. "Computer Network Measurements: Techniques and Experiments," *Report UCLA-ENG-7165,* School of Engineering and Applied Science, University of California, Los Angeles, 1971.

[11] COHEN, D. "A Protocol for Packet Switching Voice Communication," *Proceedings of the Symposium on Computer Network Protocols*, Liège, Belgium, February 1978.

[12] COVIELLO, G., and P. VENA, "Integration of Circuit/Packet Switching by a SENET (*Slotted Envelope NET* work) Concept," *Proceedings of the NETC 75*, New Orleans, December 1975.

[13] CROWTHER, W. et al., "Issues in Packet Switching Network Design," *Proceedings of the AFIPS National Computer Conference,* Anaheim, Calif., May 1975.

[14] DANET, A. et al., "The French Public Packet Switched Service: The Transpac Network," *Proceedings of the 3rd International Conference on Computer Communications,* Toronto, August 1976.

[15] DANZIG, G. B. *Linear Programming and Extensions*, Princeton University Press, Princeton, N.J., 1963.

[16] DAVIES, D. W. "The Control of Congestion in Packet-switching Networks," *IEEE Transactions on Communications*, **COM-20**(3) January 1972.

[17] FAYOLLE, G. et al., "An Analytical Evaluation of the Performance of the 'Send and Wait' Protocol," *IEEE Transactions on Communications*, **COM-26**(3) (1978). March 1978.

[18] FORGIE, J., and A. NEMETH, "An Efficient Packetized Voice/Data Network Using Statistical Flow Control," *Proceedings of the International Conference on Communications,* Chicago, June 1977.

[19] FOSCHINI, G., and J. SALZ, "A Basic Dynamic Routing Problem and Diffusion," *IEEE Transaction on Communications*, **COM-26**(3) (1978) March 1978.

[20]　FRANK, H. et al., " Packet Radio System, Network Considerations," *Proceedings of the AFIPS National Computer Conference*, Anaheim, Calif., May 1975.

[21]　FRATTA, L., M. GERLA, and L. KLEINROCK, "The Flow Deviation Method: An Approach to Store-and-Forward Computer-Communication Network Design," *Networks*, **3**, pp. 97–133 1973.

[22]　FULTZ, G. L., and L. KLEINROCK, "Adaptive Routing Techniques for Store-and-Forward Computer Communication Networks," presented at *IEEE International Conference on Communications*, Montreal, June 14–16, 1971.

[23]　FLUTZ, G. L. "Adaptive Routing Techniques for Message Switching Computer Communications Networks," *UCLA Eng. Report* 7252, July 1972.

[24]　GALLAGER, R. G. "A Minimum Delay Routing Algorithm Using Distributed Computation," *IEEE Transactions on Communications*, **COM-25**(1), January 1977.

[25]　GERLA, M. "The Design of Store-and-Forward Networks for Computer Communications," Ph.D. dissertation, School of Engineering and Applied Science, University of California, Los Angeles, January, 1973.

[26]　GERLA, M. "Deterministic and Adaptive Routing Policies in Packet-switched Computer Networks," presented at the *ACM-IEEE 3rd Data Communications Symposium,* Tampa, Fla., November 13–15, 1973.

[27]　GERLA, M., W. CHOU, and H. FRANK, "Computational Considerations and Routing Problems for Large Computer Communications Networks," *Proceedings of the National Telecommunications Conference,* Atlanta, Ga., November 1973.

[28]　GERLA, M., W. CHOU, and H. FRANK, "Cost-Throughput Trends in Computer Networks Using Satellite Communications," *Proceedings of International Conference on Computer Communications,* Minneapolis, Minn., June 1974.

[29]　GERLA, M., H. FRANK, W. CHOU, and J. ECKL, "A Cut-Saturation Algorithm for Topological Design of Packet-switched Communications Networks," in *Proceedings of National Telecommunications Conference,* San Diego, Calif., December 2–4, 1974.

[30]　GERLA, M., and L. KLEINROCK, "Closed Loop Stability Controls for S-ALOHA Satellite Communications," *Proceedings of the 5th Data Communications Symposium,* Snowbird, Utah, September 1977.

[31]　GERLA, M., and G. DE STASIO, "Integration of Packet and Circuit Transport Protocols in the TRAN Data Network," *Proceedings of the Symposium on Computer Network Protocols*, Liège, Belgium, February, 1978.

[32]　GERLA, M., and D. MASON, "Distributed Routing in Hybrid Packet and Circuit Data Networks," COMPCON, September 1978.

[33]　HUYNH, D., H. KOBAYASHI, and F. KUO, "Optimal Design of Mixed-Media Packet-switching Networks: Routing and Capacity Assignment," *IEEE Transactions on Communications*, **COM-25**(1), January 1977.

[34]　IRLAND, M. "Buffer Management in a Packet Switch," *IEEE Transactions on Communications*, **COM-26**(3), March 1978.

[35] JACOBS, I. M., R. BINDER, and E. V. HOVERSTEN, "General Purpose Packet Satellite Networks," *Proceedings of the IEEE*, **66**(11), November 1978.

[36] JUENEMAN, R. R., and G. S. KERR, "Explicit Path Routing in Communications Networks," *Proceedings of the 3rd International Conference on Computer Communications*, Toronto, August 1976.

[37] KAHN, R. E., and W. R. CROWTHER, "A Study of the ARPA Computer Network Design and Performance," *Report* 2161, Bolt, Baranek, and Newman, Inc., August 1971.

[38] KAHN, R., "The Organization of Computer Resources into a Packet Radio Network," *IEEE Transactions on Communications*, **COM-25**(1), January 1977.

[39] KAMOUN, F. "Design Considerations for Large Computer Communications Networks," Ph.D. dissertation, *Engineering Report* 7642, UCLA, Los Angeles, Calif., April 1976.

[40] KERMANI, P., "Switching and Flow Control Techniques in Computer Communications Networks," Ph. D. dissertation, *Engineering Report* 7802, UCLA, Los Angeles, Calif., February 1978.

[41] KLEINROCK, L., and S. LAM, "Packet Switching in a Slotted Satellite Channel," *Proceedings of the AFIPS National Computer Conference*, **42** 1973.

[42] KLEINROCK, L., *Queueing Systems, Vol. 2, Computer Applications*, Wiley-Interscience, New York, 1976.

[43] KLEINROCK, L., and M. GERLA, "On the Measured Performance of Packet Satellite Access Schemes," *Proceedings of the 4th International Conference on Computer Communications*, Tokyo, September 1978.

[44] LAM, S., and L. KLEINROCK, "Dynamic Control Schemes for a Packet Switched Multi-access Broadcast Channel," *Proceedings of the AFIPS National Computer Conference*, **44**, 143–153, 1975.

[45] LAM, S., and M. REISER, "Congestion Control of Store and Forward Networks by Buffer Input Limits," *Proceedings of the National Telecommunications Conference*, Los Angeles, December 1977.

[46] LAM, S. "An Analysis of the Reservation ALOHA Protocol for Satellite Packet Switching," *Proceedings of the International Conference on Communications*, Toronto, Canada, June 1978.

[47] MANNING, E. "On Datagram Service in Public Packet Switched Networks," *Computer Networks*, **2**, 1978.

[48] McQUILLAN, J. M. et al., "Improvements in the Design and Performance of the ARPA Network," *Proceedings of the AFIPS Fall Joint Computer Conference*, **41**, 1972.

[49] McQUILLAN, J. M., "Adaptive Algorithms for Distributed Computer Networks," *Report* 2831, Bolt, Beranek and Newman, Inc., Cambridge, Mass., May 1974.

[50] METCALFE, R. M., and D. R. BOGGS, "Ethernet: Distributed Packet Switching for Local Computer Networks," *Communications of the ACM*, **19,**(7), 1976.

[51] NAYLOR, W., and L. KLEINROCK, "On the Effect of Periodic Routing Updates in

Packet-switched Networks,'' *Proceedings of the National Telecommunications Conference*, Dallas, Tex., November 1976.

[52]   PENNOTTI, M., and M. SCHWARTZ, "Congestion Control in Store and Forward Tandem Links," *IEEE Transactions on Communications*, **COM-23**(12), December, 1975.

[53]   POUZIN, L., "Another Idea for Congestion Control in Packet-switching Networks," *Technical Memorandum*, Réseau Cyclades, January 1973.

[54]   POUZIN, L., "Virtual Circuits vs. Datagrams: Technical and Political Problems," *Proceedings of the AFIPS National Computer Conference*, June 1976.

[55]   POUZIN, L., "Flow Control in Data Networks—Methods and Tools," *Proceedings of the 3rd International Conference on Computer Communications*, Toronto, Canada, August 1976.

[56]   PRICE, W. L., "Data Network Simulation Experiments at the National Physical Laboratory," *Computer Networks*, **1**, 1977.

[57]   RAUBOLD, E., and J. HAENLE, "A Method of Deadlock-free Resource Allocation and Flow Control in Packet Networks," *Proceedings of the 3rd International Conference on Computer Communications*, Toronto, August 1976.

[58]   RINDE, J., "Routing and Control in a Centrally Directed Network," *Proceedings of the AFIPS National Computer Conference*, Dallas, Tex., June 1977.

[59]   RUDIN, H., "On Routing and Delta Routing: A Taxonomy and Performance Comparison of Techniques for Packet-switched Networks," *IEEE Transactions on Communications*, **COM-24**(1), January, 1976.

[60]   SCANTLEBURY, R., and P. WILKINSON, "The National Physical Laboratory Data Communications Network," *Proceedings of the International Conference on Computer Communications*, Stockholm, August 12–14, 1974.

[61]   SEGALL, A., "The modeling of adaptive routing in Data Communications Networks," *IEEE Transactions on Communications*, **COM-25**(1), January 1977.

[62]   SILK, D. J., "Routing Doctrines and Their Implementation in Message Switching Networks," *Proceedings of the Institute Electrical Engineering*, **116,** pp. 1631–1638, October 1969.

[63]   STERN, T. "Approximations of Queue Dynamics and Their Application to Adaptive Routing in Computer Networks," *Proceedings of the National Telecommunications Conference,* December 1978.

[64]   SUNSHINE, A. C., "Interconnection of Computer Networks," *Computer Networks* **1,** 1977.

[65]   SUNSHINE, C., "Source Routing in Computer Networks," *Computer Communications Review,* ACM, SIGDC, January 1977.

[66]   TOBAGI, F., "Packet Switching in Radio Channels: Part IV—Stability Considerations and Dynamic Control in Carrier Sense Multiple Access," *IEEE Transactions on Communications*, **COM-25**(10), October 77.

[67]   TOMLIN, J. A., "Minimum Cost Multi-commodity Network Flows," *Operations Research*, **14,** pp. 45–47, January 1966.

[68] Wong, J. W., and M. S. Unsoy, "Analysis of Flow Control in Switched Networks," *Proceedings of the IFIP*, August 1977.

[69] Yum, T., and M. Schwartz, "Comparison of Adaptive Routing Algorithms for Computer Communications Networks," *Proceedings of the National Telecommunications Conference*, December 1978.

5

PACKET PROTOCOLS FOR BROADCAST SATELLITES

RICHARD BINDER

LINKABIT Corporation

5.1 INTRODUCTION AND PRELIMINARIES

This chapter describes some protocols that have been developed for data communications using broadcast satellites. The emphasis of the chapter is on demand assignment techniques, applicable to either an autonomous satellite network or mixed-media applications in which a satellite is used in conjunction with terrestrial circuits. Considerable attention is also given to fixed assignment access prior to discussion of demand assignment, however, since many performance characteristics of fixed assignment are common to the demand assignment systems.

5.1.1 Satellite and Earth Station Assumptions

The protocols to be described all assume a geosynchronous satellite. A single communication transponder, or portion thereof is accessed by all stations in a manner determined by the particular protocol; these uplink transmissions are amplified and broadcast on the downlink to these same stations. Where the full transponder bandwidth is not required, frequency division is assumed used to provide a single channel of smaller bandwidth for use by the set of stations. This

175

channel (or the entire transponder) is shared by the stations through use of either synchronous or asynchronous time-division multiple access (TDMA), in which each station transmits at a particular time on the same uplink frequency as all other stations, and receives on the same downlink frequency as all other stations. The uplink and downlink frequencies differ from each other, however, allowing simultaneous transmission and reception by each station. Thus, each station has a full duplex hardware interface to what is in fact a single uplink plus downlink channel, with the transponder acting as a frequency translator.

Figure 5.1 identifies the major system functions assumed performed by the station. The satellite channel protocol is the topic of this chapter; the user interface and network level protocols refer to things such as host access protocols (e.g., X-25) and station-to-station flow-control protocols used to regulate the acceptance of particular host traffic into the system. While the design of these protocols may be optimized to some extent by considering the particular channel protocol being used, their selection is reasonably separable from that of the channel protocol itself.

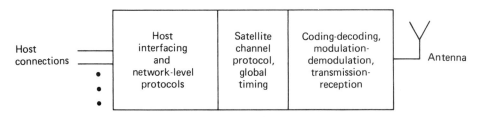

FIGURE 5-1   *Major station functions.*

The coding–decoding,[1] modulation–demodulation, and transmission–reception functions are somewhat less separable from the channel protocol design. This is in part due to the dependence of particular channel protocols on realizable bit error rates, full duplex transmitter–receiver equipment, and tolerance of these components (and the satellite transponder) to factors such as simultaneous multiple transmissions by several stations [1]. We will assume here that these functions are designed to provide a constant environment to the different channel protocols being discussed.

5.1.2   Traffic and Performance Factors

The choice of an efficient satellite protocol depends strongly on both the nature of the traffic and the performance demanded by users. If the traffic at each station has a high degree of predictability with respect to its bandwidth require-

---

[1]   This is not a required function.

ments at any particular point in time, relatively simple techniques can be used to coordinate efficient use of the satellite channel by each station. On the other hand, a low predictability implies either less efficient use of available bandwidth or more sophisticated allocation techniques. Similarly, a user delay requirement of less than 0.5 s per message excludes protocols that require at least two hops[2] for delivery. In fact, as we shall see in later sections, relaxing this delay requirement allows significant improvements in bandwidth efficiency to be made.

Data communications traffic generated by an individual terminal user or process tends to be bursty, that is, relatively unpredictable in its moment-to-moment bandwidth requirements. If many such traffic sources are concentrated into a single flow for satellite access purposes at a station, however, the station bandwidth requirement becomes more predictable. From the point of view of satellite protocol selection, highly concentrated data traffic at each station thus represents one extreme in which little or no demand assignment may be needed, at least on a short-term basis. The other extreme is represented by a station supporting a single interactive terminal user, providing a high degree of source burstiness.

In addition to burstiness, a related factor that strongly impacts protocol performance is individual message lengths. If messages tend to be short and sufficient concentration does not exist at a station, channel allocation overhead may be large relative to the channel time being allocated. On the other hand, concentration provides the opportunity for a station to ''pack'' short messages together for channel transmission as if they were a single long message.

In addition to message delay and bandwidth efficiency, other performance factors that must be considered are *fairness* in use of the channel by competing stations, *priority* traffic handling, *robustness* in the presence of noise and other degradations, and *flexibility* with respect to system growth.

5.1.3 Packetizing

As the title of this chapter implies, we are concerned with protocols for packetized data. Although this packetizing may typically be performed by a higher-level protocol prior to arrival at a station, further packetizing will in general need to be performed by the station to satisfy the requirements of the satellite protocol. To avoid confusion we will refer to all traffic arriving at a station from user sources as messages, and each data segment transmitted in the satellite channel as a packet.

Each packet contains addressing and other control information and has a maximum allowed length, chosen according to the dictates of the protocol being used. If a message is less than this maximum, the packet length is assumed to be only as long as required to contain the message.

---

[2] A ''hop'' is one uplink plus downlink propagation time, or approximately 0.27 s for a geosynchronous satellite.

5.1.4 Global Timing

An assumption common to most of the protocols to be described is that each station is synchronized to a time reference, allowing transmissions by each station to arrive at the satellite at a time agreed upon by all stations. For accuracy, this requires two items of information at each station: a common clock reference and the station's uplink plus downlink propagation time (or a related correction factor). The latter allows each station to compensate for differences between its distance to the satellite and the distances of the other stations, which becomes increasingly important for timing accuracy in higher-data-rate channels.

There are many techniques for accomplishing this global timing; the interested reader is referred to [2] for a survey of the subject. The important point we wish to make here is that, at least for channel data rates below a few Mbits/s, this timing can be achieved with a relatively simple and inexpensive implementation. For example, an accuracy to within one bit time at 64 kbits/s has been achieved using inexpensive crystal oscillators and a small amount of hardware to augment the satellite protocol processor I/O interface used in the experimental system of [3].

5.2. FIXED ASSIGNMENT TDMA

5.2.1 Protocol Considerations

In this protocol channel time is administratively assigned to each station according to its anticipated traffic requirements. In its simplest form a single *frame time T* is defined as shown in Fig. 5.2, large enough to contain one time assignment for each station.[3] Notice that the times assigned to each station can in general be of different durations.

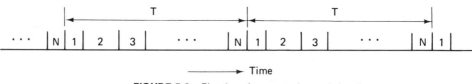

FIGURE 5-2 *Fixed assignment channel timeline.*

The transmission protocol associated with the timeline of Fig. 5.2 consists simply of each station noting the occurrence of its assigned time in each frame relative to global timing, and of transmitting any waiting packets at these times. All stations constantly monitor the satellite downlink, checking each received

---

[3] In this and all figures to follow, time is referenced to the satellite.

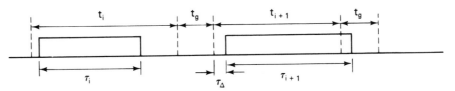

FIGURE 5-3 *Slot, burst, and guard times.*

packet to see if it is addressed to them. If it is, a station delivers it to its user destination; otherwise, it discards it.

A more detailed view of how channel time is used is given in Fig. 5.3, in which the adjacent time assignments for two stations are shown. The first station is assigned time t_i, the second time t_{i+1}. Each assignment is separated by a guard time t_g which allows for errors due to the global timing inaccuracies in the starting times of adjacent transmissions. The figure shows a transmission burst τ_i from station i which does not occupy the full-time assignment t_i, and a burst of length τ_{i+1} from station $i + 1$ which equals its assigned time t_{i+1}. Note that the τ_{i+1} burst starts t_Δ later than the end of the t_g interval preceding it and overlaps the next t_g interval, illustrating how the guard time absorbs the transmission timing error $t\Delta$ of station $i + 1$.

Figure 5.4 illustrates the transmission of several short data packets in a single burst to more efficiently use the assigned time. Each packet contains addressing information which allows delivery by the appropriate destination station, just as if they were sent in separate bursts.

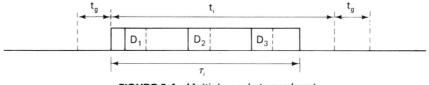

FIGURE 5-4 *Multiple packets per burst.*

Figure 5.5 illustrates a more complex framing structure using fixed assignments. In this case station 1 is assigned relatively frequent time slots, which recur with a frame time T_1. Each of the other stations has a frame time T_j between successive slots. This assignment might be made if station 1 had a greater bandwidth *and* shorter access delay requirement than the other stations (see below). Although this arrangement appears more complicated, it is important

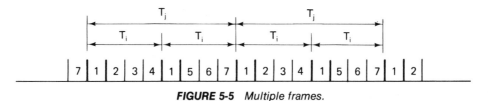

FIGURE 5-5 *Multiple frames.*

179

to note that the protocol executed by each station is identical to that used with Fig. 5.2.

5.2.2 Performance

As indicated in Sec. 5.1.2, station traffic characteristics play a large role in determining resulting performance. For fixed assignments, a particular station's performance is affected by other station traffic only through the frame time T seen by the station. Within the structure imposed by these assignments, however, only its own traffic characteristics will determine the delay of its messages and the efficiency with which it uses its assigned time.

For example, referring to Fig. 5.2 we see that if each station's traffic consists of a single message per frame always arriving just prior to the station's assigned transmission time, and each message burst fully occupies the assigned time t_i, then we will achieve the minimum possible delay (for the given channel bandwidth) and the maximum possible channel efficiency (for a system using a channel time-sharing technique and packetized messages).

On the other hand, if message arrivals are random with an average time between arrivals considerably larger than T, each message will experience an average delay of at least $T/2$ more than in the previous example, and efficiency will be low owing to unused time assignments. More generally, for Poisson-distributed message arrivals of constant length, the average message delay for each station i with frame time T_i is given by

$$D_i = \frac{T_i}{2} + Q_i + \tau_i + T_p \qquad (5.1)$$

where T_p is the propagation time, τ_i the message burst time, and Q_i the queueing delay encountered by the message in addition to the $T_i/2$ waiting time.[4] Since Q_i is a function of the utilization of the assigned time t_i, (5.1) provides the delay-efficiency trade-off relation for Poisson traffic. (Efficiency is taken here and in subsequent sections to be the fraction of channel bandwidth occupied by message bits. Packet and burst overhead bits introduced by the sending station and guard time thus provide an upper bound on achievable efficiency.)

The parameters that determine T_i in (5.1) are the number of stations N, the maximum message length L to be sent in a single burst by each station, and the channel data rate R. If each station has the same assignement t_i, then

$$T_i = Nt_i \qquad (5.2)$$

---

[4] For a detailed analysis, see [4].

where

$$t_i = \frac{L + B}{R} \tag{5.3}$$

and B is the total overhead bits of a message, including guard bits.

Figure 5.6 illustrates the delay-efficiency trade-off of (5.1) for $R = 100$ kbits/s, $L = 1000$ bits, and total overhead $B = 100$ bits. The value of each curve at zero channel efficiency represents the minimum average delay for a random message arrival when the station queue is empty, and illustrates an important characteristic of fixed assignment TDMA systems: *the minimum achievable average delay increases directly porportional to N for fixed values of L and R.* The behavior of the curves as the message arrival rate increases, reflected by increasing channel efficiency, shows the influence of the queuing delay within the station.

Figure 5.7 shows the results of Fig. 5.6 in a different form to illustrate a principle common to all protocols to be considered: *if users are willing to tolerate*

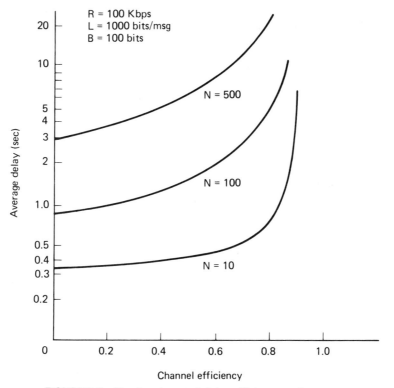

FIGURE 5-6 *Fixed assignment delay-efficiency performance.*

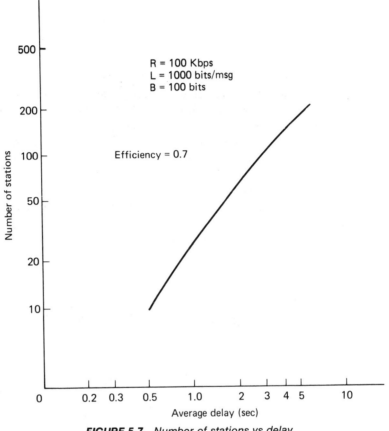

FIGURE 5-7 *Number of stations vs delay.*

greater message delay, more stations can share a given channel bandwidth. This is important to keep in mind when bandwidth cost is a significant factor in the protocol selection; because of the large lower bound on delay imposed by the satellite channel propagation time, a significant increase in the number of users can be obtained with only a relatively small increase in the delay observable by a human user.

5.2.3 Traffic Concentration

The benefits resulting from concentrating more traffic per station can be seen by expressing frame time in (5.1) as a function of *average traffic per station K*. For a desired channel efficiency E, the channel data rate required to support N stations each with average traffic K is

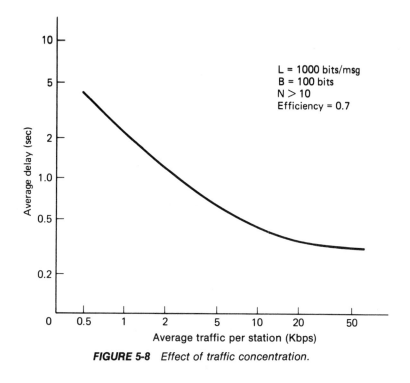

FIGURE 5-8 *Effect of traffic concentration.*

$$R = \frac{NK}{E} \tag{5.4}$$

Using this in (5.3) and substituting the result in (5.2) gives

$$T_i = \frac{E}{K}(L + B) \tag{5.5}$$

Figure 5.8 shows the delay given by (5.1) and (5.5) as a function of K for an efficiency $E = 0.7$ and a constant message length $L = 1000$ bits, for $N \geq 10$.[5] Notice that for traffic concentrations greater than about 20 kbits/s per station, average delay is close to the minimum one-hop delay. Thus, *for sufficient traffic concentration we can have an arbitrarily large number of stations and still have an average delay approaching the one-hop value.*

[5] For $N < 10$, the delay in Fig. 5.8 is slightly greater because of the larger values of burst time τ relative to the other delay components.

183

5.2.4 Variable Message Lengths

The curves in Figs. 5.6 to 5.8 are based on constant-length messages, with assigned channel time t_i chosen to match this length. The choice of t_i is not as simple if traffic consists of variable-length messages. Suppose, for example, that messages at each station have two different lengths, L and mL, with m an integer. Should t_i match L, mL, or some value between the two?

The answer depends on the desired delays for each message length, the amount of traffic concentration at each station, and the importance of channel efficiency.

Consider first the effects of sending the longer messages of length mL in m separate bursts of length L. Channel efficiency is reduced due to the higher ratio of burst overhead bits to burst data bits. In addition, average message delay is increased, which can be seen from the following argument. For a random message arrival that finds the station queue empty, the average delay when the message is sent in a single burst is

$$D_1 = \frac{T}{2} + \frac{T}{N} + T_p \tag{5.6}$$

where each of the N stations is assumed to have the same time assignment $t_i = T/N$. If the messages are sent in m bursts of duration t_i, the average message delay (ignoring additional burst overhead) is

$$D_m = \frac{T}{2m} + (m - 1)\frac{T}{m} + \frac{T}{mN} + T_p \tag{5.7}$$

where the first term of (5.7) is the average waiting time for the first time assignment, the second term is the subsequent waiting time for the last burst of the message to be sent, and the third term is the transmission time of the last burst. Taking the difference $D_\Delta = D_m - D_1$ gives

$$D_\Delta = \left(\frac{1}{2} - \frac{1}{N}\right)\left(1 - \frac{1}{m}\right)T \tag{5.8}$$

This, in fact, also holds when the queue is not empty [4].

Figure 5.9 shows D_Δ in terms of the frame time T for different N and m. As N grows large, the worst-case delay difference is seen to be between $T/4$ and $T/2$, according to the value of m. Thus, if $N = 100$, $R = 100$ kbits/s, $L = 10,000$ bits, and $m = 10$, then $T = 10$ s and the average delay in the D_m system is about 5 s greater than in the D_1 system. If the channel efficiency is 0.7, this represents an increase of about 30% over the D_1 delay of 17.4 s.

The preceding shows that the messages of length mL will suffer degraded performance if smaller time assignments are used. However, if the time assignments are chosen such that the messages of length mL are sent in a *single burst*, the short messages of length L will suffer a greater delay due to the larger frame size. Depending on the concentration of messages queued at each station, channel efficiency will also suffer—whenever a short message is sent and other messages (or portions thereof) cannot also be sent to fill out the time assignment, only $1/m$ of the assigned time will be used.

Thus, a compromise value of t_i must be chosen which satisfies message delay requirements while providing reasonable channel efficiency. This can be difficult to do if message-length variance is high and station traffic concentration is low, conditions which, among others, lead us to investigate some of the protocols in the following sections.

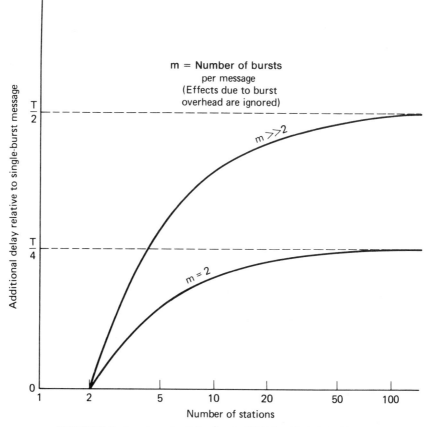

FIGURE 5-9 *Increase in delay for multiple-burst messages.*

5.3 RANDOM-ACCESS PROTOCOLS

The results of Section 5.2 showed that, for random message arrivals, fixed assignment performance tends to become poor as station traffic concentration becomes small and the number of stations becomes large. Even when this is not the case, fixed assignment does not allow for changes in traffic flow among the stations relative to that assumed when the system is designed.

Thus several alternatives to fixed assignment have evolved for packet systems. This section describes approaches consisting either entirely or predominately of a random-access technique.

5.3.1 Unslotted and Slotted ALOHA

This approach is named after the project at the University of Hawaii, which pioneered its use [5]. In its simplest form, no synchronization of station transmissions is used—whenever a packet is ready to be sent, a station simply transmits it. If no other station is transmitting during this time (and no local noise errors occur at the receiver), the packet will be received successfully by the destination station. If one or more other stations are transmitting, a conflict occurs due to destructive interference at the satellite transponder and, with high probability, the packets are not received correctly in the downlink.[6] The satellite broadcast mode allows detection of the conflict by the sending station, which then queues the packet for retransmission. A random waiting interval is used by each station prior to its retransmission to minimize the probability of further conflicts. The resulting channel activity is shown in the timeline of Fig. 5.10. When Poisson packet arrivals are assumed with equal rates at each station and the number of stations is greater than about 20, channel efficiency has an upper bound of approximately $1/2e$, or about one-sixth the available bandwidth [5].

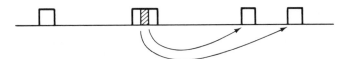

FIGURE 5-10   *Unslotted ALOHA channel timeline.*

For traffic consisting of fixed-length packets, a factor-of-2 improvement in performance can be achieved by synchronizing the burst starting times of all stations [6]. This is accomplished by "slotting" the channel using global timing in the same way as for fixed assignments in Sec. 5.2, except that a frame reference is not needed (Fig. 5.11). Under these circumstances a maximum

---

[6] Differences in station uplink powers are assumed to be sufficiently small that capture effects do not occur.

FIGURE 5-11 *Slotted ALOHA channel timeline.*

channel efficiency of approximately one-third can be achieved for traffic equally distributed among the stations.

A complication to either the unslotted or slotted method is the need to stabilize the channel. The random-access technique is inherently unstable if the retransmission intervals used are too small relative to the traffic rate. On the other hand, unnecessarily large intervals can result in excessive delays. Thus, a control mechanism is required which can adapt the rate of new transmissions and retransmissions to dynamic load changes while minimizing delay [7, 19, 20].

5.3.1.1 Performance

Unlike a fixed assignment system, the performance seen by an individual station in an ALOHA channel depends directly on the traffic sent by *all* other stations. The general efficiency-delay performance of an ALOHA channel is shown in Fig. 5.12 for the same traffic rate at each station and fixed-length packets. The lower (solid-line) portions of each curve represent the optimum achievable performance for stable operation. The dashed portions of the curves indicate typical degraded operation during instabilities, wherein efficiency decreases and delay increases due to the increased number of retransmissions in the channel.

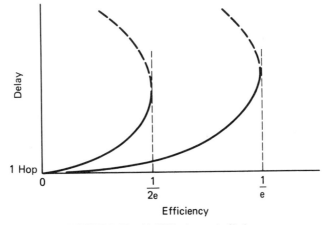

FIGURE 5-12 *ALOHA channel efficiency.*

Note that, to adequately specify the performance of an ALOHA channel without an explicit stability control mechanism, *a probability of expected stable operation time* must be given along with values of efficiency and delay [8]. This probability is in general a function of the interval used for retransmissions and the total number of stations, with longer intervals resulting in a higher probability of maintaining stable operation for a given time.

Another important aspect of ALOHA performance in a satellite channel is the average number of retransmissions associated with a given efficiency, since at least one hop of delay occurs for each retransmission. In particular, an average of 1.7 retransmissions must be made for each success at the maximim efficiency points of the curves in Fig. 5.12 ($1/2e$ and $1/e$), resulting in almost three hops in the total delay. In order to approach an average delay of one hop, channel efficiency must be substantially reduced from the maximum points. The retransmissions also result in a relatively large variance in message delays compared to a fixed assignment system.

5.3.1.2 Variable Message Lengths

The maximum achievable channel efficiency for unslotted ALOHA has been shown to be somewhat less than the $1/2e$ value when variable-length packets are sent [9]. On the other hand, the fixed-length slots of slotted ALOHA result in delay-efficiency degradations similar to those discussed in Sec. 5.2 for fixed assignment access. The choice between unslotted and slotted ALOHA thus depends on the ratio of burst overhead to message lengths, the distribution of lengths, the efficiency operating point chosen to satisfy delay and stability considerations, and the relative system cost of global timing.

5.3.1.3 Excess Capacity

One of the important features of the ALOHA approach is that a particular station can potentially use the entire channel capacity for some arbitrary period of time, depending on the needs of other stations during that time. In particular, the average channel efficiency can exceed $1/2e$ or $1/e$ when the transmission rates of the stations are unequal. This result is known as the excess capacity of an ALOHA channel [10] and can give an efficiency approaching 1 in the case of a single user with a high packet rate and all other users with a very low packet rate. However, the delay encountered by the low-rate users is significantly higher than in the homogenous case of Fig. 5.12 [11].

5.3.2 Reservation-ALOHA

While the excess-capacity effect does allow a small number of high-rate stations to use the channel, it would appear desirable to remove these stations from the random-access competition for channel time. An approach called Reservation-

ALOHA [12] was designed to do this while maintaining the relative simplicity of the basic ALOHA approach.

This protocol introduces the fixed-assignment frame concept to a slotted ALOHA channel, along with a control memory requirement at each station. The frame size is equal to or greater than the maximum uplink plus downlink propagation time, allowing each station to remember the state of a slot's previous usage at the time a new use of it must begin. Three states are distinguished by each station: whether the slot was last used successfully by itself ("Mine"), whether it was used successfully by another station ("Other"), or whether it was not used successfully by anyone ("Empty"). The random-access transmission rules are modified according to this information as follows. If a slot is marked *Empty*, use it as in the simple random-access system; if marked *Other*, do *not* use it; if marked *Mine*, it is reserved for that station's exclusive use.

Thus, if a station has a long queue of messages, once it successfully uses a slot it is guaranteed successive use of it until its queue is emptied. If traffic is equally distributed among the stations and duty cycles are high, the system behavior approaches that of fixed TDMA. If duty cycles are low, it approaches simple slotted ALOHA behavior [13].

If a significant traffic imbalance exists even for a short period of time, however, it is possible for a single station to capture the entire channel, creating long delays for the other stations. A related issue concerns whether a station should wait for its acquired slots or also use intervening empty slots. Because of these issues and the fact that decreasing processing costs have made the premise of simplicity on which Reservation-ALOHA was based less significant, subsequent work on packet demand assignment has tended to concentrate on the explicit reservation approaches discussed in the next section.

5.4 EXPLICIT RESERVATION PROTOCOLS

The desire to allow flexible sharing of the channel while achieving efficiencies comparable to those provided by fixed assignment has led to the evolution of explicit reservation techniques. The basic approach consists of transmitting a relatively small number of bits to request channel time for queued messages, which are subsequently sent in the requested time.

The reservations may be sent using fixed assignment techniques, random access, or both. Channel time may be assigned to reserved messages by any of a number of ordering algorithms (e.g., first come, first-served (FIFO) or round-robin by sending station). Control may be achieved by use of either distributed or centralized techniques, or by a mixture of the two.

Three reservation systems will now be described. The first illustrates the use of random access for reservations and a relatively simple assignment algorithm. The second uses fixed assignment for reservations and a scheduling algorithm designed to reduce access delays for short messages and provide robustness in the presence of noise. The third makes use of both random access and assigned reservation time, and is designed to satisfy a wide variety of traffic sources and operating conditions.

5.4.1 Roberts' Reservation System

Roberts' reservation system, like reservation-ALOHA, was designed to keep processing bandwidth requirements reasonably small while providing relatively efficient use of the satellite channel [14]. At any particular time the channel is in one of two states, as shown in Fig. 5.13, a reservation state or an ALOHA state. The channel is in the reservation state whenever one or more reservations are being serviced, and otherwise is in the ALOHA state.

In the ALOHA state, time is divided into small equal-sized slots in which reservation packets are sent using the slotted ALOHA protocol described in Section 5.3.1. A distributed control algorithm is used in which each station monitors all channel traffic; when a reservation is heard successfully in the ALOHA state, all stations enter the reservation state (after allowing time for the reservation to be heard by the stations most distant from the satellite).

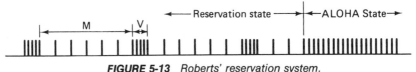

FIGURE 5-13   *Roberts' reservation system.*

In the reservation state, channel time is divided into a data subframe consisting of M equal-sized data slots, followed by V small reservation slots. The data slots are used by the stations that have made a successful reservation, while other stations can make new reservations in the V small slots of each frame.

A FIFO scheduling discipline is used for the reservations. Each reservation consists of a number between one and eight, representing the number of data slots requested. When heard, this number is simply added to a total count J, which represents the total reservations to be serviced. Each station tracks the current value of J and in addition remembers the value of J that exists at the time its own reservation is added to the total—this value is the number of data slots it must then count off to determine when it should send its reserved packets.

To allow stations to detect the fact that they have missed a reservation due to a local reception error, and to allow new stations to enter the system, each station sends its value of J in its transmitted packets. If a station hears a value of J larger than its own, it uses the new value and remakes any reservations it has outstanding.

5.4.2 Reservation-TDMA

In contrast to Roberts' system, reservation-TDMA (R-TDMA) uses fixed assignments to make reservations [3].[7] Channel time is divided as shown in Fig. 5.14, with N small reservation slots of duration τ' and $k \cdot N$ large slots of duration τ in each frame. One reservation slot in each frame is preassigned to each of the N stations. Each station is also preassigned one data slot in each of the k subgroups and is called the "owner" of its slot—this data slot ownership is included to provide robustness in the presence of noise, as explained below.

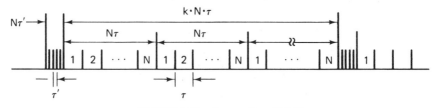

FIGURE 5-14 *Reservation-TDMA.*

Reservations are made as follows. Each station sends a "new reservation" count in its reservation slot to announce its need for new data slots; this count represents message arrivals that have occurred since its reservation packet transmission of the preceding frame. If no new arrivals have occurred, it sends a value of zero. Every station monitors the channel for these reservation packets and, at a globally agreed-upon time (the *update slot*), adds the received values to a reservation table which is used to assign the data slots.

The reservations are used to assign the data slots by all stations as follows. If a slot's owner has one or more reservations in the table, the slot is assigned to the owner. Slots whose owners have a zero table entry are assigned in a round-robin manner among those stations with nonzero entries. Each time an assignment is made, the assigned station's table entry is decremented. If the reservation table is empty, a station is allowed to send immediately in its own slot.

To allow initial acquisition of outstanding reservations (reservation synchronization), each station also sends its own current total reservation count in its reservation packets. To acquire synchronization, a station uses these received counts to determine the outstanding reservations as of the time the reservations were sent. It then determines which reservations were honored in each subsequent slot until the update slot, by repeatedly executing the assignment algorithm for each slot. It then applies the new reservation counts from each reservation packet as described above.

---

[7] This system is a modified version of one designed to use a mixture of fixed assignment and random access for reservations [15].

If a station misses one or more reservation packets, it reverts to using only its own slots until it can reacquire reservation synchronization. (Since the other nodes assign the station its own slots whenever it has an outstanding reservation, the R-TDMA algorithm tends to perform well even when channel errors cause frequent missing of reservation packets.) After hearing a subsequent complete set of reservation packets, the station performs the steps above to reacquire reservation synchronization.

5.4.3   Priority-Oriented Demand Assignment (PODA)

PODA [16–18] is a demand assignment protocol designed to efficiently satisfy the requirements of a general-purpose network, including support of both block data (datagram) and packetized voice (stream) traffic, multiple delay classes and priorities, and variable message lengths. Its design represents an integration of both circuit- and packet-switched demand assignment techniques:

- Explicit reservations are used for datagram messages, generally resulting in delays of at least two satellite hops.

- A single explicit reservation is used to set up each stream, with subsequent packets automatically scheduled at predetermined intervals to give essentially one-hop delays.

- High availability and improved performance are achieved by the use of distributed control techniques.

- Robustness and mixed receiving-rate operation are achieved by the integrated use of both distributed and centralized control techniques.

Channel time is divided into two basic subframes, an information subframe T_I and a control subframe T_C (Fig. 5.15). The information subframe is used for

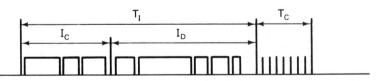

FIGURE 5-15   *Priority-oriented demand assignment (PODA).*

scheduled datagram and stream transmissions, which also contain control information such as reservations and acknowledgments in their headers. The information subframe is further divided into a section for centralized assignments I_C and a section for distributed assignments I_D. The control subframe is used to send reservations that cannot be sent in the information subframe in a timely manner.

5.4.3.1 Control Subframe

The control subframe must be used for initial reservation access by a station that has no impending scheduled transmissions, and may also need to be used at times to make reservations for traffic whose urgency does not allow waiting for the next opportunity to use the header of a scheduled message.

The access method used for this subframe depends on the particular characteristics of the system in which PODA is being used. If the total number of stations is small, fixed assignments of one slot per station are used within the control subframe (as in R-TDMA), and the system is referred to as FPODA. For large populations of low-duty-cycle stations, mixed station populations, or situations in which traffic requirements are not well known, contention access is used (as in Roberts' protocol), and the system is referred to as CPODA. Combinations of fixed assignment and random access in the control subframe are also possible. In either case subframe time is divided into fixed-sized slots equal to the (constant) length of the control packets.

In CPODA, the size of the control subframe is varied according to current scheduling requirements. If no reservations are outstanding, the control subframe occupies almost the entire CPODA frame in order to reduce contention probability; as loading increases, the control subframe is reduced to a value determined by the urgency of the messages being scheduled until a minimum value is reached. In this state new reservation transmissions are constrained at all stations, allowing only higher-priority traffic to compete in the contention subframe when the channel is heavily scheduled.

5.4.3.2 Reservations and Scheduling

All datagram reservations received successfully in the satellite downlink are entered into a scheduling queue maintained by all stations performing distributed scheduling. These entries are ordered according to reservation urgency, which is a function of potential lateness (relative to the user-specified delay class) and priority. Reservations with the same urgency are further ordered to provide fairness to the stations involved. Channel time in the information subframe is then assigned to messages according to the ordering of reservations in the scheduling queue.

A reservation for a stream is made only once, at the beginning of the stream use, and is retained at each station in a separate stream queue when received in the downlink. Each stream reservation contains information defining the stream repetition interval, desired maximum delay relative to this interval, and priority. Whenever the interval starting time is near, a reservation is created for that stream's next message and entered into the scheduling queue; the reservation urgency is calculated according to the stream queue information and is treated the same as datagram reservation urgency. Thus, all channel time requests, whether for datagrams for streams, are ordered according to a single set of rules.

In particular, high-priority datagram traffic can preempt lower-priority stream allocations for an indefinite period, possibly resulting in termination of streams.

To maximize channel efficiency while satisfying urgency constraints, each reservation in the scheduling queue may actually be for a group of several distinct datagrams. The maximum burst-length request allowed per group reservation represents a trade-off between satisfying system urgency constraints for competing stations, which argues for a smaller maximum, and reducing relative burst overhead by using a larger maximum.

Of course, a station must have several messages queued in order to make a single group reservation for them. Furthermore, at certain times a station may have more than one message group being scheduled within the same frame. Overhead can be further reduced by scheduling these message groups contiguously to allow a single burst transmission.

5.4.3.3 Centralized Assignments

To achieve the reduced delay of distributed control (at least one hop less than centralized control) while also making centralized assignments for stations unable to participate in the scheduling, the information subframe is partitioned as shown in Fig. 5.15 and an integrated control technique used. Since the centralized assignments cannot be acted on until the assigned stations are informed, they are scheduled for a frame at least one hop in the future. Thus, the centralized assignment section of the information subframe in Fig. 5.15 represents assignments made at least one hop in the past, while the distributed assignment section represents assignments being made from the scheduling queue in the current frame.

Note that all stations which perform distributed scheduling can also make the centralized assignments, so that the high system availability resulting from distributed control is maintained. To avoid introducing unnecessary burst overhead in sending the assignments, they are sent by a station transmitting a scheduled burst in the distributed assignment section. A separate control burst is thus necessary for this function only when no messages are otherwise scheduled for the distributed assignment section.

5.4.3.4 Scheduling Synchronization for Distributed Scheduling

As in the other reservation systems, the use of distributed control introduces potential synchronization problems due to local receiving errors at each station performing scheduling. To prevent increased reservation errors in PODA due to reservations piggybacked on long data bursts, all global control information is sent with a separately checksummed header in each burst.

The synchronization acquisition and maintenance process consists of three states: (1) the initial acquisition state, (2) the out-of-sync state, and (3) the in-sync state, with the transition into or out of a particular state based upon consistency checks. Each station compares its own scheduling decisions against the transmission actually taking place in the channel; if a discrepancy is noted, the station detecting it does some further checks and if necessary adjusts its scheduling queue.

When a station is first turned on, it enters the initial acquisition state, in which it has no information about the state of the scheduling queue in the other stations. In this state it listens for new reservations and observes the packets being transmitted in the channel, but does not itself send any data messages or reservations. Since each reservation has a maximum lifetime in the scheduling queue, a station can build up a reservation list compatible with other stations within a reasonable period. When a certain number of correct consistency checks have been made, the station enters the out-of-sync state.

In the out-of-sync state, the station schedules the received reservations and monitors for consistent schedulings, but it does not send any data packets or make reservations. If several consecutive consistent schedulings are made within a certain period of time, the station enters the in-sync state.

While in the in-sync state, the station can send reservations and scheduled messages. Whenever it detects a transmission in the channel that it has not scheduled for the same time, it readjusts its scheduling queue using the header information contained in the transmission. If a certain number of consecutive inconsistent checks are detected within a given time period, the station enters the out-of-sync state, preventing possible subsequent disturbance of transmissions made by other stations due to its own incorrectly sent data packets.

5.4.4 Performance Considerations

The general delay–efficiency behavior of an explicit reservation system relative to a slotted ALOHA system is shown in Fig. 5.16. The ALOHA method has a maximum achievable channel efficiency of $1/e$ but provides one-hop average delays at low loading values, while the reservation approach has a minimum average delay of two hops[8] but can typically achieve efficiencies of 0.7 to 0.9.

The upper bound α on reservation system efficiency shown in Fig. 5.16 represents the fraction of channel bandwidth required for making reservations. This efficiency can in general be increased at the expense of longer access delays, since the larger data subframe time associated with more efficient operation means that random message arrivals must wait longer on the average for the occurrence of the next reservation subframe. A second factor affecting efficiency is the average message length of system traffic; since the number of reservation bits required to specify the message length being reserved is small

---

[8]   However, some reservation systems can achieve lower delays under certain loading conditions by the use of special mechanisms (e.g., the immediate access via an owned slot in R-TDMA when the reservation table is empty).

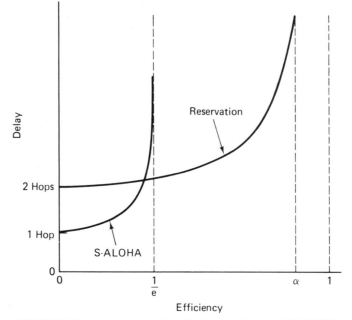

FIGURE 5-16 *Comparison of explicit reservation and S-ALOHA.*

compared to the total burst overhead for the reservation packet, efficiency increases with increasing message length.

Figure 5.17 shows some delay–efficiency measurement and simulation results for the CPODA protocol in a 64-kbits/s channel for two and 10 stations [21]. Notice that delay at first *decreases* with increased loading—this is due to the increase in piggybacking opportunities for making reservations as traffic increases. Figure 5.18 shows the effect of increasing α in the CPODA system by increasing the frame size. The lower curve is for a channel with two reservation slots out of 14 total slot times per frame, while the other curve is for two reservation slots out of 58 total slot times.

An important property of all the reservation systems considered in this chapter is the effective creation of a single "global queue" into which all data messages (i.e., their reservations) are placed, with the queue serviced by a channel capacity of αC, where α is the fraction of total capacity C available for data messages as in Fig. 5.16. This allows the well-known performance improvements resulting from combining a number of single-server queues into a single queue with a faster server to be achieved for the αC portion of the channel [22].

In particular, for a fixed channel data rate R, the increased delay for larger numbers of stations N shown in Fig. 5.6 for fixed TDMA applies only to the reservation portion of the channel in a fixed-assignment-reservation system such as R-TDMA—that is, for an increase ΔN in the number of stations, frame size

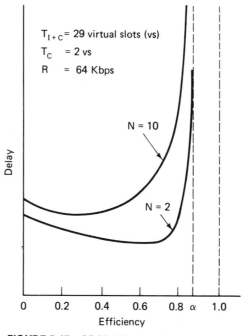

FIGURE 5-17   CPODA Delay-efficiency results.

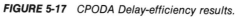

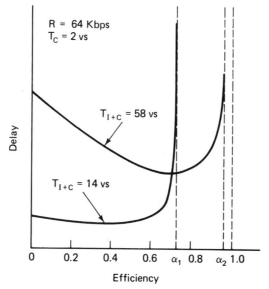

FIGURE 5-18   CPODA-Effects of frame size.

increases by only $(1 - \alpha) \Delta N$, since the size required for the global queue portion of the channel is independent of N for a given total rate.

The global queue performance benefits also apply to systems using random access for making reservations, as far as the αC portion of the channel is concerned. However, the random-access portion of the channel has different scaling properties than both the global-queue portion and a fixed-assignment-reservation portion. When the random-access portion is lightly loaded, its performance properties are essentially dependent only on total traffic, as in the case of the global-queue portion of the channel. As its loading approaches $1/e$, however, the need for stability control introduces a dependence on the number of stations [8], and the benefits of a combined queue are not realized.

More generally, the use of fixed assignment versus random access for making reservations involves a number of performance trade-offs. The choice that gives the best overall efficiency–delay performance depends essentially on the same factors that determine the choice between the fixed-assignment and random-access systems of Sections 5.2 and 5.3 (e.g., number of stations and traffic burstiness). The same performance problems also apply—while average delay may be minimized and efficiency maximized by using a random-access reservation subframe for large numbers of bursty traffic stations, the delay variance resulting from this choice may be unacceptable for some applications. In addition, stability and fairness problems may be introduced if suitable control mechanisms are not provided.

The problems associated with variable-length message traffic discussed in Section 5.2.2 apply directly to the reservation systems using fixed-size data slots, such as Roberts' and R-TDMA. In contrast, one of the significant advantages of the PODA approach is that its scheduling algorithm allows it to assign exactly as much time as is needed for each message, reducing the fragmentation problem to only the occurrences of frame boundaries. (The other significant advantage of the PODA scheduling algorithm is, of course, its ability to assign channel time according to message priorities on a completely flexible basis.)

The use of distributed scheduling in the reservation systems of this chapter has a significant impact on performance for downlink channel error rates above a certain value, since time spent out of synchronization represents either reduced or zero throughput for the station in question. The basic property determining this performance degradation is the average rate at which errors occur at a station.[9] Since it takes at least one hop to hear the consequence of a missed reservation and thus be able to resynchronize, an upper bound on the acceptable control information error rate is on the order of one error each 0.27 s. For a given bit error rate, this control error rate increases with channel data rate (since more reservations are sent per unit time).

Figure 5.19 shows some measurement results for a two-station network using the CPODA protocol and a 64-kbits/s channel [21]. The bit error rate was

---

[9]   A more detailed discussion of reservation synchronization issues is given in [18].

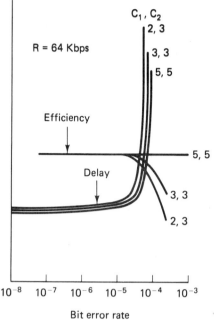

R = 64 Kbps

Efficiency

Delay

C_1, C_2
2, 3
3, 3
5, 5

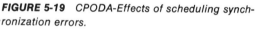
5, 5

3, 3

2, 3

10^{-8} 10^{-7} 10^{-6} 10^{-5} 10^{-4} 10^{-3}

Bit error rate

FIGURE 5-19 *CPODA-Effects of scheduling synchronization errors.*

introduced artificially at each station for the measurements; the parameters C_1 and C_2 associated with each curve are the number of consecutive good or bad checks that must be detected to move into or out of synchronization, as described in Section 5.4.3. The results show that the system performs well for bit error rates smaller than 1×10^{-5}; for error rates above this value, performance deteriorates rapidly.

5.5 CONCLUSIONS

We have examined several representative packet protocol approaches for use in a multiple-access broadcast satellite channel. While connectivity considerations make the use of the general TDMA approach attractive for packet networks, it seems clear that several access techniques must be considered within this framework to satisfy the performance requirements of widely differing network design parameters such as the number of earth stations and the traffic concentration at each station.

When high traffic concentrations and nonvarying loads exist at most or all stations in a network, fixed capacity assignments will in general give the best overall performance. Where bursty station traffic or variable loading prevails, a demand assignment protocol will provide significant improvements in both efficiency and delay. Except where very small message sizes are sent by a large number of very bursty stations, an explicit reservation protocol provides significant performance improvements relative to simple ALOHA protocols. To the extent that processing cost is small relative to other system costs, a generalized protocol such as PODA should be optimum for a wide range of traffic and station contexts.

REFERENCES

[1] JACOBS, I. M., R. BINDER, AND E. V. HOVERSTEN, "General Purpose Packet Satellite Networks," *Proceedings of the IEEE*, **66**(11), pp 1448–1467, November 1978.

[2] NUSPL, P. P., K. E. BROWN, W. STEENAART, and B. GHICOPOULOS, "Synchronization Methods for TDMA," *Proceedings of the IEEE*, **65**(3), pp. 434-444, March, 1977.

[3] WEISSLER, R., R. BINDER, R. BRESSLER, R. RETTBERG, and D. WALDEN, "Synchronization and Multiple Access Protocols in the Initial Satellite IMP," *Fall COMPCON*, September 1978.

[4] LAM, S. S. "Delay Analysis of a Packet-switched TDMA System," *Proceedings of the National Telecommunications Conference*, December 1976.

[5] ABRAMSON, N. "The ALOHA System—Another Alternative for Computer Communications," *Proceedings of the AFIPS Fall Joint Computer Conference*, **37,** Fall 1970.

[6] ROBERTS, L. "ALOHA Packet System with and without Slots and Capture," ACM SIGCOMM *Computer Communications Review*, **5**(2), April 1975.

[7] LAM, S. S., and L. KLEINROCK, "Packet Switching in a Multiaccess Broadcast Channel: Dynamic Control Procedures," *IEEE Transactions on Communications*, **COM-23**(9), pp. 891-905, September 1975.

[8] KLEINROCK, L., and S. S. LAM, "Packet Switching in a Multiaccess Broadcast Channel: Performance Evaluation," *IEEE Transactions on Communications*, **COM-23,** pp. 410-423, April 1975.

[9] FERGUSON, M. "A Study of Unslotted ALOHA with Arbitrary Message Lengths," *Proceedings of the 4th Data Communications Symposium*, Quebec City, Canada, October 1975.

[10] N. ABRAMSON, "Packet Switching with Satellites," *Proceedings of the AFIPS National Computer Conference Proceedings*, **42** June 1973.

[11] KLEINROCK, L., and S. S. LAM "Packet-Switching in a Slotted Satellite Channel," *Proceedings of the AFIPS National Computer Conference*, **42,** June 1973.

[12] CROWTHER, W. R., R. RETTBERG, D. WALDEN, S. ORNSTEIN, and F. HEART, "A System for Broadcast Communication: Reservation-ALOHA," *Proceedings of the Sixth Hawaii International Conference on System Sciences*, January 1973.

[13] LAM, S. S. "An Analysis of the Reservation-ALOHA Protocol for Satellite Packet Switching," *Proceedings of the International Conference on Communications*, Toronto, June 1978.

[14] ROBERTS, L. "Dynamic Allocation of Satellite Capacity through Packet Reservation," *Proceedings of the AFIPS National Computer Conference*, **42**, June 1973.

[15] BINDER, R. "A Dynamic Packet Switching System for Satellite Broadcast Channels," *Proceedings of the International Conference on Communications*, San Francisco, June 1975.

[16] JACOBS, I. M., et al, "CPODA—A Demand Assignment Protocol for SATNET," *Proceedings of the 5th Data Communications Symposium*, Snowbird, Utah, September 1977.

[17] JACOBS, I. M., and L.-N. LEE, "A Priority-oriented Demand Assignment (PODA) Protocol and an Error Recovery Algorithm for Distributively Controlled Packet Satellite Communication Network," *EASCON '77 Convention Record*, pp. 14-1A to 14-1F, 1977.

[18] HSU, N., and L. LEE, "Channel Scheduling Synchronization for the PODA Protocol," *Proceedings of the International Conference on Communications*, Toronto, June 1978.

[19] METCALFE, R. M. "Packet Communication," *MIT Project MAC Technical Report* 114, Cambridge, Mass., December 1973.

[20] GERLA, M., and L. KLEINROCK, "Closed Loop Stability Controls for S-ALOHA Satellite Communication," *Proceedings of the 5th Data Communications Symposium,* Snowbird, Utah, September 1977.

[21] CHU, W. W., and W. E. NAYLOR, "Measurement and Simulation Results of C-PODA Protocol Performance," *Proceedings of the National Telecommunications Conference*, December 1978.

[22] KLEINROCK, L. *Queueing Systems*, Vols. 1 and 2, Wiley, New York, 1974.

6

MIXED-MEDIA PACKET NETWORKS

*DIEU HUYNH**

IBM Systems Communications Division

FRANKLIN F. KUO

University of Hawaii

6.1 INTRODUCTION

In a message or packet-switching radio network, each user is directly linked to the others via a multiaccess broadcast channel; that is, all users transmit packets at the same frequency and all receive on a second common frequency. The broadcast packet can be heard by all users, including the sender. A user picks out packets addressed only to itself.

In this chapter, the radio networks that we are concerned with are satellite networks. The satellite is characterized as a high-capacity channel with a fixed propagation delay of approximately 0.26 s, which is large compared to the packet transmission time.

There have been many operational schemes proposed for packet-broadcasting radio networks. We describe here two basic ones: pure ALOHA and slotted ALOHA [1, 2].

---

* The views expressed in the chapter are those of the authors and the authors alone, and do not reflect in any way, IBM policy. The work was done while Dr. Huynh was working at the University of Hawaii.

In pure ALOHA, users transmit any time they desire. If they hear their own transmissions and no errors are detected, they assume that the transmission is successful. If errors are detected, such as when packets interfere with each other, the packets have to be retransmitted after a random delay to avoid further interference.

In slotted ALOHA, the channel time axis is segmented into a contiguous sequence of time slots. Users are still allowed to transmit packets at random epochs, but a packet must be of fixed length with a transmission duration equal to the slot size and it must fall exactly into one of the time slots. The slotted ALOHA scheme certainly requires a more costly implementation than the pure ALOHA, but enjoys a gain in efficiency, since collisions are now restricted to a single slot duration.

Pure ALOHA has been implemented in an existing operational ground radio network called the ALOHANET [3–5].

6.1.1 Characteristics of Terrestrial and Satellite Packet-Switching Networks

As described earlier, both the store-and-forward terrestrial networks and the ALOHA satellite networks achieve the goal of sharing and better utilizing scarce communications facilities and geographically scattered computer resources. The major disadvantages of these networks are the problems of reassembling of packets to form the original message at the destination and the added overhead due to acknowledgments, source and destination addresses, sequence number, and other control information. If a user has a long file requiring continuous transmission, the repetition of the overhead in each packet can be costly; in this case it would be better to use a dedicated link to send the long file. This problem can be remedied for a satellite network by introducing scheduled usage of the satellite channel such as that proposed in the various reservation ALOHA schemes [6–9]. Let us now examine the performances of the terrestrial and satellite networks as compared with each other.

The advantages of the ground network over the satellite network are as follows:

1. Faster response under light to moderate input traffic load.

2. Higher channel utilization.

3. Greater stability.

4. Less vulnerability.

In a terrestrial store-and-forward packet-switching network using leased lines such as the ARPANET, the average transcontinental point-to-point delay under light to moderate traffic load is generally required to be less than 0.1 s, whereas in a satellite network, the intrinsic propagation delay alone amounts to 0.26 s.

Advantages 2 and 3 are related. For a terrestrial network, the utilization of all channels can be high (say greater than 50% of the channel capacity) without causing the deterioration of the system in the sense that the throughput rate of the system is still equal to its input rate and the response times are finite. For a satellite network operating in the ALOHA or slotted ALOHA mode, analysis and simulation experiments have shown that as the channel utilization approaches a certain limit, the transmissions interfere with each other so frequently that only a few packets ever get through the channel without conflict. As a result, the number of backlog packets grows and the channel is jammed with retransmissions, which, in turn, cause more conflicts. Eventually, the channel utilization approaches 100%, but no packets get through the channel and reach their destinations. The response time becomes infinite.

Note that for the ground network, even if all channels are under heavy traffic loads, packets have to wait longer in queues before being transmitted, and the response times get large, the packets still keep reaching their destinations at a relative fixed rate as long as no packets have to be rejected by the nodes due to lack of memory buffer space.

Since nodes of a terrestrial network should be at least two-connected, for reliability, damage to one node or channel does not destroy the connectivity of the network. Moreover, even if a part of the network is out of service, the remaining part can still be used for local transmissions. This is not necessarily true in the satellite network. If the satellite channel is somehow destroyed either due to breakdown of the satellite transponder, or the "jamming" of the channel by some interfering signal(s), the whole network is out of service.

The advantages of the ALOHA satellite network over store-and-forward terrestrial networks are as follows:

1. Low-cost, high-bandwidth channel.
2. Elimination of complex topological design and routing problems.
3. Wide geographical coverage.
4. Mobility of users.
5. Design insensitive to the addition of new users.
6. Statistical load averaging.
7. Reliability.

Many of these have been suggested by Lam [10].

Although the terrestrial communication cost appears to dominate the future cost of packet-switching computer communication networks, many researchers have predicted [11, 12] that the cost of satellite channel bandwidth will decrease in keeping with the general cost trend of electronics. Roberts [11] estimated that the rate of technological improvement in the cost performance of satellites is about 40.7% per year, or a factor of 10 every 6.7 years.

Also, with a domestic satellite system, a high-bandwidth channel with data rates ranging up to tens of megabits per second will be available, whereas the data rates of terrestrial links are fixed and limited. Leased lines may sometimes be obtained at a variety of data rates, but at a premium cost.

Topological design and routing problems are very complex in large ground networks. On the other hand, for a satellite network, the satellite channel used in the multiaccess broadcast mode provides a fully connected network topology.

In addition, landline communications becomes expensive over long distances (say over 100 miles), whereas satellite communications costs are relatively independent of distance.

As for the mobility of users, since radio is a multiaccess broadcast medium, it is possible for users to move around freely. This is crucial in the development of personal hand-held terminals in the future.

The insensitivity to the addition of new users is evidenced by the fact that the user population in the satellite communication system can be made bigger or smaller without major changes in the basic system design and operational schemes. This is not true in the ground subnet; the addition of a node requires the addition of channels, the modification of the routing, and so on.

The statistical load average results from the fact that at any given time, users transmit data at the full channel processing rate and the application of random-multiaccess packet-switching techniques permits the total traffic from the whole user population to be statistically averaged at the channel. At any given instant, there may still be unused channel capacity in some parts while congestion exists in other parts of the networks.

As for reliability, the normal bit error rate of a satellite channel using forward error-correction techniques is estimated to be 10^{-9} or better, compared to 10^{-5} for typical terrestrial links [13].

6.1.2 Mixed-Media Network

In Section 6.1.1 we discussed some pros and cons of ground and satellite packet-switching networks. Probably the most undesirable features of the satellite network are its slow response and the vulnerability of the satellite transponder. However, its potentially good cost/performance, its broadband data communication capability, and other unique characteristics, such as its multiaccess and broadcast features, are not to be given up so easily. We thus seek to combine these two into a single entity so that they can complement each other.

The possibility indeed has triggered the interest of the network planners. Recently, ARPA has augmented its terrestrial network with packet satellite communication between the United States and the United Kingdom via INTEL-

SAT IV using satellite interface message processors or SIMPs [14] built by BBN (Bolt Beranek and Newman, Inc.). This multiple-access broadcast system was initiated in September 1975 and now includes four ground stations [15]. TELE-NET Communications Corporation, one of the new value-added carriers [16], announced a plan to offer public packet-switched data service in which, initially, terrestrial and, eventually, satellite links will be available. Therefore, it is of great interest and importance to investigate such a mixed-media packet-switched computer communication network. It is our goal in this chapter to model, analyze, and investigate some of the design problems related to the mixed-media network. To do that we first define our model and describe how it functions. Then we analyze this model mathematically to obtain optimal design parameters.

6.2   DESCRIPTION OF THE PROPOSED MIXED-MEDIA PACKET-SWITCHING NETWORKS

In this section we introduce the proposed mixed-media packet-switching computer communications networks and discuss the topology, routing, and other operational aspects of the network.

6.2.1   Network Topology

Consider a computer communications network that consists of clusters of host computers linked together by a mixed-media communications network shown in Fig. 6.1. The communication network is composed of two subnetworks: one is the ground subnet, the other the satellite subnet. Physically, the network consists of clusters of nodes; these clusters are geographically scattered and relatively far apart from each other; each of these clusters is called a *region*. The nodes are the locations of interface message processors (IMPs) linked together by landlines, such as cables, to form a distributed, connected ground subnet. Inside each region there is a special node where a satellite IMP (SIMP) also resides. The SIMPs of different regions are linked together by a multiaccess/broadcast radio channel via a satellite transponder in a star configuration to form a fully connected satellite subnet. An IMP cannot access any SIMP other than its regional SIMP. In addition, there exists at most a full duplex line directly connecting any IMP pair. Since both landlines and satellite links are used as the connecting media, it is called a mixed-media network. Such a network configuration is shown in Fig. 6.2.

The nodes (IMPs and SIMPs), landlines, and radio channels all have limited processing capacities which are allocated by our design according to the traffic

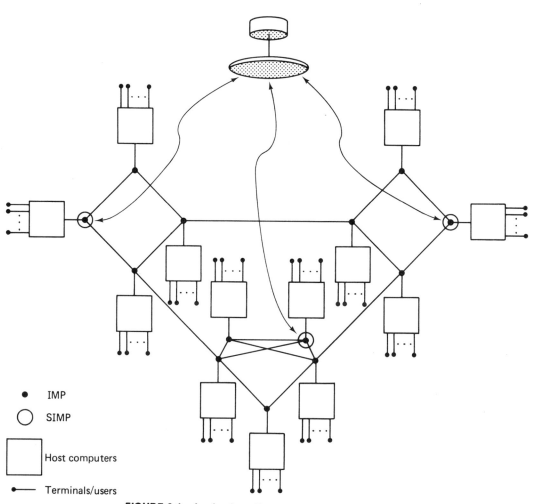

FIGURE 6-1 *A mixed-media computer communication network.*

loads placed on them and the allowable cost designated to build the network. Also, the IMPs and SIMPs all have buffer storage for queueing and scheduling transmissions.

6.2.2 Network Operations

The host computers and their related facilities represent the resources to be shared by local and networkwide users. Each host computer can receive messages and generate responses. If a request message is from a local user, the host computer answers the request directly. If a user requests services of another

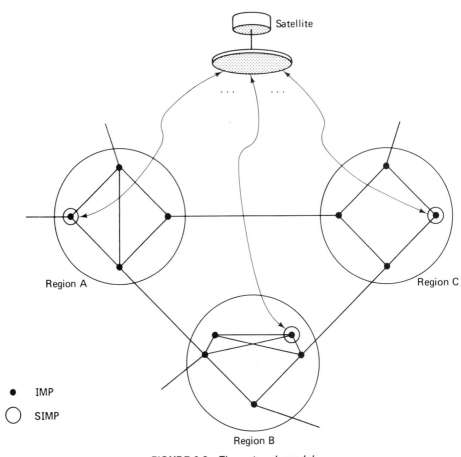

FIGURE 6-2 *The network model.*

host in the network, usually the length of the messages from that user is kept intact; however, if it is longer than a certain length, it is segmented into smaller blocks. Each of these blocks is less than a maximum allowable length.

To the message (if less than the maximum allowable length), or each of the segmented submessages, are added source and destination addresses plus routing and other control information as a *header* and error-detection information (or checksum) as a *trailer*. The message or submessage together with the attached information is called a *packet*. A message is sent, packet by packet, from a host to its adjacent IMP. The host keeps a replica of every forwarded packet in its buffer and will not discard it until a positive acknowledgement (or *ACK*, itself a short packet) is received from the IMP. In some rare cases, if an ACK fails to arrive within a fixed time period (the timeout period), the backlog packet will be retransmitted.

208

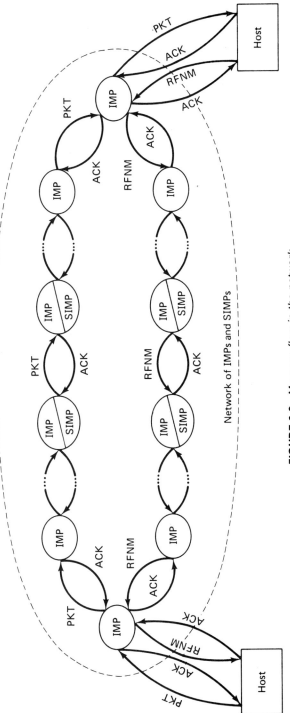

FIGURE 6-3 *Message flow in the network.*

209

The IMPs and SIMPs help relay the packet by passing it along from one node to the other until it gets to its destination[1] in a manner as shown in Fig. 6.3. At their destination IMPs, packets are forwarded to their destination hosts. When a host receives a packet, it determines whether that received packet is a full message or a segmented submessage with the aid of the control information. If it is a full message, a response is generated. Otherwise, it is stored in a buffer. The host reassembles each message upon the arrival of all of its components and then responds to it.

At the completion of a message at the destination host, an ACK is generated and relayed back to the origin host, by the network of IMPs and SIMPs, to Request For Next Message (RFNM of ARPANET). The described message flows are also shown in Fig. 6.3. Note that the two paths shown in Fig. 6.3 are not necessarily distinct: they may be the same path, or they may coincide at some nodes, depending on the topology and the routing procedure being used.

From the description above we see that the hosts only handle and process data, whereas the IMPs and SIMPs perform the network communication procedures. It is the network of IMPs and SIMPs that we concern ourself with throughout this chapter. We will look at some issues that help in the design of a packet-switching communication network with as fast a response time as possible for a given traffic load and network cost, in which the switching, routing, and control are transparent to the users.

6.2.2.1 Ground Subnet Operations

Upon the receipt of a packet from its host, an IMP has to decide where and how to send this newly arrived packet according to the attached source and destination addresses and control information. Obviously, it can send the packet either through the ground subnet or the satellite subnet as shown in Fig. 6.4. If the packet goes through the ground subnet, it is transmitted from one IMP to another until it reaches the destination IMP in the following fashion: when an IMP receives a correct packet with no detectable bit errors, it sends an ACK back to the previous IMP and *forwards* the received packet to one of its neighboring IMPs according to the routing procedures while storing a replica of that packet in its buffer. If an ACK arrives, it discards the replica from its buffer storage. If for some reason an ACK fails to arrive at the end of a *timeout period*, a retransmission is initiated and the process repeats until the receipt of an ACK. The ground subnet is said to be operated in a store-and-forward mode.

---

[1] Throughout this chapter, an IMP where a packet enters the network is called the origin of that packet; an IMP where a packet leaves the network is termed the destination of that packet. A region where an origin (destination) IMP resides is called the origin (destination) region and its regional SIMP is referred to as the origin (destination) SIMP. Every (SIMP, region) can be the origin (SIMP, region) of some input packets as well as the destination of others.

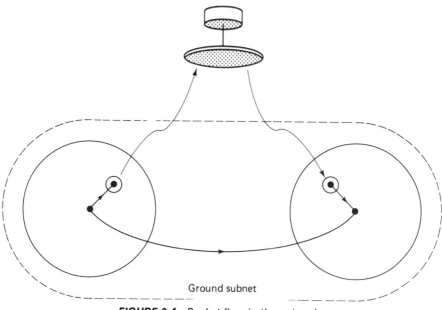

FIGURE 6-4 *Packet flow in the network.*

6.2.2.2 Satellite Subnet Operations

If a packet is sent through the satellite subnet, it goes through the ground subnet from its origin IMP to the regional SIMP, is then transmitted through the satellite channel to its destination SIMP, and finally through the ground subnet to its destination IMP (see Figs. 6.3 and 6.4).

From the description above it is clear that only the interregional traffic will ever go through the satellite channel; the intraregional traffic will use landlines exclusively.

The operation of the satellite subnet remains to be described. The satellite subnet uses the ALOHA technique of random-access asynchronous time-division multiplexing [2–4]. All SIMPs access the satellite transponder at the same frequency; the satellite transponder broadcasts its received signal, which is the sum of all the transmitted signals, to all the SIMPs (including the sender itself) via a different frequency. If at any time a SIMP has a packet ready to send, it transmits that packet into the random-access channel.

If the packet occupies the channel by itself for the entire duration of the packet transmission, it will be successfully received by the destination SIMP. If, during the transmission time of a packet, other users also transmit packets, all these packets interfere with each other in the channel. This phenomenon is called *channel collision*. All the packets involved are transmitted unsuccessfully and have to be retransmitted. The scheme outlined above is completely asynchronous, since SIMPs can initiate packet transmissions at arbitrary moments.

Another way of operating the channel is to segment the channel time into contiguous "time slots" and have every packet transmission fall in one of these time slots. We call this scheme slotted random multiaccess whereas the former is unslotted random multiaccess. Packets may still collide with each other in the slotted scheme, but this occurs less frequently, since any given two packets will never partially overlap each other.

In both the slotted and unslotted cases, retransmissions are a major concern: if they are not handled properly, the satellite channel may be jammed with retransmission traffic. Note that the retransmission process is initiated whenever a SIMP detects a channel collision by observing the downlink signal. In addition, in the rare event that even the downlink signal is error-free but for some reason an ACK fails to arrive at the end of a timeout period, the retransmission process is also initiated as in the ground subnet.[2]

6.2.2.3 *Retransmission Routing Procedures*

A way to lighten the traffic load on the satellite channel is to divert the retransmissions through the ground subnet. Thus, we have two options to exercise to resolve the backlog traffic: (1) to retransmit all backlog traffic again through the satellite channel after some randomly chosen delay time; and (2) to reroute all backlog traffic through the ground subnet as soon as the SIMPs sense the occurrence of channel collisions, or ACKs fail to arrive at the end of the timeout periods.

In the first scheme the retransmission delays are randomized to help keep interfering transmissions from repeating their collisions. If the satellite channel is unslotted, this scheme is called unslotted ALOHA or simply ALOHA; if the channel is slotted, it is called slotted ALOHA. The term ALOHA is used since this technique was first introduced in The ALOHA System at the University of Hawaii [3, 17].

The second scheme is called Multi-Access Satellite with TErrestrial Retransmissions, or MASTER (slotted or unslotted).

---

[2] In practice, for both ground and satellite subnet, there is a limit on the number of retransmissions of a packet due to the absense of ACKs at the end of the timeout periods. If that limit is exceeded, the receiving node is proclaimed dead. Then proper measures must be taken to reroute the backlog packet via a different path if the topology and the routing procedures of the network allows. If not, the origin IMP is notified of the switching failure and the backlog packet is discarded.

The IMP that detects the failure keeps sending test packets to its malfunctioning neighbor IMP at regular intervals until the receipt of an ACK for a test packet, which signals the recovery of its faulty neighbor. Proper measures are taken to put the network back to the normal operation.

Another way of putting the network back to the normal operation is by having the recovered node send a packet to each of its neighboring nodes, informing them of its recovery. This scheme is most suitable for the satellite subnet because of its broadcast feature.

The distinction between these two options is as follows. Under ALOHA, once a packet joins the satellite subnet, it stays there until it gets through the satellite channel successfully; whereas under MASTER, after the first unsuccessful transmission, the packet is rerouted through the ground subnet to its destination directly without going through the destination SIMP.

ALOHA and MASTER can be combined to form a generalized scheme that includes ALOHA and MASTER as special cases. That is, when a channel collision occurs, retransmissions can go either through the satellite subnet, as in ALOHA, or through the ground subnet, as in MASTER. This scheme is termed (slotted or unslotted) Multi-Access Satellite with MIxed Retransmissions, or MASMIR.

For MASTER or MASMIR, retransmission traffic on the ground subnet can either be treated as ordinary traffic and queued for transmissions on a first-come, first-served (FCFS) basis, or as high-priority traffic and be the next to be transmitted on an available channel. Under the priority scheduling scheme, the IMPs should be equipped with facilities to manipulate traffic with priority classes.

6.2.2.4 Routing

Routing is a decision process by which an IMP chooses one of its neighboring IMPs to which to forward its received packet. In other words, routing is the decision as to which path a packet should travel from its origin to its destination.

Routing in a Mixed-Media Network: For our mixed-media network model, the routing decision consists of two major portions: (1) splitting of the input traffic between ground and satellite subnets; and (2) routing on the ground subnet.

The first portion of the routing decision, as noted above, is for the interregional traffic only. The splitting is done for each interregional node pair according to a traffic splitting factor for that pair. This traffic splitting factor indicates the percentage of the input traffic to be sent through the ground subnet. The determination of the set of traffic splitting factors for all interregional node pairs in the network is a prime concern in routing design.

Note that there is no routing problem for the satellite subnet because of the broadcasting feature associated with the satellite radio channel. However, the specific paths between IMPs and regional SIMPs are determined by ground routing rules.

Routing on the Ground Subnet: The ground subnet routing determines the paths packets take to travel from their origins to destinations, or in the case of packets to be sent through the satellite channel, between their IMPs and regional SIMPs, via landlines.

Central to the routing decision is a routing table stored at each node (IMP or SIMP) of the communication network. The routing table of a node is just a list or table which shows, for each origin and destination (O-D) node pair, those neighboring nodes where a packet associated with the O-D node pair will visit next after being processed at the current node. The neighboring nodes are those with direct channels linking to that node.

The structure of the routing table and the ways the information contained therein are to be used vary according to the individual routing procedure. For example, if fixed routing is used, only one path links each O-D node pair; therefore, only a single neighboring node associated with each node pair is listed in the routing table.

The design of routing is a process of determining the structure of routing tables and specifying the procedures of using them.

The choice of routing depends on many factors, such as network topology, available facilities, throughput and delay requirements, and so on.

Adaptive routing techniques are ruled out in this chapter. Gerla has shown that the difference between designing a network with a nonadaptive routing policy and operating it with an adaptive policy are not great [18].

For more extensive and exhaustive descriptions of routing techniques, interested readers are referred to the literature [19–24].

6.2.3 Important Network Performance Indices

The important network performance indices are the network cost, throughput rate, and average delay.

6.2.3.1 *Network Cost*

Cost tops the list of design considerations of any system; it affects the design in significant ways. In this chapter, each channel is assigned a cost that is linearly proportional to the capacity. The network cost is then defined as the sum of the channel capacity costs. The cost of channel capacities are different for ground and satellite subnets, with ground channel capacities being more expensive than satellite channel capacities, measured in terms of cost units per unit capacity. Currently, the cost ratio between ground and satellite channels is about 2:1 or 3:1. As the cost of the satellite channel bandwidth continues to decline [12], the cost ratio may become as high as 10:1 or more.

6.2.3.2 *Network Throughput Rate*

The throughput rate of a network is defined as the average number of packets delivered to all destinations per unit time. In steady state, the throughput rate of a network is given by the sum of the input traffic rates of all the O-D (origin–destination) node pairs. To be able to operate in steady state, a network must have enough nodal processing and channel capacity to handle the incoming traffic. The satellite channel usually has high capacity not only because it is inexpensive relative to the ground links and is shared by a number of SIMPs, but also because it is operated in a contention mode: channel collisions seriously reduce the effective satellite channel capacity [10].

6.2.3.3 Network Average Delay

The average delay of a network is the average time a packet spends in the network traveling from its origin to its destination.

At this point, it is appropriate to identify the delay characteristics of both ground and satellite subnets. A packet going from one IMP (or SIMP) to another encounters delay from several sources:

1. Queueing for transmission.

2. Propagation.

3. Retransmission.

4. Nodal processing.

5. Reception.

Queueing for transmission is the time spent waiting for transmission on an available channel. The choice of a channel is dictated by routing and flow-control rules.

Propagation delay is the delay for a packet to traverse the portion of channel from the output of the transmitter to the input of the receiver.

Retransmission delay is the delay incurred when an ACK is not received, for some reason, after a timeout period, or, in the case of the satellite channel, a channel collision is detected.

Nodal processing delay is the time spent in error checking (information provided by checksum), source and destination identification (source and destination addresses), routing and flow-control decision making, and so on. Note that we assume that the nodal processing unit has sufficient processing capacity so that no incoming packets need to wait in a buffer before being processed. This means that the nodal processing queueing delay is zero.

Reception delay is the time spent in the receiver unit.

For the ground subnet the first component is dominant. The propagation delay on the ground subnet is small since the landlines are relatively short. The reception and nodal processing delays are also small, since the transceiver and packet processor handle packets at a high speed. Finally, the retransmission delay on the ground subnet is insignificant since the IMPs and landlines are highly reliable and the transmission error rates on the ground channels are relatively low.

For the satellite subnet, the first delay is significant; however, the propagation and retransmission delays are now the dominant components. The one-way propagation delay of the satellite channel is about 0.26 s, which is usually larger than the other delay components. The retransmission delay is even more important: the satellite channel is operated in a random multiaccess mode, so channel collisions are unavoidable. Each retransmission requires a randomization delay if the ALOHA technique is used, plus queueing, transmission, and propagation delays totaling more than 0.26 s.

In short, the ground subnet is a low-delay subnet, whereas the satellite subnet is a high-delay subnet.

6.2.3.4   Trade-offs among Network Cost, Throughput Rate, and Average Delay

Obviously, both the network throughput rate and average delay are functions of the input traffic loads and the network processing capacities or cost. In fact, if the network processing capacities are fixed and large enough so that the

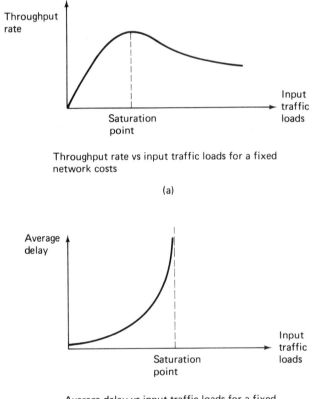

Throughput rate vs input traffic loads for a fixed network costs

(a)

Average delay vs input traffic loads for a fixed network cost

(b)

FIGURE 6-5

network can be operated in a steady state, then the larger the input traffic loads, the higher the throughput rate and the average delay, since packets have to wait longer to be transmitted at IMPs. Figure 6.5a and b shows the possible throughput rate and average delay of a mixed-media network as a function of input traffic loads. The drop in throughput rate results from the fact that the mixed-media network has a satellite subnet which operates in the contention mode; such a component reduces the throughput rate substantially under heavy traffic loads. Occasionally, the drop in throughput rate may also be a result of packet losses due to infrequent node and line failures.

On the other hand, if the input traffic loads are fixed, then as the network cost increases, the throughput rate also increases, until it reaches the point where it is equal to the sum of input traffic rates and stays there, as shown in Fig. 6.6a; whereas the average delay decreases down to a limit that is approximately equal to the average end-to-end propagation delay, as shown in Fig. 6.6b.

If the network cost is smaller than the critical level, the network cannot

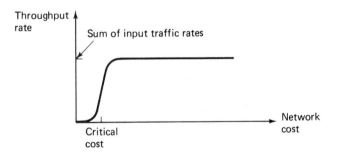

Throughput rate vs cost for fixed input traffic loads

(a)

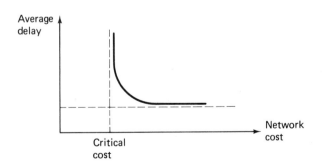

Average delay vs cost for fixed input traffic loads

(b)

FIGURE 6-6

support the input traffic loads; the average delay becomes arbitrarily large and the throughput rate drops to zero.

In this chapter, the latter problem is our concern. We fixed the input traffic loads placed on the network by assuming as given the set of input traffic rates between all node pairs. Since in steady state, the throughput rate can be computed by summing the input traffic rates, we are mainly interested in obtaining the cost–delay trade-offs, as shown in Fig. 6.6b. Since in addition to the cost and input traffic loads the average delay is greatly affected by the routing and retransmission strategies, the latter two also play a part in our design.

6.2.4 The Design Problem

6.2.4.1 Design Issues

Assuming that the network topology is given and the traffic characteristics can be estimated for all O-D node pairs, we concentrate on the following problems.

1. The splitting of packets between ground and satellite channels.

2. Capacity assignments for ground and satellite channels.

3. Retransmission strategies.

As stated earlier, traffic enters the communication network from the hosts. This traffic consists of $N(N - 1)$ packet streams going from every node to every other node with different input rates. Some of the interregional traffic goes through the satellite channel while the rest travels on the ground links. A nonadaptive routing is adopted for the ground subnet and any deterministic or probabilistic routing technique can be used [25].

Our main routing concern here is to decide how input traffic can be split between the two subnets. That is, we want to find a set of traffic splitting factors which tells what percentage of the traffic one should send through the ground or satellite subnet in such a way that the average delay of the network is kept minimal. Since the ground subnet is a low-delay subnet whereas the satellite subnet is a high-delay subnet, to achieve minimal average delay, all input packets should go via the ground subnet if the ground subnet has enough channel and nodal processing capacity. However, if our budget is limited, we have to compromise between the inexpensive high-delay satellite subnet and the expensive low-delay landlines.

The splitting of the interregional traffic and the capacity assignments depends substantially on the satellite operating scheme being used. For the same set of traffic splitting factors, the satellite channel under ALOHA has both transmission and retransmission traffic going through it, so more capacity should be allocated to compensate for the reduction in effective capacity due to retransmissions through the ALOHA channel. On the other hand, the MASTER channel diverts all backlog traffic to the ground subnet, so additional capacity should be allocated to the interregional ground links to account for the added traffic load. MASMIR combines the features of both ALOHA and MASTER. One of our objectives in this chapter is to provide means to compare the performances of the proposed satellite subnet operational schemes: slotted and unslotted ALOHA, MASTER, and MASMIR.

6.2.4.2 Design Problem Statement

Our design problem can now be stated. We are given a network topology, a set of input traffic rates, a ground routing procedure, and a total budget; we want to minimize the average delay of the network over the set of traffic splitting factors, nodal processing, and link capacities. Our objective here is to find the delay–cost trade-offs and use these as indicators to compare the ALOHA, MASTER, and MASMIR schemes proposed earlier.

6.3 DERIVATION OF A SIMPLIFIED AVERAGE-DELAY EXPRESSION

In [26] the exact, mathematical modeling and analysis of the mixed-media network are carried out in detail. Some highlights are listed in the following:

- The input traffic processes are characterized by Poisson point processes that give rise to a traffic rate matrix with elements the rates of packet arrivals.

- The input traffic processes can be decomposed into classes, each class having certain properties in common. (e.g., same origin and destination, backlog traffic, etc.)

- The routing of packets is defined by using a set of routing transition probabilities which provide a unified mathematical description for a large class of routing rules.

- For the purpose of studying the delay performance, the mixed-media network is modeled by a network of queues. Both slotted and unslotted cases are treated, and ALOHA, MASTER, and MASMIR are embedded in a unified model.

- Under appropriate assumptions [26], the joint queue length distributions of the network can be decomposed into a product of the individual marginal distributions by applying the results of the work pioneered by Jackson [27]; extended by Baskett, Chandy, Muntz, and Palacios [28]; and later further enhanced by Kobayashi and Reiser [29]. The application of this decomposition theorem and Little's formula [30] provides the average-delay expression.

The sheer complexity of the modeling and analysis prohibits their inclusion in this chapter. In the following, we shall present a heuristic derivation of the simplified average-delay expression used in our design of the mixed-media network.

6.3.1 Derivation Details

We seek to derive a simplified average-delay expression, including those factors that seriously affect the delay performance of the network while neglecting those terms which have only a minor effect on system performance. We go even further and adopt some approximations to permit closed-form analytical solutions to be part of our design problem. This allows us to get a quick estimate of the optimum solution to our problem.

In the design we assume that the network is fed from Poisson packet sources with rates equal to the rates of the traffic during certain peak hours. Since channel capacities are expensive and scarce resources, queueing delays contribute significantly to the overall average network delay. For the satellite subnet, the channel queueing delay is even more important because of the channel collisions. Moreover, for each transmission or retransmission, the satellite channel propagation delay is a major part of the delay of the satellite subnet and thus cannot be neglected.

On the other hand, IMPs and SIMPs are assumed to have comparatively large processing power; thus, the delays contributed by the processing times of these nodal facilities are small and are neglected. The propagation delays on the ground channels can also be disregarded in comparison with the queueing delays of the channels during peak traffic hours since the ground channels are relatively short. Finally, the transmission errors of the channels are assumed to be so small that the added delay of the retransmissions due to transmission errors can be ignored.

Suppose that we are given a network of N nodes linked by L ground links of capacities C_l (bits/s), $l = 1, 2, \ldots, L$ in a specified topology. The network is partitioned into M regions, each having a SIMP. These M SIMPS are linked together via a satellite channel of capacity C_s (bits/s). A traffic rate matrix $[\gamma_{ij}]$ specifies, in packets/s, the average rates of messages flowing between all possible IMP pairs i and j, $i, j = 1, 2, \ldots, N$.

Let g_{ij} be the traffic splitting factor which specifies the fraction of the traffic, originating at node i and destined for node j, going through the ground subnetwork. It is clear that $g_{ij} = 1$ if IMPs i and j are in the same region. Define

$$\bar{g}_{ij} \triangleq 1 - g_{ij}$$

This fraction ($\bar{g}_{ij}$) of the traffic is first routed to the regional SIMP of IMP i, sent through the satellite channel to the regional SIMP of IMP j, and finally directed to the destination IMP j. Of course, this sequence of steps takes place only when the transmission over the satellite channel is successful. If a channel collision takes place, two possible courses of action follow, depending on the scheme assumed. In case of MASMIR, the retransmission of a packet from SIMP σ will be attempted through the ground subnet with probability d_σ, and through the satellite channel with probability $\bar{d}_\sigma = 1 - d_\sigma$. Observe that $d_\sigma = 0$ corresponds to ALOHA scheme, whereas $d_\sigma = 1$ is the case of MASTER scheme. The probabilities d_σ, $\sigma = \sigma_1, \sigma_2, \ldots, \sigma_M$, can also be referred to as *retransmission splitting factors*.

The average delay T of a packet traveling from its origin to destination is the weighted sum of the individual delays in each channel in the network. Thus, we can write

$$T = \frac{1}{\gamma}\left(\sum_{l=1}^{L} \lambda_l T_l + \sum_{\sigma=\sigma_1}^{\sigma_M} \lambda_\sigma T_\sigma \right) \tag{6.1}$$

where $\gamma = \displaystyle\sum_{i,j=1}^{N} \gamma_{ij}$ = total traffic rate in the network

λ_l = traffic rate on channel l

λ_σ = traffic rate from SIMP σ

T_l = average delay experienced by a packet in channel l

T_σ = average delay experienced by a packet sent from SIMP σ through the satellite channel

$l = 1, 2, \ldots, L$

$\sigma = \sigma_1, \sigma_2, \ldots, \sigma_M$

The link traffic rates λ_l and λ_σ are uniquely determined by the traffic rate matrix $[\gamma_{ij}]$, the ground routing rules, and retransmission strategy [25, 26]. Under the assumptions of Poisson arrivals, exponential packet lengths with mean $1/\mu$ (bits/packet), and independence of retransmissions, the average delay or channel l can be given by the $M/M/1$ formula:

$$T_l = \frac{1}{\mu C_l - \lambda_l} \tag{6.2}$$

The average delay T_σ for packets from SIMP σ can be found as follows. Each transmission through the satellite channel incurs a queueing delay τ_σ and a propagation delay τ_{min}. Because of the possibility of channel collisions, on the average, more than one transmission is required before a packet leaves the satellite subnet. A packet leaves the satellite subnet only if the transmission is successful, or if it is not successful, it is retransmitted through the ground subnet.

Define P_σ as the probability of a successful transmission from SIMP σ and, $\overline{P}_\sigma = 1 - P_\sigma$. The probability of departure Q_σ from the satellite subnet at SIMP σ can be found as

$$Q_\sigma = P_\sigma + \overline{P}_\sigma d_\sigma = d_\sigma + \overline{d}_\sigma P_\sigma$$

Note that the inverse of the probability of departure, $1/Q_\sigma$ represents the number of satellite transmissions attempted before a packet departs from the subnet, and the product $(1 - Q_\sigma)(1 - d_\sigma) = \overline{Q}_\sigma \overline{d}_\sigma$ denotes the probability that a packet is to be retransmitted through the satellite channel. Furthermore, each satellite retransmission from SIMP σ incurs an additional randomization delay, with mean τ'_σ, to avoid further collision. Hence, the average delay T_σ experienced by a packet from SIMP σ can be written as

$$T_\sigma = \frac{1}{Q_\sigma}(\tau_\sigma + \tau_{min} + \overline{Q}_\sigma \overline{d}_\sigma \tau'_\sigma) \qquad (6.3)$$

Again, under the assumptions of Poisson arrivals, exponential packet lengths and independence of retransmissions the queueing delays τ_σ, $\sigma = \sigma_1, \sigma_2, \ldots,$ σ_M, on the satellite channel can readily be found.

- For unslotted channel it is given by the $M/M/1$ formula

$$\tau_\sigma = \frac{1}{\mu C_s - \lambda_\sigma/Q_\sigma} \qquad (6.4a)$$

- For slotted channel, it is given by the $M/D/1$ forumla

$$\tau_\sigma = \frac{1}{\mu C_s} + \frac{\lambda_\sigma/Q_\sigma}{2(\mu C_s - \lambda_\sigma/Q_\sigma)\mu C_s} \qquad (6.4b)$$

Notice that λ_σ/Q_σ is the aggregated satellite traffic rate due to both retransmission and original transmissions from SIMP σ.

Substituting the expressions for T_l and T_σ into (6.1), we finally get

- For unslotted satellite channel

$$T = \frac{1}{\gamma}\left[\sum_{l=1}^{L} \frac{\lambda_l}{\mu C_l - \lambda_l} + \sum_{\sigma=1}^{M} \frac{\lambda_\sigma}{Q_\sigma}\left(\frac{Q_\sigma}{\mu C_s Q_\sigma - \lambda_\sigma}\right) + \tau_{min} + \overline{Q}_\sigma \overline{d}_\sigma \tau'_\sigma\right] \qquad (6.5a)$$

- For slotted satellite channel

$$T = \frac{1}{\gamma}\left\{ \sum_{l=1}^{L} \frac{\lambda_l}{\mu C_l - \lambda_l} + \sum_{\sigma=1}^{M} \frac{\lambda_\sigma}{Q_\sigma}\left[\frac{1}{\mu C_s} + \frac{\lambda_\sigma}{2\mu C_s(\mu C_s Q_\sigma - \lambda_\sigma)}\right] + \tau_{\min} + \overline{Q}_\sigma \overline{d}_\sigma \tau'_\sigma \right\}$$

(6.5b)

A more rigorous derivation of (6.5a) and (6.5b) can be found in [26].

Note that the average-delay expressions in both the unslotted and slotted cases are similar. Since the following design is based on the average-delay expression, any design principle, approach, and procedures applicable to the slotted case are also applicable to the unslotted case. Thus, to avoid repetition, we shall concentrate on the design of a slotted subnet. For a slotted satellite subnet, the probability Q_σ of a packet departing from SIMP$_\sigma$ becomes

$$Q_\sigma = d_\sigma + \overline{d}_\sigma \prod_{\substack{\nu = \sigma \\ \nu \neq \sigma_1}}^{\sigma_M} \left(1 - \frac{\lambda_\nu}{\mu C_s}\right)$$

(6.6)

If each of the input and retransmission rates and retransmission splitting factors are approximately equal to their respective arithmetic means:

$$\lambda_\sigma \approx \frac{\sum_{\nu=\sigma_1}^{\sigma_M} \lambda\nu}{M} \triangleq \frac{\lambda_s}{M}$$

$$\frac{1}{\tau'_\sigma} \approx \frac{\sum_{\nu=\sigma_1}^{\sigma_M} 1/\tau\gamma}{M} \triangleq \frac{1}{\tau'}$$

$$d_\sigma \approx \frac{\sum_{\nu=\sigma_1}^{\sigma_M} d_\nu}{M} \triangleq d_\nu$$

then the average delay T of the network can further be approximated by [26]

$$T = \frac{1}{\gamma}\left\{ \sum_{l=1}^{L} \frac{\lambda_l}{\mu C_l - \lambda_l} + \lambda_s \left[\tau_{\min} + \frac{1}{\mu C_s}\left(1 + \frac{b(M, d)\lambda_s}{2[a(M, d)\mu C_s - \lambda_s]}\right)\right]\right\}$$

(6.7)

[3]   The last two conditions can be viewed as the results of the first, since if the arrival rates are equal, the design would lead to the choice of randomization rates and retransmission splitting factors satisfying the last two conditions.

Let us denote the term inside the brackets by T_s:

$$T_s = \tau_{\min} + \frac{1}{\mu C_s}\left(1 + \frac{\lambda_s b(M, d)}{2[\mu C_s a(M, d) - \lambda_s]}\right) \tag{6.8}$$

where the constants $b(M, d)$ and $a(M, d)$ depend only upon the number of SIMPs M and the retransmission splitting factor d for a suitably chosen value of mean time τ' between satellite retransmissions:

- For MASTER, we have

$$b(M, 1) = 1$$
$$a(M, 1) = M$$

- For ALOHA, we get

$$b(M, O) = b(M)$$
$$a(M, O) = a(M)$$

the values of $b(M)$ and $a(M)$, for a given M, are given in Table 6.1.
- For MASMIR, the values of $b(M, d)$ and $a(M, d)$ can be solved from (6.5b) and (6.6). See [26] for more details.

Typical plots of the average delay T_s versus throughput rate $s = \lambda_s/\mu C_s$ are shown in Fig. 6.7.

The throughput–delay trade-offs of the network under ALOHA are bounded between those of the infinite population and those corresponding to $M = 2$. On the other hand, under MASTER they are bounded between those corresponding to $M = 2$ and those of the infinite population. Under MASMIR they are bounded between those of the infinite population model under ALOHA and MASTER. Furthermore, for a given M, the throughput–delay trade-offs of the subnet under MASMIR are bounded between those under MASTER and ALOHA with the same value of τ'.

Note that for a given throughput rate S, the average delay of the subnet under MASTER decreases as M increases. This observation may be surprising at first

TABLE 6-1

Number of SIMPs, M	$a(M)$	$b(M)$
1	1	1 ·
2	0.531	3.059
3	0.528	4.674
5	0.494	5.871
10	0.489	7.219

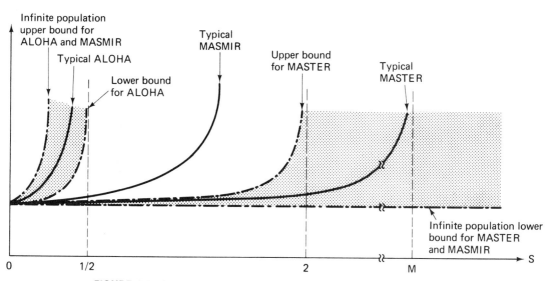

FIGURE 6-7 *Delay-throughput tradeoffs of the slotted satellite subnet under ALOHA, MASTER and MASMIR.*

glance, but it becomes reasonable after some thought: for the subnet under MASTER, the average delay is the sum of the queueing, transmission, and propagation delay. Given a value of S, the increase in M means smaller input rate from each SIMP; thus, the queueing delay at each SIMP is smaller. This explains the decrease in delay.

This is not true under ALOHA. Under ALOHA, for a given S, the increase in M not only means smaller input rates from the SIMPs but also the increase in collisions, which, in turn, results in more retransmissions, causing the reduction of the channel capacity. The analysis shows that the reduction in the effective channel capacity is larger than the decrease in the individual input rates of the SIMPs.

6.4 DESIGN OF MIXED-MEDIA PACKET NETWORKS

In this section we deal with the problem of optimizing the traffic splitting factors and channel capacities, and finding the cost–delay trade-offs for the mixed-media network. In particular, we shall focus our attention on the mixed-media network with a slotted subnet, although the design approach can also be applied to the unslotted subnet case. Those efforts will not be duplicated here.

As discussed in Secs. 6.2.4 and 6.2.5, cost tops the list of design considerations of most systems. Here each channel is assigned a cost that is linearly proportional to the capacity, and the network cost is defined as the sum of the capacity costs of all channels in the network. The costs of channel capacities are different for ground and satellite subnets with ground channel capacities assumed to be more expensive than the satellite channel capacities, measured in terms of cost per unit capacity. Currently, the cost ratio between ground and satellite channels is about 2:1 or 3:1. As the cost of the satellite channel bandwidth continues to decline [12], the cost ratio may become as high as 10:1 or more.

The other important performance index is the average delay. In the design, we fix the throughput rate of the network and minimize the delay for various costs. The result is then expressed in terms of the delay–cost trade-offs.

In addition to the cost and input traffic rates, since the average delay is also greatly affected by the routing and retransmission strategies, the latter two also play a part in our design.

Let b_s and b_l be the unit costs of the capacities of the satellite channel and ground channel l, respectively. The cost function B may be described by the following equation:

$$B = \sum_{l=l_1}^{l_L} b_l C_l + b_s C_s \qquad (6.9)$$

where C_l is the channel capacity of the ground channel l and C_s is the satellite channel capacity. The budget B represents the total number of dollars available to spend in supplying the $L + 1$ channel network with the set of capacities $\{C_l, l = l_1, \ldots, l_L\} \cup \{C_s\}$.

The particular form of cost function as given by (6.9) associates the entire network cost with the channels themselves. This represents no loss of generality, since other network costs may be embedded in the channel costs [26].

6.4.1 Design Problem

The combination of the high-delay, low-cost satellite subnet that operates in a contention mode and the low-delay, high-cost ground subnet that operates in a store-and-forward mode into an overall system presents many interesting problems. Here we consider a few of them.

After assuming that the network topology is given and the traffic characteristics can be estimated for all O-D node pairs, we concentrate on the following problems:

1. The routing of packets via ground and satellite channels.

2. The capacity assignments for the ground and satellite channels.

3. Retransmission strategies.

The network is fed from statistically independent Poisson sources which constitute $N(N - 1)$ packet streams going from every node to $N - 1$ other nodes with different input rates. Some of the interregional traffic goes through the satellite channel while the rest travels on the ground links. A nonadaptive routing is adopted for the ground subnet and any routing that can be described by a set of routing transition probabilities.

The part of the routing that we are concerned with here is to decide how input traffic can be split between the two subnets. That is, we want to find a set of traffic splitting factors $\{g_{ij}|i, j = 1, 2, \ldots, N\}$ that minimizes the average delay of the network. Since the ground subnet is a low-delay subnet whereas the satellite subnet is a high-delay subnet, all input traffic should go via the ground if the ground subnet has enough channel and nodal processing capacities to achieve minimal average delay. However, if our budget is limited, we have to compromise between the inexpensive, high-delay satellite channel and the expensive, low-delay landlines.

The splitting of the interregional traffic and the capacity assignments depends substantially on the satellite operating scheme being used. For the same traffic splitting factors, the satellite channel under ALOHA has both transmission and retransmission traffic going through it; thus more capacity should be allocated to compensate for the reduction in effective capacity due to retransmissions through the ALOHA channel. On the other hand, the MASTER channel diverts all backlog traffic to the ground subnet, additional capacity should be allocated to the interregional ground links to account for the added traffic load.

To investigate the problems proposed above, we first find a solution to the following problem. Given a network topology, a set of input traffic rates, a ground routing procedures, a satellite retransmission strategy, and a total budget as given by (6.9), we want to minimize the average delay of the network over the set of traffic splitting factors and channel capacities:

$$
\begin{array}{lll}
\underset{\{g_{ij}\}}{\text{Minimize } T} & \text{subject to} & \displaystyle\sum_{l = l_1}^{l_L} b_l C_l + b_s C_s \leq B \\
\{C_l\}, C_s & \text{and} & 0 \leq g_{ij} \leq 1 \quad \forall\, i, j
\end{array}
\tag{6.10}
$$

By solving the problem several times with different values of the budget B, we can obtain the trade-offs between the B and the minimum delay T^*.

Next we change the satellite retransmission strategy and repeat the solutions to (6.10). This results in another functional relationship between the budget B and the minimum delay T^* having the form $T^* = f(b)$. These trade-offs provide a means to compare the performance of the network under different satellite retransmission schemes.

6.4.2 Solution

Let us first consider the problem given in (6.10), where T is given by (6.5) or (6.8) if the input rates are approximately equal, and B is as defined in (6.9). The constraint on each of the g_{ij}'s comes from the definition of the traffic splitting factors.

To minimize the average network delay T over the set of traffic splitting factors $\{g_{ij}\}$ and the set of channel capacities C_s, C_l, $l = l_1, l_2, \ldots, l_L$ would be difficult; we thus choose to solve the problem by using an iterative numerical procedure. Each iteration is a two-stage optimization: In the first stage we fix the set of channel capacities C_s, C_l, $l = l_1, l_2, \ldots, l_L$, and we minimize T over the set of traffic splitting factors $\{g_{ij}\}$. In the second stage, we fix the optimum set of the traffic splitting factors $\{g_{ij}\}$ and minimize T over the set of channel capacities C_s, C_l, $l = l_1, l_2, \ldots, l_L$.

Thus, in the first stage, for the fixed set of channel capacities and the other given parameters listed in Sec. 6.4.1, we solve the following traffic splitting problem:

$$\underset{\{g_{ij}\}}{\text{Minimize } T} \quad \text{subject to} \quad 0 \leq g_{ij} \leq 1 \quad \forall\, i, j \tag{6.11}$$

If the optimization algorithm used to solve this problem converges, an optimum set of the traffic splitting factors $\{g*_{ij}\}$ can be found, and the optimization reaches the second stage. In the second stage, for the fixed set of the traffic splitting factors and the other given parameters listed in Sec. 6.4.1, we solve the following capacity assignment problem:

$$\underset{\{C_l\},\, C_s}{\text{Minimize } T} \quad \text{subject to} \quad \sum_{l=l_1}^{l_L} b_l C_l + b_s C_s \leq B \tag{6.12}$$

Again, if the optimization algorithm used to solve this problem converges an optimum set of channel capacities C_s, C_l, $l = l_1, l_2, \ldots, l_L$ is obtained and the next iteration of the two-stage optimization is initiated.

The two-stage optimization described above is iterated over and over again until there is very little change in the average network delay T; that is, if the change in T does not exceed a preset constant ϵ, we then stop the numerical procedures and accept the final solution as the optimum solution. For a complete discussion of the iterative numerical procedures summarized above, the reader is referred to [26].

The delay–cost trade-offs can be obtained by repeating the joint optimization described above for different values of the budget B. Each value of B corresponds to a (sub-)minimum attainable average delay. The repetition of the joint optimization procedure thus provides a functional relationship between cost and delay.

6.4.3 Design Examples

Let us now look at some design examples in which not only the sets of optimal traffic splitting factors and channel capacities are found but also are the delay–cost trade-offs, which provide a means of evaluating the performances of ALOHA and MASTER relative to each other.

Example 6.1: As a first example of the joint optimization and delay–cost trade-offs, let us consider the network model depicted in Fig. 6.8.

In solving the capacity assignment problem we need to know the total allowable budget and unit cost of ground and satellite channel capacities. We assume that the unit cost of the ground channel capacities are identical, so we

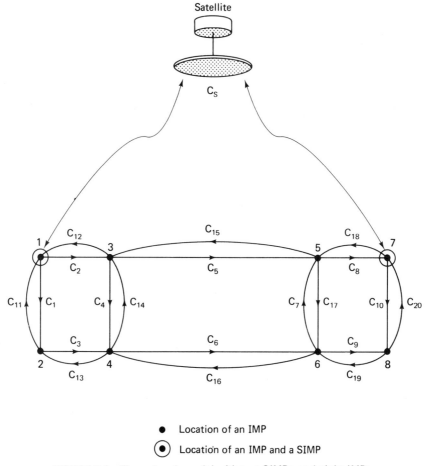

FIGURE 6-8 *The network model with two SIMPs and eight IMPs.*

can normalize all costs by the unit cost of ground channel capacity. In obtaining the following results, we further assume a ratio of 1 to 10 for satellite-to-ground channel capacity costs. Our computer program is general enough so that we can assume any ratio between satellite capacity and ground capacity costs. Perhaps a more realistic ratio to use today is a 1 : 3 proportion.

The traffic rate matrix is assumed to be uniform with $\gamma_{ij} = 20$ packets/s for all $i = j$ and $\gamma_{ii} = 0$ for all $i = 1, 2, \ldots, 8$, and the average packet length is assumed to be 512 bits on all ground channels. The packet lengths on the satellite channel are 1 kbits. The ground link capacities are all initially assumed to be 50 kbits/s i.e., $C_l = 5 \times 10^4$ bits/s for $l = 1, 2, \ldots, 20$, and the satellite capacity to be $C_s = 1.5 \times 10^6$ bits/s.

For the capacity assignment in the joint optimization, the input data also include the assumed total budget B and the unit ground and satellite channel capacity costs of $b_l = 1$ and $b_s = 0.1$, all expressed in ground channel cost units.

The final results for optimum channel capacities C^* and link traffic rates for $B = 10^6$ cost units are given in Table 6.2, and those for $B = 1.7 \times 10^6$ cost units are given in Table 6.3. By comparing Tables 6.2 and 6.3 we observe that under

TABLE 6-2: *Optimum link traffic rates and channel capacities for B = 1,000,000 cost units.*

		MASTER		ALOHA	
		λ *(packets/s)*	C *(kbits/s)*	λ *(packets/s)*	C *(kbits/s)*
Satellite channel:		293.67	160.391	270.13	525.054
Ground channel:	1	95.79	50.341	93.61	49.877
	2	92.54	48.675	79.67	42.672
	3	91.49	48.138	88.29	47.132
	4	82.76	43.654	77.50	41.548
	5	90.79	47.778	81.71	43.727
	6	96.96	50.946	102.99	54.718
	7	82.96	43.758	77.61	41.603
	8	92.70	48.760	82.43	44.100
	9	91.52	48.154	86.86	46.391
	10	95.88	50.389	93.62	49.886
	11	95.92	50.408	91.26	48.663
	12	91.98	48.389	82.50	44.137
	13	91.62	48.205	85.94	45.916
	14	82.70	43.624	79.97	42.827
	15	90.29	47.521	82.07	43.913
	16	97.04	50.982	103.11	54.780
	17	82.64	43.596	79.97	42.825
	18	92.52	48.665	80.43	43.065
	19	91.28	48.029	89.34	47.672
	20	96.12	50.513	91.14	48.605
Minimum delay (s)		0.41872		0.33112	

TABLE 6-3: *Optimum link traffic rates and channel capacities for B = 1,700,000 cost units.*

		MASTER		ALOHA	
		λ* (packets/s)	C* (kbits/s)	λ* (packets/s)	C* (kbits/s)
Satellite channel:		1.64	11.249	2.15	15.966
Ground channel:	1	67.54	54.942	67.95	55.196
	2	119.82	88.110	120.06	88.238
	3	119.71	88.040	119.80	88.082
	4	92.38	70.947	92.43	70.967
	5	159.52	112.295	159.54	112.292
	6	159.42	112.237	159.43	112.226
	7	92.44	70.984	92.46	70.985
	8	119.99	88.213	120.00	88.201
	9	119.64	87.996	119.81	88.088
	10	67.97	55.223	67.80	55.097
	11	67.75	55.077	67.81	55.109
	12	120.20	88.341	120.09	88.259
	13	119.91	88.166	119.67	88.001
	14	92.48	71.010	92.46	70.984
	15	159.79	112.460	159.55	112.295
	16	159.73	112.420	159.33	112.163
	17	92.45	70.995	92.46	70.987
	18	120.25	88.373	120.00	88.203
	19	119.96	88.193	119.71	88.025
	20	67.65	55.013	67.90	55.165
Minimum delay (s)		0.03676		0.03690	

both schemes, ALOHA and MASTER, the optimum satellite capacity decreases and the ground channel capacities increase as the total allowable budget increases. This is because we have assumed a 10 : 1 ratio between the cost of unit ground capacity and that of unit satellite capacity; as the budget grows, we have more money to spend on the relatively more expensive ground channel capacities. As ground channel capacities become large, packets tend to go via the ground subnet, since the minimum satellite propagation delay is comparatively high (0.26 s). For a total budget of $B = 1.7 \times 10^6$ cost units, the minimum overall average delay is $T = 0.037$ s for both ALOHA and MASTER schemes. Whereas for $B = 10^6$, $T = 0.331$ s for the network under ALOHA and 0.419 s for the network under MASTER.

We have performed a number of runs with different values of budget B and the results are given in Table 6.4 and Fig. 6.9. We see that the throughput–delay trade-off curves are hyperbolic. As shown in Fig. 6.9, ALOHA tends to perform better than MASTER. Notice that the delay differences between ALOHA and MASTER are negligible for budget ranging from $B = 1.3 \times 10^6$ cost units to $B = 1.7 \times 10^6$ cost units. As B drops below 1.3×10^6 cost units, the delay curve of

TABLE 6-4: *Delay–cost trade-offs for network with eight IMPs and two SIMPs.*

	DELAY		Percentage Delay Difference
BUDGET	MASTER	ALOHA	Relative to MASTER
950,000	≫1	1.43478	
1,000,000	0.41872	0.33112	21
1,100,000	0.21072	0.16549	21
1,300,000	0.09281	0.08674	7
1,500,000	0.05651	0.05715	−1
1,700,000	0.03676	0.03690	−0.4

MASTER departs from that of ALOHA. A reasonable explanation for these outcomes is as follows. When the budget B is sufficiently large, one has money to spend on the more expensive ground channel capacities; therefore, most traffic goes through the lower delay ground subnet. (Recall that the satellite subnet delay is at least 0.26 s.) Since satellite channel traffic is small (see satellite

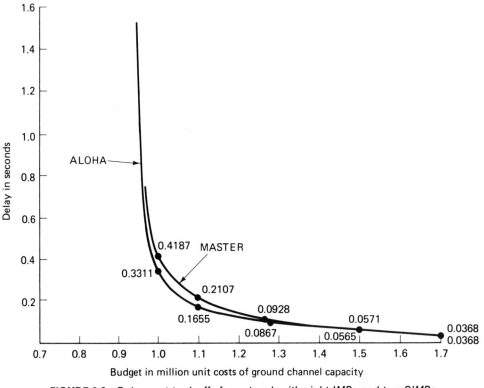

FIGURE 6-9 *Delay-cost tradeoffs for network with eight IMPs and two SIMPs.*

232

traffic rates in Table 6.3, the difference between ALOHA and MASTER disappears; their performances are thus similar. When the budget becomes small, the ground subnet alone cannot support the entire traffic load; more and more traffic is diverted to the satellite channel, and the distinction between MASTER and ALOHA becomes apparent. Since we have assumed a 10 : 1 cost ratio in favor of the satellite channel, more capacity is assigned to the satellite subnet and less to the ground subnet (again, see Tables 6.2 and 6.3). As we know, the larger the satellite channel capacity, the better ALOHA performs, whereas the smaller the ground channel capacities, the poorer MASTER performs. Altogether these make ALOHA outperform MASTER.

Example 6.2: To further clarify the problem, let us consider the eight-node network shown in Fig. 6.10 with the same configuration as the previous example,

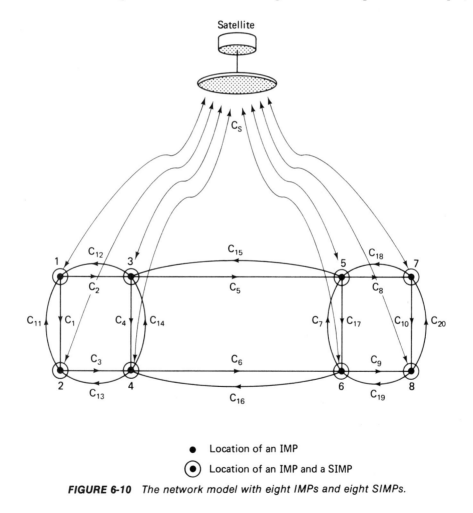

FIGURE 6-10 *The network model with eight IMPs and eight SIMPs.*

●   Location of an IMP

◉   Location of an IMP and a SIMP

TABLE 6-5: *Delay–cost trade-offs for network with eight IMPs and eight SIMPs and 10:1 cost ratio*

| | DELAY | | Percentage Delay Difference |
BUDGET	MASTER	ALOHA	Relative to MASTER
900,000	0.99657	0.39165	60
1,100,000	0.17009	0.10026	41
1,300,000	0.08959	0.07522	16
1,500,000	0.05626	0.05649	−.8
1,700,000	0.03691	0.03668	.6

but each node now has an IMP and SIMP. It is now a network with eight IMPs and eight SIMPs. We assume that the traffic rate matrix, mean packet lengths, and unit-cost ratio remain the same as before. For ALOHA, however, $a(M)$ and $b(M)$ are now estimated to be 0.492 and 6.724, respectively. Results for this network model are summarized in Table 6.5 and depicted in Fig. 6.11. It is seen that this network model has generally smaller delay than the previous one. This is because of the addition of six more SIMPs. ALOHA is again superior to MASTER, and the difference is more substantial. This is a general trend: as the number of SIMPs is increased, more traffic goes through the satellite channel,

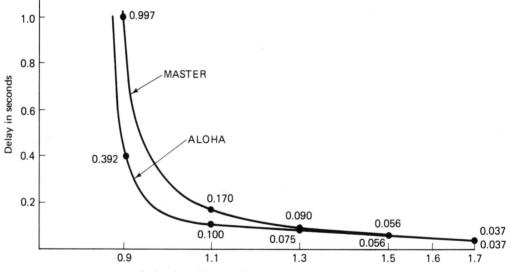

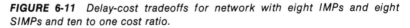

FIGURE 6-11 *Delay-cost tradeoffs for network with eight IMPs and eight SIMPs and ten to one cost ratio.*

BUDGET	DELAY		Percentage Delay Difference Relative to MASTER
	MASTER	ALOHA	
1,150,000	0.547	0.831	−52
1,200,000	0.239	0.281	−18
1,300,000	0.104	0.122	−17
1,500,000	0.058	0.058	0
1,700,000	0.039	0.039	0

which draws more capacity from the total, and the ground subnet gets less of its share. This puts MASTER in a disadvantageous position relative to ALOHA. For the same network (shown in Fig. 6.10) and parameters, if we now reduce the cost ratio to 3:1, we obtain different results, which are summarized in Table 6.6 and depicted in Fig. 6.12. As seen in Fig. 6.12, again, when the budget $B > 1.5 \times 10^6$ cost units, no distinction exists between ALOHA and MASTER, but when $B < 1.5 \times 10^6$ cost units, MASTER is slightly better than ALOHA, since now the cost ratio is advantageous for the ground subnet, ground channels get more of their share of the total capacity, and excessive capacity in the ground subnet favors MASTER.

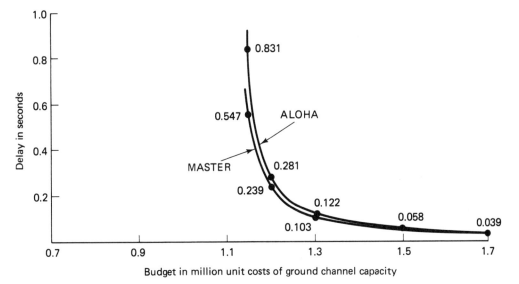

FIGURE 6-12 *Delay-cost tradeoffs for network with eight IMPs and eight SIMPs and three to one cost ratio.*

6.4.4 Extended Design Problem

Note that although numerical results have not been obtained for MASMIR, since it includes both ALOHA and MASTER, it would be the best system. The reason is as follows: since the retransmission splitting factors can take any values between 0 and 1,

$$0 \leqslant d_\sigma \leqslant 1 \qquad \forall\, \sigma$$

there are not one but a family of infinitely many MASMIR schemes, each with a different set of the retransmission splitting factors $\{d_\sigma\}$. Note that both ALOHA and MASTER belong to this family. Among the infinitely many MASMIR schemes there must be at least one which gives better delay performance for a given cost, input traffic rates, ground routing rules, and so on. Each optimal MASMIR is associated with an optimal set of the retransmission splitting factors $\{d^*_\sigma\}$. One way of obtaining the optimal set $\{d^*_\sigma\}$ is by solving the following extended designed problem:

$$\text{Minimize } T \qquad \text{subject to} \qquad \sum_{l=l_1}^{l_L} b_l C_l + B_s C_s \leqslant B$$
$$\{g_{ij}\}, \{d_\sigma\}$$
$$\{C_l\}, C_s$$
$$0 \leqslant g_{ij} \leqslant 1 \qquad \forall\, i, j$$
$$0 \leqslant d_\sigma \leqslant 1 \qquad \forall\, \sigma$$

This design problem can readily be solved by using the iterative numerical procedures similar to the one discussed in Sec. 6.4.2. Each iteration of the joint optimization procedure is again a two-stage optimization. In the first stage we fix the set of the channel capacities and solve the problem:

$$\text{Minimize } T \qquad \text{subject to} \qquad 0 \leqslant g_{ij} \leqslant 1 \qquad \forall\, i, j$$
$$\{g_{ij}\}, \{d_\sigma\}$$
$$0 \leqslant d \leqslant 1 \qquad \forall\, \sigma$$

In the second stage we fix the set of the optimal traffic splitting obtained from the first stage and solve the problem:

$$\text{Minimize } T \qquad \text{subject to} \qquad \sum_{l=l_1}^{l_L} b_l C_l + b_s C_s \leqslant B$$
$$\{C_l\}, C_s$$

which can be solved by using the numerical procedure such as in [26].

6.5 CONCLUSIONS

In this chapter we have presented some of the important design issues for mixed-media packet-switching networks. Satellite packet switching has considerable promise for low-cost, high-bandwidth data communications. However, there is inherent high delay in satellite links which do not appear in ground links. Therefore, a mix of the two communication media seems to offer the best of both worlds. The trade-offs considered in this chapter should offer guidelines for the design and optimum utilization of mixed-media networks.

Since the satellite channel has potentially excellent cost performance, which, as the results of Section 6.4.3 show, is a favorable factor for the ALOHA scheme, ALOHA needs more study to improve its performance.

The most salient feature of ALOHA is "random access," which allows users to transmit at the full data rate of the satellite channel at any time. Unfortunately, it is also this feature which results in channel collisions that seriously reduce the satellite channel capacity. Some reservation schemes such as reservation ALOHA [15, 31], priority reservation ALOHA [15], and CPODA [15] have been proposed to remedy this problem. Each of these schemes can be implemented in the satellite subnet.

Note that although greatly reduced, channel collisions still exist in both the reservation ALOHA and priority reservation ALOHA; thus, the reservation MASTER or MASMIR and priority reservation MASTER or MASMIR may further improve the network performances.

Because of the long propagation delay of the satellite channel, it takes at least 0.26 s before s SIMP knows if its reservation is granted. To speed up the process, reservation information can be sent via the ground subnet as high-priority traffic.

Although the satellite channel has a large propagation delay, its wide bandwidth and low transmission error rate make it suitable for transmission of bulk data, such as long files, weather data, and so on. This can be done in conjunction with the use of some sort of reservation scheme. If, as a result of reservation, a long file can be transmitted continuously, the average delay experienced by a bit traveling through the satellite subnet can be lower than that on the packet-switching ground subnet, since the long satellite channel propagation delay is averaged out by the enormous number of bits in a file.

REFERENCES

[1] ABRAMSON, N. "The ALOHA System," in *Computer-Communication Networks* (N. Abramson and F. F. Kuo eds.), Prentice-Hall, Inc., Englewood Cliffs, N.J., 1973, pp. 501–518.

[2] Roberts, L. G. "ALOHA Packet System with and without Slots and Capture," *ARPANET Satellite System Note 8 (NIC 11290)*, Stanford Research Institute, June 1972.

[3] Kuo, F. F., and N. Abramson. "Some Advances in Radio Communications for Computers," *Digest of Papers—COMPCON '73*, San Francisco, pp. 57–60, February 1973.

[4] Kuo, F. F., and R. Binder. "Computer-Communications by Radio and Satellite: The ALOHA System" in *Computer Communication Networks* (R. L. Grimsdale and F. F. Kuo eds.), Nato Advanced Study Institute Series, P. Noordhoff, Leyden, Netherlands, pp. 397–407, 1975.

[5] Binder, R. et al., "ALOHA Packet Broadcasting—A Retrospect," *Proceedings of the AFIPS National Computer Conference*, **44**, pp. 203–215, 1975.

[6] Metcalfe, R. M. "Packet Communication," *MAC TR-114, Project MAC*, Massachusetts Institute of Technology, Cambridge, Mass., December 1973.

[7] Roberts, L. G. "Multiple Computer Networks and Intercomputer Communications," *ACM Symposium on Operating Systems Principles*, Gatlinburg, Tenn., October 1967.

[8] Kemeny, J. G., and T. E. Kurtz. "Dartmouth Time-Sharing," *Science*, 162(3850), 223, 1968.

[9] Kleinrock, L. *Queueing Systems*, Vol. 2, *Computer Applications*, Wiley-Interscience, New York, 1976, p. 294.

[10] Lam, S. S. "Packet-Switching in a Multi-access Broadcast Channel with Application to Satellite Communication in a Computer Network," Ph.D. thesis, UCLA. (Also available as *UCLA-ENG-7429*, UCLA Computer Science Department, April 1974.)

[11] Roberts, L. G. "Data by the Packet," *IEEE Spectrum*, **11**(2), pp. 46–51, February 1974.

[12] Abramson, N., and E. R. Cacciamani, Jr., "Satellite Data Communications," *ALOHA System Technical Report B75-14*, University of Hawaii, April 1975.

[13] Cacciamani, E. R. "Data Services—American Satellite Corporation," *Proceedings of the 7th Hawaii International Conference on System Sciences, Computer Nets*, pp. 66–69, January 1974.

[14] Butterfield, S., R. Rettberg, and D. Walden. "The Satellite IMP for the ARPA Network," *Proceedings of the 7th Hawaii International Conference on System Sciences, Computer Nets*, pp. 70–73, January 1974.

[15] Jacobs, I. M., R. Binder, and E. V. Hoversten, "General Purpose Packet Satellite Networks," *Proceedings of the IEEE*, **66**, pp. 1448–1467, November 1978.

[16] Wessler, B. D., and R. B. Hovey, "Public Packet-switched Networks," *Datamation*, pp. 85–87, July 1974.

[17] Abramson, N. "The ALOHA System—Another Alternative for Computer Communications," *Proceedings of the AFIPS Fall Joint Computer Conference*, **37**, pp. 281–285, 1970.

[18] GERLA, M. "Deterministic and Adaptive Routing Policies in Packet-switched Computer Networks," *Proceedings of the 3rd Data Communications Symposium*, Tampa, Fla., pp. 23–28, November 1973.

[19] KLEINROCK, L. *Communication Nets: Stochastic Message Flow and Delay,* Dover Publications, Inc., New York, 1964.

[20] FULTZ, G. L. "Adaptive Routing Techniques for Message Switching Computer-Communication Networks," Ph.D. thesis, UCLA. (Also available as *UCLA-ENG-7252,* UCLA Computer Science Department, July 1972.)

[21] CANTOR, D. G., and M. GERLA. "Optimal Routing in a Packet-switched Computer Network," *IEEE Transactions on Computers*, C-**23**(10), pp. 1062–1069, October 1974.

[22] McQUILLAN, J. M. "Adaptive Routing Algorithms for Distributed Computer Networks," Ph.D. thesis, Harvard University. Also available as *BBN Report* 2831, May 1974.

[23] FRANK, H., and W. CHOU, "Routing in Computer Networks," *Networks*, **1**(2), pp. 99–112, 1971.

[24] GALLAGER, R. G. "A Minimum Delay Routing Algorithm Using Distributed Computation," *IEEE Transactions on Communications*, vol. COM-**25**(1), pp. 73–85, January 1977.

[25] HUYNH, D., H. KOBAYASHI, and F. F. KUO, "Optimal Design of Mixed Media Packet-switching Networks: Routing and Capacity Assignment," *IEEE Transactions on Communications,* COM-**25**(1), pp. 158–169, January 1977.

[26] HUYNH, D. "Ground-Satellite Packet Switching Networks," Ph.D. dissertation, University of Hawaii, Department of Electrical Engineering, December 1976.

[27] JACKSON, J. R. "Job Shop-like Queueing Systems," *Management Science*, **10**(1), p. 131, October 1963.

[28] BASKETT, F., K. M. CHANDY, R. R. MUNTZ, and F. G. PALACIOS, "Open, Closed, and Mixed Networks of Queues with Different Classes of Customers," *Journal of the Association of Computing Machinery*, **22**(2), pp. 248–260, April 1975.

[29] KOBAYASHI, H., and M. REISER, "On Generalizations of Job Routing Behaviour in a Queueing Network Model," *IBM Research Report RC* 5679, IBM Thomas J. Watson Research Center, Yorktown Heights, N.Y., pp. 248–260, October 1975.

[30] LITTLE, J. D. C. "A Proof for the Queueing Formula: $L = \lambda w$," *Operations Research*, **9**, pp. 383–387, 1961.

[31] BINDER, R. "A Dynamic Packet Switching System for Satellite Broadcast Channels," *ALOHA System Technical Report B74-5,* University of Hawaii, August 1974.

[32] TOBAGI, F. A., M. GERLA, R. W. PEEBLES, and E. G. MANNING. "Modeling and Measurement Techniques in Packet Communication Networks," *Proceedings of the IEEE*, **66**, pp. 1423–1447, November 1978.

7

CODING FOR RELIABLE DATA TRANSMISSION AND STORAGE

SHU LIN

University of Hawaii

DANIEL J. COSTELLO, JR.

Illinois Institute of Technology

7.1 INTRODUCTION

In recent years, the demand for efficient and reliable digital data transmission systems has been accelerated by the increasing use of automatic data processors. One of the serious problems in any high-speed data transmission system is the occurrence of errors. A major concern to the communications engineer is the control of these errors such that reliable transmission of data can be obtained. In 1948, Shannon [1] demonstrated that, by proper encoding and decoding of data, errors induced by a noisy channel can be reduced to any desired level without sacrificing the data transmission rate. Since the appearance of this result, a great deal of effort has been expended on the problem of devising efficient encoding and decoding schemes for error control over noisy channels. Recent developments in error-correcting codes have contributed toward achieving the reliability required by today's high-speed digital systems, and the use of coding techniques for error control has become an integral part in the design of modern communication systems and digital computers. This chapter is intended as an introduction to error-correcting codes.

The transmission and storage of digital data have much in common. They both accomplish the transfer of digital data from an information source to a destination (or user). A typical data transmission system (or a data storage system) may be represented by the block diagram as shown in Fig. 7.1. The first element is the information source that may be a person or a machine (e.g., a digital computer). The output of the source may be a continuous waveform or a sequence of discrete symbols. The source encoder transforms the source output into a sequence of binary symbols called the *information sequence*, denoted by *x*. The source encoder should be designed in such a way that (1) the number of binary digits per unit of time required to represent the source output is small, and (2) the source output can be reconstructed from the information sequence *x* without ambiguity. Typical examples of transmission channels are telephone lines, high-frequency radio links, telemetry links, microwave links, satellite links, and so on. Typical storage media are core and semiconductor memories, magnetic tapes, drums, disk files, or optical memory units. The transmission channel (or storage medium) is usually subject to various types of noise disturbances, natural or human-made. For example, on a telephone line, the disturbance may come from switching impulse noise, thermal noise, crosstalk from other lines, or lightning. On a magnetic tape, surface defects are regarded as a disturbance. The *channel encoder*, according to some rules, transforms the information sequence *x* into a longer binary sequence *y* that is called the *code word* of *x*. This transformation is referred to as *channel encoding*. The channel encoder is implemented to cope with the noisy condition in which the resulting code sequence is to be transmitted or stored. The binary digits are not suitable for transmission over the physical channel. The function of the modulator is to encode each output digit of the channel encoder into one of two physical waveforms of duration T seconds. For example, a "1" may be encoded into a positive pulse of duration T. The output signal of the modulator enters the channel and is disturbed by noise. The *demodulator* makes a decision for each received signal of duration T to determine whether a 1 or 0 was transmitted (this is called a *hard decision*). Thus, the output of the demodulator is a sequence *r* of binary digits. The sequence *r* is called the *received sequence*. Because of the channel noise disturbance, the received sequence *r* might not match the code word *y*. The places where they differ are called *transmission errors* (or simply errors). For example, if $y = (1\ 1\ 0\ 0\ 1\ 1\ 0\ 0\ 1\ 1\ 1\ 0\ 1\ 1)$ is transmitted and $r = (1\ 1\ 0\ 0\ 0\ 1\ 0\ 0\ 1\ 0\ 1\ 0\ 1\ 1)$ is received, then errors occur at the fifth and eleventh places. The channel encoder should be designed such that its output code words have the capability of combatting the transmission errors. The *channel decoder*, based on the received sequence *r*, the rules of channel encoding, and the channel characteristics, does the following two things: (1) It attempts to correct the transmission errors in *r* and produces an estimate $\hat{y}$ of the actual

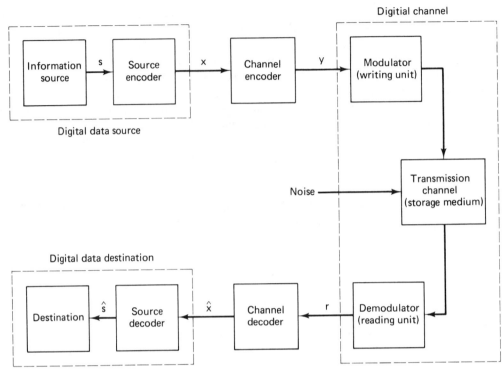

Information source — s — Source encoder — x — Channel encoder — y — Modulator (writing unit)

Digital data source

Noise — Transmission channel (storage medium)

Digital data destination

Destination — $\hat{s}$ — Source decoder — $\hat{x}$ — Channel decoder — r — Demodulator (reading unit)

FIGURE 7-1 *Block diagram of a typical data transmission or storage system.*

transmitted code word y; and (2) it transforms $\hat{y}$ into an information sequence $\hat{x}$ which is an estimate of the transmitted information sequence x. The *source decoder*, based on the rules of source encoding, transforms $\hat{x}$ into an estimate $\hat{s}$ of the actual source output s and delivers it to the user. If the channel is quiet, $\hat{y}$, $\hat{x}$, and $\hat{s}$ are reproductions of y, x, and s, respectively. If the channel is very noisy, $\hat{s}$ might be quite different from the actual source output.

To focus our attention on the properties of channel encoder and channel decoder, the source and source encoder are combined into a binary source; the modulator, channel, and demodulator are combined into a discrete coding channel; and the source decoder and user are combined into a binary data sink as shown in Fig. 7.1.

A major engineering problem is to design the channel encoder–decoder pair such that (1) the binary data can be transmitted over the noisy channel as *fast* as possible; and (2) *reliable reproduction* of the information sequence x can be obtained at the output of the channel decoder. The design of the channel encoder–decoder pair is primarily based on the channel characteristics.

7.1.1 Types of Codes

Basically, there are two different types of error-correcting codes, *block codes* and *convolutional codes*. The encoder for a block code segments the continuous sequence of information digits into message blocks; each message block *m* consists of *k* information digits. There are a total of 2^k distinct messages. The encoder transforms each input message *m* independently into a longer binary sequence *y* of *n* digits, which is a code word. Therefore, corresponding to the 2^k possible input messages, there are 2^k possible code words at the output of the encoder. This set of 2^k code words is called a *block code*. The $n - k$ digits added to each message block by the encoder are called *redundant digits*. These redundant digits carry no new information and their function is to provide the code with the capability of correcting (or detecting) errors made in transmission. How to form these redundant digits such that the code has good error-correcting (or -detecting) capability is a major concern in designing the encoder. The ratio $R = k/n$ is called the *code rate*, which is interpreted as the number of information digits entering the encoder per transmitted channel digit. An example of a block code is given in Table 7.1, where $k = 4$ and $n = 7$. This code uses 3 redundant bits for correcting any single error over the block of seven digits (this will be shown later).

A convolutional encoder operates on the information sequence without breaking it up into independent blocks. Rather, the encoder processes the information sequence continuously and produces a code sequence. At any time

TABLE 7-1: Block code with $k = 4$ and $n = 7$.

Messages	Code Vectors
(0 0 0 0)	(0 0 0 0 0 0 0)
(1 0 0 0)	(1 1 0 1 0 0 0)
(0 1 0 0)	(0 1 1 0 1 0 0)
(1 1 0 0)	(1 0 1 1 1 0 0)
(0 0 1 0)	(1 1 1 0 0 1 0)
(1 0 1 0)	(0 0 1 1 0 1 0)
(0 1 1 0)	(1 0 0 0 1 1 0)
(1 1 1 0)	(0 1 0 1 1 1 0)
(0 0 0 1)	(1 0 1 0 0 0 1)
(1 0 0 1)	(0 1 1 1 0 0 1)
(0 1 0 1)	(1 1 0 0 1 0 1)
(1 1 0 1)	(0 0 0 1 1 0 1)
(0 0 1 1)	(0 1 0 0 0 1 1)
(1 0 1 1)	(1 0 0 1 0 1 1)
(0 1 1 1)	(0 0 1 0 1 1 1)
(1 1 1 1)	(1 1 1 1 1 1 1)

unit, the encoder accepts a small block of b information digits (called a message block) and produces a block of v code digits (called a *code block*), where $b < v$. The v-digit code block depends not only on the b-digit message block of the same time unit but also on the previous m message blocks.

7.1.2 Maximum Likelihood Decoding

Suppose that $y = (y_0, y_1, y_2, \ldots, y_{n-1})$ is the transmitted code word and $r = (r_0, r_1, r_2, \ldots, r_{n-1})$ is the sequence received at the channel output. The received sequence might differ from the transmitted code word y because of channel noise disturbance. On the basis of r and the channel characteristics, a decision is made at the decoder concerning the transmitted code word. This decision process is called *decoding*. An error in decoding is committed if the decoder fails to reproduce the actual transmitted code word. The probability of an error in decoding depends on the code used, the channel characteristics, and the decoding strategy employed at the decoder. If all the code words have the same likelihood of being transmitted, the best decoding scheme is as follows. Upon receiving the sequence r, the decoder computes the conditional probability $P(r|y_\ell)$ for all 2^k code words y_ℓ. The code word y_t is identified as the transmitted word if the conditional probability $P(r|y_t)$ is the largest. This decoding scheme is known as *maximum likelihood decoding*.

The most important and most striking result on transmission of information over a noisy channel is *Shannon's coding theorem*. The theorem says that every channel has a fixed capacity C, and that for any rate R less than C, there exists codes of rate R which, with maximum likelihood decoding, have an arbitrarily small probability of decoding error $P(\epsilon)$. More specifically, for any given rate $R < C$ and length n, there exists a block code such that the probability of decoding error

$$P(\epsilon) \le e^{-nE(R)}$$

where $E(R)$ is a positive function of R for $R < C$ and is specified by the channel characteristics. Therefore, the probability of decoding error can be made as small as we desire by increasing the code length n and keeping rate R less than the channel capacity C. Shannon's theorem only shows the existence of codes that give arbitrarily small probability of decoding error, but does not indicate how these codes can be constructed. We are thus faced with the problem of how to construct these good codes of large n promised by Shannon.

As shown in the inequality, the code length n must be large for a code to guarantee error-free decoding. If we implement this code with an encoder that stores 2^{nR} ($= 2^k$) code words and a decoder that performs maximum likelihood decoding, both encoder and decoder would be prohibitively complex. As for the decoder, it has to compute 2^{nR} conditional probabilities $P(r|y_\ell)$. Therefore, one is faced with the following three problems: (1) to find good long codes, (2) to find a practical method of encoding, and (3) to find a practical method of decoding.

7.1.3 Types of Errors

For certain channels, noise affects each transmitted digit independently. These channels are referred to as *discrete memoryless channels*. An example of a discrete memoryless channel is the *binary symmetric channel* (BSC), as shown in Fig. 7.2, where q is the probability that the same symbol as transmitted will be received, and $p = 1 - q$ is the probability that the opposite symbol will be received. The BSC is a good model for channels that are disturbed by white Gaussian noise (e.g., a space channel). Transmission errors induced in a discrete memoryless channel are called *random errors*. The codes devised for correcting random errors are called *random-error-correcting codes*. A different situation arises when the noise does not affect each transmitted digit independently; in this case the errors tend to occur in *bursts* or *clusters*. Channels of this type are said to have memory. The most common cause of errors in telephone lines, for example, is switching impulse noise. The duration of such impulses is on the order of milliseconds, resulting in short error bursts. For microwave and radio links, typical fading or dropouts may last from milliseconds to seconds, resulting in longer error bursts. In storage media, such as magnetic tapes, bursts may last up to several mils. The observation of these phenomena led to the development of codes for correcting burst errors. Codes of this type are called *burst-error-correcting codes*.

7.1.4 Error-Control Techniques

There are basically two techniques for controlling errors in a data transmission system: the automatic-repeat-request (ARQ) scheme and the forward-error-correction (FEC) scheme. The ARQ scheme is used in conjunction with an error-

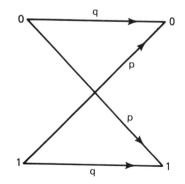

FIGURE 7-2 *A binary symmetric channel.*

detecting code. When errors are detected at the receiver, the transmitter is instructed, via a return channel, to retransmit the corrupted message. There are two types of ARQ: *stop and wait* ARQ and *continuous* ARQ. With stop-and-wait ARQ, the transmitter sends a code word to the receiver and waits for a positive (ACK) or negative (NAK) acknowledgment from the receiver. If the acknowledgment is positive (no errors being detected), it sends the next code word. If a negative acknowledgment is received, the transmitter resends the previous code word. When noise is persistent, the same word may be retransmitted several times before it is accepted by the receiver.

With continuous ARQ, the transmitter sends code words to the receiver continuously and receives acknowledgments continuously. When a negative acknowledgment is received, the transmitter begins retransmission. The transmitter may back up to the code word in error and retransmit that word and those words which follow it. This is called a *pullback scheme*. Alternately, the transmitter may simply resend the code word in error but not those words which follow it. This is known as *selective-repeat* ARQ. Selective-repeat continuous ARQ is more efficient than the pullback continuous ARQ. However, it requires more logic and buffering.

Continuous ARQ is more efficient than the stop-and-wait ARQ; however, it is also more expensive. In a situation such as a satellite communication system where the transmission rate is high and the round-trip delay is long, continuous ARQ is normally used. Stop-and-wait ARQ is normally used in a system where the time taken to transmit a code block is long compared to the time taken to receive an acknowledgment. Stop-and-wait ARQ is designed for use on a half-duplex channel, whereas continuous ARQ is designed for use on a full-duplex channel.

Forward error correction (FEC) is used in conjunction with an error-correcting code. When errors are detected, they are corrected at the receiver. This technique is normally used in situations where a return channel is unavailable or retransmission is not possible or inconvenient. FEC is more difficult to implement than ARQ. When the error rate is high and the retransmission time is long, ARQ will lower the throughput of the channel. In this situation, a combination of forward correction of the most frequent error patterns and detection coupled with retransmission for less frequent error patterns is often more efficient than either FEC or ARQ alone.

7.2 LINEAR BLOCK CODES [2–7]

For a block code with 2^k code words and length n, unless it has certain special structure, the encoding and decoding apparatus would be prohibitively complex for large k since the encoder has to store the 2^k code words in a dictionary and the decoder has to perform a table (with 2^n entries) look-up to determine the transmitted code word. Therefore, we must restrict our attention to block codes that can be implemented in a practical manner.

A desirable structure for a block to possess is the *linearity*. A block code (binary) C of length n and 2^k code words is called a linear (n, k) code if and only if its 2^k code words form a k-dimensional subspace of the vector space of all the n-tuples over the binary field GF(2). In fact, a binary block code is linear if and only if the modulo-2 sum of two code words is also a code word. The block code given in Table 7.1 is a (7, 4) linear code. We can easily check that the sum of any two code words in this code is also a code word. For example, (1 0 0 0 1 1 0) and (0 0 1 0 1 1 1) are two code words, the sum of them is

$$(1\ 0\ 0\ 0\ 1\ 1\ 0) + (0\ 0\ 1\ 0\ 1\ 1\ 1) = (1\ 0\ 1\ 0\ 0\ 0\ 1)$$

which is also a code word, where + denotes modulo-2 addition. If we take the sum of a code word with itself, we obtain the all-zero code word (0 0 0 0 0 0 0). A linear code contains the all-zero vector as a code word.

It is also desirable to require a code word to have the format as shown in Fig. 7.3 where a code word is divided into two parts, the information part and the redundant checking part. The information part consists of the k *unaltered message digits* and the redundant checking part consists of $n - k$ *parity-check digits*. A linear code with this feature is referred to as a *linear systematic code*. The (7, 4) code given in Table 7.1 is a linear systematic code; the rightmost four digits of each code word are identical to the corresponding message digits.

A linear systematic (n, k) code is completely specified by a $k \times n$ matrix G with binary entries as in

$$
G = \begin{bmatrix} g_0 \\ g_1 \\ g_2 \\ \cdot \\ \cdot \\ \cdot \\ g_{k-1} \end{bmatrix} = \begin{bmatrix} p_{00} & p_{01} & \cdot & p_{0, n-k-1} & 1 & 0 & 0 & \cdots & 0 \\ p_{10} & p_{11} & \cdot & p_{1, n-k-1} & 0 & 1 & 0 & \cdots & 0 \\ p_{20} & p_{22} & \cdot & p_{2, n-k-1} & 0 & 0 & 1 & \cdots & 0 \\ & \cdot & & & & & & & \\ & \cdot & & & & & \cdot & & \\ & \cdot & & & & & & & \\ p_{k-1, 0} & p_{k-1, 1} & \cdots & p_{k-1, n-k-1} & 0 & 0 & 0 & \cdots & 1 \end{bmatrix} \tag{7.1}
$$

$$\underbrace{\hspace{4cm}}_{P \text{ matrix}} \quad \underbrace{\hspace{4cm}}_{\substack{k \times k \text{ identity} \\ \text{matrix}}}$$

Each code word is a linear combination of the rows of G and every linear combination of rows of G is a code word. Let $m = (m_0, m_1, \ldots, m_{k-1})$ be the message block to be encoded. Then the corresponding code word is

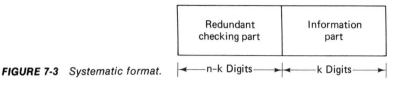

Redundant checking part	Information part

FIGURE 7-3 *Systematic format.* |◄────n-k Digits────►|◄────k Digits────►|

$$u = (u_0, u_1, u_2, \ldots, u_{n-1})$$

$$= m_0 g_0 + m_1 g_1 + \ldots + m_{k-1} g_{k-1} \qquad (7.2)$$

$$= mG$$

It follows from (7.1) and (7.2) that we obtain the code word digits as

$$u_{n-k+i} = m_i \qquad \text{for } i = 0, 1, \ldots, k-1 \qquad (7.3a)$$

$$u_j = m_0 p_{0j} + m_1 p_{1j} + \ldots + m_{k-1} p_{k-1,j} \qquad \text{for } j = 0, 1, \ldots, n-k-1 \quad (7.3b)$$

Equation (7.3a) shows that the rightmost k digits of a code word are identical to the message digits to be encoded, and (7.3b) shows that the leftmost $n - k$ redundant digits are linear combinations of the message digits and the $n - k$ equations of (7.3b) are referred to as *parity-check equations* of the code. The matrix G of (7.1) is called the *generator* matrix of the code. The linear code specified by (7.3a) and (7.3b) is also referred to as the *systematic parity-check code*. The generator matrix of the (7, 4) code given in Table 7.1 is

$$G = \begin{bmatrix} g_0 \\ g_1 \\ g_2 \\ g_3 \end{bmatrix} = \begin{bmatrix} 1 & 1 & 0 & 1 & 0 & 0 & 0 \\ 0 & 1 & 1 & 0 & 1 & 0 & 0 \\ 1 & 1 & 1 & 0 & 0 & 1 & 0 \\ 1 & 0 & 1 & 0 & 0 & 0 & 1 \end{bmatrix}$$

Let $m = (m_0, m_1, m_2, m_3)$ be the message to be encoded. Then the digits of the corresponding code word are

$$u_6 = m_3$$

$$u_5 = m_2$$

$$u_4 = m_1$$

$$u_3 = m_0 \qquad (7.4)$$

$$u_2 = m_1 + m_2 + m_3$$

$$u_1 = m_0 + m_1 + m_2$$

$$u_0 = m_0 + m_2 + m_3$$

The code word corresponding to the message (1 0 1 1) is (1 0 0 1 0 1 1).

Based on the equation of (7.3a) and (7.3b), the encoding circuit can be implemented easily. The encoding circuit is shown in Fig. 7.4 where →☐→ denotes a shift register stage, ⊕ denotes a modulo-2 adder, and →(p_{ij})→ denotes a connection if $p_{ij} = 1$ and no connection if $p_{ij} = 0$. The message to be encoded is shifted into the message register and simultaneously into the channel. As soon as the message has entered the message register, the $n - k$ parity-check bits are formed at the outputs of the $n - k$ modulo-2 adders. These parity-check bits are then serialized and shifted into the channel. The encoding circuit for the (7, 4) code given by Table 7.1 is shown in Fig. 7.5. The connection is based on equations of (7.4).

Let $u = (u_0, u_1, u_2, \ldots, u_{n-1})$ and $v = (v_0, v_1, v_2, \ldots, v_{n-1})$ be two n-tuples. The *inner product* of u and v is defined as the following sum:

$$u \cdot v = \sum_{i=0}^{n-1} u_i v_i \tag{7.5}$$

(The sum is modulo-2 sum.) If the inner product $u \cdot v = 0$, u and v are said to be *orthogonal* to each other. A linear (n, k) code can also be specified by an $(n - k) \times n$ matrix H of rank $n - k$ in the following manner. Let $u = (u_0, u_1, \ldots, u_{n-1})$ be an n-tuple. *Then u is a code word if and only if the inner product of u and any row of H is equal to zero* (i.e., $u \cdot H^T = 0$). This H matrix is called the *parity-check matrix* of the code. If the generator matrix is of the form of (7.1), the parity-check matrix may take the following form:

$$H = \begin{matrix}
1 & 0 & 0\cdots 0 & p_{ij} & p_{ij} & \cdots & p_{ijk-1,0} \\
0 & 1 & 0\cdots 0 & p_{ij} & p_{ij} & \cdots & p_{ijk-1,1} \\
0 & 0 & 1\cdots 0 & p_{ij} & p_{ij} & \cdots & p_{ijk-1,2} \\
\cdot & & & \cdot & & & \\
\cdot & & & \cdot & & & \\
\cdot & & & \cdot & & & \\
0 & 0 & 0\cdots 1 & p_{0,n-k-1} & p_{1,n-k-1} & \cdots & p_{k-1,n-k-1} \\
\underbrace{\qquad\qquad}_{I_{n-k \times n-k}} & & & \underbrace{\qquad\qquad}_{P^T} & & &
\end{matrix} \tag{7.6}$$

where P^T is the *transpose* of matrix P in (7.1). Let $m = (m_0, m_1, \ldots, m_{k-1})$ be the message to be encoded. In systematic form, the corresponding code word would be

$$u = (u_0, u_1, \ldots, u_{n-k-1}, m_0, m_1, \ldots, m_{k-1})$$

Using the fact $uH^T = 0$, we will obtain the same parity-check equations as (7.3b). The parity-check matrix of the (7, 4) code given in Table 7.1 is

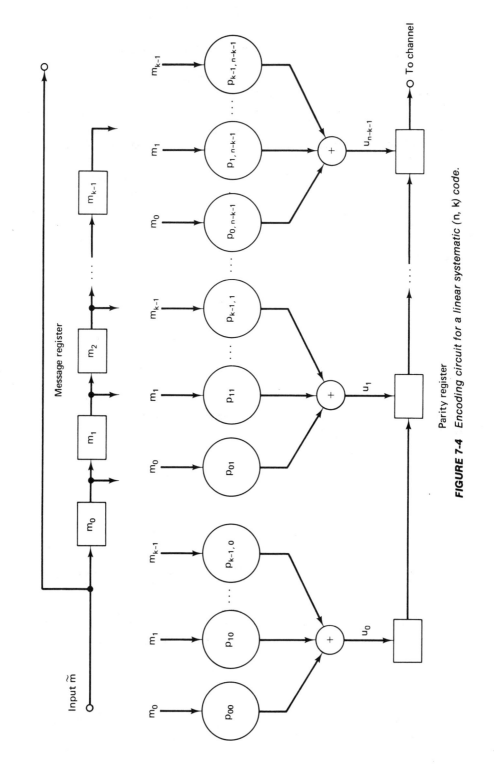

FIGURE 7-4 *Encoding circuit for a linear systematic (n, k) code.*

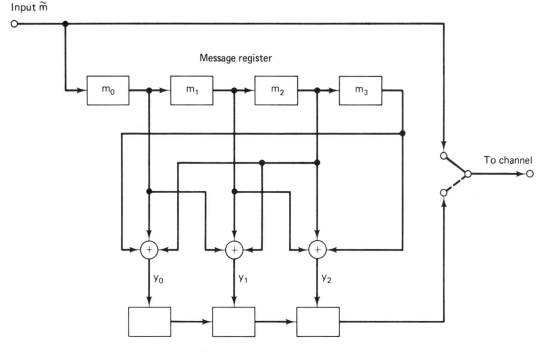

Input $\widetilde{m}$

Message register

m_0 m_1 m_2 m_3

To channel

y_0 y_1 y_2

Parity register

FIGURE 7-5 *An encoding circuit for the (7,4) systematic code given in Table 3.1.*

$$H = \begin{bmatrix} 1 & 0 & 0 & 1 & 0 & 1 & 1 \\ 0 & 1 & 0 & 1 & 1 & 1 & 0 \\ 0 & 0 & 1 & 0 & 1 & 1 & 1 \end{bmatrix} \qquad (7.7)$$

7.2.1 Syndrome and Error Detection

Let $u = (u_0, u_1, \ldots, u_{n-1})$ be the transmitted code word over the noisy channel. Let $r = (r_0, r_1, \ldots, r_{n-1})$ be the received vector. Then $r + u$ is the vector that contains a 1 in each position in which r and u differ. This vector is called the *error vector* (or *error pattern*) e. The 1's in e are the transmission errors introduced by the channel noise. Upon receiving r, the decoder must first determine whether there are transmission errors in r. If there are errors, the decoder will take actions to correct the errors (FEC) or ask for retransmission (ARQ). To check whether the received vector r is a code word, the decoder computes the $(n - k)$-tuple defined as following:

251

$$s = (s_0, s_1, \ldots, s_{n-k-1})$$

$$= rH^T \tag{7.8}$$

Then r is a code word *if and only if* $s = (0 \quad 0 \quad \ldots \quad 0)$, and r is not a code word *if and only if* $s \neq (0 \quad 0 \quad \ldots \quad 0)$. Therefore, s is used for detecting the existence of errors. For this reason, we call s the *syndrome* of the received vector r. Certain patterns of transmission errors are not detectable. For example, if a code word u is transmitted and the noise disturbs u into another valid code word, say w, then the syndrome $s = wH^T = 0$. In this case, the decoder would assume no transmission errors and take no action to correct them. Error patterns of this type are called *undetectable* error patterns. In the design of a linear (n, k) code, we would like the code to be able to detect as many probable error patterns as possible.

Based on (7.6) and (7.8), the syndrome digits are

$$s_0 = r_0 + r_{n-k} P_{00} + r_{n-k+1} P_{10} + \ldots + r_{n-1} P_{k-1,0}$$

$$s_1 = r_1 + r_{n-k} P_{01} + r_{n-k+1} P_{11} + \ldots + r_{n-1} P_{k-1,1}$$

$$\vdots \tag{7.9}$$

$$s_{n-k-1} = r_{n-k-1} + r_{n-k} P_{0,n-k-1} + r_{n-k+1} P_{1,n-k-1} +$$

$$\ldots + r_{n-1} P_{k-1,n-k-1}$$

Suppose that the $(7, 4)$ linear code given in Table 7.1 is used and $r = (r_0, r_1, r_2, r_3, r_4, r_5, r_6)$ is the received vector. Then the syndrome digits are obtained from r and (7.7) as follows:

$$s_0 = r_0 + r_3 + r_5 + r_6$$

$$s_1 = r_1 + r_3 + r_4 + r_5 \tag{7.10}$$

$$s_2 = r_2 + r_4 + r_5 + r_6$$

Based on (7.9), we can implement the syndrome computation circuit easily. For the $(7, 4)$ code given in Table 7.1, the syndrome computation circuit is shown in Fig. 7.6.

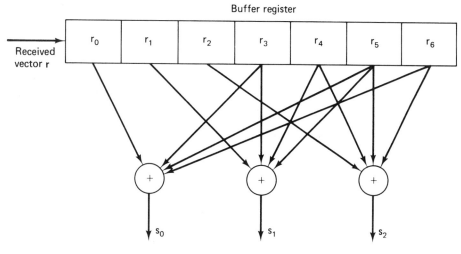

Buffer register

Received vector r

r_0 r_1 r_2 r_3 r_4 r_5 r_6

s_0 s_1 s_2

Syndrome

FIGURE 7-6 The syndrome circuit for the (7,4) code given in Table 7.1.

7.2.2 Hamming Distance, and Error-Detecting and Error-Correcting Capabilities

In this section we will discuss what determines the *error-detecting* and *error-correcting* capabilities of a block code. Let $u = (u_0, u_1, \ldots, u_{n-1})$ be a binary n-tuple. The *Hamming weight* of u, denoted $w(u)$, is defined as the number of nonzero components (or 1's) in u. For example, the Hamming weight of $u = (1\ 0\ 0\ 1\ 0\ 1\ 1)$ is 4. Let u and v be two binary n-tuples. The *Hamming distance* between u and v, denoted by $d(u, v)$, is defined as the number of places where they differ. For example, if $u = (1\ 0\ 0\ 1\ 0\ 1\ 1)$ and $v = (0\ 1\ 0\ 0\ 0\ 1\ 1)$, the Hamming distance between them is 3. Given a linear code, we can compute the Hamming distances between all possible pairs of code words; the smallest distance is called the *minimum distance* of the code, denoted by $d_{\min}$. We can easily check that the minimum distance of the (7, 4) code given in Table 7.1 is 3.

It is clear that a single error results in a Hamming distance 1 between the transmitted code word and the received vector. If a block code has minimum distance $d_{\min}$, it is capable of detecting all error patterns of $d_{\min} - 1$ or fewer errors because no error pattern of $d_{\min} - 1$ errors can change one code word into another. However, it cannot detect all the error patterns of $d_{\min}$ errors because there exists some pair of code words at distance $d_{\min}$ apart and there is an error pattern of $d_{\min}$ errors that will carry one into the other. The same argument is applied to error patterns of more than $d_{\min}$ errors. Based on the analysis above, we define the *random-error-detecting capability* of a block code with minimum distance d_{min} as $d_{min} - 1$.

Even though a block code with minimum distance d_{min} guarantees detecting all the error patterns of $d_{min} - 1$ or fewer errors, it is also capable of detecting a large fraction of error patterns with d_{min} or more errors. In fact, an (n, k) linear code is capable of detecting $2^n - 2^k$ error patterns of length n. This can be shown as following. Among the $2^n - 1$ possible error patterns, there are $2^k - 1$ error patterns, which are identical to the $2^k - 1$ nonzero code words. If each of these $2^k - 1$ error patterns occurs, it alters the transmitted code word u into another code word v. Thus, v will be received and its syndrome is zero. In this case the decoder accepts v as the transmitted code word and thus commits an incorrect decoding. Therefore, there are $2^k - 1$ *undetectable* error patterns. If an error pattern is not identical to a nonzero code word, the received vector r will not be a code word and the syndrome will not be zero. In this case, an error will be detected. There are exactly $2^n - 2^k$ error patterns which are not identical to the code words of an (n, k) linear code. These $2^n - 2^k$ error patterns are *detectable* error patterns. For large n, $2^k - 1$ is in general much smaller than 2^n. Therefore, there is only a small fraction of error patterns that pass through the decoder without being detected.

When we choose a linear block code for error detection only, it is important to choose one which is capable of detecting those error patterns that occur most frequently. For a BSC as shown in Fig. 7.2, the probability of occurrence of an error pattern with ℓ errors is $p^\ell q^{n-\ell}$. Assuming that $p < q$, this probability decreases monotonically with increasing ℓ. Thus, an error pattern with smaller number of errors is more likely to occur than an error pattern with larger number of errors.

When an (n, k) linear code is used only for error detection on the BSC, the probability $P(E)$ that the decoder fails to detect an error can be computed as following. Let A_i be the number of code words with weight i. An undetectable error occurs only when the error pattern is identical to a nonzero code word; therefore,

$$P(E) = \sum_{i=1}^{n} A_i \, p^i q^{n-i}$$

For the (7, 4) linear code given in Table 7.1, the probability of an undetected error is

$$P(E) = 7p^3q^4 + 7p^4q^3 + p^7$$

With $p = 10^{-2}$, this probability is approximately 7×10^{-6}. In other words, if 1 million code words are transmitted over the BSC with $p = 10^{-2}$, there are on average seven corrupted code words passing through the decoder without being detected. If a long powerful code is used, the probability of an undetected error can be made very small.

If a linear code with minimum distance $d_{\min}$ such that $2t + 1 \leq d_{\min} \leq 2t + 2$ is used for random-error correction, it is capable of correcting all the error patterns of t or fewer errors. This can be justified as follows. For any received vector with $t' \leq t$ errors, it differs from the transmitted code word in t' places but from every other code word in at least $t + 1$ places. Thus, the received vector is closer to the actual transmitted code word than to any other code word. By maximum likelihood decoding, the decoder will make a correct decoding. However, the code is not capable of correcting all the error patterns of ℓ errors with $\ell \geq t + 1$, because there is at least one case where an ℓ-fold error results in a received vector at least as close to an incorrect code word as to the transmitted code word. Therefore, the *random-error-correcting capability* of a block code with minimum distance $d_{\min}$ is $t = (d_{\min} - 1)/2$, where $[q]$ denotes the integer part of the number q. The (7, 4) code given in Table 7.1 has minimum distance 3; therefore, it is a single-error-correcting code.

A block code with random-error-correcting capability t is usually capable of correcting many error patterns of $t + 1$ or more errors. In fact, it is capable of correcting a total of 2^{n-k} error patterns, including all those with t or fewer errors. If a random-error-correcting (n, k) linear code with error-correcting capability t is used on a BSC, the probability that the decoder commits an erroneous decoding is upper-bounded by

$$P(E) \leq \sum_{i = t + 1}^{n} \binom{n}{i} p^i q^{n-1}$$

By a similar argument, it can be seen that a block code with minimum distance $d_{\min}$ is capable of correcting λ errors and simultaneously detecting d errors $(d > \lambda)$ if and only if $d_{\min} \geq \lambda + d + 1$. From the foregoing analysis, we realize that the (random) error-detecting and error-correcting capabilities of a block code are determined by its minimum distance. Obviously, in the construction of a random-error-detecting/error-correcting code with fixed n and k, we would like to obtain an (n, k) code with minimum distance as large as possible (besides the implementation considerations).

As we pointed out earlier, there are channels that are affected by noise that cause transmission errors to cluster into bursts. In general, codes for correcting random errors are not efficient for detecting or correcting burst errors. Therefore, it is desirable to design codes specifically for detecting or correcting burst errors. Codes of this kind are called burst-error-correcting/burst-error-detecting codes. A burst of length ℓ is defined as a vector whose nonzero components (1's) are confined to ℓ consecutive digit positions, the first and last of which are nonzero. For example, the vector $u = (0\ 0\ 0\ 1\ 1\ 0\ 1\ 0)$ is a burst of length 4. A number of theorems related to the burst-error-detecting and burst-error-correcting capabilities of a block code are stated in the following:

1. For detecting all burst errors of length ℓ or less with a linear block code of length n, ℓ parity-check symbols are necessary and sufficient.

2. In order to correct all burst errors of length b or less, a linear block code must have at least $2b$ parity-check symbols.

3. In order to correct all bursts of length b or less and simultaneously detect all burst of length $\ell \geqslant b$ or less, a linear code must have at least $b + \ell$ parity-check symbols.

7.2.3 Decoding of Linear Codes

Now, we want to show how the syndrome of a received vector can be used for error correction. Let $u = (u_0, u_1, \ldots, u_{n-1})$, $e = (e_0, e_1, \ldots, e_{n-1})$ and $r = (r_0, r_1, \ldots, r_{n-1})$ be the transmitted code, the error vector, and the received vector, respectively. Then

$$r = u + e$$

and the syndrome is

$$s = rH^T = (u + e)\,H^T = uH^T + eH^T$$

Since $uH^T = 0$, we have

$$s = eH^T \tag{7.11}$$

From (7.6) and (7.11), we obtain

$$
\begin{aligned}
s_0 &= e_0 + e_{n-k}\,p_{00} + e_{n-k+1}\,p_{10} + \cdots + e_{n-1}\,p_{k-1,0} \\
s_1 &= e_1 + e_{n-k}\,p_{01} + e_{n-k+1}\,p_{11} + \cdots + e_{n-1}\,p_{k-1,1} \\
&\;\;\vdots \\
s_{n-k-1} &= e_{n-k-1} + e_{n-k}\,p_{0,n-k-1} + e_{n-k+1}\,p_{1,n-k-1} + \\
&\qquad \cdots + e_{n-1}\,p_{k-1,n-k-1}
\end{aligned}
\tag{7.12}
$$

From (7.12), we see that the syndrome digits are actually linear combinations of the error digits. Therefore, they contain information about the error digits. Any decoding circuit will use the syndrome digits to estimate the error digits. A general decoder for a linear (n, k) block code is shown in Fig. 7.7.

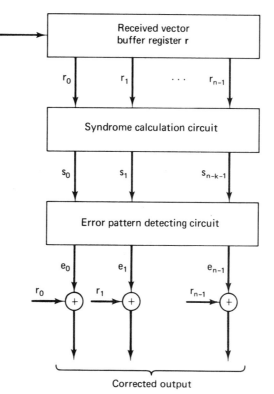

FIGURE 7-7 *A general decoder for a linear block code.*

We pointed out in Sec. 7.2.2 that an (n, k) linear code is capable of correcting 2^{n-k} error patterns. Each of these correctable error pattern corresponds to a unique $(n - k)$-bit syndrome. This one-to-one correspondence between a correctable error pattern and an $(n - k)$-bit syndrome can be used for designing the error pattern detecting circuit of a decoder. This is best explained by an example. The $(7, 4)$ code given in Table 7.1 is a single-error correcting code (i.e., it is capable of correcting any single transmission error over the span of seven digits). The parity-check matrix of this code is given in (7.7). Suppose that a single transmission error occurs. The seven single-error patterns are listed in Table 7.2 together with their corresponding syndromes. Table 7.2 shows that there is a one-to-one correspondence between a single-error pattern and its syndrome. If a single error occurs, from the syndrome we would be able to locate the error. For example, if the syndrome computed from the received vector is $s = (1 \quad 1 \quad 1)$, then, from the table, we know that the transmission error is at the fifth-digit position. Knowing the error location, we can correct the received digit. A combinational logic circuit for error pattern detection can be designed based on

TABLE 7-2: *Single-error patterns and their corresponding syndromes for the (7, 4) code given in Table 7-1.*

Error Patterns	Syndrome
$e = (e_0, e_1, e_2, e_3, e_4, e_5, e_6)$	$s = (s_0, s_1, s_2)$
(1 0 0 0 0 0 0)	(1 0 0)
(0 1 0 0 0 0 0)	(0 1 0)
(0 0 1 0 0 0 0)	(0 0 1)
(0 0 0 1 0 0 0)	(1 1 0)
(0 0 0 0 1 0 0)	(0 1 1)
(0 0 0 0 0 1 0)	(1 1 1)
(0 0 0 0 0 0 1)	(1 0 1)

the truth table given in Table 7.3. A complete decoding circuit for the (7, 4) code given in Table 7.1 is shown in Fig. 7.8. The (7, 4) code is not capable of correcting double errors. This can be seen easily. Suppose that there are two transmission errors, say $e_1 = 1$ and $e_5 = 1$. The error vector is $e = (0 \ 1 \ 0 \ 0 \ 0 \ 1 \ 0)$. The corresponding syndrome will be

$$s = (0 \ 1 \ 0 \ 0 \ 0 \ 1 \ 0) \begin{bmatrix} 1 & 0 & 0 \\ 0 & 1 & 0 \\ 0 & 0 & 1 \\ 1 & 1 & 0 \\ 0 & 1 & 1 \\ 1 & 1 & 1 \\ 1 & 0 & 1 \end{bmatrix} = (1 \ 0 \ 1)$$

However, syndrome (1 0 1) also corresponds to the single error pattern with $e_6 = 1$. Therefore, the decoder of Fig. 7.8 will decode the double errors as a single error and make an incorrect decoding. This is true when there are two or more transmission errors.

TABLE 7-3: *Truth table for the single-error pattern for the (7, 4) code given in Table 7-1.*

Syndrome			Error Pattern						
s_0	s_1	s_2	e_0	e_1	e_2	e_3	e_4	e_5	e_6
0	0	0	0	0	0	0	0	0	0
1	0	0	1	0	0	0	0	0	0
0	1	0	0	1	0	0	0	0	0
0	0	1	0	0	1	0	0	0	0
1	1	0	0	0	0	1	0	0	0
0	1	1	0	0	0	0	1	0	0
1	1	1	0	0	0	0	0	1	0
1	0	1	0	0	0	0	0	0	1

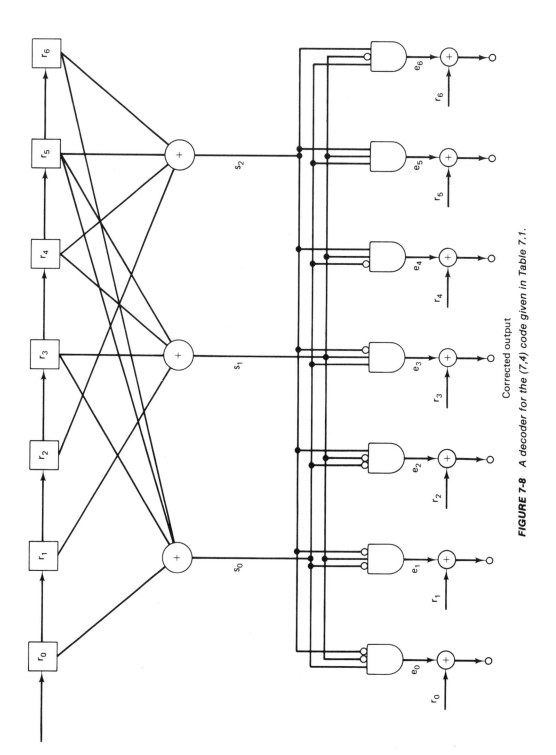

Corrected output

FIGURE 7-8 A decoder for the (7,4) code given in Table 7.1.

In principle, we can design a decoder for an (n, k) linear code which corrects all the 2^{n-k} correctable error patterns based on the one-to-one correspondence between a correctable error pattern and an $(n - k)$-bit syndrome. However, for large $n - k$, the decoder becomes prohibitively complex and impractical. If we only intend to correct those error patterns that occur most frequently but not all the 2^{n-k} correctable error patterns, the complexity of the decoder can be greatly reduced. Several practical decoding methods which are refinements of the decoding scheme described above are available. Each of these decoding methods requires additional properties in a code other than just the linear property.

7.2.4 Average Probability of an Undetected Error for a Linear Code over the BSC

If an (n, k) linear code is used only for error detection over the BSC, the probability of an undetected error can be computed from (7.11) if we know the weight distribution of the code (i.e., A_i for $i = 1, 2, \ldots, n$). Theoretically, we can determine the weight distribution by simply examining all the 2^k code words. However, for large n and k, this becomes practically impossible. To overcome this difficulty, we consider the average probability of an undetected error over an ensemble of (n, k) linear codes.

As we pointed out earlier, a systematic (n, k) linear code is completely specified by a matrix G of form given by (7.1). The submatrix P consists of $k(n - k)$ entries. Since each entry p_{ij} can be either a "0" or a "1," there are $2^{k(n-k)}$ distinct linear systematic (n, k) codes. Let Γ denote the ensemble of these codes. Suppose that we choose a code randomly from Γ and use it for error detection. Let C_j be the chosen code. Then the probability of C_j being chosen is

$$P(C_j) = 2^{-k(n-k)} \tag{7.13}$$

Let A_{ji} denote the number of code words in C_j with weight i. Then the probability of an undetected error for C_j is given by

$$P(E/C_j) = \sum_{i=1}^{n} A_{ji} p^i q^{n-i} \tag{7.14}$$

The average probability of an undetected error for a code in Γ is defined as

$$\overline{P(E)} = \sum_{j=1}^{|\Gamma|} P(C_j)P(E/C_j) \tag{7.15}$$

Combining (7.13) to (7.15), we obtain

$$\overline{P(E)} = 2^{-k(n-k)} \sum_{i=1}^{n} p^i q^{n-i} \sum_{j=1}^{|\Gamma|} A_{ji} \tag{7.16}$$

It can be shown that a nonzero binary vector of length n is either contained in exactly $2^{(k-1)(n-k)}$ codes in Γ or contained in none of the codes. Since there are $\binom{n}{i}$ binary vectors of length n with weight i, we have

$$\sum_{j=1}^{|\Gamma|} A_{ji} \leqq \binom{n}{i} 2^{(k-1)(n-k)} \tag{7.17}$$

Combining (7.16) and (7.17), we obtain

$$\overline{P(E)} \leqq 2^{-(n-k)} \sum_{i=1}^{n} \binom{n}{i} p^i q^{n-i}$$

$$= 2^{-(n-k)} (1 - q^n) \tag{7.18}$$

The foregoing analysis indicates that the probability of an undetected error for an (n, k) linear code decreases exponentially with the number of parity-check digits. For a linear code with 24 parity-check digits, the probability of an undetected error will be in the order 10^{-8}.

7.3 CYCLIC CODES [3–7]

A linear (n, k) code is said to be cyclic if any cyclic shift of a code word is another code word. That is, if

$$\boldsymbol{u} = (u_0, u_1, u_2, \ldots, u_{n-1})$$

is a code word, then

$$\boldsymbol{u}^{(1)} = (u_{n-1}, u_0, u_1, \ldots, u_{n-2})$$

obtained by shifting $\boldsymbol{u}$ cyclically one place to the right, is another code word. Cyclic codes are attractive for two reasons. First, encoding and syndrome calculation can be implemented easily by employing simple shift registers with feedback connection (or linear sequential circuits). Second, because they have considerable inherent algebraic structure, it is possible to find various simple and efficient decoding methods.

In discussing cyclic codes, we represent a code word $\boldsymbol{u} = (u_0, u_1, u_2, \ldots, u_{n-1})$ by a polynomial of degree $n - 1$ or less as following:

$$u(X) = u_0 + u_1 X + u_2 X^2 + \ldots + u_{n-1} X^{n-1}$$

We call $u(X)$ as a code polynomial. A number of important properties of cyclic codes are discussed in the following. In an (n, k) cyclic code, every nonzero code polynomial must have degree at least $n - k$ but not greater than $n - 1$. There exists one and only one code polynomial $g(X)$ of degree $n - k$ of the following form:

$$g(X) = 1 + g_1 X + g_2 X^2 + \ldots + g_{n-k-1} X^{n-k-1} + X^{n-k} \qquad (7.19)$$

Every code polynomial $u(X)$ is a multiple of $g(X)$ [i.e., $u(X) = m(X) g(X)$]. Moreover, every polynomial of degree $n - 1$ or less that is a multiple of $g(X)$ is a code polynomial. Therefore, an (n, k) cyclic code is completely specified by the polynomial $g(X)$ of (7.19). The polynomial $g(X)$ is called the *generator polynomial* of the cyclic code. The degree $n - k$ of $g(X)$ is equal to the number of parity-check digits of the code.

Consider the $(7, 4)$ code given by Table 7.4. It is easy to check that a cyclic shift of any code word results in another code word. Therefore, it is a $(7, 4)$ cyclic code. Since $n - k = 3$, the generator polynomial is a code polynomial of degree 3. By examining the code words, we find that the code word $(1\ 1\ 0\ 1\ 0\ 0\ 0)$ corresponding to the generator polynomial $g(X)$. Hence,

$$g(X) = 1 + X + X^3$$

TABLE 7-4: *(7, 4) cyclic code generated by $g(X) = 1 + X + X^3$.*

Message	Code Word	Code Polynomial
(0 0 0 0)	(0 0 0 0 0 0 0)	$0 = 0 \cdot g(X)$
(1 0 0 0)	(1 1 0 1 0 0 0)	$1 + X + X^3 = g(X)$
(0 1 0 0)	(0 1 1 0 1 0 0)	$X + X^2 + X^4 = Xg(X)$
(1 1 0 0)	(1 0 1 1 1 0 0)	$1 + X^2 + X^3 + X^4 = (1 + X)g(X)$
(0 0 1 0)	(1 1 1 0 0 1 0)	$1 + X + X^2 + X^5 = (1 + X^2)g(X)$
(1 0 1 0)	(0 0 1 1 0 1 0)	$X^2 + X^3 + X^5 = X^2 g(X)$
(0 1 1 0)	(1 0 0 0 1 1 0)	$1 + X^4 + X^5 = (1 + X + X^2)g(X)$
(1 1 1 0)	(0 1 0 1 1 1 0)	$X + X^3 + X^4 + X^5 = (X + X^2)g(X)$
(0 0 0 1)	(1 0 1 0 0 0 1)	$1 + X^2 + X^6 = (1 + X + X^3)g(X)$
(1 0 0 1)	(0 1 1 1 0 0 1)	$X + X^2 + X^3 + X^6 = (X + X^3)g(X)$
(0 1 0 1)	(1 1 0 0 1 0 1)	$1 + X + X^4 + X^6 = (1 + X^3)g(X)$
(1 1 0 1)	(0 0 0 1 1 0 1)	$X^3 + X^4 + X^6 = X^3 g(X)$
(0 0 1 1)	(0 1 0 0 0 1 1)	$X + X^5 + X^6 = (X + X^2 + X^3)g(X)$
(1 0 1 1)	(1 0 0 1 0 1 1)	$1 + X^3 + X^5 + X^6 = (1 + X + X^2 + X^3)g(X)$
(0 1 1 1)	(0 0 1 0 1 1 1)	$X^2 + X^4 + X^5 + X^6 = (X^2 + X^3)g(X)$
(1 1 1 1)	(1 1 1 1 1 1 1)	$1 + X + X^2 + X^3 + X^4 + X^5 + X^6 = (1 + X^2 + X^3)g(X)$

Table 7.3 shows the $(7, 4)$ code in polynomial form and that each code polynomial is a multiple of $g(X)$.

7.3.1 Encoding of Cyclic Codes

The encoding of an (n, k) cyclic code with generator polynomial $g(X)$ can be accomplished as following. Suppose that the message to be encoded is $\boldsymbol{m} = (m_0, m_1, \ldots, m_{k-1})$. The corresponding message polynomial is

$$\boldsymbol{m}(X) = m_0 + m_1 X + \ldots + m_{k-1}X^{k-1}$$

Multiplying $\boldsymbol{m}(X)$ by X^{n-k}, we obtain

$$X^{n-k}\boldsymbol{m}(X) = m_0 X^{n-k} + m_1 X^{n-k-1} + \ldots + m_{k-1}X^{n-1}$$

which is a polynomial of degree $n - 1$ or less. Dividing $X^{n-k}\boldsymbol{m}(X)$ by $g(X)$, we have

$$X^{n - k}\boldsymbol{m}(X) = q(X)g(X) + \rho(X) \tag{7.20}$$

where $q(X)$ and $\rho(X)$ are the quotient and remainder, respectively. Since the degree of $g(X)$ is $n - k$, the degree of $\rho(X)$ must be $n - k - 1$ or less and of the following form:

$$\rho(X) = \rho_0 + \rho_1 X + \rho_2 X^2 + \ldots + \rho_{n-k-1}X^{n-k-1}$$

Rearranging (7.20), we obtain

$$\rho(X) + X^{n-k}\boldsymbol{m}(X) = q(X)g(X)$$

This indicates that $\rho(X) + X^{n-k}\boldsymbol{m}(X)$ is a multiple of $g(X)$ and has degree $n - 1$ or less. Hence $\rho(X) + X^{n-k}\boldsymbol{m}(X)$ is a code polynomial corresponding to the message $\boldsymbol{m}(X)$. Writing out $\rho(X) + X^{n-k}\boldsymbol{m}(X)$, we have

$$\rho(X) + X^{n-k}\boldsymbol{m}(X) = \rho_0 + \rho_1 X + \ldots + \rho_{n-k-1}X^{n-k-1} + m_0 X^{n-k} + m_1 X^{n-k+1}$$
$$+ \ldots + m_{k-1}X^{n-1}$$

which corresponds to the code word

$$\boldsymbol{u} = (\rho_0, \rho_1, \rho_2, \ldots, \rho_{n-k-1}, m_0, m_1, \ldots, m_{k-1})$$

$$|\longleftarrow \text{Parity-check digits} \longrightarrow|\longleftarrow \text{Message digits} \longrightarrow|$$

The code word consists of the unaltered message m followed by $n - k$ parity-check digits. The $n - k$ parity-check digits are just the coefficients of $\rho(X)$. Clearly, the code word is in systematic form. In summary, the encoding consists of three steps:

1. Multiply the message $m(X) = m_0 + m_1X + \ldots + m_{k-1}X^{k-1}$ by X^{n-k}.

2. Obtain the remainder (parity-check digits) from dividing $X^{n-k}m(X)$ by $g(X)$.

3. Combine $\rho(X)$ and $X^{n-k}m(X)$ to obtain the code word $\rho(X) + X^{n-k}m(X)$.

The above encoding can be implemented by using a dividing circuit that is a shift register with feedback connections according to the generator polynomial $g(X)$ as shown in Fig. 7.9.

Note that shifting the message $m(X)$ into the register from the right end of the register is equivalent to multiplying the $m(X)$ by X^{n-k}. The encoding procedure is accomplished as follows: (1) The k message digits are shifted into the register and simultaneously into the channel. As soon as the k message digits have entered the register, the $n - k$ parity-check digits are formed in the register. (2) Shift the $n - k$ parity-check digits out of the register and into the channel. Using the encoding circuit given above, it requires a total of n shifts to form a code word. The encoding circuit for the $(7, 4)$ code generated by $g(X) = 1 + X + X^3$ is shown in Fig. 7.10.

Another important property of an (n, k) cyclic code is its generator polynomial $g(X)$ is a factor of $X^n + 1$:

$$X^n + 1 = g(X)h(X)$$

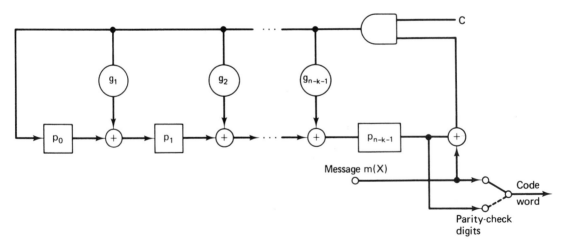

FIGURE 7-9 *An encoding circuit for an (n, k) cyclic code.*

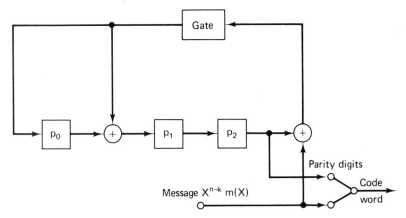

FIGURE 7-10 *An encoder for the (7,4) cyclic code generated by g(X) = 1 + X + X³.*

The polynomial $h(X)$ is usually called the *parity polynomial* of the code and has the following form:

$$h(X) = 1 + h_1X + h_2X^2 + \ldots + X^k \qquad (7.21)$$

Knowing $h(X)$, we can determine $g(X)$ uniquely. Therefore, the parity polynomial also completely specified the code. An encoding circuit based on $h(X)$ is shown in Fig. 7.11.

The encoding procedure is described as following (1) Set $C_1 = 0$ and $C_2 = 0$. The message m is shifted into the register and simultaneously into the channel. (2) Set $C_1 = 0$ and $C_2 = 1$. Shift the register $n - k$ times to form $n - k$ parity-check digits. Comparing the two encoding circuits of Figs. 7.9 and 7.11, we see

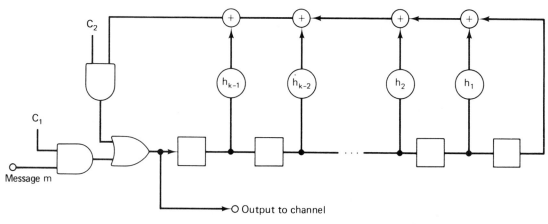

FIGURE 7-11 *Another encoding circuit for an (n, k) cyclic code.*

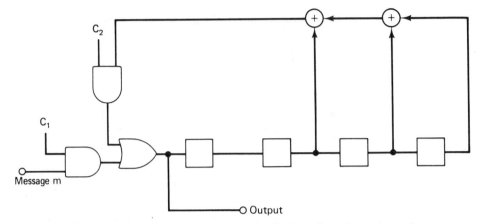

FIGURE 7-12 *The encoding circuit for the (7, 4) cyclic code on the parity polynomial h(X) = 1 + X + X² + X⁴.*

that, for codes with more information digits than the parity-check digits, the circuit of Fig. 7.9 is more economical; otherwise the circuit of Fig. 7.11 is preferable.

Consider the (7, 4) cyclic code given by Table 7.4. The parity polynomial of this code is

$$h(X) = \frac{X^7 + 1}{1 + X + X^3}$$

$$= 1 + X + X^2 + X^4$$

The encoding circuit based on $h(X)$ is shown in Fig. 7.12.

7.3.2 Construction of Cyclic Codes

At this point, we would like to ask the question whether, for any n and k, there exists an (n, k) cyclic code. This is answered by the following theorem. If $g(X)$ is a polynomial of degree $n - k$ and is a factor of $X^n + 1$, then $g(X)$ generates an (n, k) cyclic code. As a matter of fact, any factor of $X^n + 1$ with degree $n - k$ would generate an (n, k) cyclic code. For example, $X^{15} + 1$ can be factored as following:

$$X^{15} + 1 = (X^4 + X + 1)(X^4 + X^3 + 1)(X^4 + X^3 + X^2 + X + 1)$$

$$\cdot (X^2 + X + 1)(X + 1)$$

Each factor of degree 4 generates a (15, 11) cyclic code. The factor

$$g_1(X) = (X^4 + X + 1)(X^4 + X^3 + 1)$$
$$= X^8 + X^7 + X^5 + X^4 + X^3 + X + 1$$

generates a (15, 7) cyclic code. The factor

$$g_2(X) = (X^4 + X^3 + 1)(X^4 + X^3 + X^2 + X + 1)$$
$$= X^8 + X^4 + X^2 + X + 1$$

generates another (15, 7) cyclic code.

For large n, $X^n + 1$ may have many factors of degree $n - k$. Some generate good codes and some generate bad codes. How to select generator polynomials to produce good cyclic codes is a very hard problem. For the past 18 years, much effort has been expended in searching good cyclic codes. A number of classes of good cyclic codes have been discovered, such as Hamming codes, BCH codes, Reed–Solomon codes, geometry codes, Fire codes, and so on. These codes can be practically implemented.

7.3.3 Syndrome Calculation and Error Detection

For cyclic codes, syndrome computation is extremely easy. Let $u(X)$ and $r(X)$ be the transmitted code polynomial and received polynomial, respectively. Dividing $r(X)$ by the generator polynomial $g(X)$, we obtain

$$r(X) = q(X)\,g(X) + s(X) \tag{7.22}$$

where $q(X)$ and $s(X)$ are the quotient and the remainder, respectively. If $s(X) \equiv 0$, the received polynomial is a multiple of the generator polynomial and therefore is a valid code polynomial. If $s(X) \neq 0$, then $r(X)$ is not a code polynomial and contains transmission errors. Therefore, the remainder $s(X)$ obtained from dividing the received polynomial by the generator polynomial is the syndrome. The syndrome $s(X)$ has the following form:

$$s(X) = s_0 + s_1 X + \ldots + s_{n-k-1} X^{n-k-1}$$

It is clear that the syndrome calculation circuit is just a dividing circuit, as the encoding circuit of Fig. 7.9. The received polynomial may be shifted into the register either from the right end or from the left end. A syndrome calculation circuit is shown in Fig. 7.13.

Cyclic codes are extremely suitable for error detection. The detection circuit is just the syndrome circuit with a single OR gate with the syndrome digits as inputs. If the syndrome is not identical to zero, the output of the OR gate is 1 and errors have been detected.

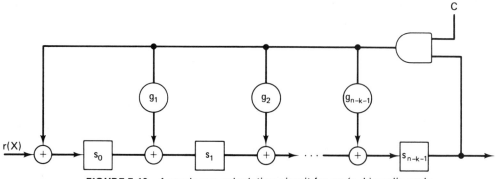

FIGURE 7-13 *A syndrome calculation circuit for an (n, k) cyclic code.*

Let $e(X) = e_0 + e_1 X + \ldots + e_{n-1}X^{n-1}$ be the error polynomial. Then the received polynomial is

$$r(X) = u(X) + e(X) \tag{7.23}$$

Combining (7.22) and (7.23), we obtain

$$e(X) = u(X) + q(X)\,g(X) + s(X)$$

Since $u(X)$ is a code polynomial, it is a multiple of $g(X)$ i.e., $u(X) = m(X)g(X)$. Therefore,

$$e(X) = [m(X) + q(X)]\,g(X) + s(X) \tag{7.24}$$

From (7.24), we see that the syndrome $s(X)$ is actually the remainder resulting from dividing the error polynomial by the generator. Since the syndrome $s(X)$ may be obtained from the received polynomial $r(X)$. The function of decoder is to estimate the error polynomial $e(X)$ from the syndrome $s(X)$.

Since $g(X)$ has degree $n - k$, it is a code vector with burst of length $n - k + 1$. If the error polynomial $e(X)$ is a burst of length $n - k$ or less, we can see from (7.24) that the syndrome is never equal to zero. This implies that an (n, k) cyclic code is capable of detecting any burst error of length $n - k$ or less. In fact, a large percentage of longer burst can also be detected. The fraction of undetectable burst errors of length $n - k + 1$ is $2^{-(n-k-1)}$, and the fraction of undetectable burst errors of length $\ell > n - k + 1$ is $2^{-(n-k)}$. The foregoing analysis shows that cyclic codes are very powerful for error detection.

7.3.4 General Decoder for Cyclic Codes

The basic function of a decoder is to associate the syndrome of the received polynomial to an error pattern. The association can be completely specified by the decoding table. A straightforward approach to the design of a decoder is via a combinational logic circuit that implements the table-lookup procedure. When decoding delay must be minimized, the logic-circuit approach in decoding can be very attractive. However, the limit to this approach is that the complexity of the decoding circuit tends to grow exponentially with the capability of the code used.

Since cyclic codes have considerable inherent algebraic and geometric structure, simplification in decoding circuit is possible. A general decoder for a cyclic code is shown in Fig. 7.14. The error-correction procedure is described as following:

- *Step 1.* The syndrome is formed by shifting the entire received vector into the syndrome register. At the same time, the received vector is stored into the buffer.

- *Step 2.* The syndrome is read into the detector and is tested for the corresponding error pattern. The detector is a combinational logic circuit which is designed in such a way that its output is "1" if and only if the syndrome in the syndrome register corresponds to a correctable error pattern with an error at the highest-order position, X^{n-1}. That is, if a "1" appears at the output of the detector, the received symbol in the rightmost stage of the buffer register is assumed to be erroneous and must be corrected; if a "0" appears at the output of the detector, the received symbol at the rightmost stage of the buffer register is assumed to be correct and no correction is necessary. Thus, the output of the detector is the estimated error value for the symbol to come out of the buffer.

- *Step 3.* The first received symbol is read out of the buffer. At the same

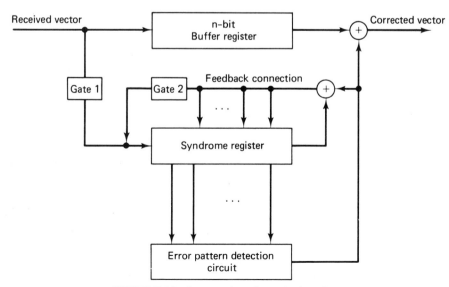

FIGURE 7-14 *A general cyclic code decoder.*

time, the syndrome register is shifted once. If the first received symbol is detected to be an erroneous symbol, it is then corrected by the output of the detector. The output of the detector is also fed back to the syndrome register to modify the syndrome (i.e., to remove the error effect from the syndrome). This results in a new syndrome, which corresponds to the altered received vector shifted one place to the right.

- *Step 4.* The new syndrome formed in step 3 is used to detect whether or not the second received symbol (now at the rightmost stage of the buffer register) is an erroneous symbol. The decoder repeats steps 2 and 3. The second received symbol is corrected in exactly the same manner as the first received symbol was corrected.

- *Step 5.* The decoder decodes the received vector symbol by symbol as described above until the entire received vector is read out of the buffer.

After the entire received vector is read out, the errors will have been corrected if they correspond to an error pattern built into the detector, and the syndrome register will contain all 0's. *If the syndrome register does not contain all 0's at the end of the process, an uncorrectable error has been detected.* The decoder above corrects errors in a sequential manner. A total of n shifts is required. For large n, it may cause undesirable delay.

The decoder described above applies in principle to any cyclic code. But whether or not this decoder is practical depends entirely on its combinational logic circuit. There are cases in which the logic circuits are simple. Several of these cases will be described later.

7.3.5 Shortened Cyclic Codes

In system design, if a code of suitable natural length or suitable number of information digits cannot be found, it may be desirable to shorten a code to meet the requirements. A technique of shortening a cyclic code is described in the following. This technique leads to simple implementation of encoding and decoding for the shortened code.

Given an (n, k) cyclic code. Consider the set of code vectors whose ℓ ($\ell < k$) leading high-order information digits are zeros. There are 2^{k-l} such code vectors. If the ℓ zero information digits are deleted from those code vectors, we obtain a set of 2^{k-l} vectors of $n - \ell$ digits. It is easy to see that this set of shortened code vectors form an $(n - \ell, k - \ell)$ linear code. This code is called a *shortened cyclic code* and is not cyclic. A shortened cyclic code has at least the same error-correcting capability as the code from which it is derived. The encoding and syndrome calculation for a shortened cyclic code can be accomplished by the same circuits as employed by the original cyclic code. This is so because the deleted ℓ leading zero information digits do not affect the parity-check calculations. The decoder for the original cyclic code can be used for decoding the shortened cyclic code simply by prefixing each received vector with n zeros. This prefixing can be eliminated, however, by modifying the feedback connections of the syndrome register.

Cyclic codes and shortened cyclic codes are sometimes referred to as *polynomial codes*, since each code is uniquely specified by a generator polynomial.

7.4 HAMMING CODES

Hamming codes were discovered by R. W. Hamming of Bell Labs in 1950 [8]. This class of codes and their variations have been widely used for error-control purpose in digital systems. For this reason, these codes deserve a detailed discussion. Hamming codes were first constructed as linear (noncyclic) codes, and later coding theorists discovered that Hamming codes can be arranged into cyclic form. In the following, we will present Hamming codes in cyclic form.

A polynomial $p(X)$ of degree m with coefficients from $\{0, 1\}$ is said to be *irreducible* if $p(X)$ is not divisible by any polynomial with binary coefficients of degree less than m and greater than zero. An irreducible polynomial $p(X)$ of degree m is said to be *primitive* if and only if it divides $X^n + 1$ for no n less than $2^m - 1$. Mathematicians have shown that for any positive integer m there exists at least one primitive polynomial of degree m. Moreover, every binary primitive polynomial of degree m is a factor of $X^{2^m - 1} - 1$. A list of primitive polynomials is given in Table 7.5.

A *cyclic Hamming code* is a code whose generator polynomial is a primitive polynomial $p(X)$ of degree m. This code has the following parameters:

$$\text{Code length:} \quad n = 2^m - 1$$
$$\text{Number of information symbols:} \quad k = 2^m - m - 1$$
$$\text{Number of parity-check symbols:} \quad n - k = m$$
$$\text{Error-correcting capability:} \quad t = 1 \ (d_{\min} = 3)$$

Let

$$p(X) = 1 + p_1 X + p_2 X^2 + \ldots + X^m$$

The encoding can be accomplished easily based on $p(X)$. In the following, we will discuss the decoding of a Hamming code and we will do so by using an example.

Consider the (7, 4) cyclic code given in Table 7.4. The generator polynomial $g(X) = 1 + X + X^3$ is a primitive polynomial of degree 3. Therefore, the code is a Hamming code. Now, we want to show how to use its cyclic structure to decode it. There are seven ($n = 7$) single-error patterns, which, in polynomial

TABLE 7-5: *List of primitive polynomials.*

m	*Primitive Polynomials*
3	$1 + X + X^3$
4	$1 + X + X^4$
5	$1 + X^2 + X^5$
6	$1 + X + X^6$
7	$1 + X^3 + X^7$
8	$1 + X^2 + X^3 + X^4 + X^8$
9	$1 + X^4 + X^9$
10	$1 + X^3 + X^{10}$
11	$1 + X^2 + X^{11}$
12	$1 + X + X^4 + X^6 + X^{12}$
13	$1 + X + X^3 + X^4 + X^{13}$
14	$1 + X + X^6 + X^{10} + X^{14}$
15	$1 + X + X^{15}$
16	$1 + X + X^3 + X^{12} + X^{16}$
17	$1 + X^3 + X^{17}$
18	$1 + X^7 + X^{18}$
19	$1 + X + X^2 + X^5 + X^{19}$
20	$1 + X^3 + X^{20}$
21	$1 + X^2 + X^{21}$
22	$1 + X + X^{22}$
23	$1 + X^5 + X^{23}$
24	$1 + X + X^2 + X^7 + X^{24}$

form, are represented as $e_0(X) = X^0$, $e_1(X) = X^1$, $e_2(X) = X^2$, $e_3(X) = X^3$, $e_4(X) = X^4$, $e_5(X) = X^5$, and $e_6(X) = X^6$. If the transmitted code polynomial is $u(X) = 1 + X^3 + X^5 + X^6$ and the error polynomial is $e_4(X)$, the received polynomial is

$$r(X) = u(X) + e_4(X) = 1 + X^3 + X^4 + X^5 + X^6$$

[or the received vector is (1 0 0 1 1 1 1)]. Dividing the seven single-error patterns by the generator polynomial $g(X) = 1 + X + X^3$, we obtain their corresponding syndromes as following:

Error, $e(X)$	Syndrome, $s(X)$	Syndrome Vector, (s_0, s_1, s_2)
$e_0(X) = X^0$	$s(X) = X^0$	(1 0 0)
$e_1(X) = X^1$	$s(X) = X^1$	(0 1 0)
$e_2(X) = X^2$	$s(X) = X^2$	(0 0 1)
$e_3(X) = X^3$	$s(X) = 1 + X$	(1 1 0)
$e_4(X) = X^4$	$s(X) = X + X^2$	(0 1 1)
$e_5(X) = X^5$	$s(X) = 1 + X + X^2$	(1 1 1)
$e_6(X) = X^6$	$s(X) = 1 + X^2$	(1 0 1)

We notice that there is a one-to-one correspondence between a single-error pattern and its syndrome. Knowing the syndrome, we can locate the single error.

The syndrome $s(X)$ is computed from the received polynomial $r(X)$ by a dividing circuit as shown in Fig. 7.10. The combinational logic circuit that determines the error from the syndrome is the same as shown in Fig. 7.8. The decoding circuit for the (7, 4) cyclic Hamming code is shown in Fig. 7.15. This decoding circuit is very similar to the decoding circuit of Fig. 7.8 except that the syndrome computation circuit is simpler. Both circuits perform parallel correction, which minimizes the decoding delay.

A simpler decoding circuit for the (7, 4) Hamming code may be obtained by fully employing the cyclic structure. Suppose that a single error occurs at X^i. After the entire received vector has shifted into the syndrome register, the syndrome in the register corresponds to the error at X^i. Now, if we shift the received vector cyclically once in the buffer register and simultaneously shift the syndrome register, the error will be at the X^{i+1} and the contents in the syndrome register will be the syndrome corresponding to the error at X^{i+1}. We keep on shifting the buffer register and the syndrome register until the error digit is shifted to *rightmost stage* of the buffer register; at this point the error is at the location X^6 and the contents in the syndrome register will be the syndrome for the error at X^6. When the syndrome corresponding to the error at X^6 is detected, we know that the next digit comes out from the buffer register in an erroneous digit and must be corrected. Based on this reasoning, we may obtain a decoding circuit as shown in Fig. 7.16. This decoder performs error correction in a sequential manner. After correction the buffer register must continue shifting until the entire received vector is shifted back to its original position. The syndrome register must be also reset to zero after the correction. To carry out the correction, a total of seven shifts ($n = 7$) is required. This decoding circuit is clearly simpler than the circuit of Fig. 7.15; however, it has a longer decoding delay. If speed and simplicity cannot be achieved at the same time, a trade-off between them must be made. Figure 7.17 illustrates the error-correction process. Suppose that the code word $u(X) = 1 + X^3 + X^5 + X^6$ [or (1 0 0 1 0 1 1)] is the transmitted code word and $e(X) = X^3$ is the error polynomial. Then the received polynomial is $r(X) = 1 + X^5 + X^6$ [or the received vector is (1 0 0 0 0 1 1)]. When the entire received vector has shifted into the syndrome and buffer registers, the syndrome register contains (1 1 0), which is the syndrome for error at X^3. In Fig. 7.17 the contents in the syndrome register and the contents in the buffer register are recorded after each shift. Also, there is a pointer to indicate the error location after each shift.

The parity-check matrix H of a Hamming code can be formed easily. For a Hamming code of length $2^m - 1$ generated by a primitive polynomial $p(X)$ of degree m, the parity-check matrix consists of $2^m - 1$ columns that are the $2^m - 1$ nonzero m-tuples. Therefore, it is an $m \times (2^m - 1)$ binary matrix. Since the code is cyclic, the $2^m - 1$ nonzero m-tuples (columns) must be arranged in certain specific order. Dividing X^i by the generator polynomial $p(X)$ for $i = 0$, $1, \ldots , 2^m - 2$, we obtain a remainder $\rho_i(X)$ of degree $m - 1$ or less in the following form:

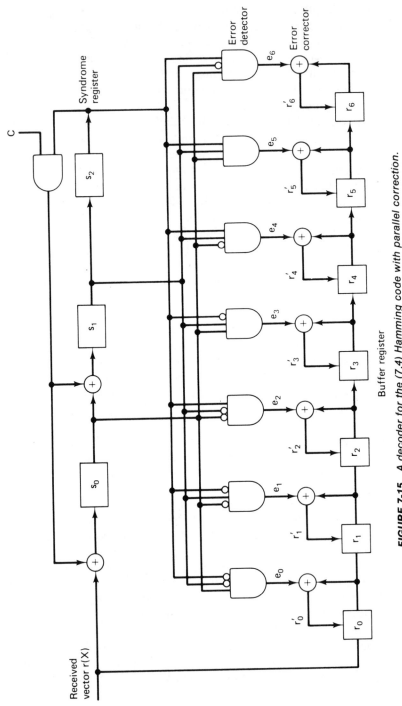

FIGURE 7-15 A decoder for the (7,4) Hamming code with parallel correction.

274

$$\rho_i(X) = \rho_{i0} + \rho_{i1}X + \rho_{i2}X^2 + \ldots + \rho_{i,m-1}X^{m-1}$$

The coefficients of $\rho_i(X)$ form an m-tuple

$$(\rho_{i0}, \rho_{i1}, \rho_{i2}, \ldots, \rho_{i,m-1})$$

For $i = 0, 1, \ldots, 2^m - 2$, we obtain $2^m - 1$ of these nonzero m-tuples. Now, we use these $2^m - 1$ m-tuples as columns of the parity-check matrix. The columns are arranged in the order of increasing power of X as shown below:

$$\text{Location numbers} \quad
\begin{matrix} X^0 & X^1 & X^2 & \cdots & X^{2^m-2} \end{matrix}$$

$$H = \begin{bmatrix}
\rho_{00} & \rho_{10} & \rho_{20} & \cdots & \rho_{2m-2,0} \\
\rho_{01} & \rho_{11} & \rho_{21} & & \rho_{2m-2,1} \\
\rho_{02} & \rho_{12} & \rho_{22} & & \rho_{2m-2,2} \\
\cdot & \cdot & \cdot & & \cdot \\
\cdot & \cdot & \cdot & & \cdot \\
\cdot & \cdot & \cdot & & \cdot \\
\rho_{0,m-1} & \rho_{1,m-1} & \rho_{2,m-1} & & \rho_{2m-2,m-1}
\end{bmatrix} \quad (7.25)$$

For $i = 0, 1, 2, \ldots, m - 1$, the remainder vectors are

$$\rho_0 = \quad (1 \quad 0 \quad 0 \quad 0 \quad \cdots \quad 0 \quad 0)$$

$$\rho_1 = \quad (0 \quad 1 \quad 0 \quad 0 \quad \cdots \quad 0 \quad 0)$$

$$\rho_2 = \quad (0 \quad 0 \quad 1 \quad 0 \quad \cdots \quad 0 \quad 0)$$

$$\cdot$$
$$\cdot$$
$$\cdot$$

$$\rho_{m-1} = \quad (0 \quad 0 \quad 0 \quad 0 \quad \cdots \quad 0 \quad 1)$$

Therefore, the **H** matrix of (7.25) actually has the following form:

$$
\begin{matrix} X^0 & X^1 & X^2 & \cdots & X^{m-1} & X^m & X^{m+1} & \cdot & X^{2^m-2} \end{matrix}
$$

$$H = \begin{bmatrix}
1 & 0 & 0 & \cdots & 0 & p_{m,0} & p_{m+1,0} & \cdot & p_{2m-2,0} \\
0 & 1 & 0 & \cdots & 0 & p_{m,1} & p_{m+1,0} & \cdot & p_{2m-2,1} \\
\cdot & & & & & & & & \cdot \\
\cdot & & & & & & & & \cdot \\
\cdot & & & & & & & & \cdot \\
0 & 0 & 0 & \cdots & 1 & p_{m,m-1} & p_{m+1,m-1} & \cdot & p_{2m-2,m-1}
\end{bmatrix} \quad (7.26)$$

$$\underbrace{\qquad\qquad}_{\substack{m \times m \text{ identity} \\ \text{matrix } I_m}} \qquad \underbrace{\qquad\qquad\qquad}_{\textbf{\textit{P}} \text{ matrix}}$$

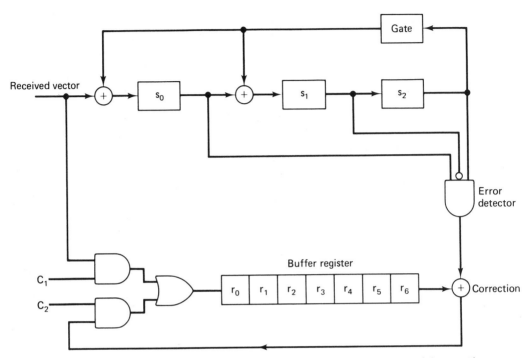

FIGURE 7-16 *A decoder for the (7, 4) Hamming code with sequential correction.*

Using this process, the parity-check matrix for the (7, 4) Hamming will be just the matrix of (7.7).

We may delete ℓ columns from the P submatrix of H to obtain an $n \times (2^m - \ell - 1)$ matrix H'. Using H' as a parity-check matrix, we would obtain a linear (in general, not cyclic) code with the following parameters:

$$\text{Code length:} \quad n = 2^m - \ell - 1$$

$$\text{Number of information symbols:} \quad k = 2^m - m - \ell - 1$$

$$\text{Number of parity-check symbols:} \quad n - k = m$$

$$d_{\min} \geqslant 3$$

This code is called a *shortened Hamming code*. If we delete columns from P properly, we may obtain shortened codes that are capable of correcting single error and simultaneously detecting double errors. For example, with $m = 8$, there exists a (255, 247) Hamming code. Let $\ell = 183$. We may shorten the (255, 247) Hamming code to a (72, 64) linear code with $d_{\min} = 4$ that is a single-error-correcting and double-error-detecting code. A (72, 64) shortened Hamming code is used in the IBM 370 Models 145, 155, and 165 processor storages.

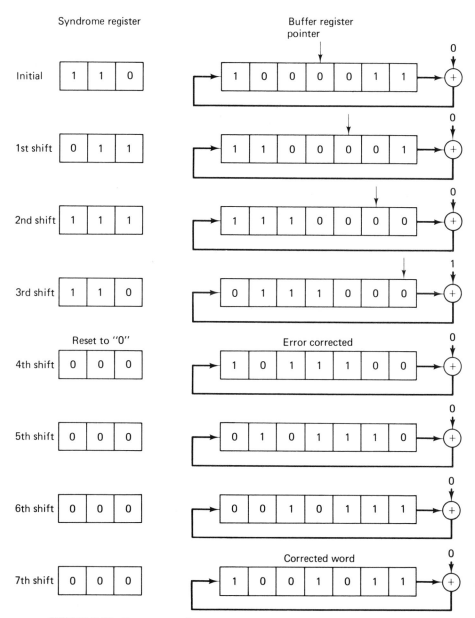

FIGURE 7-17 *Error correction process of the circuit shown in Figure 7-16.*

7.5 MAJORITY-LOGIC-DECODABLE CYCLIC CODES [5, 9]

The complexity of a cyclic code decoder depends on the structure of the code. There are subclasses of cyclic codes which can be decoded easily; one such subclass is the class of *majority-logic-decodable codes*. In the following, we will use an example to illustrate the concept of majority-logic-decoding scheme.

Consider a (21, 11) cyclic code which is generated by the following polynomial:

$$g(X) = 1 + X^2 + X^4 + X^6 + X^7 + X^{10}$$

This code has minimum distance 6 and is capable of correcting *two* or *fewer* errors. The generator matrix in systematic form for this code can be constructed easily. For $i = 0, 1, 2, \ldots, 10$, we form 11 code words for 11 messages of the following form:

$$m_i(X) = X^i$$

These code words are formed by using the encoding scheme described in Sec. 7.3.2. Then the generator matrix $\mathbf{G}$ is obtained by using these 11 code words as its rows:

$$\mathbf{G} = \begin{bmatrix}
1 & 0 & 1 & 0 & 1 & 0 & 1 & 1 & 0 & 0 & 1 & 0 & 0 & 0 & 0 & 0 & 0 & 0 & 0 & 0 & 0 \\
0 & 1 & 0 & 1 & 0 & 1 & 0 & 1 & 1 & 0 & 0 & 1 & 0 & 0 & 0 & 0 & 0 & 0 & 0 & 0 & 0 \\
0 & 0 & 1 & 0 & 1 & 0 & 1 & 0 & 1 & 1 & 0 & 0 & 1 & 0 & 0 & 0 & 0 & 0 & 0 & 0 & 0 \\
1 & 0 & 1 & 1 & 1 & 1 & 1 & 0 & 0 & 1 & 0 & 0 & 0 & 1 & 0 & 0 & 0 & 0 & 0 & 0 & 0 \\
1 & 1 & 1 & 1 & 0 & 1 & 0 & 0 & 0 & 0 & 0 & 0 & 0 & 0 & 1 & 0 & 0 & 0 & 0 & 0 & 0 \\
0 & 1 & 1 & 1 & 1 & 0 & 1 & 0 & 0 & 0 & 0 & 0 & 0 & 0 & 0 & 1 & 0 & 0 & 0 & 0 & 0 \\
0 & 0 & 1 & 1 & 1 & 1 & 0 & 1 & 0 & 0 & 0 & 0 & 0 & 0 & 0 & 0 & 1 & 0 & 0 & 0 & 0 \\
0 & 0 & 0 & 1 & 1 & 1 & 1 & 0 & 1 & 0 & 0 & 0 & 0 & 0 & 0 & 0 & 0 & 1 & 0 & 0 & 0 \\
0 & 0 & 0 & 0 & 1 & 1 & 1 & 1 & 0 & 1 & 0 & 0 & 0 & 0 & 0 & 0 & 0 & 0 & 1 & 0 & 0 \\
1 & 0 & 1 & 0 & 1 & 1 & 0 & 0 & 1 & 0 & 0 & 0 & 0 & 0 & 0 & 0 & 0 & 0 & 0 & 1 & 0 \\
0 & 1 & 0 & 1 & 0 & 1 & 1 & 0 & 0 & 1 & 0 & 0 & 0 & 0 & 0 & 0 & 0 & 0 & 0 & 0 & 1
\end{bmatrix}$$

It follows from (7.6) that we obtain the following parity-check matrix for the codes:

$$\mathbf{H} = \begin{bmatrix} h_0 \\ h_1 \\ h_2 \\ h_3 \\ h_4 \\ h_5 \\ h_6 \\ h_7 \\ h_8 \\ h_9 \end{bmatrix} = \begin{bmatrix}
1 & 0 & 0 & 0 & 0 & 0 & 0 & 0 & 0 & 0 & 1 & 0 & 0 & 1 & 1 & 0 & 0 & 0 & 0 & 1 & 0 \\
0 & 1 & 0 & 0 & 0 & 0 & 0 & 0 & 0 & 0 & 0 & 1 & 0 & 0 & 1 & 1 & 0 & 0 & 0 & 0 & 1 \\
0 & 0 & 1 & 0 & 0 & 0 & 0 & 0 & 0 & 0 & 1 & 0 & 1 & 1 & 1 & 1 & 1 & 0 & 0 & 1 & 0 \\
0 & 0 & 0 & 1 & 0 & 0 & 0 & 0 & 0 & 0 & 0 & 1 & 0 & 1 & 1 & 1 & 1 & 1 & 0 & 0 & 1 \\
0 & 0 & 0 & 0 & 1 & 0 & 0 & 0 & 0 & 0 & 1 & 0 & 1 & 1 & 0 & 1 & 1 & 1 & 1 & 1 & 0 \\
0 & 0 & 0 & 0 & 0 & 1 & 0 & 0 & 0 & 0 & 0 & 1 & 0 & 1 & 1 & 0 & 1 & 1 & 1 & 1 & 1 \\
0 & 0 & 0 & 0 & 0 & 0 & 1 & 0 & 0 & 0 & 1 & 0 & 1 & 1 & 0 & 1 & 0 & 1 & 1 & 0 & 1 \\
0 & 0 & 0 & 0 & 0 & 0 & 0 & 1 & 0 & 0 & 1 & 1 & 0 & 0 & 0 & 1 & 0 & 1 & 0 & 0 \\
0 & 0 & 0 & 0 & 0 & 0 & 0 & 0 & 1 & 0 & 0 & 1 & 1 & 0 & 0 & 0 & 1 & 0 & 1 & 0 \\
0 & 0 & 0 & 0 & 0 & 0 & 0 & 0 & 0 & 1 & 0 & 0 & 1 & 1 & 0 & 0 & 0 & 1 & 0 & 1
\end{bmatrix}$$

Now, let us form the following linear combinations of rows of the parity-check matrix H:

$$w^{(1)} = h_0 + h_5 + h_7 = (1\ 0\ 0\ 0\ 0\ 1\ 0\ 1\ 0\ 0\ 0\ 0\ 0\ 0\ 0\ 0\ 0\ 1\ 0\ 0\ 1)$$

$$w^{(2)} = h_1 \qquad\qquad = (0\ 1\ 0\ 0\ 0\ 0\ 0\ 0\ 0\ 0\ 0\ 1\ 0\ 0\ 1\ 1\ 0\ 0\ 0\ 0\ 1)$$

$$w^{(3)} = h_2 + h_3 + h_8 = (0\ 0\ 1\ 1\ 0\ 0\ 0\ 0\ 1\ 0\ 1\ 0\ 0\ 0\ 0\ 0\ 0\ 0\ 0\ 0\ 1)$$

$$w^{(4)} = h_4 + h_6 \qquad = (0\ 0\ 0\ 0\ 1\ 0\ 1\ 0\ 0\ 0\ 0\ 0\ 0\ 0\ 0\ 0\ 1\ 0\ 0\ 1\ 1)$$

$$w^{(5)} = h_9 \qquad\qquad = (0\ 0\ 0\ 0\ 0\ 0\ 0\ 0\ 0\ 1\ 0\ 0\ 1\ 1\ 0\ 0\ 0\ 0\ 1\ 0\ 1)$$

The vectors above have the following properties: (1) the rightmost component of each vector is a "1"; and (2) no two vectors have a "1" at any other location.

Let $r = (r_0, r_1, \ldots, r_{20})$ be the received vector. Then r is the sum of a code word $u = (u_0, u_1, \ldots, u_{20})$ and an error vector $e = (e_0, e_1, \ldots, e_{20})$:

$$r = u + e \tag{7.27}$$

Taking the inner products of r and the vectors $w^{(1)}$, $w^{(2)}$, $w^{(3)}$, $w^{(4)}$, and $w^{(5)}$, we obtain the following sums of received digits:

$$A_1 = r \cdot w^{(1)} = r_0 + r_5 + r_7 + r_{17} + r_{20}$$

$$A_2 = r \cdot w^{(2)} = r_1 + r_{11} + r_{14} + r_{15} + r_{20}$$

$$A_3 = r \cdot w^{(3)} = r_2 + r_3 + r_8 + r_{10} + r_{20} \tag{7.28}$$

$$A_4 = r \cdot w^{(4)} = r_4 + r_6 + r_{16} + r_{19} + r_{20}$$

$$A_5 = r \cdot w^{(5)} = r_9 + r_{12} + r_{13} + r_{18} + r_{20}$$

Since u is a code word, the inner product of u and any row of the parity-check matrix is zero. Hence, $u \cdot w^{(i)} = 0$ for $1 \le i \le 5$. Using this fact and (7.27), we obtain the following relations between the sums A_i and the error digits:

$$A_1 = e_0 + e_5 + e_7 + e_{17} + e_{20}$$

$$A_2 = e_1 + e_{11} + e_{14} + e_{15} + e_{20}$$

$$A_3 = e_2 + e_3 + e_8 + e_{10} + e_{20} \tag{7.29}$$

$$A_4 = e_4 + e_6 + e_{16} + e_{19} + e_{20}$$

$$A_5 = e_9 + e_{12} + e_{13} + e_{18} + e_{20}$$

Thus, each A_i is simply a sum of certain error digits. These sums are referred to as *checksums*. An error digit e_ℓ is said to be checked by A_i if e_ℓ is contained in A_i. We notice that the error digit e_{20} is checked by all the checksums of (7.29), and no other error digit is checked by more than one checksum. We say that these checksums are *orthogonal* on e_{20}. Since these orthogonal checksums are obtained from the vectors $w^{(1)}$, $w^{(2)}$, $w^{(3)}$, $w^{(4)}$, and $w^{(5)}$, we call these vectors *orthogonal vectors*. The checksums orthogonal on e_{20} will be used to decode e_{20} based on a *majority* decision scheme.

The code given above is capable of correcting two or fewer errors. Suppose that there are two or fewer errors in the error vector e (i.e., two or fewer digits of e are "1"). If $e_{20} = 0$, the nonzero digits of e can distribute among at most two checksums of (7.29). Hence, there are at least three checksums which are equal to $e_{20} = 0$. If, on the other hand, $e_{20} = 1$, there are at least four checksums of (7.29) that are equal to "1." Thus, e_{20} is equal to the value which is assumed by a *clear majority* of the checksums orthogonal on e_{20}. Based on the preceding facts, we can decode e_{20} in the following manner. The error digit e_{20} is decoded as "1" if a clear majority of the checksums orthogonal on e_{20} is "1"; otherwise, e_{20} is decoded as "0." Correct decoding of e_{20} is guaranteed if two or fewer errors occur in the error vector e. Since the code is cyclic, the decoding of the other error digits is the same as the decoding of e_{20}. The decoding scheme described above is called *majority-logic decoding*.

Based on (7.28), a majority-logic-decoding circuit for the example code is shown in Fig. 7.18. The error-correction procedure is described as follows:

- *Step 1.* The received vector is read into the buffer register with gate 1 on and gate 2 off.

- *Step 2.* The checksums orthogonal on e_{20} are formed by summing appropriate received digits based on (7.28).

- *Step 3.* The orthogonal check sums are inputed to a majority-logic gate (The output of this gate is "1" if and only if majority of its inputs are "1"; otherwise, the output is "0"). The received digit r_{20} is read out of the buffer (with gate 1 off and gate 2 on) and is corrected by the output of the majority-logic gate.

- *Step 4.* After step 3, the buffer register has been shifted cyclically one place to the right. Now the second received digit is in the rightmost stage of the buffer register and will be corrected in exactly the same manner as the first received digit was. The decoder repeats steps 2 and 3.

The received vector is decoded digit by digit in the manner described above until a total 21 digits have been decoded. Correct decoding is guaranteed, provided that two or fewer errors occur in the received vector.

A code that can be decoded in the foregoing manner is said to be *majority-logic-decodable*. For an (n, k) cyclic code, if J checksums orthogonal on the error digit e_{n-1} can be formed, it is capable of correcting $[J/2]$ or fewer errors by using the majority-decoding scheme. Let d_{min} be the minimum distance of the code. The code is said to be *completely orthogonalizable* if $J = d_{min} - 1$. Majority-logic decoding is simple and can be implemented easily. Many efficient

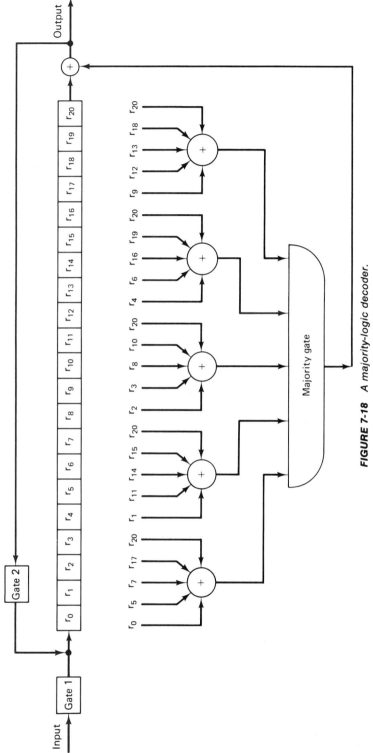

FIGURE 7-18 A majority-logic decoder.

281

majority-logic-decodable cyclic codes have been found, some codes require multilevel majority decision for decoding.

There is another subclass of powerful random-error-correcting cyclic codes known as Bose–Chaudhuri–Hocquenghem (BCH) codes. The construction and decoding of BCH codes are based on the finite fields. It is beyond the scope of this introductorial chapter to discuss the theory of finite field. An excellent treatment of BCH codes can be found in Berlekamp [4], Peterson and Weldon [3], and MacWilliams and Sloane [6].

7.6 BURST-ERROR CORRECTING CODES

Cyclic codes are not only effective for burst-error detection, they are also very effective for burst-error correction. Many effective cyclic codes for correcting burst errors have been discovered for the past 20 years. The first class of cyclic codes, which is constructed systematically for correcting a single burst of errors over a span of n digits, is the class of *Fire codes* [3, 10]. Fire codes can be decoded in a very simple manner. In the following, we will give a brief discussion of these codes.

Let $p(X)$ be an irreducible polynomial of degree m. Let e be the smallest positive integer such that $X^e + 1$ is divisible by $p(X)$. This integer e is called the period of $p(X)$. A Fire code that is capable of correcting all error bursts of length b or less is generated by the following polynomial:

$$g(X) = p(X)(X^{2b-1} + 1)$$

where $b \leq m$ and $2b - 1$ is not divisible by e. The length of this code is the least common multiple of e and $2b - 1$:

$$n = \text{LCM}(e, 2b - 1)$$

The number of parity-check digits is $m + 2b - 1$. For example, $p(X) = 1 + X + X^4$ is an irreducible polynomial of degree 4 whose period is $e = 15$. Let $b = 4$. Clearly, $2b - 1 = 7$ is not divisible by $e = 15$. Consider the Fire code generated by

$$g(X) = (1 + X + X^4)(1 + X^7)$$
$$= 1 + X + X^4 + X^7 + X^8 + X^{11}$$

The length of this code is

$$n = \text{LCM}(15, 7) = 105$$

Hence, it is a (105, 94) cyclic code which is capable of correcting any single error burst of length 4 or less.

Fire codes can be most easily decoded by the error-trapping technique. We will use the (105, 94) code described above to illustrate the error-trapping decoding. Suppose that an error burst of length 4 or less has occurred starting at location X^i and ending at location X^{i+l} with $\ell \leq 3$. Thus, the error burst has the following form:

$$e(X) = X^i(1 + b_1X + b_2X^2 + b_3X^3)$$

where $b_j = 0$ or 1, $B(X) = 1 + b_1X + b_2X^2 + b_3X^3$ is the burst pattern, and X^i indicates the location of the burst. Once $B(X)$ and i are determined, the correction is accomplished by adding $X^iB(X)$ to the received polynomial $r(X)$.

The error-trapping decoder for the (105, 94) is shown in Fig. 7.19. The received polynomial $r(X)$ is shifted into the syndrome register from the right end with gate 1 being opened and gate 2 being closed. Shifting $r(X)$ into the syndrome register from the right end is equivalent to premultiplying $r(X)$ by X^{11}. The contents in the syndrome register are the syndrome of the vector $r^{(11)}(X)$ obtained by cyclically shifting $r(X)$ *eleven* times. Suppose that the error burst is confined to the first four highest-order positions X^{101}, X^{102}, X^{103}, and X^{104} of $r(X)$ [i.e., $e(X) = X^{101}B(X)$]. Then the burst is confined to the positions X^7, X^8, X^9, and X^{10} of $r^{(11)}(X)$ [i.e., $e^{(11)}(X) = X^7B(X)$]. Since the syndrome $s(X) = s_0 + s_1X + \ldots + s_{10}X^{10}$ in the syndrome register is the remainder of $r^{(11)}(X)$ divided by the generator polynomial $g(X)$, we have

$$s(X) = X^7B(X)$$
$$= b_0X^7 + b_1X^8 + b_2X^9 + b_3X^{10}$$

In this case, the first seven stages of the syndrome register contain only zeros and the burst $B(X)$ is *trapped* in the last four stages.

Suppose that the burst is not confined to the positions X^{101}, X^{102}, X^{103}, and X^{104} of $r(X)$ but are confined to four consecutive positions of $r(X)$ *(including the end-around case)*. When the entire received polynomial $r(X)$ has been read into the syndrome register, the burst is *not contained* in the last four stages of the syndrome register and the first seven stages *do not contain* all zeros. However, if we cyclically shift $r(X)$ in the buffer register and the syndrome register simultaneously with gates 1 and 4 opened and gate 2 closed, eventually after certain number of shifts, say i, the burst will be confined to the highest-order positions X^{101}, X^{102}, X^{103}, and X^{104} of $r^{(i)}(X)$ in the buffer register, and at the same time the burst is trapped in the last four stages of the syndrome register. This event is detected when the first *seven* stages of the syndrome register *contain* only zeros. When this event occurs, gate 1 is closed and gate 2 is opened. The burst is shifted out of the syndrome register and is added to the received polynomial coming out from the buffer register.

The operation of the error-trapping decoder shown in Fig. 7.19 is described in the following:

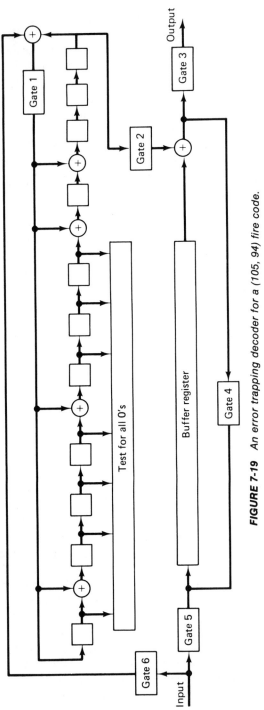

FIGURE 7-19 An error trapping decoder for a (105, 94) fire code.

1. The entire received polynomial $r(X)$ is shifted into the syndrome register and the buffer register simultaneously with gate 1 opened and gate 2 closed.

2. After the entire received polynomial $r(X)$ has been shifted into the syndrome and buffer registers, both registers are shifted one bit at a time with no input: gates 1 and 4 opened, gates 2 and 3 closed.

3. As soon as all zeros appear in the first seven stages of the syndrome register, the error burst is trapped in the last four stages. The next four digits to come out from the buffer register are erroneous digits and must be corrected. At this time, gate 1 is closed, gate 2 is opened, and the burst in the syndrome register is shifted out to correct the erroneous digits coming out from the buffer register.

4. After a total n shift, gate 3 is opened and the received vector in the buffer is then read out one bit at a time.

7.7 CONVOLUTIONAL CODES

As we have just seen, a block encoder accepts k-bit message blocks and generates n-bit code words. The encoder must buffer the entire k-bit message block before a code word is generated. Hence, code words are produced block by block in an intermittant fashion. The encoder itself requires no memory (other than the buffer) and hence can be implemented with a combinational logic circuit.

A *convolutional encoder*, on the other hand, processes message bits continuously in a serial fashion. At each time unit, b message bits enter the encoder and v code-word bits are generated, where b and v are typically small integers and $b < v$. The v code word bits generated at a given time depend on the b message bits at that time plus the message bits at the previous m time units. Hence, the encoder requires an m time-unit memory, and must be implemented with a sequential logic circuit.

The total number of code-word bits that can be affected by a single message bit is given by $N = (m + 1)v$ and is called the code *constraint length*. Since the encoder generates v code-word bits for each b message bits, $R = b/v$ is called the *code rate*. An encoder for an $R = \frac{1}{3}$ code with $m = 2$ is shown in Fig. 7.20. x_i represents the message bit entering the encoder at time i, and y_{1i}, y_{2i}, and y_{3i} represent the code word bits generated at time i. Note that the encoder is a linear sequential circuit.

To understand the operation of the encoder we must introduce a little terminology. To simplify the notation, we will assume that $b = 1$ (i.e., only one message bit enters the encoder per unit time). We stress, however, that all of the analysis techniques and decoding methods presented in this section also apply to codes with $b > 1$.

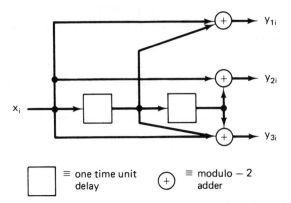

FIGURE 7-20   *A convolutional encoder for an R = 1/3 code with m = 2.*

Let $x = (x_0, x_1, x_2, \ldots)$ be the *information sequence* (message). x can also be represented by the polynomial $X(D) = x_0 + x_1 D + x_2 D^2 + \ldots$, where D denotes a one-time-unit delay. A rate $R = 1/v$ code with constraint length $N = (m + 1)v$ is described by a set of v *generator sequences* $g_j = (g_{j0}, g_{j1}, \ldots, g_{jm})$, $j = 1, 2, \ldots, v$. These can also be represented as polynomials, $G_j(D) = g_{j0} + g_{j1}D + \ldots + g_{jm}D^m$, of degree m. The generator sequences can be interpreted as the v "impulse responses" of the encoder [i.e., the output sequences when the information sequence is $x = (1 \quad 0 \quad 0 \ldots)$]. For the encoder of Fig. 7.20, $g_1 = (1 \quad 1 \quad 0)$, $g_2 = (1 \quad 0 \quad 1)$, and $g_3 = (1 \quad 1 \quad 1)$. The generator polynomials are $G_1(D) = 1 + D$, $G_2(D) = 1 + D^2$, and $G_3(D) = 1 + D + D^2$. Note that each generator sequence can be determined directly from the sequence of connections from the delay units to the corresponding output, a "1" representing a connection and a "0" no connection.

The encoder outputs are represented by a set of v *transmitted sequences* $y_j = (y_{j0}, y_{j1}, y_{j2}, \ldots), j = 1, 2, \ldots, v$, which can also be written as polynomials, $Y_j(D) = y_{j0} + y_{j1}D + y_{j2}D^2 + \ldots$. The *encoding equations* are given by

$$y_j = x \star g_j \qquad j = 1, 2, \ldots, v \tag{7.30}$$

where $\star$ denotes discrete convolution and all operations are over the binary field:

$$y_{ji} = x_i g_{j0} + x_{i-1} g_{j1} + \ldots + x_{i-m} g_{jm} \tag{7.31}$$

For the encoder of Fig. 7.20,

$$y_{1i} = x_i + x_{i-1} \tag{7.32a}$$

$$y_{2i} = x_i + x_{i-2} \tag{7.32b}$$

$$y_{3i} = x_i + x_{i-1} + x_{i-2} \tag{7.32c}$$

It can easily be shown that (7.30) is equivalent to

$$Y_j(D) = X(D)G_j(D) \qquad j = 1, 2, \ldots, v \tag{7.33}$$

Hence, the generator polynomials can be interpreted as the v "transfer functions" of the encoder.

Finally, the v transmitted sequences are multiplexed into a single sequence prior to transmission, resulting in the *code word*

$$y = (y_{10}y_{20} \ldots y_{v0}, y_{11}y_{21} \ldots y_{v1}, y_{12}y_{22} \ldots y_{v2}, \ldots)$$

or $\qquad Y(D) = Y_1(D^v) + DY_2(D^v) + \ldots + D^{v-1}Y_v(D^v)$

As an example, consider the code of Fig. 7.20 with $x = (1\ 0\ 1\ 1\ 1)$. Then

$$y_1 = x \star g_1 = (1\ 0\ 1\ 1\ 1) \star (1\ 1\ 0) = (1\ 1\ 1\ 0\ 0\ 1\ 0) \tag{7.34a}$$

$$y_2 = x \star g_2 = (1\ 0\ 1\ 1\ 1) \star (1\ 0\ 1) = (1\ 0\ 0\ 1\ 0\ 1\ 1) \tag{7.34b}$$

$$y_3 = x \star g_3 = (1\ 0\ 1\ 1\ 1) \star (1\ 1\ 1) = (1\ 1\ 0\ 0\ 1\ 0\ 1) \tag{7.34c}$$

Using the polynomial representation yields

$$Y_1(D) = X(D)G_1(D) = (1 + D^2 + D^3 + D^4)(1 + D) = 1 + D + D^2 + D^5 \tag{7.35a}$$

$$Y_2(D) = X(D)G_2(D) = (1 + D^2 + D^3 + D^4)(1 + D^2) = 1 + D^3 + D^5 + D^6 \tag{7.35b}$$

$$Y_3(D) = X(D)G_3(D) = (1 + D^2 + D^3 + D^4)(1 + D + D^2) = 1 + D + D^4 + D^6 \tag{7.35c}$$

The code word is given by $y = (1\ 1\ 1, 1\ 0\ 1, 1\ 0\ 0, 0\ 1\ 0, 0\ 0\ 1,$ $1\ 1\ 0, 0\ 1\ 1)$ or $Y(D) = 1 + D + D^2 + D^3 + D^5 + D^6 + D^{10} + D^{14} + D^{15} + D^{16} + D^{19} + D^{20}$.

Since a convolutional encoder is a linear sequential circuit, it can be described by a *state diagram*. The state diagram for the encoder of Fig. 7.20 is shown in Fig. 7.21. The encoder state at time i is the set $x_{i-1}, x_{i-2}, \ldots, x_{i-m}$ of delay unit outputs at time i (i.e., the past m information bits). Hence, there is a total of 2^m states in the state diagram. Each input causes a transition to a new state. There are two branches leaving each state, one corresponding to the input $x_i = 0$ and the other to $x_i = 1$. Each branch is labeled with the encoder input (x_i) and the v outputs $(y_{1i}y_{2i} \ldots y_{vi})$ corresponding to that state transition.

Assuming that the all-zero state is the initial state, the code word corresponding to any given information sequence can be determined by tracing the indicated path through the state diagram, and then returning to the all-zero state. For example, from Fig. 7.21 if $x = (1\ 1\ 1\ 0\ 1)$, then $y = (1\ 1\ 1, 0\ 1\ 0,$ $0\ 0\ 1, 1\ 1\ 0, 1\ 0\ 0, 1\ 0\ 1, 0\ 1\ 1)$. Note that the last m blocks of any code word are produced while the encoder is returning to the all-zero state after accepting the last nonzero information bit.

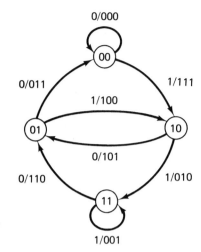

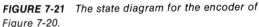

FIGURE 7-21   *The state diagram for the encoder of Figure 7-20.*

7.7.1   Distance Properties of Convolutional Codes

We have already seen that for block coders, the minimum-distance properties of the code play an important role in determining its performance in a noisy environment. This is also true for convolutional codes. The distance measure of most interest in convolutional codes is the minimum *free distance* d_f, defined as the minimum value of the Hamming distance $d_H(y, y')$ between all pairs of distinct code words y and y':

$$d_f = \min_{y \neq y'} d_H(y, y') \tag{7.36}$$

Since each code word bit y_{ji} is a linear combination of information bits [see (7.31)], a convolutional code is a linear code, and hence

$$d_f = \min_{y \neq y'} d_H(y, y') = \min_{y \neq 0} w_H(y) \tag{7.37}$$

where $w_H(y)$ is the Hamming weight of y. From Fig. 7.21 it can be seen that the nonzero code word with minimum weight is $y = (1\ 1\ 1, 1\ 0\ 1, 0\ 1\ 1)$, and hence $d_f = 7$ for this code.

Following the work of Viterbi [11], we will now use a modified state diagram to provide a complete description of the weights of all nonzero code words (i.e., a weight enumerator for the code).[1] The all-zero state is split into an initial state

[1]   Only code words that diverge from and remerge with the all-zero state once will be considered. Code words that remerge more than once can be considered as a sequence of shorter code words.

and a final state, the self-loop around the all-zero state is deleted, and each branch is labeled with W^i, where i is the weight of the v code word bits on that branch. W^i is called the *branch gain*. The modified state diagram for the encoder of Fig. 7.20 is shown in Fig. 7.22.

Each path connecting the initial state to the final state represents a nonzero code word. The *path gain* is the product of the branch gains along the path, and the weight of a code word is the exponent of W in its path gain. For example, the path represented by the state sequence 0 0, 1 0, 0 1, 0 0 in Fig. 7.22 has path gain $W^3 \cdot W^2 \cdot W^2 = W^7$, and the corresponding code word has weight 7.

The set of weights of all nonzero code words can be determined by considering the modified state diagram as a signal flow graph and applying Mason's gain formula [12] to compute its "generating function" $T(W)$. For the code of Fig. 7.22,

$$T(W) = \frac{W^7(1 - W) + W^8}{1 - (W + W^3 + W^4) + (W \cdot W^3)} = \frac{W^7}{1 - W(1 + W^2)}$$

$$= W^7[1 + W(1 + W^2) + W^2(1 + W^2)^2 + W^3(1 + W^2)^3 + \ldots] \quad (7.38)$$

$$= W^7 + W^8 + W^9 + 2W^{10} + \ldots$$

Hence, there is one code word of weight 7, one of weight 8, one of weight 9, two of weight 10, and so on. Note that the free distance d_f (7 in this example) is the weight of the lowest-order term in $T(W)$.

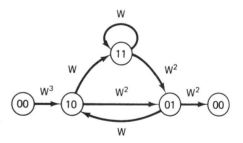

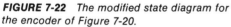

FIGURE 7-22 *The modified state diagram for the encoder of Figure 7-20.*

The modified state diagram can be augmented by labeling each branch corresponding to a nonzero information bit with B. The "generating function" $T(W, B)$ will then give the weight of each information sequence as well as the weight of each code word. The modified state diagram of Fig. 7.22 is shown augmented in Fig. 7.23. The "generating function" is given by

$$T(W, B) = \frac{W^7B(1 - WB) + W^8B^2}{1 - (WB + W^3B + W^4B^2) + (WB \cdot W^3B)} = \frac{W^7B}{1 - WB(1 + W^2)}$$

$$= W^7B[1 + WB(1 + W^2) + W^2B^2(1 + W^2)^2 + W^3B^3(1 + W^2)^3 + \ldots] \quad (7.39)$$

$$= W^7B + W^8B^2 + W^9B^3 + W^{10}(B^2 + B^4) + \ldots$$

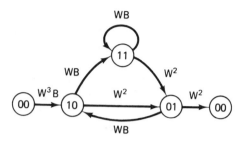

FIGURE 7-23 *The augmented modified state diagram for the encoder of Figure 7-20.*

Hence, the code word of weight 7 has a weight 1 information sequence, and so on. Note that one code word of weight 10 has a weight 2 information sequence and the other has a weight 4 information sequence.

This generating function approach to finding the weights of all nonzero code words and their corresponding information sequences is severely limited by the number of states in the encoder. For $m > 4$, this approach becomes much too unwieldly. Fortunately, as we shall see in Sec. 7.7.3, it is primarily the lowest-order term (the free-distance term) in the generating function which determines the performance of a code when used with maximum likelihood decoding.

Another important distance measure for convolutional codes is the *column distance function* (CDF). The column distance function of order i, $d_c(i)$, is the minimum Hamming distance between the first $i + 1$ blocks of any two code words y and y' which differ in block zero:

$$d_c(i) = \min d_H([y]_i, [y']_i) = \min w_H([y]_i)$$
$$[y]_0 \neq [y']_0 \qquad\qquad [y]_0 \neq 0$$

(7.40)

where $[y]_i = (y_{10}y_{20} \cdots y_{v0}, y_{11}y_{21} \cdots y_{v1}, \ldots, y_{1i}y_{2i} \cdots y_{vi})$.

The CDF for the code of Fig. 7.20 is plotted in Fig. 7.24. Note that $d_c(i)$ is a monotonically nondecreasing function of i.

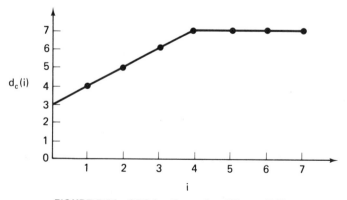

FIGURE 7-24 *CDF for the code of Figure 7-20.*

The CDF determines the computational performance of a code when used with sequential decoding, as will be seen in Sec. 7.7.4. Two specific values of the CDF assume additional interest: $d_c(m)$ (sometimes denoted d_m), the minimum distance over one constraint length, and $\lim i \to \infty \ d_c(i)$, which is just the free distance d_f. It can be seen from Fig. 7.24 that $d_m = 5$ for the code of Fig. 7.20. We will see in Sec. 7.7.5 that d_m determines the performance of a code when used with threshold decoding.

7.7.2 Maximum Likelihood Decoding

In discussing maximum likelihood decoding, it is convenient to expand the state diagram in time (i.e., to represent each time unit with a separate state diagram). The resulting structure is called a *trellis diagram* and is shown in Fig. 7.25 for the code of Fig. 7.20 and an information sequence of length $L = 5$. For an information sequence of length L, the trellis diagram contains $L + m$ levels, the last m levels corresponding to the encoder's return to the all-zero state. Since the encoder always starts in the all-zero state and returns to the all-zero state,

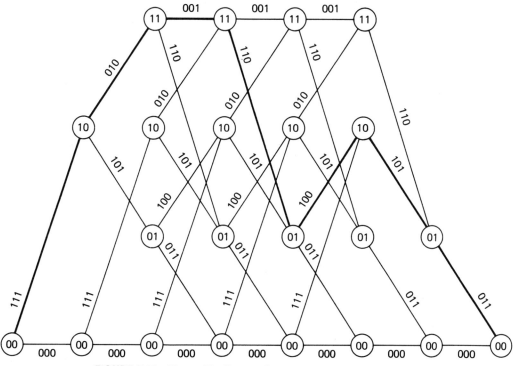

FIGURE 7-25 *The trellis diagram for the encoder of Figure 7-20 and L = 5.*

not all states are possible in the first m or the last m trellis levels. However, in between all states are possible and each trellis level is a replica of the state diagram. Of the two branches leaving each state, the upper one always represents $x_i = 1$ while the lower one represents $x_i = 0$, and each branch is labeled with the v corresponding outputs. Note that each of the 2^L code words of length $n = v(L + m)$ is represented by a unique path through the trellis. For example, the code word corresponding to $x = (1 \ 1 \ 1 \ 0 \ 1)$ is shown highlighted in Fig. 7.25.

Now assume that an information sequence $x = (x_0, x_1, \ldots, x_{L-1})$ of length L is encoded into a code word $y = (y_0, y_1, \ldots, y_{n-1})$ of length $n = v(L + m)$, and that a Q-ary sequence $r = (r_0, r_1, \ldots, r_{n-1})$ is received over a Q-ary output *discrete memoryless channel* (DMC), such as illustrated in Fig. 7.26. The transition probabilities shown in Fig. 7.26 are defined by

$$P(j \mid i) = P(j \text{ received} \mid i \text{ transmitted}) \tag{7.41}$$

If $Q = 2$, r is a binary sequence, and the demodulator output is said to be *hard quantized*. If $Q > 2$, the demodulator output is said to be *soft quantized*. It is well known (see, e.g., Wozencraft and Jacobs [13]) that for channels disturbed by *additive white Gaussian noise* (AWGN), the digital channel can be modeled as a DMC and soft quantization yields a 2 to 3 dB performance improvement over hard quantization. In other words, a "soft decoder" gives the same error probability as a "hard decoder" with 2 to 3 dB less signal power at the transmitter.

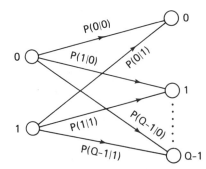

FIGURE 7-26 *A Q-ary output DMC.*

The decoder must produce an estimate $\hat{y}$ of the code word y based on the *received sequence r*. We define an optimum decoder as one that minimizes the *sequence error probability* $P(E)$ given by

$$P(E) = P(\hat{y} \neq y) \tag{7.42}$$

$P(E)$ can be rewritten as

$$P(E) = \sum_r P(E, r) = \sum_r P(E \mid r) P(r) \tag{7.43}$$

Since $P(r)$ is independent of the decoding rule, an optimum decoder must minimize $P(E \mid r)$, or equivalently maximize $P(C \mid r)$, for all r, where

$$P(C \mid r) = P(\hat{y} = y \mid r) \tag{7.44}$$

is the probability that the decoder makes a correct decision given that r is received. Hence, the optimum decoding rule chooses $\hat{y}$ as the code word y which maximizes

$$P(y \mid r) = \frac{P(r \mid y)\, P(y)}{P(r)} \tag{7.45}$$

or, since $P(r)$ is independent of the decoding rule, the optimum decoder maximizes $P(r \mid y)\, P(y)$.

A *maximum likelihood decoder* (MLD) is one that maximizes $P(r \mid y)$. Clearly, a MLD is optimum when all code words are equally likely [i.e., $P(y)$ is the same for all y]. Maximizing $P(r \mid y)$ is equivalent to maximizing

$$\log P(r \mid y) = \log \prod_{i=1}^{n} P(r_i \mid y_i) \tag{7.46}$$

For a *binary symmetric channel* (BSC, $Q = 2$) with crossover probability $P(1 \mid 0) = P(0 \mid 1) = p$, (7.46) reduces to

$$\log P(r \mid y) = \log p^{d_H(r,\,y)}(1-p)^{n \,-\, d_H(r,\,y)}$$

$$= d_H(\mathbf{r}, \mathbf{y}) \log \frac{p}{1-p} + n \log (1-p) \tag{7.47}$$

Since $\log [p/(1-p)] < 0$ for $p < \frac{1}{2}$ and $n \log (1-p)$ is a constant for all y, a MLD for a BSC

> chooses $\hat{y}$ as the path through the trellis (code word) which is closest to r in Hamming distance

The following algorithm, due to Viterbi [14], when applied to the received sequence r from a BSC, finds the path through the trellis which is closest to r in Hamming distance (i.e., the maximum likelihood path).

Viterbi Algorithm (BSC)

- *Step 0.* Beginning at the first level of the trellis for which two paths enter each state, compute the distances from r to the two paths entering each state, and store for each state the path closest to *r* (the *survivor*) along with its distance from *r* (the *metric*).

- *Step 1.* Repeat step 0 for each level in the trellis. The metric for a path (its distance from *r*) is computed by adding the metric of the survivor at the previous level to its distance from *r* on the next branch.

Note that there are 2^m survivors at each level (the best path into each state) up to the last *m* levels, but that there is only one survivor when the algorithm terminates since all paths return to the all-zero state. We now prove that the final survivor is the maximum likelihood (ML) path. First assume that the ML path is eliminated by the algorithm at some point, as illustrated in Fig. 7.27. This implies that the initial portion of the survivor along with the remainder of the ML path is closer to *r* than the ML path. But this contradicts the definition of the ML path, and hence the ML path is never eliminated and must be the final survivor.

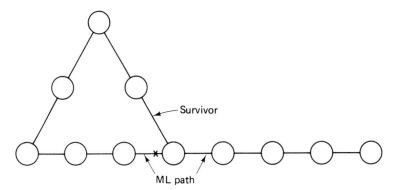

FIGURE 7-27 *Path elimination in the Viterbi algorithm.*

In Fig. 7.28 we show an example of the application of the Viterbi algorithm to the trellis of Fig. 7.25 for a received sequence $r = (1 \ 0 \ 1, 1 \ 1 \ 0, 0 \ 0 \ 1, 1 \ 1 \ 0, 1 \ 1 \ 1, 1 \ 1 \ 1, 1 \ 0 \ 1)$. The numbers above each state represent the metric of the survivor for that state, and the paths eliminated by the algorithm are shown crossed out on the trellis diagram. Note that at some states neither path is crossed out, indicating a tie in the metric values. If the final survivor goes through any of these states, there must be more than one ML path. From an implementation point of view, whenever a tie in metric values occurs, one path is arbitrarily selected as the survivor, because of the impracticality of storing a variable number of paths. This arbitrary resolution of ties has no effect on *P(E)*.

In this example the final survivor is $\hat{y}$ = (1 1 1, 0 1 0, 0 0 1, 1 1 0, 1 0 0, 1 0 1, 0 1 1), which is the highlighted path in Fig. 7.28. $\hat{y}$ differs from r in seven positions, and since it is the ML path, no other path through the trellis differs from r in fewer than eight positions. The information sequence corresponding to $\hat{y}$ is given by $\hat{x}$ = (1 1 1 0 1).

The Viterbi algorithm can also be used as a MLD for soft-quantized channels. For a DMC with $Q > 2$, a MLD maximizes [see (7.46)]

$$\log P\,(r\mid y) = \log \prod_{i=1}^{n} P(r_i\mid y_i) = \sum_{i=1}^{n} \log P(r_i\mid y_i) \tag{7.48}$$

and $\log P(r_i\mid y_i)$ can be used as the metric for the ith bit in the code word y. As an example, consider the 4-ary output DMC shown in Fig. 7.29. Using logarithms to the base 10, the metric table for this channel is shown in Fig. 7.30. The Viterbi algorithm for DMCs with $Q > 2$ now follows.

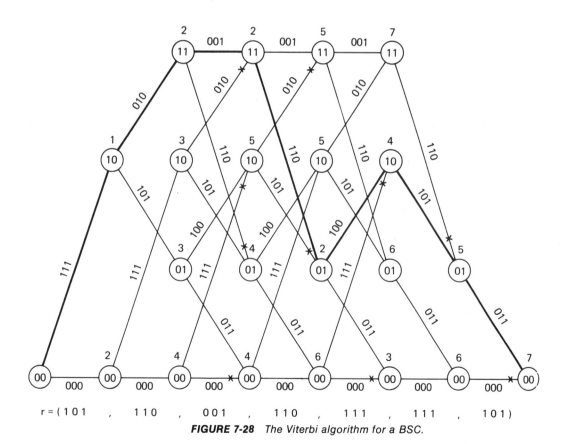

$r = (1\ 0\ 1 \quad , \quad 1\ 1\ 0 \quad , \quad 0\ 0\ 1 \quad , \quad 1\ 1\ 0 \quad , \quad 1\ 1\ 1 \quad , \quad 1\ 1\ 1 \quad , \quad 1\ 0\ 1)$

FIGURE 7-28 *The Viterbi algorithm for a BSC.*

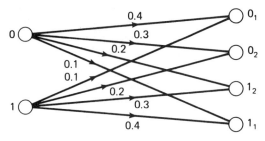

FIGURE 7-29 *A 4-ary output DMC.*

Viterbi Algorithm (DMC)

- *Step 0*. Beginning at the first level of the trellis for which two paths enter each state, compute the metrics of the two paths entering each state, and store for each state the path with the largest metric (the survivor) along with its metric.

- *Step 1*. Repeat step 0 for each level in the trellis. The metric for a path is computed by adding the metric of the survivor at the previous level to its metric on the next branch.

In terms of implementation, it is more convenient to use positive integers as metrics. Following the suggestion of Massey [15], the bit metric $\log P(r_i \mid y_i)$ can be replaced by $c_2[\log P(r_i \mid y_i) + c_1]$, where c_1 is any real number and c_2 is any positive real number. If c_1 is chosen to make the smallest metric zero, c_2 can then be chosen so that all metrics can be approximated by integers. For the metric table of Fig. 7.30, choosing $c_1 = 1$ and $c_2 = 17.3$ yields the integer metric table shown in Fig. 7.31. Clearly, there are many integer metric tables possible for a given channel depending on the choice c_2. The performance of the Viterbi algorithm, which is now slightly suboptimum due to the metric approximation by integers, has been shown by Heller and Jacobs [16] to be quite insensitive to the choice of an integer metric table.

r_i / y_i	0_1	0_2	1_2	1_1
0	−0.4	−0.52	−0.7	−1
1	−1	−0.7	−0.52	−0.4

FIGURE 7-30 *Metric table for the channel of Figure 7-29.*

r_i / y_i	0_1	0_2	1_2	1_1
0	10	8	5	0
1	0	5	8	10

FIGURE 7-31 *An integer metric table for the channel of Figure 7-29.*

As an example of the application of the Viterbi algorithm to a soft-quantized channel, consider again the trellis of Fig. 7.25, the 4-ary output DMC of Fig. 7.29, the integer metric table of Fig. 7.31, and a received sequence

$$r = (1_1 \ 1_2 \ 0_1, \ 1_1 \ 1_1 \ 0_2, \ 1_1 \ 1_1 \ 0_1, \ 1_1 \ 1_1 \ 1_1, \ 0_1 \ 1_2 \ 0_1, \ 1_2 \ 0_2 \ 1_1, \ 1_2 \ 0_1 \ 1_1)$$

The result is shown in Fig. 7.32, with the final survivor $\hat{y} = (1 \ 1 \ 1, 0 \ 1 \ 0,$ $1 \ 1 \ 0, 0 \ 1 \ 1, 0 \ 0 \ 0, 0 \ 0 \ 0, 0 \ 0 \ 0)$ shown as the highlighted path. The information sequence corresponding to $\hat{y}$ is given by $\hat{x} = (1 \ 1 \ 0 \ 0 \ 0)$.

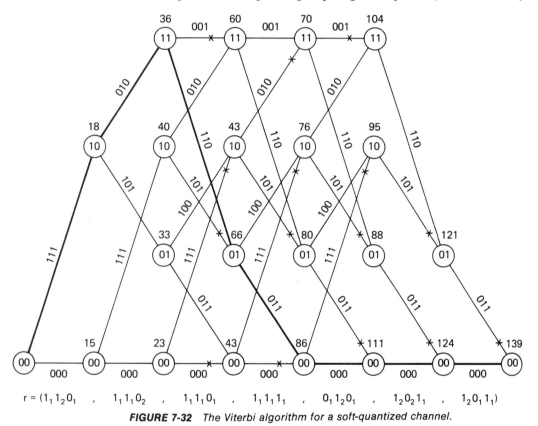

FIGURE 7-32 *The Viterbi algorithm for a soft-quantized channel.*

Implementation of the Viterbi algorithm requires that storage be provided for 2^m L-bit survivors and their metrics, and that 2^m path comparisons (computations) be made per decoded information bit. Hence, the algorithm is limited in practice to values of m less than about 10. In addition, since typically $L \gg m$, storing the entire path history for each survivor is not practical. Fortunately, it has been shown by Forney [17] that with high probability all survivors have the same path history up to within about $5m$ branches of the present decoding level. Hence, a decoder with a path memory of about $5m$ bits, which decodes the oldest bit on an arbitrary path each time it proceeds one level further into the trellis, will provide very close to maximum likelihood performance. Such a decoder is called a *truncated Viterbi decoder*. Additional information on the performance characteristics and implementation requirements of the Viterbi algorithm can be found in papers by Heller and Jacobs [16] and Forney [18].

7.7.3 Error Probability Bounds

In this section we analyze the performance of convolutional codes over a BSC with maximum likelihood decoding using Viterbi's [11] generating function approach. First assume, without loss of generality, that the all-zero code word is transmitted from the $v = 3$, $m = 2$ code of Fig. 7.20. We say that a *first event error* is made at an arbitrary level j if the all-zero path (the *correct path*) is eliminated *for the first time* in favor of the other path (the *incorrect path*) entering the all-zero state. If the incorrect path is the weight 7 path, a first event error will be made if, in the seven positions in which the correct and incorrect paths differ, the received sequence agrees with the incorrect path in four or more of these positions. If the BSC crossover probability is p, this probability is

$$P_7 = \sum_{e=4}^{7} \tbinom{7}{e} p^e (1-p)^{7-e} \tag{7.49}$$

If the weight 8 path is the incorrect path, a first event error is made with probability

$$P_8 = \tfrac{1}{2}\tbinom{8}{4} p^4 (1-p)^4 + \sum_{e=5}^{8} \tbinom{8}{e} p^e (1-p)^{8-e} \tag{7.50}$$

since if the metrics of the correct and incorrect paths are tied, an error is made with probability $\tfrac{1}{2}$. In general, if the incorrect path has weight k, a first event error is made with probability

$$P_k = \begin{cases} \displaystyle\sum_{e=(k+1)/2}^{k} \tbinom{k}{e} p^e (1-p)^{k-e} & k \text{ odd} \\[4mm] \displaystyle\frac{1}{2}\tbinom{k}{k/2} p^{k/2}(1-p)^{k/2} + \sum_{e=(k/2)+1}^{k} \tbinom{k}{e} p^e (1-p)^{k-e} & k \text{ even} \end{cases} \tag{7.51}$$

Since all incorrect paths of length j branches or less can cause a first event error at level j, the first event error probability at level j, $P_E(j)$, can be overbounded, using the union bound, by the sum of the error probabilities of each of these paths. If all incorrect paths of length greater than j branches are also included, $P_E(j)$ is overbounded by

$$P_E(j) < \sum_{k=7}^{\infty} N_k P_k \tag{7.52}$$

where N_k is the number of code words with weight k. Since this bound is independent of j, the *first event error probability*, P_E, is bounded by

$$P_E < \sum_{k=7}^{\infty} N_k P_k \tag{7.53}$$

Now note that for k odd,

$$
\begin{aligned}
P_k &= \sum_{e=(k+1)/2}^{k} \binom{k}{e} p^e (1-p)^{k-e} \\
&< \sum_{e=(k+1)/2}^{k} \binom{k}{e} p^{k/2}(1-p)^{k/2} \\
&= p^{k/2}(1-p)^{k/2} \sum_{e=(k+1)/2}^{k} \binom{k}{e} \\
&< p^{k/2}(1-p)^{k/2} \sum_{e=0}^{k} \binom{k}{e} \\
&= 2^k p^{k/2}(1-p)^{k/2}
\end{aligned}
\tag{7.54}
$$

It can also easily be shown that (7.54) is an upper bound on P_k for k even. Hence,

$$P_E < \sum_{k=7}^{\infty} N_k (2\sqrt{p(1-p)})^k = T(W)\big|_{W=2\sqrt{p(1-p)}} \tag{7.55}$$

Clearly, the same bound applies to an arbitrary convolutional code with generating function $T(W)$. For small p, the bound is dominated by its first term, so that

$$P_E \simeq N_{d_f}(2\sqrt{p(1-p)})^{d_f} \simeq N_{d_f} 2^{d_f} p^{d_f/2} \tag{7.56}$$

For example, for the code of Fig. 7.20 and $p = 10^{-2}$,

$$P_E \simeq 2^7 p^{7/2} = 1.28 \times 10^{-5} \tag{7.57}$$

The final decoded path can diverge from and remerge with the correct path any number of times; that is, it can contain any number of event errors, and each event error contains at least one *information bit error*. After one or more event errors have occurred, the two paths compared at the all-zero state will both be incorrect paths, one of which has diverged from and remerged with the correct path at least once. This is illustrated in Fig. 7.33. Assume that the correct path y has been eliminated for the first time at level $j - 1$ by the incorrect path y', and that at level j y' is compared to the incorrect path y''. If the metric for y'' exceeds the metric for y', it must also exceed the metric for y, since y' has a better metric than y. Hence, if y'' were compared to y at level j, a first event error would be made, and P_E is therefore an upper bound on the probability of an event error at level j. At each level, then, the probability of an event error (i.e., the probability of at least one bit error) is upper-bounded by (7.53).

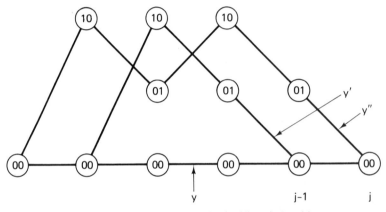

FIGURE 7-33 *Path comparison in the Viterbi algorithm.*

Since the kth term in (7.53) corresponds to all incorrect paths of weight k, the expected number of bit errors at each level can be upper-bounded by weighting P_k in (7.53) with the total number of nonzero information bits (bit errors) in all incorrect paths of weight k. Hence, the *bit error probability*, P_B, is bounded by

$$P_B < \sum_{k=7}^{\infty} B_k P_k \tag{7.58}$$

where B_k is the total number of nonzero information bits in all code words of weight k. Using (7.54) and noting that the B_k's can be computed by differentiating $T(W, B)$ with respect to B and then setting $B = 1$, we see that P_B is bounded by

$$P_B < \sum_{k=7}^{\infty} B_k (2\sqrt{p(1-p)})^k = \left. \frac{dT(W, B)}{dB} \right|_{\substack{B=1 \\ W = 2\sqrt{p(1-p)}}} \tag{7.59}$$

Again the same bound applies to an arbitrary convolutional code with generating function $T(W, B)$. For small p, the bound is dominated by its first term, so that

$$P_B \simeq B_{d_f}(2\sqrt{p(1-p)})^{d_f} \simeq B_{d_f} 2^{d_f} p^{d_f/2} \tag{7.60}$$

For the code of Fig. 7.20 and $p = 10^{-2}$,

$$P_B \simeq 2^7 p^{7/2} = 1.28 \times 10^{-5} \tag{7.61}$$

the same as P_E. This implies that for this code, each time an event error occurs, typically it is caused by the weight 7 path and only one bit error is made.

It is well known (see, e.g., Wozencraft and Jacobs [13]) that for binary antipodal modulation, an AWGN channel, and binary output quantization, the resulting digital channel is a BSC with crossover probability

$$p = \frac{1}{2}\operatorname{erfc}\left(\sqrt{\frac{RE_b}{N_0}}\right) \tag{7.62}$$

where E_b is the transmitted energy per information bit, N_0 is the (one-sided) noise power spectral density, and

$$\operatorname{erfc}(x) = \frac{2}{\sqrt{\pi}}\int_x^\infty e^{-u^2}\, du \simeq e^{-x^2} \qquad \text{for large } x \tag{7.63}$$

Note that since erfc (x) is a monotonically decreasing function, large values of the *signal-to-noise ratio* (SNR) E_b/N_0 correspond to small values of p. Using (7.62) and (7.63) in (7.60) yields

$$P_B \simeq B_{d_f} 2^{d_f/2}\, e^{-(Rd_f/2)\cdot(E_b/N_0)} \tag{7.64}$$

If binary antipodal modulation is used over an AWGN channel with *no coding*, the error probability (see [13]) is given by

$$P_e = \frac{1}{2}\operatorname{erfc}\left(\sqrt{\frac{E_b}{N_0}}\right) \simeq \frac{1}{2}e^{-E_b/N_0} \tag{7.65}$$

Comparing (7.64) and (7.65), we see that for a fixed SNR, the exponent with convolutional coding is larger by a factor of $Rd_f/2$ than the exponent with no coding. Since the exponential term dominates the error probability expressions for large SNR, the factor $Rd_f/2$, in decibels, is called the *asymptotic coding gain*:

TABLE 7-6: *Coding gains of best short constraint-length codes with rates $R = \frac{1}{2}, \frac{1}{3}$, and $\frac{1}{4}$.*

R	m	Generator		Sequences			d_f	Coding Gain (dB)
½	2	5	7	—	—		5	0.97
½	3	15	17	—	—		6	1.76
½	4	23	35	—	—		7	2.43
½	5	53	75	—	—		8	3.01
½	6	133	171	—	—		10	3.98
½	7	247	371	—	—		10	3.98
½	8	561	753	—	—		12	4.77
½	9	1167	1545	—	—		12	4.77
⅓	2	5	7	7	—		8	1.25
⅓	3	13	15	17	—		10	2.22
⅓	4	25	33	37	—		12	3.01
⅓	5	47	53	75	—		13	3.36
⅓	6	133	145	175	—		15	3.98
⅓	7	225	331	367	—		16	4.26
⅓	8	557	663	711	—		18	4.77
⅓	9	1117	1365	1633	—		20	5.23
¼	2	5	7	7	7		10	0.97
¼	3	13	15	15	17		13	2.11
¼	4	25	27	33	37		16	3.01
¼	5	53	67	71	75		18	3.52
¼	6	135	135	147	163		20	3.98
¼	7	235	275	313	357		22	4.39
¼	8	463	535	733	745		24	4.77
¼	9	1117	1365	1633	1653		27	5.28

$$\text{coding gain} = 10 \log_{10} \frac{R d_f}{2} \quad \text{dB} \tag{7.66}$$

Table 7.6 gives the asymptotic coding gains of the best short constraint-length convolutional codes with rates $R = \frac{1}{2}, \frac{1}{3}$, and $\frac{1}{4}$. These codes were taken from a table prepared by Larson [19]. The generator sequences are given in octal notation.

7.7.4 Sequential Decoding

We have seen that Viterbi decoding is practically limited by its computational and storage requirements to values of m less than about 10. It follows from Table 7.6 that Viterbi decoding can achieve coding gains of at most about 5 dB, with an additional 2 to 3 dB gain possible through the use of soft quantization. If larger coding gains are desired, codes with larger values of d_f, and therefore larger m, must be used. This requires a decoding algorithm whose computational and storage requirements are independent of m.

Sequential decoding is a decoding method for convolutional codes, originally due to Wozencraft [20], whose computational and storage requirements are independent of m, and which can therefore be used with codes having large values of d_f. In discussing sequential decoding it is convenient to represent the 2^L code words of length $n = v(L + m)$ as paths through a *binary code tree* containing $L + m$ levels. The code tree is just an expanded version of the trellis diagram in which every path is totally distinct from every other path. The code tree for the code of Fig. 7.20 and an information sequence of length $L = 5$ is shown in Fig. 7.34. Of the two branches leaving each node of the tree, the upper one represents $x_i = 1$ while the lower one represents $x_i = 0$, and each branch is labeled with the v corresponding outputs. Each of the 2^L code words is represented by a unique path through the code tree. For example, the code word corresponding to $\mathbf{x} = (1 \quad 1 \quad 1 \quad 0 \quad 1)$ is shown highlighted in Fig. 7.34.

The decoder searches the code tree according to one of a variety of sequential decoding algorithms in an attempt to find the ML path. In general, the paths under consideration at any step in an algorithm are of different lengths, and hence a sequential decoder does not use the same metric as a Viterbi decoder. The metric that has proved to be the best compromise between decoding error probability and computational requirements is the *Fano metric* [21], given by $\Sigma_i Z_i$, where

$$Z_i = \log_2 \frac{P(r_i \mid y_i)}{P(r_i)} - R \tag{7.67}$$

and the sum is over the length of the path $\mathbf{y}$ being compared to $\mathbf{r}$. For a BSC with crossover probability p,

$$Z_i = \begin{cases} \log_2 p - R & \text{if } r_i \neq y_i \\ \log_2 2(1 - p) - R & \text{if } r_i = y_i \end{cases} \tag{7.68}$$

For example, for $R = \frac{1}{3}$ and $p = 0.10$,

$$Z_i = \begin{cases} -2.65 & \text{if } r_i \neq y_i \\ 0.52 & \text{if } r_i = y_i \end{cases} \tag{7.69}$$

Scaling these bit metrics by a factor of $1/0.52$ and rounding to the nearest integer yields the integer metric table shown in Fig. 7.35.

As was mentioned above, several versions of sequential decoding have been proposed in the literature. Only one of these will be discussed in detail here. It is the *stack* or *ZJ* algorithm discovered independently by Zigangirov [22] and

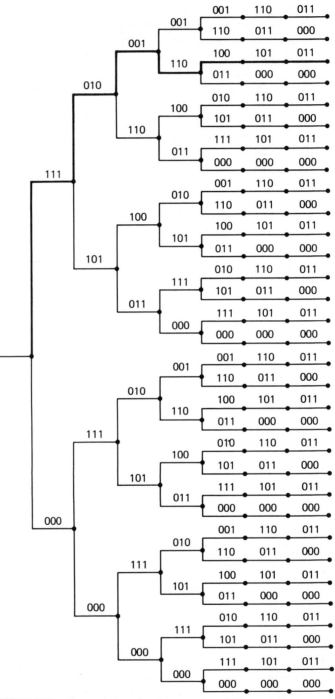

FIGURE 7-34 The code tree for the encoder of Figure 7-20 and L = 5.

Jelinek [23]. In this algorithm an ordered list or stack of various-length paths through the code tree is formed. Each entry in the stack contains a path along with its metric, the path with the largest metric being placed on top, and the others listed in order of decreasing metric. Each step consists of extending the top path in the stack by computing the metrics of its two succeeding branches in the tree and adding them to the metric of the extended path to form two new paths. The extended path is then deleted from the stack and the two new paths inserted in order according to their metric values.

ZJ Algorithm

- *Step 0.* Load the stack with the origin node in the tree, whose metric is taken to be zero.

- *Step 1.* Compute the metrics of the successors of the top path in the stack, and insert the new paths in the stack in order according to their metric values.

- *Step 2.* Delete from the stack the path whose successors were just inserted.

- *Step 3.* If the top path in the stack is a terminal node in the tree, stop. Otherwise, return to step 1.

When the algorithm terminates, the top path in the stack is taken as the decoded path.

As an example, consider the application of the ZJ algorithm to the tree of Fig. 7.34 for a received sequence $r = (1 \quad 0 \quad 0, 0 \quad 1 \quad 0, 0 \quad 1 \quad 1, 1 \quad 1 \quad 1, 1 \quad 0 \quad 0, 1 \quad 0 \quad 1, 0 \quad 1 \quad 1)$ and the integer metric table of Fig. 7.35. The contents of the stack after each step of the algorithm are shown in Fig. 7.36. Note that in general the stack size increases by 1 after each step, except when the extended path is in the last m branches (the "tail") of the tree, since here only one branch leaves each node. The algorithm terminates after 10 steps and the final decoded path is given by $\hat{x} = (1 \quad 1 \quad 1 \quad 0 \quad 1)$. (The last two zeros are not included, since they do not represent information bits.) This corresponds to the highlighted path in Fig. 7.34. In this example, ties in the metric values were resolved by placing the most recently extended path on top.

The major problem in implementing the ZJ algorithm is the reordering of the stack, which must be done after each step. This problem can be alleviated by dividing the range of possible metric values (from $+n$ to $-5n$ in the example) into a fixed number of metric "buckets." Paths are then placed in buckets according to their metric values. Paths within a bucket are not ordered, and an arbitrary path from the top bucket is chosen to be extended. This modification of the ZJ algorithm was first proposed by Jelinek [23], and its performance is almost equivalent to that of the unmodified algorithm.

Forney [24] has shown, using random coding arguments, that the final

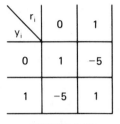

FIGURE 7-35

Stack Contents of the ZJ Algorithm for a BSC.

Step 1	Step 2	Step 3	Step 4	Step 5
0 (-3)	00 (-6)	001 (-9)	1 (-9)	11 (-6)
1 (-9)	1 (-9)	1 (-9)	0010 (-12)	0010 (-12)
	01 (-12)	01 (-12)	01 (-12)	01 (-12)
		000 (-15)	000 (-15)	000 (-15)
			0011 (-18)	0011 (-18)
				10 (-24)
111 (-9)	1110 (-12)	11101 (-9)	111010 (-6)	1110100 (-3)
0010 (-12)	0010 (-12)	0010 (-12)	0010 (-12)	0010 (-12)
01 (-12)	01 (-12)	01 (-12)	01 (-12)	01 (-12)
110 (-15)	110 (-15)	110 (-15)	110 (-15)	110 (-15)
000 (-15)	000 (-15)	000 (-15)	000 (-15)	000 (-15)
0011 (-18)	1111 (-18)	1111 (-18)	1111 (-18)	1111 (-18)
10 (-24)	0011 (-18)	0011 (-18)	0011 (-18)	0011 (-18)
	10 (-24)	10 (-24)	10 (-24)	10 (-24)
		11100 (-27)	11100 (-27)	11100 (-27)

FIGURE 7-36 *Integer metric table for a code with R = 1/3 and a BSC with p = 0.10.*

decoded path is with high probability the ML path (i.e., that the error probability of sequential decoding is almost the same as Viterbi decoding). Also, Chevillat and Costello [25] have shown that for a specific code, the event error probability P_E for sequential decoding is upper-bounded by a function that decreases exponentially with d_f and increases linearly with N_{d_f}, just as for Viterbi decoding.

Unlike Viterbi decoding, however, the number of computations (path extensions) for sequential decoding is a random variable and is independent of m. Typically, the average number of computations per decoded information bit for sequential decoding is much less than the fixed number 2^m required by the Viterbi algorithm. Hence, sequential decoding normally enjoys a speed advantage over Viterbi decoding.[2] However, if the received sequence is very noisy (i.e., if r

[2] The Viterbi algorithm can be implemented by having 2^m separate but identical metric computers and comparators operating in parallel. This results in only one computation per decoded information bit, but requires a 2^m-fold duplication of hardware.

contains a relatively large percentage of transmission errors), the sequential decoder may require many more computations than the Viterbi algorithm, sometimes resulting in an *erasure* (a failure to decode) due to an overflow of the input buffer storing the received sequence.

The computational distribution of sequential decoding has been studied by many authors, including Savage [26], Jacobs and Berlekamp [27], Jelinek [28], and Forney [24]. Using random coding arguments, they have shown that

$$P(C > N) < \beta \cdot N^{-\psi} \tag{7.70}$$

where C is the number of computations per decoded information bit, and β and ψ are functions of the BSC crossover probability p and the code rate R only. Inequality (7.70) is referred to as the *Pareto distribution*. Since (7.70) implies that $P(C > N)$ decreases only algebraically, rather than exponentially, with N, this results in a relatively large (typically between 10^{-2} and 10^{-4}) probability of buffer overflow or *erasure probability*. This is the major disadvantage of sequential decoding. In some applications, however, this may be a desirable property, since if a very noisy sequence is decoded, it is likely to be decoded incorrectly, even by a MLD. In other words, a sequential decoder in some sense trades errors for erasures.

Chevillat and Costello [25] have also shown that for a specific code,

$$P(C > N) < \sigma \cdot n' \cdot e^{-\mu \cdot d_c(\log_2 N) + \phi \cdot \log_2 N} \tag{7.71}$$

where σ, μ, and ϕ are functions of p and R only, and n' denotes the number of code words of length $\log_2 N$ with weight $d_c(\log_2 N)$. Inequality (7.71) implies that a rapidly decreasing computational distribution requires a rapidly increasing CDF. The logarithm in the argument of the CDF has the effect of enhancing the significance of the initial portion of the CDF.

In summary, we can say that the achievement of low error probabilities, fast decoding speeds, and low erasure probabilities with sequential decoding requires the selection of codes with large d_f and rapid initial column distance growth. Such codes have been constructed and reported by Chevillat and Costello [29] and Johannesson [30].

We are now in a position to understand that the reason for the "bias term" $-R$ in the definition of the bit metric in (7.67) is to achieve a reasonable balance between error probability and decoding speed. For example, using the integer metric table of Fig. 7.35, a path of length 12 having 10 agreements ($r_i = y_i$) and 2 disagreements ($r_i \neq y_i$) would have a metric value of zero, the same as a path of length 6 having 5 agreements and 1 disagreement. This is intuitively satisfying since both paths contain the same percentage of transmission errors. If no bias term were used in the definition of Z_i, the length 12 path would have a considerably larger metric value, because it is longer. This "bias" in favor of longer paths would result in less searching for the ML path, and hence faster decoding speeds at a cost of a substantial increase in error probability. On the other hand, if a larger bias term were used, each disagreement would cause a larger metric drop. This would result in more searching for the ML path, and hence a slight decrease in error probability at a cost of slower decoding speeds.

There are several sequential decoding alternatives to the ZJ algorithm. The *Fano algorithm* [21] requires more path extensions than the ZJ algorithm, but uses no storage and thereby avoids the stack ordering problem of the ZJ algorithm. A thorough comparison of the ZJ and Fano algorithms has been published by Geist [31]. The *multiple stack algorithm* (MSA), due to Chevillat and Costello [32], modifies the ZJ algorithm in such a way that erasures are eliminated and every transmission is completely decoded. Comparisons of the MSA with the Viterbi algorithm (see [32]) indicate that for a given error probability, the MSA decodes considerably faster than the Viterbi algorithm (at least in the absence of parallel processing), at the expense of a substantial increase in stack and buffer storage. Another modification of the ZJ algorithm, due to Haccoun and Ferguson [33], extends several paths simultaneously and achieves a reduced error and erasure probability at a cost of a higher average number of computations (i.e., slower decoding).

7.7.5 Threshold Decoding

Both Viterbi decoding and sequential decoding are essentially optimum decoding techniques which are capable of achieving very low error probabilities at a considerable cost in decoding complexity. In many applications, with more modest error probability requirements, a much simpler decoding technique is desired.

Threshold decoding is a decoding method for convolutional codes, originally due to Massey [9], whose performance is suboptimum compared to maximum likelihood decoding, but which can be implemented using simple threshold logic gates. In discussing threshold decoding, we will restrict attention to a subclass of rate $R = 1/v$ convolutional codes called *systematic codes*. In a systematic code, the generator polynomial $G_1(D) = 1$. Hence, $Y_1(D) = X(D)$ (i.e., the information bits appear directly as the first transmitted sequence) and $Y_1(D)$ is called the *information sequence*. The other $v - 1$ transmitted sequences are then called *parity sequences*.

For a BSC, the polynomial notation can be extended to include the sequence of transmission errors and the received sequence. Specifically, for $v = 2$ we can write

$$R_1(D) = Y_1(D) + E_1(D) \tag{7.72a}$$

$$R_2(D) = Y_2(D) + E_2(D) \tag{7.72b}$$

where

$E_1(D) = e_{10} + e_{11}D + e_{12}D^2 + \ldots$ is the *information error sequence*

$E_2(D) = e_{20} + e_{21}D + e_{22}D^2 + \ldots$ is the *parity error sequence*

$R_1(D) = r_{10} + r_{11}D + r_{12}D^2 + \ldots$ is the *received information sequence*

$R_2(D) = r_{20} + r_{21}D + r_{22}D^2 + \ldots$ is the *received parity sequence*

All sequences are binary, and addition is over the binary field.

At the receiver, the sequence

$$S(D) = G_2(D)\,R_1(D) + R_2(D) \tag{7.73}$$

can be formed by "encoding"[3] the received information sequence and adding it to the received parity sequence. Using (7.72) in (7.73) yields

$$\begin{aligned} S(D) &= G_2(D)[Y_1(D) + E_1(D)] + Y_2(D) + E_2(D) \\ &= G_2(D)\,E_1(D) + E_2(D) \end{aligned} \tag{7.74}$$

since $G_2(D)Y_1(D) + Y_2(D) = Y_2(D) + Y_2(D) = 0$. Clearly, then, $S(D)$ depends only on the error sequences $E_1(D)$ and $E_2(D)$ and not on the particular code word transmitted, and $S(D) = \mathbf{0}$ if and only if a code word is received. Hence, $S(D) = s_0 + s_1D + s_2D^2 + \ldots$ is called the *syndrome sequence*. It is well known (see, e.g., Massey [9]) that knowledge of $S(D)$ is equivalent for decoding to knowledge of the received sequences $R_1(D)$ and $R_2(D)$ [i.e., a decoder can be designed to operate on $S(D)$ rather than on $R_1(D)$ and $R_2(D)$]. Such a decoder is called a *syndrome decoder*.

Threshold decoding is based on the concept of an *orthogonal parity check*. From (7.74) we see that any single syndrome bit, or any sum of syndrome bits, represents a particular set of error bits whose sum is known, and is called a *parity check* A_i. A set $\{A_i\}$ of parity checks is *orthogonal* on an error bit e_j if each parity check includes e_j, but no other error bit appears in more than one parity check. For example, consider finding a set of orthogonal parity checks on e_{10}, the first information error bit, for the $R = \frac{1}{2}$ systematic code with $G_2(D) = 1 + D + D^4 + D^6$. First note that e_{10} can affect only the first constraint length $[s]_6 = (s_0, s_1, \ldots, s_6)$ of syndrome bits. The equations for $[s]_6$ [see (7.74)] can be rewritten using matrix notation as

---

[3] Since the parity sequence $Y_2(D) = G_2(D) \cdot X(D) = G_2(D) \cdot Y_1(D)$, the operation $G_2(D) \cdot R_1(D)$ is equivalent to encoding.

$$[s]_6^T = \begin{bmatrix} s_0 \\ s_1 \\ s_2 \\ s_3 \\ s_4 \\ s_5 \\ s_6 \end{bmatrix} = \begin{bmatrix} 1 \\ 1\ 1 \\ 0\ 1\ 1 \\ 0\ 0\ 1 \\ 1\ 0\ 0\ 1 \\ 0\ 1\ 0\ 1\ 1 \\ 1\ 0\ 1\ 0\ 1\ 1 \end{bmatrix} \begin{bmatrix} e_{10} \\ e_{11} \\ e_{12} \\ e_{13} \\ e_{14} \\ e_{15} \\ e_{16} \end{bmatrix} + \begin{bmatrix} e_{20} \\ e_{21} \\ e_{22} \\ e_{23} \\ e_{24} \\ e_{25} \\ e_{26} \end{bmatrix} = G[e_1]_6^T + [e_2]_6^T \tag{7.75}$$

where G is called a *parity triangle*. Note that the first column of G is just the generator sequence g_2, which is shifted down by one and truncated in each succeeding column. From (7.75) we can recognize the syndrome bits

$$A_1 = s_0 = e_{10} \qquad\qquad\qquad\qquad + e_{20} \tag{7.76a}$$

$$A_2 = s_1 = e_{10} + e_{11} \qquad\qquad\qquad + e_{21} \tag{7.76b}$$

$$A_3 = s_4 = e_{10} \qquad\quad + e_{13} + e_{14} \qquad + e_{24} \tag{7.76c}$$

$$A_4 = s_6 = e_{10} \quad + e_{12} \quad + e_{15} + e_{16} + e_{26} \tag{7.76d}$$

as a set of four parity checks orthogonal on e_{10}, since e_{10} appears in every parity check and no other error bit appears more than once. It is not possible to obtain more than four orthogonal parity checks on e_{10} in this example. This follows from the fact that only four syndrome bits "check" e_{10}, and no syndrome bit can be used in more than one orthogonal parity check, since then a parity error bit would appear more than once. This is called a *self-orthogonal code* since the orthogonal parity checks are syndrome bits themselves, not sums of syndrome bits. Robinson and Bernstein [34] have constructed an extensive list of self-orthogonal codes.

As a second example, consider the $R = \frac{1}{2}$ code with $G_2(D) = 1 + D^3 + D^4 + D^5$. The parity triangle for this code [compare with (7.75)] is given by

```
1                          ←———
0   1                      ←——— ┐
0   0   1                        │
1   0   0  [1]             ←———   │
1  [1]  0   0  [1]         ←———   │
1   1  [1]  0   0  [1]  ←─────────┘
```

where the arrows indicate the syndrome bits, or sums of syndrome bits, which are selected as orthogonal parity checks on e_{10}, and the boxes indicate which information error bits, other than e_{10}, are checked. We see that $\{s_0, s_1 + s_5, s_3, s_4\}$ is a set of four orthogonal parity checks on e_{10}. The orthogonal parity checks in this example were found by trial and error. Massey [9] has constructed a large number of *trial-and-error codes*. For a given number of orthogonal parity checks, trial-and-error codes require shorter constraint lengths than self-orthogonal codes.

Given a set of $2t$ orthogonal parity checks on an error bit e_j, the *threshold decoding rule*

> chooses $\hat{e}_j = 1$ if and only if more than half of the $2t$ parity checks orthogonal on e_j have value 1

If the error bits included in the $2t$ orthogonal parity checks contain t or fewer 1's (errors), this decoding rule will correctly estimate e_j. This follows from the fact that if $e_j = 0$, then at most t errors can cause at most t of the $2t$ parity checks to have value 1, resulting in $\hat{e}_j = 0$, which is correct. On the other hand, if $e_j = 1$, then at most $t - 1$ other errors can cause no more than $t - 1$ of the $2t$ parity checks to have value 0, so that at least $t + 1$ will have value 1, resulting in $\hat{e}_j = 1$, which is again correct. For the self-orthogonal code above, there are a total of 11 error bits included in the four orthogonal parity checks of (7.76). Hence, the threshold decoding rule will correctly estimate e_{10} whenever two or fewer of these 11 error bits are 1's (errors).

A threshold decoder must, of course, be capable of estimating not only e_{10}, but all other information error bits also. Consider again the example of the self-orthogonal code. If, after e_{10} has been correctly estimated, it is subtracted from each syndrome bit it affects, the *modified syndrome bit* $s_1' = s_1 - e_{10}$, along with syndrome bits s_2, s_5, and s_7, form a set of four orthogonal parity checks on e_{11}:

$$A_1 = s_1' = e_{11} \qquad\qquad\qquad\qquad\qquad\qquad + e_{21} \qquad (7.77a)$$

$$A_2 = s_2 = e_{11} + e_{12} \qquad\qquad\qquad\qquad\quad + e_{22} \qquad (7.77b)$$

$$A_3 = s_5 = e_{11} \qquad\quad + e_{14} + e_{15} \qquad\quad + e_{25} \qquad (7.77c)$$

$$A_4 = s_7 = e_{11} \qquad + e_{13} \qquad + e_{16} + e_{17} + e_{27} \qquad (7.77d)$$

From this orthogonal set, e_{11} can be correctly estimated if there are two or fewer errors among the 11 error bits included in (7.77). In general, if, after each information error bit has been correctly estimated, it is subtracted from each syndrome bit it affects, then the equations

$$A_1 = s_{i-6}' = e_{1,i-6} \qquad\qquad\qquad\qquad\qquad\qquad + e_{2,i-6} \qquad (7.78a)$$

$$A_2 = s_{i-5}' = e_{1,i-6} + e_{1,i-5} \qquad\qquad\qquad\qquad + e_{2,i-5} \qquad (7.78b)$$

$$A_3 = s_{i-2}' = e_{1,i-6} \qquad\qquad + e_{1,i-3} + e_{1,i-2} \qquad + e_{2,i-2} \qquad (7.78c)$$

$$A_4 = s_i = e_{1,i-6} \qquad + e_{1,i-4} \qquad\qquad + e_{1,i-1} + e_{1,i} + e_{2,i} \qquad (7.78d)$$

form a set of four orthogonal parity checks on $e_{1,i-6}$. From this orthogonal set, $e_{1,i-6}$ can be correctly estimated if there are two or fewer errors among the 11 error bits included in (7.78). Hence, each information error bit can be estimated using exactly the same decoding rule as long as the decoder calculates the syndrome bits in succession and modifies them by subtracting the effect of past estimates.

A complete encoder–decoder block diagram for the self-orthogonal code with threshold decoding is shown in Fig. 7.37. The threshold element produces an output of 1 only when three or four of its inputs are 1's. The "feedback" in the syndrome circuit subtracts each estimate from the syndrome bits it affects. Hence, this is called a *feedback decoder*. (It is not necessary to subtract $\hat{e}_{1,i-6}$ from s'_{i-6}, since this syndrome bit is not used in any future estimates.)

In the foregoing discussion of feedback decoding, specifically in (7.77) and (7.78), it was assumed that the past estimates subtracted from the syndrome were all correct. This is, of course, not always true. When an incorrect estimate is fed back to the syndrome, it has the effect of an additional transmission error and can cause further decoding errors that would not otherwise occur. This is called the *error propagation effect* of feedback decoders. For example, letting $\tilde{e}_{1j} = e_{1j} + \hat{e}_{1j}$ be the result of adding $\hat{e}_{1j}$ to a syndrome equation containing e_{1j}, (7.78) becomes

$$A_1 = s'_{i-6} = \tilde{e}_{1,i-12} + \tilde{e}_{1,i-10} + \tilde{e}_{1,i-7} + e_{1,i-6} \qquad\qquad + e_{2,i-6}$$

$$A_2 = s'_{i-5} = \qquad\quad \tilde{e}_{1,i-11} + \tilde{e}_{1,i-9} + e_{1,i-6} + e_{1,i-5} \qquad\qquad + e_{2,i-5} \qquad (7.79)$$

$$A_3 = s'_{i-2} = \qquad\qquad\qquad \tilde{e}_{1,i-8} + e_{1,i-6} + e_{1,i-3} + e_{1,i-2} \qquad + e_{2,i-2}$$

$$A_4 = s_i \quad = \qquad\qquad\qquad\qquad e_{1,i-6} + e_{1,i-4} + e_{1,i-1} + e_{1,i} + e_{2,i}$$

Clearly, if all past estimates are correct (i.e., $\tilde{e}_{1j} = 0, j = i - 12, \ldots, i - 7$) then (7.79) reduces to (7.78). However, if any $\tilde{e}_{1j} = 1$, it "looks like" an additional transmission error in the preceding equations, and can cause error propagation.

There are two approaches generally taken to reducing the effects of error propagation. One is to select codes with automatic recovery properties, codes for which the decoder recovers from a decoding error if the channel is free from transmission errors over some relatively short span of received bits. Sullivan [35] has studied the automatic recovery properties of several important classes of threshold decodable codes.

The other approach to limiting error propagation is simply not to use feedback in the decoder. This is called *definite decoding* and was first proposed by Robinson [36]. For the self-orthogonal code, if past decoding estimates are not fed back to modify the syndrome, (7.78) becomes

$$A_1 = s'_{i-6} = e_{1,i-12} + e_{1,i-10} + e_{1,i-7} + e_{1,i-6} \qquad\qquad + e_{2,i-6}$$

$$A_2 = s'_{i-5} = \qquad e_{1,i-11} + e_{1,i-9} + e_{1,i-6} + e_{1,i-5} \qquad + e_{2,i-5}$$

$$A_3 = s'_{i-2} = \qquad e_{1,i-8} + e_{1,i-6} + e_{1,i-3} + e_{1,i-2} \qquad + e_{2,i-2}$$

$$A_4 = s_i \quad = \qquad e_{1,i-6} + e_{1,i-4} + e_{1,i-1} + e_{1,i} + e_{2,i} \tag{7.80}$$

This still forms a set of four orthogonal parity checks on $e_{1,i-6}$, and hence $e_{1,i-6}$ can be correctly estimated if there are two or fewer errors among the 17 error bits included in (7.80). Hence, we see that while definite decoding is not subject to error propagation, the error-correcting capability of the code is reduced since the *decoding constraint length*[4] N' is increased (from 11 to 17 in this example). (With trial-and-error codes the number of orthogonal parity checks is also reduced.) Morrissey [37] has compared the effect of error propagation with feedback to the reduced error-correcting capability without feedback and has concluded that feedback decoders generally outperform definite decoders.

An estimate of the bit error probability P_B of threshold decoding on a BSC can be made by noting that a decoding error can occur only when more than t errors occur within the error bits in one decoding constraint length. Hence, P_B can be upper-bounded by

$$P_B \leqq \sum_{i=t+1}^{N'} \binom{N'}{i} p^i (1-p)^{N'-i} \tag{7.81}$$

For small p, this bound is dominated by its first term, so that

$$P_B \simeq \binom{N'}{t+1} p^{t+1}(1-p)^{N'-t-1} \simeq \binom{N'}{t+1} p^{t+1} \tag{7.82}$$

For the self-orthogonal code and feedback decoder of Fig. 7.37 and $p = 10^{-2}$,

$$P_B \simeq \binom{11}{3} p^3 = 1.65 \times 10^{-4} \tag{7.83}$$

(Note that this simple approximation ignores the effects of error propagation.)

Massey [9] has shown that the maximum number of orthogonal parity checks which can be formed on each information error bit is one less than the minimum distance of the code (i.e., $d_m - 1$). If $2t = d_m - 1$, the code is said to be *completely orthogonalizable*. (It is important to note that most convolutional codes are not completely orthogonalizable.) For the self-orthogonal code of Fig. 7.37, $d_m = 5$, and hence this code is completely orthogonalizable.

If d_m is odd, (7.82) reduces to

[4]   The decoding constraint length N' is simply the number of error bits included in the orthogonal parity-check equations.

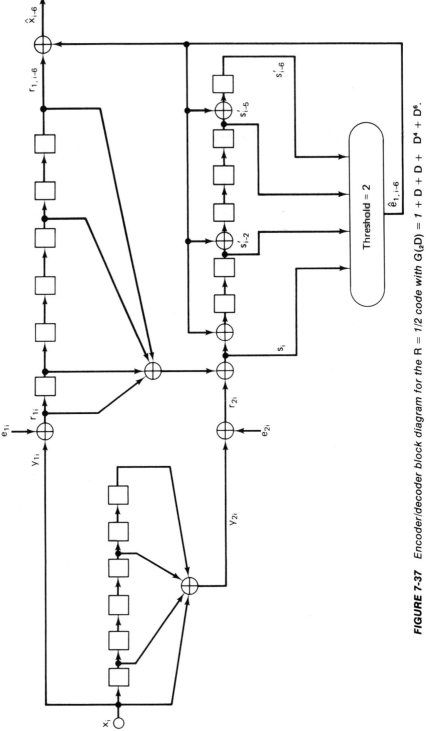

FIGURE 7-37 Encoder/decoder block diagram for the R = 1/2 code with $G(_2D) = 1 + D + D + D^4 + D^6$.

$$P_B \simeq \left(\frac{N'}{(d_m + 1)/2}\right) p^{(d_m + 1)/2} \tag{7.84}$$

for completely orthogonalizable codes. For binary antipodal modulation, an AWGN channel, and binary output quantization, (7.84) becomes

$$P_B \simeq \left(\frac{N'}{(d_m + 1)/2}\right)(1/2)^{(d_m + 1)/2} e^{-[R(d_m + 1)/2] \cdot (E_b/N_0)} \tag{7.85}$$

for large values of E_b/N_0. Comparing (7.85) for feedback threshold decoding to (7.64) for maximum likelihood decoding shows that their performance is roughly equivalent only if $d_m + 1 = d_f$. For the best systematic codes, it is well known that $d_f \simeq d_m$. However, for the best *nonsystematic codes* [i.e., codes for which $G_1(D) \neq 1$], Costello [38] has shown that $d_f \simeq 2d_m$. Hence, threshold decoding is a suboptimum decoding technique for convolutional codes.

7.7.6 Summary

In the preceding sections we have introduced the fundamental properties of convolutional codes and discussed the three major approaches to decoding. We have also given some basis for comparing the performance, speed, and implementation complexity of the three decoding methods. In summary, Viterbi decoding achieves optimum performance, but must provide storage for 2^m paths and their metrics and requires 2^m path comparisons per decoded information bit (unless parallel processing is used). Soft-decision Viterbi decoders have been implemented which achieve coding gains of up to 6 dB at speeds of 10 Mbits/s [39]. More recent experience with analog implementations promises similar gains at speeds in excess of 50 Mbits/s [40]. The performance of sequential decoding is nearly optimum, but the decoding effort is variable and sometimes results in erasures. The amount of storage needed depends on the particular version of sequential decoding employed. Hard-decision sequential decoders have been implemented that achieve coding gains of up to 6 dB at speeds of 50 Mbits/s [39]. Threshold decoders require only one decoding cycle per decoded information bit and are particularly simple to implement, but their performance is decidedly suboptimum.

In terms of applications, the large coding gains and high decoding speeds achievable with Viterbi and sequential decoders make them best suited for space and satellite channels. Threshold decoders, on the other hand, are most often used in conjunction with data scrambling or interleaving to protect against bursts of errors for telephone, high-frequency, or troposcatter channels or for digital magnetic tape recording.

REFERENCES

[1] SHANNON, C. E., "A Mathematical Theory of Communication," *Bell System Technical Journal*, **27**, 1948.

[2] SLEPIAN, D., "A Class of Binary Signaling Alphabets," *Bell System Technical Journal*, **35**, 203–234, 1956.

[3] PETERSON, W. W., and E. J. WELDON, JR., *Error-correcting Codes*, 2nd ed., The MIT Press, Cambridge, Mass., 1972.

[4] BERLEKAMP, E. R., *Algebraic Coding Theory*, McGraw-Hill Book Company, New York, 1968.

[5] LIN, S., *An Introduction to Error-correcting Codes*, Prentice-Hall, Inc., Englewood Cliffs, N.J., 1970.

[6] MACWILLIAMS, F. J., and N. J. A. SLOANE, *The Theory of Error-correcting Codes*, North-Holland Publishing Co., New York, 1977.

[7] MCELIECE, R. J., *The Theory of Information and Coding*, Addison-Wesley Publishing Co., Inc., Reading, Mass., 1977.

[8] HAMMING, R. W., "Error Detecting and Error Correcting Codes," *Bell System Technical Journal*, **29**, 147–160, 1950.

[9] MASSEY, J. L., *Threshold Decoding*, The MIT Press, Cambridge, Mass., 1963.

[10] FIRE, P., "A Class of Multiple-Error-correcting Binary Codes for Nonindependent Errors," *Sylvania Report RSL-E-2*, Sylvania Electronic Defense Lab., Reconnaissance System Division, Mountain View, Calif., March 1959.

[11] VITERBI, A. J., "Convolutional Codes and Their Performance in Communication Systems," *IEEE Transactions on Communication Technology*, **COM-19,** pp. 751–771, October 1971.

[12] MASON, S. J., and H. J. ZIMMERMAN, *Electronic Circuits, Signals, and Systems*, John Wiley & Sons, Inc., New York, 1960.

[13] WOZENCRAFT, J. M., and I. M. JACOBS, *Principles of Communication Engineering*, John Wiley & Sons, Inc., New York, 1965.

[14] VITERBI, A. J., "Error Bounds for Convolutional Codes and an Asymptatically Optimum Decoding Algorithm," *IEEE Transactions on Information Theory*, **IT-13**, pp. 260–269, April 1967.

[15] MASSEY, J. L., class notes for a course in digital communications, Department of Electrical Engineering, University of Notre Dame, Notre Dame, Ind., 1974.

[16] HELLER, J. A., and I. M. JACOBS, "Viterbi Decoding for Satellite and Space Communication," *IEEE Transactions on Communication Technology*, **COM-19,** pp. 835–848, October 1971.

[17] FORNEY, G. D., JR., "Convolutional Codes II: Maximum-Likelihood Decoding," *Information and Control*, **25**, pp. 222–266, July 1974.

[18] FORNEY, G. D., JR., "The Viterbi Algorithm," *Proceedings of the IEEE*, **61**, pp. 268–278, March 1973.

[19] LARSON, K. J., "Short Convolutional Codes with Maximal Free Distance for Rates 1/2, 1/3 and 1/4," *IEEE Transactions on Information Theory*, **IT-19**, pp. 371–372, May 1973.

[20] WOZENCRAFT, J. M., and B. REIFFEN, *Sequential Decoding*, The MIT Press, Cambridge, Mass., 1961.

[21] FANO, R. M., "A Heuristic Discussion of Probabilistic Decoding," *IEEE Transactions on Information Theory,* **IT-9**, pp. 64–74, April 1963.

[22] ZIGANGIROV, K., "Some Sequential Decoding Procedures," *Problemy Peredachi Informatsi*, **2**, pp. 13–25, 1966.

[23] JELINEK, F., "A Fast Sequential Decoding Algorithm Using a Stack," *IBM Journal of Research and Development*, **13**, pp. 675–685, November 1969.

[24] FORNEY, G. D., JR., "Convolutional Codes III: Sequential Decoding," *Information and Control*, **25**, pp. 267–297, July 1974.

[25] CHEVILLAT, P. R., and D. J. COSTELLO, JR., "An Analysis of Sequential Decoding for Specific Time-Invariant Convolutional Codes," *IEEE Transactions on Information Theory,* **IT-24**, pp. 443–451, July 1978.

[26] SAVAGE, J. E., "Sequential Decoding—The Computation Problem," *Bell System Technical Journal*, **45**, pp. 149–175, January 1966.

[27] JACOBS, I. M., and E. R. BERLEKAMP, "A Lower Bound to the Distribution of Computation for Sequential Decoding," *IEEE Transactions on Information Theory,* **IT-13**, pp. 167–174, April 1967.

[28] JELINEK, F., "An Upper Bound on Moments of Sequential Decoding Effort," *IEEE Transactions on Information Theory*, **IT-15**, pp. 140–149, January 1969.

[29] CHEVILLAT, P. R., and D. J. COSTELLO, JR., "Distance and Computation in Sequential Decoding," *IEEE Transactions on Communications*, **COM-24**, pp. 440–447, April 1976.

[30] JOHANNESSON, R., "Robustly-Optimal Rate One-Half Binary Convolutional Codes," *IEEE Transactions on Information Theory*, **IT-21**, pp. 464–468, July 1975.

[31] GEIST, J. M., "An Empirical Comparison of Two Sequential Decoding Algorithms," *IEEE Transactions on Communication Technology,* **COM-19**, pp. 415–419, August 1971.

[32] CHEVILLAT, P. R., and D. J. COSTELLO, JR., "A Multiple Stack Algorithm for Erasurefree Decoding of Convolutional Codes," *IEEE Transactions on Communications,* **COM-25**, pp. 1460–1470, December 1977.

[33] HACCOUN, D., and M. J. FERGUSON, "Generalized Stack Algorithms for Decoding Convolutional Codes," *IEEE Transactions on Information Theory*, **IT-21**, pp. 638–651, November 1975.

[34] ROBINSON, J. P., and A. J. BERNSTEIN, "A Class of Binary Recurrent Codes with Limited Error Propagation," *IEEE Transactions on Information Theory*, **IT-13**, pp. 106–113, January 1967.

[35] SULLIVAN, D. D., "Control of Error Propagation in Convolutional Codes," *Technical*

Report EE-667, Department of Electrical Engineering, University of Notre Dame, Notre Dame, Ind., November 1966.

[36] ROBINSON, J. P., "Error Propagation and Definite Decoding of Convolutional Codes," *IEEE Transactions on Information Theory*, **IT-14,** pp. 121–128, January 1968.

[37] MORRISSEY, T. N., JR., "A Unified Markovian Analysis of Decoders for Convolutional Codes," *Technical Report EE*-687, Department of Electrical Engineering, University of Notre Dame, Notre Dame, Ind., October 1968.

[38] COSTELLO, D. J., JR., "Free Distance Bounds for Convolutional Codes," *IEEE Transactions on Information Theory*, **IT-20,** pp. 356–365, May 1974.

[39] Error Control Products Brochure, Linkabit Corporation, San Diego, Calif.

[40] ACAMPORA, A. S., and R. P. GILMORE, "Analog Viterbi Decoding for High Speed Digital Satellite Channels," *IEEE Transactions on Communications*, **COM-26,** pp. 1463–1470, October 1978.

8

SYNCHRONIZATION
IN SNA NETWORKS

JAMES P. GRAY

IBM Corporation

8.1 INTRODUCTION

This chapter describes the functions within an SNA network from a uniform viewpoint: synchronization among cooperating processes. Synchronization is a familiar theme in the description of operating systems; its relevance to SNA derives from the fact that, just as OS/VS2-MVS (operating system/virtual storage 2—multiple virtual storage) is an operating system for tightly coupled S/370 multiprocessors, so SNA is an operating system for the loosely coupled multiple processor computer systems formed by interconnection of the diverse IBM products that support SNA.

Process-to-process communication is a rich topic. SNA represents a shaping of this richness to the specific environment of computer networks. In this environment delays range from seconds to tenths of seconds, speeds range from megabits to 600 bits/s, distance from thousands of kilometers to zero. Cost-effective systems must be configurable across these broad ranges of parameters; this goal has dictated SNA's structure and differentiates its protocols from more specialized interprocess protocols.

Processes exist at several levels within SNA, but, they all exist to serve the communication needs of *end users*. To do this, a connection must be established, synchronization of the parties obtained, messages passed, and the inevitable errors recognized and corrected. The lower-level processes, then, convert a wide variety of dispersed computers and transmission facilities capable of sending signals between these computers, into a large number of communication linkages between end-user processes.

The conversion of computer-to-computer transmission into communication is accomplished by synchronization, which is discussed in basic forms in the next section. More material is presented in Chapter 7.

Following a short introduction to the structure, terminology, and functions of SNA, the SNA elements are discussed in more detail, showing how each contributes to the system as a whole. Some of the material that follows has been adapted from [1] and [2]. For a description of extensions to SNA announced after this chapter was written, see [5].

8.2 SYNCHRONIZATION AS THE MEANING OF COMMUNICATIONS

In technology, the narrow sense of the verb "to synchronize" is "to cause to have the same period or, to cause to have the same period and phase." This definition applies directly to clocks and to oscillators; by simple extension it applies to machinery such as electric generators. It is this sense of the verb which applies in the phrases "synchronous detection" (demodulation) or "synchronous sequential machine" (digital logic). The broader sense is "to cause to happen at the same time, or to cause to happen at a known time." It is this sense that is of particular interest for communication: the receiver's operations must occur at a known time (precisely: in a predictable order) relative to the transmitter's operations in order for communication to take place. This thought will be developed more fully within the framework of a model based on synchronous finite-state machines [1].

8.2.1 Simplex Communication System

In Fig. 8.1, two sequential machines are connected in a simplex communication system. Machine A is the originator and transmitter of the information; machine B is the receiver. The output of A connects to the input of B, and, for the present example, they share a common clock TA (the clock used to drive machine B will be discussed again later). Since A and B already share the same clock, their clocks are synchronized, but machine A may not know what state machine B is in at a given instant, even assuming error-free transmission. For some machines B, A can drive B into a known state. After B has entered a known state, any further transmission by A will have the effect of changing B's state vector in a known way. In this simplex communication situation, synchronization amounts to control: the goal of the system is to allow A to establish and maintain control over B's state.

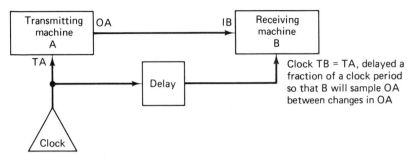

FIGURE 8-1 *A simplex communication system.*

8.2.2 Reset Signals

When the receiving machine in a simplex communication system is designed, it is possible to include signals (over a separate wire if parallel inputs are possible; else via a specific bit pattern, or message) to quickly and specifically force *B* to a known (reset) state. This kind of design enhances the usefulness of machine *B* as a part of a larger system. That is, when an error occurs that cannot be fixed by some other procedure, a reset signal can establish a known point for restarting operations. SNA contains reset signals at many levels.

8.2.3 Synchronization as Communication

In systems network architecture (SNA), both the sending and receiving nodes (finite-state machines) are highly decomposed to obtain the advantages of a structured, modular design. The elements of the architecture that directly attach to the physical links between SNA nodes are called data link control (DLC) elements. While the purpose of data link control within SNA is to convert transmission into communication by acquiring and maintaining synchronism between separated machines, there are higher levels of processing, higher-order users of the node-to-node communication facility. In this perspective, each DLC element does not so much convert transmission into communication as it acquires and maintains synchronism for the benefit of the higher-level users. These users transform transmitted messages into communication through themselves being synchronized by the information contained in the messages. In this view, DLC elements must act as conduits for some of the transmitted data the content of which should not affect, or be affected by, DLC.

SNA, then, views DLC elements as paired finite-state machines (alternatively, as paired algorithms) which acquire and maintain synchronization in order to pass messages between higher-level users. Subsequent layers of SNA will apply this principle recursively. At each level, synchronization is established and maintained by the transmission of signals that establish and maintain a known state in the corresponding element in the remote layer. The higher-level users of each layer are themselves synchronized (driven into a known state) by the message contents, and in this sense communication means synchronization.

8.3 STRUCTURE AND FUNCTION OF SNA

SNA is divided into six layers, following accepted principles of modularization in the design of large-scale systems. Above each layer, some amount of inner detail is hidden; each layer introduces an appropriate abstraction. A given SNA network is comprised of many SNA nodes, each of which has an external behavior that can be modeled by some subset of the structure shown in Fig. 8.2.

At the lowest level lie the *data link control* (DLC) elements. Their task is to convert the specific physical facilities which connect two adjacent SNA nodes into a reliable, efficient, full-duplex transmission path. Above DLC, physical details (e.g., transmission speed, or two-wire versus four-wire transmission facility) are not visible. Next, the path control element abstracts from DLC's next node connections and creates a reliable, full-duplex connection between origin and destination nodes. Within each node, path control multiplexes and demultiplexes into finer destinations, called sessions.

The *transmission control* (TC) elements lie on each end of a session and ensure isolation of sessions from each other. TC elements also provide session flow control and session-level data encryption. The reliable FDX properties of the connection are maintained.

Data flow control (DFC) modulates the FDX flows provided by TC. Each half of the session (half-session) also contains a DFC element, and creates through it an end-to-end protocol suited to the use of that session. Protocols include chaining of message packets, called *request units* (RU), restriction of flow to be strictly one-way alternate (HDX-flip-flop) or two-way with races (HDX-contention) or two-way-simultaneous (FDX). In addition, a session sub-protocol, *Brackets*, is used to synchronize the connection and disconnection of processes to the half-session.

Above DFC, within the attached processes just mentioned, lie a variety of *function management* (FM) modules (data manipulating), ranging from customer-provided programs to microcode entirely supplied by the product. Simple terminals, for instance, contain microcoded processes that provide subsets of SNA-defined protocols. Further, collections of related half-sessions are grouped together into *logical units* (LUs); it is the LU that is the target of a request to build a session. Some half-sessions have specialized uses; control of the network is provided by *systems services control points* (SSCPs) and SSCPs in turn control network resources within SNA nodes via sessions with *physical units* (PUs). SSCPs are optional elements of a node.

Apart from the half-session structure just discussed, there are additional

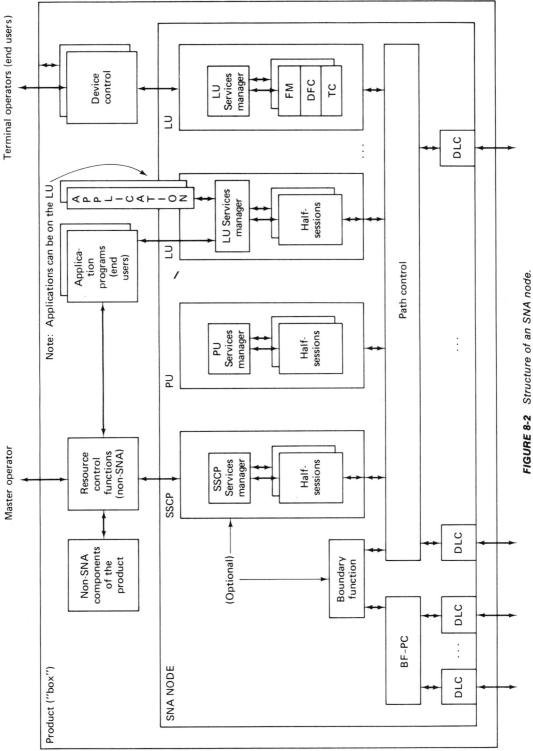

FIGURE 8-2 *Structure of an SNA node.*

323

algorithms within individual nodes that are coupled to the states of several half-sessions at one time. These processes are called *services managers*; each node contains one PU services manager, optionally one SSCP services manager, and one LU services manager for each LU.

The final elements of an SNA node provide an optional boundary facility where address and certain protocol transforms are performed. Although every SNA node implemented by a product is definable as a subset of the architected node, some subsets (e.g., path control for cluster controllers and terminals) have been explicitly included in the *SNA Formats and Protocol Reference Manual* [3]. Additional material on SNA has been published in many places (e.g., [4–9]).

SNA has evolved over time; different levels of implementation are available at any given time. The level of SNA described in this chapter corresponds to that implemented by ACF/VTAM version 1, release 2 [10]; ACF/NCP version 1, release 2 [11]; and ACF/TCAM version 2, release 1 [12].

We now turn to a more detailed discussion of each of the SNA elements. Two data link controls are supported by SNA. One is SDLC, for bit-serial transmission facilities; the other is a S/370 channel protocol for character-parallel transmission. Here we will discuss SDLC.

8.4 SDLC

8.4.1 Serialization

Conceptually, each message is an indivisible unit of communication, and if messages were fixed length they could be transmitted as 500 or 1000 bits in parallel. Of course, that many parallel transmission channels would be very expensive, and messages are usually of variable length anyway, so, for practical reasons, messages are serialized into character streams even for communication via local transmission facilities. These character-serial cables include a separate clock line, often called a *sample line* or *deskewing* line, which is used by the receiver to tell precisely when, and just how often, to sample the receive data lines. The separate clock and data lines in Fig. 8.1 illustrate the usefulness of an explicit clock.

Remote transmission links are more expensive than local ones, so a single channel is used and character streams are serialized into bit streams. This bit-level serialization creates problems of clock recovery at the receiver: if a data-independent bit clock is not recovered by the modem (so-called "modem clock") or supplied by the digital transmission facility (e.g., X.21), the transmitter clock has to be recovered from the single serial bit stream, which implies that there must be transitions in the received raw data. That, in turn, implies that certain characters will not be allowed, or that additional bits will be embedded in the transmission to ensure an adequate number of transitions for reliable clock recovery. An additional requirement created by the serialization is for an agreed upon speed of transmission, since the clock recovery algorithm and the bit-embedding or code-sensitivity problems are greatly simplified by knowing the approximate bit rate a priori.

8.4.2 Practical Simplex Synchronization

For simplex communication, synchronization is the receiver's problem in a practical sense: it does not have, but needs, clocks at the bit, character, and message levels of transmission. Table 8.1 summarizes the methods of bit and character clock recovery that can be used in SDLC, and shows their relationship to the methods that can be employed for transmission.

To allow higher-speed transmission than start-stop methods [1], SDLC uses a synchronous clock recovery method. There are two methods of interest. In the first, the bit clock is derived by the modem from data-independent signals on the

TABLE 8-1: Relationship between SDLC and DCEs.

DCE	SDLC
Asychronous modems (e.g., FSK and baseband): DTE clock*	Useful, but a terminal with a sync. DLC can often justify a higher-speed modem
Synchronous DCEs: DCE clock derived from the data	Natural design point
Synchronous DCEs: DCE clock independent of the data	Natural design point

*DTE (data terminal equipment) clock means that the bit clock is generated (on transmission) and recovered (on reception) by the DTE. DCE (data communication equipment) clock means that the bit clock is generated and recovered by the DCE (modem, or equivalently, by a digital transmission facility). A DCE clock channel looks as shown in Fig. 8-1.

line; this case is equivalent to a separate clock channel. In the other case, the bit clock is derived from the serial data stream itself, either within the modem or within the business machine, depending upon the form of detection that the modem uses (see Table 8.1). In either case, once the bit clock has been started, it is not stopped until the transmission is complete and all signals disappear from the line. In the case of a data-derived clock, the clock is corrected periodically, usually after every transition on the line. Clearly, there must be enough line transitions to keep the local clock in sync with the transmitter's bit clock or else a dropped or inserted bit will result (which is a form of code sensitivity). For this purpose, special bit patterns (described below) are inserted within the message text.

Once bit clock has been recovered, character clock must still be obtained. This is done by prefixing the transmission with a unique bit pattern generated by bit insertion on transmission and bit deletion on reception. A ''0'' is added after five consecutive ''1's,'' making six consecutive ''1's'' with a leading and trailing zero a unique control character (called a *flag*) at the receiver. Every transmission block (called a *frame*) sent in SDLC starts with one of these flags, which serve to establish character synchronism as well as message synchronism. The receiver, of course, must delete every zero that follows five consecutive ''1's'' in order to recover the proper message text.

Once the transmission of a frame has been started and the receiver has sync at the bit, character, and start of frame levels, the termination of the frame must by synchronized, too. SDLC uses a terminal flag for this purpose. Some SNA message formats contain a message length that is used to further strengthen end of frame synchronization.

Modem sensitivity to the transmitted code is possible with data-dependent synchronous bit clock recovery. Just which bit patterns are disallowed depends on the modem design; modern modems often include a scrambler circuit to make the sensitive pattern a highly unlikely one in normal data streams. Synchronous operation with asynchronous modems can mean that the clock is sensitive to long strings of zeros or long strings of ones. In SDLC, long strings of ones cannot occur because of the bit stuffing that creates the unique flags, and long strings of zeros can be prevented by encoding the line signal in a Non-Return to Zero, Invert to transmit a zero format (NRZI encoding). This just means that transmission of a one is accomplished by not changing the line signal, while transmission of a zero is accomplished by inverting the line signal. Basically, the width of the zero intervals is sent as a series of transitions in the line signal. At the receiver, a differentiation extracts impulses which are used to repeatedly trigger a timing circuit, which emits a zero bit for one bit time when triggered. This restores the data to true data form.

Another modem-related sensitivity of all line controls is the need to pad a transmission at the end of transmission. This is needed because some half-duplex asynchronous modems turn off abruptly when told to stop sending and start listening, so abruptly that a portion of the trailing flag may be lost if a pad is not added at the end of the frame. It follows that separate bit clocks to overlap transmission of the pad with reception of the next received frame are required in SDLC implementations that support two-way alternate operation with such modems. Separate bit clocks are also required when DTE clock is used and two-way simultaneous operation of the DCE is being used.

8.4.3 Duplex Synchronization

Duplex transmission consists of transmission in both directions at once (full duplex or FDX) or alternately (half duplex of HDX), but in either case it is more than just two simplex links. The something more lies in the *sequential coordi-*

nation between the transmission and reception operations on both ends of the link. We will concentrate on HDX since it is easier to understand, yet contains all the essential elements of duplex operation.

At the initiation of transmission, two HDX DLC elements (called stations in SDLC) may be "equals," meaning that their respective finite-state machines are identical so far as the DLC behavior is concerned. If this is the case, and both wish to transmit, a race condition can develop. Thus when A sends its initiation sequence, since it is HDX, it will not see B's initiation sequence and will try again. In practice, this try-again effort is done after a timeout, so that when A and B try again, with the same timeout (they are identical, remember), a race or contention will again exist on the line. Sooner or later, of course, the asynchronous nature of their local clocks will get them out of the race, but it can be a long time (experiments have demonstrated races lasting several hours), so a primary–secondary mode of communication is desirable, and is used in SDLC. That is, one of the stations is designated the primary, and in case of a race, only the primary tries again. FDX operation solves this start of transmission condition. However, other aspects of FDX operation, especially system cost, motivate primary–secondary architecture for SDLC.

In the fixed primary system of SDLC, one station is more equal than the others, and when in doubt about races or other error-induced asynchronisms, the primary reestablishes the connection and the synchronism. In older rotating primary systems, the station that initiated the transmission was responsible for the health of the link until that transmission had been acknowledged. This increased the cost of the secondary stations and complicated the error-recovery procedures (but it was a natural outgrowth of experience with earlier terminal-to-terminal networks).

In HDX systems, during the course of connection, both ends may have occasion to wait for a transmission by the other. If this occurs at the same time, each waiting for the other, a deadlock occurs, which can only be broken by timeouts or by some outside intervention. With SDLC such deadlocks are broken by asymmetric timeouts: the primary station has a short timer and retransmits upon its expiration. The secondary station has a long timer, which is used only to detect a broken line; it is not used to initiate retransmission.

8.4.4　Reverse Interrupt Facilities

HDX operation with reverse interrupt (RVI) is an extension of the HDX mode to allow interruption of transmission by the receiving station, or to allow a slave to signal "attention" to the master station. It is added to HDX protocols and engineered into the communications equipment primarily for human-factor (or application-level efficiency) reasons since the interrupt or control functions are freely available when the line is turned around at the end of a transmission. On Teletypewriters this function is called "break," while on IBM 2741 terminals it is called "attention." The exact meaning of the interrupt must be assigned by application logic (hardware and software). SDLC does not contain this kind of reverse interrupt, since that level of protocol is supplied by SNA sessions. One kind of reverse interrupt that is used internally to SDLC is RNR, or Receive-Not-Ready. This is issued to a transmitter when the receiver is temporarily unable to receive any additional messages because of a buffer full condition or some other condition that requires a delay. Reverse interrupt signals have also been used in locally attached equipment to signal error or emergency situations, but this is not done in SDLC, because errors have to be handled locally anyway when the link fails.

8.4.5 Errors

Error rates on common carrier channels generally range from one error in 10,000 to one in 10,000,000 bits transmitted, while in specialized applications such as mobile radio channels, the rate may be as high as one error in 10 bits. Errors include bit insertion and deletion due to faulty synchronization, single bit errors, and burst errors. Short-term outages may occur, and if short enough, these will appear to be burst errors; if the outage is on the order of a frame length, an entire frame can be lost. Line quality can change abruptly for a few bits or frames or longer periods as the carrier's equipment fails, degrades, and is manually or automatically reconfigured. The complexity and variability of the carrier channels available to the data user make prediction of data channel error rates and error behavior impossible and survey data very expensive to obtain and of limited value once obtained. Error considerations have also made it necessary for limits to be placed on the number of drops engineered for some multipoint leased lines.

Although how many errors a particular communications channel will introduce into a data stream cannot be predicted exactly, such a large fraction of the ones that do occur are detected by SDLC that, with retransmission, as few as one frame in 20 billion will contain an undetected error for frames of about 600 bits. If the raw error rate is so high that the probability of transmitting a frame correctly is appreciably less than 1, some forward error-correcting codes (FEC) may have to be employed to obtain satisfactory throughput. These codes do not have to be nearly as elaborate or as expensive to implement as some FEC codes, which theoretically speaking, would allow transmission with arbitrarily low error rates without retransmission (see Chapter 7).

Error detection is based on some kind of redundancy built into the transmitted information. While the transmission of a duplicate copy of the data is the simplest redundancy, it is not efficient, nor is a parity check across some group of bits sufficiently strong. To obtain better checking while still maintaining transmission efficiency, checking must be done across the whole frame. SDLC uses cyclic redundancy checking, the most powerful and efficient error-detection method in general use today. The general theory of the behavior of these check codes is well known, but somewhat involved, so it will not be repeated here, except to note that the checking polynomial used in SDLC (the V.41 recommendation of the CCITT) is among the best known for commonly observed error statistics.

8.4.6 Half-Duplex Error-Recovery Algorithms

Once an error has been detected by the SDLC element, a retransmission of the erroneous frame must be agreed upon. The transmitter and receiver finite-state machines must be properly designed to avoid frame duplication or loss occasioned by cascaded errors. The basic principle is based on two ideas: first, number the frames so that the receiver can tell if a correctly received frame has been previously received, and second, have the receiver acknowledge every frame received, replying positively when the frame was received correctly and negatively when the frame was received incorrectly. Since SDLC allows more than one frame to be outstanding before acknowledgment, the acknowledgments must be numbered to correspond to the frames.

Whenever a frame is received, it is checked for errors. If in error, a request for retransmission is made, by responding with the old receive count. If no error is detected, the frame send number is checked. If it is $n + 1$, where n was the last frame accepted, it is accepted by responding with the send number in the received frame. If it is n, it is accepted but is thrown away by the receiving station, since it must have been a duplicate transmission caused by an error in one of the responses. If it is anything else, such as $n + 2$, it is negatively acknowledged with the old count.

At the transmitter, each response is also checked for errors. If an erroneous response is received, the most recent frame(s) sent is (are) retransmitted (this would be message number n). If the response received is free of errors, it is either n or $n - 1$, where n is the last number transmitted; and if it is n, frame $n + 1$ is transmitted, while if it is $n - 1$, frame n is retransmitted.

This set of linked algorithms can be seen to provide perfect transmission under all conditions of detected errors. Undetected errors can still cause trouble, however. For instance, if an n is changed, without being detected into $n + 1$, a message will be dropped, while the reverse undetected error will cause no problem. In this context, the checking of control characters used in SDLC greatly strengthens it vis-à-vis line controls that have unchecked control characters.

Implicit in this discussion has been the assumption that no frames are totally lost on the line, but this can happen due to a short-term outage of some portion of the communications channel. If a frame is lost without detection of this fact, then the DLC elements may become deadlocked, with the receiver waiting for the next frame, say, and the transmitter waiting for the response to the previous frame, the response having been lost. SDLC avoids this deadlock by the timeouts previously described.

8.4.7 Full-Duplex Error Recovery

If a FDX channel is operated in the FDX mode, line control protocols sufficient for HDX operation will no longer work, or will not work efficiently. The central issue in extending HDX protocols to FDX usage is sequence numbering: are there two sequence numbers, one for transmission A to B and another independent number for transmission B to A, or is there only one sequence number used for both directions of transmission? SDLC uses two independent sequence numbers, so that the error-recovery actions in the two directions can be independent. Further, with two sequence numbers the sequence number modulus p can be independent of the delay in the channel without affecting throughput, as long as p messages overfill the channel round-trip delay (this is also a function of frame length).

8.4.8 Multipoint Systems

Simplex operation of a link can be point-to-point, as we have already discussed, or it can be multipoint-tandem, commonly called just multipoint. This means that there are more than two stations on the link and that the connections are engineered so that when one of the stations transmits, all other stations receive the transmission. To operate such a link in a simplex mode one station would be the transmitter and the others the receivers. Thus, SDLC needs to include selection by address for the receiving (secondary) stations to allow frames to be directed to individual stations. SDLC uses 1-byte addresses; this is many more stations than can be reliably engineered onto a single multipoint line. Notice that multipoint lines provide a form of physical multiplexing and concentration; logical (i.e., session-level) multiplexing and concentration are provided in SNA by path control.

Multipoint FDX operation is similar to simplex in that selection or addressing is required. But since the tributary stations can also transmit inbound, some method of babel control is required. If traffic is light, so that the probability that two tributary stations will want to transmit at the same time is small, pure contention might be used. When a contention (race) situation does develop, the primary would calm the line by issuing quiesce orders and then asking each station in turn if it had something to send. This latter procedure is called *polling* or *serial selection with enable*. Mixtures of contention (group enable) and polling (serial enable) are also possible. Since SNA is designed for all ranges of traffic, contention is not used in SDLC.

Polling is controlled by the primary; one station at a time is given the opportunity to send by sending it a frame with the poll bit on. When that station has completed its transmission, it returns the poll bit (called the final bit when it comes from a secondary).

The use of serial enable or polling involves a certain amount of transmission that transfers no useful data; that is, it involves inefficiencies in the use of the transmission capacity of the line and in the primary station's CPU cycles. SDLC addresses this problem in three ways; one is through the use of cluster controllers. Clustering several work stations at a single controller creates concentrated traffic so that unproductive polling is greatly reduced. The second is through the use of SDLC's multi-multipoint configuration. This refers to the use of a FDX primary station on a two-day simultaneous line with HDX secondary stations. The result is HDX costs with FDX performance and throughput, since the primary station can schedule output traffic while waiting for a previous poll to be acknowledged on the input leg of the line. A third way is to use a loop configuration.

A benefit of loop operation is that the loop structure, in effect, wires in a priority among the terminals (the terminals upstream nearest the controller receive control frames first), so that loop systems can utilize a group poll operation without contention resulting. While the links are simplex, the primary station both sends and receives, so that the operation is full duplex at the central and either full or half duplex at the secondary stations. Furthermore, SDLC secondary stations can be built that will work as either multipoint secondary, multi-multipoint secondary, or loop secondary stations.

Secondary stations on a loop facility might be connected to the loop in a variety of ways, but if the loop bit rate is low, then even 1 bit of delay per connected terminal could make the loop delay too long for many applications. So SDLC uses a method that involves a minimum insertion delay. First, the primary station follows every poll with a series of "go-ahead" markers; in fact, these are close to flags: zero followed by seven ones. A terminal wishing to respond to the poll simultaneously reads and writes into the last bit of the octet. It always writes a zero, trying to build an initial flag for a frame, but if it also reads a zero, it looks for the next go-ahead to try and capture. If, however, it reads a one, it has built a flag and can insert its data, writing over the following go-aheads. The primary continues to send go-aheads until they are received at the primary station. Their reception indicates that no further frames will be received, since secondary stations can only respond at the first go-ahead following a poll. Zero-delay-loop connection is possible, but does not allow for regeneration and retiming of the bits as they are repeated around the loop. Therefore, either the length of an SDLC loop must be limited, or regeneration equipment with delay (between ½-bit and 1-bit times for most modulation schemes) must be inserted at each station.

8.4.9 Scheduling

The primary SDLC station is responsible for efficient scheduling of the line. To this end implementations define various parameters, while SNA imposes various others. One of these is MAXOUT: the maximum number of I-frames a station can receive before being polled (mutatus mutandus: before receiving the Final bit). Another is PASSLIM: the maximum number of I-frames a station can receive before the next station in the polling list is polled (at the primary) or an RR (Final) is returned without I-frames (at a secondary).

8.4.10 Inoperative

In SNA, the primary SDLC station executes a retry, pause, retry algorithm when attempting to recover from errors. The number of retries before a pause, the length of the pause, and the number of retry, pause repetitions are customer-selected network definition parameters. When the entire series of retries (including pauses) has been exhausted without successfully transmitting or receiving a frame, the primary declares that secondary station to be inoperative. This inoperative event is conveyed to PU Services for the node in which the primary status resides; from there it is conveyed to the SSCP currently in session with the PU via an INOPERATIVE message. The SSCP notifies the network operator of the failure; he or she can take recovery action as appropriate. For instance, a switched network connection may be activated to back up a nonswitched line. For links to cluster controllers and terminals, the SSCP also notifies LUs that have been using this link of the failure of their sessions.

At the secondary station an inoperative condition is declared based upon inactivity on the line. Other processing is similar.

Other implications of inoperative events are discussed under path control.

8.4.11 Other SDLC Topics

SDLC is a subset of high-level data link control (HDLC) defined by ISO standards [13]. The performance benefits of SDLC have been thoroughly studied [14]. One result has been to show that use of Selective Reject only appreciably improves throughput on lines that are severely degraded. Thus, SDLC DLC elements easily provide FIFO delivery of messages by not using Selective Reject.

8.4.12 Summary of SDLC Synchronization

In summary, SDLC synchronizes adjacent nodes at the:

1. Physical connection level. In conjunction with the node's PU services, a switched connection is established or a nonswitched connection is verified to exist.

2. Bit, character, and frame levels. Errors are removed by retransmission. Multidropped or loop-connected adjacent nodes are scheduled in an efficient way.

3. Path control–to–path control level. The XID command, pause–retry logic, and I-frame transmission establish and maintain the ability of adjacent PC elements to exchange messages. SDLC also helps to synchronize the network users of a given link with the state of that link by:

    (a) Passing XID data to the local PU. From there it is sent to the SSCP that requested activation of the link.

    (b) Passing CONTACTED to the local PU. From there it is sent to the SSCP that asked for CONTACT synchronization with that station. See the network service section below for more information on contact synchronization.

    (c) Passing INOPERATIVE to the local PU. From there it is sent to the SSCP that activated the link or station.

    (d) Passing INOPERATIVE to the local PU, which, for links between subarea nodes, broadcasts this information to adjacent subarea nodes. See Sec. 8.5 for more detail.

8.5 PATH CONTROL

8.5.1 Routing

Path control (PC) is responsible for delivering messages from origin-to-destination *transmission control elements* (TCE). To do this, PC employs several levels of multiplexing/demultiplexing. Both levels of multiplexing result in a merger of messages on the link queues served by DLC elements. Each link queue contains all messages destined for a specific adjacent node; this is the primary station if the queue is served by a secondary station, and vice versa. Path control, however, does not see this detail of DLC operation.

The first level of demultiplexing, or routing, occurs when the high-order bits (subarea portion) of the destination address held in the transmission header are examined to identify messages destined for this node. Those not so destined are sent to the link queue named in the subarea routing table. Those which do remain are demultiplexed on the remaining bits (element portion) of the address so as to arrive at a particular destination. Then, the third level of demultiplexing is applied on the origin address field to reach an individual transmission control element.

The pairing of transmission control elements described above has important properties, as seen above the path control interface. The immediate result is that every SNA network-level connection, or session, is identified by a pair of network addresses (origin address, destination address). Another consequence is the static partitioning of the total network address space that results. That is, each node need only coordinate the size of its subarea with other nodes: the number of element addresses used is a local node property. Further, as additional sessions are built, more local addresses are not used; rather, origin address routing is invoked. This ensures that network addresses do not have to be allocated as a scarce resource during network operation. Since individual sessions between large LUs (e.g., major subsystems such as IMS or CICS) could become a bottleneck, multiple sessions are allowed between LUs. This requires that LUs with parallel session capability be assigned multiple addresses. More detail can be found in [3] and [5].

Sessions are established by requests, called BIND for LU-LU sessions, that contain the network addresses of both TCEs. The TCE from which it is sent is part of the *primary half-session* (PHS), while the other TCE is part of the *secondary half-session* (SHS).

Path control uses a *static routing* algorithm between subareas but a dynamically defined, statically executed algorithm for the connection of clusters and terminals to the subarea network. This choice has avoided the performance losses that would be induced by dynamically updated routing schemes, as well as their tendency to behave badly under heavy load. More important, statically executed routing makes it simple to preserve FIFO deliver of messages and establish reset states for routes, properties required by the TC elements that use PC. See [5] for discussion of multiple active routes.

8.5.2 Segmenting and Blocking

Path control adapts the messages sent by TC elements to the performance constraints of links and the buffer-size constraints of adjacent nodes. The methods used are segmenting, in which a message is divided into smaller pieces (one version of packetizing) and blocking, in which (small) messages are combined into a large block in order to more efficiently use the resources of a given link. As performance-oriented features of SNA, these tools are applied selectively in current SNA products; for instance, blocking is only supported for the S/370 channel DLC, where it saves significant numbers of CPU cycles.

8.5.3 Path Control Synchronization

Path control provides reliable FDX, FIFO delivery service for sessions. Reliability means that the session ends are notified if a message may not have been delivered. To fulfill this responsibility, path control algorithms in every node broadcast notification of loss of connectivity when a DLC inoperative event occurs. For links between subareas, this is done with a LOST SUBAREA request, which is sent to all adjacent nodes and rebroadcast when received. See the later discussion of network failure. Each PC needs a routing table to direct messages between TC elements. These tables, or states, are synchronized in several ways: initially, the states of all PC elements are established by a coordinated system definition and IPL of all subarea nodes in the network; subsequently, the network can be reconfigured through re-IPL of some nodes or through sending SET CONTROL VECTOR (subarea routing) commands from the SSCPs to the PUs of the network. Each SSCP is able to synchronize the subarea nodes under its control since these (in the implemented SNA products) are IPL'ed from the SSCP.

8.5.4 Summary of PC Synchronization

In summary, PC synchronizes the half-sessions of the network through:

- Routing. Messages are routed to the destination node based on the subarea portion of their destination address. Within a node, messages are delivered to specific TC elements based on the message's origin address, destination address pair (the session ID). Messages are kept in order.

- Buffer-size coordination. Messages are segmented to match buffer-size constraints in destination nodes.

- Loss of connectivity events. When connectivity is lost, all affected subarea nodes are notified.

8.6 TRANSMISSION CONTROL

Transmission control forms the third functional layer of SNA. Transmission control elements (TCEs) exist at the origin and destination to protect the path control network from unauthorized or mistaken synthesis of destination addresses when sending, and to limit or pace the amount that each origin can send into the shared path control network. Both of these functions are corollaries of the fact that PC does not provide message queueing. Thus, the path control network only provides in-transit buffering for messages that are enroute from one TCE to another. The TCEs provide short-term buffering, while long-term queueing or storage is provided by the LUs.

In addition to providing the essential protective functions, the TCEs provide closely related services for their users: message headers are built, sequence numbers or unique identifiers are added when sending and checked when receiving, and TCEs are bound together dynamically. For LUs the permission to bind to a named destination is acquired through cooperation with LU services and the SSCP; the SSCP resolves the destination name into a network address and passes this address through LU services to a TCE. By acquiring destinations by name, the LUs are isolated from changes in the address structure within the network.

8.6.1 Boundary Function

SNA had conflicting design goals: on the one hand, cluster controllers should be attachable with full participation in the network; on the other hand, changes in the network configuration should not impact the cluster controllers. This conflict was resolved by defining several transmission header formats and introducing a *boundary function* between the cluster controllers and the global network. This boundary function translates globally addressed headers to locally addressed headers. Since the cluster controllers and terminals only deal with local addresses, changes in the global routing tables do not cause changes in these products. The boundary function acts as a transducer between the global network and the cluster controllers or terminals in other ways as well. One of these, buffer allocation, is discussed in Sec. 8.6.2.

The boundary function's address translation tables need to be synchronized with the SSCP's name to address resolution tables so that sessions can be built to the LUs in the cluster controllers. This is done through a coordinated system definition or through a flow of initialization commands from the SSCP to the boundary function. See the subsequent discussion of the SSCP.

8.6.2 Logical Units, Data Flow Control, and Pacing

Logical units act as ports to the network for end users. They provide data mapping and protocol enforcement services for the end users (either application programs or terminal operators). LUs exist in two forms, primary and secondary; LU services at a primary LU has more interaction with the SSCP than LU services at a secondary LU. Customers can supply their own LUs by writing programs that use access method macros.

Each session experiences, in general, a variable transmission delay that depends on the physical configuration of the network, the location of the LUs, and the network load. Because of this variability, the LU-to-LU protocols in SNA are designed to provide good performance over a wide range of session delays. This has been achieved by avoiding the polling mode of operation commonly used between application and device when data link and application functions were mixed, and using instead an asynchronous sending mode of operation between LUs. This is possible since all sessions are point-to-point: primary LU to secondary LU. In addition, long messages are sent as chains of smaller blocks (or packets), so that processing or printing can overlap transmission. Chaining, synchronization of asynchronous sending when required, and other controls over the flow of data on the session between two LUs are handled by data-flow-control (DFC) elements within each LU.

The TCEs provide a queue management service, called pacing. Queues can form within a session when the data-generation rate of the sending LU exceeds the data-handling rate of the receiving LU. Pacing synchronizes the data rates of the LUs and keeps these queues from getting too long, which would clog the intermediate network nodes and lead to reduced network throughput, or too short, which would cause the receiving LU to become idle while waiting for more data. Pacing consists of service messages generated by the network that ask for additional elements of the queue to be moved forward. It is performed in two stages. One stage goes from the sending TCE out to the boundary function; the second stage goes from the boundary function to the receiving TCE. This allows the number of buffers in the cluster controllers and terminals to be designed based on a fixed delay, that of the single data link to the boundary function.

The buffers at the boundary function, on the other hand, are allocated according to the network delay back to the sending LU, which varies depending upon the configuration. Increasing the buffers allocated at the boundary function can also reduce the number of cycles used in the sending LU's node by moving groups of messages to the boundary rather than moving them one at a time.

8.6.3 Summary of TCE Synchronization

In summary, TC elements synchronize LUs at the:

- Processing speed level, through pacing.

- Protection level, by building transmission headers and preventing synthesis of network addresses.

- Session protocol level, by enforcing the proper sequence of session control commands (e.g., BIND request cannot be sent unless the half-session is in a session reset state).

8.7 NETWORK SERVICES

This section discusses the services provided by the network to the network users. Session services, provided by the network's SSCPs in conjunction with LU services at each LU, are concerned with the initiation and termination of sessions under normal and failure conditions. Session services are supplied to the terminal operator or the person who controls the session behavior of the LU. This "person" is often a combination of system programmers at system definition time and subsystem (i.e., LU such as IMS) operator at run time.

Configuration services, provided by the network's SSCPs in conjunction with PU services at each PU, are concerned with the control of physical network

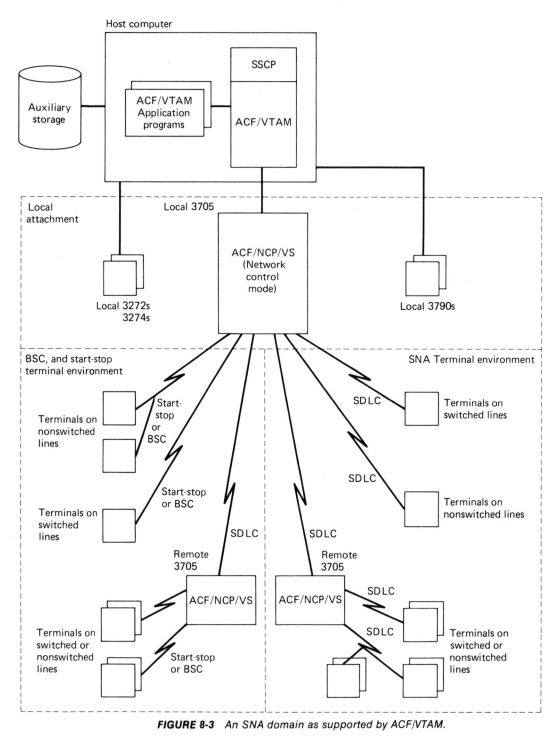

FIGURE 8-3 *An SNA domain as supported by ACF/VTAM.*

resources, notably nodes and links between them, under normal and failure conditions.

The SSCPs form the second level in a series of feedback structures that control the network. The path control network and sessions form the first level and can continue in operation without SSCP intervention.

Management services in the SSCPs and PUs of the network provide coupling between the communications network management (CNM) application(s) in the network and the CNM services in each node of the network. CNM constitutes the third level of feedback control for the network. A major CNM function is network problem determination, both preventive and recuperative [15, 16].

8.7.1 SSCP

The SSCP is the central point of control for an SNA network domain, one example of which is shown in Fig. 8.3. An SNA network consists of one or more domains. Within the domain defined to the SSCP at the time of system definition are a variety of nodes and resources connected to or residing in these nodes. At one extreme are simple terminals, such as the 3767, which contain a single LU and whose PU services are partially performed (to the extent that any are needed) by the boundary function. A slightly more complex terminal, such as the 3775, contains its own PU services. It supports a single LU. There are a variety of larger cluster controllers that support multiple LUs.

The communication controllers for the network are 370X nodes with NCP/ VS. These nodes contain extensive PU services functions to allow the SSCP to control and be informed about the lines, terminals, cluster controllers, and communication controllers that are attached.

In Fig. 8.4, the internal structure of an SSCP is shown in schematic form. Configuration services consist of command processors that control the physical resources of the network. The activation and deactivation of network logical resources (LUs) is included under configuration services. The process of setting up sessions (allocating secondary LUs to primary LUs) and taking them down (deallocating) is performed by session services (see Sec. 8.7.4). The character-coded system services component is also discussed in Sec. 8.7.4.

Figure 8.5 illustrates three domains in the middle of a larger network. Since the scope of a domain is dynamically controllable by the network operator, a wide variety of operational modes are possible. Backup of one SSCP by another is one example; control of all terminals and communication controllers by one or two SSCPs is another. Figure 8.5 also illustrates the ability for an SNA node to be shared by several SSCPs simultaneously.

8.7.2 PU Services

As the remotely located subordinate of the SSCP, PU services consist primarily of independent function groups. There are groups of commands to control nonswitched lines, an extended set to control dial ports and boundary function

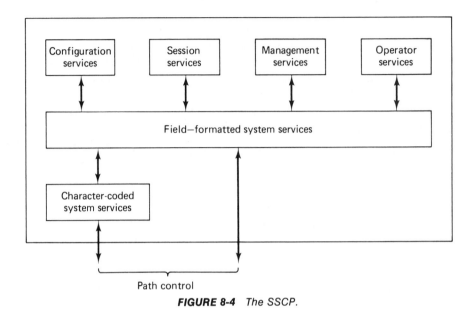

Configuration services · Session services · Management services · Operator services

Field—formatted system services

Character-coded system services

Path control

FIGURE 8-4 *The SSCP.*

resources for dial connections, and another set to control PC routing tables. There are also commands that report the existence of exception conditions, such as a link or station failure. Statistics about the error rates on links are collected and periodically transferred to the SSCP. Finally, an increase in buffer utilization past a threshold is signaled to the SSCP, as is the corresponding decrease in buffer utilization past a lower threshold.

8.7.3 Configuration Control

PU services contains many command processors for the control of the lines and dial ports that are attached to the communication controller. To illustrate the kinds of functions that are performed, the sequence of commands to control a dial-in connection from a cluster controller or terminal is shown in Fig. 8.6.

The sequence begins after the activation of the communication controllers in the network. The SSCP first enables a dial-in port at the request of the network operator. The syntax of the character-coded operator command is not defined by SNA; the semantic is: vary on (resource name). In this example the resource is a dial port, and the SSCP first translates the name into an address, then sends ACTIVATE LINK (line 1) to verify that the link is operational. When the +response is returned from the ACTLINK command processor in the controller's PU, the ACTIVATE CONNECT IN command is sent to enable the port to receive calls. If the port were to be used for dial-out (which might be triggered by a request from a primary LU to initiate a session with a secondary LU in a cluster controller), CONNECT OUT would be sent. The connect-in and connect-out command interpreters are synchronized so that the use of a port to connect-out will override a preestablished use for connect-in (if a connection has not already been made), and when that connection is dropped the port will again be enabled for connect-in.

A successful ACTIVATE CONNECT IN results in the port being enabled for auto-answer operation. Typically, this means raising *data terminal ready* (DTR) and operating the modem according to CCITT Recommendation 108.2. After some period of time, a connection is established (line 3 in Fig. 8.6), and *data set ready* (DSR) is raised by the modem. The SDLC action is to send an XID (exchange ID) nonsequenced command. The calling station replies with XID. Since the communication controller answers as a primary station, there is potential to extend SNA to include dial-in operation of fan-out modems.

The data carried in the XID are returned to the SSCP via REQUEST CONTACT and enable the SSCP to match the station to a resource name that has been previously defined to the SSCP. Thus, while the XID identifier does not have to be unique in all the world, it does have to be unique within the domain of the SSCP. At line 5 an ABANDON CONNECTION (not shown in Fig. 8.6) can be sent if the XID is not known to the SSCP. Assuming that the calling station is known to the SSCP, a SET CONTROL VECTOR (STATION) is sent

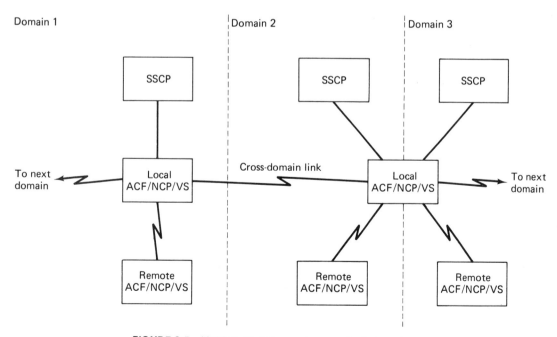

FIGURE 8-5 *Multiple domains and convenient shared control.*

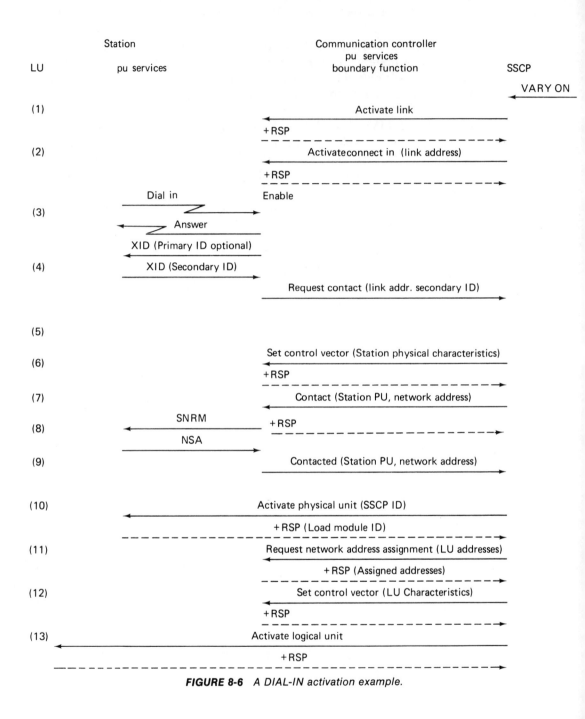

FIGURE 8-6 *A DIAL-IN activation example.*

to the PU. It contains the parameters necessary to adapt the link scheduler and boundary function to the station characteristics. Parameters include the following:

1. Transmission header type (FID value of 2 or 3).

2. Maximum number of frames that can be accepted by this station before it is polled (MAXOUT in the system definition).

3. Maximum number of frames to be sent to this station before selecting another station (PASSLIM in the system definition).

4. Pause and retry parameters (see subsequent section on maintenance, failure, and repair).

5. Maximum segment size.

This is followed (line 6) by CONTACT (also used on nonswitched lines), which instructs DLC to issue a *set normal response mode* (SNRM) command. The *nonsequenced acknowledgment* (NSA) is returned, and CONTACTED synchronizes the SSCP with this event. Note that this synchronization uses a separate command, CONTACTED, rather than the +response to CONTACT. This is done because the CONTACT procedure can take a long time to complete (e.g., the remote station's power is off on a nonswitched line). Lengthy CONTACT completion is further covered by sending SNRM from a slow-poll list so as not to use up all the line capacity in unacknowledged contact polls. Note that since NSA was reported in CONTACTED instead of *request initialization* (RQI), the down-the-link IPL sequence is omitted by the SSCP. If RQI were reported, the SSCP would send IPL INITIAL, several IPL TEXT commands, and an IPL FINAL command to the PU, which would send them to the remote node while the remote node's DLC was in initialization mode.

In line 10 the SSCP sends ACTIVATE PHYSICAL UNIT to the PU in the newly connected and contacted node. The network address for this ACTPU is, by convention, the link network address plus one. This eliminates a REQUEST NETWORK ADDRESS ASSIGNMENT command which would otherwise be needed. The ACTPU establishes a session between the SSCP and the PU and also further identifies the PU by returning a load module ID on the ACTPU response. This name establishes the identity of the connected station and completes the contents synchronization of the PU with the SSCP. This can be summarized by saying that the catenated string XID, LOAD MODULE ID is unique within each domain with which the station can be connected. Thus, the same station can have different contents at different times, and the same load module can be used simultaneously in many nodes.

Now, in line 11, the SSCP requests enough network addresses be assigned to this station to allow all the LUs in the cluster to be activated. Immediately following this command comes a series of SET CONTROL VECTOR commands for the LUs. Finally, in line 13, ACTIVATE LOGICAL UNIT, which creates the supervisory LU-SSCP session, is sent to each LU.

With the cluster or terminal synchronized with the network at the DLC, PC, and SSCP services levels, normal operation can proceed. LU-LU sessions will be established (see Sec. 8.7.4), used, and terminated. Sooner or later the connection will be dropped. This is done in an orderly manner under control of the SSCP, which monitors the number of sessions in progress to this station and when the count goes to zero, deactivates the LUs, PU, and station. The station deactivation uses the SDLC DISC (DISCONNECT) command, which causes the secondary station to release the connection (put the phone on-hook), typically by dropping DTR.

This disconnection process is not exercised indiscriminately. The network operator can ask the SSCP to put the PU in either of two states: disconnect when session count drops to zero, or hold connection. If in the disconnect at zero state, the connection can still be held if session termination is done with a TERMINATE (HOLD). Also, the PU can send the SSCP a REQUEST DIS-CONTACT command which can change the PU's state from hold to disconnect. Note that breaking the connection at the terminal ("hanging up the phone") is not a desirable operation, since this looks like a failure to the primary station.

8.7.4   LU Services and Session Initiation

Just as PU services are subordinated to the SSCP, LU services are subordinated to the SSCP. The location of LU services is analogous to the location of PU services: on the LU-SSCP session and above the transmission subsystem. However, LU services are not usually exposed above access method interfaces. The data that pass between LU services and the TCE on a given session include parameters, such as pacing counts and session addresses, which if synthesized by the program above the access method could result in damage to the network as a whole.

Figure 8.7 illustrates the general structure of an LU: there can be multiple end users (most likely, application programs) and multiple sessions. FM consists of presentation services and scheduling within the half-session. Each session is supported by individual DFC and presentation service components (other FM function interpreters, e.g., for FM headers, may exist but are not shown in Fig. 8.7). The half-session scheduling and multiplexing algorithm attaches end users to sessions, detaches end users from sessions, creates sessions through LU services, and destroys sessions through LU services. An LU at a low-function terminal is a subset of this picture: single session, single end user (e.g., the 3767 keyboard-printer terminal).

Figure 8.8 illustrates the role of LU services in initiating a session (lines 1 through 4). The SSCP is the focal point of this process; it is at the SSCP that

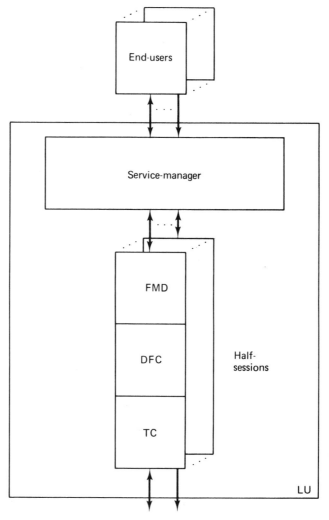

FIGURE 8-7 The LU.

network names are mapped into network addresses. It is at the SSCP that synchronization of conflicting requests for sessions is achieved.

The process of starting a session is begun when an INITIATE command arrives at the SSCP from the primary LU or the secondary LU or another authorized source (e.g., the network operator may INITIATE-OTHER). This command carries the network name of the target LU (for INITIATE-SELF; two names for INITIATE-OTHER), which LU is to be primary for this session (issuer of INITIATE or target of INITIATE; a mode for the session (e.g., batch

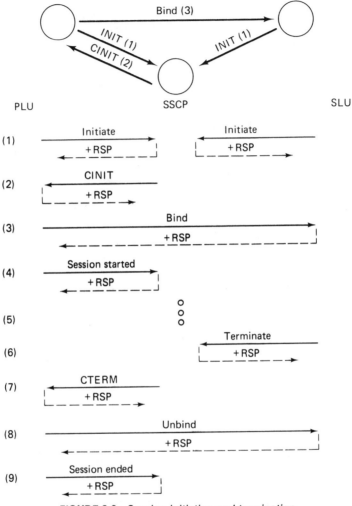

FIGURE 8-8 *Session initiation and termination.*

or interactive), and user data. Assuming that the INITIATE is accepted, a CONTROL INITIATE (CINIT) command is built by the SSCP and sent to LU services at the PLU. The CINIT carries enough information (e.g., the network address of the SLU) to enable LU services to construct a BIND command. Parameters in the BIND can be modified and added by the primary LU and then the BIND is sent by common session control for a newly activated TCE (see Fig. 8.8). The BIND is processed by the secondary LU's session control (also by the boundary function if present). If all the BIND parameters are acceptable to the secondary LU (including the primary LU's name), a positive response is returned to the primary LU and the session participants have been synchronized. The SSCP is synchronized with the successful binding of the secondary LU to the primary LU via the SESSION STARTED command.

The binding process can be divided into two levels of synchronization: allocation of use and tailoring of behavior. The basic allocation function requires only the translation of network name(s) into network addresses; on this basis, the CINIT command would merely carry the network address of the secondary LU to which a BIND was to be sent. After BIND, the primary LU and secondary LU could tailor their behavior to any session local protocols that they needed. This basic approach suffers from defects which prevent its exclusive adoption. To understand these, consider that there are *m* primary LU and *n* secondary LU implementations of SNA, and the matrix of which primary LUs have a requirement to go into session with which secondary LUs is dense.

Thus, one of several alternatives must obtain:

1. The primary LUs design interfaces matched to individual secondary LUs and conversely: behavior is tailored at product design. In effect, all LUs in the network keep a table indexed by LU name which contains a description of the command and data sequences and data formats to be used when in session with that LU. Since primary LUs might share an entry, the table might be indexed with a mode name distinct from the LU name. This scheme can be used in SNA when one end of the session contains a customer-written LU. The BIND carries both MODE name and PLU name parameters.

2. The primary LUs could all work with the same fixed set of command and data sequences (i.e., protocols) and data formats: behavior tailored at architecture specification. The secondary LUs would be fixed-function. This scheme was considered for the SNA fixed-function LUs (such as LU type 1; see below for more about LU types) but was rejected when it was clear that it implied poor performance in a networking environment. In particular, the various primary LUs had intrinsically different requirements for the protocols on a session; the secondary LU would have had to operate in a strict HDX mode; the keyboard being locked when a chain was completely sent and only unlocked upon explicit command from the primary LU. Primary LUs that did not want to lock the keyboard so often (e.g., CICS) would have generated extra traffic and created unnecessary session turnaround delays just to manage the keyboard lock.

3. The secondary LUs in the terminals could keep a table of alternative protocols, a mode table as in 1. When a primary LU wanted to operate in a particular way, it would send a mode name in the BIND, thus

adapting the SLU to its requirements. This variation of option 1 replaces the user-written LUs with microcoded LUs designed into the product. The problem with this approach is that it is not very open-ended. What if a primary LU with a new mode comes along? Are a whole series of new hardware products to be designed? Another way of describing this approach is that it results in a very tight interlock between the development cycles of the primary LUs (usually software products) and secondary LUs (usually hardware products). This approach was rejected because of this interlock.

4. Instead of a table indexed by mode names, the LUs could synchronize by sharing the same syntax and semantics for the entries in the mode tables. The entries, rather than their names, could be sent in BIND. This implies an architected structure for the the protocols and data formats on LU-LU sessions, but has the advantage of stability of the interface once it is established. This is, in fact, the approach that was adopted for SNA.

To return to the BIND command itself, we see that it carries the architected parameters needed to establish the operating mode specified by the mode name in INITIATE. These parameters could be built by the primary LU based on tables indexed by mode names. In this case the mode names would be local to the primary LUs; the same mode name might have different meanings for different primary LUs. Also, each primary LU would have to provide a means to create the mode table contents. This approach would have resulted in sizable costs for the primary LUs and inconveniences for the customer's system programmers, so the mode tables were moved into the SSCP. There, the mode tables are associated with the SLUs in the network; that is, the same mode name may have different meanings for different secondary LUs. When the SSCP is building the CINIT command, the mode name is used to index the mode tables and extract a partial BIND image which contains the architected parameters that are to be fixed for the duration of the session.

In addition to the primary LUNAME and a mode name, an INITIATE from a secondary LU can carry user data. The SSCP does not modify the secondary LU's user data in any way but passes it directly to the primary LU, where it acts as an extension to mode or may carry authorization data. The primary LU puts its own user data in the BIND and it acts as an extension to the BIND image at the secondary LU.

Notice that the session initiation triangle keeps all three parties to the process in synchronism. It would not do, for instance, for the SSCP to send BIND commands to both LUs simultaneously, since this could result in the arrival of data at the SLU before the BIND.

8.7.5 Negotiable BIND and Reducing SYSDEF

While the BIND triangle described above solved many problems, it left unsolved certain others. The most pressing of these concerns was the need to SYSDEF ("define to the system") the LOGMODE tables. SYSDEF (in all its many forms) has benefits: it allows widely used, hence low-cost products to be tailored to unique customer requirements. But it should be minimized whenever possible. Consider, for instance, the parameter variations ("features") that occur in terminals; these have to be specified when the terminal is ordered; when it is used with an SNA network the terminal should be able to tell the network about itself rather than being specified to the network's components another time.

Some parameters [e.g., the LUNAME(s) and PUNAME for a terminal] cannot be included in a node's microcode since they must be synchronized with all other network names and may change. Rather, they have to be SYSDEFed to the SSCP(s) whose domains include the node. Other parameters (e.g., what kind of transmission header is used) can be passed to the network in XID. These are data link control or path control parameters; the binding time is the connection and activation time of the node. What about the parameters that describe the LUs in a node? These, too, could be passed to the SSCP at activation (perhaps on the LU-SSCP session), but to do so would cause an early binding of these parameters. To be useful, it would also force the SSCP to contain an algorithm for the dynamic construction of mode table entries. In some fashion these entries would have to be correlated to the customer-specified mode names themselves.

Fortunately, a better solution exists: the BIND parameters can be negotiated. That is, the same fields that exist in BIND can be included in the BIND response, thus creating a "Session ID and Parameter" exchange that is similar to the XID exchange.

The SLU is then given a convenient and late binding method to synchronize the PLU with the current capabilities of the SLU. The BIND triangle is still useful for establishing initial values for the negotiation. If, through some mistake (e.g., the operator logs on to an application that does not support the terminal), a satisfactory BIND cannot be established, the PLU UNBINDs the session.

8.7.6 Character-Coded LU Services Commands

The commands in SNA are constructed in field-formatted form, each field being a data type (binary, bit string, character string) suitable for easy program processing. Cluster controllers (e.g., the IBM 3791) construct commands such as INITIATE in field-formatted form from character strings entered by terminal operators, or from data passed to the controller's LU services from an application program. While the syntax analysis of a string that is to be parsed into INITIATE is not difficult, it constitutes more function than a fixed-function terminal (e.g., IBM 3767) can contain. Thus, the SSCP is provided with a syntax analyzer which translates between the field-formatted commands used by the SSCP (see Fig. 8.4) and the character-coded input and output adapted to the terminal's LU-SSCP session. The DFC and presentation services on these character-coded system services sessions are architecturally defined, as are the semantics of the commands made available to the terminal operator on this session. The syntax of this language is not architecturally defined but is left up to each SSCP implementation for definition. For instance, the character-coded verb Logon might be mapped into the SNA-defined INITIATE.

8.7.7 Session Termination and Other Services

Sessions can be torn down via the SSCP, as shown in Fig. 8.8. The secondary LU can send TERMINATE-SELF (Logoff) or the network operator can send TERMINATE-OTHER (Vary Net Deactivate) to the SSCP. The SSCP expands this into a CONTROL TERMINATE (CTERM on line 7) and sends it to LU services at the PLU. If the TERMINATE specifies unconditional (i.e., forced), UNBIND is sent immediately. If the type is conditional, LU services does not UNBIND immediately but waits until the primary LU agrees to end the session.

This latter kind of terminate can also be accomplished through a DFC command called REQUEST SHUTDOWN, which is sent from SLU to PLU and asks for an orderly termination of the session. In this case, or when the PLU decides to UNBIND the session on its own, the PLU can send UNBIND and SESSION ENDED or it can send TERMINATE-SELF and receive a CTERM in reply. The choice of method depends upon the detailed product-dependent interface between the LU and LU services. The SSCP may optionally supply additional services to the LUs. These include queueing of INITIATE requests as well as access to the network operator commands. A detailed discussion of these optional services is beyond the scope of this chapter.

8.7.8 Cross-Domain Session Services

SNA allows networks to be configured with one or more SSCPs. When there are two or more, each SSCP controls its own domain. These may overlap since certain PUs (e.g., ACF/NCP/VS) support concurrent control by multiple SSCPs.

When an LU in one domain desires a session with an LU in another domain, the SSCPs work together to build the session while still maintaining the LU's view of the network as a single domain. Basically, the record of a session maintained by a single SSCP for same-domain sessions is maintained in each of the SSCPs involved in a cross-domain session. Before the SSCPs can cooperate, they need to be connected. This is done by sending ACTIVATE CROSS-DOMAIN-RESOURCE-MANAGER (ACTCDRM) from one SSCP to the other. A race can result if both send ACTCDRM at the same time; such a race is resolved in favor of the SSCP with the larger SSCP-ID (a parameter in ACTCDRM). ACTCDRM is negotiated analogously to negotiable BIND. SSCP to SSCP sessions are terminated by DEACTIVATE CDRM. Both ACTCDRM and DEACTCDRM are typically sent as a result of network operator commands.

The CROSS-DOMAIN synchronization methods are illustrated by the BIND quadrangle in Fig. 8.9. Just one of many possible cross-domain session services sequences, it illustrates most of the principles involved. In line 1, the SLU has issued an INITIATE, asking for a session between itself and *B*. This request is transformed into a cross-domain initiate (CDINIT) and sent to *B*'s SSCP for resolution of *B*'s network address. SSCP-A, while it knows *B*'s network name, does not know *B*'s address; indeed, if SSCP-B has to dynamically activate *B* (e.g., by auto-dial to the node containing *B*), *B*'s network address may not be determined until it is needed.

The positive response to CDINIT contains *B*'s network address as well as a

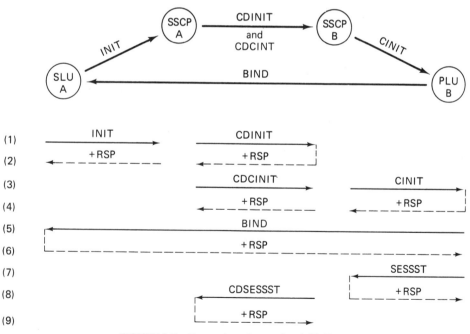

FIGURE 8-9 *Cross-domain session initiation.*

decision about which LU will be the PLU (if this was not specified by the INIT or by SSCP-A). The +RSP to CDINIT is transformed into a +RSP to INIT; the session initiation has been approved by both SSCPs. If B's name were unknown to SSCP-A, or if SSCP-B had not been activated, or if B was not available, and so on, the response to the INIT would be negative, with a sense code detailing the reason for the rejection.

In this example, A is the SLU for the session, so its SSCP sends a CDCINIT (line 3) containing the partial BIND image extracted from A's mode table. SSCP-B constructs a complete BIND image and sends CINIT to B. When this is accepted, the responses to CINIT and CDCINIT are returned in line 4. Since which LU will be primary is not known until the +RSP to CINIT, and since CINIT can originate on either side, MODE is carried in CINIT. To eliminate, by design, protocol errors caused by multiple transmission of different MODE values, the CDCINIT does not carry MODE. Instead, it is saved by SSCP-B and inserted in the CINIT.

In lines 5 and 6 the BIND flows, followed in lines 7, 8, and 9 by SESSION-STARTED and CD-SESSION-STARTED. At this time the session initiation procedure is complete; the SSCPs will not get involved again until the session terminates or fails. Since there is only one session connecting the SSCPs, and there may be many session initiation or termination procedures active at once, a procedure-correlation-ID is generated (e.g., by SSCP-A while building CDINIT) and carried in each CD message of the procedure. In this respect (allowing multiplexing of multiple activities over a single session) it resembles the use made of the link network address in the configuration requests such as ACTLINK.

8.7.9 Summary of Network Services Synchronization

In summary, network services in the SSCPs, PUs, and LUs serve to synchronize the elements of the network in these ways:

- Coordination of network physical configuration with network address assignments.

- Correlation of network addresses with network names.

- Modification of physical configuration in response to session initiation requests and session termination requests.

- Resolution of conflicting session requests; allocation of access to LUs.

- Tailoring of session protocols to those mutually desired by the LUs.

- Translation between character-coded and formatted request forms.

8.8 NETWORK MAINTENANCE: FAILURE AND REPAIR

8.8.1 Maintenance and Problem Determination

The maintenance of an SNA network can be divided into two pieces: node repair and line repair. In general, the approach to node repair is to localize the repair action to minimize the number of customer engineers required to make the repair. This contrasts with the remote maintenance philosophy used for pre-SNA terminals and reflects the decreasing cost of microcode relative to service costs. Node repair, then, involves resident microcode diagnostics and maintenance statistics which can be used by the customer to determine if a problem exists before the customer engineer is called. Indeed, it is possible in many cases to verify that the terminal or cluster is operating correctly, thus suggesting that the problem is in the common carrier equipment. The PU-SSCP session is used to carry maintenance statistics records back through the SSCP to the communications network management application (CNMA), where they can be used for problem localization. See [15, 16] for more discussion.

A similar situation exists for the lines. RECORD MAINTENANCE STATISTICS (RECMS) commands are generated at each communication controller PU and routed through the SSCP to the CNMA, where the statistics are filed. The logs can be scanned periodically to detect marginally satisfactory lines, modems, and line interface hardware.

8.8.2 Detection of Failures

The RECMS command is generated as a by-product of the primary SDLC station's retransmission attempts. In fact, counts of the number of retries and the number of successful transmission are kept; when the counters fill, their contents are reported and they are reset. A brief digression into the observed failure properties of common carrier facilities will motivate the structure of this algorithm.

During the development of SNA, studies were made [17] that revealed an interesting fact about line failures; many of them were of short duration and were observed to heal without any repair action on the part of the computer system operator. It appears from these data that there are two distinct groups of sources for failures: a short-repair-duration group and a long-repair-duration group. In the first group are such things as carrier fade with automatic switchover or loss of signal introduced by service and reconfiguration efforts at a common carrier wire center or switching center. In the long-duration group are such things as repair of a cable severed by a road construction crew.

SNA adopted a pause-and-retry algorithm at the primary station which can be used to maintain synchronization during short-duration failures. The algorithm contains three parameters R, P, and M. R is the number of immediate retransmissions to be attempted to a given station before a pause of P seconds is entered. M is the number of times to repeat the retries-and-pause sequence before declaring that the station is inoperative. Depending upon the application, R, P, and M can be set to allow continued operation of the line in a larger or smaller fraction of the failures. Once the station (or line, when the modem drops DSR unexpectedly) is declared inoperative, an INOP command is sent to the SSCP followed by an RECMS (to report the final status of the counters).

The ability to tailor the SDLC pause, retry logic to particular environments is one of the benefits of the asymmetric error-recovery responsibility built into SDLC: the primary station, not the sending station, is responsible for retransmission timeouts. This can be contrasted with the BSC design, in which the secondary stations have to timeout and retransmit (or send ENQ). When the secondary station algorithm is in hardware or microcode, this implies a fixed number of retries.

At the SDLC secondary station, a nominally 20-s link inactivity timer is operating, so if the line has really been severed, the secondary station will declare an inoperative condition after 20 s. In this case, the secondary station will be in normal disconnected mode (NDM) when the pause-and-retry algorithm finally succeeds. The SDLC response to a poll when in NDM is disconnected mode (DM). This, too, will cause an INOP to be returned to the SSCP from the primary station. A cold activation (e.g., Vary Net Activate cluster name) is necessary to recover from a failure that has proceeded to the point of an INOP, while no recovery action above the link level is required for failures recovered prior to an INOP. Of course, before the cold activation can succeed, a physical configuration change (repair or switched alternate) is necessary. After reactivation, individual sessions reestablish synchronism.

8.8.3 Failure of Sessions

Sessions fail as a result of physical failures. Either half-session can fail, or the path between them can fail. The network elements cooperate to ensure that each surviving half-session is notified of the failure; this ensures that the interface between half-sessions is an event-driven interface, not only during normal operation, but during failures. Repair of session failures proceeds according to customer procedures:

- The failed session may be restarted, the half-sessions resynchronized, and work resumed. See the discussion of sync point that follows.

- The failed session may be restarted with the half-sessions initialized to reset states. The end users (typically a terminal operator and a program) may then resynchronize through non-SNA means. For instance, if a session between a printer and an RJE LU fails, the work station's operator can issue a "backspace N pages" command before resuming the printing. Or if a data-base record was being updated when the session failed, the operator can inquire into the data base to see if the update was completed. If not, the update can be repeated. This, of course, constrains the design of the data base; the absence of this constraint is one of the benefits of the sync point technique.

- For sessions involving distributed application programs, the work that was proceeding on the failed session may be performed (in a degraded fashion) in a local fashion. For instance, a credit inquiry into a central master file might be handled locally with the aid of general guidelines and a negative credit list when the central positive credit file is unavailable.

- The work on the failed session might proceed via an alternative session. For instance, if an RJE job cannot be submitted to a failed CPU, it may be possible to submit it to an alternative CPU.

8.8.4 Route Extension Failures

The path between two half-sessions is composed of a route defined by the subarea routing tables in one or more nodes and, optionally, a route extension between a boundary function and attached cluster controller. When the route extension fails, it is detected by the primary DLC at the boundary function; an INOP (STATION|LINK) is sent to the SSCP that contacted the station. Of course, station failure is undistinguishable (at the primary station) from failure of the attached node itself.

The SSCP notifies (synchronizes) all its own LUs that are affected by the failure; it also notifies any other SSCPs and they notify their affected LUs. The network operator of the original SSCP is also notified. The operator can initiate repair action or can activate a backup switched line to the affected node. The switched backup, if successful, results in the lost LUs being rejoined to the network under the same names as they had prior to the failure. Of course, if the route extension was switched prior to the failure, it can be reestablished.

The LUs inside the attached node are also notified of the failure of the route extension. Session restart proceeds from the reset state for the session.

8.8.5 Transit Link Failures

When a DLC element (primary or secondary) detects a failure of a transit link an INOP (link|station) is sent to the owning SSCP(s) just as is the case with the route extension links. The SSCP(s) notify their operators of the damage. The operators take appropriate repair or reconfiguration action; a SET CONTROL VECTOR (SUBAREA routing) can be used to establish an alternate backup link, or re-IPL of one or more nodes can be used to reconfigure the network's connectivity. See [5] for multiple route usage.

The affected sessions have yet to be notified; this is accomplished by notifying all affected subarea nodes and their owning SSCP(s) of the loss of connectivity to the subarea nodes that were routed to via the lost transit link.

The PU on each end of the failed link scans its subarea routing table and builds a LOST SUBAREA (LSA) command that is broadcast to all adjacent subarea nodes. Their PUs prune the subarea list in the LSA command by deleting

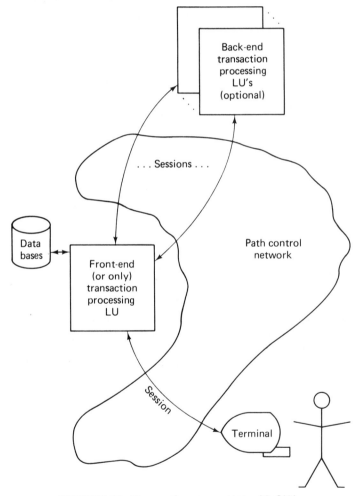

FIGURE 8-10 *Transaction processing with SNA.*

those subareas to which they retain connectivity. Then they rebroadcast the LSA to all adjacent subarea nodes except the one from which they received the LSA. Notice that this algorithm requires that each message received by path control from data link control carry a pointer to the link over which it was received.

As each PU receives an LSA, It also sends it to all its active SSCPs. They are able to scan their list of LU-LU sessions and notify those LUs that have been affected by the failure. See also reference [5]

8.8.6 Transaction Processing and Sync Point

A transaction processing system (TPS) presents to its application programs an environment that allocates ownership of various system resources (e.g., a terminal, data base, queueing facility, etc.) for the duration of a process. This process is normally created by the transaction processing system at the direction of a terminal operator who includes the identity (transaction code) of the process (e.g., an application program) within a message.

The duration of a process and therefore ownership of a terminal or device is typically very short (in some systems one message in and one message out). Thus, the setup time for this ownership is as important as the normal operation. Thus, in SNA, a transaction processing system is an LU; it multiplexes access to SNA sessions over multiple application programs (end users). See Fig. 8.10 for an illustration of the relationship among a transaction processing LU, terminal operators, and optional "back-end" transaction processing LUs.

A transaction processing LU normally presents a high-level interface for data communications that allows flexibility of operation with various otherwise incompatible devices and that also considerably eases migration problems.

Part of the environment usually presented to the application program includes recovery facilities that allow the effects of a failing process to be backed out to a previously identified point. Facilities may also be provided to restart a process at the identified point.

8.8.7 Sync-Point Recovery

In connecting multiple transaction processing LUs together with SNA sessions, it was desirable to maintain this same environment for currently written application programs (in which the customers have a heavy investment). In addition, it was also desirable to extend the environment so that new application programs might avail themselves of the benefits of distributed processing.

While a transaction is running, its access to system resources (e.g., a session, or data-base entries) is monitored by the LU. As changes are made (updating or deleting a data-base entry; sending a message on a session), the resource is locked for exclusive use and a record is made of the change. When the transaction is complete (more precisely, when all the related processing, or work, is finished), these records are erased, the locks released, and the work is thereby committed.

If a failure occurs (e.g., the program fails, the LU fails, or the session fails), the change records are used to undo the partial results. This restores the state of the protected resources to that in which they began at the start of this atomic unit of work ("atomic" since it either completely succeeds or completely fails). This synchronizing service (sync pointing) by an LU really creates a kind of high-level computer instruction out of a customer-defined set of lower-level instructions. Just as the state of a CPU is not observable (to application programs) during the middle of an ADD REGISTER instruction, so the state of the LU is not visible (to the application programs) during the middle of an atomic unit of work.

Since SNA supplies facilities (sessions) to connect two application programs, some means was needed to synchronize the sync points on each side of the session, thus creating a distributed atomic unit of work. The sequence numbers in requests, together with the responses correlated by carrying the same number, create this synchronization. Thus, when one transaction comes to sync point, a special request (request sync point, coded as a definite response requested) is made to the other half-session. If the application protocols have operated successfully, the other transaction will also be ready to take a sync point and a positive response will be returned. If the sync point fails, a negative response is returned and the initial requestor backs out to the beginning of the atomic unit of work.

It is now easy to see that a session failure appears to the sync-point requestor as a missing sync-point response if the failure occurs after a sync-point request but prior to receipt of the response. This response can be reconstructed at session restart by exchanging and testing the values of the sequence numbers on each flow (primary to secondary and secondary to primary). This is done by sending the SET-AND-TEST-SEQUENCE-NUMBERS (STSN) request and response after BIND but prior to the beginning of the use of the session.

With the half-session states resynchronized, useful work can proceed, perhaps with a restart of the transaction-processing application program that was running at the time of the failure.

8.8.8 Summary of Maintenance: Failure and Repair Synchronization

To summarize, the network components create synchronization in these areas:

- Maintenance data are recorded and made available for inquiry into the state of the network and its components.

- Failures of links and nodes are detected and reported to all affected operators.

- Damaged sessions are synchronized with failures through failure notification.

- Network services can be used to restructure the network for backup and recovery.

- Restarted sessions begin with resynchronization of the half-sessions.

8.9 LU-LU PROTOCOLS

In previous sections we have discussed the synchronization that is established and maintained across various portions of an SNA network. However, all these discussions have dealt with only the foundation of the structure: SNA exists to allow LUs to communicate with one another and to thereby perform useful work. In the language we have favored, this means to create synchronization between end users and thereby create desired changes in end-user states. Operators are informed, data bases are updated, computations are performed, and so on.

LUs share certain things in common with PUs and SSCPs: they contain both half-sessions and a service manager that connects them all together and connects them to the end user(s) of the LU (see Fig. 8.7).

8.9.1 Data Flow Control

The data-flow-control (DFC) elements in LU-LU half-sessions contain considerably more function than they do in LU-SSCP, PU-SSCP, SSCP-SSCP, or PU-PU sessions. The first and most basic fact about DFC is its initimate relationship to the attach manager, a subtask (or process) within the LU. DFC maintains states that are used by the attach manager to connect one program (from a library of possible programs) at a time to the half-session. In fact, the request to attach the program can come in a message received from the other half-session, or it can come from a source outside the SNA LU structure but within the product or system component that is implementing the LU. Actual implementations of this structure include:

1. JES2 as the LU and device processors as the programs.

2. IMS/VS as the LU and the MIDs or MODs (interpreted programs) as the programs.

3. CICS/VS as the LU and transaction processors as the programs.

4. The IBM 3767 as the LU with a single microcoded program permanently attached.

This ability to attach one of a number of programs leads immediately to race conditions, one of which is illustrated in Fig. 8.11. A session is shown with a primary half-session (PHS) and a secondary half-session (SHS). In this example both half-sessions try to start a unit of work (i.e., a bracket) by asking the other half-session to attach a program. The message on line 1 carries a BB indicator and the name, x, of the desired program in the SHS. The SHS is already in a bracket at the time this request is received, so cannot honor the request. It is rejected with a negative response carrying a sense code indicating the reason for the rejection. X′0813′ means a bracket race was the cause, while X′0814′ means a bracket race caused the rejection, but when the SHS will honor a BB, a READY-TO-RECEIVE DFC command will be sent to the PHS. Following an X′0813′ the PHS must try the BB following the end of each bracket.

In line 3 the BB from the SHS is received and honored. Several things are happening here. First, the SHS in this example is the Bracket First Speaker, and

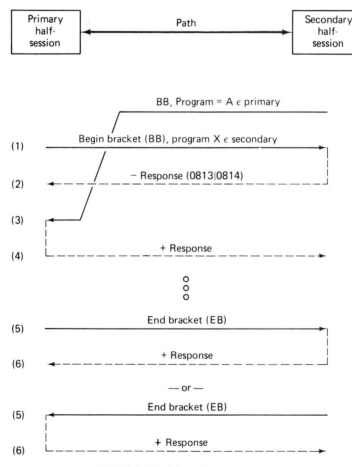

FIGURE 8-11   *A bracket race.*

is allowed to win all begin bracket races. Second, the PHS, the bidder in the bracket protocol, has used the nonqueued option for the response mode to its BB request. This allowed line 2 to be processed ahead of line 3, since line 2 will bypass the pacing queues in the TC elements of the session.

After program *A* has been attached to the half-session, messages are ex-

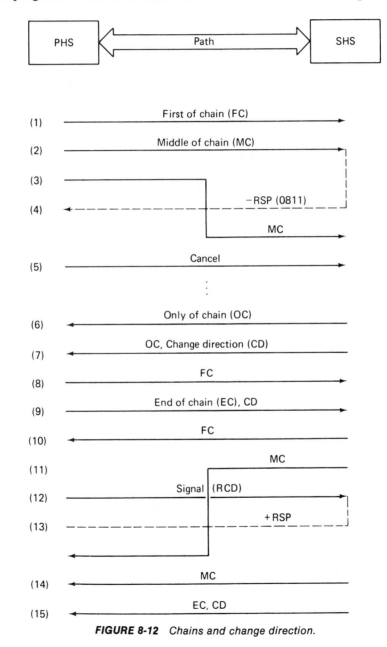

FIGURE 8-12 *Chains and change direction.*

changed between the half-sessions. Finally, the work is completed and one program or the other ends. End Bracket is sent to the other half-session to detach the program at that end.

The use of brackets allows efficient access to multiple destinations within a single LU. Sessions, which also address multiple destinations (LUs), cannot be efficiently used in this range of applications because of the overhead involved in establishing and breaking the sessions themselves. Nor are parallel sessions an answer; since the transaction lifetime is (usually) short, sessions have to be used by many transactions to make them economical. But this need for several levels of multiplexing is not new; sessions are analogous to dial connections to time-sharing systems and brackets are analogous to command invocations.

The messages that are exchanged may be rather long. To allow efficient transport through the path control network, and in order to match the buffer sizes within the half-sessions, long messages are broken up into chains of individual message units, called *request units* (RUs) in SNA.

In order to allow the data sent by the programs to be arbitrary, the BB, EB, and chaining indicators are carried in a *request header* (RH) in front of each RU. Some of the communications between DFC elements is not frequent enough to justify using separate bits in the RH. These are carried as DFC commands (the RH distinguishes between FM data and DFC RUs). CANCEL, used to prematurely end a chain, is one example of a DFC command; RTR is another.

Figure 8.12 lines 1 through 5 illustrate one use of CANCEL. A chain being received at the SHS is found to carry unneeded data. A −response (0811), perhaps generated by the CANCEL key on a printer, is returned to the PHS, and this forces the chain to be ended prematurely. If line 4 had been EC, CANCEL would not have been needed. CANCEL is also used in a "forward" cancel of chain (e.g., without having been solicited by a −RSP). The CANCEL key on the IBM 3767 generates such a CANCEL request when the terminal is in the middle of sending a chain.

Figure 8.12, lines 6 through 9, illustrate the use of the change direction (CD) indicator in the RH to control the direction of data flow on the session. Although not all sessions are run in this half-duplex (with brackets) fashion, many are. Of course, it may be necessary (perhaps due to data content) to retrieve the right to send. This can be done with the Request Change Direction command, coded as a SIGNAL DFC command with the signal code X'0001'. SIGNAL, flowing expedited, bypasses the pacing queues and is received (e.g., through an exit) even if the pacing queue in the receiving half-session is not being read. The current chain is ended as quickly as possible and the CD bit returned.

8.10 LU TYPES

The FM component in the half-session and the LU's services manager cooperate to present an appearance to their session partner. When this appearance has been defined by the architecture, it is called an LU type; LU types are similar in concept to network virtual terminals. The definition of LU types has allowed more products to support each other for a given investment than would otherwise have been the case. This is so because the number of products is much greater than the number of LU types. For generality, LU type 0 is available for product- and customer-defined uses.

LU type 1 presents the appearance of a keyboard-printer console with optional alternate data destinations within the half-session, such as printers, punches, and diskettes. With suitable use of negative responses, a product can build a receive-only printer under LU type 1. LU type 2 presents the appearance of a keyboard display with optional local copy capability. LU type 3 is a display data-stream receive-only printer, while LU type 4 is similar to LU type 1 but with a different choice of data streams. LU type 7 is similar to LU type 2, but with a different data stream.

LU type 6 provides a general-purpose transaction program–to –transaction program, distributed processing capability. Programs can be invoked remotely (see the discussion of the attach manager, above). Certain of these programs, called models, are architecturally defined. Models exist for remote access to queues, subsystem operators, time scheduled execution of programs, and DL/1 data bases. Product-supplied models exist for a variety of file access methods.

LU type 6 has been used to implement complete function shipping for transaction processing programs [18]. In this application of SNA protocols, an application program accesses facilities (e.g., queues, DL/1, etc.) as if they were locally attached when they are in fact in another node.

8.10.1   Data-Stream Synchronization

LU-LU data streams provide a variety of synchronizing commands. Some of these are encoded as structured parameter fields called FM headers. The attach header used by the attach manager in LU type 6 is an example. The destination selection header used in LU types 1 and 4 is another. Other synchronization is encoded within the data stream. For instance, SNA character strings are oriented to the control of an output presentation surface (e.g., a printer). Controls are included to establish margins, page depth, and line density; others move the presentation position to new lines or columns.

8.10.2   Contention for Destinations

Each LU can have multiple sessions and multiple active destinations. When contention occurs for access to a single destination, the LU's services manager grants one request and denies the others. The protocol units at which contention can occur may be a bracket, already described; a chain, in which case a retry event is generated that is similar to RTR following −RSP(0814) for brackets; or it may be managed merely by withholding pacing (e.g., a printer's paper is being changed by an operator).

8.10.3 Summary of LU to LU Synchronization

To summarize, LU-LU synchronization is performed in these areas:

- Brackets initiation and termination; selection of programs to be attached; synchronization of bracket initiation with session termination.
- Chain size, RU size, and direction of flow.
- Selection of parameters to be used by an output destination.
- Resolution of contention for access to destinations.
- And many other ways in specific LU types and attached models.

8.11 SUMMARY

This chapter has stressed the multiple levels of synchronization created by and between components of an SNA network for the benefit of the network's users. As needs occur in a brief exposition, many details have been suppressed. Often, synchronizing behavior was described with synonymous words such as "notification" or "race resolution." This reflects the specialized language that has grown up to describe different applications of the underlying primitive: synchronization.

GLOSSARY

ACF: Advanced Communication Function. *See* NCP, TCAM, and VTAM.

BB: Begin Bracket; a flag used by DFC and carried in the RH.

BIND: The SNA command that activates a session between LUs.

CCITT: The international standards body of the common carriers.

CD: As a prefix, Cross Domain; as in CD-INITIATE or CDINIT.

CD: As an RH flag used by DFC; Change Direction.

CICS: An IBM program product that provides a transaction-processing environment for application programs. It also implements most of the functions of an SNA LU, the TC functions of the LU being implemented in the access method (e.g., VTAM). CICS provides shared access to other SNA LUs for its applications. It also provides shared access to data bases for its applications.

CTERM: Control Terminate; a command sent by the SSCP to a primary LU to tell it to UNBIND a session.

DCE: Data Communications Element (e.g., a modem or carrier facility).

DFC: Data Flow Control; the SNA component that maintains states that are used to synchronize the local half-session's send/receive protocols with its session partner.

DL/1:   Data Language One; a data base supported by IMS and CICS.

DLC: Data Link Control.

DTE: Data Terminal Equipment (e.g., an SNA node).

EB: End Bracket; a flag used by DFC and carried in the RH.

EC: End Chain; a flag in the RH that marks the end of a chain of RUs.

FDX: Full DupleX; two-way simultaneous transmission.

FID: Format Identifier; a field in the SNA transmission header that determines its format.

FM: Function Management; the SNA component that deals with data streams and other protocols above the DFC level.

FSK: Frequency Shift Keying; a form of signaling used by modems.

HDLC: High Level Data Link Control; the international standard definition of data link control. SDLC is a subset of HDLC except for functions, such as commands to control loop configurations, that are not defined in HDLC.

HDX: Half-DupleX; one-way transmission at a time.

IMS: An IBM program product that provides data-base and data communication services to its application programs. Its data communications services implement all but the TC portion of an SNA LU. *Compare* CICS.

INIT: INITiate a session; a bit encoded as opposed to a character-string form of a LOGON request. The target of the LOGON is an LU.

IPL: Initial Program Load.

ISO: International Standards Organization.

JES2:   Job Entry Subsystem 2; an RJE system that runs with MVS.

LU: Logical Unit; an SNA component that provides a port into the network for end users.

MID: Message Input Descriptor; an interpreted program in IMS that provides much of the SNA LU function for a session to IMS. The MID processes messages received from a session and typically puts them on a queue that is read by a specific application program.

MOD: Message Output Descriptor; an interpreted program in IMS that takes messages off of an output queue and sends them into an SNA session.

MVS: An IBM operating system that runs on large system/370 CPUs and on the 303X series of processors.

NCP: Network Control Program; the SNA software for the IBM 3705 communication controllers. NCP is used in conjunction with an SNA access method such as VTAM or TCAM.

NCP/VS: The program product version of NCP.

PC: Path Control; the component of SNA that does routing.

PHS: Primary Half-Session; the half-session in the PLU.

PLU: Primary Logical Unit; the LU that sent BIND.

PU: Physical Unit: the component of SNA that receives commands from an SSCP and executes them against the local resources under the PU's direct control (e.g., against links).

RH: Request Header; flags with each RU, used by TC, DFC, and FM.

RJE: Remote Job Entry.

RNR: Receive Not Ready; an HDLC/SDLC supervisory frame that means that further information frames cannot be accepted at this time.

RR: Receive Ready; an HDLC/SDLC supervisory frame that means that information frames can now be accepted.

RSP: Response; as in positive (+RSP) or negative (−RSP) response.

RTR: Ready To Receive; a DFC command used with bracket protocol to indicate that the sender of RTR can now accept a begin bracket.

RU: Request Unit; request or response message unit. Each RU has an associated RH that immediately precedes it when the RU is transmitted between nodes.

SDLC: Synchronous Data Link Control; SNA's serial-by-bit DLC protocol.

SHS: Secondary Half-Session; the half-session within the SLU.

SLU: Secondary Logical Unit; LU that receives BIND. Note that a single LU can contain both primary and secondary half-sessions and therefore can be both a primary and a secondary LU on different sessions.

SNA: Systems Network Architecture.

SSCP: System Services Control Point; a centralized point of control and supervision for an SNA network. There can be multiple SSCPs within a single network, each responsible for its own domain.

TC: Transmission Control; the SNA component that interfaces a half-session to path control.

TCAM: TeleCommunications Access Method; one SNA access method that runs on large System/370 and all 303X processors. *Contrast* VTAM.

TCE: Transmission Control Element; an instance of TC.

TPS: Transaction Processing System (e.g., IMS or CICS).

VTAM: Virtual Telecommunications Access Method; an SNA access method that runs in all System/370 and 303X and 403X processors. *Contrast* TCAM.

X.21: A DCE-to-DTE interface standard issued by the CCITT.

XID: Exchange Identification; an HDLC/SDLC frame used by SNA to exchange data that identify nodes that are being added to a network.

REFERENCES

[1] GRAY, J. P. "Line Control Procedures," *Proceedings of the IEEE*, **60**(11), pp. 1301–1312, November 1972.

[2] GRAY, J. P. "Network Services in Systems Network Architecture," *IEEE Transactions in Communications* **Com-25**(1), pp. 104–116, January 1977. A description of network services at the SNA 2 level.

[3] *Systems Network Architecture Formats and Protocol Reference Manual: Architecture Logic,* IBM Systems Library, order number SC30-3112. This is the definitive reference for details of SNA.

[4] GRAY, J. P., and C. R. BLAIR, "IBM's System Network Architecture," *Datamation*, pp. 51–56, April 1975. An overview of SNA that stresses user requirements and benefits at a SNA 2 level.

[5] GRAY, J. P., and T. B. MCNEIL, "SNA Multiple-System Networking," *IBM Systems Journal*, **18**(2), 1979. A description of the multiple-domain, multiple-host features of SNA.

[6] EADE, D. J., P. HOMAN, and J. H. JONES, "CICS/VS and Its Role in Systems Network Architecture," *IBM Systems Journal*, **16**(3), pp. 258–286, 1977. SNA's advantages to CICS/VS.

[7] *Systems Network Architecture: Logical Unit Types,* IBM Systems Library, order number GC20-1868. This contains definitions of LU types.

[8] SUSSENGUTH, E. H. "Systems Network Architecture: A Perspective," *Proceedings of the 4th International Conference on Computer Communications*, Kyoto, Japan, pp. 353–358, September 1978. Covers the rationale for SNA, its future, and its relationship to public networks and services around the world.

[9] DEATON, G. A., JR., and D. J. FRANSE, "A Computer Network Flow Control Study," *Proceedings of the 4th International Conference on Computer Communications,* Kyoto, Japan, pp. 135–140, September 1978. Results of a simulation study of SNA flow control at the SNA 3 level.

[10] *ACF/VTAM Release 2: Program Summary,* IBM Systems Library, order number GC27-0457.

[11] *ACF/NCP/VS Release 2: Network Control Program and System Support Programs General Information,* IBM Systems Library, order number GC30-3058.

[12] *ACF/TCAM Version 2: Program Summary,* IBM Systems Library, order number GC30-9520.

[13] *IBM Synchronous Data Link Control General Information*, IBM Systems Library, order number GA27-3093. An introduction to SDLC.

[14] TRAYNHAM, K. C., and R. F. STEEN, "Data Link Control and Contemporary Data Links," *IBM Technical Report TR29.0168*, June 1977, (Available from K. C. TRAYNHAM, IBM E95/B629, P.O. Box 12195, Research Triangle Park, N.C. 27709.) Performance data on SDLC and related line controls for a wide range of parameters.

[15] GILES, H. L., "Successful Network Management Hinges on Control," *Data Communications*, pp. 33–41, August 1978. A general discussion of the role and importance of network management.

[16] *Network Communications Control Facility General Information Manual*, IBM Systems Library, order number GC27-0429.

[17] MARKOV, J. D., M. W. DOSS, and S. A. MITCHELL, "A Reliability Model for Data Communications," *Proceedings of the International Conference on Communications*, Toronto, Canada, **1**, pp. 03.4.1–03.4.5.

[18] *CICS/VS Version 1: Release 4: System Programmer's Guide (OS/VS)*, IBM Systems Library, order number SC33-0071.

9

SECURITY IN COMPUTER NETWORKS

STEPHEN T. KENT

M.I.T. Laboratory for Computer Science
and
Bolt Beranek and Newman, Inc.
Cambridge, Massachusetts

9.1 INTRODUCTION AND PERSPECTIVE

Network security is a complex topic involving not only communication security but also authentication and access control measures, as well as more conventional physical, electromagnetic emanation, procedural, and personnel security controls. Recent research in computer systems security has focused attention on several of these problems (e.g., the development of theory and techniques of authentication and access control [1–7]), while the adoption of the National Bureau of Standards Data Encryption Standard (DES) [8], and the subsequent development of hardware implementing this standard, has spurred work on communication security for nonclassified applications. This chapter examines the topic of network security through the presentation of communication security, authentication, and access control techniques, and through the discussion of the integration of these techniques with computer system security measures to provide a coherent framework for network security.

There are several trends that emphasize the need to develop network security measures. The increased use of networks to provide remote access to computer facilities, coupled with improved physical security measures at computer sites, make attacks on networks more attractive to an intruder. The growth in the quantity and value of information made vulnerable by breaches of network security, exemplified by the development of electronic funds transfer systems [9], further enhances the attractiveness of networks as intruder targets. Computer systems connected by networks are more likely to cooperate in various ways to provide resource sharing for a user community, and in so doing the security of information on a given host may become dependent on the security measures employed by the network and by other hosts. Finally, the development of new network technologies makes certain types of attacks on communication systems easier (e.g., passive wiretapping attacks are easily mounted against satellite and radio networks).

Problems in network security are closely related to those in other areas. Many of the models and mechanisms developed in the course of research in computer system security are directly applicable to or easily adapted for use in the network environment. This relationship is not one-sided, however, since the security mechanisms incorporated in a computer system accessed via a network can be rendered largely ineffective if the network fails to provide a secure communication path between each user and the computer system. The interface between network and computer system security measures must be carefully designed to provide a coherent security policy across this interface and to permit the interaction of these measures in a synergistic fashion. The design of communication protocols, especially end-to-end protocols, is another area in which careful coordination with network security measures is required if the resulting system is to be both effective and efficient.

Networks span the spectrum from collections of heterogeneous, autonomous hosts, as in the ARPANET [10], to groups of hosts operating under the auspices of a single authority and cooperating to provide a coherent, supracomputer interface, as in the case of the Distributed Computer System (DCS) developed at the University of California at Irvine [11]. Correspondingly, the types of measures provided for network security purposes vary over a wide range, depending on the network environment. As is the case with computer systems, the selection of an appropriate set of network security measures begins with an evaluation of the threat environment and an assessment of risks in that environment. Once this procedure has been completed, appropriate techniques can be selected for use in that particular environment. Although this chapter examines a variety of threats to network security and presents techniques to counter these threats in a wide range of environments, it is not a substitute for a thorough risk assessment.

9.2 PHILOSOPHY AND PRINCIPLES

This chapter examines the topic of network security by employing principles of information protection developed in the course of research on computer system security. Although the specific mechanisms employed to protect information in computer systems are not always directly applicable in the network context, the categorization of potential security violations and the design principles developed in the computer system security context can be applied to networks. Recent work in the mathematical modeling of security policies [1, 2] is an example of research that is applicable in both computer system and network security contexts.

Potential security violations can be categorized in terms of unauthorized release of information, unauthorized modification of information, or unauthorized denial of use of resources. In the context of communication, attacks of the first type correspond to passive wiretapping, while attacks of the second and third type correspond to active wiretapping. The term *unauthorized* used in describing the three categories of attacks implies that the release, modification, or denial of use takes place contrary to some security policy. The *intruder* in this environment may be a wiretapper outside of the user community or may be an otherwise legitimate user of the network. Communication security techniques have traditionally been employed to counter attacks by the former type of intruder while authentication and access control techniques provide the finer granularity of protection required in the latter case.

9.2.1 Principles

The development of secure, general-purpose computer systems has been extremely difficult, and no such systems exist at the time of this writing. In the absence of a complete methodology for the production of such systems, experience in the development of protection mechanisms for computer systems has provided a number of useful principles that can guide the design of such mechanisms. Even when networks composed solely of proven, secure computer systems become a reality, the security mechanisms in the network must take into account the possibility that individual components of the network could be physically subverted, thus violating some of the premises upon which the secure system proofs are based. Therefore, the design principles presented in Table 9.1 will remain appropriate in the network context even after the development of proven, secure systems.[1]

The first of these principles, *economy of mechanism*, dictates the use of the simplest possible design that achieves the desired effect. Although this principle applies to many aspects of system design, it is especially appropriate in the development of protection mechanisms, since design and implementation errors that result in unintended access paths may not be noticed during normal use. Adherence to this principle makes practical techniques such as line-by-line

---

[1] These design principles are revised versions of material published in the *Proceedings of the IEEE* by J. H. Saltzer and M. D. Schroeder [5]. Design principles 2, 4, 6, and 8 originally appeared in the *Communications of the ACM* in an article by J. H. Saltzer [12].

TABLE 9–1: *Secure system design principles.*

1. Economy of mechanism
2. Fail-safe defaults
3. Complete mediation
4. Open design
5. Separation of privilege
6. Least privilege
7. Least common mechanism
8. Psychological acceptability

inspection of software and physical examination of hardware that implements protection mechanisms.

The second and third principles are complementary. The second requires that access decisions be based on permission rather than exclusion, and the third requires that every access to every object be checked against an access control data base. The second results in a conservative design approach in which arguments must be made as to why objects should be accessible, rather than why they should not, while the third enforces a system-wide view of access control. The application of these principles becomes evident in the discussion of network-level access control in Sec. 9.4.

The fourth principle states that the design of the protection mechanisms should not be secret, and this principle was proposed early in consideration of communication security [13]. Mechanisms should not depend on the ignorance of potential attackers, but rather on the possession of specific, more easily protected keys or passwords. The decoupling of protection mechanisms from protection keys permits the mechanisms to be reviewed by many potential users without the concern that the review itself will compromise the safeguards. This principle is especially relevant in the network environment, where standards must be developed and disseminated to a large user community to permit the interconnection of systems. It should be noted that the principle of open design is not universally accepted, especially in the context of military security. In that context, the argument is made that a secret design may have the additional advantage of significantly raising the price of penetration, especially the risk of detection. However, this approach does not seem acceptable in the common user network environment examined in this chapter.

The principle of *separation of privilege* is based on the concept that a protection mechanism that requires two keys to unlock it is more robust and flexible than one that allows access based on the presentation of a single key. A physical analog of this principle often appears in the design of bank safe-deposit boxes. This principle can be applied to several aspects of network security, including the distribution and use of encryption keys and the interaction among communication security techniques, authentication procedures, and access control mechanisms at the network level.

The principle of *least privilege* requires that every program and every user of a system should operate using the least set of privileges necessary to perform a required task. This principle serves to limit the damage that can result from an accident, error, or subversion of a component of a system. The military security rule of "need-to-know" is an example of this principle. The application of this principle to establish "fire walls" is evident in the use of connection-oriented communication security measures (see Sec. 9.3.2.3) and in the use of selective encryption techniques (see Sec. 9.3.6.2).

The principle of *least common mechanism* implies that the amount of mechanism common to more than one user and depended on by all users should be minimized. Every shared mechanism represents a potential information path between users and must be designed with great care to ensure that it does not unintentionally compromise security. Further, any mechanism serving all users must be certified to the satisfaction of every user, a job presumably harder than satisfying only one or a few users. This principle motivates the use of connection-oriented communication security measures and influences the positioning of encryption modules in a communication hierarchy.

Finally, the principle of *psychological acceptability* emphasizes that the human interface be designed for ease of use so that users routinely and automatically apply the protection mechanisms available. Also, to the extent that the user's mental image of his protection goals matches the mechanisms he must use, mistakes will be minimized. This principle is important in discussing the suitability of various authentication procedures and access control models, and motivates the use of the simple connection model for discussing communication security measures.

9.3 COMMUNICATION SECURITY

The techniques and mechanisms presented in this chapter are applicable to a wide variety of environments. In this section, contexts in which various threats may arise are examined and the range of applicability of countermeasures to these threats is discussed. In order to provide a context in which some details of proposed mechanisms can be explored, some specific, though widely applicable, models are employed. A network model that encompasses packet-switched and packet broadcast network configurations is introduced as a context for discussion.[2] Emphasis is placed on techniques that are applicable to connection-oriented applications and a simple model of full-duplex connections is introduced. The NBS DES, a *conventional cryptosystem*, and a newly developed algorithm by Rivest [14], an example of *public-key cryptosystem* [15, 16], are introduced in

---

[2]　Although circuit-switched networks are not explicitly discussed in the chapter, most of the analysis of threats and development of countermeasures described therein are applicable to such networks.

this section. Many of the communication security mechanisms developed are not particularly sensitive to the use of a particular algorithm, and encryption algorithms with similar external characteristics can be easily interchanged.

A suitable protocol must be employed to discuss the details of combining encryption techniques and protocols to provide connection-oriented communication security. The X.25 (level 3) interface specification [26] for public packet-switched networks is used throughout this chapter as a sample network-level protocol. The choice of X.25 is motivated by its widespread adoption in the public packet network arena, the corresponding availability of equipment designed to meet the interface standard, and by its relative simplicity.[3] Finally, the salient characteristics of X.25 with respect to network security are representative of protocols encountered in the commercial sector in various networks.

9.3.1 Models

Before discussing classification of threats and countermeasures for threats in a general communication network, we introduce a simple model of a network and of a connection in a network to provide a context for this discussion. These models are shown in Figs. 9.1 and 9.2 and the components of the models are discussed below.

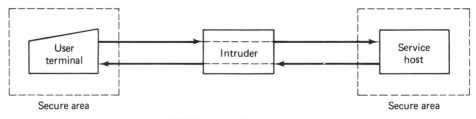

FIGURE 9-1 *A connection model.*

9.3.1.1 Network Model

The basic component of the network is the *communication subnet*, which, for our purposes, can be viewed simply as a transmission medium. Thus, in an Ethernet [20], this transmission medium is a coaxial cable, while in the Distributed Computer System (DCS) ring network [11], it consists of a twisted pair with the necessary network interface repeaters along the ring. In the ARPANET the transmission medium consists of packet switches (TIPs or IMPs) connected by leased phone lines or satellite channels.

---

[3] Note that X.25 should not be directly compared with the transmission control protocol (TCP) described in Chapter 7, since they are designed for different contexts and they provide different services (e.g., X.25 is not an end-to-end protocol like TCP).

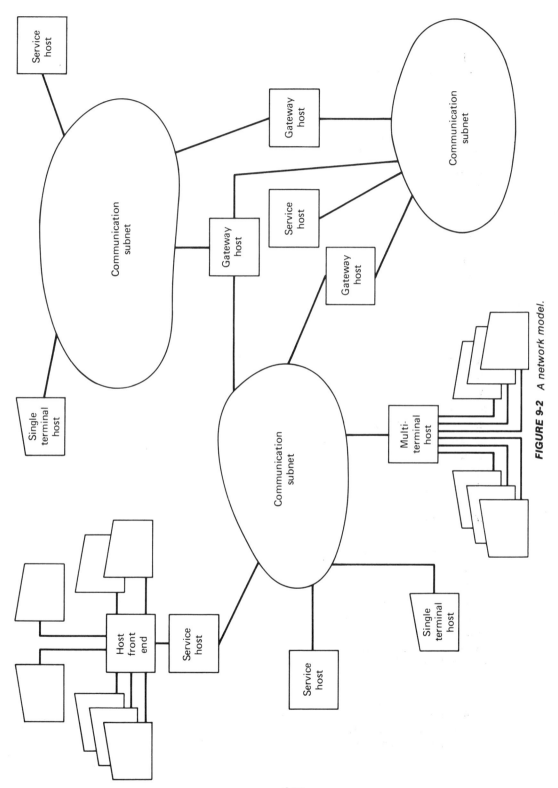

FIGURE 9-2 A network model.

The communication subnet serves to connect the hosts on the network. Four types of hosts are distinguished in the model: *single-terminal hosts, multiterminal hosts, service hosts,* and *gateway hosts.* A single-terminal host serves to connect an individual user terminal to the network and might be implemented by a microprocessor contained within the terminal. A multiterminal host (network access machine) serves to connect several terminals to the network. Such a host might be implemented by a microprocessor or by a minicomputer, depending on the number of terminals being served and the level of service provided. The distinction between a single-terminal host and a multiterminal host is important because the latter is an instance of a multiplexed communication facility in which we may be concerned about the mixing of data streams from the various terminals served.[4] The terminals connected to a multiterminal host may be directly wired to it or may access it by dialing through the telephone network.

The service hosts on the net consist of conventional computers providing information-processing utility functions as well as special-purpose hosts providing specialized functions, (e.g., ILLIAC IV on the ARPANET). These service hosts, especially information-processing utilities, may have terminals connected to them by means other than the communication network (i.e., directly wired or dialed terminals). Finally, gateway hosts [17, 18] serve to interconnect two or more networks. The services provided by a gateway include routing of packets from one network to another, fragmenting packets that are too large for a destination network, and embedding of internetwork packets in the packet formats of those local networks for which the gateway provides an interface. There may be more than one gateway path between two networks.

Terminals form the final component of the network model. Terminals are important as distinct entities in the network because they provide the most direct interface to the human users of the network. Since a user is frequently the ultimate source or destination of the information we are trying to protect, the terminal provides the earliest point in the system at which we can begin this job of protection. Now that we have introduced this network model, we can examine several examples of existing or planned networks to see how they fit in with it.

A number of packet-switched networks follow this model quite closely (e.g., ARPANET and CYCLADES [21]). Using the ARPANET as an example, [5] we note that the communication subnet consists of packet switches (IMPs and TIPs) connected by leased telephone lines or satellite channels. Terminal access to the ARPANET is provided via multiterminal hosts (TIPs) to which terminals may be connected either by direct or by dialed lines, and via the many service hosts on the network. Terminal access to service hosts is varied, including dedicated and dialed lines. Several other networks are connected to the ARPANET via

---

[4] A similar concern arises if a network front end is employed in interfacing hosts and terminals to the subnet.

[5] We will employ the ARPANET as a reference point throughout the chapter, since it is so well known and since many other networks are based on the architecture of the ARPANET.

gateways of varying sophistication (e.g., the ALOHA system [22] and the Xerox PARC Ethernet). Correspondence with the components of this model can similarly be established for CYCLADES, Telenet [23], and several military networks now being developed (e.g., AUTODIN II [19]).

The salient features (with respect to security) of packet broadcast networks (e.g., Ethernet, Packet Radio Network [24], and the DCS Ring Network) are represented by the simple network model presented above. The Packet Radio Network provides examples of single-terminal hosts and an elaborate communication subnet, employing repeater nodes that track the mobile packet radio terminals and perform routing functions. Hosts on the Ethernet at Xerox PARC are primarily personal computers, which may be viewed as extremely sophisticated single-terminal hosts, although more general service hosts also exist on the net. The DCS constructed at the University of California at Irvine using a ring network connects minicomputer hosts, some acting purely as network-accessible service hosts and others acting as conventional hosts with terminals directly attached.

9.3.1.2 Connection Model

For generality, we consider a *(full) duplex connection* between two processes (e.g., a user terminal and a computation on a service host). The connection is composed of two *independent simplex channels*, each capable of transmitting messages in a single direction. In most applications the connection is viewed as transitory (e.g., existing for the duration of a single login session). Although the connection is embedded in a common user network, details of the connection related to its physical realization are not a part of this model.

Both ends of the connection are assumed to terminate in secure areas, while the remainder of the connection may be subject to physical attack. If a terminal forms one end of the connection, it may, at different times, be used by various individuals over a range of authorization levels. A host that provides one end of the connection may provide services to a diverse user community, not all of whose members employ communication security measures. We postulate the existence of an intruder, represented by a computer under hostile control, situated in the communication path between the ends of the connection. Thus, all messages transmitted on the connection must pass through the intruder. Figure 9.2 depicts this configuration in the context of a connection between a user terminal and a service host. This model is employed in the discussion of attacks and connection-oriented countermeasures presented in Sec. 9.3.3.

9.3.2 Types of Communication Security Measures

In viewing the problems of communication security, there are two basic approaches: *link-oriented security measures* and *end-to-end security measures*. The former measures provide security by protecting message traffic independently on each communication link while the latter provide uniform protection for each message from its source to its destination. These two approaches differ not only in their internal implementation characteristics, but also in the nature of security provided and the type of external interface presented to users of the communication network. Below we examine some of the characteristics and implications of using both link-oriented and end-to-end security measures.

9.3.2.1 Link-Oriented Measures

There are several places in our network model where communication links can be readily identified. Here we have used the term *link* in the same context as data link control protocols (e.g., SDLC [25] and X.25 (level 2) [26]). In this sense we usually expect to find such links connecting the switching nodes in a packet-switched network. Thus, the satellite channels and telephone lines that connect IMPs are examples of communication links in the ARPANET. In most cases, the connection between a host and the communication subnet also involves a link. Finally, a link usually exists between a terminal and the host to which it is connected.

In each of the examples presented above, the communication link may be physically unprotected and thus subject to attack. Link-oriented protection measures provide security for all the message traffic passing over an individual communication link between two nodes, independent of the ultimate source and destination of the messages. In providing protection of this sort, the assumption is made that it is much easier to attack communication links than to attack the nodes. However, often it may not be possible or economically feasible to physically secure nodes in the communication subnet as readily as the terminal and host nodes. Yet subversion of one of the subnet nodes results in exposure of all the message traffic passing through that node despite physical security precautions still in effect at the source and destination nodes.

Even if all subnet nodes are located physically near the hosts attached to them, and thus are afforded the same level of physical security as those hosts, subversion of a single subnet node can result in exposure of message traffic between other hosts on the network. In a network where adaptive routing strategies are employed (e.g., ARPANET) a subverted packet switch could cause packets to be routed through it almost independently of their source and destination hosts. Thus, link-oriented protection in the communication subnet suffers from the defect that subversion of one of the subnet nodes could result in exposure of substantial amounts of message traffic. There is also the problem that in packet broadcast networks, link-oriented measures are generally inapplicable because there are no readily identifiable communication links within the communication subnet.

If the only unsecured communication links in a network occur within the communication subnet, link-oriented measures have an advantage in that they can provide a transparent form of communication security for the hosts attached to the network. If only some of the communication links between terminals and hosts (or between hosts and the communication subnet) need to be protected, security measures for these links can be implemented without affecting the other hosts on the network. The cost of providing link-oriented protection on terminal-to-host and host-to-communication subnet links can be borne by the directly affected parties while the overall cost of link-oriented measures within the communication subnet can be amortized over all its users. Of course, in a common user network, some users may not perceive the need for the security measures provided by the communication subnet and thus may feel unjustly charged for this service. Finally, in many network environments, the subscribers may not wish to rely on the authorities controlling the communication subnet to provide security services.

9.3.2.2 End-to-End Measures

Rather than viewing a network as a collection of nodes joined by communication links, each of which can be independently protected, one can view a network as a medium for transporting messages in a secure fashion from source to destination. From this perspective, end-to-end security measures protect messages in transit between source and destination nodes in such a way that the subversion of any of communication links between the source and destination does not result in exposure of message traffic. There is some flexibility in defining the points at which end-to-end security measures are implemented: from host to host, from terminal to terminal or service host, or from terminal to process on a service host. By extending the domain of end-to-end security measures, more of the communication path between a user and his computation, or between a pair of users, is protected by these security measures. However, as the domain of such measures is extended, the range of hardware and software that must interface with these measures may increase.

Since end-to-end security measures usually extend beyond the communication subnet, these measures sometimes require a greater degree of standardization of interfaces and protocols for subscribers to the network. However, such standardization is already coming about for technical, economic, and political reasons and thus should not be a serious impediment to the adoption of end-to-end security measures in networks. A major advantage of end-to-end security measures is that individual users and hosts can elect to employ them without affecting other users and hosts, and thus the cost of employing such measures can be more accurately apportioned. Moreover, these measures can be employed not only in packet-switched networks but also in packet broadcast networks, where link-oriented measures are often not applicable.

9.3.2.3 Connection-Oriented Measures

In many applications, a communication network is viewed as providing its users with a medium for establishing connections or *virtual circuits* from source to destination. This view suggests that security services be connection-oriented (i.e., that each connection or virtual circuit be protected individually). Thus, *connection-oriented security measures* constitute a refinement of end-to-end measures. As is the case with end-to-end security measures, there is considerable flexibility in choosing the points that are to act as the ends of the connection for security purposes.

Connection-oriented security measures not only protect that portion of a communication path that lies between the security-defined ends of the connection, but also significantly reduce the probability of undetected *cross-talk,* whether induced by hardware or software, over that interval. In many respects, connection-oriented measures provide the greatest degree of communication security and they are applicable in a wide variety of environments.

Although both link-oriented and connection-oriented security measures have advantages and disadvantages peculiar to themselves, connection-oriented security measures generally afford greater overall protection in a wide range of environments and are more naturally suited to a user's perceptions of his or her own security requirements. This stems from the fact that connection-oriented measures rely on the security of equipment only at the source and destination of a connection, while link-oriented measures may require that each node in the communication subnet be secure. However, there are situations where both types of measures can be useful and can be employed to provide an economic level of protection that is higher than that which could be achieved using either class of measures alone.

9.3.3   Classification of Attacks on Communication Security

Using the context of the network connection models presented in Sec. 9.3.1, we can classify the types of attacks that can be mounted by an intruder. We assume that the intruder can position himself at some point in the network through which all information of interest must pass. For example, in an internetwork environment, the intruder could take the form of a gateway in some intermediate network that provides the only communication path between the two processes that are at the ends of the connection of interest, as illustrated in Fig. 9.3. Here, even though the source (A) and destination (D) networks are secure, the intruder can attack the connection as it passes through the gateway connecting networks B and C. In general, the intruder is assumed to be in a position to mount both active and passive wiretapping attacks.

9.3.3.1   Passive Wiretapping

In *passive wiretapping*, the intruder merely observes messages passing on a connection without interfering with their flow. Intruder observation of the (application level) data in a message can be termed *release of message contents* and is the most fundamental type of passive wiretapping. The intruder can also

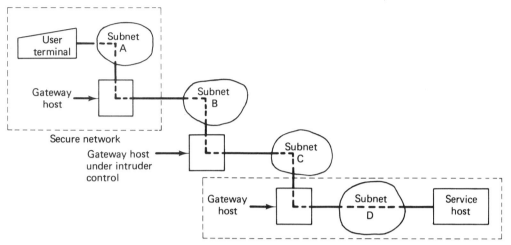

FIGURE 9-3 *Intruder in internetwork context.*

observe portions of the message headers, even if the application-level data are not intelligible to him, to learn the location and identities of the communicating processes. Finally, the intruder can examine the lengths of messages and their frequency of transmission to gain knowledge of the nature of the data being exchanged. These latter types of passive wiretapping attacks are usually referred to as *traffic analysis* or *violations of transmission security*.[6]

9.3.3.2 Active Wiretapping

The intruder can also engage in *active wiretapping*, performing a variety of processing on messages passing on the connection. These messages can be selectively modified, deleted, delayed, reordered, duplicated, and inserted into the connection at a later point in time, or may pass through unaffected. He can also synthesize bogus messages and insert them into the connection. Acts such as these can be designated *message stream modification* attacks [30].

Since we have assumed that the intruder can be positioned so that all

---

[6] Although traffic analysis is usually viewed as a means of inferring information by observing legitimate message traffic, this form of attack can also be used in conjunction with a *Trojan Horse* [27] program operating in a user process at a service host. The Trojan Horse program could perform some legitimate function within the process while clandestinely modulating message destination, length, or frequency of transmission in order to use the connection as a covert channel for transmitting to the intruder data legitimately accessible by the process [28, 29]. In an interactive communication environment, if the bandwidth of the communication network is high relative to the speed of user terminal equipment, modulation of message length and frequency could be carried out by a Trojan Horse program and still be completely undetected by a user.

messages of interest flow through his location, the intruder can discard all messages or, in a less drastic action, can delay all messages going in either or both directions on a connection. Acts of this nature can be classified as *denial of message service* attacks [30].[7] In the context of message deletion or delay, the difference between message stream modification and denial of message service attacks is subtle and is a function both of the degree of the attack and of the state of the connection. The distinction is made because different types of countermeasures can be employed for each type of attack.

In the preceding discussion, intruder attacks were viewed in the context of existing connections. A further requirement of communication security is that connections be initiated in a fashion that supports secure identification of the principles (users, terminals, hosts) at each end and establishes the time integrity of the connection. Although verification of identity is a complex issue that interacts with authentication and security controls above the level of the connection model, a portion of the identification problem is relevant at the connection level itself. The role of connection initiation in the more general context of authentication and access control is discussed in Sec. 9.4.

Verification of the time integrity of the connection counters *playback* attacks by an intruder using recordings of previous connection initiation message sequences. Attempts by an intruder to violate these constraints can be classified as *spurious connection initiation* attacks. Such attacks are similar in nature to message stream modification attacks, but the context of connection initiation prompts the use of a somewhat different set of countermeasures.

9.3.4 Communication Security Goals

From this discussion, we note that active and passive wiretapping attacks are in some sense duals. Although message stream modification, denial of message service, and spurious connection initiation attacks cannot be prevented, we will see that they can be reliably detected. Conversely, release of message contents and traffic analysis attacks cannot usually be detected,[8] but they can be

---

[7] Depending on the communication medium employed, measures can be used that make it extremely difficult for an intruder to severely disrupt the communications (e.g., spread spectrum techniques in radio networks). Such *tamper-free* techniques are of interest in any environment where disruption of communication cannot be tolerated (e.g., military communication networks [13]). In many ways, such techniques are more akin to reliability measures than to the communication security measures discussed here, and in many communication environments, economic or technical considerations will prohibit the use of such techniques. Thus, in this chapter, the generally applicable assumption will be made that an intruder cannot be prevented from disrupting communication services in the network.

[8] In some communication media, techniques can be employed to detect passive wiretapping attacks (e.g., careful measurement in changes in inductance over circuits). However, recent trends in network technology involve media in which such detection cannot be carried out. Moreover, in most environments, preventing the release of information in the face of passive wiretapping is more important than detecting such wiretapping. Thus, no discussion of detection of passive wiretapping attacks is included in this chapter.

effectively thwarted. Mindful of these limitations, we can establish five goals for the design of mechanisms that provide communications security:

1. Prevention of release of message contents.

2. Prevention of traffic analysis.

3. Detection of message stream modification.

4. Detection of denial of message service.

5. Detection of spurious connection initiation.

Historically, encryption has been employed extensively as a countermeasure against passive wiretapping, thus addressing the first and second goals [31].[9] Encryption can be used in conjunction with protocols to obtain the third, fourth, and fifth goals [29, 30, 32, 33]. With respect to message stream modification, denial of message service, and spurious connection initiation attacks, we can further require that communication security measures not only detect these attacks, but also automatically recover from them if they are of a transient nature. In each case, attainment of the goals is based on the inability of the intruder to subvert the encryption algorithm employed, and the goals are achieved only in a probabilistic sense.

9.3.5 Data Encryption

As noted above, encryption serves both as a countermeasure to passive wiretap-ping attacks and as a foundation on which to construct countermeasures to active wiretapping attacks. The design and analysis of encryption algorithms is beyond the scope of this chapter, but an understanding of some characteristics of such algorithms is critical to the development of all the countermeasures. Thus, we will briefly describe some general characteristics of conventional ciphers and the newly developed class of public-key ciphers.

As a Federal Information Processing Standard, the DES forms the basis for cryptographic communication security measures applied to nonclassified govern-ment information. Since it appears that the DES will become a *de facto* industry standard as well, it has been selected as the primary example of a conventional encryption algorithm for use in this chapter. Rivest's algorithm is described since it is the first published and most widely known example of a public-key cipher. At various points throughout this chapter, footnotes will be used to indicate how the use of public-key ciphers would affect the mechanisms being proposed.

---

[9] Encryption has also been employed in *Identification Friend or Foe* (IFF) systems that verify the identity of approaching aircraft [31]. Such systems encompass some of the aspects of the fifth goal.

A *cipher* is an algorithmic transformation performed on a symbol-by-symbol basis on any data. Although there are technical distinctions between the terms *encipherment* and *encryption* [31, 34], the two terms will be used interchangeably throughout this chapter to refer to the application of a cipher to data. An *encryption algorithm* is any algorithm that implements a cipher. The input to an encryption algorithm is referred to as *cleartext* or *plaintext*, and the output from the algorithm is designated as *ciphertext*. The transformation performed on the cleartext to encipher it is controlled by a *key*. For use in the communication context we are examining, the encryption algorithm must be invertible (i.e., there must be a matching decryption algorithm that reverses the encryption transformation when presented with an appropriate key).

In conventional ciphers the key used to decipher a message is the same as the key employed in enciphering it. Such a key must be kept secret, known only to users authorized to transmit messages under it and to decipher messages enciphered using it. Figure 9.4 illustrates these aspects of a conventional cipher. In contrast, in a public-key cipher, the ability to encipher messages under a given key is separable from the ability to decipher those messages. This is accomplished by using pairs of transformations (E, D) each of which is the inverse of the other, neither of which is readily derivable from the other. The use of such "trapdoor" functions provides a form of multiaccess cipher in which one key is made public (E), for use in enciphering messages for a given user, while a corresponding key (D) is kept secret, for use in deciphering messages sent to the user under the public key. The implications of this for key distribution and management are discussed in Sec. 9.3.10, where we see that the need for authentication in the distribution of public keys results in there being few differences between conventional and public-key key distribution mechanisms in many communication network contexts.

Since, in a public-key cipher, anyone can transmit a message to a user (i) under the public key of that user (E_i), some additional mechanism is needed to securely identify the sender. This problem is solved by having the sender (j) 51encrypt his message under the secret key (D_j), then under the public key of the intended receiver (E_i). The receiver can then strip off the outer layer of encryption using the secret key (D_i) and complete the deciphering using the

FIGURE 9-4 *Conventional cipher.*

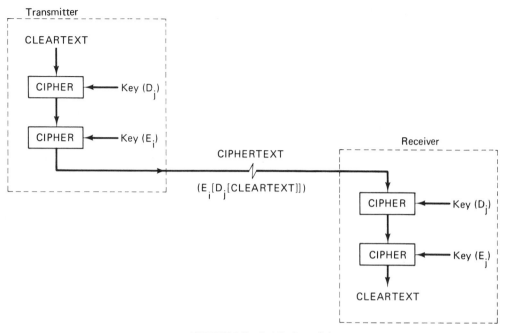

FIGURE 9-5 *Public-key cipher.*

public key of the sender (E_j). This is illustrated in Fig. 9.5. The essential requirements for public-key systems are that the encryption and decryption transformations are easy to compute and are inverses, and that the key pairs (E_i, D_i) are easy to generate. Moreover, it should not be feasible to derive D_i from E_i, nor to invert the transformations, without the proper keys.

9.3.5.2 *Attacks on Cryptosystems*

A cryptographic system that would succumb to an attack mounted with unlimited computational power is considered *computationally* or *practically* secure if the computational cost makes such a task infeasible, while a cipher that can resist any analytical attack, regardless of the computational power and time available, is considered *unconditionally* or *theoretically* secure [16, 34]. Even without examining in detail the techniques employed in cryptanalysis, three hierarchic classes of cryptanalytic attack can be identified: *ciphertext-only*, *known-plaintext*, and *chosen-plaintext*.

In ciphertext-only attack, the cryptanalyst employs only a knowledge of the statistical properties of the language in use (e.g., the relative frequency of occurrence of letters in a natural language or the use of parity bits in the transmission of ASCII characters) and a knowledge of "probable" words (e.g., standard salutations in letters or common variable names in program text). At

385

the next level of difficulty, a known-plaintext attack can be mounted by a cryptanalyst whenever matching plaintext and ciphertext are available. This attack occurs frequently in a network environment, since well-known fixed-format messages are issued by software systems (e.g., stylized login greetings, and system-wide messages on time-sharing systems). Finally, in a chosen-plaintext attack, the cryptanalyst not only possesses matching plaintext and ciphertext, but the plaintext is selected by him. This form of attack can be mounted in a variety of ways, (e.g., through transmission of "network mail") and thus constitutes a very real threat in a general network environment.[10] Hence, any cipher proposed for use in a network environment should be resistant to known and chosen plaintext attacks as well as ciphertext-only attacks.

Two major classes of encryption techniques have been employed in modern nonvoice telecommunications and digital computer applications: stream and block ciphers. The former method performs bit-by-bit (or byte-by-byte) transformations on cleartext under the control of a stream of key bits, usually using some easily reversible operation (e.g., addition modulo 2). The latter method enciphers fixed-sized blocks of bits under the control of a key that is often approximately the same size as the blocks being encrypted.

9.3.5.3 Stream Ciphers

Stream ciphers can be constructed so that they operate on the stream of cleartext in real time, enciphering each bit (byte) as it is generated by combining it with a bit (byte) from the key stream. A stream cipher in which the key stream consists of a random bit string as long as the combined length of all messages that are ever transmitted using this stream, a *Vernam cipher*, is theoretically and practically unbreakable [31, 34]. In practice, the volume of communication traffic, and the logistic difficulties associated with providing each user with a sufficient quantity of key stream, causes most stream ciphers to utilize pseudo-random bit streams with very long periods. Unlike the Vernam cipher, such stream ciphers are susceptible to cryptanalysis [35].

Various techniques may be used in stream ciphers to generate the key stream. The source of the key bits may be completely independent of the cleartext stream (e.g., a pseudo-random-number generator primed with a small initial key). With such an independent key stream, changes to individual bits in the ciphertext do not propagate to other portions of the ciphertext stream. Although this is an advantage in that transmission errors that alter the value of bits of the ciphertext do not affect the ability of the receiver to correctly decipher subsequent transmissions, undetected insertion or removal of bits from the ciphertext stream still results in a loss of deciphering ability in ciphers of this sort [32]. Stream ciphers of this sort are generally unacceptable for our purposes because the lack

---

[10] Public-key ciphers are easily subjected to such attacks, since the public keys are generally available (see Sec. 9.3.10.3).

of error propagation hampers development of mechanisms to detect (length-preserving) message-modification attacks.

Autokey ciphers are stream ciphers in which the key stream is a function of the cleartext, ciphertext, or the key stream itself and some initial, *priming* key [34]. Ciphers employing this approach can achieve interbit dependence that can be used to detect errors in transmitted ciphertext, since such errors interfere with the correct decipherment of subsequent transmissions. In *ciphertext autokey* (CTAK) *ciphers*, transmitted ciphertext is used as input for key-stream generation. These self-synchronizing ciphers achieve interbit dependence, but resume correct operation following transmission errors, after some fixed number of unaffected ciphertext bits are received [36].

9.3.5.4 Block Ciphers

In contrast to stream ciphers, block ciphers transform entire blocks of bits under the control of a key. A block cipher maps the space of cleartext blocks into the space of ciphered text blocks. If the block size is n bits, the size of the cleartext space (the range of cleartext block values) and the size of the ciphertext space (the range of ciphertext block values) is 2^n. In order that the deciphering of a block yield an unambiguous cleartext block, the mapping must be invertible, hence one-to-one and in this case onto, since the sizes of the spaces are equal. Thus, we can view a block cipher under the control of a single key as defining one of the $2^n!$ permutations on the set of n-bit blocks. In practice, it is not feasible to implement a block cipher that realizes all the possible permutations, because of the size of the key required and the logical complexity of the cipher.

For all values of n, the block size, a block cipher is equivalent to a classical simple substitution cipher. When n is 7 or 8, the block corresponds to an individual character from a small alphabet and this equivalence becomes very apparent. This system is known to be very weak, not because of the structure of the system, but because of the small size of the blocks used. The cipher is subject to analysis by comparing the frequency distribution of individual blocks, with the known frequency distribution of characters in large samples of cleartext. If the size of the block is increased and the cipher is constructed so that the frequency characteristics of the components of the block are concealed by mixing transformations, such frequency distribution and analysis become infeasible because the size of the effective alphabet has been increased and the resulting cryptographic system is thought very good [32].

9.3.5.5 DES

The DES is basically a block cipher operating on 64-bit blocks, using a 56-bit key. This means of using the DES is referred to as the *electronic code book* (ECB) mode in an analogy to conventional code books. Each key parameterizes the cipher, defining a permutation on the space of 64-bit blocks. Each bit of ciphertext in a block generated by use of the ECB mode is a function of each bit of the key and each bit of the cleartext block from which it was generated. A change of as little as one bit in either the key or the cleartext results in ciphertext in which each bit is changed with approximately equal probability. Conversely, a change in one bit either of the key or ciphertext will result in changes in an average of 50% of the bits of deciphered cleartext. Although this error propagation is extensive, it is strictly limited to the block in which the error occurs and decryption of other blocks is unaffected by such an error. Thus, in the ECB mode, the cryptographic synchrony required for correct deciphering of messages is achieved when both sender and receiver employ the same key and blocks are correctly delimited. Figure 9.6 illustrates this mode of using the DES.

The DES, like other conventional ciphers, can also be used, in several ways, as part of a key-stream generator for a CTAK cipher. The *cipher feedback* (CFB) mode of operation transforms the DES into a self-synchronizing stream cipher which operates on cleartext strings of 1 to 64 bits in length. The cleartext is combined, by addition modulo 2, with a matching number of key-stream (output) bits generated by the DES block cipher (any extra DES output bits are discarded). The transmitted ciphertext is fed into 64-bit shift registers that form the input to

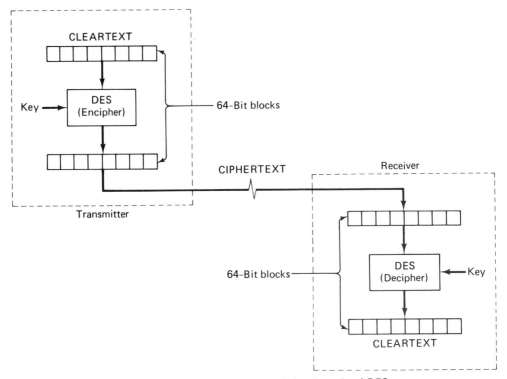

FIGURE 9-6 *Electronic code book mode of DES.*

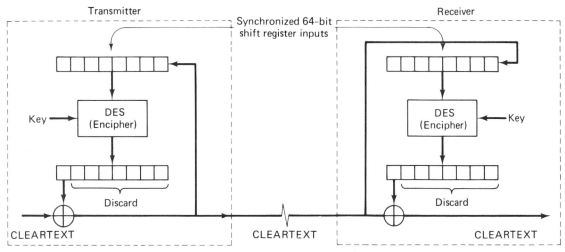

FIGURE 9-7 *Cipher feedback mode of DES.*

the basic DES at both ends of the connection, making the key stream a function of all transmitted ciphertext. Figure 9.7 displays this configuration of the DES for use with 8-bit bytes.

In CFB mode, cryptographic synchrony is achieved only if the sender and receiver use the same key and both shift registers contain the same bit pattern. If an error occurs in the ciphertext stream, a portion of the received cleartext will be garbled, but receipt of 64 bits of error-free ciphertext automatically resynchronizes the cipher. While the number of bits actually garbled by a single bit error is constant at 65, the number of cleartext bits that might be rendered useless by such an error depends on the length of the cleartext bit strings employed and the granularity of error detection employed in higher-level protocols.

The data encryption standard appears to be resistant to conventional cryptanalysis [37], although it is *breakable* in a theoretical sense and it may be susceptible to "brute-force" attacks employing a large, special-purpose, highly parallel device [38]. Both the ECB and CFB modes of the DES provide a basis for achieving the first goal, prevention of release of message contents, by application to the data to be concealed. Both modes also provide a foundation for the construction of countermeasures to achieve the other goals.

9.3.5.6 *Rivest Algorithm*

The Rivest algorithm, the first published realization of a public-key cipher, is also a block cipher. Suggested block sizes for this algorithm range from 80 digits (about 256 bits) to 200 digits (over 650 bits), depending on the level of security desired.[11] The algorithm enciphers a message (M), viewing it as an integer, by raising it to power e (modulo n) and deciphers the resulting ciphertext (C) by raising it to a power d (modulo n). The encryption key is the pair (e, n) and the decryption key is (d, n). The values d, e, and n are computed from a pair of large prime numbers (p, q). The rules for calculating d, e, and n and techniques for selecting p and q are provided by Rivest [14]. The algorithm is based on the apparent difficulty of factoring large composite numbers. Unlike the DES, there appears to be no way of transforming this algorithm into a stream cipher while preserving the public-key characteristics of the algorithm.

9.3.5.7   *Comparison of Block and Stream Encryption Modes*

While both block and stream ciphers provide a foundation on which other countermeasures can be constructed, each has characteristics that must be taken into account in designing such countermeasures. This section examines these characteristics and extends the basic cipher modes to better meet the requirements of secure message transmission in networks.

There are several problems associated with using the basic block (ECB) mode of operation of a conventional or public-key cipher. Generally, the length of a message will not correspond to the block size of the cipher, and some means of resolving this mismatch must be employed. One approach is to fragment the logical message (e.g., an X.25 packet) into as many block-sized pieces as required, padding the message to occupy an integral number of blocks. This padding results in wasted bandwidth (half the block size on the average) on each message. Since each block is enciphered independently of others, two cleartext blocks consisting of the same bit pattern result in identical ciphertext blocks. This exposure of block-size data patterns that fall on block boundaries is often unacceptable. In this mode, error propagation is strictly intrablock, and this has implications for the type of message-modification detection techniques that can be employed (see Sec. 9.3.8). Because of these characteristics, ECB mode is not well suited to use with general message text. However, this mode can be employed in some circumstances with fixed-format message fields that are well matched to the block size (e.g., transmission of a new encryption key).

An enhanced version of this mode, which is usable with both conventional and public-key ciphers, is the *chained block cipher* (CBC) mode, illustrated in Fig. 9.8. As with ECB mode, a message is first fragmented into block-sized pieces and padded to occupy an integral number of blocks, if necessary. The first block is enciphered as in ECB mode. This ciphertext block is then combined via addition modulo 2 with the second message block and the result is enciphered as

---

[11]   A block for the Rivest algorithm would have to be approximately 320 to 380 bits in length to provide security comparable to the 56-bit DES key, assuming that DES keys can be recovered only via exhaustive search and Rivest keys can be recovered via factoring.

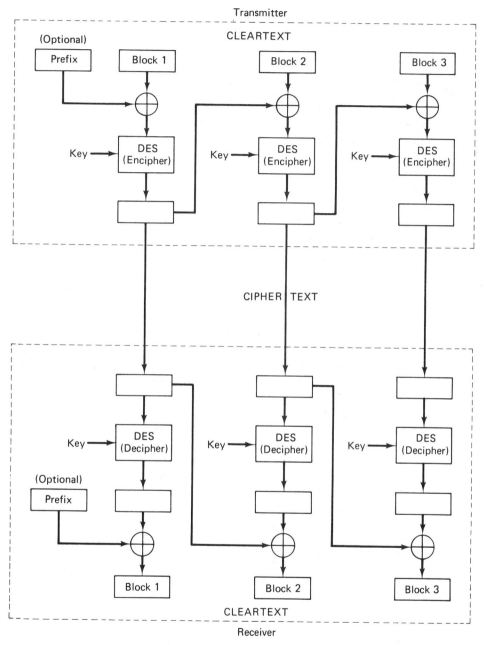

FIGURE 9-8 *Chained block cipher (on 3 blocks).*

in ECB mode. This process is repeated until all of the message is enciphered. An error occurring in a ciphertext block propagates throughout that block and a portion of the following block, but subsequent blocks are not affected.

Because the ciphertext form of each block after the first is a function of all the preceding blocks in the message, the problem of block-aligned data pattern exposure is greatly reduced. In this mode, identical cleartext blocks in two messages result in identical ciphertext blocks only if the prefixes of the blocks in their respective messages are identical. Often this apparent deficiency poses no problem, as protocol data such as unique sequence numbers will form the beginning of the message and will thus result in a unique prefix for the text that follows. Alternatively, a time-varying quantity can be used as a prefix for each message and communicated in the clear (or encrypted in ECB mode) at the head of each message.[12]

CTAK stream ciphers such as the CFB mode of the DES provide a key stream that can be matched exactly to the length of the text to be enciphered, thus avoiding the problems associated with padding of cleartext to match block sizes. This flexibility is usually attained by establishing a basic quantum of text operated on by the cipher (e.g., 8-bit bytes). The disadvantage of this approach is that the throughput of a block encryption algorithm can be substantially reduced by this mode of operation (e.g., throughput of the DES operating on 8-bit bytes in CFB mode is reduced by a factor of eight or more). This problem can be overcome by employing two quanta in enciphering each message; the block size of the underlying cipher and the length of the message modulo this block size. This results in throughput comparable to that of CBC mode yet eliminates padding.[13]

Another characteristic of CTAK ciphers is the need for an *initial fill* to synchronize the shift registers at both ends of the connection. This fill can be handled in several ways and is analogous to the prefix discussed in conjunction with the CBC mode. Options include carrying the fill with each message, or making the fill a function of previously transmitted messages. This last option is generally untenable, as it poses serious difficulties in situations where messages arrive out of order (see Sec. 9.3.8.2) and in the event of errors. The characteristics of the other options have already been discussed in the context of CBC mode. Finally, because CFB and CBC modes are self-synchronizing, error propagation is limited and this must be considered in designing message-modification detection mechanisms.

---

[12] The use of a message prefix that is constant over the lifetime of a connection, but distinct for each connection, provides a means of serially using a single key for more than one connection while being able to distinguish among messages from each connection. An obvious candidate for such a prefix is a binary encoding of the time and date at which the connection is established.

[13] This technique can also be applied to the CBC mode of operation to eliminate padding by switching to CFB mode to encipher the end of a message if the message is not an integral number of blocks long.

9.3.6 Release of Message Contents

As noted earlier, protection measures can be link-oriented or connection-oriented (end to end), and this distinction is often made in discussing encryption. Both encryption approaches can be used to prevent release of message contents, although link encryption can also provide protection from traffic analysis (see Sec. 9.3.7). The characteristics of both approaches are examined below, with particular emphasis on end-to-end countermeasures.

9.3.6.1 Link-Oriented Techniques

Link encryption can be performed independently on each of the communication links in a network as discussed earlier. Usually, a different key is employed for each link so that subversion of one link does not necessarily result in release of information transmitted on other links. Stream ciphers are generally employed in link encryption, and a continuous stream of ciphertext bits is maintained between nodes. Because switching (routing) functions are performed only at nodes in a network, both the headers and the data of packets can be enciphered on links. Since many of the links in the network are multiplexed (e.g., links connecting packet switches in the communication subnet), no segregation of connections on a link is enforced.

Since information is enciphered only on the links and not within the nodes connected by links, these nodes must be secure. Although the origin and destination nodes in the network (hosts or terminals) are assumed to be physically secure, link encryption requires the extension of this physical security to all intermediate nodes as well (e.g., packet switches and gateways). Not only must these intermediate nodes be physically secure, but the hardware and software components of these nodes must be certified to isolate the information on each of the connections passing through it. Secure communication processors of this form will be employed in military networks now under development [40]. Even in contexts where intermediate nodes are secure, the use of link encryption as the primary defense against release-of-message-contents attacks violates the principle of least privilege when there is no need to expose the contents of messages at any point between the origin and destination.

9.3.6.2 End-to-End Techniques

In *end-to-end encryption,* each message, with the exception of certain header information that must be examined en route, is enciphered at its source and not deciphered until it reaches its destination. A unique key can be used for each connection or a coarser granularity of key distribution can be employed (e.g., a different key can be used between each pair of communicating hosts or a single key can be used over an entire secure subnet). The latter schemes afford end-to-end protection but do not provide the connection segregation of the former approach. As the range of use of a single key increases, the amount of information exposed in the case of disclosure of that key also increases, but the task of distributing keys becomes easier.

In accordance with the principle of least privilege, messages should be enciphered so that each module that processes a message has available to it only the information necessary in performing its task. The information in a message can be hierarchically categorized based on whether the information must be accessible to gateways and *data circuit-terminating equipment* (DCE), hosts, or the processes at the end of the connection.[14] Gateways must access header fields, indicating the destination network as well as any fields associated with internet services (e.g., priority routing). The gateway into the destination network must also be able to access the address of the destination host. Finally, if error indications are to be routed to the source host from gateways, the complete source address must be available to them. Thus, information at the gateway level cannot be encrypted on an end-to-end basis but can be protected on a gateway-to-gateway basis.

Upon arrival at a host, messages must be sorted by connection. This sorting is generally based on examination of the *source* and *destination port (socket) fields,* as well as the *source network* and *host fields.* If the latter information does not have to be available at the gateway level for error-reporting purposes, then it, along with the source and destination port fields, can be enciphered at the host level just to hide this level of addressing (see Sec. 9.3.7.2). If this precaution is employed, then after this level of decryption takes place, all of the source and destination address fields are available and can be used to determine the connection to which the message belongs. The remainder of the information in the message, per-connection control information and text, can be enciphered under a key used only for that connection.

In the case of X.25, most of the connection parameters are fixed at the time of *virtual-circuit establishment* and thus do not appear in subsequent *data packets.* Moreover, since X.25 is an *interface specification* rather than an *end-to-end protocol,* all the data in X.25 headers and most of the information in control packets must be accessed by the source DCE and thus cannot be encrypted on an end-to-end basis. As we shall see later, additional information must be embedded in X.25 data packets to provide end-to-end security features (see Secs. 9.3.8 to 9.3.10).

This hierarchical use of encryption can be achieved either by *selective encipherment* of appropriate information fields or by *embedding* the information from each level in a protocol layer for the next level and performing encryption on the layered message at each level, this latter approach possibly resulting in

---

[14] The distinction between *host-level* and *process-level* encryption may not be present, depending on the granularity of key distribution employed in the network and the information fields present in a particular protocol.

superencryption. In practice, variations on these techniques are employed, using some aspects of selective encryption and protocol layering.

9.3.6.3 Red–Black Separation

In dealing with release of message contents, a technique referred to as *red–black separation* is often employed. Red–black separation attempts to construct a barrier between the secure (*red*) and unsecure (*black*) facilities in a communication network. Ideally, red–black separation prevents the transmission of cleartext across the barrier from the red side to the black side, forcing all the information that crosses the barrier from red to black to pass through an encryption unit. Information flow in the reverse direction, from black to red, either passes through the decryption unit or through a *bypass* around it. In practice, this barrier is implemented by physically imposing an encryption unit on the information path between red and black processing components.

Red–black separation provides a barrier not only to explicit red-to-black information flow but, through the use of optical isolators and appropriate filtering and shielding, to electromagnetic emanations as well. In the network context, complete red–black separation generally is not achieved because address and control information must be passed around the sender's encryption unit from the red side to the black side for routing and flow-control purposes. A suitably constrained, low-bandwidth, red-to-black channel can be provided for the transmission of such information.[15]

Red–black separation has been used extensively in link-oriented encryption devices and can be used in end-to-end encryption as well by placing the communication security device between the host (or terminal) and the communication subnet. Although red–black separation provides a context in which it is easier to certify that only enciphered information (with the exception of limited amounts of addressing and flow-control information) crosses the boundary from red to black, this context does not appear to greatly simplify certification of the isolation of connections back to their origins or destinations in processes. Different levels of encryption can be most easily implemented in a red–black separation context by protocol layering and supercipherment.

9.3.7 Traffic Analysis

Traffic analysis countermeasures center around masking the frequency, length, and origin–destination patterns of message traffic. The precision with which an intruder can carry out such pattern analysis directly influences the amount of

[15] The private line interfaces (PLIs) constructed by Bolt Beranek and Newman for use in the ARPANET operate in this fashion [41]. Each PLI employs two minicomputers, one red and one black, an encryption unit, and appropriate electromagnetic emanations countermeasures. A PLI is positioned between host and the IMP or TIP to which the host would normally be connected.

information that can be gained from the analysis. This precision is a function of several factors, including the protocols employed in the network, transmission medium of the communication subnet, and operating characteristics of the hosts. For example, analysis can take place at several levels in the network environment, enabling an intruder to determine the origin and destination of messages at the level of the network(s), the hosts, the processes, or the specific user(s) involved. The difficulty associated with countering attacks at each level depends heavily on the specific protocol being used and on the network environment. As is the case with the use of encryption as a countermeasure against release of message contents attacks, traffic analysis countermeasures can be employed on a link-by-link or end-to-end basis.

9.3.7.1 Link-Oriented Techniques

If link encryption is employed, a continuous stream of ciphertext bits can be maintained between nodes in the communication environment, thus masking the frequency and length patterns of connections.[16] In situations where communication links are multiplexed among several connections, link encryption also provides origin–destination masking as message routing information is not visible on the link. This approach does not have to degrade the effective bandwidth of the network because it does not require transmission of any additional data, but it may entail continuous key-stream generation at each node. However, if a node is subverted, all the message traffic passing through the node is now subject to traffic analysis. In an internetwork environment, gateway hosts must examine and act upon routing information, and thus *unfriendly* gateways can engage in traffic analysis despite the use of link encryption. Finally, there is the problem noted earlier that some network technologies do not lend themselves to link encryption, as there are no identifiable links within the communication subnetwork.

9.3.7.2 End-to-End Techniques

If end-to-end encryption is employed, *dummy messages* of various lengths can be generated and actual messages can be padded to meet artificially selected frequency and length patterns that can be maintained for each connection. An enciphered length field can be used to indicate to the receiver extraneous padding and dummy messages to be discarded. The encrypted protocol layering approach described earlier is especially well suited to the maintenance of artificial frequency

---

[16] It is not strictly necessary for link encryption devices to maintain a continuous stream of ciphertext on a link; ciphertext may be transmitted only when messages are available for transmission. In this latter context the overall frequency of message transmission and lengths of messages can still be detected, even though it may not be possible to associate these statistics with individual logical message streams.

and length patterns. The sequence numbers and length information contained in the outer layer protocol can be used to hide actual frequency and length patterns, as dummy messages can be discarded and padding can be stripped away before the inner message is delivered to the next protocol layer for processing.

We have already seen that the source and destination port fields can be enciphered up to the point of reception by the destination host. Although the identity of the communicating process can be explicitly masked in this fashion, it is much more difficult to mask the host-level origin–destination patterns of message traffic. In a broadcast network environment, host-level addresses can be enciphered using a network-wide key. An intruder with access only to the transmission medium would then be unable to determine host-level origin–destination patterns. Techniques for dynamically varying the logical addresses of the communicating parties in a broadcast network have been developed [28, 42] and could be effectively used to mask process-level and host-level patterns, hiding them from legitimate hosts not involved in the connection as well as from *outside* intruders. However, these techniques are capable of providing origin–destination pattern masking only if the network utilizes a broadcast medium for the communication subnet. In a general network environment it appears that completely effective end-to-end traffic analysis countermeasures would require both message embedding and transmission to all possible hosts. Thus, depending on the network configuration and the protocols involved, end-to-end traffic analysis countermeasures could be very wasteful of processing power and could substantially reduce effective network bandwidth.

In many environments, release of information through traffic analysis may be deemed a secondary threat, and no specific countermeasures may be instituted. End-to-end countermeasures are easily implemented and can be tailored to reduce the bandwidth of these covert channels provided by traffic analysis by trading off bandwidth and processing power. However, the cost of masking the host-level origin–destination patterns using end-to-end techniques seems prohibitive in nonbroadcast networks. In such networks, the use of link encryption and secure communication processors provides a feasible basis for traffic analysis countermeasures, while end-to-end techniques can be used to achieve the other protection goals. Thus, a combination of end-to-end and link-oriented security measures may prove appropriate in some environments.

9.3.8 Message Stream Modification

To achieve the third goal, detection of message stream modification, mechanisms must be employed to determine message *authenticity*, *integrity*, and *ordering*. In the context of our model, *authenticity* implies that the source of a message can be reliably determined (e.g., that a received message was transmitted by the other end of the connection). *Integrity* implies that a message has not been modified enroute, and *ordering* implies that a message can be properly located in the stream of information being transmitted from the source to the destination.

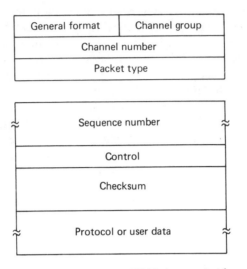

FIGURE 9-9 *Enhanced X.25 data packet format.*

Although these functions are usually provided by a communication protocol for reliability purposes, here they must be provided in the face of attacks by a malevolent intruder, as opposed to failures by benign components. Message authenticity and ordering requirements interact with secure connection initiation and motivate the use of distinct encryption keys for each connection. More important, the protocol data that provide the basis for authentication and ordering must be bound to application data in a fashion that precludes undetected modification of any portion of the resulting message (i.e., through the use of encryption and error-detection fields). Figure 9.9 illustrates one way in which the necessary additional fields could be incorporated into X.25 data packets. Note that these new fields added for network security purposes reside in the user data area of the packet and are transparent to the X.25 protocol.

For suitably robust protocols, message-stream-modification attacks resulting in deletion, reordering, duplication, modification, or delay of messages pose no problems in terms of recovery. However, in the context of X.25, provisions must be made for recovering from these types of attacks and for maintaining or restoring cryptographic synchrony in the face of such attacks.[17] An example of such provisions in the context of a simple protocol design to provide communication security in interactive environments is given in Kent [30].

While the need to provide protection from passive wiretapping attacks is

[17] The flow-control mechanisms employed in X.25 (RR, RNR, REJ, Reset Request, and Reset Confirmation packets) cannot be protected on an end-to-end basis and deal only with the outer-level sequence numbers; hence, they are not adequate for these purposes. The existence of two independent mechanisms for these purposes may lead to synchronization problems between the two levels.

apparent, it may be argued that most users and many application programs can easily detect message-stream-modification attacks without the assistance of a protocol, especially when an encryption scheme with suitable error propagation characteristics is employed. However, not all application programs are prepared to detect attacks of this sort, and not all message streams contain the proper kind of redundant information for such detection. Even messages directed to a user may admit a wide range of "meaningful" contents when they represent answers to a new problem or when they consist of random numbers. Thus, there is good reason to provide detection measures in a communication security protocol. Moreover, provision of this protection by the communication protocol frees the applications programmer of responsibility for determining how to counter such attacks.

9.3.8.1 *Message Authenticity*

For reliability purposes, messages usually contain explicit information associating them with a particular connection. If a single encryption key is used in conjunction with more than one connection, it is critical that this explicit connection identification information be bound to the remainder of the message in a fashion that precludes undetected tampering. However, if a distinct key is associated with each connection, this provides implicit identification of the connection with which the message is associated. Further information is required to associate a message with one of the two simplex channels that make up a single connection, identifying the end of the connection that transmitted the message. This channel isolation could be accomplished by using distinct keys for the channels or by using distinct, per-channel, constant prefixes with CFB or CBC mode and a per-connection key. As there are only two possible sources for messages on a single connection, a single bit suffices to distinguish them if cryptographic isolation techniques are employed only on a per-connection basis [30].

9.3.8.2 *Message Ordering*

Secure message ordering does not imply that messages arrive at their destination in order, or even that they are always delivered to the application program at the destination in order. In some application environments (e.g., real-time transmission of audio or video), messages that arrive ahead of some of their logical predecessors may be delivered immediately, while those arriving after some of their logical successors may be discarded. In interactive environments, some "high-priority" messages may arrive at a service host out of order with respect to the regular message stream, and the user process may wish to be notified of their arrival immediately. In still other environments (e.g., some types of transaction processing) programs are prepared to accept messages independent of their order of transmission and the application system will perform detection of duplicate messages. In general, however, applications require that messages be delivered in a fashion that preserves both the order of transmission and continuity (i.e., there are no missing messages).

To fulfill these requirements, messages can be labeled with consecutive sequence numbers, indicating the order of transmission. Sequence numbering allows messages to be delivered in order to a process, independent of order of arrival, allows detection of missing messages, and permits detection and rejection of duplicate messages. Sequence numbering also supports delivery of the ''most recent'' message to arrive, even if some of its logical predecessors have not yet arrived, and supports rejection of those predecessors should they arrive later. If messages are sometimes delivered out of order to processes, each message must also be independently decipherable. Techniques for achieving the cryptographic synchrony required in this context were discussed in Sec. 9.3.5.7.

When encryption techniques are employed that allow messages to be deciphered independent of their order of arrival, it is critical that the sequence numbers assigned to messages not be reused during the lifetime of the key employed in enciphering messages. If sequence numbers were reused under these circumstances, an intruder would be able to insert copies of old messages into the connection in an undetectable fashion. To counter this threat, keys can be changed automatically if the sequence numbers used on a connection are about to cycle [30]. An alternative approach is to employ an extensible sequence number field that expands as the sequence numbers increase past selected thresholds. This technique has been proposed by Dennis Branstad in conjunction with the development of protocol standards for use with the DES.[18]

The description of message ordering was given in the context of an existing connection; thus, the numbering of messages was relative to that connection. In a larger context, we must ensure that messages are ordered not only within a single connection, but also that messages from previous connections can be distinguished. Here again, the use of a distinct key for each connection simplifies the task by ensuring that messages transmitted on previous connections, even between the same parties, cannot be confused with messages transmitted on a current connection.

9.3.8.3 High-Priority Messages

The handling of high-priority messages in an interactive environment provides an example of a combination of requirements of message ordering. Simple examples of high-priority messages include the Multics *quit* [43] and the Telnet *interrupt process* signal [10]. Although both the semantics of such messages and the manner in which they are handled by specific protocols vary widely, the

---

[18]   The sequence numbers employed in X.25 for message ordering and flow control, P(R) and P(S), are too small for security purposes since cycling under a key is not acceptable and rekeying at the rate required by the X.25 sequence number size would be very inefficient.

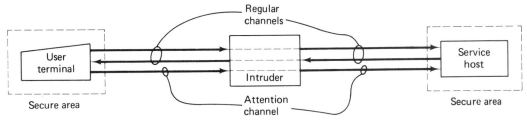

Regular
channels

User
terminal

Intruder

Attention
channel

Service
host

Secure area

Secure area

FIGURE 9-10 *Connection model augmented with attention channel.*

transmission of high-priority messages can be modeled by assuming that any text associated with the message is transmitted on the regular terminal-to-host channel along with other application-level data and that a *high-priority-message processing facility* (HPMP) at the host scans all these data for high-priority messages and acts upon them. Because the host communication system may employ buffering between the HPMP and the rest of the connection, it is frequently necessary to provide some means of alerting that facility that a high-priority message has been transmitted. For this purpose, a separate *virtual attention channel* can be added to the connection model, as illustrated in Fig. 9.10.[19]

This channel need carry only one type of message, an *attention message*, to signal the host that a high-priority message has been transmitted on the regular terminal-to-host channel, and thus it is a relatively low bandwidth channel.[20] Since this channel is logically separate from the other channels, messages transmitted on it should be independently sequenced and the cryptographic synchrony of this channel should be independent of the other channels.

The end of the high-priority message text on the regular terminal-to-host channel can be delimited with a distinguished *data mark message* that contains the sequence number of the attention message corresponding to it. In this way, the two terminal-to-host message streams are tied together but attention messages do not have to contain any information that makes them dependent on the context of regular terminal-to-host message traffic.

The use of a separate logical channel with independently sequenced and enciphered attention messages permits high-priority-message processing to be carried out despite the difficulty associated with recognizing and authenticating

[19] This model is offered because of its wide applicability, encompassing environments as simple as asynchronous terminals connected to multiterminal hosts. In the context of X.25, one can view the attention channel as being multiplexed with the regular data channel and can use the *Interrupt packet* to alert the destination process. Because of the limited space available for user data in the Interrupt packet, it cannot be used to transmit secure attention messages.

[20] Whether the attention channel is implemented as a separate physical channel or shares the regular terminal-to-host channel through the use of an out-of-band signal or through some form of software multiplexing depends on the available hardware and the protocol employed. This model attempts to be very general and applicable even in environments where this third simplex channel can be implemented only as a very low bandwidth channel.

enciphered messages that arrive asyncronously with respect to regular message traffic. This mechanism can be employed even in environments where the two logically separate terminal-to-host channels are multiplexed on a single physical channel and only low levels of the communication system at the service host are available to perform the attention message recognition function [30].

9.3.8.4 *Message Integrity*

For purposes of reliability and security, an *error-detection field* must be included in each message to provide a basis for determining the integrity of the message. In the security context, the combination of encryption and an error-detection field also provides a means of indivisibly binding application-level data and the protocol information needed for authentication and ordering of messages. The point here is to ensure, with high probability, that an intruder cannot tamper with either the data or header information in an undetectable fashion. Two basic approaches can be employed in meeting this requirement, each of which depends on the error-propagation characteristics of encryption algorithms.

In the first approach, a conventional error-detection code [e.g., a *cyclic redundancy check* (CRC)] is applied to the protocol information and data and is enciphered along with the message. This technique can be used with all of the cipher modes described in Sec. 9.3.5. If an n-bit error-detecting code is employed, the probability of an intruder undetectably modifying a message can be reduced to $(1/2)^n$. For example, in the case of a 16-bit CRC this would result in a probability of undetected modification of approximately 1.5×10^{-5}.

An alternative approach to detecting attacks on message integrity relies more heavily on the error-propagation characteristics of encryption techniques. Instead of using an error-detection code that is a function of the message text, the error-detection field can consist of a value that is predictable by the receiver of the message. The advantage here is that no CRC need be computed and the predictable field may already be needed as part of the protocol (e.g., a sequence number field). This value must be positioned within the message at a point where any modification of the enciphered message will, with high probability, result in modification of the value. Using the interblock error-propagation characteristics of certain forms of block chaining (not CBC mode), the inclusion of a predictable n-bit field at the end of a message results in a probability of undetected modification on the order of $(1/2)^n$. This technique provides not only integrity checking but also ordering if the field varies over time in a suitable fashion (e.g., sequence numbers). Note that this approach cannot be employed with the CFB or CBC modes because of the limited error propagation of those modes.

9.3.9 Denial of Message Service

The fourth protection goal, detection of denial of message service, can be achieved through the use of a *request-response protocol* [30]. Such a protocol, built on top of message authentication and ordering, involves the exchange of a pair of messages that establish the time integrity and status of the connection. At each end of the connection a timer is used to periodically trigger the transmission of a request message that forces a response from the other end of the connection. Each of these messages conveys the status of its transmitter in terms that permit detection of any messages missing from the connection. In X.25 an acknowledgment function is provided by the packet send and receive numbers but, as noted earlier, these numbers are too small for security purposes. An explicit request-response protocol can be provided by defining a pair of end-to-end control messages (sent using X.25 data packets) containing both a sequence number and an acknowledgment field along with an error-detection code. These messages could be periodically exchanged by the DTEs to verify the time integrity and status of the connection and could trigger end-to-end retransmission or other mechanisms for recovering from lost or damaged packets not detected by X.25.

In some environments there is also a need for a mechanism to permit a process that has no estimate of the arrival time of the next message on a quiescent connection, to detect denial of message service taking place on that connection. This characterizes the case in which a user at a remote terminal is editing text in a process on a service host. In this context the editor process cannot rely on positive acknowledgment of messages to detect denial of message service because it is not transmitting any messages. The request-response protocol proposed above for X.25 detects this type of attack.

Again, it must be noted that while many interactive applications provide implicit checking for denial-of-message-service attacks because of the command-response nature of the application, general-purpose protocols for interactive and other types of applications cannot rely on such application-dependent character-istics. Moreover, in many instances the application program in execution at a service host is unable to predict when a user will make an additional request, especially when that request may be to abort the current operation. Thus, we must provide automatic detection and reporting of denial of message service attacks.

9.3.10 Spurious Connection Initiation

Countermeasures for accomplishing the fifth goal, detection of spurious connec-tion initiation, are designed to provide a secure basis for verifying the identities of the *principals*[21] at each end of the connection and verifying the time integrity of the connection. Verification of the time integrity of the connection protects against playback attacks, in which an intruder uses a recording of a previous, legitimate connection to mislead or confuse a user or cause a service host process to perform redundant activities, possibly resulting in errors.

---

[21] The term "principal" refers to the entity held accountable by the security policy in force [5]. Depending on the granularity of the protection measures employed, a process, user, terminal, host, or network could be a principal.

Mechanisms for verifying the time integrity of the connection initiation procedure should not require human intervention, so as not to restrict their applicability and to avoid dependence on and inconvenience to users. An example of such a mechanism is easily derived from the detection of denial-of-message-service mechanism outlined in Sec. 9.3.9. Each end of the connection generates a unique challenge (e.g., a binary time and date value) and transmits it to the other end. The challenges are then returned to the senders (perhaps modified in some predetermined fashion) to verify that the procedure is taking place in real time. Receipt of the matching responses by each end completes this procedure. In X.25 a pair of simple end-to-end control messages embedded in data packets could be used for this purpose once the connection has been established at the X.25 level.

Verification of the identities of the principals at the ends of the connection during the connection initiation procedure provides the basis on which the authenticity of subsequent message traffic is founded. Maintenance of this association between the principals identified during connection initiation and the connection involves appropriate key distribution techniques and other measures (e.g., physical security for a terminal in use or protection mechanisms that bind a connection to a process within a host). In the following section we examine key distribution techniques and their relation to authentication during connection initiation.

9.3.10.1 Granularity of Key Distribution

In both conventional and public-key cryptographic systems, the ability to encipher messages under a specific key carries with it an implicit form of authentication in that the transmitter must possess a secret encryption key.[22] If a single key is employed by a subset of the principals of a network, these users form a secure virtual subnet and the ability to initiate a secure connection implies membership in this subset without differentiating among the principals. If a different key is used for communication between each pair of principals (pairwise disjoint key distribution), these keys serve to authenticate the identities of the principals. These observations apply to the use of keys on a per-terminal, per-user, or per-process level. Any pattern of key distribution that is coarser than pairwise disjoint distribution of distinct keys among the principals that form the ends of connections violates the principle of least privilege.[23]

---

[22] In a public-key cipher this cryptographic authentication is achieved by the transmitter using the secret key, and the secrecy of the message is provided by using the public key of the intended recipient in enciphering the message. In such ciphers authentication and secrecy are separable, independent functions, whereas these functions are closely integrated in conventional ciphers.

[23] Public-key ciphers achieve the authentication effect of pairwise disjoint distribution of keys by using the secret key of the sender and the public key of the intended recipient to super-encipher messages. For purposes of secrecy, the multiple-access nature of public-key ciphers provides the effect of pairwise disjoint distribution of keys.

9.3.10.2 Multilevel Key Distribution

In the discussion above there was no mention of per-connection keys, even though it has been emphasized that the use of a distinct key (or equivalent mechanism) for each connection minimizes the amount of information exposed in case of disclosure of a key and simplifies the design of countermeasures used to detect message-stream-modification attacks. In order for a per-connection key to be employed, each end of the connection must possess the key. Secure distribution of a new key for each connection involves some sort of boot-strapping technique. If the initiator of a connection possesses a key known exclusively by himself and the other participant in the connection, the keys used over the duration of a single connection can be generated and transmitted enciphered under this long-term key.

Keys held for long periods of time and used exclusively for the transmission of per-connection keys are referred to as *primary* keys [30]. One or more keys used during the course of a single connection are referred to as *secondary* or *working* keys [29, 33].[24] The use of a primary key as a boot-strapping mechanism in the distribution of secondary keys is referred to as *multilevel key distribution*. Primary keys thus serve as an explicit form of authentication based on the granularity of key distribution employed (assuming pairwise disjoint distribution), while secondary keys are used exclusively for encryption of messages on a single connection.

If pairwise disjoint distribution of conventional cryptographic keys is carried out at the level of individual hosts, complete communication among n hosts requires on the order of n^2 keys. If this form of key distribution is carried out at the level of terminals, as in the case of multiterminal hosts, or at the level of individual users, the number of primary keys involved can become staggering. For an individual user, a convenient way of carrying a personal, primary key would be on a magnetic stripped card much like many credit cards in use today. The number of distinct keys that can be recorded on such a card limit the number of hosts a user could directly contact using the primary keys on the cards. Although this problem can be mitigated through the use of higher recording densities, the inclusion of more magnetic material in the card, and by carrying multiple cards, this is but one aspect of the problem of the use of multiple primary keys. To ameliorate this problem of primary-key proliferation we can employ trusted intermediaries as active *key distribution centers* (KDCs) [33, 44].[25]

---

[24] In public-key ciphers, only primary keys need be employed and some additional mechanism (e.g., a per-connection initial fill or prefix) can be used to achieve the effect of secondary keys. Alternatively, it has been proposed that public-key ciphers could be employed solely for distribution of secondary keys for conventional ciphers such as the DES.

[25] Key distribution centers are needed for public-key ciphers as well. Although it has been suggested that telephone-book listings of public keys would suffice [14], the frequency of key changes one might expect to encounter in a large network and other logistic problems motivate the use of KDCs for public keys.

9.3.10.3 Key Distribution Centers

A KDC can be implemented by a secure host, perhaps a minicomputer, dedicated solely to the task of acting as a trusted intermediary in establishing secure connections. A KDC holds one primary key for each principal that requires its services in establishing connections. The initiator of a connection first contacts the KDC and indicates the target of the connection. The KDC generates a secondary key to be used for the connection and sends this key to the initiator of the connection and to the target of the connection. The copy of the secondary key sent to the initiator of the connection is enciphered under the primary key of the initiator, while the copy sent to the target of the connection is enciphered under the primary key of the target.[26] In this fashion, each connection participant need only hold one primary key that identifies it to a KDC and yet mutually suspicious participants are protected in the same fashion as if pairwise disjoint key distribution had been employed.[27]

To minimize the impact of successful attacks on KDCs, this concept can be extended [15] to include multiple KDCs, each addressed using a different primary key. Connection initiation would involve communication with at least three of the KDCs, and both the initiator and the target of the connection would receive three secondary keys, one from each of the KDCs. The actual secondary key used for the connection is formed by combining, via addition modulo 2, the secondary keys provided by each KDC. By using three or more KDCs in this fashion, the subversion of a single KDC need not result in exposure of user data. In addition to this use of multiple KDCs for security purposes, KDCs may be pooled for load sharing and reliability. Establishment of connections across KDC pools introduces the need for KDC–KDC connections and may require a hierarchy of KDCs to handle distribution of KDC primary keys. The use of multiple KDCs also arises as a result of jurisdictional boundaries associated with the authorities that operate KDCs. Such boundaries become increasingly important in the context of authentication and access control mechanisms.

---

[26] This is but one of several possible scenarios for a KDC. The secondary-key copy enciphered under the primary key of the target could be sent to the initiator and then forwarded to the target as part of the first connection initiation message. This approach eliminates synchronization concerns from the key distribution protocol and is appropriate in the X.25 environment because the charges associated with connection establishment may make it inappropriate for the KDC to contact the target of the call.

[27] A public-key distribution center provides a tamper-free channel for the distribution of public keys. The initiator of a connection contacts the KDC to retrieve the public key of the target. The KDC responds by transmitting this key to the user enciphered under the secret key of the KDC, along with the name of the target. The requestor uses the public key of the KDC (which is distributed outside the system just like primary keys in conventional ciphers) to decipher this response. The KDC keys (public and secret) must be employed to prevent spoofing or tampering during the distribution of the other public keys. The target, upon receiving the message from the initiator, engages in a similar exchange to retrieve the public key of the initiator.

Note that the use of KDCs does not imply the level at which primary keys are held: network, subnet, host, terminal, user, or process.[28] If primary keys are used to segregate networks or virtual subnets, the role played by a KDC may be referred to as that of a *communication security gateway*. Within a given network, even within the establishment of a single connection, primary keys at several levels may come into play (e.g., host, terminal, and user keys). Each of the hosts within a network can use its primary key in establishing a long-term connection with the KDC. The information exchanged over this connection could include requests to establish individual connections and responses to such requests, both for the initiators and targets of connections. In this fashion origin–destination analysis during connection initiation can be reduced.

It is instructive to examine in some detail the use of KDCs for conventional and public-key ciphers. For conventional ciphers a KDC provides the security of pairwise disjoint distribution of keys while requiring each principal to hold only one secret primary key. In the context of public-key ciphers a KDC provides a tamper-free repository and distribution facility for public keys while requiring each principal to hold only one secret primary key plus the public key of the KDC. Both types of KDCs require an initial "face-to-face meeting" between each user and the KDC.[29] In the case of a conventional cipher the user receives from the KDC (or presents to the KDC) his secret primary key and establishes the association between this key and his identity at this meeting. In a public-key cipher the user presents the public key that corresponds to the secret key, establishes the correspondence between this public key and his identity, and receives the public key of the KDC at this meeting. The essential distinction between these two procedures is that while both entail a tamper-free key exchange, only the former requires secrecy in the exchange.

Once this initial meeting has been carried out, a user can establish a connection with any other user with the assistance of the KDC, as described earlier in this section. The message exchange between the user and the KDC to receive a secondary key or to retrieve the public key for another user must employ a unique identifier on both messages so that the response from the KDC can be reliably associated with the request. Failure to employ such a mechanism may expose the user to attacks in which recordings of prior user-KDC interactions

---

[28]   Terminal-level keys can be used in authenticating individual terminals connected to a multiterminal host and may be quite useful when the identity of the terminal indicates its location as well. Note that the distinction between host and terminal-level keys is lost in the case of single-terminal hosts. User-level keys can be employed to "personalize" (in a security sense) a terminal that may be accessed by a number of different users. Processes on service hosts, especially processes providing widely applicable services to the user community, may similarly deserve their own primary keys.

[29]   Depending on the security requirements of the network and the overall environment, the face-to-face meeting may be replaced by an equivalent procedure (e.g., use of a bonded courier or registered mail).

are played back. Since primary keys change over time to reduce the quantity of data exposed in the face of inadvertent key disclosure, in the event of such disclosure, recordings of old exchanges could result in use of old, exposed keys and subsequent masquerading and/or data release.

One of the major advantages of a KDC is its ability to handle the implications of a limited primary-key lifetime. A user can change his primary key through a procedure equivalent to the initial user-KDC meeting. Other procedures, ones based on use of the current primary key, should be avoided since they could be exploited by an intruder in the event of key disclosure. Once a primary-key-replacement procedure has been carried out, the whole network will automatically employ the new key in establishing connections to the affected user. If a less centralized key distribution approach were employed, notification of affected users in the event of key disclosure could be a time-consuming and difficult task. Note that this discussion has implications for schemes that rely on caching of keys to reduce calls on a KDC, both for conventional and public-key ciphers. In the communication security context, the result of using an encached key that is no longer valid may include data exposure and masquerading by an intruder. Thus, the cost of caching keys includes not only storage space but also mechanisms for timely propagation of key changes to all affected parties in the network.

Finally, one can evaluate the vulnerability of KDCs used with conventional and public-key ciphers. Attacks on KDCs can be classified based on whether key data are released or modified. Release of a primary key from a KDC used with a conventional cipher results in potential exposure of all data transmitted under that key, including other keys distributed under this primary key. It also permits an intruder to pose as the user whose key has been compromised or to pose as the KDC in interactions with that user. Modification of an entry in the key data base can permit an intruder to pose as the user whose entry has been modified, whether the KDC uses a conventional or public-key cipher.[30]

Release of public keys in a KDC has no ill effects, since these keys are freely provided to requestors anyway.[31] The important point here is that release of these keys cannot result in release of any data transmitted under them. However, if the secret key of the KDC is compromised, an intruder could pose as the KDC, and transitively, as any user. This could result in release of information as well as masquerading. If the secret key of the KDC is compromised, it is necessary to notify all users and distribute a new KDC public key, a possibly

---

[30]   In practice the primary keys of principals would not be stored in the clear at a KDC but would be encrypted under a single "master key" [39] held in an encryption device. Thus, disclosure or modification really involves obtaining the master key and using it to obtain or modify primary keys.

[31]   Note that a KDC could be selective in releasing public keys [e.g., it may distribute keys only to legitimate users of a network as an access control measure (see Sec. 9.4.2.7)], and this would contradict the statement above.

formidable task requiring a tamper-free channel (a face-to-face meeting) between the KDC and each user.

9.4 AUTHENTICATION AND ACCESS CONTROL IN NETWORKS

Although authentication and access control mechanisms are logically and functionally separate, they are related in that the decisions made by access control mechanisms are based on information supplied by authentication mechanisms. Both types of mechanisms are, in turn, dependent on the communication security measures described in Sec. 9.3, since violations of communication security can result in circumvention of the security policies implemented by the authentication and access control mechanisms.

Authentication and access control mechanisms have been studied extensively in the context of individual computer systems, and many of the techniques and much of the terminology developed in that context are applicable in a network environment as well. However, the desire to provide flexible and controlled sharing of resources in networks introduces the need for additional authentication and access control techniques. This section examines authentication and access control in networks and discusses the relationship between these mechanisms and host security controls.

9.4.1 Authentication

In a security context, the term *authentication* applies to procedures for verifying the claimed identity of a principal, whether this principal is embodied as an individual, a terminal, or a network. A variety of techniques have been developed for personal authentication, including various password schemes, the use of badges and keys, and physical characteristic measurements (e.g., fingerprints and voiceprints [6, 7, 45]). With the exception of the use of encryption keys for authentication purposes, in a network environment all these techniques are eventually reduced to the transmission of a stream of identifying bits to the site performing the authentication. Therefore, authentication mechanisms are dependent on communication security measures to prevent the release of authentication information and to maintain the integrity of communication paths after authentication has been performed. The first of these requirements is achieved by release of message contents countermeasures, while the second, which addresses attacks such as *piggyback* infiltration and *between-lines entry*, is effected by message-stream-modification countermeasures.

9.4.1.1 Lifetime of Authentication Information

One way of characterizing authentication techniques is based on the lifetime of the information transmitted during the authentication procedure. This lifetime, expressed either in terms of the number of occasions on which the information is used or in terms of a time interval over which the information is acceptable, ranges from unbounded to a single use. At one end of the spectrum are fingerprints, hand geometry analysis, and passwords for which there are no enforced lifetime, while at the other end are one-time passwords and unique challenge–response schemes in which the authentication data are a function of a challenge issued by the host.[32] Between these two extremes are techniques in which passwords, badges, and encryption or physical keys have an enforced lifetime.

Characterization of authentication techniques according to the lifetime of the information transmitted provides one measure of the damage that may result in the event of exposure of this information. If relatively *static authentication information* is exposed, it will enable an intruder to masquerade as an individual for some (perhaps very long) time, while more *dynamic authentication information* may not prove useful to an intruder at all. One-time password or encryption key schemes in which the next password or key is transmitted as an epilogue to the authentication procedure are examples of a "chained" form of authentication and do not provide the desired limited-lifetime characteristics. However, these techniques are superior to more static authentication procedures in that they intrinsically prevent spoofing attacks and they alert a user to the disclosure of authentication information by causing his subsequent authentication attempts to fail once the intruder makes use of the exposed authentication information.

9.4.1.2 Centralized Authentication Services

In the simplest context, authentication procedures already in force at service hosts can be used in conjunction with the communication security measures described in Sec. 9.3. Almost independent of the authentication techniques employed, the addition of the communication security measures will protect against release of authentication information, ensure the integrity of connections, and protect against spoofing attacks. However, in a network environment, there are several reasons for considering centralized authentication services.

---

[32] A response can involve manipulation of challenge text under a secret transformation known only to the user, or can take the form of the digitized signature or voiceprint produced by a user in writing or pronouncing a word or phrase supplied by the host.

Since networks provide convenient access to large numbers of service hosts, users may find it appropriate to have accounts on multiple service hosts. If, for a given user, the same authentication criteria are employed at each host, subversion of any one of these hosts would permit an intruder to masquerade as the user in communicating with all the other hosts with which he has an account. In the case of dynamic authentication schemes such as one-time passwords, it could be difficult to maintain synchrony among the corresponding password lists on each of the hosts.

As an alternative, the user could employ different authentication information for each host he accesses, but it could prove difficult for a user to maintain all of this information. Moreover, several types of authentication techniques do not permit the maintenance of independent authentication information at multiple sites (e.g., fingerprints or voiceprints). If authentication is based on information that is kept secret, as opposed to information about physical characteristics of the user, the task of reissuing such information on a periodic basis or in the face of possible disclosure can be complicated when a number of hosts are involved.

Personal authentication in a network context may be carried out not only for the benefit of access control mechanisms on service hosts, but also for access control and accounting purposes at the network level. If personal authentication is required by the network, independent of authentication requirements of service hosts, a central authentication service can simplify this procedure even for individuals who access only a single host via the network, since it dispenses with the need for multiple authentication procedures.

Since we have already noted that encryption keys can be used as an implicit form of authentication and that, to a great extent, the effectiveness of authentication mechanisms is dependent on the effectiveness of underlying communications security measures, one may question the need for authentication mechanisms other than encryption keys. There are several environments in which the use of encryption keys for personal authentication may not be appropriate. Although inclusion of an encryption module in every terminal can provide a very high degree of security, the cost of retrofitting existing terminals may be deemed prohibitively expensive in some cases. Even if encryption facilities are available in individual terminals, provision for per-user rather than (or in addition to) per-terminal keys could further increase the cost and complexity of such facilities. For those users who access the network via terminals attached to server hosts, providing an encrypted communication path from the network through the server host and back to the terminal may prove difficult. Thus, although primary keys provide an extremely powerful and inexpensive mechanism, they should be viewed only as one of several static personal authentication mechanisms that can be employed.

This points out the dichotomy between the distribution of keys at the device (terminal or host) level for purposes of communication security, and the use of encryption keys or other information for personal authentication purposes. This dichotomy, and the principles of separation of privilege and least privilege, suggest that key distribution and personal authentication services be provided independently. However, encryption keys do constitute an excellent mechanism for personal authentication and the KDC approach can be applied to the problems of managing authentication information. A designated, secure *authentication server host* can act as a trusted intermediary, carrying out user authentication procedures and forwarding the results to service hosts. In this fashion the problems associated with proliferation of authentication information can be managed.

The analogy between a KDC and an authentication server extends to all of the limitations of KDCs noted earlier (e.g., each authentication server host has a corresponding domain over which it provides services to users and hosts). Authentication server hosts can be grouped to provide load sharing and reliability and different groups can be provided to parallel jurisdictional boundaries and provide fire walls. As with KDCs, if the authentication server groups trust one another, simple protocols can be employed to handle cross-jurisdictional authentication. However, when jurisdictions view one another with mutual suspicion, providing authentication services across these boundaries can become quite complex.

Techniques can be employed to minimize the release of authentication information in the event of subversion of an authentication server. For example, if passwords are employed, instead of storing the password at the authentication server the image of the password under a one-way transformation can be stored and this transformation can be applied to a text string submitted as the password during an authentication procedure [46]. If the application of the transformation to the candidate password results in a match with the image of the password under the transformation, the authentication procedure succeeds. In this fashion, subversion of an authentication server would result in release of authentication information only for those users actively engaged in an authentication procedure, since the transformed passwords are useless to an intruder.

As an alternative to this approach, an authentication server could store for each user the authentication information required by each host accessed by that user. In this context, a user would employ a single means of identifying himself to the authentication server, which, in turn, would act as the user's agent in carrying out appropriate authentication procedures for the host the user wishes to access. An advantage of this scheme is that it does not require service hosts to distinguish between connections established using an authentication server and those in which the user provides the authentication information directly to the host. A user could "program" different authentication procedures for each host he accesses, and have the authentication server carry out these procedures on his behalf. An authentication server functioning in this fashion would appear as a user to each service host, and thus no special provision need be made for users employing this technique as opposed to those who use "direct" authentication.

The discussion above has treated the problem of user authentication from a terminal host. Another problem arises when a user's process on a service host (*B*) attempts to establish a connection to another service host (*C*), as illustrated in Fig. 9.11. Connections of this sort may come about because the user's only means of accessing the network is via the local service host *B*, because the connection from *B* to *C* is a necessary part of the task being performed on *B*, or simply because the user would like to perform some task on *C* while maintaining his connection to *B* and his terminal facilities (*A*) are capable of maintaining only one direct connection at a time. The problem of authentication in conjunction with establishing the connection from *B* to *C* is an example of what has been termed the *third-party authentication problem*. The difficulty here lies in carrying out an authentication procedure for the connection to host *C* in a fashion that will not permit host *B* to masquerade as the user in establishing connections to host *C* in the future.

Solutions to this problem must consider the possibility that there are Trojan Horse programs operating in the user's process on host *B* and, in consideration of the principle of least privilege, host *B* should not have any ability to masquerade as the user in future interactions with host *C*. In one approach to this problem, an authentication server host would be invoked in the course of establishing the connection from host *B* to host *C*, and this server would establish a connection directly to the user at terminal *A* to request confirmation of the legitimacy of the connection from host *B* to host *C*. However, this approach requires that a secure connection can be established directly between the

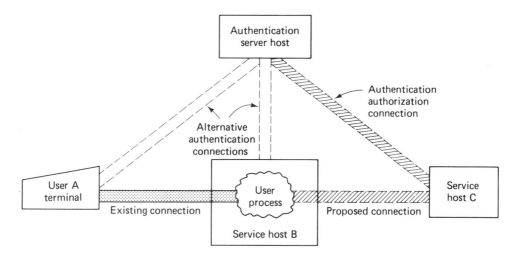

FIGURE 9-11 *Third party authentication example.*

413

authentication server and terminal A without destroying the connection from terminal A to host B.

If this type of connection configuration cannot be established, the authentication server can request user authorization of the proposed connection by conducting an authentication procedure over a connection that passes through host B. If the authentication procedure employed involves a time-varying response that is not predictable based on examination of previous responses (e.g., one-time password lists or unique challenge–response schemes), no information is released to host B that can be used for illegitimate authentication purposes later.

While both of these approaches minimize the exposure of authentication information subject to the constraints imposed by network configuration, the first requires sophisticated connection management facilities, the second restricts the type of authentication information that can be used, and both impose a burden on the user that could become intolerable should his task on host B require a substantial number of connections to other hosts. The use of a proxy login scheme for authentication forwarding has been discussed by Karger [28], but it was pointed out that such schemes offer no advantage for protection from Trojan Horse attacks over simple schemes such as storing authentication information at service hosts.

Another consideration in discussing personal authentication is the points in time at which a user is required to provide authentication information. A user may be required to authenticate his identity only when he begins using a terminal to access the network, or he may be required to supply authentication information in conjunction with opening each connection or every time a connection is established to a different host. By requiring reauthentication every time the user's range of access changes, a form of containment is provided for the exposure or damage that could result if the terminal is left unattended for any reason or in the event of loss of the control message, indicating the end of a terminal session. Whether a user is required to provide personal authentication can be a function of the terminal employed and/or the service host being accessed. If the terminal being employed is located in a room protected by a guard who admits only selected individuals, only terminal (rather than personal) authentication may be required.

9.4.2 Access Control

As is the case with personal authentication at the network level, there are various reasons for employing network-level access control and several methods for effecting this control. In the simplest case, access control can be used to determine whether or not an individual is allowed to access any of the resources on the network. The granularity of access control exercised at the network level can be refined so that access to individual hosts can be selectively granted or denied to specific users or hosts. Finally, network-level access control mechanisms can be extended to include subhost entities (e.g., processes or files), although enforcement of access policies at this level is beyond the purview of such mechanisms [47, 48]. In general, the theory of access control in networks is derived from research on the protection of information in computer systems. This section briefly describes the two primary models of access control that have evolved from such research and describes how these models can be implemented at the network level. The discussion of these two models is drawn from Karger [28].

9.4.2.1 Access Matrix Model

The *access matrix model* proposed by Lampson [3] provides a general representation of access control policies in which the *access privileges* of each *subject* to each *object* are defined as entries in a matrix. In a network context, subjects could be individuals, terminals, hosts, or individuals qualified by the terminal or host through which they gain access to the network. Correspondingly, the objects to which access is controlled are usually the hosts and terminals on the network, although subhost objects for which the individual hosts actually control access may be included in the matrix as a service to hosts.

Subjects are usually represented by rows of the matrix and objects by columns. The access rights that appear in the entries of the matrix correspond to the operations that can be performed on the objects. Thus, with respect to hosts, permission to establish a connection is an appropriate access attribute, while for files, permission to read or write is appropriate. By introducing attributes such as *owner* or *control*, the matrix can define not only access rights to objects, but also access rights to change entries in the matrix itself.

An access matrix is usually sparse, and in practice one of two generic implementations is employed. The matrix can be decomposed by columns, yielding an *access control list system*, or by rows, resulting in a *capability system*.[33] In the former approach, the access control list associated with each object enumerates the subjects that have access rights to the object and indicates those rights, while in the capability approach, associated with each subject is a list that describes the objects to which the subject has access rights and indicates those rights. In an access control list system, when a subject attempts to gain access to an object, the access control list is examined to determine whether the access is permitted. In a capability system, each capability held by a subject implies the access rights of that subject to the object designated by that capability. The protection mechanisms available in most computers can be represented by this access matrix model.

---

[33] The third potential implementation, decomposition by access rights, is rarely used.

9.4.2.2 *Discretionary Access Control*

Usually, both access control lists and the capability systems are implemented as *discretionary access control systems* (i.e., access to an object can be granted or denied to any subject at the discretion of the "owner" of the object). In a discretionary access control system, changes to the access control list of an object are determined by the owner of the object, and the holder of a capability for an object is usually free to pass that capability to other subjects. The basic disadvantage of discretionary access controls in computer systems is the vulnerability of such controls to attack by Trojan Horse programs. Access control lists and capabilities are usually manipulated by programs, on behalf of a user, and these programs may not always be trustworthy (i.e., they may be Trojan Horse programs). Such programs, in addition to performing their legitimate functions, can surreptitiously modify access control lists or distribute capabilities without being detected by the user.

The limitations of discretionary access controls have been formally modeled [4] and it has been shown that, for a fully general access matrix, certain security questions are undecidable. One such security question that is undecidable in a general access matrix is the *confinement problem* [49]. The problem is to eliminate every means by which a subject that is authorized to access an object can release the information contained in that object to some subjects not authorized to access that information. If, for a particular security system, it can be demonstrated that no such mechanism exists, that security system is not susceptible to Trojan Horse attacks. The results developed by Harrison [4] demonstrate that discretionary access control systems based on general access matrices may be vulnerable to Trojan Horse attacks and that, in general, it is impossible to determine if unauthorized information flows of the type described above exist.

9.4.2.3 *Lattice Model*

Although the confinement problem is undecidable in the case of a general access matrix, it has been shown that this problem is decidable in the context of a *lattice security model* [1, 2, 4]. The lattice model is a *nondiscretionary access control system*, originally derived from the military classification system, although it can also be used to describe nonmilitary security systems (e.g., corporate proprietary systems or personal privacy protection systems [50]). In a lattice model, objects are assigned classifications and subjects are assigned clearances. Whether a subject is allowed to access an object is a function of the clearance of the subject and the classification of the object.

The basis of the lattice model, and the origin of its name, is a set of partially ordered access classes from which subject clearances and object classifications are selected. The semantics associated with the access classes are not a part of the model; it is necessary only that a partial ordering can be imposed on the access classes and that the set contains a highest access class and lowest access

416

class under this ordering, so that the partially ordered set forms a lattice. Since only a partial ordering is required by the model, two arbitrarily selected access classes are either comparable (less than, greater than, or equal) or incomparable (disjoint).

As an example, consider how the military classification system can be represented in the lattice model. In this context, an access class consists of two components: a sensitivity level and a category set. The sensitivity levels are UNCLASSIFIED, CONFIDENTIAL, SECRET, and TOP SECRET. Within some sensitivity levels, categories serve to compartmentalize collections of information that require special access permission. In order to access information in a given category a subject must have a clearance not only for the sensitivity level of the information, but also must possess an authorization for the category (i.e., a "need-to-know" determination that access is essential to the accomplishment of official Government duties or contractual obligations). Examples of formalized need-to-know categories (called "Special Access Programs") include NUCLEAR and NATO. Thus, a subject holding a TOP SECRET clearance could not access an object classified as CONFIDENTIAL-NUCLEAR unless the subject also possessed a NUCLEAR authorization. Figure 9.12 illustrates this lattice example.

The partial ordering defined on access classes in this example uses the total ordering on sensitivity levels and the partial ordering of set inclusion on category sets. Hence, access class A is less than or equal to access class B if and only if the sensitivity level of A is less than or equal to that of B and the category set of A is a subset of that of B. The lowest access class in this lattice is UNCLASSIFIED-no categories and the highest access class is TOP SECRET-all categories. As noted earlier, the military security lattice is just an example, and more complex lattices can be developed to model other types of security policies.

Extensive research on lattice-model access control systems has resulted in the isolation of two properties the enforcement of which assures invulnerability to Trojan Horse attacks [1, 2]. The first of these, the *simple security property*, requires the clearance of a subject to be greater than or equal to the classification of an object if the subject is to read (or execute) that object. The second property, the **-property* (pronounced "star property"), requires the clearance of a subject to be less than or equal to the classification of an object if the subject is to write in the object. Thus, a Trojan Horse program can never release information by writing it at a "lower" access class than the object or the objects from which the information was gathered.

9.4.2.4　*Role of Access Control in Networks*

Before considering how discretionary and nondiscretionary access controls can be implemented in networks, it is appropriate to place the use of such controls in perspective. First, it is important to remember that the mechanisms described below can enforce a security policy only within the confines of the

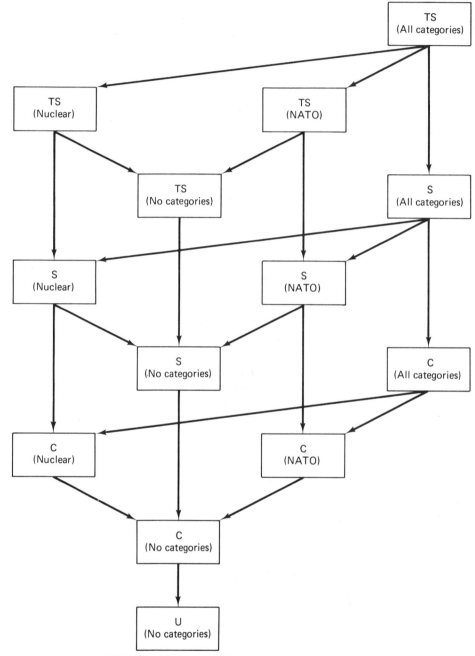

FIGURE 9-12 *Example lattice for military classification.*

network; they cannot control the flow of information among users along channels outside the network. The extension of these policies to the actions of individuals or groups in the environment encompassing the network requires appropriate physical, procedural, and judicial measures. The dependence of internal access control mechanisms on external security controls is exemplified by the fact that all access control mechanisms depend on some form of authentication (personal or otherwise) at the interface between external and internal controls.

It is important to remember that the effectiveness of access control mechanisms depends on the effectiveness of the communications security measures employed in a network environment, since active and passive wiretapping attacks can be used to circumvent access control mechanisms. Thus, the realization of a security policy implemented by access control mechanisms within a network is dependent on communication security measures, authentication techniques, physical controls, and procedural policies.

9.4.2.5 *Network-Level Access Control*

The first level of access control that can be carried out in a network is a simple binary decision of whether a given subject is allowed to access the network facilities as a whole. In most networks, this level of access control for hosts is implicitly implemented by physically restricting the connection of hosts to the communication subnet. This approach can also be applied to individual terminals that are directly connected (not dialed) to hosts. However, without the application of communication security measures, this simple approach is subject to several forms of attack. Depending on the communications technology employed in the subnet, it may be possible for an intruder to be positioned on the link between two subnet nodes and masquerade as the immediate neighbor of each of the nodes. Again, depending on the routing and addressing techniques employed, the intruder may then be able to provide access to the network for illegitimate or counterfeit hosts or terminals. Wiretapping of a communications link between the subnet and a host or between a host and a terminal similarly permits an intruder to introduce counterfeit network resources.

The need to employ communication security measures as a means of enforcing even this simple access control policy becomes especially apparent in broadcast and internetwork environments and in situations where terminals may be dialed to hosts, since in these contexts, physical control over attachment to the communication subnet is not generally available. One can easily imagine a situation in which access to a local network must be selectively provided to only a subset of the terminals or hosts that can potentially communicate with the local network via a gateway. This situation is analogous to the problem of granting network access to a selected subset of all terminals capable of being dialed to terminal hosts, or to the authorized subset of all users capable of accessing terminals on such hosts.

This type of problem can be solved by providing a secure communication path from the subject to the target network and by authenticating the identity of the subject. If encryption keys are used as the basis of authentication, which is especially appropriate when the subjects are terminals or hosts, authentication and access control functions are implicitly subsumed by the key distribution aspect of the communication security measures. In an internetwork context the target network usually cannot rely on the security measures in force in foreign networks, and thus end-to-end communication security measures should be employed from the subject at least as far as the gateway to the target network and preferably to the target host.

9.4.2.6 *Host-Level Access Control*

The next level at which access control can be carried out in a network involves controlling access to individual hosts rather than the network as a whole. Access control at this level can be enforced either by the individual hosts or by the network itself. In the former approach, each host may provide its own key distribution and authentication functions or may avail itself of network-supplied services for these purposes, while in the latter case, the network must carry out the key distribution and authentication functions. From a network security standpoint, host-enforced access control mechanisms provide a basis for (host-level) discretionary security controls while network-enforced access control can implement discretionary or nondiscretionary security policies. The ability of network-enforced access controls to impose nondiscretionary security policies on the flow of information between hosts in a single network permits sharing of this network by a collection of hosts in which subsets of the collection process information at different access classes.

The ARPANET, as currently configured, provides examples of host-enforced (host-level) discretionary access controls, and network-enforced nondiscretionary controls. Most service hosts on the ARPANET enforce discretionary access control policies by requiring a user to provide a password as part of a login sequence. At each host a system administrator can exercise individual discretion in granting a subject access to the host. The ARPANET also serves as a carrier for a secure virtual subnet consisting of a number of hosts at several sites. The hosts that make up this virtual subnet are interfaced to the ARPANET via private line interfaces (PLIs) that provide end-to-end encryption and control the hosts to which packets can be addressed.[34] In this fashion, all message traffic (excluding ARPANET headers) between PLIs is cryptographically isolated from regular ARPANET message traffic.

Because of limitations of the equipment employed by PLIs, cryptographic isolation on a per-host or per-connection basis is not available. The PLI network

---

[34] Multiple hosts can be connected to a single PLI, and message traffic among them is not controlled by the PLI. The encryption here is really PLI-to-PLI, not host-to-host, but it is end-to-end rather than link encryption.

can be segregated into disjoint subnets cryptographically using manual key distribution techniques. To provide a finer granularity of access control when subnets are not disjoint, the red and black sides of each PLI contain access control tables that constrain the addressing range of the PLI. Thus, the PLI network imposes nondiscretionary controls on host access through cryptographic and addressing restriction mechanisms.

9.4.2.7 *Network Security Controllers*

A centralized approach to providing network-enforced host-level access control has been proposed [33, 47, 48] in which key distribution and authentication functions are combined with an access control data base in a secure host termed a *network security center* (NSC). In this approach, each host is connected to the network through a *cryptographic interface unit* (CIU) controlled by the NSC. The NSC enforces access control policies through key distribution on a per-connection basis. As an example, consider the scenario in which a user at a terminal establishes a connection to a service host. First, a secure connection is established between the terminal host and the NSC so that the user can authenticate his or her identity to the NSC. The user then requests a connection to the desired service host and the NSC, based on its access control data base, either approves or rejects this request. If the request is approved, the NSC initiates the establishment of a logical connection between the terminal host and the service host by generating and distributing a secondary key for this connection to the CIUs at both hosts. It has been suggested that access control be based on the access matrix model and that changes to this data base could be effected either by a system security officer at the NSC (nondiscretionary access control) or by protocols between the NSC and service hosts (discretionary access control).

While this NSC approach to network access control has a number of advantages, it also has limitations. As described by Heinrich, multiterminal hosts (network front ends) would employ a single CIU for the host rather than providing units for each of the terminals supported by the host. This permits the multiterminal host to provide various support functions for the terminals connected to it and may be more cost-effective than providing cryptographic interface units for each of the terminals, but it requires that the multiterminal host be secure so that no misrouting or unauthorized copying of messages can take place. However, this design can logically be extended to utilize encryption units on individual terminals, even terminals connected to a network through multiterminal hosts.

If the NSC implements a discretionary access control scheme in which changes to an access matrix can be authorized via communication with hosts, the access control mechanisms will be subject to Trojan Horse attacks. In fact, since the service hosts in this context are not presumed to be secure, the NSC cannot guarantee that the correspondence between a connection and a subject will be maintained within any of the hosts. This can lead to further problems with respect to forwarding of authentication and attempts to enforce the security policy defined by the access matrix. It must be emphasized that the granularity of access control that can be enforced by an NSC is that of an entire host, even if the access matrix at an NSC contains entries for subhost objects as a service to the host. The centralized access control provided by an NSC may be precluded by judicial or administrative policy or by reliability and load-distribution constraints. Finally, as proposed, the NSC approach does not support lattice-model nondiscretionary access control, including the *-property.

As is the case with key distribution and authentication, the problem of providing NSC-based access control across jurisdictional boundaries is also a complex task.[35] In one approach to this problem, each jurisdiction is served by an NSC, and the CIUs for the hosts within that jurisdiction are under the exclusive control of that NSC. To establish a cross-jurisdictional connection in this approach, the NSCs in the origin and target jurisdiction must both concur in their access control decisions and must cooperate in distribution of the secondary key to the CIUs at the source and target hosts. If the NSCs trust one another, the NSC in the local jurisdiction could carry out the authentication procedure and forward the results of this procedure to the NSC in the target jurisdiction. However, if the authorities represented by the NSCs in each jurisdiction interact with one another in a mutually suspicious fashion, it becomes difficult to implement this type of interaction using this approach.

To a great extent, problems arise in the mutually suspicious jurisdictions context because of the use of centralized access control enforced via conventional key distribution. Using the NSC paradigm, the problem could be approached by providing each CIU with multiple primary keys, corresponding to the jurisdictions with which the hosts attached to the unit may interact, so that the CIU can establish secure connections to NSCs outside its own jurisdiction. However, this approach engenders a primary-key distribution problem, as the number of jurisdictions increases, if no hierarchy of key distribution facilities is available.

Abandoning the NSC approach, one can imagine a scheme in which the (possibly centralized) access control policy is enforced in a decentralized fashion, using more sophisticated CIUs, each of which contains the portion of the access control data base relevant to the host or hosts attached to the CIUs. Key distribution could be decoupled from the access control function through the use of public-key KDCs. Personal authentication services could be based on the public-key distribution or provided by authentication server hosts. Centralized facilities under the control of an authority for a jurisdiction could manage the

[35] Within a single jurisdiction, multiple NSCs can be provided for reliability and load-distribution purposes without encountering these problems, since within a jurisdiction, the key distribution, authentication, and access control data bases can be shared among multiple NSCs. As these data bases are relatively static, the maintenance of duplicate copies at several sites is relatively straightforward, and the use of such copies simplifies the inter-NSC protocols used in conjunction with load-distribution and reliability measures.

distribution and maintenance of the access control data-base components in CIUs within the jurisdiction. The use of a decentralized access control mechanism, the decoupling of this mechanism from authentication and key distribution services, and the use of public-key ciphers simplifies the task of establishing cross-jurisdictional connections in which both jurisdictions independently perform authentication and exercise access control.

9.4.2.8 Secure Communication Processors

With respect to nondiscretionary access control in networks, consider as an example service hosts classified either as single-level or multilevel hosts [51]. A single-level host processes information at only one access class (or security classification category) and is not trusted to correctly label outgoing messages with that access class, while a multilevel system can support concurrent processing of information in various access classes. In a network environment, nondiscretionary access control mechanisms should permit dedicated hosts operating at the same level to establish full-duplex connections between one another and should permit the establishment of simplex connections from hosts operating at one level to hosts operating at a higher level in support of the *-property. Similar observations about permissible connections can be made with respect to communication between processes on different multilevel hosts and communication between processes on multilevel hosts and dedicated hosts. In this environment, terminal hosts can be assigned maximum and minimum access classes, with the constraint that all connections established from these hosts must be to processes that lie within that range of access classes. This constraint is understandable when one recalls that the primary purpose of nondiscretionary access controls in computer systems and networks is to prevent disclosure of information by Trojan Horse attacks.

The simple security property requirement that two-way communication be permitted only between principals in the same access class can be enforced using an NSC approach in which the access control data base describes the access classes of all the dedicated hosts and the access class ranges of all multilevel hosts in the network. Alternatively, because of the simplicity of the lattice model and the relatively static nature of the data base describing this model, a decentralized approach can be used. In a decentralized scheme, secure communication processors enforce correct access class labeling of messages based on a table of the access class characteristics of the hosts that are attached to them. Delivery of messages to hosts is governed by a comparison of the access class label of the message and the table describing the access classes of the hosts served by the processor.

The secure communication processors can be implemented as interface units for the individual hosts or could be part of the communication subnet (e.g., packet switches). In the latter case, and in the former case when servicing multilevel hosts, the communication processors must be multilevel secure hosts themselves. Both nondiscretionary, decentralized access control in networks and link-oriented traffic analysis countermeasures generate a requirement for such multilevel secure communication processors.

One-way communication involving dedicated hosts is a more difficult problem because of the problems of providing flow control and error control without a reverse communication channel.[36] It has been suggested [28] that a multilevel secure communication or front-end processor could be equipped with suitable mass storage so that messages from a low-access-class host can be acknowledged and stored until they are delivered to and acknowledged by a high-access-class host. In this fashion, a one-way communication path from a low-access-class host to a high-access-class host can be constructed using two-way communication paths from the low-access-class host to the secure communication processor and from that processor to the high-access-class host.[37]

9.4.2.9 Interfacing Network and Host Security Mechanisms

Network and host security mechanisms must be carefully interfaced to provide a coherent security policy. The use of a secure front-end processor provides this interface in the case of nondiscretionary network access control for dedicated hosts. This type of interface can be employed with minimal impact on the host operating system and the communication subnet. The use of PLIs in the ARPANET illustrates the simplicity of this approach. Each PLI appears as a packet switch to the host(s) it serves and as a host to the subnet. Discretionary controls can be implemented using CIUs, as presented in Sec. 9.4.2.7, or through integration of these controls with protection mechanisms within the host, as described later in this section.

Interfacing nondiscretionary network controls and multilevel host security mechanisms presents a more interesting challenge. There the goal is to minimize the amount of code that constitutes a common mechanism for all users and thus must reside in the security kernel of the host [52]. One possibility is to employ a single data path between the subnet and the host and to use a multiplexed cryptographic unit either on this path or accessed from within the host. Using this approach, a single facility in the security kernel would perform multiplexing and demultiplexing of logical connections on the host–network data path. Additional code to provide security protocol functions (and to handle cryptographic transformations if they are controlled from within the host) can be

[36] One-way communication between multilevel hosts can be enforced because the operating system in multilevel hosts can provide the reverse channel for flow control and error control without violating the *-property. The difficulty arises in providing one-way communication between a pair of dedicated hosts or from a multilevel host to a dedicated host.

[37] The PLIs used in the ARPANET provide the foundation for one-way communication between hosts based on two-way communication between the black sides of PLIs, one-way communication from the red to the black side at the source, and one-way communication from the black to the red side at the destination.

provided for each active access class in the system independently, as distinct protected subsystems. Additional study is required in this area, and no secure multilevel systems connected to multilevel networks yet exist on which to evaluate these proposals. The details of interfacing in this context also depend on the structure of the multilevel host operating system.

As noted earlier, one of the major advantages of end-to-end or connection-oriented security measures is that the protection provided by such measures is applied uniformly from origin to destination, independent of the characteristics of the path between the ends. Although the importance of using end-to-end security measures to protect a communication path, portions of which are physically unsecured, is generally agreed upon, the extension of such measures to include portions of the path that are physically secured but multiplexed among several users is not so widely accepted.

A fundamental principle in the design of secure systems is the avoidance of unnecessary common mechanisms, for mechanisms that are common to more than one user provide a potential path for unauthorized interaction. If connection-oriented security measures are employed, encryption modules can be associated with individual logical connections and need not be implemented in a multiplexed facility of the communication system. Thus, the encryption provided by the modules can ensure the logical separation of individual connections as they pass through various multiplexed facilities, and the verification of the secure operation of these facilities can be simplified.[38] In the context of interactive communication between a user at a terminal and his computation on a service host, this positioning strategy results in placing the encryption modules in the terminal and in the user's computation at the service host. Figure 9.13 illustrates this positioning strategy.

One objection to using this strategy with respect to terminals is that it eliminates the ability of a multiterminal host to provide support functions involving processing of cleartext. It can also be argued that it is more cost-effective to provide an encryption module at a multiterminal host rather than in each of the terminals connected to it. The continuing decline in the cost of hardware and the corresponding increase in the sophistication and processing power of terminals indicates that both of these objections can be overcome. The inclusion of encryption modules in individual terminals also supports the use of per-user keys for personal authentication purposes.

With respect to service hosts, this positioning strategy has a number of implications for the security policy. This strategy clearly contrasts with the use of red–black separation and with the proposed use of CIUs or secure front-end processors for access control purposes. The use of secure communication or

---

[38] Examples of hardware facilities that are frequently multiplexed among many connections, and thus should be positioned between the modules, are multiterminal hosts and host front-end processors, while buffer management modules for multiplexed channels provide a similar example in software.

front-end processors supporting red–black separation is appropriate in the context of enforcing nondiscretionary access controls with dedicated hosts or in enforcing centralized, discretionary controls on a collection of hosts without effective internal access controls. However, the red–black separation positioning strategy may be inappropriate in contexts where no network-level access control policy is being enforced (i.e., each host employs independent internal access control policies) or in contexts where nondiscretionary controls are applied to collections of multilevel hosts. In these environments it is important not only to prevent cleartext information but also to prevent leakage of information between logical connections within the host from appearing in the physically unsecured environment. The former positioning strategy can be justified in these environments because of the simplification in design and verification of multiplexed components resulting from the use of the strategy. The strategy also appears reasonable in environments where not all of the user community employs communication security techniques in accessing the service host.

In those contexts where encryption can be performed inside the service host, the encryption is constrained to be performed "beyond" the portion of the communication system that engages in syntactic processing of message contents. With respect to output from the host, encryption cannot be performed until transformations such as device-specific code conversion have taken place. With respect to input to the host, messages must be deciphered before such transformations as translation, character echoing, and high-priority-message recognition can be performed. The host modules that implement communication security functions can be implemented in software, although hardware support for encryption is generally required for efficient operation.[39] Host memory protection machinery can be used to provide a private environment for the execution of the module for each connection, and the modules should be beyond any multiplexed buffers managed by the host operating system software. The host memory protection machinery can also be used to protect the modules from user-level programs that might damage or circumvent them. The user-level programs might inflict damage as a result of errors, or they might be Trojan Horse programs.

Communication systems connecting users to interactive computations must deal with the fundamental problem of synchronizing the arrival of messages from a user with the demand for input from a computation. Many systems achieve this necessary synchronization by providing one or more buffers in the connection between the user and the computation, thus allowing the user to work ahead of the demands for input by the computation. Since some of these buffers may be multiplexed among several users, incoming messages in these buffers will still be

---

[39] In the future, encryption/decryption instructions may be included in the host instruction repertoire, whereas current systems could achieve the effect by providing an input/output type of device interface for these purposes. Design of appropriate key storage and management mechanisms within hosts is a topic requiring further study.

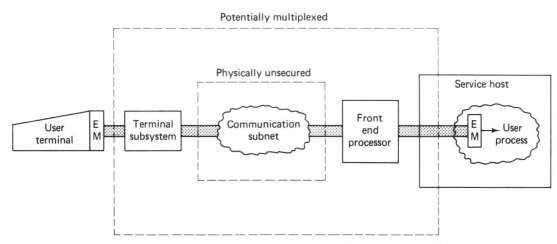

FIGURE 9-13 *Positioning strategy for encryption modules.*

encrypted according to the module positioning strategy described earlier. This has implications for message-processing functions that must be performed immediately upon receipt of a message (e.g., high-priority message processing and character echoing).

High-priority messages can be handled through the use of the techniques described in Sec. 9.3.8.3. Character echoing in networks poses problems with respect to delays and bandwidth utilization regardless of the use of communication security measures. Mechanisms such as the *remote-controlled transmission and echoing* (RCTE) option in the ARPANET TELNET protocol [10] promise to mitigate these problems. RCTE was developed for use in situations where the time delay associated with conventional remote echoing is considered unacceptably long (e.g., over satellite connections from users in the continental United States to the ALOHA system in Hawaii) or when a service host does not wish to be burdened with the extra processing required by echoing. Telenet [23] includes a host-level protocol option for such local echoing, and the use of microprocessors for such purposes has been suggested in connection with packet radio networks [24].

9.5 SUMMARY AND CONCLUSIONS

This chapter has examined the topic of network security, emphasizing the relevant communication security, authentication, and access control aspects of the topic. Communication security techniques provide the foundation on top of which authentication procedures and access control mechanisms can be constructed. In turn, authentication procedures provide essential input to the decision process performed by access control mechanisms in carrying out security policy. The chapter has examined various threats to network security and proposed countermeasures to these threats. The interactions among these countermeasures and the problems of integrating them and host security controls were examined.

The communication security techniques presented in Sec. 9.3 can be employed independently of the use of any network-level authentication or access control measures. A wide range of techniques was presented and particular options can be selected in tailoring a communication security system to a particular environment. The techniques employed in any given situation depend on a number of factors, including the perceived threat environment, the intended applications, and some aspects of the communication media employed. Although conventional ciphers such as the NBS DES were employed as the cryptographic paradigm in presenting most of the communication security techniques, public-key ciphers can be employed with only minor differences in the resulting protocols and procedures.

The use of encryption in conjunction with communication security provides the added bonus that encryption keys can provide a form of static authentication that is superior to the password schemes in use in most computer systems today. Although much more sophisticated user-authentication mechanisms are being developed, use of an encryption key that is, for example, a function of a bit string recorded on a magnetic stripped card and a memorized password, provides a powerful and economical form of personal authentication that may see widespread use. The use of network-level authentication techniques, encryption-based or otherwise, provides a means for users to access multiple hosts without the fear that subversion of one of those hosts will lead to disclosure of information at other hosts. These authentication procedures can be used in conjunction with access control mechanisms provided by individual hosts or organized on a network level.

Network-level access control mechanisms are appropriate in situations where a collection of hosts is operated under the auspices of a single authority or where the autonomous authorities controlling individual hosts delegate part of their authority to some trusted intermediary. In both cases, this approach permits the extension of access control policies employed within hosts to be applied to interactions between hosts. This approach is especially attractive in environments where the individual hosts do not have effective security controls, but where a "macro" access control policy can be applied to the flow of information among these hosts.

The concept of jurisdiction arises in discussing centralized key distribution, authentication, and access control. Interjurisdiction interactions are easily implemented as long as the jurisdictions involved are not mutually suspicious. Mutual suspicion complicates matters, requiring a hierarchy of jurisdictions or complex protocol and key distribution arrangements. It seems likely that the hierarchic approach will prove more attractive, but government regulation may influence the choice of configuration or may even prohibit substantial centralization of these functions.

Acknowledgments

A number of individuals at the M.I.T. Laboratory for Computer Science and at Bolt Beranek and Newman, Inc., have contributed helpful comments and suggestions during the preparation of this chapter. I would especially like to thank John Davidson, Doug Hunt, Tony Lake, Buz Owen, Karen Sollins, and Liba Svobodova. Preparation of the manuscript was a long, occasionally arduous process, and I am grateful to Nathalie Graham and Donna Jamieson for their outstanding work in transcribing, typing, and correcting the text, and to my wife Rachel for proofreading the manuscript. Finally, I wish to acknowledge the support of Bolt Beranek and Newman, Inc., during the preparation of this chapter.

REFERENCES

[1] WALTER, K. et al., "Primitive Models For Computer Security." Case Western Reserve University, *ESD-TR-74-117*, HQ Electronics Systems Division, Hanscom AFB, Mass., January 1974.

[2] BELL, D., and L. LaPADULA, "Computer Security Model: Unified Exposition and Multics Interpretation," The Mitre Corp., *ESD-TR-75-306*. HQ Electronic Systems Division, Hanscom AFB, Mass., June 1975.

[3] LAMPSON, B., "Protection," *Proceedings of the 5th Princeton Conference on Information Sciences and Systems*, Princeton University, pp. 18–24, January 1974.

[4] HARRISON, M., W. RUZZO, and J. ULLMAN. "Protection in Operating Systems," *CACM*, **19**(8), pp. 461–471, August 1976.

[5] SALTZER, J., and M. SCHROEDER, "The Protection of Information in Computer Systems," *Proceedings of the IEEE*, **63**(9), pp. 1278–1308, September 1975.

[6] COTTON, I., and P. MEISSNER, "Approaches to Controlling Personal Access to Computer Terminals," *Proceedings of the 1975 Symposium on Computer Networks: Trends and Applications*, IEEE Computer Society, pp. 32–39, 1975.

[7] WOOD, H., The Use of Passwords for Controlled Access to Computer Resources, *NBS Special Publication 500-9*, May 1977.

[8] National Bureau of Standards, Data Encryption Standard, *Federal Information Processing Standard Publication 46*, January 1977.

[9] KAUFMAN, D., and K. AUERBACH, "A Secure, National System For Electronic

Funds Transfer," *Proceedings of the AFIPS National Computer Conference*, **45,** pp. 129–138, 1976.

[10] FEINLER, E., and J. POSTEL, "ARPANET Protocol Handbook," *NIC 7104,* Network Information Center, Stanford Research Institute, Menlo Park, Calif., April 1976.

[11] FARBER, D., and K. LARSON, "The Structure of a Distributed Computer System— Communications," *Proceedings of the Symposium on Computer-Communications Networks and Teletraffic,* Microwave Research Institute of Polytechnic Institute of Brooklyn, Brooklyn, N.Y., pp. 21–27, April 1972.

[12] SALTZER, J., "Protection and the Control of Information Sharing in Multics," *CACM,* **17**(7), pp. 388–402, July 1974.

[13] BARAN, P., Distributed Communications: Volume 9, Security, Secrecy, and Tamper-free Considerations," *Rand Memo RM-3765-PR,* August 1964.

[14] RIVEST, R., A. SHAMIR, and L. ADLEMAN, "A Method for Obtaining Digital Signatures and Public-Key Cryptosystems," *CACM,* **21**(2), pp. 120–126, February 1978.

[15] DIFFIE, W., and M. HELLMAN, "Multiuser Cryptographic Techniques," *Proceedings of the AFIPS National Computer Conference,* **45,** pp. 109–112, 1976.

[16] DIFFIE, W., and M. HELLMAN, "New Directions in Cryptography," *IEEE Transactions on Information Theory,* **IT-22**(16), pp. 644–654, November 1976.

[17] CERF, V., and R. KAHN, "A Protocol For Packet Network Intercommunication," *IEEE Transactions on Communications*, **COM-22**(5), pp. 637–648, May 1974.

[18] CERF, V. G., and P. T. KIRSTEIN, "Issues in Packet-Network Interconnection," *Proceedings of the IEEE,* **66**(11), pp. 1386–1408, November 1978.

[19] U.S. Department of Defense, Defense Communications Agency, System Performance Specification for AUTODIN II, Phase I, February 1977.

[20] METCALFE, R., and D. BOGGS, "Ethernet: Distributed Packet Switching For Local Computer Networks," *CACM,* **19**(7), pp. 395–404, July 1976.

[21] POUZIN, L., "Presentation and Major Design Aspects of the Cyclades Computer Network," *Proceedings of the 3rd Data Communications Symposium,* pp. 80–85, November 1973.

[22] ABRAMSON, N., "The Aloha System," *Proceedings of the AFIPS Fall Joint Computer Conference,* **37,** pp. 281–285, 1970.

[23] Telenet Communications Corporation, Host Interface Specifications, Washington, D.C., March 1975.

[24] KAHN, R., "The Organization of Computer Resources into a Packet Radio Network," *Proceedings of the AFIPS National Computer Conference,* **44,** pp. 177–186, 1975.

[25] IBM, Synchronous Data Link Control General Information, IBM Corp. System Reference Library, *GA27-3093-O,* March 1974.

[26] CCITT Recommendation X.25, Interface between Data Terminal Equipment and Data Circuit-terminating Equipment for Terminals Operating in the Packet Mode on Public Data Networks, Geneva, 1976.

[27] ANDERSON, J., Computer Security Technology Planning Study, James P. Anderson & Company, *ESD-TR-73-51,* Vols. 1 and 2, HQ Electronics System Division, Hanscom AFB, Mass., October 1972.

[28] KARGER, P., Non-discretionary Access Control for Decentralized Computing Systems, S.M. Thesis, MIT Department of Electrical Engineering and Computer Science, May 1977. (Also available as *MIT/LSC/TR-179,* Laboratory for Computer Science, Massachusetts Institute of Technology, Cambridge, Mass., May 1977.)

[29] KENT, S., "Encryption-based Protection for Interactive User/Computer Communication," *Proceedings of the 5th Data Communications Symposium*, pp. 5–7 to 5–13, September 1977.

[30] KENT, S., Encryption-based Protection Protocols for Interactive User-Computer Communication, S.M. thesis, MIT Department of Electrical Engineering and Computer Science, May 1976. (Also available as *MIT/LCS/TR-162,* Laboratory for Computer Science, Massachusetts Institute of Technology, Cambridge, Mass., May 1976.)

[31] KAHN, D., *The Code Breakers*, Macmillan Publishing Co., Inc., New York, 1967.

[32] FEISTEL, H., W. NOTZ, and J. SMITH, "Cryptographic Techniques for Machine to Machine Data Communications," *Proceedings of the IEEE*, **63**(11), pp. 1545–1554, November 1975.

[33] BRANSTAD, D., "Encryption Protection in Computer Data Communication," *Proceedings of the 4th Data Communications Symposium,* pp. 8–1 to 8–7, October 1975.

[34] SHANNON, C., "Communication Theory of Secrecy Systems," *Bell Systems Technical Journal,* **28**(4), pp. 656–715, October 1949.

[35] MEYER, C. and W. TUCHMAN, "Pseudorandom Codes Can Be Cracked," *Electronic Design*, **23**(11), pp. 74–76, November 1972.

[36] SAVAGE, J., "Some Simple Self-synchronizing Data Scramblers," *Bell Systems Technical Journal*, **42**(2), pp. 449–487, February 1967.

[37] HELLMAN, M. et al., "Results of an Initial Attempt to Cryptanalyze the NBS Data Encryption Standard," Stanford University Center for Systems Research, *SEL 76-042,* September 1976.

[38] DIFFIE, W., and M. HELLMAN, "Exhaustive Cryptanalysis of the NBS Data Encryption Standard," *Computer*, **10**(6), pp. 74–84, June 1977.

[39] ESHRAM, W., S. MATYAS, C. MEYER, and W. TUCHMAN, "A Cryptographic Key Management Scheme for Implementing the Data Encryption Standard," *IBM Systems Journal*, **17**(2), pp. 106–125, 1978.

[40] CHANDERSEKARAN, C., and K. SHANKAR, "Towards Formally Specifying Communication Switches," *Trends and Applications 1976: Computer Networks,* IEEE Computer Society, pp. 104–112, November 1976.

[41] Bolt Beranek and Newman, Inc., Specifications for the Interconnection of a Host and an IMP, *BBN Report 1822,* December 1974.

[42] FARBER, D., and K. LARSON, "Network Security via Dynamic Process Renaming,"

Proceedings of the 4th Data Communications Symposium, pp. 8–13 to 8–18, October 1975.

[43] SALTZER, J., "Traffic Control in a Multiplexed Computer System," Sc.D. thesis, MIT Department of Electrical Engineering, 1966.

[44] BRANSTAD, D. "Security Aspects of Computer Networks," *Proceedings of the AIAA Computer Network Systems Conference*, Paper 73-427, April 1973.

[45] MEISSNER, P., "Guideline on Evaluation of Techniques for Automated Personnel Identification," *Federal Information Processing Standard Publication 48*, 1977.

[46] WILKES, M., *Time-Sharing Computer Systems*, 2nd ed., American-Elsevier Publishing Co., Inc., New York, 1972.

[47] HEINRICH, F., and D. KAUFMAN, "A Centralized Approach to Computer Network Security," *Proceedings of the AFIPS National Computer Conference*, **45**, pp. 85–90, 1976.

[48] HEINRICH, F., "The Network Security Center: A System Approach to Computer Network Security," *NBS Special Publication 500-21*, **2**, January 1978.

[49] LAMPSON, B., "A Note on the Confinement Problem," *CACM*, **16**(10), pp. 613–615, October 1973.

[50] TURN, R., "Classification of Personal Information for Privacy Protection Purposes," *Proceedings of the AFIPS National Computer Conference*, **45**, pp. 301–307, 1976.

[51] *ADP Security Manual: Techniques and Procedures for Implementing, Deactivating, Testing, and Evaluating Secure Resource-Sharing ADP Systems*, DOD5200.28-M Department of Defense, Washington, D.C., January 1973.

[52] MILLEN, J., "Security Kernel Validation in Practice," *CACM*, **19**(5), pp. 243–250, May 1976.

10

DATA-BASE MANAGEMENT IN DISTRIBUTED NETWORKS[1]

JAMES B. ROTHNIE, JR.

NATHAN GOODMAN

THOMAS MARILL

Computer Corporation of America

10.1 INTRODUCTION

A distributed data-base management system (DBMS) offers three major advantages over a centralized system:

1. It is more reliable, being constructed from multiple computers at multiple locations. Consequently, it is not susceptible to total failure when one computer breaks down.

2. In the distributed system, one may store data in locations in which the data are frequently used. As a result, access may be faster and communication costs lower than in a centralized system.

3. A distributed system lends itself more readily to incremental upward

[1] The present chapter is based closely on an earlier presentation. This research was supported by the Advanced Research Projects Agency of the Department of Defense under contract N00039-77-0074. The views and conclusions contained in this document are those of the authors and should not be interpreted as necessarily representing the official policies, either expressed or implied, of the Advanced Research Projects Agency or the U.S. government.

scaling of data-base capacity. If more power is needed to accommodate increases in data-base size or usage, this power can be added incrementally through the addition of new sites to the network. By contrast, a centralized system is often difficult to upgrade without service disruption and conversion costs.

These advantages, coupled with the maturation of the necessary technology, have generated a substantial amount of interest in distributed data-base management. A number of implementations have been reported in the past year: Champine [13] describes six recently implemented distributed data-base systems; Foster [19, 20], Heller and Osterer [25], Pliner et al. [42], and Wiseman [64] describe others.

These systems represent the state of the art. Many are quite large and serve to validate the soundness of the approach. Nevertheless, each of them is a *special-purpose*, one-of-a-kind system, designed to handle the particular needs of a single enterprise.

Complementing these efforts is a growing body of research and development whose aim is the development of *general-purpose* distributed DBMSs. Such systems, like conventional non-distributed DBMSs, are envisioned as off-the-shelf items capable of solving a wide range of data management problems. No such system yet exists, and many technical problems remain to be overcome before one can come into existence. This chapter examines the significant research and development (R&D) efforts directed at such general-purpose distributed systems.

10.2 DATA-BASE MANAGEMENT SYSTEMS

A *distributed* DBMS is, functionally, a data-base management system. The operations such a system performs on behalf of users are precisely those performed by a centralized DBMS. It is only below the surface, in the implementation of the system, that differences arise. Hence, to understand the technology of distributed data-base management it is first necessary to understand those functions which are common to data-base systems in general. This section briefly reviews certain basic DBMS concepts and introduces notation that is necessary for understanding the distributed-system concepts presented in subsequent sections.

A data-base management system is a tool for storing and retrieving formatted data. The collection of stored formatted data (called a data base) is usually accessed by a community of users, and many of the facilities of DBMS are designed to facilitate fruitful and interference-free sharing of this common resource.

The term *formatted* data is meant to imply that the collection of data has an internal structure which is known to the system and which can be used in retrieving data from the data base. The nature of the "format" of a data base, which is called its data model, differs from system to system and has been the focus of a long-standing controversy among data-base practitioners. (A general discussion of this controversy appears in Michaels et al. [37].) Here we will sidestep the controversy, since it is not particularly germane, and make an arbitrary choice of a data model to use in examples throughout this chapter.

The data model we choose is the relational model. It is a simple but powerful logical form which was introduced by Codd [14] in 1970 and which has been the basis of substantial and widespread research since that time. Two excellent tutorial introductions can be found in Date [16] and Chamberlin [12]. Here we will present a very brief overview of the model, to establish its basic terminology and concepts.

A data base in the relational model is a set of *relations*. One can think of a relation as a table such as that pictured in Table 10.1. (These example relations are drawn from Chamberlin [12].) The rows are called the *tuples* of the relation and the columns are termed *attributes*.

Formally, the data-base object called "relation" corresponds to a mathematical construct of the same name. This mathematical notion is defined as follows:

TABLE 10-1: Example relations.

ELECTIONS-WON	YEAR	WINNER-NAME	WINNER-VOTES
	1952	Eisenhower	442
	1956	Eisenhower	447
	1960	Kennedy	303
	1964	Johnson	486
	1968	Nixon	520
PRESIDENTS	NAME	PARTY	HOME-STATE
	Eisenhower	Republican	Texas
	Kennedy	Democrat	Mass.
	Johnson	Democrat	Texas
	Nixon	Republican	Calif
ELECTIONS-LOST	YEAR	LOSER-NAME	LOSER-VOTES
	1952	Stevenson	89
	1956	Stevenson	73
	1960	Nixon	219
	1964	Goldwater	52
	1968	Humphrey	191
	1968	Wallace	46
	1972	McGovern	17
LOSERS	NAME	PARTY	
	Stevenson	Democrat	
	Nixon	Republican	
	Goldwater	Republican	
	Humphrey	Democrat	
	Wallace	Am. Indep.	
	McGovern	Democrat	

Given sets $D_1, D_2, \ldots, D_n$ (the *domains*), a relation R is a set of n-tuples each of which has its first element from D_1, second from D_2, and so on.

It is important to note that relations are *sets* in the precise mathematical sense and hence have no duplicate members (i.e., all tuples of a relation must differ from each other in at least one attribute).

A fundamental operation of all data-base management systems is the selection of a subset of the data base based on a precisely specified criterion. In relational systems such criteria are usually expressed in a form of predicate calculus called relational calculus. An example of a language based on relational calculus is DSL-ALPHA (Codd [14]). Its key characteristics are illustrated by the following examples.

Consider the query: "What was the home state of President Kennedy?" Using the relations of Table 10.1, a DSL-ALPHA expression for this question would be:

RANGE PRESIDENTS P
GET W P.HOME-STATE: (P.NAME = "KENNEDY")

The first statement, a "RANGE statement," defines the variable P to range over the relation Presidents. The second statement requests the system place in the work space W the HOME-STATE attribute from all those tuples P in which the attribute NAME equals KENNEDY. The expression P.HOME-STATE is called the "target list" and it identifies the attributes to be extracted from the selected tuples. In general, the target list can be a list of attribute names enclosed in parentheses, as, for example, (P.PARTY, P.HOME-STATE).

The expression P.NAME = KENNEDY is called the "qualification." The qualification is a predicate on the tuple variables such as P. It instructs the system to select those tuples in the range of the tuple variables which, when substituted into the predicate, yield a value of true. So, for example, when the tuple (KENNEDY, DEMOCRAT, MASS.) is substituted into our sample qualification, the predicate yields true, and hence the tuple is selected. In general, qualifications may include Boolean combinations of conditions, as, for example, (P. NAME = "KENNEDY" AND P. PARTY = "DEMOCRAT").

A more complicated DSL-ALPHA expression is required to deal with the problem: "List the election years in which a Republican from Illinois was elected." This would be expressed as:

RANGE PRESIDENTS P SOME
RANGE ELECTIONS-WON E
GET W E.YEAR: (P.NAME = E.WINNER-NAME
  AND P.PARTY = "REPUBLICAN,"
  AND P.HOME-STATE = "ILLINOIS")

There are several differences from the previous query which should be noted. First, there are two tuple variables, *P*, corresponding to PRESIDENTS, and *E*, corresponding to ELECTIONS-WON. This is because both relations are involved in answering the question. Second, the RANGE statement defining *P* includes the key word SOME. This indicates that *P* is "existentially quantified." The effect of this construct is that we choose an *E* tuple in our result if there exists *some* tuple *P* which makes the qualification true. Note that the qualification involves both tuple variables. The meaning of such an expression is that *pairs* of tuples corresponding to *P* and *E* are selected by the qualification. In English the intent of this query is the following:

> Extract the YEAR attribute from any ELECTION-WON tuple whose NAME attribute matches the NAME attribute of a PRESIDENTS tuple if that PRESIDENTS tuple has a HOME-STATE of ILLINOIS and a PARTY equaling REPUBLICAN.

A very wide range of questions can be expressed using these constructs. In addition to these query capabilities, all relational languages include facilities for updating, inserting, and deleting tuples as well as defining the data base. This is the sort of user interface we will assume for the distributed DBMSs we will discuss in this chapter. With this very brief description of the externals, we can proceed to consider the means by which this functionality is achieved in a distributed system.

10.3 BACKGROUND

The field of distributed data-base management is not yet based on a foundation of well-developed and generally accepted concepts and assumptions. Different researchers in the field make varying assumptions on issues like the following:

- Whether the distributed structure of the data base is visible or invisible to users.

- The characteristics of the communication network that interconnects the distributed DBMS sites.

- The nature of typical distributed applications.

- The data model supported by the system.

Often, these assumptions are not explicitly stated, and the different approaches taken by various researchers hinge on the disparity of their assumptions. This section reviews the major assumptions that underlie work in the field. To the extent possible, it also identifies the impact of different assumptions on the work of different persons.

1. One area of agreement within the R&D community is the general system architecture of a distributed DBMS (see Fig. 10.1). The system consists of a collection of independent computers, each of which supports a portion of the overall data base. These computers are interconnected by a communication network. Users are permitted to enter transactions at any of the computers. The users' transactions may reference data stored at a remote site, in which case the system accesses the data through the network.

2. Within this general system architecture an important distinction can be drawn between systems which permit data redundancy and those which do not. In a nonredundant system the data base may be partitioned among the various sites in the network but no data item may be stored at more than one site. In the redundant case, the subsets of the data base stored at different sites may overlap. That is, a data item may be stored at more than one site in the network.[2]

    The advantage of the nonredundant approach is that it simplifies the system design problem significantly. For this reason, most special-purpose implementations to date have adopted this approach. Unfortunately, however, this advantage is bought at a substantial cost. Redundancy offers substantial improvements over the nonredundant case in all of the dimensions (discussed in Sec. 10.2) which we seek to enhance through distributed DBMS. Specifically:

    (a) Reliability. Without redundant data, the failure of a particular database site must cause the failure of all applications that require data stored there, even though other nodes of the distributed DBMS are up and running.

    (b) Communications Efficiency. Without redundancy, each data item must be stored at exactly one node. If a data item is accessed frequently from geographically dispersed locations, substantial communications costs will be incurred in accessing this data item regardless of where it is stored. A system that supports redundancy can reduce this cost *on retrieval* by storing the data item at several sites. For example, in an inventory application, a file of standard

---

[2] One special case of a redundant system which has appeared repeatedly in the literature is the totally redundant system. In this case the entire data base is stored at every site. This sort of system has been discussed by Alsberg and Day [3], Bernstein et al. [6], Ellis [18], Thomas [61, 62], and Rothnie and Goodman [46]. This approach, however, becomes impractical as data bases become large. Some authors have viewed this approach as a pedagogic simplification of the more general redundant approach. (See Bernstein et al. [6] and Rothnie et al. [48].)

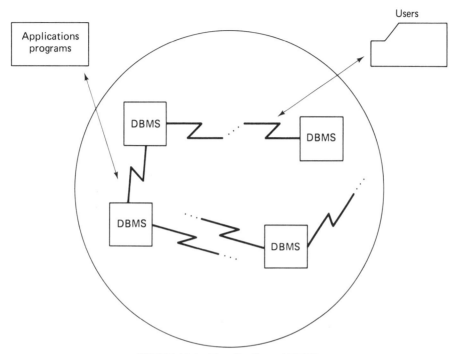

FIGURE 10-1 *The distributed DBMS.*

part descriptions might receive frequent accesses from both New York and Los Angeles. If the file is stored in any *one location*, there will be a substantial amount of long-distance communication. In a redundant system, the file could be stored at both locations and all retrieval accesses to these data are then local.

(c) Finally, the redundant-data approach permits more flexibility in increasing data-base capacity to support very large data bases. Portions of the data base that are accessed frequently can be stored at many small sites using relatively fast secondary storage. Other portions of the data base that are needed only occasionally could be stored at an archival site on inexpensive, but slow, tertiary storage. Moreover, the redundant approach allows additional data-base sites to be added to accommodate increases in data-base *activity*, whereas in a nonredundant system, increases in activity against a selected subset of a large data base could require an upgrade of the site at which that subset were stored.

Most ongoing research assumes that redundant data are permitted. (See Alsberg et al. [1, 2], Bernstein et al. [7], Rothnie and Goodman [46], and Stonebraker and Neuhold [58].)

3. Another question concerns the visibility or invisibility of the distribution to users. In much of the literature, it is assumed that users who access or update data are not required (or able) to specify the location of the data or of redundant copies. In these systems users enter queries and updates into the distributed DBMS in precisely the same manner as in a nondistributed system. The motivation for keeping data distribution invisible is that distribution is a data-base design issue similar to the choice of secondary indices, and for reasons of data independence users should not and need not be aware of it. With respect to redundant updates the motivation for invisibility is even stronger: consistency of the data base depends on keeping all redundant copies of data up to date and identical to each other (see Sec. 10.4); if responsibility for this function were entrusted to users, serious integrity problems could ensue.

    Of the major current R&D efforts, the only one in which data distribution is not strictly invisible to users is that of Stonebraker and Neuhold [58]. The system described by these authors supports two modes, one in which distribution is invisible and one in which users must specify data locations in their transactions. The motivation for the latter mode is to improve performance.

4. Assumptions regarding characteristics of the computer network vary widely, and those assumptions are rarely stated in the published work. The types most frequently postulated are

    (a) "Ethernet" [40]-like networks: high-bandwidth, low-delay networks suitable over short distances.

    (b) Packet-switched networks such as ARPANET [10, 38]: these have lower bandwidth and higher delay than Ethernet-like media and are usable over much longer distances.

    (c) Point-to-point leased circuit configurations: such networks would typically support lower bandwidth than the Arpanet but would incur lower delay.

    Additionally, one should expect to see in the forthcoming literature:

    (d) Broadcast networks, either radio broadcast networks such as ALO-HA [8, 29], or broadcast networks employing satellites.

These communication channels span three orders of magnitude in bandwidth and over six orders of magnitude in delay! Needless to say, the assumptions made here have a significant effect on distributed DBMS design. Among the issues affected are the following:

*   The feasibility of propagating control information to all data-base sites in real time.

- The feasibility of posting updates to all copies of redundant data in real time.

- The trade-off between the cost of moving data from site to site in processing complex queries and the cost of performing extra local computations.

Most of the literature takes as a given some particular type of network and proceeds to design a distributed DBMS within the confines of that network environment. The converse approach of designing a network to meet the goals of the distributed DBMS is rarely addressed, although such work could be fruitful (see Sec. 10.5).

10.4 SYNCHRONIZING UPDATE TRANSACTIONS

In developing a distributed DBMS, perhaps the single most difficult problem is the synchronization of update transactions. It is necessary to develop techniques for controlling concurrent transactions so that

- Data-base consistency is preserved, while

- Excessive overload in propagating control information among the nodes of the distributed DBMS is avoided.

The problem has been addressed by numerous authors including Alsberg et al. [1, 2], Alsberg and Day [3], Bernstein et al. [6, 7], Ellis [18], Johnson and Thomas [28], Lampson and Sturgis [31], Rosenkrantz et al. [44], Rothnie et al. [48], Rothnie and Goodman [46, 47], Stearns et al. [57], Stonebraker and Neuhold [58], and Thomas [61, 62].

The simplest method for synchronizing distributed updates is to *lock* those portions of the data base being read or written by the active transaction. Indeed, locking is the usual mechanism employed for update synchronization in conventional, nondistributed DBMSs. However, in a distributed data-base environment, an appreciable and often intolerable delay is introduced as locking information is propagated to the many computers in the data-base network.

For example: a straightforward distributed locking algorithm described by Rothnie and Goodman [46] requires $5n$ intercomputer messages in order to synchronize a transaction among n nodes of a distributed data-base system:

n lock request messages, n lock grant messages, n messages to transmit the update, n update acknowledgments, and n messages to release the locks.

Furthermore, the delay in executing the update is lengthy, engendering:

the maximum delay encountered in setting the locks, plus
the maximum delay encountered in performing the update.

The communication delay that would be encountered if the system used a communication network such as the Arpanet for these messages could easily be as much as 0.1 to 1 s. This delay is some *two to three orders of magnitude greater* than the delay typically encountered when setting locks in a centralized system. The net effect of this locking delay on total transaction time will depend on the details of the processing algorithm. Conservatively, the effect is likely to reduce update processing throughput by an order of magnitude. There are few application systems that can accommodate this sort of performance degradation.

For these reasons the straightforward locking approach is inadequate for a general-purpose distributed DBMS, and other methods must be sought.

A variety of solutions to this problem have been proposed. Certain of these solutions are closely related to the locking approach in concept, seeking to find more efficient algorithms for propagating lock information through the data-base network. For example, Lampson and Sturgis [31] describe a method involving "two-phase commit," in which only $4n$ messages are needed to propagate locking information to n sites of a distributed DBMS. It is possible to reduce this cost even further by piggybacking "update transmission" messages on "lock request" messages, thereby reducing the cost of locking to $3n$ (although this only reduces communication volume if the update transmission messages are short or if most lock requests are granted). Ellis [18] describes an algorithm which further reduces communication volume to $2n$. This method is similar to Lampson and Sturgis's two-phase-commit approach, but uses a sequential-daisy-chain communication procedure for propagating synchronization messages from site to site. Although this method reduces communication *volume* by 50% over the Lampson and Sturgis method, its sequential communication procedure greatly increases communication delay.

As a final example, Thomas [62] has described a solution that employs daisy-chain communication and a "voting" protocol to enable lock setting by a *majority* of data-base sites rather than requiring unanimous approval. This method reduces communication volume to about $1.5n$, but, like Ellis's algorithm, it introduces lengthy communication delays.

Although the savings achieved by the foregoing algorithms are substantial, in many cases these methods still require a large amount of intercomputer communication to perform updates. It appears, therefore, that these methods will perform unacceptably in networks containing large numbers of sites and high transaction volumes.

Other approaches seek to reduce synchronization costs by introducing some degree of *centralized control* in the distributed system. Alsberg et al. [1, 2], Alsberg and Day [3], and Stonebraker and Neuhold [58] have proposed "primary-site" methods, which require that all update activity for a given file (or in some cases, subfile) be funneled through a single data-base site called the primary site. This approach appears to be quite good for simple data-base applications, in which it is possible to effectively partition data-base activity by geographic region. In more complex situations, though, this method cannot avoid the need for global data-base locking with concomitant high communication cost and delay. In particular, transactions that access multiple files with different primary sites must perform locking to guarantee that the files are consistent with each other. *This is true for retrieval transactions as well as for updates!*

Another approach to the update synchronization problem that is qualitatively different from the preceding methods is described by Bernstein et al. [6, 7], Rothnie et al. [48], and Rothnie and Goodman [46]. Rather than merely trying to improve the efficiency of global data-base locking, this method seeks to avoid global locking whenever possible. The method is based on a formal analysis of the ways in which transactions in a distributed DBMS can interfere with each other and the ways in which this interference can be avoided. The methodology described by these authors is being implemented for SDD-1, A System for Distributed Databases, under development by Computer Corporation of America.

The SDD-1 methodology achieves update synchronization by means of several different "synchronization protocols," which vary in cost and which offer varying levels of synchronization control. Each synchronization protocol is an algorithm that specifies what to do to ensure the correct processing of a given transaction. The most efficient of the protocols specifies no intercomputer synchronization whatever; a transaction run under this protocol need only perform *local locking* to ensure the atomicness of its read and write operations at each *individual* site. Each of the other protocols introduces some degree of nonlocal synchronization, with the strongest protocol achieving even greater control than global data-base locking.

Not all transactions may be run under the most efficient protocol. Correct operation of the system depends critically on the correct selection by the data-base system of the protocol to use in processing each transaction entered by users.

The decision as to which transactions must use which protocols is made *off-line*, for example, during data-base design. The decision process begins with the data-base administrator defining "classes of transactions" that are commonly executed in the data-base application. Then using rules presented in Bernstein et al. [6, 7] and Rothnie et al. [48], the defined transaction classes are algorithmically analyzed, yielding a specification of which transaction classes must use each protocol. Those results can then be summarized in tables which are stored at each data-base site for later use at run time.

The run-time protocol selection function operates by first mapping each transaction entered into the DBMS into the class(es) of which it is a member. Then for each class the function looks up the correct protocol for transactions in that class, using the table stored at the local data-base site. If the transaction is a member of several classes, the selection function chooses the most efficient one; if the transaction is not a member of any defined class, the function selects the strongest protocol defined for the system.

It is important to note that the run-time operation of the protocol selection function does not itself require any intercomputer communication. This is because all the intelligence needed to ensure correct synchronization of transactions in each class is already compiled into the protocol selection tables.

It appears that the SDD-1 update methodology permits faster and lower-cost execution of update transactions than using any alternative method yet proposed (see notes in Sec. 10.6).

10.5   DISTRIBUTED QUERY PROCESSING

In this section we consider the problem of processing a query that accesses data at multiple sites of the distributed DBMS. How does this problem differ from query processing in a nondistributed DBMS? There are two significant differences to consider. First, there is a substantial new element of processing delay, the time required to communicate among the sites involved in the query. Second, there is an opportunity for parallel processing, since there are several computers involved in handling the query. We will begin with an example which illustrates these differences and then proceed to a discussion of research efforts that attempt to deal with them.

Consider the relations of Table 10.2. These relations provide information about supply relationships among certain suppliers and the projects they supply. *Projects* contains project identifiers (J#) and the location (J-Location) of each project. *Suppliers* indicates the identifiers of suppliers (S#) and their locations (S-Location). *Parts* tells the name (P-Name) and length (P-Length) of each part. Finally, *Supply* ties these objects together by indicating which suppliers (S#)

TABLE 10-2: *Example relations.*

Relation Name	Attributes	Bits per Tuple	Number of Tuples	Site
Projects	J#	100	10,000	A
	J-Location			
Suppliers	S#	100	1,000	B
	S-Location			
Parts	P#	100	100,000	C
	P-Name			
	P-Length			
Supply	S#	100	1,000,000	A
	P#	100		
	J#			

supply which parts (P#) to which projects (J#). Table 10.2 also indicates the size of each relation and the site where each is stored.

We will assume an ARPANET-like communications facility with a transmission delay of 1 s and a bandwidth of 10,000 bits/s. As we shall see, the relatively long transmissions delay has a substantial impact on the choice of a strategy for query processing: it favors strategies characterized by a small number of bulk transmissions rather than a large number of short interactions.

Now, consider a query that selects the identifiers of projects in Boston that use 10-in. bolts. A DSL-ALPHA expression for this query is:

RANGE J PROJECTS
RANGE Y SUPPLY SOME
RANGE P PARTS SOME
GET W J.J#WHERE J.J-LOCATION="BOSTON" AND
J.J#=Y.J# and Y.P#=P.P# AND
P.P-NAME="BOLT" AND P.P-LENGTH=10

To calculate the costs of various strategies for processing this query, we need to estimate the sizes of three intermediate results:

1. The number of projects located in Boston: Count(J,where J.J-Location="Boston") Estimate=1,000

2. The number of supply tuples for projects located in Boston: Count(Y,where Y.J#=J.J# and J.J-Location="Boston") Estimate=100,000

3. The number of parts are 10-in. bolts: Count(P,where P.P-name="Bolt" and P.P-Length=10) Estimate=10

With this preliminary information we will proceed to consider (briefly) six alternative strategies for handling this query, and we will calculate the communications delay incurred by each strategy. Delay in seconds will be computed by the formula

$$\text{delay} = \text{number of interactions} \times 1 \text{ s} + \frac{\text{volume}}{10,000}$$

Strategies 1 and 2 involve an initial step of rendering the query local by moving all relations involved to a single site. When this step is completed, the query is processed by some nondistributed algorithm.

Strategy 1 involves moving the Parts relation to site A. This entails 1 interaction and 10^7 bits of total volume for a delay of 10^3 or 16.6 min. Strategy 2 involves moving Supply and Projects to site C at a cost of two messages and about 10^8 bits of data transfer for a delay of more than 2.7 hr.

Strategies 3 and 4 mimic a strategy that is sometimes used in single-site relational query processing, called tuple substitution. In this scheme a multivariable query is processed as a sequence of one-variable queries by repeatedly substituting tuples for certain variables into the query.

Strategy 3 will substitute tuples from Supply and Project to generate a sequence of queries to process against the Parts relation. For example, if the Supply tuple (7036, 152475, 1567) and the Project tuple (1567, Boston) were substituted into the original query, the resulting one-variable query to process at site C would be

(P,where P.P.#=152475 and P.P-name="Bolt" and P.P-Length=10)

In essence the process has found a project in Boston which uses part 152475, and we are now asking if this part is a bolt. Using the estimated sizes provided above, there will be 100,000 questions of this form to ask. (This number can be reduced by using query feedback techniques of the form described by Rothnie [45], but these will not be considered here.) Each of these queries to site C will require a separate interaction in each direction. This will generate a delay of 55.5 hr.

Strategy 4 involves substitution of Parts tuples into the original query to produce two-variable queries involving the relations Supply and Projects. Such queries can be processed entirely at site A. Our estimates indicate that 10 such queries will be generated for a delay of about 20 s.

Strategies 5 and 6 involve the initial computation of subsets of the relations at sites A and C and then moving the subset at one of these sites to the other one to complete the query processing.

Strategy 5 computes at site A all of the P# and J# pairs for projects located in Boston. This relation is then moved to site C to determine which of the P#'s correspond to 10-in. bolts. At site A this involves processing the query

Get W (J.J#, Y.P#), where (J.J#=Y.J# and J.J-Location="Boston")

W will contain about 100,000 tuples of (say) 100 bits each. This will be transmitted to C in one interaction, with a delay of about 10^3 s or 16.6 min.

Strategy 6 involves the computation at site C of the P#'s for parts which are 10-in. bolts and transmitting these P#'s to site A. Our estimates indicate that there will be 10 such values and hence that they will be transmitted to A in less than 1 s.

Table 10.3 summarizes the delay incurred by each of these strategies. There are four points to observe from this example:

1. There is a very great variation in communication cost among a set of plausible distributed query-processing schemes.

2. The absolute magnitudes of the communication delays are very great for the poor strategies and seem likely to dominate the total query-processing delay in these cases.

3. The two dimensions of communication delay, end-to-end delay and bandwidth, are both important in choosing a distributed query-processing strategy. For the parameters used in this example, it is better to employ a strategy that transmits a batch of data at once (as in strategies 5 and 6) than small amounts of data in each of many separate messages (as in strategies 3 and 4).

4. Although the communication delays we have computed do not reflect this, the best strategy (strategy 6) provides opportunities for parallel processing which can reduce the total elapsed time for handling this query. Specifically, at site A we can compute the (J#, P#) pairs for Boston projects while at site C computing the set of P#'s for 10-in. bolts. Then when the P#'s are moved to site A, the solution to the query can be obtained by taking the join of these intermediate results. For some queries this effect will be significant and can result in elapsed processing times for distributed queries which are actually less than for single-site queries.

The literature contains few reports of work in this area of distributed query processing. Results that have been published describe algorithms which are similar in their approach to algorithms invented for use in handling relational queries. This approach involves: first, the definition of a family of strategies that

TABLE 10-3: Communications delay for various example strategies.

Strategy	Description	Messages	Volume	Delay (s)
1	Move Parts to A	1	10^7	10^3
2	Move Supply and Projects to C	1	10^8	10^4
3	Substitute tuples from Supply and Projects	2×10^5	10^7	2×10^5
4	Substitute tuples from Parts	20	10^3	20
5	Move restricted join of Supply and Projects to C	1	10^7	10^3
6	Move restriction of Parts to A	1	10^3	10^{-1}

can be applied to compute the result of a query and second, an optimization scheme to choose the least costly member of this family. Each of the schemes to be mentioned here adopts this approach.

Wong [65] has proposed an algorithm for use in SDD-1 in which each member of the family of strategies consists of a sequence of two types of actions: local processing performed in parallel at several sites, and parallel moves of subrelations from site to site. This sort of strategy is rather similar in concept to the decomposition scheme that Wong developed for use in INGRES [58, 66]. Wong's decomposition attempts to handle a difficult problem (multivariable relational queries) as a sequence of easier problems (one-variable queries) and actions which transform the multivariable query into one-variable queries (tuple substitution). For SDD-1, the Wong approach is to solve a difficult problem (distributed query processing) as a sequence of easier problems (local query processing) and actions that transform the distributed query into local queries (subrelation moves).

The optimization scheme in SDD-1 begins with a proposed solution consisting of performing all local processing that can be performed without any data moves and then moving the results to a single site where the query processing is completed. The single site is selected to minimize the costs of the data moves.

In our example, strategy 6 would be the starting-point solution for this algorithm. From there the optimization scheme looks for an improvement involving one set of moves and local processing to be performed prior to the movement of subrelations to the site selected in the initial solution. Sometimes this prior move will reduce the subrelations to be moved to the final site substantially and result in a lower cost for the complete query.

If some improvement is gained, the optimization scheme is applied recursively to determine if any further gains can be obtained. The algorithm can be characterized as a "greedy" one because it always looks for immediate gains and hence will always terminate on a local optimum but not necessarily a global one.

Of the distributed query-processing algorithms reported in the literature, Wong's is the only one to consider communications costs as a key element of query-processing cost. Hence, it is the most strongly oriented toward the distributed DBMS environment. As we shall see, the other algorithms represent smaller perturbations from local query-processing techniques.

Schneider [50] has attacked a broader query-processing problem than the other authors we consider here. He treats the issue of processing a query in a network where the data base may be distributed over a set of dissimilar data handlers. The proposed solution uses the data-representation tools of DIAM to deal with heterogeneity and its generalized search-path selection schemes to handle the optimization problem. The technique does not consider communication cost issues. Schneider also deals with the query transformations which are necessary to process a query at a local site when the data there represent a projection, restriction, or join of the relation the user has referenced.

Stonebraker and Neuhold [58] have proposed an extension to INGRES to deal with distributed data bases. This extension uses a straightforward modification of Wong's decomposition to deal with distributed query processing. The scheme preserves tuple substitution as a basic strategy and hence is vulnerable to the type of phenomenon observed in strategies 3 and 4 of the example. While the volume of communication may not be particularly large, the needs for a long series of separate interactions across the network can lead to long processing times because of transmission delay. It is this effect which Wong attempted to avoid in replacing tuple substitution by subrelation moves in SDD-1.

10.6 HANDLING FAILURES

One of the key motivations for distributed data-base systems is a requirement for high data-base availability, that is, a need to ensure that a data base is nearly always accessible. Distributed data-base systems seem to offer this characteristic, since availability is not limited by the reliability of any single component but rather by the reliability of combinations of components (processing nodes and communication links in the network). These combinations can be configured to achieve arbitrarily high availability. Belford et al. [5] present an analysis that determines availability as a function of the configuration of a distributed data-base system.

To achieve this reliability potential, however, it is necessary that the distributed system be able to cope with the failures of individual components and continue operation. In this section we outline the problems inherent in constructing a system of this sort and briefly describe the solutions that have been proposed. The central problem in reliable operation of a distributed data-base system is maintaining data-base consistency in the presence of failures during update transactions. Such failures threaten to destroy the "atomicness" of these transactions by causing the update to be only partially accomplished in the data base. Consider, for example, a transaction T_1 which updates portions of a data base stored at nodes N_1 and N_2. If a failure occurs during the execution of T_1 which prevents the update from being recorded at N_2, the data base has been made inconsistent. A later transaction which reads the results of T_1 will see an anomalous data base with unpredictable results. The system-updating algorithms must therefore be aware of the possibility of component failure and avoid these partial results.

The avoidance of data-base inconsistencies of this type is the major objective of failure-handling mechanisms, but it is clear that there are other desiderata which are important to the design of these algorithms. Perhaps first on the list is efficiency. We desire that the responsiveness and throughput of the system be "good" both during normal operation and in the presence of failure. This is an important consideration because it eliminates a very simple mechanism which preserves consistency but introduces intolerable delay in the presence of failures.

This simple algorithm specifies that any transaction that would normally communicate with a failed node must wait until that node has recovered from the failure before it can proceed. Clearly, this sort of approach can lead to indefinite delays and is therefore unacceptable. An effective distributed DBMS must employ a different type of mechanism: one that attempts to execute to completion any transaction that can proceed without a resource (such as a data item) which is *exclusively* available at the failed node.

The problems to be solved by efficient failure-recovery algorithms can be partitioned into the following subproblems:

1. Reliable Broadcast. Consider a distributed data-base system which is executing a transaction T. Suppose that the execution is being "controlled" from one node in the network, N_1, and that the results of T will have an effect on the fragments of the data base stored on nodes N_1, N_2, N_3, and N_4. Let us further suppose that nodes N_2, N_3, and N_4 have received instructions indicating what changes are to be made in their data-base fragments but are awaiting a signal, W, from N_1 before actually writing the changes. To ensure that the results of T are completely installed in the data base, the system must guarantee that W will either reach everyone of N_2, N_3, and N_4 or none of them. This guaranteed delivery at multiple sites we will refer to as *reliable broadcast*.

Requirements for this sort of characteristic arise frequently in the distributed data-base systems designed to date. It is a difficult characteristic to achieve because the communication networks supporting these systems typically offer pairwise communication only. Thus, to send W to N_2, N_3, and N_4, N_1 must send three distinct messages. There is, of course, a finite probability that N_1 will fail after the message has been sent to N_2 but not before it has been sent to N_4. If this occurs, reliable broadcast has not been achieved. This problem can be handled in a variety of ways. Lampson and Sturgis [31] try to minimize the reliable broadcast window (e.g., the time between sending W to N_2 and sending W to N_4) and hence minimize the likelihood of a failure during that inconvenient period. If a failure does occur during that time, the data base is not left inconsistent, but locks set during the execution of T will remain set until the failed node is recovered.

In the SDD-1 design, Hammer and Shipman [24] try to ensure that reliable broadcast is achieved even when N_1 fails during the broadcast window. This is accomplished by requiring that the first few recipients of W also send the message on to the other addressees. (This requires that all recipients be capable of handling duplicate messages.) In addition, each node is warned when a reliable broadcast is about to be sent, and any node that does not receive the message in a reasonable period will ask the other addressees if they have received it. By selecting the parameters of this scheme appropriately, the likelihood of a breakdown in the reliable broadcast can be made arbitrarily small.

2. Operation with Missing Nodes. A second subproblem in failure handling is continuing operation of the system when one or more nodes in the network are known to be down or otherwise unavailable. The objective here is to avoid

having the absence of these nodes cause trasactions to be delayed until the missing nodes are recovered. All the existing system designs try to accomplish this objective by acting (almost) as if the missing nodes never existed. Non-existent nodes cannot be allowed to cause any delays, of course. It is necessary, however, to take some note of these failed nodes to prepare for their recovery and to deal with any incomplete actions they have left behind.

Thomas [62], Ellis [18], and Hammer and Shipman [24] each prepare for a failed module's recovery by continuing to send relevant updates to the node so that they can be applied when the node is restarted. As we indicate below, these updates are held at some other site pending the recovery.

Another way in which the Thomas algorithm recognizes the existence of a failed site is in determining the number of nodes in the majority which is required to finally accept a transaction. This majority is computed on the basis of the full original network and not only on the currently active sites.

The Lampson and Sturgis scheme will sometimes have a lingering recollection of a failed node in the form of locks that cannot be released until the node recovers.

3. Restarting a Node. A third subproblem is reintegrating a node into the system when the cause of the node's failure has been corrected. Since the fragment of the data base stored at the node may be out of date, it is necessary for the node to find out what has happened during its absence prior to continuing its active participation in the system. The principal mechanism for accomplishing this task might be called *persistent communication*, after the persistent processes of Sutherland [60]. Persistent communication guarantees the delivery of a message to a node even if the addressee is down when the message is sent and even if the sender is down when the addressee recovers. This sort of mechanism is a very clean way of achieving recovery, since the restarting node simply acts on its old messages in almost the same way it does in normal operation. Thus, few new facilities are needed to accomplish node recovery. Thomas, Ellis, and Hammer and Shipman use forms of persistent communication for restarting failed nodes.

4. Failure Detection. The mechanisms discussed under "Operation with Missing Nodes" and "Restarting a Node" both depend on knowing when a node has failed. The methods used for detecting failure are all variations on a single time-honored technique called timeout. Under this scheme, a node that is suspected of having failed is probed with a message to which an active node will respond. If the response does not arrive within some prescribed time period, the probed site is assumed to have failed.

5. Partitioning. The final subproblem is a serious one for which no adequate technical solution has been proposed. This problem arises when communication failures break all connections between two or more active segments of the network. When this occurs, each isolated segment will continue its operation, including processing updates, but there is no way for the separate pieces to coordinate their activities. Hence, the fragments of the data base in the separated

pieces will become inconsistent. This divergence is unavoidable if the segments are permitted to continue general updating operations, and in many situations it is essential that these updates proceed. However, a problem arises when the partition is repaired and communications resume. How are the inconsistencies to be reconciled?

This problem is not amenable to solutions that attempt to construct a new and consistent data base by somehow interleaving the transactions run in the separate segments. This approach will not work because some of the transactions run in the partitioned network are simply not correct in the context of a connected network. Consider the following example.

Suppose that there is a distributed DBMS serving a fleet of naval ships, with nodes located on each ship. The data base includes the location of every ship in the fleet. Further, suppose that a portion of the fleet becomes separated from the rest and communications are lost. The separated body might decide to assume that the rest of the fleet will move according to the original operations plan and update its data base accordingly. Meanwhile, the main body might choose a different course and update its data base with the correct locations. Furthermore, some guess about the locations of the separated ships might be made and recorded. When the fleet is reintegrated, the data base will be inconsistent. The appropriate action to take at this point is to construct a new consistent data base by taking certain fragments from each of the separated segments and discarding the rest.

In general, the correct action to take when a partition is repaired depends on the semantics of the data base, the topology of the partition, and the transactions that have been run during the partition. The integration process is likely to require human decision making assisted by automatic conflict detection and some limited automatic conflict resolution.

10.7   DIRECTORY MANAGEMENT

An important characteristic of modern data-base management systems is that they employ a directory (often called a schema) to define the data base being managed. This frees the user or application program from the need to supply this information, and it simplifies many types of data-base structural changes. A directory typically contains four types of information:

1.   Logical structure definition (e.g., the names of relations and their domains).

2.   Physical structure definition (e.g., data field formats, inverted fields).

3.   File statistics (e.g., size).

   4. Accounting data (e.g., who has accessed the file, who owns the file).

For a distributed data base we must add an additional category of directory information: the location of each piece of the data base in the network.

   The DBMS must have access to this information in order to parse user requests, choose and execute an accessing strategy, and account for the resources used. The following question therefore arises: Where should the directory be stored?

   There are many possible answers to this question and the best answer varies with the data base and particular accessing pattern. Furthermore, within a single system the entire directory need not be handled uniformly. Some types of information, such as the logical structure definition and location information, will be needed frequently and may be handled differently from less frequently accessed data, such as accounting data.

   The principal directory management schemes can be divided into two categories: nonredundant approaches, in which each directory entry is stored in only one location, and redundant approaches, in which each entry may appear in several places. Among the nonredundant schemes the principal alternatives are the following:

   1. Centralization. The complete directory is stored at exactly one site. This requires access to the directory site for every retrieval or update to the directory.

   2. Distribution. Each site has the directory entries for the data stored at that site. Competely local access can proceed using the local directory. Any request requiring access to remote data must be broadcast so that other sites can determine whether or not they have relevant data.

   3. Combinations. An intermediate approach is to partition the network into several pieces and employ a centralized directory in each piece.

The redundant approaches include the following alternatives:

   1. Centralization. A redundant but centralized approach might be a combination of the centralized and distributed nonredundant alternatives. That is, each site has the entries for its local data, but a central site has a complete directory. In this way, nonlocal references can appeal to a single site to determine the location of the remote data.

   2. Distribution. Each site has the complete directory stored locally. All user transactions can be started into execution without a remote reference, but all directory updates must be posted to every site.

   3. Combinations. Many combinations are possible. The most general would

permit an arbitrary subset of the directory to exist at each site. This permits a great deal of flexibility, but it requires a more complicated "directory directory" to tell the system what piece of the directory is stored where.

The factors that determine the choice of a directory management scheme are these:

1. Directory retrieval frequency. High frequency of directory retrievals encourages redundant directories and distribution, so that most retrievals will not require access to remote nodes of the network. Since *every* user transaction requires a directory retrieval, directory redundancy is nearly always desirable.

2. Directory update frequency. High frequency discourages redundancy and encourages centralization. This is because every copy of the directory must have the change posted. Since this requires the kind of concurrency control discussed in Sec. 10.4, directory updates can be expensive to process.

3. Reliability. A requirement for high reliability encourages redundancy and distribution for obvious reasons.

Stonebraker and Neuhold [58] propose to use a redundant-directory approach to INGRES. In this scheme each site stores the directory entries for local data as well as locator information for remote data. In addition, they suggest the use of a local cache at each site which holds the directory entries for recently accessed data.

Rothnie and Goodman [46] propose a more general mechanism for SDD-1. They observe that the storage options and criteria of choice for directories are exactly the same as those of user files. Hence, they suggest that directories be treated exactly as the user data. This permits arbitrary subsets of the directory to be stored at each site. It also makes other system features, such as security, integrity, reliability, and concurrency control, available for directory management. Decisions concerning allocation of the directory to physical sites can therefore be deferred until data-base design rather than being built into the structure of the distributed DBMS itself. The decisions at data-base design time are amenable to the techniques discussed in the next section.

10.8 DATA-BASE DESIGN

The discussion concerning directories in Sec. 10.7 addressed the issue of system access to a description of a data base. In this section we consider the problem a user faces in creating such a description: the problem of data-base design. In particular, we will discuss the data-base design issue peculiar to the distributed environment: the allocation of pieces of the data base to sites in the network. This problem is frequently referred to as *file allocation*.

There is considerable literature concerning file allocation [11, 15, 32, 33, 35, 63], much of which has been reviewed by Levin and Morgan [34]. These research efforts have applied classical mathematical programming techniques to variants of the following problem:

- Given: a description of user demand for service stated as the volume of retrievals and volume of updates from each node of the network to each file.

- Given: a description of the resources available to supply this demand stated as the network topology, link capacities, and costs, and the node capacities and costs.

- Determine: an assignment of files to nodes that does not violate any capacity constraints and minimizes total costs.

The variations on this problem that have been explored include:

- Consideration of time-varying and uncertain demand.

- Consideration of the dual problem of constraining costs and determining capacities.

- The use of heuristics to reduce the computational complexity of finding an acceptable solution.

This work on file allocation has led to substantial understanding of the data-base design problem stated above. Unfortunately, however, this problem is only a small piece of the file allocation problem in a distributed DBMS of the sort discussed in this paper. There are three specific shortcomings of the existing body of research in this field which limit the usefulness of these results in the context of our problem:

1. The user demand model is stated as a set of requirements to access a given file from a given node. This model does not adequately reflect user demand for data-base access involving more than one file. Consider the example problem treated in Sec. 10.5. This problem involved the join of relations at two sites. The bulk of the communication costs for that problem incurred between the nodes that stored the relations involved. This cost is not reflected in a model that considers only user node–to–file node communication. In particular, the model cannot represent the fact that a file allocation scheme which places all the relations involved in the query at a single site will be cheaper for this

query than one in which they are distributed. This is a serious shortcoming, since it seems likely that the clustering of relations into allocated groups will be a more important determinant of accessing cost than the assignment of each group to a particular node.

2. A second serious problem with existing file allocation results is the complete neglect of synchronization costs in updating redundantly stored data. As previous sections indicated, this cost is likely to dominate update costs (particularly for cost measured as delay), it will vary substantially with the synchronization scheme, it will vary with the mix of update traffic, and it will vary in a complex way with the data-base design.

3. The assumption that complete files should be the unit of assignment of data to nodes seems inflexible. There are many situations in which permitting a vertical or horizontal partitioning of files will reduce data accessing and storage costs. Furthermore, two prototype distributed DBMSs currently being developed will permit this sort of partitioning. Of course, if a subfile partitioning were *given*, the existing results could be used for distribution. However, this begs the question of determining what the partition should be. Answering this question seems to be an important element of data-base design.

The discussion above is not intended to say that existing results in file allocation are useless. On the contrary, when user behavior is accurately modeled as interaction with single files, these well-developed results are valuable indeed. However, in the context of a modern DBMS in which multifile transactions are important, existing research results do not provide adequate tools for data-base design.

REFERENCES

[1] ALSBERG, P.A., G. G. BELFORD, S. R. BUNCH, J. D. DAY, E. GRAPA, D. C. HEALY, E. J. MCCAULEY, and D. A. WILCOX, "Synchronization and Deadlock," *CAC Document Number 185, CCTC-WAD Document Number 6503,* Center for Advanced Computation, University of Illinois at Urbana-Champaign, Urbana, Ill., March 1, 1976.

[2] ALSBERG, P.A., G. G. BELFORD, S. R. BUNCH, J. D. DAY, E. GRAPA, D. C. HEALY, E. J. MCCAULEY, and D. A. WILCOX, ibid. (See also "Research in Network Data Management and Resource Sharing: Final Research Report," *CAC Document Number 210, CCTC-WAD Document Number 6508,* Center for Advanced Com-

putation, University of Illinois at Urbana-Champaign, Urbana, Ill., September 30, 1976.

[3] ALSBERG, P. A., and J. D. DAY, "A Principle for Resilient Sharing of Distributed Resources," Report from the Center for Advanced Computation, University of Illinois at Urbana-Champaign, Urbana, Ill., 1976. (Also accepted for *Proceedings of the 2nd International Conference on Software Engineering.*)

[4] BAKKOM, D. E., and T. A. BEHYMER, "Implementation of a Prototype Generalized File Translator," *Proceedings of 1975 ACM SIGMOD International Conference on the Management of Data,* pp. 99–110, 1975.

[5] BELFORD, G. G., P. M. SCHWARTZ, and S. SLUIZER, "The Effect of Backup Strategy on Database Availability," *CAC Document Number 181, CCTC-WAD Document Number 5515,* Center for Advanced Computation, University of Illinois at Urbana-Champaign, Urbana, Ill., February 1, 1976.

[6] BERNSTEIN, P. A., N. GOODMAN, J. B. ROTHNIE, and C. A. PAPADIMITRIOU, "Analysis of Serializability in SDD-1: A System for Distributed Databases (the Fully Redundant Case)," *First International Conference on Computer Software and Applications (COMPSAC 77),* IEEE Computer Society, Chicago, November 1977. Also available from Computer Corporation of America, 575 Technology Square, Cambridge, Mass. 02139, as *Technical Report CCA-77-05.*

[7] BERNSTEIN, P. A., J. B. ROTHNIE, D. W. SHIPMAN, and N. GOODMAN, "The Concurrency Control Mechanism of SDD-1: A System For Distributed Databases (The General Case)," *TR-77-09,* Computer Corporation of America, 575 Technology Square, Cambridge, Mass. 02139.

[8] BINDER, R., N. ABRAMSON, F. F. KUO, A. OKIMAKA, and D. WAX, *Proceedings of the AFIPS National Computer Conference,* **44** pp. 203–215, 1975.

[9] BIRSS, E. W., and J. P. FRY, "Generalized Software for Translating Data," *Proceedings of the AFIPS National Computer Conference,* **45,** pp. 889–899, 1976.

[10] BBN, "Specification for the Interconnection of a Host and an IMP," *Report 1822,* Bolt, Beranek and Newman, Inc., Cambridge, Mass., January 1976 revision.

[11] CASEY, R. G. "Allocation of Copies of Files in an Information Network," *Proceedings of the AFIPS Spring Joint Computer Conference,* **40,** pp. 617–625, 1972.

[12] CHAMBERLIN, D. D. "Relational Data-Base Management Systems," *Computing Surveys,* **8**(1), March 1976.

[13] CHAMPINE, G. A. "Six Approaches to Distributed Databases," *Datamation,* **23**(5), pp. 69–72, May 1977.

[14] CODD, E. F. "Further Normalization of the Database Relational Model," in *Database Systems,* Courant Computer Science Symposium 6 (R. Rustin, ed.), Prentice-Hall, Inc., Englewood Cliffs, N.J., p. 3364, 1972.

[15] CHU, W. W. "Optimal File Allocation in a Computer Network," in *Computer-Communication Networks* (N. ABRAMSON and F. F. KUO, eds.) Prentice-Hall, Inc., Englewood Cliffs, N.J., 1973.

[16] DATE, C. J. *An Introduction to Database Systems,* Addison-Wesley Publishing Company, Inc., Reading, Mass., 1976.

[17] DEEPE, M. E., and J. P. FRY, "Distributed Databases: A Summary of Research," *Computer Networks*, **1**(2), pp. 130–138, 1976.

[18] ELLIS, C. A. "A Robust Algorithm for Updating Duplicate Databases," *Proceedings of the 1977 Berkeley Workshop on Distributed Data Management and Computer Networks*, Lawrence Berkeley Laboratory, University of California, Berkeley, Calif., May 1977.

[19] FOSTER, J. D. "The Development of a Concept for Distributive Processing," *Proceedings of the 12th IEEE Computer Society International Conference (COMPCON 76)*, San Francisco, Calif., 1976.

[20] FOSTER, J. D. "Distributive Processing for Banking," *Datamation*, **22**(7) July 1976.

[21] FRY, J. P., R. L. FRANK, and S. HERSHEY, III, "A Developmental Model for Data Translation," *Proceedings of the ACM 1972 SIGFIDET Workshop on Data Description, Access, and Control,* Denver, Colo., pp. 77–105, 1972.

[22] FRY, J. P., D. P. SMITH, and R. W. TAYLOR, "An Approach to Stored Data Definition and Translation," *Proceedings of the ACM 1972 SIGFIDET Workshop on Data Description, Access, and Control,* Denver, Colo., pp. 13–55, 1972.

[23] FRY, J. P., D. P. SMITH, and R. W. TAYLOR, "Stored-Data Description and Data Translation," *Information Systems*, **2**(3), pp. 95–163, 1977.

[24] HAMMER, M. M., and D. W. SHIPMAN, "Resiliency Mechanisms in SDD-1: A System for Distributed Data Translations," *Technical Report CCA-78-01,* 1977, Computer Corporation of America, 575 Technology Square, Cambridge, Mass. 02139.

[25] HELLER, J., and L. OSTERER, "The Design and Data Model of the BNL Archive and Dissemination System," *Proceedings of the 1977 Berkeley Workshop on Distributed Data Management and Computer Networks,* Lawrence Berkeley Laboratory, University of California, Berkeley, Calif., pp. 161–181, May 1977.

[26] HOUSEL, B. C., V. Y. LUM, and N. C. SHÚ, "Architecture for an Interactive Migration System (AIMS)," *Proceedings of the ACM 1974 SIGMOD Workshop on Data Description, Access, and Control,* Ann Arbor, Mich., pp. 157–169, May 1974.

[27] HOUSEL, B. C., D. P. SMITH, N. C. SHU, and V. Y. LUM, "DEFINE—A Non-procedural Data Description for Defining Information Easily," *Proceedings of the ACM Pacific 75,* San Francisco, pp. 65–70, April 1975.

[28] JOHNSON, P. R., and R. H. THOMAS, "The Maintenance of Duplicate Databases," *Network Working Group RFC 677 NIC 31507,* January 27, 1975. Available from Network Information Center, Stanford Research Institute, Menlo Park, Calif. 94025.

[29] KLEINROCK, L., and L. TOBAGI, "Random Access Techniques for Data Transmission over Packet-Switched Radio Channels, *Proceedings of the AFIPS National Computer Conference,* **44,** pp. 187–201, 1975.

[30] LAMPORT, L. "Time, Clocks and Ordering of Events in a Distributed System," *Massachusetts Computer Associates Report CA-7603-2911,* March 1976. Also submitted to *CACM.*

[31] LAMPSON, B., and H. STURGIS, "Crash Recovery in a Distributed Data Storage System," unpublished paper, Computer Science Laboratory, Xerox Palo Alto Research Center, Palo Alto, Calif., 1976.

[32] LEVIN, K. D. "Organizing Distributed Databases in Computer Networks," *Technical Report 74-09-01,* Department of Decision Sciences, The Wharton School, University of Pennsylvania, 1974 (Ph.D. dissertation).

[33] LEVIN, K. D. "Optimizing Distributed Databases—A Framework for Research," *Proceedings of the AFIPS National Computer Conference,* **44,** pp. 473–478, 1975.

[34] LEVIN, K. D., and H. L. MORGAN, "Dynamic File Assignment in Computer Networks under Varying Access Request Patterns," *Technical Report 75-04-01,* Department of Decision Sciences, The Wharton School, University of Pennsylvania, April 1975.

[35] LUM, V. Y., N. C. SHUAND, and B. C. HOUSEL, "A General Methodology for Data Conversion and Restructuring," *IBM Journal of Research and Development,* **20**(5), pp. 483–497, May 1976.

[36] MAHMOUD, S., and J. S. RIORDAN, "Optimal Allocation of Resources in Distributed Information Networks," *ACM Transactions on Database Systems,* 1(1), pp. 66–78, March 1976.

[37] MICHAELS, S., B. MITTMAN, and C. R. CARLSON, "A Comparison of Relational and CODASYL Approaches to Data-Base Management," *ACM Computing Surveys,* 8(1) March 1976.

[38] MERTEN, A. G., and J. P. FRY, "A Data Description Language Approach to File Translation," *Proceedings of the ACM 1974 SIGMOD Workshop on Data Description, Access, and Control,* Ann Arbor, Mich., pp. 191–205, May 1974.

[39] METCALFE, R. M. "Packet Communication," *Technical Report TR-114,* MIT Laboratory for Computer Science, Cambridge, Mass., December 1973.

[40] METCALFE, R. M., and D. R. BOGGS, "Ethernet: Distributed Packet Switching for Local Computer Networks," *Technical Report,* Xerox Palo Alto Research Center, Palo Alto, Calif. 1976. Abstract also appears in *Proceedings of the 1976 Berkeley Workshop on Distributed Data Mangement and Computer Networks,* Lawrence Berkeley Laboratory, University of California, Berkeley, Calif., May 1976, p. 238.

[41] NAVATHE, S. H., and J. P. FRY, "Restructuring for Large Databases: Three Levels of Abstraction," *ACM Transactions on Database Systems,* 1(2), pp. 138–158, June 1976.

[42] PLINER, M., L. McGOWAN, and K. SPALDING, "A Distributed Data Management System for Real-Time Applications," *Proceedings of the 1977 Berkeley Workshop on Distributed Data Management and Computer Networks,* Lawrence Berkeley Laboratory, University of California, Berkeley, Calif., pp. 68–86, May 1977.

[43] RAMIREZ, J. A., N. A. RIN, and N. S. PRAWES, "Automatic Generation of Data Conversion Programs Using a Data Description Language," *Proceedings of the ACM 1974 SIGMOD Workshop on Data Description, Access, and Control,* Ann Arbor, Mich., pp. 207–225, May 1974.

[44] ROSENKRANTZ, D. J., R. E. STEARNS, and P. M. LEWIS, "A System Level

Concurrency Control for Distributed Database Systems," *Proceedings of the 1977 Berkeley Workshop on Distributed Data Management and Computer Networks,* Lawrence Berkeley Laboratory, University of California, Berkeley, Calif., May 1977.

[45] ROTHNIE, J. B. "Evaluating Inter-Entry Retrieval Expressions in a Database Management System," *Proceedings of the AFIPS 1975 National Computer Conference,* **44,** pp. 417–424, 1975.

[46] ROTHNIE, J. B., and N. GOODMAN, "A Study of Updating in a Redundant Distributed Database Environment," *Technical Report CCA-77-01,* February 15, 1977, Computer Corporation of America, 575 Technology Square, Cambridge, Mass., 02139.

[47] ROTHNIE, J. B., and N. GOODMAN, "An Overview of the Preliminary Design of SDD-1: A System for Distributed Databases," *Proceedings of the 1977 Berkeley Workshop on Distributed Data Management and Computer Networks,* Lawrence Berkeley Laboratory, University of California, Berkeley, Calif., May 1977. Also available from Computer Corporation of America, 575 Technology Square, Cambridge, Mass., 02139, as *Technical Report CCA-77-04.*

[48] ROTHNIE, J. B., N. GOODMAN, and P. A. BERNSTEIN, "The Redundant Update Algorithm of SDD-1: A System for Distributed Databases (the Fully Redundant Case)," *First International Conference on Computer Software and Applications (COMPSAC 77),* IEEE Computer Society, Chicago, Ill., November 1977. Also available from Computer Corporation of America, 575 Technology Square, Cambridge, Mass., 02139, as *Technical Report CCA-77-02.*

[49] SCHNEIDER, G. M., and E. J. DESAUTELS, "Design of a File Translation Language for Networks," *Information Systems,* 1(1), pp. 23–31, January, 1975.

[50] SCHNEIDER, L. S. "A Relational Query Compiler for Distributed Heterogeneous Databases," unpublished paper, Martin Marietta Corporation, Denver, Colo., 1977.

[51] SHOSHANI, A. "A Logical-Level Approach to Database Conversion," *Proceedings of the ACM 1975 SIGMOD Conference on the Management of Data,* San Jose, Calif., pp. 112–122, 1975.

[52] SHOSHANI, A., and K. BRANDON, "On the Implementation of a Logical Database Converter," *Proceedings of the First International Conference on Very Large Databases,* Framingham, Mass., pp. 529–531, September 1975.

[53] SHU, N. C., B. C. HOUSEL, and V. Y. LUM, "CONVERT: A High Level Translation Definition Language for Data Conversion," *Communications of the ACM,* 18(10), pp. 557–567, October 1975.

[54] SHU, N. C., B. C. HOUSEL, R. W. TAYLOR, S. P. GHOSH, and V. Y. LUM, "EXPRESS: A Data Extraction, Processing and Restructuring System," *ACM Transactions on Database Systems,* 2,(2), pp. 134–174, June 1977.

[55] SIBLEY, E. H., and R. W. TAYLOR, "A Data Definition and Mapping Language," *Communications of the ACM,* 16(12), pp. 750–759, December 1973.

[56] SMITH, D.P. "A Method for Data Translation Using the Stored Data Definition and

Translation Task Group Languages," *Proceedings of the ACM 1972 SIGFIDET Workshop on Data Description, Access, and Control,* Denver, Colo., pp. 107–124, 1972.

[57] STEARNS, R. E., P. I. LEWIS, II, and D. J. ROSENKRANTZ, "Concurrency Controls for Database Systems," *Proceedings of the 17th Annual Symposium on Foundations of Computer Science,* IEEE, pp. 19–32, 1976.

[58] STONEBRAKER, M., and E. NEUHOLD, "A Distributed Database Version of INGRES," *Proceedings of the 1977 Berkeley Workshop on Distributed Data Management and Computer Networks,* Lawrence Berkeley Laboratory, University of California, Berkeley, Calif., May 1977.

[59] STONEBRAKER, M., N. McDONALD, and E. WONG"The Design and Implementation of INGRES," *ACM Transactions on Database Systems,* 1(3), pp. 189–222, September 1976.

[60] SUTHERLAND, W. R. "Distributed Computation Research at BBN," **111,** *BBN Technical Report 2976,* December 1974.

[61] THOMAS, R. H. "A Resource Sharing Executive for the Arpanet," *Proceedings of the AFIPS National Computer Conference,* **42,** pp. 155–163, 1973.

[62] THOMAS, R. H. "A Solution to the Update Problem for Multiple Copy Databases Which Uses Distributed Control," *BBN Report 3340,* Bolt, Beranek and Newman Inc., Cambridge, Mass., July 1975.

[63] WHITNEY, V. K. M. "A Study of Optimal File Assignment and Communication Network Configuration in Remote-Access Computer Message Processing and Communication Systems," Ph.D. Dissertation, Department of Electrical Engineering and College of Engineering, University of Michigan, September 1970.

[64] WISEMAN, T. "Ambitious EFT: Quintet of Banks, Quartet of Vendors," *Computerworld,* 11(23), pp. 1-6, June 6, 1977.

[65] WONG, E. "Retrieving Dispersed Data from SDD-1: A System for Distributed Databases," *Proceedings of the 1977 Berkeley Workshop on Distributed Data Management and Computer Networks,* Lawrence Berkeley Laboratory, University of California, Berkeley, Calif., May 1977. (Also available from Computer Corporation of America, 575 Technology Square, Cambridge, Mass. 02139, as *Technical Report CCA-77-03.*)

[66] WONG, E., and K. YOUSSEFI K. "Decomposition—A Strategy for Query Processing," *ACM Transactions on Database Systems,* vol. **1,**(3), pp. 223–241, September, 1976.

INDEX